Computer Studies

Fourth Edition

Geoffrey Knott BA, AIB, Cert Ed

Nick Waites BSc, MSc, Cert Ed

Business Education Publishers

1998

©Geoffrey Knott and Nick Waites 1998
ISBN 1-901888-09-6

First published 1987
Reprinted 1988 (twice)
Reprinted 1989 (twice)
Second Edition 1990
Reprinted 1990
Reprinted 1991
Reprinted 1992
Third Edition 1993
Fourth Edition 1999
Reprinted 2000
Reprinted 2001

Cover Design by Tim Murphy Creative Solutions
Graphical illustrations by Nick Waites and Geoffrey Knott
Production and Editing by Geoffrey Knott

Published in Great Britain by

Business Education Publishers Limited
The Solar Building
Doxford International
Sunderland
SR3 3XW

Tel: 0191 525 2410
Fax: 0191 520 1815

British Cataloguing-in-Publications Data
A catalogue record for this book is available from the British Library

Printed in Great Britain by Athenaeum Press, Gateshead

To Carolyn and Anne with love

The Authors

Geoffrey Knott and Nick Waites have long experience in Computing and IT education and have been producing highly successful course text books for over a decade, beginning in 1987 with the first edition of this book. They are authors of GNVQ Advanced Information Technology, Information Processing, Computing, Small Business Computer Systems, Information Technology Skills - A Student Guide, GCSE Information Systems and co-authors of Business GNVQ Advanced and Core Skills for GNVQ.

Acknowledgements

We would like to thank our friend and colleague Jim Morton for his meticulous proofing of several of the more technical chapters in this book.

Preface

The Fourth Edition of Computer Studies has been thoroughly revised and updated to keep students aware of the most recent changes and developments in this subject. For example, the increasing importance of networking and data communications is recognised with extended coverage of these topics and a new chapter which deals solely with the Internet. The sections on program design and testing have been completely revised and improved. The COBOL chapter has been rewritten to reflect COBOL 85 standards and the example programs are implementations of detailed examples provided in the section on program design.

This book has been written primarily for BTEC National Courses in Computer Studies and covers:

Core Units

        Information Systems

        Introduction to Programming

        Computer Systems

        Quantitative Methods

Programming Stream

        Concepts and Practice Units

Each chapter is followed by exercises designed to test the reader's retention of facts and understanding of ideas and techniques developed within the text.

The Assignment Programme at the end of the book provides assessment coverage of all the BTEC Units listed above. Unit tables at the beginning of the Assignment Programme list the assignments, and for each one, the Principal Objectives it covers and the chapters which are of particular use for its completion.

Although the book meets the particular requirements of BTEC National Courses in Computer Studies, it is also suitable for first year higher education programmes which do not assume prior knowledge of the subject.

Contents

Chapter 17
Categories of Software

Chapter 18
Computer Systems

Chapter 19
Peripherals

Chapter 20
Number Systems

Chapter 21
Data Representation

Chapter 22
Computer Logic

Chapter 23
Computer Instructions

Chapter 24
Computer Networks and Distributed Systems

Chapter 37
Program Testing, Debugging and Documenting

Chapter 38
COBOL

Chapter 1
Organisations

Need for organisations

The society in which we live is complex and sophisticated. As consumers we demand a variety of goods and services to enable us to maintain the quality of life we enjoy. In order to satisfy these demands, suppliers must produce the goods and services which the consumer wants by combining factors of production such as land, labour and capital in the most efficient manner. By this we mean producers must hire workers, rent or buy premises, perhaps invest in plant and machinery and purchase raw materials, and then organise the manufacture of the final product in such a way that they will make a profit. Society may also gain, as its scarce resources are being used in the way consumers wish rather than being wasted in producing things people do not need. Suppliers under such a system are known as commercial organisations. Many public sector organisations also provide goods and services to society and, in the same way as commercial organisations, these public sector bodies must employ staff, occupy premises and raise capital. The fundamental difference between these two types of organisation lies in the objectives they seek to fulfil. The private sector tends to be motivated by profit, while public sector organisations will often have a much less mercenary motive, such as providing for the public good and improving the state of society.

If we wish to see society ordered and governed in such a way that individuals are free to express their demands and producers are able to meet such wants, it becomes necessary to form organisations to control and regulate society through a variety of administrative structures. These are the bodies which make up the organisations of the state. In the UK, these are Parliament, the Government and its Executive, the Civil Service, the Local Authorities and the Courts and justice system. These bodies are required to carry out legislative, administrative and judicial functions.

If you examine the nature and range of individual demands in an industrialised society you soon realise that most of them cannot be met other than by organisations. Individually we lack the knowledge, skills and physical resources to manufacture products that fulfil our needs, whether these are simple or sophisticated. It would be as difficult for us to make a biro or a floppy disk as it would a television or a computer. Admittedly, some goods and services can be supplied by an individual working alone. A farmer may be able to grow sufficient food to satisfy himself and his family without any help from others. But what if he requires other goods and services? It is unlikely that the farmer will also have the ability or resources to produce his own combine-harvester or tractor. If he did not have such products which are manufactured by others, his life would be much simpler, but no doubt much harder.

A similar situation exists in the supply of services. A strong and resourceful individual may try to protect himself and his property from the dangers imposed by thieves or vandals. If he cannot, however, then he may turn to the state to demand protection. Recognising that a failure to respond to such demands from its citizens would lead to an anarchic system, the government must accept the responsibility and establish a legal system incorporating law enforcement agencies to provide the protection being sought.

How, then, are these goods and services produced? It is clear that individuals working independently would be unable to meet our complex physical and social needs. Therefore society has developed a system where people join together to form organisations. These bodies are extraordinarily diverse. They manufacture products, which they distribute and sell. They also provide all the services that we need. Thus, both the BBC and the Ford Motor Company are organisations, although their products are very different.

Clearly, then, if individuals within society are to have all their various needs satisfied, there must be co-operation between workers. Each must specialise in a certain aspect of the supply process. These workers must be organised and allocated a specific role in which to perform co-ordinated tasks. These tasks are normally organised with the aim of producing a given product or service, although there are some organisations which do not specialise and which make an extremely diverse range of products. In the private sector of the economy, such businesses will usually have the objective of making a profit for their owners. Of course, this is just one example of an organisation. As we have already noted, the state is another form of organisation which is clearly more complex than a business, and it has a variety of objectives, such as increasing the wealth of citizens, improving their quality of life and protecting them if they are threatened. We are all members of organisations, some of which are formal while others are informal. Your family is an example of an informal organisation, as is the group of friends you mix with. Other more formal organisations to which you may belong or may have belonged are the school you attended as a child, your employing body, or your trade union.

The tendency to form groups is a characteristic of human nature. Human beings are highly socialised, they need to 'belong' and will generally find it uncomfortable and disturbing if they cannot find 'acceptance' within a social group. An employee who is capable and confident in his or her job, and who is in turn regarded by the employer and the rest of the work force as a professional, gains a 'role' satisfaction through identifying as a vital part of the group. So organisations have an important role to fulfil in meeting the social needs of man. However, perhaps more important in the context of this course of study is the function of organisations as the satisfiers of needs. They allow individual workers to develop their specialist skills, and this in turn allows productive capacity to increase.

Since differing organisations concentrate on the supply of different goods and services, there must be a system established whereby products can be distributed to the consumers. Thus shops, wholesalers, transport companies and so on must all be involved. The fabric of the social and economic environment is based on a process whereby individuals form organisations which are dependent upon other organisations to survive. In just the same way as the needs of the individual cannot be met by that individual alone, so the same also holds true for organisations. They are interdependent. Organisational activity involves a perpetual interaction, one organisation with another, as society steadily evolves in a direction that individually and collectively we try to guide. However, as we shall see, even though the overall aim of society is the advancement of our physical well-being, the methods for achieving this are the subject of much disagreement.

Characteristics common to all organisations

The specific reasons for the formation of organisations are many and varied, and may not, of course, always be clearly defined. Some are the result of the need for individuals to find company for a social or leisure reason, for example by forming a sporting or working-men's club. Others are formed with a more precise economic objective in mind, such as the desire to make a profit for the person who has established a business organisation. Some, such as the organisations which make up the state and government, evolve as a result of the emergence of particular needs in society which require government intervention. For example, the Government established the National Health Service in 1946 to meet the needs of society for a high standard of free health care, available to all.

Nevertheless, most formal organisations have some common characteristics. These may be simply stated as follows:

(i)   The establishment of an organisation is usually for a specific purpose.

For example, the Automobile Association was founded with the precise objective of promoting the interests of motorists within this country. Other organisations may be launched with one prime aim, but may later diversify in order to follow alternative causes or objectives. For instance, Guinness, the brewery company, was established to produce alcoholic drinks, but now has subsidiaries making a variety of products such as fishing tackle boxes and cassette cases. This illustrates how a business may try to evolve as the commercial environment changes and new commercial opportunities emerge.

(ii) Organisations usually have a distinct identity.

People belonging to a specific organisation can identify themselves as being part of a group either as a result of where they work or of what they do. A Manchester United footballer wears a red shirt to show he is part of the particular organisation. A member of a trade union is given a membership card to signify he belongs to that union. Manufacturing companies promote their brand names through advertising. This sense of identity, which we have already seen is an important need for most people, can produce extreme loyalty to the organisation.

(iii) Most organisations require some form of leadership.

We have seen that organisations are normally formed for a specific purpose. In order to achieve this purpose, it is necessary to co-ordinate the efforts of the members of the organisation. This requires management, or leadership. Formal organisations such as companies or a club have a specified management hierarchy which may be appointed by the owners of the organisation. For instance, the shareholders of a company appoint the directors. Alternatively, the leadership may be elected, as in the case of a club or society where the members vote to have a chairman, secretary and committee. However, once appointed this management team has the responsibility for ensuring the organisation achieves its objectives.

(iv) Organisations are accountable.

Such accountability applies both to those the management team deals with and those it employs.

Objectives of organisations

The objectives of an organisation are the targets it hopes to achieve. Clearly the objectives which are set will vary considerably between different types of organisation. As we shall see later in this section, the objectives of commercial organisations will largely be based around the goal of profit. For organisations within the public sector, profit may not be the sole aim. Factors such as benefit to the community or the creation of jobs may also feature as targets for the public sector. It should be noted, however, that the profit motive is growing substantially in importance in the current economic and political climate.

A classification of organisations

Initially, it is convenient to categorise organisations as follows:

❑   public service;

❑   commercial and industrial.

Public service organisations

Many public services are provided by central and local government (the public sector) Central government takes responsibility for a wide range of services and has specific organisations, referred to as Departments, to manage each. Thus, there are separate departments, each responsible for the provision of, amongst others, health, education, defence and social welfare services. The role of local government is continually changing as successive governments pursue policies which tend to centralise power, or devolve it to locally elected council bodies. The provision of water, electricity and gas services used to be provided by 'public utilities', but they have been 'privatised' and now operate as commercial and industrial businesses. Some services, traditionally provided by the public sector, are now partly in the private sector; for example, some prisons are privately owned and private companies may carry out the work of refuse collection. Even so, overall control of such services is still the responsibility of central and local government departments.

Table 1.1 lists some major central government organisations and briefly describes the responsibilities of each. Table 1.2 does the same, in respect of local government.

Government departments	Responsibilities
Education	Schools
Transport	Road and building
Home Office	Law and order, police and prison services policy
Health	Hospitals,
Trade and Industry	Business and industrial policy
Social Security	Benefits such as income support.
Treasury	Economic policy
Defence	Armed Forces

Table 1.1. *Central Government Departments and areas of responsibility*

Local Government departments	Responsibilities
Social Services	Home helps, children's homes, meals on wheels, day nurseries, residential homes and day centres for the mentally ill.
Education	Nursery, and secondary schools.
Housing	Council housing provides affordable accommodation for those who cannot buy their own homes.
Environmental Services	Refuse collection and disposal, street sweeping and pollution control.
Police and Fire Services	Although there is co-operation between forces, these services are still locally controlled.
Planning and Building Control	Consider applications for local building and enforce regulations on building standards.

Table 1.2. *Local Government Departments and areas of responsibility*

It should be noted that although the government departments retain overall responsibility for the areas listed in Table 1.1, private companies carry out some of the work. For example, some hospitals, prisons and schools are privately owned. As part of the government's 'privatisation' programme, local councils have to allow private businesses to tender for (compete for) work traditionally carried out by their own departments; this is called Compulsory Competitive Tendering (CCT).

For example, private businesses can tender for contracts to carry out street sweeping or refuse collection. In addition, some schools have 'opted out' and receive their funding directly from central governments.

Industry and commerce

The term 'industry' covers a wide range of organisations which form part of a country's economy. We tend to link factories with the idea of industry, but the term also covers: *extraction* industries, such as coal-mining and fishing; *manufacturing* businesses which take raw materials and process them into finished products, such as cars and clothing, as well as those assembling ready-made components into, for example, computers and televisions; *retail* and *wholesale* businesses, concerned with buying, selling and distributing goods for personal and business consumption; *service* industries, such as hotel, catering, travel and banking. The word 'commerce' overlaps with 'industry' and includes all forms of trading organisation and those which support trade, such as banking and insurance.

Organisational structures

A structure can be defined as having component parts, which are connected in a particular way. Structures are designed to fulfil purposes. For example, a house is a structure, consisting of rooms, windows, floors, ceilings, doors and connection passages; the mix of these component parts and the way they are put together determines the design of the house. Two main types of organisational structure are considered here: *hierarchical*; *flat*.

Hierarchical structure

An organisation with a hierarchical structure includes different levels of authority and responsibility. Heads of Department may be directly responsible to one of the Directors. For example, the Accounts Department Head may be subject to the authority of the Financial Director. Such authority relates to the operation of the organisation and enables tasks to be completed. There may be Section Supervisors who are responsible to their respective Heads of Department for particular functions within departments. Each section supervisor may have authority over a number of clerks. Generally, there are more 'indians' than 'chiefs', so a hierarchical structure can be viewed as a pyramid, as shown in Figure 1.1; the lower down the pyramid you descend, the larger the number of staff you are likely to find employed. The jobs at the top of the pyramid carry the most authority and the greatest responsibility for the success or failure of the organisation. Operatives and clerical staff are unlikely to have any authority in the organisation, but they have responsibility for the completion of their own jobs.

Downward communication

Figure 1.1, shows that, within the pyramid, communications go up and down. Policy decisions taken at board level by the directors are implemented by instructing the relevant departmental heads to see that the policy is carried out. The heads of department brief their middle managers and the final stage in the process is the communication between middle managers and their subordinates.

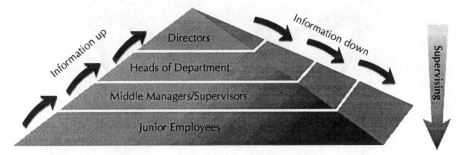

Figure 1.1. *Hierarchy of authority and responsibility and information flow*

Upward communication

The communication also passes from the bottom upwards. Staff provide feedback to their seniors. This may take many forms; it may involve monitoring shortages of materials, absences of staff, production problems, grievances and suggestions for improving work methods. Anything which requires the authority or approval of someone further up the organisational hierarchy and which has been generated or identified below, will pass back up the system. Only in extreme circumstances is it likely that an issue arising at the bottom of the pyramid will pass right back to the top for consideration and decision. For the most part, an immediate senior is likely to have sufficient authority to make a decision; ultimately however, it is a question of the extent of *delegated* responsibility held by senior employees that determines whether they can deal with it personally, or must pass it back to their own superiors. As organisations grow bigger it is inevitable that communications have much further to travel. This is not ideal since it is likely to take longer to transmit information and there is greater distancing between the giver and the receiver, which can lead to a 'them and us' view of the organisation by junior staff. However, it is clear that as the organisation grows, so its communication system must be become increasingly refined. Information technology support is crucial to the efficiency of communications.

Flat structure

In contrast to a hierarchy, a flat structure generally has a single level of management, as shown in Figure 1.2. Except for the smallest organisations, very few will have an entirely flat structure. It is possible, that an organisation wishes to avoid a cumbersome hierarchy and attempts to keep the number of management levels to a minimum; they are thus aiming for a 'flatter' structure. As mentioned earlier, hierarchies with many levels of authority can make communication difficult. A flatter structure can encourage 'team spirit' through the avoidance of the 'them and us' feelings, which can be characteristic hierarchies.

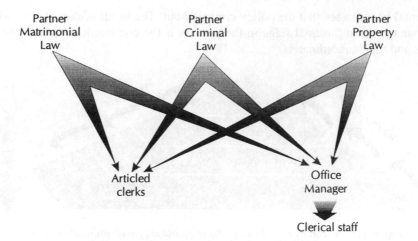

Figure 1.2. *Flatter structure for firm of solicitors*

Figure 1.2 represents a firm of solicitors, where each partner has the same level of authority and responsibility, specialises in a particular aspect of the law and has joint authority over the Office Manager and articled clerks ('apprentice' solicitors). The Office Manager is responsible for supervision of the clerical staff. Although there are hierarchical elements in the organisation, its structure is fairly 'flat'.

Exercises

1.   Choose three formal organisations with which you are familiar and for each:

   (i)   identify its main *purpose*;

   (ii)   select an aspect which gives it its distinct *identity*;

   (iii)   briefly describe how it is *lead* - its top management structure;

   (iv)   identify to whom the management are ultimately *accountable*.

2.   The water industry used to be in the public sector, but is now run by private companies, overseen by a regulator (OFFWAT). Briefly list features which allow the privatised water company to be classified as both commercial and public service.

3.   (i)   Choose a hierarchically structured organisation with which you are familiar and using Figure 1.1 as a guide, draw a pyramid structure to show the main levels of authority.

   (ii)   Identify two benefits and two drawbacks of the structure for the chosen organisation.

Chapter 2
Functional Areas of Organisations

This chapter investigates some of the main functional areas to be found in organisations, namely:

- ❑   financial accounting (sales, purchasing and general ledger);

- ❑   invoicing and stock control;

- ❑   marketing;

- ❑   payroll and personnel;

- ❑   design and production;

- ❑   IT services.

Financial accounting

Financial accounting or 'book-keeping' is the process of recording financial transactions arising from the day-to-day operation of a business. The sale of goods to a customer and the subsequent settlement of the debt are two examples of financial transactions. Apart from their function as a control mechanism over the financial transactions of a business, accounting records can be analysed to provide information on the performance of a business over a period. Typically, such information is extracted annually or every six months, in the form of a *balance sheet* and *trading and profit and loss account*. These financial statements are also required by *external agencies*, such as the Inland Revenue (for tax assessment) and the bank, if loan facilities are required.

Financial accounts need to record:

- ❑   *debtor* transactions; debtors are people or organisations who owe money to the business for goods or services provided (credit sales);

- ❑   *creditor* transactions; creditors are people or organisations to whom the business owes money, for the supply of goods (credit purchases).

These transactions are recorded in the *sales ledger* and the *purchase ledger* respectively. A third ledger, the *nominal* (or *general*) ledger is used to record the overall income and expenditure of the business, with each transaction classified according to its purpose.

Sales accounting

When credit sales are made to customers, a record needs to be kept of amounts owing and paid. Payment is normally requested with an invoice, which gives details of goods supplied, quantities, prices and VAT. Credit sales are usually made on for example, a 14, 21 or 28 day basis, which means that the customer has to pay within the specified period to obtain any discounts offered. Overdue payments need to be chased, so sales accounting systems normally produce reports analysing the indebtedness of different customers. Debt control is vital to business profitability and computerised systems can produce prompt and up-to-date reports as a by-product of the main application.

Purchase accounting

This function is concerned with controlling amounts owed and payments made to suppliers of services, goods or materials which are used in the main business of the company. For example, a car manufacturer will need to keep records of amounts owing to suppliers of car components and sheet steel manufacturers. Delayed payments to suppliers may help cash flow, but can harm an organisation's image, or even cut off a source of supply when a supplier refuses to deliver any more goods until payment is made.

General ledger

The general ledger keeps control of financial summaries, including those originating from payroll, sales and purchase accounting and acts as a balance in a double entry system. Computerised systems can automatically produce reports at the end of financial periods, including a trial balance, trading and profit and loss account and balance sheet.

Other finance-related functions

Stock control

Any organisation which keeps stocks of raw materials or finished goods needs to operate a stock control system. Although stock constitutes an asset, it ties up cash resources that could be invested in other aspects of the business. Equally, a company must keep sufficient quantities of items to satisfy customer demand or manufacturing requirements. To maintain this balance a stock control system should provide up-to-date information on quantities, prices, minimum stock levels, and re-order quantities. It should also give warning of excessively high, or dangerously low levels of stock. In the latter case, orders may be produced automatically. A stock control system may also generate valuable management reports on, for example, sales patterns, slow-moving items, and overdue orders.

Sales order processing

This function will normally be concerned with:

❑ the validation of orders, checking, for example, that the goods ordered are supplied by the business or that the customer's credit status warrants the order's completion;

❑ the identification of individual items ordered. A customer may request several different items on the same order form and any particular item will probably appear on many different order forms, so the quantities for each are totalled to produce picking lists to enable warehouse staff to retrieve the goods for despatch;

❑ the monitoring of back orders. If an order cannot be fulfilled, it may be held in abeyance until new stocks arrive, so all outstanding back orders need to be available on request.

Invoicing

This function deals with the production of customer invoices, requesting payment for goods or services delivered. Information stored in the customer files and stock files is used to produce invoices, usually on pre-printed continuous stationery.

Payroll

Payroll systems are concerned with the production of payslips for employees and the maintenance of records required for taxation and other deductions. In a manual system, the preparation of payroll figures and the maintenance of payroll records is a labour intensive task. Although tedious and repetitive, it is a vitally important task. Most employees naturally regard pay as being the main reason for work and resent delays in payment or incorrect payments, unless of course it is in their favour! The repetitive nature of the task makes it a popular candidate for computerisation, especially with organisations which employ large numbers of people. The automatic production of reports for taxation purposes also provides a valuable benefit. Smaller organisations with only several employees probably do not regard payroll as a high priority application for computerisation. The benefits are not as great if the payroll can be carried out by one or two employees who also carry out a number of other tasks.

Personnel

The personnel function is responsible for the selection (usually by interview), recruitment, training and development of staff. Personnel records will store all the information needed by Salaries and Wages to make the correct payments to employees; this will include details of, for example, gross salary, tax code, statutory sick pay and holiday entitlement. Depending on the size of the organisation, information may also be held concerning: qualifications, courses attended; personal and career development plans.

Design

The design function is present where an organisation develops its own products and services; a trader who simply buys and sells goods has no need of a design team. Design is part of the research and development (R & D) function, which is vital to organisations wishing to radically develop their product range. The nature of design teams depends on the product or service being designed. The skills and talents of a car design team are clearly very different from those of a team designing a cover for a magazine.

Production

The production function should, ideally, be driven by the market for the business's products. In other words, it should be geared to produce the necessary mix and quantities of products required by customers. If goods are perishable within a short time, and large reserve stocks cannot be held, then production should be flexible and responsive to the day-to-day sales requirements. Of course, this is an ideal and production plans cannot always be changed at short notice; ships and other large items take months or years to build. The production department must know exactly what is required and when; it must also have the staff with the necessary skills and any machinery must have the appropriate facilities and production capacity. For example, a production department which is geared to produce 1000 units of a product per day, will probably find it difficult to produce 2000 units, without modification of the system of production.

Marketing

A marketing function is a vital part of many large national and international businesses; it aims to generate information, from a wide range of data sources, to support marketing decisions. Three such decision areas are:

(i)   *strategic* and relating to, for example, expansion of the company's existing market share the identification of new marketable products;

(ii)   *tactical*, for example, planning the marketing mix;

(iii) *operational*, for example, day-to-day planning of sales calls and ad hoc promotions.

At the operational level, for example, data gathered from sales invoices, sales force staff and accounting information can be used to establish customer types. Thus, customers can be classified as 'low', 'medium' or 'high' volume users according to the frequency and volume of their orders. This information can help sales staff to target particular categories of customer and to plan the timing of sales calls. At the tactical level, a invoices provide information on sales variance between different market segments over time or sales projections based on current patterns.

Information Technology (IT) Services

Apart from small firms, most organisations need specialist staff to develop, introduce, maintain and update the various systems which make use of information technology. The term 'information technology' covers all computer-based information processing systems, plus those which make use of data communications, such as computer networks, fax machines, photocopiers and telephone systems. The responsibilities of IT Services are, therefore, much broader than those traditionally held by wholly centralised computer services or data processing departments. The development of cheaper and more powerful microcomputer systems, which can be networked with one another, as well as with larger mini and mainframe systems, has resulted in computer facilities being distributed more widely. For this reason, IT Services needs to provide a much more flexible service and support user systems at the point of use. For example, users of network workstations need support when equipment, such as a shared printer, breaks down or they may require help in the use of software on the network. This contrasts with a centralised department, which holds all the computer equipment, carries out all computer processing and restricts user access to specialised applications, run through dedicated terminals. IT Services may be known variously as Computer Services, Management Information Services or less commonly now, the Data Processing Department.

Role of IT Services

IT Services fulfils a servicing function for the whole organisation. In larger organisations, there is a centralised computer facility, possibly in the shape of a mainframe or minicomputer system, with the responsibility for major applications, such as payroll and stock control. User departments may have access to the centralised facility through attached terminals or networked microcomputers. Individual members of staff may also use stand-alone microcomputer systems or portable devices, such as notebooks and personal digital assistants (PDAs). IT Services staff need to support users in the use of these distributed facilities, as well as control the operation of any centralised system. IT Services provides facilities to satisfy both *operational* and *managerial* information needs.

Operational requirements

Each functional area has its own operational information needs. For example, Wages and Salaries need payroll details and payslips, and Sales Order Processing require the production of customer invoices. Common examples of routine operations include:

❑   keeping stock records

❏   sales accounting and purchase accounting;

❏   payroll;

❏   invoicing and production of delivery notes;

❏   routine costing;

❏   filing of customer orders.

Managerial requirements

Routine processing work forms the bulk of the activity within IT Services, but there is an increasing demand for management information. This includes assistance with functions which require management involvement and thinking, but which can be partially automated or assisted by computers. Examples of such functions include:

❏   production planning;

❏   short term and long term forecasting;

❏   setting of budgets;

❏   decision-making on financial policies;

❏   marketing decisions and sales management;

❏   factory maintenance and management;

❏   price determination;

❏   selection of suppliers.

Function of IT Services

Figure 2.1 shows the typical functions within an IT Services department.

Systems development

This function relates to the development of new computerised systems and the maintenance of existing ones. This function is staffed primarily by *systems analysts* and *programmers*. In small organisations, hybrid skills are often needed, so job titles such as *analyst programmer* may be used.

Systems analysis

Systems analysis is a process used in the design of new systems, as requested by corporate management. Systems analysis follows stages of *investigation*, *design* and *implementation*.

Each stage should involve close consultation with potential users, in the various functional areas of the organisation, to ensure that their information and operational requirements are met.

The design stage should produce a *system specification* which, rather like an architect's plans for a building, details all necessary materials and procedures needed to fulfil the specification. The specification should detail the necessary clerical procedures, hardware requirements and the inputs, processing and outputs required of the computer software.

After implementation of a system, it will require continual monitoring and probably, occasional modification, when the operational or information requirements of users change. This maintenance task is the responsibility of the systems analysts,

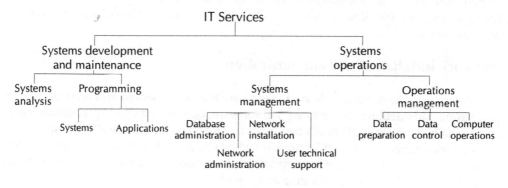

Figure 2.1. *Structure of IT Services*

Programming

Programming lacks some of the creative aspects of systems analysis and involves the use of a programming language (for example, C++, COBOL, Visual BASIC) to code the necessary computer programs. The program requirements are detailed in the *program* or *software specification*, which forms part of the system specification prepared by systems analysts.

Most programmers who work in an IT Services department are likely to be *applications programmers*, responsible for the development or modification of applications, such as stock control or payroll. Systems programmers are concerned with the development of operating systems and utilities (Chapter 17), which are normally developed by large computer manufacturers or software companies, such as Microsoft. An IT Services department may also employ *systems programmers*, but they are likely to have a more limited role than applications programmers. Much software is now in commercial package form, but not all applications can be satisfied by such means and applications programmers continue to be needed for tailoring of programs specifically for their employer. The growth of network use has created the need for *network programmers*, who have specialist knowledge of such systems.

Apart from specialising in systems, applications or network programming, a programmer is likely to be skilled in the use of one or more programming languages. An organisation seeking to employ programmers will specify the language or languages they require.

System operations

This broad function is concerned with the operational, rather than the developmental aspects of the IT systems. It is divided into *systems management* and *operations management*.

Systems management

This function deals with the general operation of all the IT systems and is not directly concerned with particular applications. There are a number of separate areas within this function: *network installation*; *network administration*; *user technical support*; *database administration*.

Network installation and administration

Computer networks (Chapter 24) are a feature of most organisations and tasks of selecting, purchasing and installing the hardware and software, both systems and applications, may be carried out by specialist staff in this area. Staff employed in this area need to be familiar with the network operating system (Chapter 17) and its utilities. They are responsible for setting up and managing network user accounts, controlling passwords, managing printer queues, allocating and maintaining and backing up network storage and monitoring the performance of the network.

User technical support

The distribution to users, of computer resources through networks, desktop and portable computer systems has hugely expanded the need for IT user support. Users often have access to a range of different devices, such as printers, scanners, plotters and fax modems and apart from needing initial training in their use, they also require occasional support when things go wrong. Support staff may also give guidance in the use of software and help trouble-shoot problems which users will inevitably encounter at some stage. User technical support is extremely important if users are to use IT resources efficiently and for the benefit of the organisation.

Database administration

If applications are implemented through a database system, then specialist staff, known as database administrators, are employed to control access to the database by applications and ensure consistency in the use of data within it. Systems analysts and programmers involved in the development of database applications need to work closely with the responsible *database administrator* (DBA).

Operations management

This function, led by an operations manager, has three main areas of responsibility: *data control*; *data preparation*; *computer operations*; *media library*. These responsibilities relate particularly to centrally controlled applications.

Data control

Data control staff are responsible for the co-ordination and control of data flowing through the operations section. For example, data received from Salaries, to update the payroll master file and produce payslips, have to be controlled to ensure their accuracy and completeness at all stages of processing. The methods of control are described in Chapter 13.

Data preparation

Batch processing systems require the transcription and encoding of data gathered from source documents, such as order forms or invoices, onto magnetic storage. The input is then effected directly from the magnetic tape or disk on which the data has been accumulated. On-line, transaction processing systems, do not usually require this data preparation stage.

Computer operations

Computer operators are responsible for the day-to-day running of the computer hardware. In the case of mainframe computer systems, their responsibilities include the loading and unloading of magnetic tape reels or magnetic disk packs, according to the on-line requirements of applications currently in use. For example, before a payroll run, the media containing the master and transaction files have to be loaded onto the relevant devices, so that they can be accessed by the computer which is running the payroll program. The computer hardware is under the control of operating system software (Chapter 17) and an operator needs to communicate with the operating system regarding jobs to be processed and to deal with error conditions which may arise. A separate terminal is normally dedicated as an *operator console* and access to it is restricted both physically and through software-controlled passwords.

Exercises

1. Machem Ltd is a large manufacturing business. It buys in raw materials from a number of suppliers and uses the raw materials to produce its range of specialist outdoor clothing and equipment, which it sells to retailers. It has a warehouse next to the factory, to store the stocks of raw materials and finished goods.

    (i)   Explain the circumstances when Machem Ltd is a *debtor* and when it is a *creditor*.

    (ii)   Explain circumstances when Machem will receive *invoices* and when it will issue them.

    (iii)   List the processes involved in invoicing a retailer and settlement of the debt.

    (iv)   Identify features of a typical *stock control* system which Machem Ltd could use to maintain sufficient, but not excessive levels of stock.

    (v)   Machem Ltd is planning to extend its range of products and needs to ensure that there will be sufficient demand for the new products to make a profit. As well as its production function, the company has its own research and development (R&D) and marketing departments. Suggest ways in which these three functions may co-operate to maximise Machem Ltd's chances of success.

2. Machem Ltd has its own *IT Services* function, employing systems analysts, programmers, network engineers, network administrators and user technical support assistants.

    Briefly outline the likely role of each of these categories of staff at Machem Ltd.

Chapter 3
Information in Organisations

Information needs

To operate, different functions within an organisation need access to particular types of information, some examples of which are briefly described below.

Design specifications; before a product is manufactured a specification is produced detailing, for example, the types, qualities and quantities of required materials, physical features, performance requirements (such as for a car) and so on. Some products, such as computer software, need to include design features concerning, for example, the user interface.

Construction drawings. As the term indicates, these are used to guide the person or persons building or constructing the product. An architect produces construction drawings for the house builder to follow; design specification details are also included, so that the builder knows the types and quantities of materials.

Market research. This information is often gathered through surveys, either using questionnaires or monitoring consumer buying patterns. A company should carry out market research before beginning the production or sale of a new product in its range.

Advertising is essential to any organisation wishing to promote its image or product range. Advertising uses market research information to target the most appropriate areas of the population. For example, market research may indicate that a product is most likely to be bought by professional people living in the south of England; advertising can be directed, perhaps through mails shots, to that section of the population.

Sales orders detail customer order requirements, including item details, quantities and delivery dates; *purchase orders* detail the organisation's purchase requirements from suppliers.

Payments and receipts. These may relate to sales orders or purchase orders. Receipts are amounts received from debtors. Payments are made by a business to settle debts with creditors (suppliers to the business).

Transport requirements. This information will detail, for example, a goods list, the delivery address, special requirements, such as refrigeration and possibly the route to be taken.

Information flow diagrams

Figure 3.1 illustrates some information flows within a typical manufacturing and wholesaling organisation.

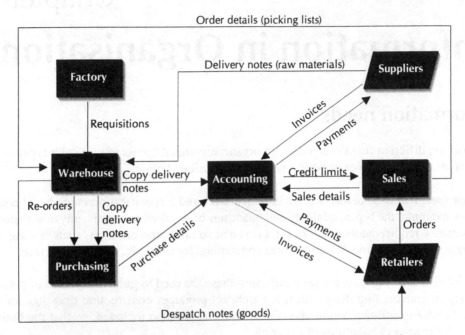

Figure 3.1. *Information flow diagram for a manufacturing and wholesale business*

An examination of Figure 3.1 shows that each functional area is dependent on one or more other areas for the information it needs to operate. For example, to charge the retail outlets (their customers) for the goods supplied, the Accounting function requires the necessary sales information, which is supplied by the Sales function. The information allows the Accounting function to prepare the necessary invoices to send to customers. Similarly, Purchasing must be kept informed by the Warehouse (stock control) of raw materials which need re-ordering from suppliers, to replenish stocks.

These examples of *operational* information allow day-to-day decisions to be made on the operation of the business. To keep the diagram in Figure 3.1 fairly simple, certain vital functions, such as Production Control and Marketing, are not shown. Obviously, their inclusion would increase the number of information flows and the complexity of the diagram. The information flows shown in Figure 3.1 are all 'triggered' by *events*. For example:

(i)   a customer order is generated when a customer orders goods;

(ii)   credit limit details flow from Accounting to Sales, when a customer order is checked;

(iii)   an invoice is raised when goods are despatched to a customer;

(iv)   a payment to a supplier is triggered when the invoice payment falls due.

IT support of information flows

To illustrate the role of IT in managing information flow, we use a simple example of a small electrical company, Wingrove Electrical Ltd, based on the outskirts of London. It employs 38 people and produces electrical components for use in central heating equipment. The following examples of activities and information flows are used to show the potential benefits of using IT.

An enquiry from a potential buyer

A telephone enquiry from a potential customer is received by the company's telephonist, who attempts to connect the caller with the company sales manager, who is out of the office. She makes a note of the caller's name and the nature of the enquiry and promises to pass these details on to the sales manager when she returns to the office. Unfortunately, the paper with the message is lost and so is the potential order. Clearly, the system could have been improved by a number of methods.

If Wingrove had a local area network, the telephonist could have obtained sufficient product information to meet the initial enquiry of the potential buyer. The message could have been transmitted through the electronic mail system, for the sales manager to access when she returned. If the sales manager used a notebook computer, she could download such messages remotely, though the telecommunications network. In any event, it is extremely likely that she would be carrying a mobile telephone or pager and could have been contacted.

Receipt of an order

Wingrove receives a substantial order by post. The manual procedures involve copying the order, sending a copy to Accounting and a copy attached to a 'job sheet' to Production. When the order is completed and despatched, Accounting will invoice the customer and await payment. Unfortunately, when the customer eventually pays, he submits a cheque for an incorrect amount, but the clerk fails to notice that the amount on the invoice and the amount on the cheque do not agree; as a result, he processes the invoice as paid. Wingrove has thus lost some of its profit.

The company could improve its financial control by installing a computerised order processing and invoice verification system. As each order is received into the company, the appropriate details, such as customer, item, quantity, price and so on, are entered into its computer, which automatically generates an invoice, statements and increasingly harshly worded reminders, until the customer settles the debt. When the cheque arrives, its value is also entered and the program automatically checks to ensure that the amount matches both the original price quoted and the invoice value. As protection against the miskeying of the cheque amount, a further check involves the automatic reconciliation, each month, of totals for paid and unpaid invoices.

Production of a quotation

Wingrove's managing director is informed that Birmingham City Council is intending to replace the central heating systems in all its public buildings, over the next three years and is seeking tenders for the component parts of the system. Wingrove would very much like to gain the contract and decide to submit a detailed quotation document. The quotation is 28 pages long and contains an extensive amount of technical detail, as well as product specifications, prices and delivery details. Typed manually, reference would have to be made to numerous files for component specifications and prices and the inevitable modifications to the tender would involve extensive re-typing. The following improvements are possible.

Using a word processor and quotation template, the task can be completed much more quickly. Layout alterations and editing can easily be done before a final copy is printed. A high quality printer, possibly with colour facility, will contribute to a highly professional appearance and improve the image of the company. Component specification and price data can be imported from the company's database of such information, directly into the document. If speed is important, the document could be faxed or e-mailed to Birmingham City Council.

Exercises

1. Study the information flow diagram in Figure 3.1 and answer the following questions.

    (i)   When a customer places an order with Sales, to which function must they refer for a credit limit?

    (ii)   When a customer order is accepted why are the details passed to Accounting?

    (iii)   What information does accounting need from the Warehouse function before paying an invoice sent from a supplier?

    (iv)   What use does the Warehouse function make of the requisitions it receives from the Factory?

Chapter 4
Filing Information

This chapter deals with the ways in which computer files are stored, organised and processed.

Files, records and fields

In data processing, it is necessary to store information on particular subjects, for example, customers, suppliers or personnel and such information needs to be structured so that it is readily controllable and accessible to the user. In traditional data processing systems, each of these 'topics' of information is allocated a file. Figure 4.1 illustrates the structure of a book file.

The *file* is a collection of *records*, one for each book. Each record contains details of the book's title, its author(s), ISBN number, publisher, date of publication and cost; each of these *data items* is allocated physical space, known as a *field*, within the record. Figure 4.1 shows a sample record, with the Title field (each one is identified by its *field name)* containing the value 'Turbo C++ for Windows' and the other fields containing values associated with that book.

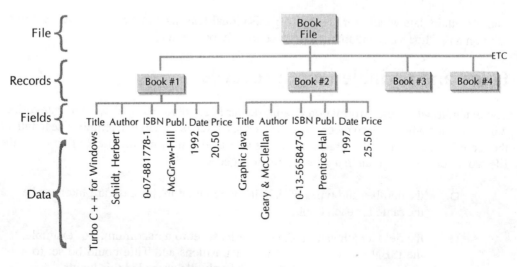

Figure 4.1. *Data file structure*

Types of file

Files can be categorised by the ways in which they are used and there are generally recognised to be four such categories.

Master files

They are used for the storage of *permanent*, or *semi-permanent*, data which is used in applications such as stock, sales or payroll. Some of the fields tend to contain data which is fairly static, for example, customer name and address, whilst data in some fields is continually changing, for example, customer balance, as transactions are applied to the file. Such *updating* is carried out, either through the direct entry (on-line) of individual transactions, or from an accumulated set of entries stored on a *transaction* file.

Transaction files

These are transient and only exist to allow the updating of master files. Each transaction record contains the *key field value* of the master record it is to update (to allow correct matching with its relevant master record), together with data gathered from source documents, for example, invoice amounts which update the balance field in customer accounts.

Reference files

These contain data used for reference or look-up purposes, such as price catalogue and customer name and address files.

Archival or historical files

These contain data which, for legal or organisational reasons, must be kept and tend to be used on an ad hoc basis and may be referred to only occasionally.

Fixed and variable length records

The extent to which the information in a particular file can be standardised and categorised will determine whether each record in the file can be fixed or variable in length. The length of the record is the number of character positions allocated to it within the file. In Figure 4.1 the file would probably contain *fixed* length records because:

- ❑   the number and types of data items required in this case are likely to be the same for each book;

- ❑   the field length can be fixed or at least set to a maximum. For example, the ISBN is fixed at 13 character positions and Title could be set to a maximum of 30, provided that no book title exceeded this length.

Variable length records may be used in files which have storage requirements markedly different from those referred to above, for instance:

❑   some records could have more fields than others. In a personnel file, for example, each record may contain details of previous jobs held and as the number of previous jobs may vary considerably from one employee to another, so the number of fields would be similarly varied;

or

❑   the number of character positions used for individual values within a field is variable. For example, in a library system each record may contain a field for data which describes the subject of the book and the amount of text needed to adequately describe this may vary from book to book.

Listed below are some of the advantages of *fixed length* records.

❑   Fixed length records are simpler to process, in that the start and end points of each record can be readily identified by the number of character positions. For instance, if a record has a fixed length of 80 character positions, a program reading the file from the start will assume that the second record starts at the 81st character position, the third at the 161st character position and so on, making easier the programming of file handling operations.

❑   Fixed length records allow an accurate estimation of file storage requirements. For example, a file containing 1000 records, each of fixed 80 characters length, will take approximately 80000 characters of storage.

❑   Where direct access files are being used, fixed length records can be readily updated 'in situ' (in other words the updated record overwrites the old version in the same position on the storage medium). As the new version will have the same number of characters as the old, any changes to a record will not change its physical length. On the other hand, a variable length record may increase in length after updating, preventing its return to its home location.

There are some instances when *variable* length records are more appropriate. For example:

❑   where records in a file contain highly variable quantities of information, variable length records may be more economical of storage space;

❑   when the saving in storage space makes the introduction of more complex file handling techniques worthwhile.

Record identification - primary and secondary keys

In most organisations, when an information system is operational it will be necessary to identify each record uniquely. In a Personnel File, for example, it might be thought that it is possible to identify each individual record simply by the employee's Surname and this would be satisfactory as long as no two employees had the same surname. In reality, many organisations will have several employees with the same surnames, so to ensure uniqueness, each employee is assigned a unique Works Number. The works number field is then used as the primary key in the filing system, each individual having his or her own unique Works Number and so a unique primary key.

There are certain circumstances when the primary key may be a *composite key*, that is, one made up of more than one field and the following example shows how a pair of fields, which individually may not be unique, can be combined to provide a unique identifier.

Table 4.1 shows an extract from a file which details suppliers' quotations for a number of different products. There is a need for a composite key because there may be a number of quotations from one supplier (in this case, SupplierNo 23783) and a number of quotations for the same part (in this instance, PartNo A112). It is necessary, therefore, to use both SupplierNo and PartNo to identify one quotation record uniquely.

SupplierNo	PartNo	Price	DeliveryDate
23783	A361	1452.75	31/01/95
37643	B452	341.50	29/01/95
23783	A112	2345.29	30/01/95
41192	A112	2474.29	28/01/95

Table 4.1. *Supplier quotations for various products*

Uniqueness is not always necessary. For example, if it is required to retrieve records which fulfil a criterion, or several criteria, *secondary keys* may be used. Thus, for example, in an information retrieval system on Personnel, the secondary key Department may be used to retrieve the records of all employees who work in, say, the Sales Department.

File storage media

This topic is examined more fully in Chapter 5. File storage media may be classified according to the kind of access they provide:

❑   serial access;

❑   direct access.

Serial access media

Serial access means that in order to identify and retrieve a particular record, it is necessary to 'read' all the records which precede it in the relevant file. The standard medium for serial access is magnetic tape. One of the difficulties with this medium is that there it has no readily identifiable physical areas which can be addressed. In other words, it is not possible to give a name or code and refer this to a particular location. It is said to be *non-addressable*. To find an individual record, the software needs to examine each record's *key field*, starting from the beginning of the file, until the required record is found.

Direct access media

Storage media such as floppy or hard disks allow *direct* access to individual records, without reference to the rest of the relevant file. They have physical divisions which can be identified by computer software (and sometimes hardware) and are *addressable*, so that particular locations can be referred to by a name or code to retrieve a record which is stored at that location. Retrieval of an individual record stored on such a medium is achieved (depending on the way the file is organised) by specifying the relevant *primary key field value*, thus providing the software with a means of finding and retrieving the specific individual record directly.

File organisation methods

Another function of the *primary key* is to provide a value which can be used by computer software to assign a record to a particular position within a file. The file organisation method chosen will dictate how individual records are assigned to particular *logical* positions within a file. Serial access media are limited in the file organisation methods they permit because they are non-addressable. Direct access media are more versatile in that they allow a variety of file organisation methods, in addition to those allowed by serial access media. The different types of file storage media are discussed in some detail in Chapter 5.

Exercises

1. Using a stock control system as an example, distinguish between *master* and *transaction files.*

2. Using the example of a criminal records system, illustrate the function of *reference* and *archive* files.

3. Using the example of a personnel system, illustrate the meaning of the terms: *field*, *record*, *file*.

4. (i) Using an example application, explain circumstances when records are likely to be of *variable* length.

   (ii) There are two ways in which the length may be varied; what are they?

5. Using an example application, explain circumstances when records are likely to be of *fixed length*.

6. A holiday company maintains a file of special discount package holidays, detailing destination, accommodation, cost, dates available and so on.

   (i) Suggest a suitable *primary key*.

   (ii) Explain, with two examples, how *secondary keys* may be used to help a customer who is undecided about where to go on holiday.

7. A medical practice maintains a patient appointments file. Each record contains the following fields: DoctorID, PatientID, AppointmentDate, AppointmentTime.

   (i) In these circumstances, why is a single field inadequate as a primary key?

   (ii) What details would enable the receptionist to identify a unique appointment?

8. Magnetic tape is a *non-addressable* storage medium; magnetic disk is *addressable*. Explain the terms in italics and their significance for the type of access each medium provides.

Chapter 5

File Storage Media

Magnetic tape - a serial access medium

Physical and logical records

The physical characteristics of magnetic tape necessitate that, to process a file, the tape unit (the device onto which a tape is loaded for processing) starts to read the tape at the beginning of the reel. The take-up spool receives the tape from the feed spool via a read/write head in the unit which can either record information onto or read information from the tape as it passes. As there are no specific physical locations on the tape which can be identified and referred to by the computer (except of course the beginning and end), the only way it can find a particular record is by reading the whole file. Unless the whole tape is to be processed, it may only be necessary to read up to the point where the specific record it is seeking is found. There may well be more than one logical file on a tape but these will have to be read in the sequence that they appear on the tape. As the tape is read, the computer will compare the key field value of each record which it comes to, with the specified key value, until the required record is found. Figure 5.1 illustrates the way in which a file is arranged on tape both *logically* and *physically*.

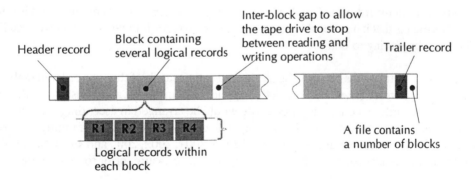

Figure 5.1. *Logical records in physical blocks on tape*

You should note from Figure 5.1 that records R1, R2, R3 and R4 are instances of logical records. For example, if this were a stock file, each logical record would relate to one commodity held in stock. On the other hand each physical record consists, in this illustration, of 4 logical records. The reason for making the distinction between logical and physical records stems from the fact that data is transferred between the computer's internal memory and the tape storage medium in manageable *blocks*, the optimum size of each depending on factors such as the size of the computer's internal memory.

Each physical record is referred to as a block of data. Between each block transfer, the tape has to stop while the previous one is processed by the computer. In order to give the tape time to stop and then restart for the next block, there is an *inter block gap* (IBG), a blank area of tape between each block. It is unlikely that the optimum block size will coincide with the actual length of a single logical record, so it is necessary to transfer a number of logical records between tape and internal memory at one time. Thus, a physical record or block will often consist of a number of logical records.

The example of a stock file is used again to illustrate this point further. Assume that each block contains 3 logical stock records (in other words three individual commodities). If the first record to be processed is stored in the fifth block, then the first four blocks have to be read in sequence into memory and each logical stock record examined for its key field value, without any records actually being used. When the fifth block is eventually read into memory each of the three logical stock records is then examined for its key field value until the required key and thus logical record, is identified.

File organisation methods on magnetic tape

There are two ways in which a file can be organised on tape:

❑   serially;

❑   sequentially.

This restriction stems from the fact that magnetic tape is a *serial* access medium. As is noted earlier, this means that it has no addressable locations, so records have to be traced by reading the file from beginning to end.

The processing of tape files can only be carried out satisfactorily if they are ordered in the sequence of their primary keys. This restriction applies to both master and transaction files. So, for example, records in a customer master file would be arranged in ascending sequence according to the Customer Reference field. If the field contain a 4 digit code, ranging from say, 2000 to 5000, the records would be sequenced 2000, 2001, 2002, 2003 and so on. Serial files, which are out of sequence, are only useful as an interim measure, prior to processing.

Generally, when a transaction file is being created on tape, for example, when customer orders are received, they are written to tape in the order in which they are received, thus creating a serial file. Before the master file can be updated, the serial transaction file has to be sorted by the computer into the same order as the master file.

Updating the master file

When a tape file is updated, a new master file must be created on a new reel of tape because the tape drive unit cannot guarantee to write an updated record to the exact position from which it was read (it is *non-addressable*). There is a danger, therefore, of adjacent records being corrupted or completely overwritten.

The following procedures are followed during the update (assuming that no new records are to be inserted). For the sake of clarity, some complexities are not mentioned.

❏   A transaction is read into memory.

❏   A master record is read into memory. If the record keys do not match, the master record is written, unchanged, to the new reel. Master records continue to be read, examined and written in the original sequence to the new reel until a match for the transaction is found.

❏   Once the match is found, the master record is updated in main memory and then written to the new reel.

These steps are repeated until all transactions have been processed and the complete updated master file has been written to the new reel. The updating process is illustrated in Figure 5.2. Note that three separate reels are involved.

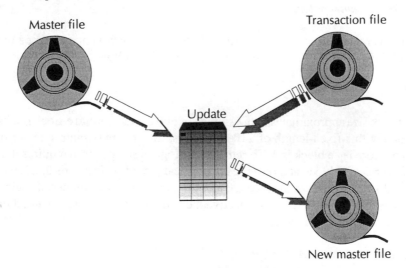

Figure 5.2. *Updating a tape master file to produce a new master file*

If the transaction files were not sorted into the same sequence as the master file, it would be necessary to rewind the master file whenever a transaction required a master record which had already passed through the system; clearly, this would be both inefficient and impractical.

Magnetic disk - a direct access medium

Addressing magnetic disk

Magnetic disk provides file storage facilities which are more flexible and
powerful than those provided by magnetic tape. As an *addressable* medium,
the surface of the disk is divided into
physical locations which are illustrated
in Figure 5.3. The address of any one
physical location on a single disk incorporates a *track* number, and within that
track, a *sector* number. A sector is the
smallest physical area on the disk which
can be addressed, each addressable unit
being referred to as a *block* or *physical*

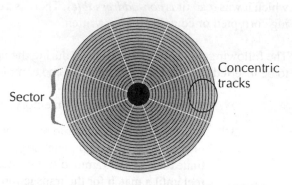

Figure 5.3. *Addressing structure of magnetic disk*

record. The size of the blocks is normally determined by the systems designer through the
use of systems software, although some disk storage systems use *hard sectoring* (the block
size cannot be altered). The number of logical records which can be accommodated in a particular block obviously depends upon the physical size of the block and the length of each
logical record. The maximum number of logical records which can be fitted into a block is
known as the *blocking factor*.

Considerations regarding the determination of block size are beyond the scope of this text,
but some of the design factors can be readily explained as follows.

Example

If a disk's block size approximates to the storage of 500 characters and a stock file has logical
records, each with a fixed length of 110 characters, then the maximum number of records
which can be stored in a block is 4. To retrieve one logical stock record requires the software
to address the relevant block and retrieve the physical record. This means that it will retrieve
all the logical stock records in the block. Therefore, the larger the number of logical records
stored in any specific block, the less selective the software can be in retrieving them but the
faster the complete file is processed.

Operational features of magnetic disk

Although there are many variations in the capacities and sizes of disk that are available, there
are certain physical characteristics which are common to all.

Commonly, a number of disks are mounted onto a central spindle as illustrated in Figure 5.4.
To transfer data to or from the disk pack it is necessary to mount it onto a disk drive unit
which rotates the pack at high speed. Data is recorded onto disk magnetically, in a similar

fashion to the recording on magnetic tape. Special read/write heads are mounted on moveable arms within the disk drive unit in such a way that they move in synchronisation across the disk surface. The software positions the heads for the writing or retrieval of records.

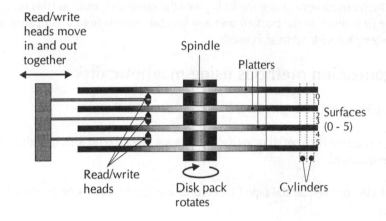

Figure 5.4. *Disk pack illustrating cylinder concept*

Further disk addressing concepts

Cylinders

If the Figures 5.3 and 5.4 are considered together it can be seen that, in a disk pack, a specified track on one disk, for example the outermost track (track 0), is vertically above other tracks on lower disks which are also specified as track 0. In other words, all the track 0s are in the same vertical plane. Such a grouping is known as a *cylinder* or *seek area*. Similarly, all track 1s form another cylinder, as do track 2s and so on. It can be seen therefore, that there are as many cylinders as there are tracks on each disk surface.

The fastest way of reading or writing records on disks is achieved by minimising the movement of the read/write arms. This is achieved by positioning associated records, which are likely to be needed as a group (they may form a complete file), into sequence (as a sequential file) on tracks in the same cylinder. Records are written to the disk pack, such that track 0 on surface 1 is filled first, followed by track 0 on surface 2 and so on, until all number 0 tracks are filled (the first cylinder). Then, if the file requires more than one cylinder, adjacent tracks are filled to form further cylinders, until the file is complete.

When access is required to the file it is quickest, in terms of keeping read/write head movement to a minimum, to deal with one cylinder of records at a time. Thus, a complete cylinder of records is processed before any head movement is required. A cylinder is also known as a seek area, because all records in a cylinder can be accessed by the read/write heads whilst they are positioned in that cylinder.

Buckets

The minimum amount of data which can be transferred between the backing store of the computer and its internal store is the *block*. However, there are occasions when a larger unit of transfer is required and on such occasions the concept of the *bucket* is used; a number of blocks (up to the maximum of one track) is given the same disk address (this is usually the address of the first block in the bucket) and any logical records held within such a bucket are retrieved when that disk address is used.

File organisation methods using magnetic disk

Magnetic disk supports the following file organisation methods.

Serial. As is the case for a serial tape file, records are placed onto disk one after another in no particular sequence.

Sequential. As for a sequential tape file, records are stored on disk ordered by each record's primary key.

Indexed sequential. Records are stored in sequence according to their primary keys and an *index* is produced when the file is created, allowing direct retrieval of individual records. The software searches different levels of the index (a *multi-level index*): cylinder index; track index; bucket (or block index), before positioning the read/write heads to retrieve the block containing the required record.

The indexes may be structured as shown in Table 5.1, using a five-digit primary key in the range 00001 to 50000. The table represents an extract only.

Cylinder index		Track index for cylinder 55		Sector index for track 3	
cylinder	highest key	track	highest key	sector	highest key
1	00452	1	26000	1	26071
2	00940	2	26063	2	26076
3	01650	3	*26120*	3	26080
.....	.....	4	26185	4	26087
55	*26500*	5	26242	5	26095
56	27015	6	26320	6	26104
.....	.....	7	26426	7	26112
115	50000	8	*26500*	8	*26120*

Table 5.1. *Extract from multi-level index*

The indexes are constructed as the records are written sequentially (according to the primary key) to the disk pack. As each sector is filled, the primary key of the last record to be placed in the sector (the highest key) is recorded in the *sector index* and once all sectors in a track have been filled, the last key to be entered is added to the *track index*, the completion of a cylinder causing the highest key field in it to be recorded in the *cylinder index*. This process is repeated with subsequent cylinders until the file is complete.

The retrieval of records requires a *serial search* to be made of the cylinder, track and sector indexes respectively, unless a complete track is to be read, in which case the sector index is not used. Referring to the Table 5.1, suppose that the record with primary key 26085 is required; the indexes may be used as follows:

❑   a serial search of the cylinder index is made until a highest key entry is found which is equal to or greater than the required key. The entry which meets this requirement is 26500, indicating that a search of the track index for cylinder 55 is needed;

❑   a serial search of that track index, again looking for an entry greater than or equal to record key 26085, reveals that the record is to be found in track 3, where the highest key field is 26120;

❑   searching the sector index for track 3 returns the entry of 26087, the highest key field entry for sector 4.

Unless record 26085 has been placed in an *overflow area*, owing to a full sector, it can be retrieved by reading in the block of data occupying the address - sector 4, track 3, cylinder 55.

The cylinder index for a given file will normally be read into main memory when the file is first opened and held there until processing is complete. Each track index is normally held in the cylinder to which it relates and will be read into main memory as required. Similarly, the sector index is usually held within its relevant track.

The preceding procedures and mechanisms only illustrate the main principles of index construction and usage, as the detail is likely to vary considerably from one system to another. To facilitate updating, space will normally be left in sectors, tracks and cylinders to allow for the insertion of new records.

This method allows the efficient sequential processing of the file as well as direct retrieval of records using the indexes. Indexes can become quite large and the file may need to be reorganised periodically so that new records can be inserted in the correct sequence. Records which are marked for deletion need to be removed from the file and the indexes then have to be reconstructed. The frequency with which such reorganisation is necessary depends on the level of file activity and the number of insertions and deletions. File reorganisation is a *housekeeping* activity.

Random organisation

This is a method which is impractical in any non-computerised situation. However, in a computerised system it is feasible to place records onto disk at random. The procedure for placing specific records in a particular position on disk may simply relate the primary key *directly* to its disk address, for example,

$$disk\ address = primary\ key$$
$$disk\ address = primary\ key + index\ value$$

With *absolute* and *indexed addressing*, each record has a unique address and can be retrieved directly with its own primary key. A major disadvantage of this method is its orientation towards the needs of the computer; the values needed for disk addressing may well be inappropriate for use as meaningful (to the user) primary keys for logical records. Further, the unique link between a disk address and a particular logical record means that any vacated space cannot be used by another record unless it adopts the same key as the previous occupant record.

Hashing algorithms

A more usual method of addressing uses a mathematical formula called a *hashing algorithm*, which generates a disk address from the record's primary key. The hashing algorithm operates on the primary keys within a given range to produce pseudo-random numbers which may then be used as bucket addresses, to which the logical records are allocated. Each pseudo-random number could refer to an address where a single record is stored, but it is more economical for it to refer to an area where a group of records is stored; thus a *bucket address* will normally contain a number of logical records. Records with the same address are known as *synonyms*.

Overflow

An uneven distribution of records means that some buckets overflow and cannot accommodate all the logical records allocated to them, whilst others remain empty or are seriously under-used. Excessive overflow slows the access time for any record which cannot be allocated to its home address. To achieve a reasonably even spread, the selection of a particular algorithm requires consideration of the following factors:

❑   the pattern and range of the primary keys within the file;

❑   the size of each bucket and the number available;

❑   the *packing density* required (number of records, divided by the total record capacity of the available buckets).

Example algorithm

Prime number division. The primary key is divided by the largest prime number which is less than the number of available buckets. The remainder of this calculation is taken as the *relative* bucket number, that is, the number of buckets after the first. For example:

> *available buckets 2000*
> *prime number 1999*
> *primary key 22316*
> *22316/1999 = 11 remainder 327*

The relative bucket number is thus 327. The same mathematical formula is used to subsequently retrieve records, which is ideal in situations where random enquiries are the norm and there is little need for sequential processing. Randomly organised files can be processed sequentially but with less efficiency than sequentially organised files. An advantage of this method is the lack of large indexes which tend to take up considerable storage space on the disk.

The aim of any randomising or hashing algorithm is to achieve an even distribution of records over the disk space allocated to a file. Most random files allow more than one logical record to occupy a single bucket, as any given algorithm will normally generate the same disk address from several different primary keys; conversely, any hashing algorithm is likely to leave some buckets with no allocated records. Any record which is stored in the address allocated to it by an algorithm is referred to as a *home record*.

Accessing disk files

Serial files

As with magnetic tape, the only way to retrieve records is serially, in other words, one after another.

Sequential files

The addressing features of disk are not used and the method is the same as that for sequential tape files.

Indexed sequential files

There are 3 methods of retrieving such records:

Sequentially. Transactions are sorted into the same sequence as the master file. This is suitable when a large proportion of the records in the file are to be processed in one run, that is, when the *hit rate* (the percentage of master records in a file, for which there are transactions) is high. Minimal use is made of the index. The cylinder index and track index may be searched, then the whole track is read into memory, sector by sector, without reference to the sector index;

Selective or **skip sequentially**. When records are sequentially organised by key, not every record needs to be read when scanning the file. The transactions are sorted into master file sequence and the indexes are used, so that only those blocks containing master records for which there is a transaction are read into memory. This is suitable when the hit rate is low;

Randomly. Transactions are not sorted. They are processed in the order in which they occur, the indexes being used to find the relevant master records as they are required. The read/write heads have to move back and forth through the file and so head movement is greater than with sequential methods of processing. This method is appropriate when records are updated immediately after the transaction occurs or, for example, when there is a need for random enquiries of a stock file.

Random files

Transactions or enquiries need not be in any logical sequence. Records are retrieved by generating the physical address from the record key. The software uses the same hashing algorithm it used to assign the record to its address in the first place.

Exercises

1. (i)   Why are the *logical records* in a sequential file usually grouped into *blocks*?

    (ii) What factors determine the block size?

2. Why must a transaction file, stored on magnetic tape, be sorted before it can update its associated master file?

3. An indexed sequential file uses a *multi-level index* to allow direct access to records.

    (i)   What index levels may exist?

    (ii) Briefly explain how each index level is used to locate a particular record, given that its primary key value has been specified.

4. In the context of random file organisation:

    (i)   Explain, with the aid of an example, the term *hashing algorithm*.

    (ii) A hashing algorithm should have two main aims. What are they?

5. What is the function of an *overflow area*?

Chapter 6
Processing Methods

Introduction

Data processing systems make use of one or more processing methods, depending on the requirements of the application. The methods can be categorised according to the ways in which data is controlled, stored and passed through the system; the major categories are: *batch* processing; *on-line* processing, which includes *real-time* and *time-share* processing; *distributed* processing and *centralized* processing; *database* systems (a separate chapter is devoted to this topic). To allow particular methods of processing a computer must have the necessary *operating system* software (Chapter 17); thus any particular computer system is equipped with, for example, a batch processing or real-time operating system, or even a combination of types, depending on the needs of the user organisation.

Batch processing

Such systems process *batches* of data at regular intervals. The data is usually in large volumes and of identical type. Examples of such data are customer orders, current weekly payroll details and stock issues or receipts. The procedure can be illustrated with the example of payroll, which is a typical application for batch processing. Each pay date, whether it is every week or every month, the payroll details, such as hours worked, overtime earned or sickness days claimed, are gathered for each employee (these details are referred to as *transactions*) and processed in batches against the payroll *master file*. The computer then produces payslips for all employees in the company. A major feature of this and similar applications is that a large percentage of the payroll records in the master file are processed during the payroll 'run'. This percentage is known as the *hit rate*. Generally, high hit rate processing is suitable for batch processing and if, as is usual, the master file is organized sequentially, then the *transaction file* will be sorted into the same sequence as the master file. In the case of magnetic tape, transactions must be sorted because the medium only allows *serial* (one record after another in their physical order) access.

The batch processing method closely resembles manual methods of data handling, in that transactions are collected together into batches, sent to the computer centre, sorted into the order of the master file and processed. Such systems are known as traditional data processing systems. There is normally an intermediate stage in the process when the data must be encoded using a *key-to-tape* or *key-to-disk* system.

A disadvantage of batch processing is the delay, often of hours or days, between collecting the transactions and receiving the results of processing and this has to be remembered when an organisation is considering whether batch processing is suitable for a particular application. Conversely, batch processing has the advantage of providing many opportunities for controlling the accuracy of data (Chapter 13) and thus is commonly used when the immediate updating of files is not crucial.

On-line processing systems

If a peripheral, such as a Visual Display Unit or keyboard, is *on-line*, it is under the control of the computer's processor or Central Processing Unit (CPU). On-line processing systems therefore, are those where all peripherals in use are connected to the CPU of the main computer. Transactions can be keyed in directly. The main advantage of an on-line system is the reduction in time between the collection and processing of data. There are two main methods of on-line processing: *real-time* processing; *time-share* processing.

Real-time processing
Process control in real-time

Real-time processing originally referred only to process control systems where, for example, the temperature of a gas furnace is monitored and controlled by a computer. The computer, through an appropriate sensing device, responds immediately to the boiler's variations outside pre-set temperature limits, by switching the boiler on and off to keep the temperature within those limits.

Real-time processing is now used in everyday consumer goods, such as video cameras, because of the development of the 'computer on a chip', more properly called the *microprocessor*. An important example of the use of the microprocessor is the engine management system, which is now standard on an increasing range of cars. A car's engine performance can be monitored and controlled, by sensing and immediately responding to, changes in such factors as air temperature, ignition timing or engine load. Microprocessors dedicated to particular functions are referred to as *embedded systems*. Further examples of the use of microprocessors can be found on the automated production lines of engineering works and car plants, where operations requiring fine engineering control can be carried out by *computer numerical controlled* (CNC) machines. The important feature common to all real-time applications is that the speed of the computer allows almost immediate response to external changes.

Information processing in real-time

To be acceptable as a real-time information processing system, the *response-time* (that is the time between the entry of a transaction or enquiry at a VDU terminal, the processing of the data and the computer's response) must meet the needs of the user. The delay or response time may vary from a fraction of a second to 2-3 seconds depending on the nature of the transaction and the size of the computer. Any delay beyond these times would generally be unacceptable and would indicate the need for the system to be updated. There are two types of information processing systems which can be operated in real-time: *transaction processing*; *information storage and retrieval*.

Transaction processing

This type of system handles clearly defined transactions one at a time, each transaction being processed completely, including the updating of files, before the next transaction is dealt with. The amount of data input for each transaction is small and is usually entered on an *interactive* basis through a VDU. In this way, the user can enter queries through the keyboard and receive a response, or the computer can display a prompt on the screen to which the user responds. Such 'conversations' are usually heavily structured and in a fixed format and so do not allow users to ask any question they wish. A typical example of transaction processing is provided by an *airline booking system* and the following procedures describe a clients enquiry for a seat reservation.

(i)   A prospective passenger provides the booking clerk with information regarding his/her flight requirements.

(ii)   Following prompts on a screen, the clerk keys the details into the system, so that a check can be made on the availability of seats.

(iii) Vacancies appear on the screen and the client can confirm the booking.

(iv)   Confirmation of the reservation is keyed into the system, usually by a single key stroke and the flight seating records are immediately updated.

(v)   Passenger details (such as name, address, etc.) can now be entered.

Such a system needs to be real-time to enable reservations to be made at once, while the client is there (or on the telephone) and so that the seating records accurately reflect availability at all times.

Information storage and retrieval

This type of system differs from transaction processing in that, although the information is updated in real-time, the number of updates and the number of sources of updating is relatively small.

Consider, for example, the medical records system in a hospital. A record is maintained for each patient currently undergoing treatment in the hospital. Medical staff require the patient's medical history to be available at any time and the system must also have a facility for entering new information as the patient undergoes treatment in hospital. Sources of information are likely to include a doctor, nurses and perhaps a surgeon, and new entries probably do not number more than one or two per day. This is an entirely different situation from an airline booking system where the number of entries for one flight record may be 200-300 and they could be made from many different booking offices throughout the world.

Time-share processing

The term *time sharing* refers to the activity of the computer's processor in allocating *time-slices* to a number of users who are given access through terminals to centralized computer resources. The aim of the system is to give each user a good *response time*. These systems are commonly used where a number of users require computer time for different information processing tasks. The processor time-slices are allocated and controlled by a time-share operating system. The CPU is able to operate at such speed that, provided the system is not overloaded by too many users, each user has the impression that he or she is the sole user of the system.

A particular computer system will be designed to support a maximum number of user terminals. If the number is exceeded or the applications being run on the system are 'heavy' on CPU time the response time will become lengthy and unacceptable. Time-share systems are possible because of the extreme speed of the CPU in comparison with peripheral devices such as keyboards, VDU screens and printers. Most information processing tasks consist largely of input and output operations which do not occupy the CPU, leaving it free to do any processing required on other users tasks.

Distributed processing

As the term suggests, a distributed processing system is one which spreads the processing tasks of an organisation across several computer systems; frequently, these systems are connected and *share resources* (this may relate to common access to files or programs, or even the processing of a single complex task) through a data communications system (Chapter). Each computer system in the network must be able to process independently, so a central computer with a number of remote intelligent terminals cannot be classified as distributed, even though some limited validation of data may be carried out separately from the main computer. Examples of distributed systems include mini or mainframe computers interconnected by way of *wide area networks*, or a number of *local area networks* similarly linked.

Distributed systems provide a number of benefits:

❑ *Economy*. The transmission of data over telecommunications systems can be costly and local database storage and processing facilities can reduce costs. The radical reduction in computer hardware costs has favoured the expansion of distributed systems against centralized systems.

❑ *Minicomputers and microcomputers*. The availability of minicomputer and microcomputer systems with data transmission facilities has made distributed processing economically viable. An increasingly popular option, in large multi-sited organisations, is to set up local area networks of microcomputers at each site and connect them through communications networks to each other and/or to a central mainframe computer at the

Head Office. This provides each site with the advantages of local processing power, local and inter-site communications through *electronic mail* and access to a central mainframe for the main filing and database systems.

❑   *Local management control.* It is not always convenient, particularly where an organisation controls diverse activities, to have all information processing centralised. Local management control means that the information systems will be developed by people with direct knowledge of their own information needs. Responsibility for the success or otherwise of their division of the organisation may be placed with local management, so it is desirable that they have control over the accuracy and reliability of the data they use.

Centralised systems

With this type of system, all processing is carried out centrally, generally by a mainframe computer. The continuing reduction in hardware costs and the increase in computer power has led the move towards distributed processing systems. This is achieved through computer networks.

Exercises

1.   Using the examples of a cinema booking system and a payroll system:

(i)   Differentiate between *batch* and *transaction processing*.

(ii)   Why is batch processing unsuitable for the cinema booking system?

(iii)   If there are 850 records in the payroll master file and 810 will be updated by transactions, what is the *hit rate*?

(iv)   Why is hit rate considered when choosing a processing method for an application?

2.   Agros uses *transaction processing* to enter stock issues and receipts into its stock control system. If the transactions are not entered until the end of each day, it is not a *real-time* system.

(i)   Explain why this is so and what Agros would need to do to employ a real-time system.

(ii)   What factors would Agros need to take into account when deciding whether to change to a real-time system?

3.   A library's computer system allows borrowers to enter key words or phrases to search for books on particular topics. The system displays a list of books which accord with the search criteria.

Describe features of the library's 'book search' application which would categorise it as an *information storage and retrieval* system

4.   (i)   Define the term *time-sharing* system.

(ii)   What circumstances may cause a time-sharing system's response time to be unsatisfactory?

5.   The Acme group has three subsidiary companies, each involved in different market areas: car production; supermarket chain; transport and distribution.

(i)   Write a list of brief arguments which would favour the use of *distributed* processing over *centralised* processing.

(ii)   Why would the Acme Group need to use *wide area network* facilities?

Chapter 7
Database Systems

Introduction

The term *database* is often used to describe any large collection of related data, but to understand the ideas which follow, it is necessary to establish a more precise definition. More specifically a database is

> *a collection of data, generally related to some subject or topic area and structured so as to allow relationships to be established between separate data items according to the various needs of users.*

From this definition it is possible to identify specific features of a database:

- ❑ A database may contain data of use in a variety of applications.

- ❑ The data are structured to allow separate data items to be connected, to form different logical records, according to the requirements of users and hence, to applications programs.

- ❑ A database will normally be used for different applications, but those applications must have some common ground concerning the data items they use. For example, sales, purchasing, stock control and production control applications are likely to use common data in respect of raw materials or finished goods. On the other hand, a database containing data on both materials and personnel may be difficult to justify; even then connections between the separate databases can be facilitated if the information requirements so justify.

The physical and logical database

A database has to satisfy the differing information needs of many users, generally through specially written applications programs. Therefore, it is often necessary to add further data items to satisfy changes in users' needs. The software which controls the database (the database management system or DBMS) must be able to relate to the data at an item, as well as a record level. This is because each application needs to group data items according to its particular, logical record requirements. Some data items are likely to be common to several applications. The physical database must be able to link data items into the various logical record structures needed by the applications.

Physical storage and data independence

Periodically, the *physical* database needs to be changed to accommodate variations in user requirements. This does not mean that all applications programs need to be changed, because the way the data is *physically* stored on the storage medium is independent of the *logical* record structures required by applications programs.

In a traditional computerised system, if a data file is changed, then any program accessing it also needs to be changed. In a database, records can be stored essentially in two different ways.

(i)   Independently - the primary key is used to decide the physical location of a record; frequently this is effected through a calculation on the primary key (see Direct Access in Chapters 4 and 5) to determine where it will be stored on the storage medium.

(ii)   In association - records are stored according to their relationship with other records and connections may be made between them with the use of *pointers*. A *physical pointer* gives the address where a record is stored and can be used to relate records anywhere in the database; a *logical pointer* is a value from which the physical address can be calculated.

Controlled redundancy

One feature, which is not specifically referred to in the earlier definition, is that of *controlled redundancy*. Effectively, this means reducing to a minimum the number of duplicated data items in a database. In traditional computerised filing systems, each department in an organisation may keep its own files, which results in a massive amount of duplication in the data that are stored. Although it is desirable to avoid data duplication and thereby minimise the storage needs of a database, there are occasions when duplication is necessary to provide efficient access to the database.

A particular type of database, known as *relational* (see later), uses duplicated items to relate data held in separate *tables*. Figure 7.1 shows two tables, created with the Access database package. Although the Product data and Supplier data are held in two separate tables, it can be combined, as required,

Microsoft Access
File Edit View Format Records Window Help

Database: STKCNTRL

Table: Product

PartCode	Description	Price	Quantity	SupplierCode
A123	Table (Cottage)	£23.50	15	KSU518
A124	Chair (Cottage)	£42.23	36	KIT518
A125	Stool (Cottage)	£28.15	6	KIT518
A133	Bar Stool	£33.55	4	KSU518

Table: supplier

SupplierCode	SupplierName	SupplierAddress
ABC123	ABC Supplies	Transit Row, Darlington
KIT518	Kitchen Systems	28 Holmeside, Sunderland, SR3 4ST
KSU518	Kitchen Supplies	112 High Street, Darlington, DL1 4SJ
PAR116	Parsons Ltd	Parsons House, Market Place, York YO4 3NS
STA436	Stapleton	36 Warwick Place, Darlington, DL4 6AJ

Figure 7.1 *Relational tables linked by SupplierCode*

through the relationship or link field, Supplier Code. For example, to produce a list of all products supplied by Kitchen Systems and headed by their name and address, requires data from both tables. The list of products would then include those with the relevant Supplier Code 'KIT518' and the supplier's name and address would be selected by the same code. The decision to store the Supplier and Product data in separate tables would be taken as part of the database design process, to avoid the repeated duplication of suppliers' names and addresses which would occur if all the data were held in one table.

Creating and manipulating the database

A special language called a *data description language* (DDL) allows the database to be created and changed and the logical data structures to be defined. A *data manipulation language* (DML) enables the contents of the database to be altered by adding, updating or deleting records. Programmers use the language to develop applications programs for users of the database. The functions of DDLs and DML languages are combined, together with a query language facility, in *Structured Query Language* (SQL).

Physical storage, schema and sub-schema

Because a database must allow various user applications programs to access it at the same time, direct access storage must be used. There are many ways of physically organising the data, but whatever method is used it must allow for the variety of logical record forms needed by applications programs. The applications programmer does not need to know how the data are physically stored. Instead, the programmer's knowledge of the data is restricted to the *logical view* required for the program. The complete or global logical database is referred to as the *schema*. The restricted, or local, view provided for an application program, is called a *subschema*.

An example database schema

The schema shown in Figure 7.2 illustrates a particular database standard, known as CODASYL. The schema can be explained as follows. There are 4 record types:

1.   DEPARTMENT

2.   STAFF MEMBER

3.   SECTION

4.   PREVIOUS JOBS

Each of 1, 2 and 3 can be retrieved directly by its *record key*, DeptNo, StaffNo and SectNo respectively. Record type 4 is only accessible through the STAFF MEMBER type record. This is reasonable as it would be unusual to search for a PREVIOUS JOBS record without first knowing the identity of the member of staff. There are 4 *sets*, each of which has an *owner* record and one or more *member* records. For example, one DEPARTMENT will have a number of STAFF MEMBERs (a one-to-many relationship). The sets are:

1.   Employees *(owner,* DEPARTMENT/ *member,* STAFF MEMBER)

2.   Sections *(owner,* DEPARTMENT/ *member,* SECTION)

3.   Staff-in-Section *(owner,* SECTION/ *member,* STAFF MEMBER)

4.   Career *(owner,* STAFF MEMBER/ *member,* PREVIOUS JOBS)

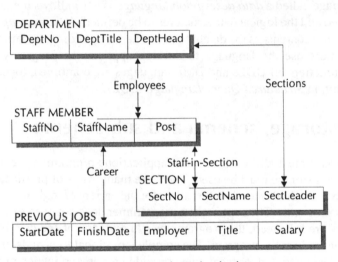

Figure 7.2. *Example Codasyl schema*

A set is an *owner* record with a number of *member* records, as illustrated in Figure 7.3. For example, Department 4 may own a number of Section (member) records. Data Manipulation Language statements could retrieve a Section record directly, using its SectNo, or through its Sections Set. If the Section is in Department No 12, it may be found through the following steps.

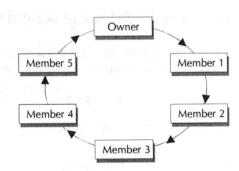

Figure 7.3. *A Codasyl set*

1.   Move 12 to DeptNo

2.   Find any Department

3.   Show Section

4.   Find next Section

5.   Show Section

Steps 4 and 5 are repeated until the correct Section record is found or the end of set is reached. It should be noticed that a PreviousJobs record can *only* be found through the Career set and the appropriate StaffMember record. As with any database, a Codasyl DBMS organises and accesses the logical database through the schema description. The structure defines the routes which can be taken through the database, but the programmer/user must know what linkages have been established to be aware of how and what data can be accessed.

Database management systems (DBMS)

So that each application program may only access the data which it needs for processing or retrieval (those data that are defined in its subschema), a suite of programs referred to as the Database Management System (DBMS) controls the database and prevents accidental or deliberate corruption of data by other applications programs. Relational DBMS examples include Access, Paradox and FoxPro. An application cannot access the database without the DBMS. Figure 7.4 illustrates the links between users, application programs, the DBMS and the database.

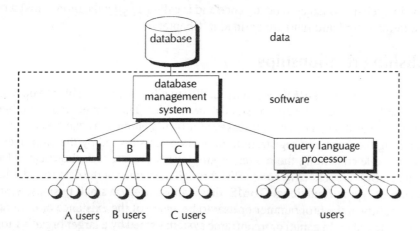

Figure 7.4. *Relationship between DBMS, database, applications and users*

A DBMS has the following functions.

    ❑   It is connects applications programs with the database.

    ❑   It facilitates the use and organisation of a database and protects the database from accidental or deliberate corruption.

    ❑   It restricts a programmer's logical view of the database to the data items needed by the program he or she is writing.

Relational database management systems

A relational DBMS is designed to handle data in two-dimensional, *table* form and a single database is likely to contain a number of separate, but related, tables. This tabular view of data is easy to understand; everyday examples include telephone directories, train timetables and product price lists. For information and clarity, when referring to other texts on relational databases, some of the jargon is defined below, by reference to the earlier Product table in Figure 7.1.

A table is sometimes referred to as a *relation* and each entry in the table is a single data item value. For example, PartCode A123 is a data item value consisting of 3 characters.

Each column in the relation contains values for a given *data item type*, or *field*. The set of values for a given data item type is called its *domain*. A domain is identified by its description, that is, the name for the data item type. For example, in Figure 7.1 the set of values in the third column is called the Price domain.

Each row in a relation is a record occurrence and is called a *tuple*; the more usual word is *record*. The terms record and field are defined in Chapter 4.

Establishing relationships

The power of a relational DBMS lies in its facility to allow separate tables to be manipulated and combined in a variety of ways to establish new tables. Thus, for example, a table containing details such as the names and addresses of a firm's employees can be combined with a table detailing the make and registration numbers of cars owned by the employees, to produce a new table containing the names of employees owning, say, Ford cars. Tables in a relational database are related *dynamically*, through the values of the data found within them. In the simplest types of relational DBMS, that is those used on small business systems, it is the responsibility of the programmer or user to be aware of the existence of common values to link tables together. In a mini or mainframe system owned by a larger organisation, this responsibility may lie with the database administrator (DBA), whose task is to control database usage by programmers and users.

The need for common values to establish relationships requires some duplication of data and thus some *controlled redundancy* (see earlier).

Benefits and drawbacks of databases in general

The following list details some of the generally accepted advantages and disadvantages.

❑   Apart from controlled redundancy, there is no unnecessary duplication of data as occurs in traditional filing systems. Apart from the economic advantage, this means that transactions can update all affected areas of the database through a single input.

❑ Because of the single input principle, there is less chance of inconsistency as may occur if the same transaction is keyed in several times to different files. Equally, of course, an incorrect entry will mean that all applications programs using the data will be working with the wrong data value.

❑ The opportunities for obtaining comprehensive information are greatly improved with a central pool of data.

❑ On-demand or ad hoc enquiries are possible through the use of a query language.

❑ Security opportunities are enhanced because access to a single database can be more readily controlled than is possible with a system based on numerous separate files. On the other hand, database design and creation is a complex process and the failure of a database affects all applications which make use of it.

Exercises

1. Suppose that the following data items are amongst those held in the personnel database of a multi-national organisation.

    Surname; Forename; DateOf Birth, Salary; Qualifications; JobTitle; Department; DepartmentAddress; HeadOfDepartment; Country.

    (i)   Suggest two, separate *logical record* structures (list the fields in each) which may be useful.

    (ii) Suggest a *primary key* for each of the logical record structures you described in (i).

    (iii) If the database is relational, how would connections be made between the two logical record structures you defined in (i)?

    (iv) What is the role of the database management system (DBMS) in relating the physical database to the logical record structures used by applications?

2. Distinguish between the terms *schema* and a *sub-schema*.

3. A database provides *data independence*. What does data independence mean and how is it beneficial for maintaining applications programs.

4. A particular company has separate departments to handle payroll and personnel information. The company operates a traditional file processing system, with each department maintaining its own files.

(i)   Give examples of data in these systems which may be duplicated

(ii)   Briefly explain how the feature of *controlled redundancy*, provided by a database system, would help reduce such duplication.

5. An academic database maintains the following information concerning students, departments, courses and tutors. Each student is assigned to a particular course and has one personal tutor. A tutor will be responsible for a number of student tutees. Each course operates in one of the five departments within the college and each department runs many courses. The system also records previous qualifications obtained by students.

(i)   Using the example in Figure 7.2 as a guide, draw a *Codasyl schema* to reflect the information held in the academic database.

(ii)   Using the example in Figure 7.3 as a guide, draw a diagram to illlustrate an *owner* and its *member* records in the academic database.

6. Pair those database terms which have the same meaning:

tuple; *domain*; *record*; *table*; *field*; *relation*.

7. A company maintains copies of customer records in two separate departments, sales and marketing.

(i)   In this context, give an example of *data inconsistency* and suggest how it might arise.

(ii)   If the customer information were held in a database and both departments used the database, how would this avoid data inconsistency?

Chapter 8
Information Technology in the Office

Introduction

This chapter looks at the ways in which Information Technology (IT) can help people, particularly those involved in office work, to operate more efficiently. The widespread use of portable computers, modems, pagers and mobile phones, for example, means that the 'office' does not have to be a fixed location and can be anywhere with access to telecommunications systems. The chapter does not deal with information processing applications such as invoicing and payroll, but with those which support staff in their work, such as document processing and electronic mail.

Document processing

Document processing systems include facilities to:

- ❑ minimise the production of *hard copy*;
- ❑ facilitate efficient *storage* and *retrieval* of documents;
- ❑ allow the incorporation of colour or monochrome text and graphics;
- ❑ allow different forms of data (*text, graphics, sound, video* or *animation*) to be inserted into the electronic version of a document;
- ❑ convert (*import* and *export*) documents into formats required by different document handling systems;
- ❑ enable *recovery* of electronic documents, either through *backup systems* of through the use of *scanning* equipment and *character recognition* software.

Document processing can be divided into:

- ❑ document production;
- ❑ document storage and retrieval.

Document production

The production of a document can involve the use of various kinds of computer software. Word processors enable the production of text, desktop publishing (DTP) packages (Chapter 17) permit the complex arrangement of text, imported from a word processor and the insertion of graphical images, such as clipart or drawings produced with another package. Many word processors have features normally associated with DTP packages and can be used for much the same purposes.

Although DTP and word processing packages often provide quite advanced drawing tools, the production of more sophisticated images may require the use of a computer-aided drawing (CAD) package.

These images can then be *embedded* in the word processor or DTP document. The most popular versions of software tend to allow the acceptance of the graphics and text *formats* of other packages. For example, CorelDRAW images can be embedded in a Microsoft Word document. Multi-tasking operating systems (Chapter 17), such as Microsoft Windows 3.x and 95 allow an embedded image to be edited by double clicking it, an action which then accesses the package which created it. Microsoft refers to this as object linking and embedding (OLE). Embedded items from other packages are often referred to as objects and other examples include spreadsheets, database tables, sound files, maps and video clips. Obviously, objects such as sound files and video clips are not of use for hard copy versions of a document.

Document production may be summarised as follows:

- ❑ text preparation;

- ❑ insertion of graphics and other objects;

- ❑ page design.

These processes are not necessarily sequential; for example, new text may be added after objects have been inserted or typographical errors may be identified and require correction after the page design process has been completed. Alternatively, page design may be tackled first, through the *setting of margins* and the creation of paragraph styles; this is often done when preparing documents such as publications, where consistency of design is paramount.

Text preparation

Dedicated word processing machines are now virtually obsolete and text preparation is carried out with a computer and word processing package. Most software is of the WIMP (Chapter 17) type and a mouse is an essential component, apart from the computer, screen, disk storage and printer. In the case of a new document, text is initially entered through the keyboard and stored on disk. Text can be automatically checked for spelling as text entry proceeds or on its completion. Errors can be corrected through keystrokes, frequently in combination with mouse-driven operations. For example, text can be marked and *copied* (leaving the original intact) or *dragged* (the original is *cut* and *pasted* into a new position in a single operation) of text to a new position. Once text entry is complete, it can be formatted in numerous ways, through the selection of alternative font styles and sizes, emboldening, italicising or underlining. Through the use of a *style palette*, pre-defined or user defined styles can be applied to paragraphs, thus avoiding the need to repeat a series of formatting operations and the possibility of inconsistency of styles throughout the document.

Insertion of graphics and other objects

Line drawings, clipart images, spreadsheet tables, sound files, database tables, maps and other images can be inserted into a document. Objects inserted, or *embedded*, from other packages can be edited, provided that the source package is installed on the same computer. Figure 8.1 shows an inserted spreadsheet object in the process of being edited.

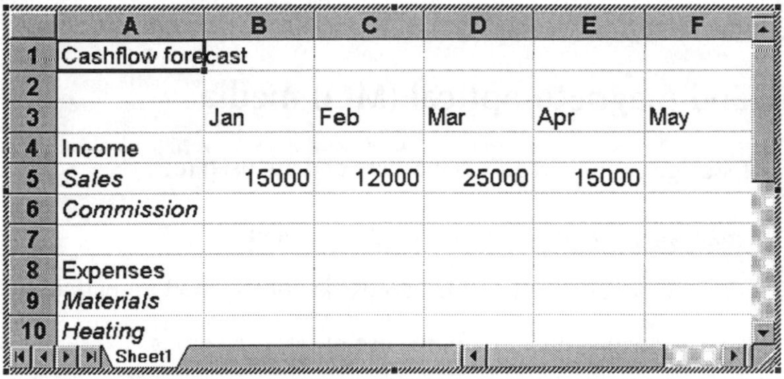

	A	B	C	D	E	F	
1	Cashflow forecast						
2							
3		Jan	Feb	Mar	Apr	May	
4	Income						
5	Sales	15000	12000	25000	15000		
6	Commission						
7							
8	Expenses						
9	Materials						
10	Heating						

Sheet1

Figure 8.1. *Editing an inserted spreadsheet object*

Inclusion of non-editable images

Not all inserted graphical images can be edited by a source package. For example, libraries of clipart held on CD-ROM can be used as a source of illustrations for any document, but are not linked to the package used to create them.

Page design

Page design facilities of word processors have been massively extended in recent years and vie with the specialised DTP package in sophistication. The following facilities are typical.

❑ Page setup. Options include setting of page size, orientation, margins, headers, footers and page numbering.

❑ Style palette. The palette holds paragraph styles for headings, main body text, bullets, numbered lists, figure and table captions, indents and so on.

A number of styles already exist and these can be altered, or new ones created and modified as required. Styles and page settings can be associated with a particular document (*style sheet* or *document template*) or be made available *globally*, to all documents.

The creation of document templates is important for an organisation, in that it ensures a consistency of corporate image.

Document storage and retrieval

The following forms of storage are commonly used:

❑   magnetic and magneto-optical media;

❑   optical media;

❑   microfilm.

Magnetic and magneto-optical (MO) media

These forms of storage provide read/write access and are used to:

❑   maintain *on-line* access to stored documents;

❑   *archive* documents to which access is not required immediately;

❑   *secure* documents through the use of backup copies.

A variety of storage media is available for *on-line* storage and rapid retrieval of document files. Most commonly, documents are held on a computer's main hard drive, although its location will depend on the system. For example, if the word processor is installed on a stand-alone microcomputer, documents are located on its internal hard drive, but in the case of a local area network (Chapter 24), documents may be stored centrally on a file server.

Not all documents need to remain immediately accessible and can be *archived* to another medium. The conventional floppy disk is adequate for most text files, but it has insufficient capacity to store graphical or other objects, unless they are stored in compressed form (the main drawback of this is the time taken to compress and decompress the files). A text file's size can be measured in kilobytes, but the insertion of graphical, sound or other images may increase its size to many megabytes. Floppy disk also provides extremely slow access times. A range of removable high capacity, quick access magnetic and magneto-optical (MO) media (Chapter 19) make ideal archive systems for documents containing graphical or other images. *Security* of storage ensures that if the main file is corrupted in anyway, a *backup* copy can be retrieved to replace it. Apart from the removable disk drives already mentioned, high capacity streamer tapes, in cassette form, are used to backup complete hard drives in a relatively short time.

Optical media

CD-ROM (compact disk, read only memory)

The CD-ROM is not used for storage of documents which require regular updating, because the medium cannot be written to by a CD-ROM drive; it is *read only*. However, the CD-ROM is widely used for reference material and training purposes, its huge capacity making it ideal for the storage of all forms of image, including video sequences, which take large amounts of storage space. The speed of CD-ROM drives is regularly being improved, although its access times cannot yet match those of magnetic hard drives. Manufacturers and traders can also store entire libraries of product details which can be accessed by organisations which buy them. Architects, technicians and designers can obtain access to libraries of specialised images for use in their work. Software is generally supplied on CD-ROM, so the CD-ROM drive is now standard equipment on computers.

CD-R (recordable compact disk)

The cost of CD-writers has fallen to an extent that even small organisations can afford to record their own CDs, perhaps in multi-media form, for training purposes. In such cases, the *authoring* process requires knowledge and skill in the use of suitable software if the multimedia aspects of CD-ROM storage are to be exploited.

A specialist company, with equipment to produce a glass master, normally carries out the production of multiple copies. Using a CD-writer to produce multiple copies is a relatively slow and expensive process and does not guarantee that every copy is identical to the original and error free.

Microform

As a celluloid medium, microform can store documentary information with textual and graphical content. The structure of the microform can be either *microfilm* (a continuous reel) or *microfiche* (a grid pattern). Microform reduces storage space requirements by approximately 95% of that required by paper documentation. There are two methods by which documentary information can be recorded on microform:

❑ by direct computer output (COM - computer output on microform). In this way, for example, text and other images can be recorded on microfilm, using a microfilm recorder;

❑ by photographic miniaturisation.

To read information stored on microform, a special projector can be used to magnify the image and display it on screen. Retrieval of documents stored on microfiche can be made more efficient, particularly where large numbers are involved, by using a computer to index, locate and retrieve individual documents, identified by unique codes. The computer uses indexing techniques to ensure an efficient search and retrieval process. This is known as computer-aided retrieval (CAR). Microform systems are becoming less popular because of the advances made in computer storage media, which can now provide the capacities needed for complex documentary information. Another reason for the decline in the use of microform is that the images cannot be edited, unless the computer version has been kept (which defeats the object of microform).

Information transmission

Documents and other types of information of electronic information, including data of all kinds and programs, can be transmitted over communication and computer networks (Chapter 24).

Telex

Telex is a long established communications system which, rather like the public telephone network, allows subscribers to communicate with one another. There are over a million subscribers in this country at present. Each subscriber is given a telex code (you will often see it at the top of business letter headings next to the telephone number) and must have a teleprinter which is a combination of keyboard and printer. There is no screen, so all messages sent or received are printed onto hard copy. The transmission rate of approximately 6 characters per second is slow compared with more modern telecommunications systems, but the limitations of keyboard entry and printer speed on the teleprinter make any faster speed unnecessary. The main benefit of telex is that a permanent record of communications is kept and the receiver does not have to be 'on the spot' when the message arrives. Its main disadvantage is that there is no storage facility for messages. Any transmission has to be printed as soon as it is transmitted so that if the receiver is faulty, the system comes to a halt. Although it is inferior to e-mail (see next section), it is still the only method (apart from telephone) of instant communication with less developed countries, where Telex machines are still widely used.

Electronic mail (e-mail)

E-mail systems based on computer networks are paper-less (except when a user requires hard copy). A major advantage is the facility for temporary message storage if a destination terminal is switched off, busy or has a temporary fault. When it is free, the terminal can receive any stored messages. Certain basic features are common to all e-mail systems:

    ❑   a terminal for preparing, entering and storing messages. The terminal will be 'intelligent', possibly a microcomputer, mainframe terminal or dedicated word processor. In any event, it should have some word processing or text editing facilities to allow messages to be changed on screen before transmission. A printer may also be available for printing out messages received over the system;

❑ an electronic communication link with other workstations in the network and with the central computer controlling the system;

❑ a directory containing the electronic addresses of all network users;

❑ a central mailbox facility (usually the controlling computer) for the storage of messages in transit or waiting to be retrieved.

Ideally, the following facilities are available to e-mail users:

❑ messages are automatically dated upon transmission;

❑ messages are automatically acknowledged as being received when the recipient first accesses it from the terminal;

❑ multiple addressing, that is the facility to address a message to an identified group, without addressing each member of the group individually;

❑ priority rating to allow messages to be allocated different priorities according to their importance.

Networks require two particular features in order to support e-mail:

❑ a message storage facility to allow messages to be forwarded when the recipient is available;

❑ compatibility with a wide range of manufacturers' equipment. Devices attached to a network have to be able to 'talk' to the communications network using protocols or standards of communication.

Benefits of e-mail

The following major benefits are generally claimed for e-mail systems:

❑ savings in stationery and telephone costs;

❑ more rapid transmission than is possible with conventional mail;

❑ e-mail can be integrated with other computer-based systems used in an organisation;

❑ all transmissions are recorded, so costs can be carefully controlled;

❑ e-mail allows staff to 'telework', that is, to work from home through a terminal;

❑ the recipient does not have to be present when a message is sent. Messages can be retrieved from the central 'mailbox' when convenient.

Voice mail

Voice Mail is a computer-based system, which answers, routes, and stores conventional phone calls. Callers' spoken messages are left in users' mail boxes, to be accessed as and when they are able. The system answers and processes calls according to the needs of the caller and the person and/or company being called. This is usually achieved with a 'voice manager', an application which provides callers with options to control the routing of their call, to leave a message, or to call another extension. The voice manager also gives the called party the option to automatically transfer or block calls. These options are selected through touch-tone buttons. The instructions and questions spoken by the automated attendant use voice processing techniques to appropriately combine a range of pre-recorded messages, including details provided by the users. The voice mail system is activated when the recipient fails to answer after a pre-determined number of rings. The caller is greeted by a pre-recorded message from the user, after which the voice mail options are provided. Organisations can use voice mail to direct callers to the correct department by asking a series of questions, to which the caller responds with touch-tone codes. If the caller does not need to speak directly to anyone, his or her recorded responses can be stored for future action. For example, callers can order goods or request product information. Some of the perceived benefits are as follows:

❑   Callers can always leave a message with a named user;

❑   Reduced call queuing for callers who do not need to speak directly to a user;

❑   A 24 hour telephone service can be provided, although outside office hours, no direct contacts are available

❑   Reduced use of message pads;

❑   Improved work-group communications;

❑   Users can manage their time more flexibly;

❑   Reduction in the number of switchboard operators;

❑   Reduced memo and business letter costs;

❑   Faster order entry, service response, etc.

❑   Increased customer service and satisfaction.

Possible disadvantages are:

❑   Temptation for users to leave the telephone unanswered and deal with recorded messages at their own convenience;

❑   Reduced caller satisfaction, if they rarely manage to speak directly to anyone and always have to leave recorded messages;

❑   Difficulties for users who receive many recorded messages, to which they have to listen and respond in batches.

❑   Tendency for users to only answer their own phone, leaving other phones in the same room to ring and then activate the voice mail system.

Teletex

Teletex is similar to Telex, except that transmissions are quicker and cheaper and text is not restricted to upper case characters. It uses the public telephone network, but can also access packet switching networks (Chapter 24) and the Telex system through *gateways*. International Teletex standards have been set and Teletex is now used in many countries throughout the world.

Electronic data interchange (EDI)

Similar to e-mail, EDI allows users to exchange business documents, such as invoices, delivery notes, orders and receipts over the telephone network. EDI can drastically reduce the volume of paperwork and business can be transacted much more quickly than is possible through the normal postal system.

UK examples of EDI systems are: Tradanet, linking manufacturers, wholesalers, distributors and retailers; Brokernet, which links insurance companies and brokers; Drugnet, linking medical practices to pharmaceutical companies, allowing the provision of current information on various products; Factornet allows firms to deal with *factors* who buy outstanding customer bills at a discount; the factors then obtain payment from the debtor. Small firms find this service particularly useful as it enables them to improve their cash flow.

Electronic funds transfer at point-of-sale (EFTPOS)

This service provides for the automatic debiting of customers' bank accounts at the checkout or point of sale. For example, many car petrol stations now have a device for reading the magnetic strip details on bank and credit cards. The system saves considerable time when contrasted with payments by cheque and, as an alternative to cash, it reduces the likelihood of theft. The retailer also has the assurance that the payment is authorised before the sale is made. Usually, a retailer will have a 'floor' limit, or amount above which a telephone call needs to be made to the credit card company for authorisation of payment.

EFT (electronic funds transfer)

This system is used to transfer money between the branches of the same bank and between different banks. In the UK, the system is known as the Banker's Automated Clearing Service (BACS). The service is not restricted to bank use; organisations can pay their employees' salaries directly into their bank or building society accounts. Business accounts can also be settled through this EFT system. Apart from the banks, other users usually link into the public switched telephone network (pstn) through a dial-up connection (unless the volume of data justifies a leased line).

Facsimile transmission (FAX)

This service allows the transmission of facsimiles or exact copies of documents or pictures through a data communications network. Using a fax machine connected to a telephone line, the user simply dials the fax number of the recipient, waits for the correct signal and the document is fed though the fax machine and transmitted. The fax machine sends picture elements or pixels obtained by scanning the document in a series of parallel lines; a synchronised fax machine at the other end prints a facsimile from those pixels. A *fax/modem*, attached to a computer can also send and receive facsimile images, with the advantage that no hard copy is required. Fax software can transmit a document directly from the word processor and when a fax is received, it can be examined with fax viewing software. Use of a fax/modem at one end of the link does not require that a fax/modem is at the other. Communications can take place with conventional fax machines, because the fax/modem is a dual-purpose component, with the ability to handle both fax transmissions and conventional computer communications, such as e-mail.

Exercises

1. A safari park is producing an electronic guide for potential visitors and publishing it on CD-ROM.

    (i)   Suggest examples of the use of vector and bit map images, sound, video and animation, in the electronic guide.

    (ii)   Explain the terms *import* and *export* and their significance for the production of the guide.

    (iii) How may object linking and embedding (OLE) be helpful when the guide needs to be updated?

    (v)   The management of the safari park have been told that they would be well advised to have a glass master of the CD-ROM produced, rather than producing multiple copies on their CD-writer. Why would they be sensible to take this advice?

2. Briefly describe the stages an e-mail message must go through, from its creation to its receipt and reading by the recipient (assuming over a wide area network).

3. Briefly describe the progress of a transaction at a supermarket checkout, from the point when the customer places the items on the conveyer belt, to the debiting of the customer's bank account.

Chapter 9
System Development

The system life cycle

In business, *systems analysis and design* is the process of investigating a business, existing or new, with a view to determining how best to manage the various procedures and information processing tasks that it involves. Though it frequently means considering the use of a computer system to replace some manual operations, this need not always be the case. The *systems analyst,* whose job it is to perform the investigation, might recommend the use of a computer to improve the efficiency of the information system under consideration, but he/she might equally well decide that a manual system is adequate, or even preferable. Thus, the intention in systems analysis is to determine how well a business copes with its current information processing needs, and whether it is possible to improve the procedures involved in order to make it more efficient, or more profitable, or both. Systems design involves planning the structure of the information system to be implemented. In other words, analysis determines what the system should do, and design determines how it should be done.

The job of the systems analyst starts with studying the current, or proposed, system; this involves collecting facts which will help the analyst to determine whether a computer would improve the information system, and if so, in what areas it would be most beneficial. Once the decision has been made to go ahead with a new or improved system, the analyst must develop a plan for putting the proposed system into practice. This includes specifying all the procedures involved, computerised or otherwise, how data is to be captured, what software will be required to process the data, what equipment will be necessary, what staff will be needed and how they will be trained, and so on. In other words, the analyst must provide a complete plan of every detail of the proposed system. A key feature of this complex task is communicating with staff, whether they are ordinary employees or managers. The people who work in the business are most likely to know what works and what does not, what causes problems and how they can be avoided, and where improvements to the current system are most necessary.

This chapter describes the *system development life cycle*, the sequence of activities involved in analysing, designing and implementing an information system. As well as systems analysts, who play key roles in the process, other personnel such as computer programmers and computer managers are also involved to a large degree. Though the steps are described separately, in practice they may be performed in a different order, or even be difficult to distinguish one from another; sometimes one part of the system will be in the process of being implemented while another is still being analysed. The cyclic nature of system development is illustrated in Figure 9.1. The system development stages illustrated in the diagram may be repeated a number of times during the life of a system. Each time a significant change or improvement is required, the cycle is repeated.

Figure 9.1. *System development life cycle*

Preliminary study

Before an organisation embarks on a costly project involving the development of a new information system, it is necessary to determine whether the system is possible to achieve and, if so, whether there will be sufficient benefits in doing so. The main part of this investigation is called a *feasibility study*. However, even before the feasibility study commences, it will be necessary to fully clarify what is being proposed. The systems analyst dealing with the proposal will talk with the people who have suggested the project in order to determine exactly what they have in mind and their reasons.

Once the proposal has been fully clarified, the feasibility study can be undertaken. The feasibility study is usually carried out by a team of people with experience in information systems techniques, with a knowledge of the type of system being proposed and who are skilled in systems analysis and design. The team will be responsible for determining whether the potential benefits of the proposed system can justify the costs involved in developing it. It may be that the consequences of not adopting the new system make the change essential. For example, if a company is unable, through volume of work, to deal with customers effectively, the latter may take their business to more efficient competitors. It then becomes essential to the company's survival to improve its information system.

The feasibility study must also establish whether the new system can operate with available technology, software and personnel. In most instances, for example where a currently manual system is to be replaced or improved by using a computer system, the existing technology will most probably exist, but a new, innovative idea might require hardware or software that don't exist. If this is the case, the feasibility study team will attempt to determine whether the new items can be developed within a reasonable time.

Finally, the team will consider how well the system will be received by the people who will have to use it. This must have been a prime concern, for instance, of the first analysts who considered the use of cash points such as those now commonly provided by banks and building societies: would customers trust them and would they be sufficiently easy to use?

Investigation and fact finding

If the feasibility study produces a favourable report, the next stage, that of making a detailed analysis of the current system, will commence. The systems analyst will investigate all aspects of the current system:

❑   what services are being offered;

❑   what tasks are being performed;

❑   how they are being performed;

❑   how frequently they are done;

❑   how well they are done;

❑   what staff are involved and the nature of their involvement

❑   what is lacking in the system;

❑   any faults with the system;

❑   how the system can be improved.

Finding the answers to these questions requires the analyst to talk to all the people involved in operating the current system, from ordinary employees to managers and directors. This will frequently involve the use of questionnaires as well as personal interviews with employees, the study of manuals and reports, the observation of current working practices, and the collection and study of forms and other documents currently used. As this process is going on, the analyst will be starting to form views on how the new system should work in order to overcome the problems with the current system. At the end of this stage, the systems analyst will thoroughly understand how the current system works and be in a position to begin to design and produce a specification for the new system.

System design

This stage produces the details of how the system will meet the requirements identified in the previous analysis stage. A major part of this stage involves identifying the inputs to the system (what they are and how they are to be captured), and the outputs from the system, such as reports, invoices, bills and statements. The designers will also specify in detail what files will be needed, their structures and what devices and media will be used to store them. All this information will be written down in the form of reports, tables and diagrams. Such diagrams as system flow charts and data flow diagrams will be used to show how the overall system is integrated. The system designers will also provide detailed specifications on what the software is required to do so that programmers in the next stage will have a clear idea of what they are expected to produce.

Software development

Depending on the system requirements, existing software may be purchased or it may be necessary to have software written specially. Software that is already available will usually be much cheaper than software that has to be custom-designed, but in many instances suitable software will not be available. Large organisations frequently employ their own systems analysts and programmers, but smaller firms may have to resort to using a software house for the necessary programs.

System testing

Before the system is put fully into operation, all aspects of it must be tested, not just the software that has been developed, but also the manual procedures involved. Personnel who have not been directly involved in developing the system will often be used to test the system after they have been given some appropriate training; such people may do things that were not anticipated by the system designers. In fact, the people testing the system will often deliberately attempt to make it fail in some way. It is vitally important to discover any serious shortcomings in the new information system before it is fully operational.

System documentation

System documentation serves much the same purposes as program documentation described briefly in the earlier section on software development. All aspects of the system's operation will need to be described in detail. The documentation will include:

- user manuals describing the operation of the system;

- technical manuals for the computer hardware;

- program documentation.

This documentation serves a number of purposes:

- ❑   To provide reference material for training purposes. This will be of value to all employees using the new system. Each task and procedure will be clearly detailed and explained to the relevant staff involved.

- ❑   To explain in detail how the system is intended to work so that the people using the system can cope with problems and unfamiliar situations. This will be of particular value to managers and supervisors responsible for organising the work.

- ❑   To specify how to test the system to ensure that it is working correctly.

- ❑   To make it easier to modify or improve the system in future.

Implementing the system

In this stage the system designers will actually install the new system, putting new equipment into operation, installing and setting up software, creating data files and training people to use the system. A common practice is to run the new system in parallel with the old one to ensure that if anything does go wrong, the business will not come to a grinding halt.

When the system has become fully operational, there will still be the possibility of unforeseen events causing problems. The system developers will therefore need to be available to deal with any problems that do arise, as well as making modifications as circumstances change. If an outside firm has developed the system, this *system maintenance,* normally will be subject to a separate financial arrangement such as an annual charge.

Monitoring and review

The final phase of the system development process is the assessment of the completed system. In this *review*, or *evaluation*, a number of factors are examined, including:

- ❑   How well the system is performing with reference to the needs that were initially identified.

- ❑   The final cost of the system compared to its original budget.

- ❑   The time taken to complete the work.

Even after the system is fully operational its performance is continually *monitored* throughout its life. At some stage, monitoring will identify needs that are no longer satisfied by the current system, and the system development process will begin once more with a preliminary study.

Exercises

1.   "The job of a systems analyst is to determine what a system should do and then design a computerised system to do it".

     Is this statement entirely correct? Give a reason for your answer.

2.   When a system is to be changed, suggest two reasons why users of the existing system should be closely consulted.

3.   (i)   What is the purpose of a *preliminary study*?

     (ii) At the *system design* stage, how do the programmers know what software they have to produce?

     (iii) "During *system testing*, the users are not involved".

           Is this statement correct? Give a reason for your answer.

4.   When the *system documentation* is produced, under what circumstances will there be no *program* documentation?

5.   Once a system is operational, it is assessed. List three features on which it may be assessed.

Chapter 10
The Feasibility Study

Introduction

The purpose of a feasibility study is to determine whether the potential benefits of a proposed system can justify the costs involved in developing it. There are many and various pressures which can 'trigger' the thought of using a computer, either for the first time or, where a computer is already installed, for other applications still operated manually. For example:

(i) The business is expanding and to cope with the increased workload it appears that the only alternative to computerisation is increased staffing.

(ii) The business is expanding at such a rate that more information is needed to manage it properly. To obtain the information manually is too time consuming and by the time it has been gathered is probably out-of-date.

(iii) Staff are being asked to work regular and increasing amounts of overtime and backlogs of work are building up.

(iv) Customers are complaining about the speed and quality of the service provided;

(v) Where stock is involved, it is difficult to keep track of stock levels and while some customer orders cannot be filled because of stock shortages, other stock is 'gathering dust' on the shelves;

(vi) a great deal of advertising literature is constantly reminding business management that they are out-of-date and at a disadvantage with their competitors;

(vii) other businesses providing a similar service use a computerised system.

Examples (i), (ii) and (iii) suggest that the business is operating successfully and needs to take on extra staff or streamline its systems. Examples (iv) and (v) may be symptomatic of generally poor business management. In such cases, computerisation alone may not solve the problems. Examples (vi) and (vii) may tempt the management to computerise simply "to keep up with the Jones's". Although a computerisation programme resulting directly from one or more such pressures may be completely successful and worthwhile, the pressure itself should not be the reason for computerisation. Instead, management should establish the business objectives they wish to achieve.

Establishing objectives for computerisation

It is important for management to establish what overall objectives they are trying to achieve, before identifying systems which contribute to their achievement. For example, two major business objectives may be to improve the delivery of customers' orders and to minimise stock levels (which tie up valuable cash resources). The achievement of these objectives may involve contributions from several different information systems. The list may include:

❑   stock control - records stock movements and controls stock levels;

❑   purchasing - responsible for the ordering of new supplies from suppliers;

❑   sales order processing - receives customers' orders and initiates the process of order fulfilment;

❑   purchase ledger - the accounting record of amounts owed and paid to suppliers of stock;

These and other applications within a business are interconnected by the information which flows between them. Such connections can be illustrated with the use of information flow diagrams.

Establishing priorities for computerisation

Although a data flow diagram may indicate the mutual involvement of several separate applications, it is not generally advisable or even practicable to attempt the computerisation of more than one or two applications at the same time. In any case, it is likely that some applications make a greater contribution to the achievement of the required business objectives than do the others. Thus, the applications which are going to bring greatest benefit to the business should be computerised first.

Establishing individual system objectives

Before any single application can be computerised, it is necessary to establish its objectives clearly because users may have become so used to its procedures that they no longer question their purpose. It is self-evident that, before any informed judgements can be made on the design of a system, the objectives of the relevant application must first be clearly understood. For example for stock control objectives may be:

❑   to maintain sufficient levels of stock to meet customer orders promptly;

❑   to provide a mechanism which removes the need for excessively high safety margins of stock to cover customer orders. This is usually effected by setting minimum stock levels which the computer can use to report variations below these levels;

- ❏ to provide automatic re-ordering of stock items which fall below mini-mum levels;

- ❏ to provide management with up-to-date information on stock levels and values of stocks held.

The Feasibility Report

The Feasibility Report should contain the following sections:

Terms of Reference. These should set out the original purpose of the study, as agreed by management and detail the business objectives to be achieved, for example:

- ❏ improvement of customer service, so that orders are delivered in 24 hours;

- ❏ the provision of more up-to-date management information on current stock levels and projected customer demand;

- ❏ a tighter control of the business's cash resources, primarily through better stock management.

Applications considered for computerisation. The applications which may assist the achievement of the business objectives set out in the Terms of Reference are listed, for exam-ple: stock control; purchasing; sales order processing; invoicing; accounts.

System investigations. For each application under consideration there should be:

- ❏ a description of the existing system;

- ❏ an assessment of its good and bad points. For example, the sales order processing system may be slow to process customer orders and this re-sults in poor delivery times, which in turn causes customers to take away their business;

- ❏ the costs of the existing system. For example, apart from the cost of staff-ing, an estimate has to be made of the cost of lost business, which could be avoided with an improved system.

Envisaged system requirements. This section should detail, in general terms, those aspects of each application which need to be improved and a broad outline of how each system may operate following computerisation. Of course, it is still possible that not all applications will benefit from computerisation and can be improved by other methods.

Costs of development and implementation. These will include both *capital* costs and *reve-nue* or running costs. Capital costs are likely to be incurred for: computer hardware; systems software and software packages; installation charges for hardware and software; staff training. Revenue costs include those for the maintenance and insurance of the system. In addition, computer specialists may need to be employed.

Time scale for implementation. This will depend on the scale of the operation, the type of application and whether packaged software is to be used.

Expected benefits. These are more difficult to quantify than the costs but may include, for example:

❑   estimated savings in capital expenditure on typewriters and photocopiers;

❑   more efficient stock management, allowing customer service to be maintained whilst keeping stock levels lower. This releases valuable cash resources and reduces possible interest charges on borrowed capital;

❑   expansion in business turnover, without the need for extra staff. Overtime requirements may also be reduced.

Other considerations. The staff have to support any development for it to be successful and this usually means consultation at an early stage in the feasibility study and the provision of a proper staff training programme. Customers must also be considered. For example, when a customer receives a computer-produced invoice it should be as easy to understand as the type it replaced. If the feasibility study concludes that computerisation is worthwhile (according to the criteria set out in the report) then more detailed investigation and design can be carried out.

Exercises

1.   The management of Bodgit plc, a DIY tools manufacturer, has identified a new *general business objective* for the next year: to cut the number of faulty units returned from retailers from 0·05% to 0·025% of their total annual production.

    (i)   List the *information systems* which are likely to contribute significantly to the achievement of that objective.

    (ii)   In respect of one of these information systems, list its specific objectives.

2.   Identify two *capital* and two *revenue costs* which may be incurred in developing and implementing a computerised system

Chapter 11
Systems Analysis and Design

Introduction

If the feasibility report supports a computerisation project, then a more detailed investigation of each candidate system begins. The facts gathered about each system will be analysed for their bearing on the design and implementation of a computerised version. The objectives of the analysis are to gain a thorough knowledge of the current way of working and to establish, in a fair amount of detail, the way in which a new system will operate. It is extremely important that the replacement system does not simply duplicate existing procedures. The design should, as far as possible, ignore existing departmental structures, which may inhibit the introduction of different and improved procedures. For example, it may be that customer credit limits are fixed by the Accounts Department and that Sales staff have to refer to the Accounts Department before accepting a customer order. A new system may allow Sales staff to access credit limits directly without reference to the Accounts Department. This method could be used in most cases and the computer could indicate any customer accounts which needed to be specially referred to the Accounts staff.

The aim of the investigation and design process is to produce a *system specification*.

Fact-finding methods

There are five main methods which can be used to gather facts about a system:

- interviewing;
- questionnaires;
- examination of records and procedure manuals;
- examination of documents;
- observation.

Each method has its own particular advantages and disadvantages. The method(s) chosen will depend on the specific circumstances surrounding the investigation. These may concern, for example, the size of the business, the number of staff employed, their location and distribution.

Interviewing

This method has much to recommend it, in that the facts can be gathered directly from the person or persons who have experience of the system under investigation. On the other hand, a business with a number of geographically distributed branches makes the process of extensive interviewing expensive and time-consuming. Further, interviewing skills need to be acquired if the process is to be effective. The interviewer needs to know how to gain the confidence of the interviewee and ensure that the information which is given is of value in the design of the new system. Questions need to be phrased unambiguously so that the interviewee supplies the required information. A checklist of points can help to ensure that all relevant questions are asked. Of course, the interview may need to 'stray' from the points in the checklist, if it becomes apparent that the interviewee is able to provide relevant information not previously considered. For example, clerical procedures may be designed quite satisfactorily but may be made less effective because of personality conflicts between staff. Such tensions may be revealed only through personal interview.

The interviewer also needs to detect any unsatisfactory responses to questions and possibly use alternative methods to glean the required information. Some possible unsatisfactory responses are given below:

□   refusal to answer. Such refusal may indicate, for example, that set procedures are not being followed and that the member of staff does not wish to be 'incriminated';

□   answer with irrelevant information. It may be that the question is ambiguous and has to be re-phrased in order to elicit the required information;

□   answer with insufficient information. If a system is to be designed which covers all foreseeable user requirements and operational circumstances, it is important that the analyst has all relevant information;

□   inaccurate answer. The interviewer may or may not be aware that an inaccurate answer has been given but it is important that other sources of information are used to cross-check answers.

Questionnaires

Questionnaires are useful when only a small amount of information is required from a large number of people. To provide accurate responses, questions need to be unambiguous and precise. The questionnaire has a number of advantages over the interview:

□   Each respondent is asked exactly the same questions, so responses can be analysed according to the pre-defined categories of information.

□   The lack of personal contact allows the respondent to feel at ease when providing information, particularly if responses are to be anonymous.

❑   Questionnaires are particularly suited to the gathering of factual information, for example, the number of customer orders received in one week.

❑   It is cheap, particularly if users are scattered over a wide geographical
area.

A number of potential disadvantages attach to the use of questionnaires.

❑   Questions have to be simple and their meaning completely unambiguous
to the respondents.

❑   If the responses indicate that the wrong questions were asked, or that they
were phrased badly, it may be difficult to clarify the information, particularly if the respondents were anonymous.

❑   Without direct observation it is difficult to obtain a realistic view of a system's operation. The questionnaire often provides only statistical
information on, for example, volumes of sales transactions or customer
enquiries.

Examination of records and procedure manuals

If existing procedures are already well documented, then the procedure manuals can provide
a ready-made source of information on the way procedures should be carried out. It is less
likely, however, that procedures will be documented in the smaller organisation. In any
event, it is important to realise that procedures detailed in manuals may not accord entirely
with what happens. The examination of current records and the tracing of particular transactions can be a useful method of discovering what procedures are carried out.

Special purpose records which may involve, for example, the ticking of a box when an activity has been completed, can be used to analyse procedures which are causing delays or are not
functioning efficiently. The use of *special purpose* records imposes extra burdens on staff
who have to record procedures as they happen and the technique should be used only when
strictly necessary.

Examination of documents

The analyst should examine all documents used in a system, to ensure that each:

(i)   fulfils some purpose, that is, it records or transmits information which is
used at some stage. Systems are subject to some inertia, for example, there
may have been a 'one-off requirement to record and analyse the geographical distribution of customers over a single month and yet the summary document is still completed because no-one told the staff it was no
longer necessary;

(ii)   is clear and satisfies its purpose. For example, a form may not indicate clearly the type of data to be entered under each heading. In any case, it may well require re-designing for any new system.

The documents, which should include, for example, source documents, report summaries, customer invoices and delivery notes, help to build a picture of the information flows which take place from input to output.

Observation

It is most important to observe a procedure in action, so that irregularities and exceptional procedures are noticed. Observation should always be carried out with tact and staff under observation should be made fully aware of its purpose, to avoid suspicions of 'snooping'. The following list details some of the features of office procedures and conditions which may usefully be observed during the investigation.

Office layout. This may determine whether the positioning of desks, filing cabinets and other office equipment is convenient for staff and conducive to efficient working;

Work load. This should indicate whether the volume of documents awaiting processing is fairly constant or if there are peak periods of activity;

Delays. These could show that there are some procedures which are constantly behind schedule;

Methods of working. A trained observer can, through experience, recognise a slow, reasonable or quick pace of working and decide whether the method of working is efficient. It is important that such observations should be followed up by an interview to obtain the co-operation of the person under observation;

Office conditions. These should be examined. Poor ventilation, inadequate or excessive temperatures or poor lighting can adversely affect staff efficiency.

Often the observation will be carried out in an informal way. It may be useful, sometimes, to work at a user's desk and observe directly the way that, for example, customer orders are processed. It is important to realise that a user may 'put on a performance' while under observation and that this reduces the value of the information gathered.

Documenting the results of analysis

A number of standard approaches, apart from narrative description, can be used to document the results of the system analysis, including:

❑   information flow diagrams;

   ❑   organisation charts;

   ❑   system flowcharts.

It is beyond the scope of this text to make a detailed examination of these standards but their use is illustrated in the following section which examines the categories of information needed to be gathered and recorded during the investigation.

Categories of system information

The major categories of information which need to be gathered involve: functional relationships and information flows; personnel and jobs; inputs; processes; outputs; storage.

The following sections examine each of these categories, which are relevant to both the analysis and design stages. The analysis of the present system naturally involves some of the design stages. In other words, while the analyst is investigating the current system, he or she is considering the design of the new system. The results of the investigation and design processes are recorded in specifications regarding, primarily, input, output and process.

Functional relationships and information flows

An organisation has a number of functional areas; typical business functions include Sales, Accounts, Stock Control and Purchasing. However, the computerisation of a system in one functional area cannot be carried out without considering its effects on the rest of the business. Information systems within a business interact with and affect one another. A business, as an entity, also interacts with and is influenced by individuals and organisations in the surrounding 'environment' and the organisation's individual information systems should be co-ordinated to allow the achievement of overall objectives.

The relationships between individual functional areas can be illustrated with the use of an information flow diagram (see Chapter 3)

Personnel and jobs

It is possible to design a computerised system without involving staff, but such a system is likely to be less successful, partly because users can provide valuable insights into the practical aspects of system operation and partly because they will feel less motivated if they have had little or no influence on the final design. A formal organisation chart can be used to gain an overall picture of staff relationships and responsibilities (an example is shown in Figure 11.1), but it should be remembered that designated and actual job responsibilities can differ radically. For example, it may turn out that a junior sales clerk is carrying out the checking of orders, which should be the responsibility of the sales supervisor.

Thus, it may be necessary for the analyst to draw an alternative informal organisation chart to show the actual working relationships of staff. Apart from identifying working relationships between staff, it is useful to draw up brief job descriptions so that consultation on individual system procedures can take place with the appropriate staff. For example, a job description for a sales clerk may include the following activities:

❑   completion of standard order forms;

❑   checking stock availability;

❑   notification of orders to Accounts.

Therefore, although the sales departmental manager may have knowledge of such procedures, the sales clerk will have practical experience of their operation and should be consulted.

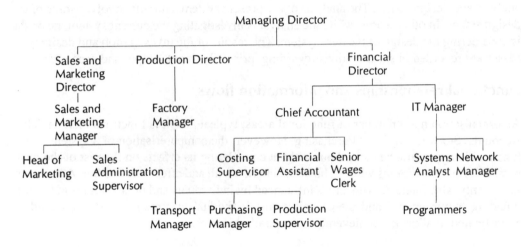

Figure 11.1. *Organisation chart*

System inputs

A number of details concerning the data inputs to a system need to be established, including the:

❑   *source* of the data. It may, for example, originate from a customer, a supplier, or another department in the organisation;

❑   *form* of the data. The data may arrive, for example, by telephone, letter, electronically (e-mail or fax) or a standard form such as an order form or supplier's invoice;

❑   *volume* of data and its *frequency*. For example, the number of orders received each day or week;

❏   *contents* of the data. For example, the individual items of data which appear on a supplier's invoice.

Such information allows the analyst to make recommendations on the most appropriate methods of computer input. The design of appropriate input methods also has to take account of several tasks involved with the collection and entry of data to a system:

❏   recording of data. For example, the completion of a customer order form following receipt of a customer order by telephone;

❏   transmission of the data for processing. For example, the order details may need to be transferred to another department or branch of the business for encoding and computer processing or they may be keyed in directly at the point of collection;

❏   checking of data for obvious errors and omissions. It may be, for example, that a customer order has no quantities entered;

❏   encoding of data into machine-readable form. Verification procedures need to be designed to prevent transcription errors when data is encoded onto a computer storage medium for processing;

❏   validation of data by computer. Data are checked by a data validation program against set limits of validity. For example, account numbers may have to fall between a particular range of values.

Thus, decisions need to be made concerning:

❏   data collection procedures;

❏   methods for the transmission of data to the place of processing;

❏   data entry, data verification and data validation procedures.

Data collection

The designer needs to be aware of the available input technologies. These can be divided into two categories, keyboard entry, and data capture technologies such as bar code reading, document scanning and optical mark reading (OMR), which allow direct input to the computer.

❏   Keyboard entry. This is the most common method of input and requires the transcription of data from source documents. These can be designed to minimise the possibility of transcription errors at the data collection stage.

❏   Direct input. Bar codes are pre-encoded and are thus immune from errors of transcription (if the bar code is correct in the first place). Optical mark reading requires that pencil marks are used to indicate particular values from a limited set on a pre-designed form. Although no keyboard entry is required, mistakes may be made by the originator of the document and good design is therefore important. Using an optical scanner (Chapter 19) and character recognition software, text can be entered into a word processor, without the need for keyboard entry (except to make corrections to the document). Voice input is also a practical option where a limited range of values needs to be entered.

Data transmission

It may be that no data transmission is necessary because the data is processed at the point of collection. For example, customer orders may be recorded on order forms at the sales desk and then taken into the next room for keying into the computer. Alternatively, the data may have to be transmitted some distance, perhaps to another floor of the building or to another building some miles away. A fundamental decision has to be made, whether to localise processing at the points of collection, or to use a central facility with data communications links from each location.

Data entry

The data entry method chosen will depend on the data collection methods used and may involve keyboard transcription from source documents or data may be captured directly (see Data Collection). Where keyboard transcription is used, verification and validation procedures (Chapter 13) are likely to be *interactive*; data entry operators have to respond to prompts on screen and make corrections whenever the system requires them. Most computer systems will be used for on-line processing, where transactions are processed immediately with master files at the data entry stage. Consequently, validation and verification have to be carried out immediately before the processing of each transaction.

On-screen verification

At the end of each transaction entry, the operator is given the opportunity to scan the data on the screen and to re-enter any incorrect entries detected. This usually takes the form of a message at the bottom of the screen which is phrased in a way such as "Verify (yes or no)".

On-screen validation

Character, data item and record checks, such as range and mode checks, can be made each time the key is pressed during data entry. For example, the screen may prompt for the entry of an account number, which must be 6 digits long and be within the range 000001 to 500000. Any entry which does not conform to these parameters is erased and the prompt re-displayed for another attempt. Appropriate screen dialogue to allow the data entry operator to enter into a 'conversation' with the computer is a crucial part of the interface design process.

Batch data entry

The type of keyboard transcription used will be affected by the type of input data. Where, for example, files need to be updated weekly, transaction data may be organised into batches and entered onto magnetic disk. Processing is carried out later in one update run.

System processes

All the clerical and machine-assisted processes, which are necessary to achieve the desired output from the given inputs, need to be identified. This will allow the systems analyst to determine the role of the computer in the new system, the programs necessary to take over the processing stages and the changes needed to clerical procedures, before and after computer processing. There are many instances when the processing requires not only the input data but also data retrieved from files. For example, to generate a customer invoice requires:

❑   input data concerning commodity codes and quantities ordered;

❑   data from the stock master file concerning prices of items ordered by reference to the input commodity codes;

❑   customer details from the customer master file.

The above processes can be completely computerised but other processes may require human intervention. For example, before a customer order is processed, the customer's credit status may need to be checked and referred to a supervisor before authorisation.

Document flow

Most processes involve the use of documents to allow the transmission of information from one stage to another. *System flowcharts* can be used to model the movement and interaction of documents and the data they record, as well as the processes involved, as they pass from one functional area or department of the business to another. So that the involvement of each section, department or personnel grouping in the processes can be identified, the system flowchart is divided into columns representing these divisions of responsibility. A system flowchart may use a range of standard symbols. some of which are illustrated in Figure 11.2.

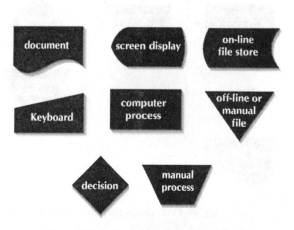

Figure 11.2. *System flowchart symbols*

The range of symbols used depends on which stage of the investigation and design process has been reached. For example, in the early stages of investigation of an existing manual system, there will be no representation of computer methods of input, processing, output or storage. At a later stage, when computer methods are considered, other symbols are needed. Figures 11.3, 11.4 and 11.5 show example system flowcharts. Figure 11.3 illustrates a manually operated order processing and invoicing system.

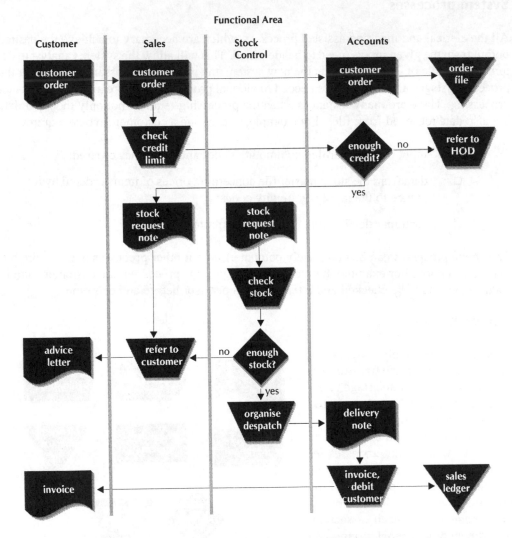

Figure 11.3. *Flowchart of manual order processing and invoicing system*

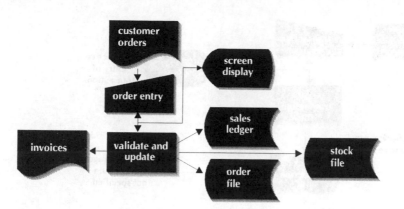

Figure 11.4. *System flowchart for on-line order processing and invoicing*

Decisions

Most business systems require alternative actions to be taken dependent upon some variable condition or circumstance. For example, 15 per cent customer discount may be allowed if the invoiced amount is paid within, say, 14 days of the invoice date, after which time all discount is lost. Figure 11.3 includes two decision symbols, one which poses the question "enough credit?" and the other "enough stock?"; the system must be able to handle the situations which arise when, for example, there is not enough stock to fulfil an order. Note that the decision box only allows two paths, one for "yes" and the other for "no".

So that computerised and non-computerised processes can be properly designed, the investigation must identify all:

❑   *decisions* made during system operation;

❑   *conditions* and circumstances which lead to alternative decisions;

❑   *actions* to be taken following a decision. Some decisions and consequent actions will need to be documented for clerical procedure guidelines. Others, which involve computer processing, will form part of program specifications used in program writing or as bases for choosing packaged software.

Figure 11.4 represents the computerised aspects of a system which fulfils a function similar to that illustrated in Figure 11.3 ; it does not detail procedures needed to prepare, for example, the data for input or the distribution of output.

A computerised system must have the necessary clerical procedures to support it. Figure 11.5 represents a batch processing update of a stock master file. Notice the sorting and validation stages which are essential to this type of system (see Chapter 13).

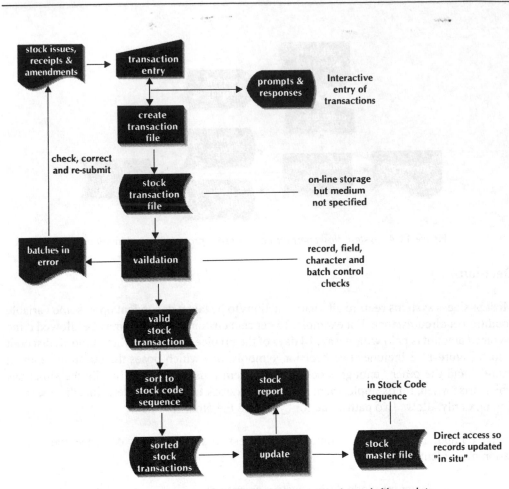

Figure 11.5. *System flowchart for batch processed, stock file update*

System outputs

Output design requires identification of the:

❑ data items required as output. Some may be revealed in the existing system, whilst others may be requested by users as being desirable in any new system;

❑ form of the output, for example, whether or not printed copy is required;

❑ volume and frequency of data with each output. This information assists decisions on the type and number of output devices required.

Using the above information, the following tasks can be carried out:

❑ selection of an appropriate output device to display or communicate the outputs. Available technologies are described in Chapter 19.

❑   designing screen and document layouts.

System storage

The storage of historical and current information is a vital part of any business system. For example, to produce a payslip requires not only transient input data, concerning hours worked and sickness days. Also needed are the relevant figures for rate of pay, tax code, deduction of tax and superannuation to date. These are held in the payroll *master file* (Chapter 4) stored on magnetic disk or tape. Information on the contents of files is gathered from existing manual files. Users should be consulted about their output requirements. If packaged software is to be used then the contents of files will be dictated by the package, in which case some data item types may be surplus to requirements, whilst others which are required may not be available.

File contents

Each file consists of a number of logical records, each of which has a number of associated data items. For example, each stock record in a stock master file may include:stock code; description; unit price; minimum stock level; re-order quantity; quantity in stock.

File sequence or organisation

This concerns the logical ordering of records within a file. Organisation methods are described in Chapter 5, but a number of possibilities and considerations are given below.

❑   The file can be organised in a particular sequence so that the output is readily available in that order. For example, it may be convenient for a file of clients paying annual subscriptions for a magazine to be stored in date order rather than client number order.

❑   The input may be presented in a particular order and sequencing the file in the same order will save re-sorting the input data.

❑   File access requirements may be entirely random so no particular sequence is needed.

File access methods

The output requirements of users and the data requirements of processes will determine the choice of access method, of which there are three:

Serial. The complete file is accessed according to its physical sequence. This is of use only when a transaction file is created immediately before it is sorted and processed against the relevant master file.

Sequential The complete file is processed according to its logical sequence. Magnetic disk allows direct access to individual records, even if they are not physically next to one another. Thus, for example, a stock file organised in stock number order may be accessed in that sequence, even though records may be physically distributed all over the disk.

Random Records are accessed in no particular sequence. Both indexed sequential and randomly organised files allow random access. Random access is appropriate where access requirements are rarely in any sequence and rapid system response is needed.

Relational database management systems (RDBMS)

An increasingly popular alternative to traditional file processing systems is to construct databases controlled by a relational DBMS. The design process requires that data is analysed according to subject area, for example, raw materials or staffing, rather than by department or functional area. Relational database systems are described in Chapter 7.

Choice of storage device

All computer systems provide direct access storage, generally in the form of magnetic disk. Even where random access files are not needed, there is little choice to be made, except in terms of capacity and speed of access. A full description of the various storage technologies is given in Chapter 19.

Exercises

1.   Universal plc has offices all over the world.

   (i)   Identify two advantages and two drawbacks for Universal of each of the following fact-finding methods: *interviewing*; *questionnaire*.

   (ii)   Suggest an IT system which may support each of these methods.

2.   Study the *systems flowchart* in Figure 11.5 and answer the following questions.

   (i)   What three types of *transaction* enter the system?

   (ii)   Why is *validation* carried out after transactions have been entered and stored?

   (iii) Are transactions applied to the master file *randomly* or *sequentially*?

   (iv)   Upon what type of *storage medium* must the stock master file be stored?

Chapter 12
System Implementation and Maintenance

System implementation

Although a new system often aims to reduce the workload of users in the long run, during the implementation period, it is usual to continue with the work of the existing system in parallel until the new system is fully tested. Additionally, staff will be occupied with activities needed to introduce the system, such as converting files to computer storage media, reading user documentation and following training programmes. There are several clearly identifiable areas of activity in the implementation of a new system:

❑ development and testing of software;

❑ conversion of files;

❑ education and training of staff;

❑ introduction of new clerical procedures;

❑ the changeover – 'going live'.

Development and testing of software

At the end of the design stage, the programmers are presented with *a program specification*, which sets out the system requirements, in terms of what the computer is required to do. Using a programming language, the programmers develop software to satisfy the requirements of the specification. The program specification also includes a *testing plan*, which uses carefully selected input data to test the working of the software for reliability and accuracy of output.

File conversion

All records to which the computer requires access have to be encoded onto magnetic media. These may include, for example, customer, stock and order records. The encoding of large files is a time-consuming process. In addition, 'live' transaction data will change the values in the master files, so encoding may need to be done in stages. In a stock control system, for example, records for certain categories of stock item may be encoded and computer processed, leaving the remainder to be processed by existing methods and encoded at a later stage. If a business has inadequate staffing to cope with the encoding exercise, a computer bureau may be used. Where possible, the bureau's staff should carry out the work on site because the records will be needed for the continued operation of the business. In favourable circumstances, a large scale encoding exercise may be undertaken initially to create the file and then, through an application program, transactions which have occurred since the encoding began, can be used to update the file to reflect the correct values. Users will have to be made aware of which records have already been encoded into the system, so that they can properly update them as transactions occur.

An additional problem is that records in their existing state may not conform with the file layouts designed for the new system and the data may have to be copied onto special-purpose input forms to assist with accurate encoding.

Education and training of staff

The education and training of the system's users is vital if it is to be operated correctly and the full benefits are to be obtained. Management staff need to be educated, so that they can recognise the ways in which the system can meet their information requirements. Generally, managerial staff do not carry out routine data entry, but often make use of computers, for example, to produce budgets, gather ad hoc reports and communicate though e-mail. The training requirements of managerial staff will differ from those of operational staff, but they will still need training.

The main categories of staff requiring training include:

- management;
- clerical;
- data control and data preparation;
- computer operations.

By the time a system is ready to 'go live', all involved staff should be competent to operate it efficiently. They should also have sufficient knowledge to assess its effectiveness, that is, answer the question, "Does it do what it is supposed to reliably and at the right time?".

Deciding when to carry out training can be difficult. If too early, some staff will have forgotten what they have been taught by the time the system is introduced. If too late, staff may feel panicked, because they have not been properly prepared. Training programmes should, as far as is possible, be designed to suit the working conditions of staff and the time-scale for implementation. It may be that residential courses will be needed for supervisory staff, who can then carry out 'in house' training of subordinate staff. This latter task may necessitate some staff working overtime, because the existing system may still have to be operated prior to implementation and for some time afterwards, during a period of 'parallel running'.

Introduction of new clerical procedures

The software only forms part of the whole information processing system. To function correctly, the correct clerical procedures need to interface with it, in a complementary way. Testing of a system's operation should also cover manual procedures, such as the preparation and handling of source documents, the batching of input and the preparation of control totals, prior to input. The system's performance in dealing with errors and the production of the planned outputs should also be tested.

System testing

Before a system is made fully operational it should be thoroughly tested, generally in stages. If reputable and popular packaged software is being used, then provided it is being used with a wholly compatible hardware configuration, its reliability can probably be assumed. It is essential, however, that the user tests the system with real data from the business. With tailor-made systems, the testing needs to be more complex and lengthy.

Once the reliability of the system has been tested, the user should run it with historical data, for which the results of processing are already known. The computerised results can then be checked for accuracy and consistency against the known manual results.

Going live

Switching from the old to the new system can be carried out in stages or all at once. There are three generally recognised approaches to going 'live':

- ❑ parallel running;

- ❑ pilot running;

- ❑ direct changeover.

Parallel running

With this approach, the old and new systems are run concurrently and the results of each are compared with the other for accuracy and consistency. The old system is not abandoned until the user has complete confidence in the reliability and accuracy of the new one.

Obviously, parallel running places a great administrative strain on the business, because staff are doing many of the jobs twice. Any inconsistencies in results have to be cross-checked and the source of errors located (they may result from the old or the new system).

The major advantage of parallel running is that the old system can be used whenever the computer system 'crashes', or fails to function as it should. However, the two systems cannot operate together indefinitely and 'Murphy's Law' may well ensure that some errors become apparent only after the old system has been abandoned.

In conclusion, it can be said that parallel running provides the safest method of going 'live' but it is extremely expensive and time consuming. It is unlikely that many businesses will use this method for any extended period, except where system failure would be completely catastrophic for the business.

Pilot running

This strategy requires that only a portion of 'live' transactions go through the new computerised system, whilst the rest are processed by the old method. Thus, for example, the transactions for one section of the business, or a sample of transactions from the whole business could be used to test the system. This is a reasonably safe strategy but again, the transactions which cause errors may be amongst those which do not pass through the computer system.

Direct changeover

This is the riskiest option in that the new system completely replaces the old, without any interim parallel or pilot running. The major benefit of this method is that there are none of the administrative costs involved with the other two methods. There is however, a severe potential cost, in that system failure could mean complete loss of data access and possible loss of business.

To minimise the risk of failure, careful system testing and thorough staff training should precede changeover. It is also helpful if the changeover is carried out during a slack period so that staff are not under pressure. The considerable cost of parallel and pilot running means that this, the riskiest strategy, is often used in small businesses.

System maintenance

After its initial introduction, a system will not remain static. Dealing with necessary changes to a system is termed 'system maintenance'. Problems will probably become apparent as the system is operated but even if they do not, the information needs of the business will probably change after a time. Some changes will come from within the business, as staff and management identify new possibilities for the system. Others may be forced upon the organisation because of changes in the external environment, for example, competitor strategies or government legislation.

The most important catalyst for change is probably the desire for better and more timely information by management, to assist their decision-making and planning.

Maintenance may concern updating of hardware or amendment of software. The hardware should be capable of being upgraded. It is unusual for commercial packages to be altered, unless they have been specially written for a business. Often, where packaged software is used the manufacturer provides free, or more usually for an additional payment, upgraded versions of the software (this can be a supplier-led method of system maintenance).

System review

The systems analyst should regularly review each system with the relevant managers, at least once a year. A system's performance should be evaluated against its current user requirements and if disparities are found, then the cause has to be identified. It may be that the system's original specification has to be changed, or it may be that the inadequacies are caused by improper implementation. There are several signs of inadequacy:

❑   output which is repeatedly behind schedule;

❑   a regular backlog of input documents awaiting attention;

❑   a significant increase in error rates;

❑   negative comments from system users, regarding its performance or effectiveness;

❑   positive suggestions for improvement from system users;

❑   related information systems being kept waiting for data from the offending system;

❑   customer complaints, or loss of business, resulting from poor service;

❑   the necessity for regular, excessive staff overtime, to clear work backlogs.

Thus, regular system reviews are necessary, if the need for system maintenance is to be identified quickly and remedial action taken.

Exercises

1. What is the function of a *test plan* in a program specification?

2. Using a sales order processing system as an example, identify two difficulties for system users at the *file conversion* stage.

3. (i)   Suggest two alternatives an organisation may choose from when considering *staff training* for a new system.

    (ii)   Identify one advantage and one drawback of each alternative.

4. Acme plc is introducing a new customer invoicing system. It is vital that there is continuity between the old and the new systems. Short-term failure of the system would cause extreme difficulty, but any extended failure would be catastrophic.

    (i)   Identify the *changeover* alternatives and select the most appropriate for Acme plc.

    (ii)   After implementation, suggest three signs which would indicate that the invoicing system needs to be *reviewed*.

Chapter 13

System Controls

Introduction

Computerised systems present particular problems for the control of data entering the system, because for much of the time, it is not in human-readable form. Even when it is stored, the data remains invisible until it is printed out or displayed on a screen. If proper system controls are not used, inaccurate data may reach master files, or unauthorised changes to data may be made, resulting in decision-making based on incorrect information. System controls can be divided into three main categories, according to the purposes they serve:

- ❑ data control;
- ❑ data security.

Data control

Controls should be exerted over:

- ❑ input;
- ❑ file processing;
- ❑ output.

Controls can be implemented by:

- ❑ clerical procedures;
- ❑ software procedures.

It is only through the combined application of both clerical and software controls that errors can be minimised. Their entire exclusion can never be guaranteed.

Input controls

Before describing the types of control, it is necessary to outline the activities which may be involved in the collection and input of data. Depending on the application, these may include the following.

❑ Source document preparation. To ensure standardisation of practice and to facilitate checking, data collected for input, for example, customer orders, are clerically transcribed onto specially designed source documents.

❑ Data transmission. If the computer centre is geographically remote from the collection point, data is transmitted through a telecommunications link.

❑ Data encoding and verification (see Verification). This involves the transcription, usually through a keyboard device, of the data onto a storage medium such as magnetic tape or disk. A process of machine verification, accompanied by a repeated keying operation, assists the checking of keying accuracy.

❑ Data input and validation. Data validation is a computer controlled process which checks data for its validity, according to certain pre-defined parameters, so it must first be input to the computer. The topic of validation is examined in more detail later.

❑ Sorting. In order to improve the efficiency of processing, input data is sorted into a sequence determined by the primary key of each record in the relevant master file (see Computer Files). This is always necessary for efficient sequential processing, but direct access files allow records to be processed by transactions in the order that they are received.

Transcription of data from one medium to another, for example, from telephone notepad to customer order form, or from *source document* (for example, an order form or requisition) to magnetic disk, provides the greatest opportunity for error. A number of strategies can be adopted to minimise input errors, including:

❑ Minimising transcription. This may involve the use of automated input methods, such as bar code reading and *turnaround* documents. These are forms which the information system produces as output and which can at a later date be returned to the system as input. For instance, a mail order book club might periodically produce a combined invoice and statement for its customers and, at the same time, attach an order form as shown in Figure 13.1. The customer completes the order form by entering the catalogue codes in the boxes provided and then returns the document together with the amount due in an addressed envelope provided by the club. Notice that the club member needs only to enter the catalogue code numbers for his or her book selections; even the membership number has been printed on the order form to prevent members from either forgetting about it or getting it wrong.

❑ designing data collection and input documents in ways which encourage accurate completion. The turnaround document in Figure 13.1 is a good example.

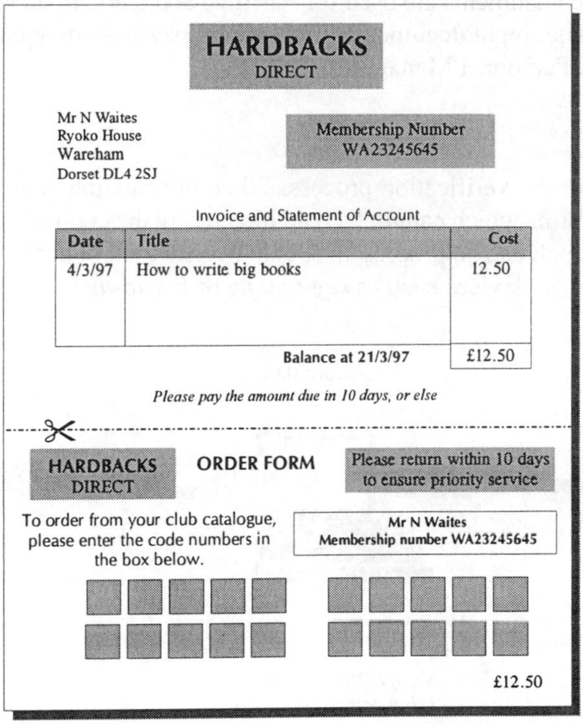

Figure 13.1. *Turnaround document example*

☐   using clerical checking procedures such as the re-calculation of totals or the visual comparison of document entries with the original sources of information;

☐   using codes of a restricted format, for example, customer account numbers consisting of two alphabetic characters, followed by six digits. Such formatted codes can easily be checked for validity;

☐   employing batch methods of input which allow the accumulation and checking of batch control totals, both by clerical and computerised methods (see Data Control in Batch Processing);

☐   using screen *verification* (visual checking of input on screen) before input data is processed and applied to computer files.

☐   checking input data with the use of batch or interactive screen validation (see Validation) techniques;

☐   ensuring that staff are well trained and that clerical procedure manuals are available for newly trained staff;

☐   controlling access to input documents. This is particularly important where documents are used for sensitive applications such as payroll. For example, input documents for changing pay rates may be available only to the Personnel Manager.

Verification

Figure 13.2 illustrates the verification process. When information is gathered using source documents such as forms which cannot be read directly by the computer, it needs to be converted into a form which can be processed. A common method of performing this task is by means of *key-to-storage* devices such as *key-to tape* or *key-to-disk*.

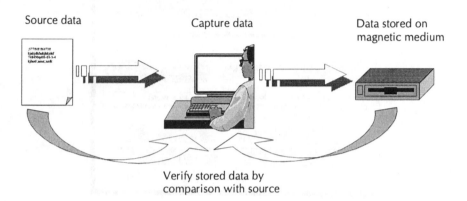

Figure 13.2. *Verifying source data*

The data are entered using a workstation consisting of a keyboard and monitor. As data are typed in they are displayed on the screen and stored on the magnetic storage medium (tape or disk). This process is error prone - it is a very easy matter for workstation operators to omit characters or type them in the wrong order - so, before the data are processed by the computer, it is usual to verify them by re-typing the data using the same source documents but with the key-to-storage device in *verify mode*. In this mode, the data is typed in a second time and compared with that typed in originally, and any differences are signalled to the operator who is then able to make the appropriate corrections.

Validation

This process is carried out after the data has been encoded onto an input medium and involves a *data vet* or *validation program*. Its purpose is to check that data falls within certain parameters defined by the systems analyst. A judgement as to whether data is valid is made possible by the validation program, but it cannot ensure complete accuracy. This can only be achieved through the use of all the clerical and computer controls built into the system at the design stage. The difference between validity and accuracy can be illustrated with a simple example. A company has established a Personnel file and each record contains a field for the Job Grade. The permitted values are A, B, C, or D. An entry in a record may be *valid* and accepted by the system if it is one of these characters, but it may not be the *correct* grade for the individual worker concerned. Whether a grade is correct can only be established by clerical checks or by reference to other files. During systems design, therefore, *data definitions* should be established which place limits on what constitutes valid data. Using these data definitions, a range of software validation checks can be carried out. Some typical validation checks are outlined below.

Size. The number of characters in a data item value is checked; for example, a stock code may consist of 8 characters only.

Range. Data must lie within maximum and minimum values. For example, customer account numbers may be restricted within the values 00001 to 10000.

Format checks. Data must conform to a specified format. Thus, a stock code designated as having 2 alphabetic characters, followed by 4 numeric digits must always be entered this way. Any other arrangement is rejected.

Consistency. Data items which are related in some way can be checked for the consistency of their relationship. For example, in a personnel file, any employee aged 25 years or over must be contributing to the company superannuation scheme. Conversely, employees under the age of 25 years cannot be members of the superannuation scheme. Any record which does not show such consistency indicates that either the age or the superannuation entry is incorrect.

Check digit. An extra digit calculated on, for example, an account number, can be used as a self-checking device. When the number is input to the computer, the validation program carries out a calculation similar to that used to generate the check digit originally and thus checks its validity. This kind of check will highlight transcription errors where two or more digits have been transposed or put in the wrong order. One of the commonest methods of producing a check digit is the modulus 11 algorithm. The following example serves to illustrate its operation.

Consider a stock code consisting of six digits, for example 462137.

The check digit is calculated as follows:

1.   Each digit of the stock code is multiplied by its own *weight*. Each digit has a weight relative to its position, assuming the presence of a check digit in the rightmost position. Beginning from the check digit (x) position the digits are weighted 1, 2, 3, 4, 5, 6 and 7 respectively as shown in Table 13.1.

Stock Code	4	6	2	1	3	7	(x)
Multiplied by Weight	7	6	5	4	3	2	(1)
Product	28	36	10	4	9	14	

Table 13.1.

2.   The products are totalled. In this example, the sum produces 101.

3.   Divide the sum by modulus 11. This produces 9, remainder 2.

4.   Subtracting the remainder 2 from11 gives a check digit of 9.

Whenever, a code is entered with the relevant check digit, the validation software carries out the same algorithm, including the check digit in the calculation. Provided that the third stage produces a remainder of zero the code is accepted as valid. This is proved in Table 13.2, using the same example as above.

Stock Code	4	6	2	1	3	7	9
Multiplied by Weight	7	6	5	4	3	2	1
Product	28	36	10	4	9	14	9

Table 13.2.

The sum of the products in Table 13.2 is 110, which when divided by 11, gives 10, remainder 0. Therefore, the number is valid.

If some of the digits are *transposed* (swapped around) the check digit is no longer applicable to the code and is rejected by the validation program because the results of the algorithm will not leave a remainder of zero. This is shown in Table 13.3.

Stock Code	6	4	1	2	3	7	9
Multiplied by Weight	7	6	5	4	3	2	1
Product	42	24	5	8	9	14	9

Table 13.3.

The sum of the products in Table 13.3 equals 111, which when divided by 11, gives 10, remainder 1. The number is, therefore, invalid.

File processing controls

Once validated data have entered the computer system, checks have to be made to ensure that they are: (i) applied to the correct files; (ii) consistent with the filed data.

Header records

Files can have header records which contain function, for example, Sales Ledger, version number and *purge date*. The purge date indicates the date after which the file is no longer required and can be overwritten. Thus, a file with a purge date after the current date should not be overwritten. Such details can be checked by the application program, to ensure that the correct file is used and that a current file is not accidentally overwritten.

File validation checks

Some validation checks can be made only after data input when reference can be made to the relevant master file data. Such checks include:

❑ new records. When a new record is to be added to a master file, a check can be made to ensure that a record does not already use the record key entered;

❑ deleted records. It may be that a transaction is entered, for which there is no longer a matching master record. For example, a customer may order a product which is no longer supplied;

❑ data consistency checks. A check is made that the transaction values are consistent with the values held on the master record which is to be updated. For instance, an entry to indicate maternity leave would obviously be inconsistent with a record for a male employee.

Data integrity

The printing of all master file changes allows the user department and auditors to check that all such changes are authorised and consistent with transaction documents. All data used by applications for *reference* purposes should be printed periodically. Price lists, for example, may be held as permanent data on master files, or in table form within computer programs.

Output controls

It might reasonably be supposed that input and file processing controls are sufficient to ensure accurate output. Nevertheless, a number of simple controls at the output stage can help to ensure that it is complete and is distributed to the relevant users on time. They include:

❑ the comparison of filed control totals with run control totals. For example, when an entire sequential file is processed, the computer counts all records processed and compares the total with a stored record total held in a *trailer record* at the end of the file;

❑ the reconciliation of control totals specific to the application with totals obtained from a related application. For example, the total sales transactions posted to the Sales Ledger in one day should agree with the total sales transactions recorded in the Sales Day book for that day;

❑ the following of set procedures for the treatment of error reports;

❑ the proper checking and re-submission of rejected transactions.

Data control in batch processing

Batch processing involves the processing of batches of input data at regular intervals. The data is generally of identical type. Examples include customer orders or payroll details. Although generally associated with large organisations using mainframe or minicomputer systems, the technique is equally applicable to microcomputer-based systems. The controls used combine both clerical and software methods and are briefly as described below.

Batch totals - clerical preparation

Batch totals allow the conciliation of clerically-prepared totals for a batch of transactions, with comparable computer-produced totals. Following the arrangement of source documents into batches, totals are calculated on add-listing machines for each value it is required to control. On an order form, for example, quantities and prices may be separately totalled to provide separate control totals. Totals may also be produced for each account number or item code, simply for purposes of control, although otherwise they are meaningless. For this reason, such totals are called 'hash' or 'nonsense' totals.

The totals are recorded on a *batch control record* (see Figure 13.3) attached to the batch, together with a value for the number of documents in the batch and a batch serial number. The batch serial number is kept in a register held by the originating department so that missing or delayed batches can be traced.

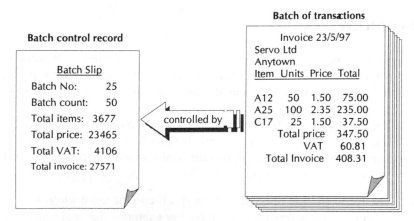

Figure 13.3. *A batch of transactions with a batch control record*

Batch totals - software checking

The details from each batch control record are encoded, with each batch of transactions, onto the storage medium. The resulting *transaction file* thus consists of a series of transactions, with each batch being preceded by the relevant batch totals. A *validation program* then reads the transaction file from beginning to end, accumulating its own comparable batch totals for each batch as it proceeds. At the end of each batch, the validation program checks its accumulated totals with the clerically-prepared totals and reports any which are in error. Rejected batches and associated batch totals must be re-checked and corrected where necessary, before re-submission. The corrections should be carried out by the originating user department. Where volumes of input are not particularly large, involving say, two staff for an hour each day, a modified version of the full-scale batch processing method may be used. Thus, when batch totals do not agree, only erroneous transactions are re-submitted. A validation program should also check individual data items against pre-defined limits. Such validation can be carried out as part of the batch processing system described above or *interactively* (through screen/keyboard dialogue between the computer and the data entry operator) as data is entered.

Security

The controls used for data security have several main functions, which are the:

☐　prevention of data loss caused by software or procedural errors, or by physical hazards;

☐　protection of data from accidental or deliberate disclosure to unauthorised individuals or groups;

☐　protection of data from accidental or deliberate corruption or modification. This is known as the maintenance of *data integrity*;

☐　to protect the rights of individuals and organisations to restrict access to information which relates to them and is of a private nature, to those entitled or authorised to receive it. This is known as data privacy.

Security against data loss

The loss of master files can bring extremely serious consequences for a business, so properly organised security procedures need to be employed. Evidence indicates that, among business organisations that have lost the major part of their information store, a large percentage subsequently fails. The main causes of data loss are as follows.

☐　Environmental hazards, such as fire, flood and other natural accidents.

☐　Mechanical problems. For example, a magnetic disk can be damaged by a faulty drive unit.

☐　Software errors resulting from program 'bugs'.

☐　Human error. For example, a wrong file may be loaded, or a disk mislaid or damaged.

☐　Malicious damage. It is not unknown for disgruntled staff to intentionally damage storage media, or to misuse programs at a terminal.

The standard solution to such problems is to take regular copies of master files and to store them in a separate, secure location. It is also necessary to maintain a record of transactions affecting a file since the last copy was taken, so that if necessary, they can be used to reconstruct the latest version of the file.

Magnetic tape file security

When a tape transaction file updates a tape master file, the physical nature of the medium makes it necessary for a new tape file to be produced. As Figure 13.4 illustrates, the updating procedure provides a built-in security system referred to as the Grandparent, Parent and Son (generation) System.

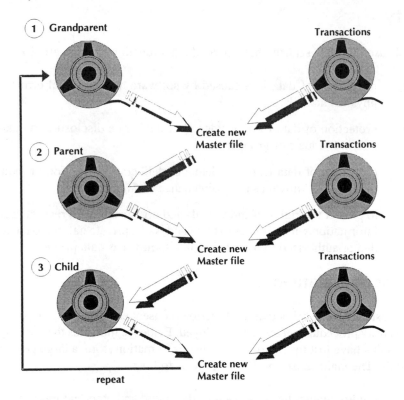

Figure 13.4. *Generation back-up system for sequential tape files*

In the first run, Master 1 is updated by the transaction file to produce Master File 2 as its son. Master File 1 is the parent. Should the son file be damaged and the data lost, it can be re-created from the parent master file and the relevant transactions. At the end of the second run, Master File 1 becomes the grandparent. Master File 2 becomes the parent and Master File 3, the child. Each generation provides security for subsequent files. The number of generations used will depend on the organisation, although three are generally regarded as providing sufficient security; the oldest files are re-used by being overwritten as each cycle of generations is completed.

Internal header labels

Internal header labels are designed to deal with two major areas of concern:

(i)   It is important that the correct file is used in a file processing operation to ensure correct results. Thus, the subject of the file and the version must be identifiable. For example, it is no good producing monthly payslips using information from a payroll master file which is three months out of date.

(ii)   A tape file must be protected against accidental erasure. This may occur because tapes are re-usable and when a file is no longer required it can be overwritten by new information.

To ensure that the correct file is used for any particular job, a tape file usually has an internal header label. The label appears at the beginning of the tape and identifies it. The identifying information in the label is usually recorded under program control or by a data encoding device.

A tape header label usually contains the following items of information:

❑   File name, for example, "Payroll", "Stock", "Sales";

❑   Date created;

❑   Purge date - the date from which the tape is no longer required and may be re-used.

The program checks the label, before the file is processed, to ensure that the correct tape is being used.

File protection ring

A device called a file protection ring can be used to prevent accidental erasure. When tapes are stored off-line, the rings are not fitted. To write to a tape, the ring must first be fitted to the centre of the reel. The computer can read a tape whether or not a ring is fitted. The simple rule to remember is "no ring, no write".

Disk file security

Security backups

Disk files can be treated in the same way as tape files in that the updating procedure may produce a new master file leaving the original file intact. On the other hand, if the file is updated 'in situ' (which in so doing overwrites the existing data), then it will be necessary to take regular backup copies as processing proceeds. The frequency with which copies are taken will depend on the volume of transactions affecting the master file. If the latest version of the master file is corrupted or lost, then it can be re-created using the previous backup together with the transaction data received since the backup.

Transaction logging

In an on-line system, transactions may enter the system from a number of terminals in different locations, thus making it difficult to re-enter transactions for the re-creation of a damaged master file. One solution is to log all the transactions onto a transaction file at the same time as the master file is updated. Thus, the re-creation process can be carried out without the need for keying in the transactions again. The systems flowchart in Figure 13.5 illustrates this procedure.

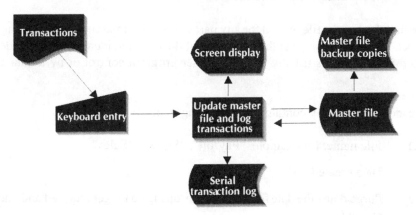

Figure 13.5. *Transaction logging and security back-up system*

Access controls

Unauthorised access to a system may:

- provide vital information to competitors;

- result in the deliberate or accidental corruption of data; allow fraudulent changes to be made to data;

- result in loss of privacy for individuals or organisations.

To avoid such hazards an information system should be protected physically, by administrative procedures and software. To detect any unauthorised access or changes to the information system:

- users should require authorisation (with different levels of authority depending on the purpose of access);

- the computer should log all successful and attempted accesses;

- ❑ users should be identifiable and their identity authenticated;

- ❑ the files should be capable of being audited;

- ❑ the actions of programmers should be carefully controlled to prevent fraud through changes to software.

Physical protection

These include the use of security staff, mechanical devices, such as locks and keys and electronic alarm/identification systems. Computer systems with terminals at remote sites present a weak link in any system and they must be properly protected and software plays an important protection role. Disk and tape libraries also need to be protected, otherwise it would be possible for a thief to take file media to another centre with compatible hardware and software.

A variety of methods may be used to identify and possibly authenticate a system user. They include the following.

Identity cards. Provided that they cannot be copied and have a photograph, they can be effective and cheap. The addition of a magnetic strip which contains encoded personal details including a personal identification number (PIN), which the holder has to key in, allows the user to be checked by machine. This method is used to allow access to service tills outside banks. Of course, the user of the card may not be the authorised holder, possession of the PIN being the only additional requirement; the following methods allow authentication as well as identification;

Personal physical characteristics. Voice recognition or fingerprint comparisons provide effective, if expensive, methods of identification and authentication.

Such methods are only effective if the supporting administrative procedures are properly adhered to.

Software protection

Ideally, before a user is given access to a system, the log-in procedures should check for:

- ❑ authorisation;

- ❑ identification;

- ❑ authentication.

Authorisation is usually provided by an account code, which must be keyed in response to a computer prompt. Similar prompts may appear for a *user name* (identification) and a *password* (authentication).

Further control can be exerted with *fixed terminal identifiers*. Each terminal and its location is physically identifiable by the controlling computer, thus preventing access from additional unauthorised locations. Such controls can also be used to restrict particular terminals to particular forms and levels of access.

Password controls

Access to files can be controlled at different levels by a series of passwords, which have to be keyed into the terminal in response to a series of questions displayed on the screen. For example, a clerk in a Personnel Department may be given authority to display information regarding an employee's career record but only the Personnel Manager is authorised to change the information held on file. Passwords should be carefully chosen, kept secure (memorised and not divulged) and changed frequently. Using people's names, for example, may allow entry by trial and error. Characters should not be echoed on screen as the password is entered.

Handshaking

This technique requires more than a simple password and may be used between two computers or a computer and a user, as a means of access control. In the latter case, the user would be given a pseudo-random number by the computer and the expected response would be a transform, of that random number. The transform may be to multiply the first and last digits of the number and add the product to a value equal to the day of the month plus 1. Provided the transform is kept secret, handshaking provides more security than simple passwords.

One-time passwords

With this method, the computer will only accept a password for one access occasion; subsequently, it will expect the user to provide a different password for each additional access, in a pre-defined sequence. Provided the password list and their expected sequence list are kept separate, then possession of one list only will not be of any assistance.

The number of attempts at logging-on should be controlled, so, for example, after three unsuccessful attempts, the user should be locked out and a record kept of the time and nature of the attempt.

Data encryption

If data signals being transmitted along the telecommunication links are not properly protected, hackers can pick up the signals and display them on their own machines. To prevent such intrusion, data encryption methods are used to protect important financial, legal and other confidential information during transmission from one centre to another. Encryption scrambles the data to make it unintelligible during transmission. As the power and speed of computers has increased, so the breaking of codes has been made easier.

Code designers have produced methods of encryption which are currently unbreakable in any reasonable time period, even by the largest and most powerful computers available. An example of such an elaborate coding system is illustrated by the operation of the Electronic Funds Transfer (EFT) system. Banks and other financial institutions use EFT to transfer vast sums of money so these transmissions are protected by the latest data encryption techniques. The Data Encryption Standard (DES) was approved by the American National Bureau of Standards in 1977, but as costs of powerful computers have fallen and come within the reach of criminal organisation, EFT makes use of the DES standard, plus additional encryption techniques.

Security to maintain data integrity

Data integrity refers to the accuracy and consistency of the information stored and is thus covered by the security methods outlined above.

Security to maintain privacy of data

The rights of individuals and organisations concerning their confidential records are similarly protected by the security controls outlined earlier. In addition, legislation by parliament (the Data Protection Act 1984) attempts to exert some control by requiring persons or organisations holding personal information on computer files to register with the Data Protection Registrar.

Computer viruses

A computer virus is program code designed to create nuisance for users, or more seriously, to effect varying degrees of damage to files stored on magnetic media. Generally, the code:

☐ is introduced via portable media, such as floppy disks, particularly those storing 'pirated' or 'shareware' programs;

☐ transfers itself from the *infected* medium into the computer's main memory as soon as the medium is accessed;

☐ transfers from memory onto any integral storage device, such as a hard disk and commonly conceals itself in the boot sector (and sometimes in the partition sector where it is less likely to be traced), from where it can readily infect any other media placed on line in that computer system, whether it be stand-alone or networked. Naturally, any write-protected media cannot be infected.

Some virus codes are merely a nuisance, whilst others are developed specifically to destroy, or make inaccessible, whole filing systems. They pose a serious threat to any computer-based information system, but a number of measures can be taken to minimise the risk:

❏   Only use proprietary software from a reliable source.

❏   Write-protect disks being used for reading purposes only.

❏   Use virus detection software, although this is only effective in respect of viruses using known storage and proliferation techniques.

❏   Use diskless workstations on networks.

❏   Control access to portable media and forbid employees to use their own media on the organisation's computer system.

Exercises

1.   A data entry operator is keying in a batch of customer orders. Order Numbers are 4 digits and range from 0001 to 5000. Old order numbers are re-used after completion. One of the Order Numbers is keyed as 3126, instead of 3216.The order entry system uses verification through a key-to-disk system.Once the orders are stored on disk, they are processed by a validation program.

   (i)   What type of error has the operator made with the Order Number?

   (ii)   Explain how the verification would work and how it may correct the mistake.

   (iii)   Describe how a check digit for the Order Number would be calculated and show how it would detect the keying error.

   (iv)   Apart from a check digit, suggest one character and one field validation check which could be made on the Order Number.

   (v)   Would either of the validation checks you suggested in (iv) pick up this particular error?

2.   The same order entry system uses batch controls. What type of batch control is created if the Order Numbers in each batch are totalled?

3.   A company holds its payroll files on magnetic tape. Name the file types used in the process.

4.   Approximately 300 transactions update (in-situ) a stock master file every hour and a master file backup is taken every 3 hours. The last backup was taken at 1.30 pm. The current master file is corrupted at 4 pm. Describe what needs to be done.

5.   Identify two software methods of preventing unauthorised access to computer data.

Chapter 14

Consequences of Computerisation

Introduction

The introduction of a computer to an organisation cannot be effective if computerisation simply means the transfer of manual files to computer storage and the automation of some of the existing clerical procedures. To achieve the full potential of computerisation, an organisation needs to implement certain changes which will affect its environment, its staff and its form of management.

Environment

Computer hardware has to be kept in a suitable environment if it is to operate correctly. Although physical protection of hardware has improved considerably over recent years, large mainframe and mini computer systems need to be maintained in a relatively dust-free atmosphere within controlled moderate temperature ranges. Microcomputers tend to be more tolerant of their surroundings and can be accommodated in the relatively basic surroundings one would expect to find in any small office. If computers have to operate in tough physical environments, for example, on warships or in battle tanks then the hardware can be designed accordingly. Fortunately, most organisations have less harsh surrounding in which to work. Nevertheless, there are generally some changes which need to be made in the *physical requirements* of the environment.

Specialist accommodation

Controlled temperature range. Most office environments will be suitable in this respect but the precise requirements will depend on the hardware to be used and the manufacturer's specification. More often than not, problems are caused by the overheating of equipment. Thus hardware should not be sited next to a radiator or in direct sunlight.

Clean surroundings. As previously indicated, the cleanliness required of the environment will depend on the type of hardware in use. In general however, dust will cause problems, particularly with storage media such as tapes and disks. For the larger organisation this may mean the installation of air conditioning within a separate room for the mainframe or mini computer system.

Electrical installation. Although computers operate from the standard electricity supply, it is essential that a separate power supply is installed to prevent problems of cut-out and possible loss of information if the circuits are overloaded. In some cases where reliability is vital, a backup power supply may be needed to cut in if the main supply fails. Magnetic storage media such as disk or tape should not be stored next to power supplies as the surrounding magnetic field may corrupt the data.

Lighting. Where natural light is at times inadequate then suitable artificial lighting will be necessary. In most office situations where manual clerical operations are already carried out, then normal electric lighting is probably sufficient. Lighting also has to be considered in terms of its possible effect on the reflective surfaces which may surround computer equipment. For this reason the casings on hardware are usually of a matt finish. Some computer screens may not have non-reflective qualities so the positioning of equipment in relation to both natural and artificial lighting will have to be taken into account to avoid reflective glare. Although most computer monitors have brightness and contrast control, direct sunlight can make the characters on a screen practically invisible. Artificial lighting which is too intense or badly positioned can also cause screen glare.

Noise control. Sources of noise from computer equipment are in the main:

(i)   printer operation;

(ii)   cooling fans built into the computer itself.

Printer noise varies with the type of printer. Where printers are part of a mini or mainframe system, noise will need to be controlled for the benefit of the computer operations staff but it is likely that a separate room will contain all the main computer resources so other parts of the organisation will be unaffected. In smaller organisation even modern laser and inkjet printers printers can lead to significant background noise levels, but sound absorbent screens and carpeted floors can help.

Cooling fans within computer equipment tend to cause a background noise to which people soon become used. It is not as loud as printer noise but it can be at a level which may result in unnecessary stress for office staff. Again sound absorbent screens around the computer can help protect staff from such noise but properly serviced equipment helps avoid worn and noisy fans.

Effects on staff

The effects on staff within an organisation will be extremely varied and the degree of effect will depend on the extent of involvement individual staff have with a computerised system.

Computerisation within an organisation tends not to be an instantaneous event affecting all functional areas at the same time. It tends to be progressive, sometimes planned and sometimes piecemeal.

Consider the following situation in a commercial trading organisation:

(i)   Assume that Sales Order Processing (SOP) is computerised and that the output includes Picking Lists (these are lists of products and quantities of each that need to be retrieved from the warehouse to satisfy customer orders).

(ii)   Assume further that Stock Control in the warehouse is not computerised but that the staff will receive computer printed picking lists.

(iii) Assume finally that the Accounting function is not computerised. Staff in Accounting will receive sales details on computer printout from SOP from which they will produce invoices to send to customers.

Effects on clerical staff

The staff in these three departments, SOP, Stock Control and Accounting are all affected by computerisation but to varying degrees. Least effected are staff in Stock Control and Accounting who only receive computer output. They have to become familiar with the reading and interpretation of computer printouts. This is not a difficult task, but one which requires some adjustment on the part of staff. At a more complex level, the staff in SOP are more significantly effected. The effects will require education and training for staff in the various parts of the computerised process as follow.

Preparation of input data

Computerisation imposes a discipline on clerical and management procedures. To deal with data correctly it needs to be presented accurately and in a form suitable for input to the computer. Usually, prior to data entry, all source data, (in this case customer orders) have to be recorded on standard, specially designed *source documents* which match the order of data requested by the computer software. For example, if the first item of data required by the computer is an order number, then this should be the first data item on the source document. The second data item required should be next and so on. Therefore, however the orders are received, by telephone, by word of mouth at the sales desk or by post, the first job is to transcribe the details onto the source document. Such tasks need to be documented in office procedure manuals and staff need to be instructed in their proper execution.

Data entry

Staff involved in this task will need to develop keyboard skills. Even if the data entry operators are already skilled typists, some training or period of familiarisation is required to use a computer terminal correctly. Training will be needed in the day-to-day operation of the software. These include 'signing on' with codes and passwords, familiarity with computer screen prompts and the correct responses to make, dealing with simple error conditions when an incorrect key is pressed and correcting or editing keying errors during data entry.

Where the volume of data entry is such that a member of staff can be fully occupied with this task there are health and safety considerations to be examined. There are for example recommended guidelines concerning time limits for personnel operating VDU's. Headaches and eye strain can result from prolonged viewing of a computer screen. Where the volume of data entry is limited, the specialist staff may not be justified and a number of clerical staff with a variety of duties may have to 'take their turn' at the keyboard. Thus more staff will need some basic training in the use of the system.

Effects on managerial staff

The day-to-day clerical routines will not usually directly involve managerial staff although this will depend on the size of the organisation and the hierarchical staffing structure. However, their necessary involvement in the development, introduction and implementation of a computerised system and their responsibilities for the efficient running of their departments mean that the effects of computerisation on the working lives of managers can be even more emphatic than the effects on clerical staff. To continue the Sales Order Processing example, the manager of that department may:

(i)   be closely involved in a consultative role with systems analysts in the analysis of the old manual system and the design of the new computerised system;

(ii)   have to maintain communication with the staff in the SOP department to ensure that:

(a) their views are taken into account;

(b) envisaged changes are reported to them.

This communication is vital if the staff are to feel 'involved'.

(iii) require some computer education and training. A prerequisite of communication between staff is that the manager has developed some computer 'awareness' and computer 'literacy' sufficiently to understand the role of the computer and the changes in procedures within his department which are necessary. A desktop or notebook computer is also likely to be an essential tool for a manager.

This educational or training need has to be satisfied if the manager is to be effective in the role of ensuring that the operational procedures are being followed and that efficiency is being maintained. Without knowledge of the powers and limitations of a computerised system a manager cannot assess its effectiveness or suggest improvements.

Other computer applications involving management

There are a number of computer applications which make use of 'content free' software. This refers to software which is not fixed to one application or type of data. Such software packages are available for spreadsheet work, and database or file management.

It is usual for microcomputers or terminals linked to a central computer to be used by managers and executive staff (although not exclusively) to aid their decision-making, with the provision of more and higher quality information. An example may illustrate this point. Spreadsheet packages can be used for the preparation of cash budgets and sales forecasting with the added facility of generating 'what if' projections. So a cash budget based on current and anticipated figures of cash due in and out of the organisation over the next few months, can be quickly modified to present the results of an alternative strategy of say, an injection of cash from a bank loan. Database packages can be used by managers for their own local information store on which they can make enquiry. In addition, where a database is held centrally, a manager could access files through the use of a Query Language (Chapter 7). To use such a language requires training, similar to that required by a programmer albeit at a simpler level.

The efficient and effective use of such packages demands a high level of knowledge and skill which will probably require some sort of training programme, perhaps with the software supplier.

Effects on managers not yet involved

The use of such facilities by one departmental manager or the issue of a general directive from top management within an organisation will place pressure on other managers to follow suit. Of course the pressure may be in the other direction where departmental managers wish to get involved and pressurise top management for training and the introduction of new computerised systems

Changes in job descriptions

It can be seen from the previous section that where computerised systems are used within an organisation and new staff are to be recruited, the job descriptions in advertisements should include a request for computer knowledge or skill, in the area which the job demands. Existing staff will have to have their job descriptions modified. In some circumstances this can mean an upgrading of the skill or professional level which may attract a higher salary. It can lead to delay in the introduction of computer systems. In local government, for example, some secretarial staff were prevented from using word processors because their union demanded an increase in their job grading. In some jobs it can lead to what is considered to be de-skilling. For example, in the newspaper industry the traditional skill of metal typesetting is now obsolete.

Effects on functional relationships

Earlier in this chapter, it is explained that computerisation effects the ways in which different functions such as Sales and Accounts relate to each other, in terms of how information flows between them and the activities in which each is engaged.

Without computers, the Sales and Accounting departments would maintain their own files. Transaction data such as a customer order would be used to update each of the department's files separately. Each department would be responsible for maintaining its own files thus creating separate autonomous areas within an organisation, each led by a Head of Department or similar executive staff member. Each department would tend to have its own working practices and provided information was presented to other departments in a form they could use, there would perhaps be little need for change.

Computerisation imposes discipline and standardisation. Information flows between departments may have to pass through a computer process and although the user requirements should take priority over what is convenient for the computer, some modifications will need to be made to the ways in which data is presented to the computer for processing. Earlier in this chapter, the example was used of customer order details being transcribed onto Source Documents designed to be compatible with the order of input to the computer. A feature of manual systems is the separateness of related operations. For example a customer order will be used to update the customer file, the stock file and to produce a customer invoice in separate operations carried out in each separate functional area. A computerised system could allow these tasks to be carried out with a single input of the data.

Inter-departmental conflict

Organisations are formed to allow a rational and coordinated approach to the achievement of certain aims which may be the provision of a service or product for which there is a profitable market. The problem is that organisations are made up of individuals who may not always be rational. Each individual has his or her own ambitions, fears and emotions. Management styles may well stem from such personal characteristics. This may lead to competition between department heads rather than cooperation in achieving the common aims of the organisation as a whole.

Personal fears

To many people, computerisation is a venture into the unknown and many individuals feel threatened because they have insufficient knowledge or experience to give them adequate control over their own futures. Being made to look a fool, or worse, the possibility of being made redundant by computerisation can be the main obstacle to the acceptance of change.

Resistance to change

Sometimes because of inter-departmental rivalry or simply incompetence, a manager may keep secret certain facts which computerisation may make available. This is another reason for resistance to the introduction of computerised systems. Managers are forced to change their style of management because of the introduction of computers and may attempt to resist the threat to their power, by doing less than they might to make the innovation work and by constantly finding fault, without making constructive suggestions.

The Enthusiast

An alternative reaction, which is usually irrational, is the whole-hearted, eager acceptance of computerisation as being the ideal solution to every problem. There are many circumstances where computerisation is inappropriate or where the immediately available standard package is far from ideal. Because organisations are made up of individuals, computer systems should be designed with the full cooperation of management and staff, enlisting their help wherever possible so as to take proper account of their individual or at least departmental information needs.

Effects on management style

Many managers work intuitively and have confidence in their own methods which have served them well. Such 'flying by the seat of the pants' often leads to a natural derision for any system designed by 'experts' and 'theorists'. Of course such confidence is usually based on previous success and the specialist in computer systems will often be young and, as far as the experienced manager is concerned, 'wet behind the ears'. Thus the computer specialist may have a difficult job in convincing existing management that a new computerised system will be an improvement on the old. The systems analyst will need to have the interpersonal skills to deal with such resistance. One feature of computerised systems is the increase in the volume of information available to a manager and the speed with which it can be obtained. A resulting danger is that the manager may become too concerned with the low level decisions within his department, thus interfering with the responsibilities of lower levels of management or supervisory staff. The problem can be more serious if it extends upwards from departmental to corporate management. Information which should have been seen by the department manager may have been seen by the chief general manager first. Too much information and the wrong type of information can be worse than insufficient information.

Effects of decentralising computer resources

Centralised and distributed systems are discussed in Chapter 6. Broadly, the development of systems using the combined technologies of computing and telecommunications have decentralised computer usage. A wide variety of systems is available to support decentralisation, including wide area and local area networks and stand-alone microcomputer systems. The main benefits for an organisation may be as follows.

- The delegation of control of some information processing to branch level management, hopefully resulting in systems which respond to local requirements.

- More rapid, up-to-date information at the local level, because it is processed locally.

- The rapid distribution of centrally produced information through network systems.

❑   Provided that the local systems are linked to a central facility, then information which is locally produced can be transmitted and stored so as to be available at a corporate level. Overall control is not lost, but enhanced.

The above benefits are not automatic and may have certain implications for an organisation. The main implications are:

❑   New hardware and software needs to be purchased, which is compatible with any existing centralised facility.

❑   Local management and workers need to be trained in the operation of any new system introduced, if the maximum benefit is to be obtained. The use of microcomputers with, for example, database and spreadsheet packages requires extensive training of users. This can be expensive.

❑   A complete re-appraisal of specialist staffing may be needed as a result of decentralisation. For example, systems analysts already familiar with the design and implementation of distributed systems may need to be recruited.

❑   Specialist personnel, including programmers and operators, may be needed at the local level.

❑   Decentralised systems present new problems in terms of controlling the security of information (Chapter 13). The added risks must be considered and covered.

Exercises

1.   A company is planning to install a mainframe computer system.

     (i)   List 5 features of its *environment* that the company should bear in mind.

     (ii)   For each feature identify the main *hazard* it is designed to avoid.

2.   When a new computerised system is to be implemented, it is important that staff are *trained* to use it effectively.

     (i)   Identify three topics you would expect to be covered on a course for new *data entry* staff

     (ii)   Identify two topics you would expect to be part of a course for *managerial* staff.

Chapter 15
Social and Organisational Effects of Computerisation

This chapter is divided into three main sections. The first looks at the applications of computer technology and considers the main benefits of computerisation for an organisation. The second section looks at the effects of computer technologies on employment patterns, working conditions, and career prospects. The final section considers some of the major effects computer technology has had and is having on society. Some possible developments for the future are also put forward for discussion.

Benefits of computerisation

Business applications such as payroll and stock control were among the earliest to be computerised. Although increasing use is being made of computers in manufacturing industry, science and medicine, business applications still constitute the greatest usage. A number of categories of computer application can be identified:

(a)   Accounting systems (see also Chapters 2 and 32)

(b)   Management Information Systems (MIS)

(c)   Decision Support Systems (DSS)

(d)   Office IT Systems (Chapter 8)

(e)   Computer-aided Design and Manufacture (CAD-CAM)

(f)   Computers in science and medicine

(g)   Artificial Intelligence

Accounting systems

Payroll

Payroll systems are concerned with the production of payslips for employees and the maintenance of records required for taxation and other deductions. In a manual system, the preparation of payroll figures and the maintenance of payroll records is a labour intensive task. Although tedious and repetitive, it is a vitally important task. Most employees naturally regard pay as being the main reason for work and resent delays in payment or incorrect payments, unless of course it is in their favour! The weekly or monthly payroll run affects almost all employee records in the payroll master file, so batch processing is normally used. This processing method provides numerous opportunities to maintain the accuracy of the information. The repetitive nature of the task makes it a popular candidate for computerisation, especially with organisations which employ large numbers of people. The automatic production of reports for taxation purposes also provides a valuable benefit. Smaller organisations with only several employees probably do not regard payroll as a high priority application for computerisation. The benefits are not as great if the payroll task can be carried out by one or two employees who also carry out a number of other jobs.

Stock control

Any organisation which keeps stocks of raw materials or finished goods needs to operate a stock control system. Although stock constitutes an asset, it ties up cash resources which could be invested in other aspects of the business. Equally, a company must keep sufficient quantities of items to satisfy customer demand or manufacturing requirements. To maintain this balance a stock control system should provide up-to-date information on quantities, prices, minimum stock levels, and re-order quantities. It should also give warning of excessively high, or dangerously low levels of stock. In the latter case, orders may be produced automatically. A stock control system can also generate valuable management reports on, for example, sales patterns, slow-moving items, and overdue orders.

Sales accounting

When credit sales are made to customers, a record needs to be kept of amounts owing and paid. Payment is normally requested with an invoice, which gives details of goods supplied, quantities, prices and VAT. Credit sales are usually made on for example, a 14, 21 or 28 day basis, which means that the customer has to pay within the specified period to obtain any discounts offered. Overdue payments need to be chased, so sales accounting systems normally produce reports analysing the indebtedness of different customers. Debt control is vital to business profitability and computerised systems can produce prompt and up-to-date reports as a by-product of the main application.

Purchase accounting

These systems control the amounts owed and payments made to suppliers of services, goods or materials used in the main business of the company. For example, a car manufacturer will need to keep records of amounts owing to suppliers of car components and sheet steel manufacturers. Delayed payments to suppliers may help cash flow, but can harm an organisation's image, or even cut off a source of supply when a supplier refuses to deliver any more goods until payment is made. A computerised system will not ensure payment, but it can provide the information that payment is due.

General ledger

The general ledger keeps control of financial summaries, including those originating from payroll, sales and purchase accounting and acts as a balance in a double entry system. Reports are generally produced at the end of financial periods, including a balance sheet. For many organisations, the systems described above can be computerised using packaged software.

Management Information Systems (MIS)

Although computers can perform routine processing tasks very efficiently, it is generally recognised that, for a business to make use of a computer solely for the processing of operational information, constitutes a waste of computer power. A MIS is designed to make use of the computer's power of selection and analysis to produce useful *management* information.

A MIS has a number of key features:

(i)   it produces information beyond that required for routine data processing;

(ii)   timing of information production is critical;

(iii)   the information it produces is an aid to decision-making;

(iv)   it is usually based on the database concept (explained in Chapter 7).

The information provided tends to be related to different levels of management (Chapter 1)

The claims for MIS are sometimes excessive. It is rarely the complete answer to all a company's information needs, but when successfully implemented, it provides a valuable information advantage over competitors.

Decision Support Systems (DSS)

A DSS aims to provide a more flexible decision tool than that supplied by a MIS. MIS tend to produce information in an anticipated, predefined form and as such, do not allow managers to make ad hoc requests for information. DSS tend to be narrower in scope than MIS, often making use of microcomputer systems and software packages. Examples of DSS are, electronic spreadsheets, for example, Microsoft Excel, file managers and relational database management systems such as Microsoft Access. The main features of these and other packages are described in some detail in Chapter 17. In addition, financial modelling (Chapter 33) and statistical packages are considered to be DSS tools. A major benefit is the independence they allow for information control by individual managers and executives. When, for example, a sales manager requires a report on sales figures for the last three months, a microcomputer with database package may provide the report more quickly than the centralised Management Information Services (Chapter 2).

Office IT systems

Information technology (IT) is now provides essential task support for most organisations. The office is viewed as an integrated whole and not necessarily in a single geographical location; many procedures are automated and much of the communication is by electronic means. The main IT support systems are described in Chapter 8, but briefly, may include the following:

- ❏ Word processing;

- ❏ Decision Support Systems (DSS) - discussed above;

- ❏ Electronic mail (e-mail);

- ❏ Bulletin boards (Chapter 25)

- ❏ Teleworking.

The last component, *teleworking*, is revolutionising working habits. Basically, it means the use of a terminal or microcomputer workstation linked to a company's computer at another location. In many cases, this removes the need for attendance at the office for workers such as programmers and typists or even executive staff. The main disadvantage is the loss of personal contact between staff, which can require considerable cultural readjustment. Such a system also has consequences for employee supervision and security of information.

Computer-Aided Design and Manufacture (CAD-CAM)

Computer-Aided Design (CAD)

With the use of a graphics terminal and cross-hair cursor (described in Chapter 19), or similar device, a designer can produce and modify designs more rapidly than is possible with a conventional drawing board. Ideas can be sketched on the screen, stored, recalled and modified. The computer can also be instructed to analyse a design for comparison with some specified criteria. Drawings can be rotated and tilted on the screen to reveal different three-dimensional views. CAD is used in the design of ships, cars, buildings, microprocessor circuits, clothing and many other products. With the use of CAD a manufacturer has a distinct advantage over non-computerised competitors, in terms of speed and flexibility of design.

Computer-Aided Manufacture (CAM)

A number of areas of computer use can be identified in the manufacturing process.

(i)   Industrial robots;

(ii)   Computer numerical control (CNC) of machine tools;

(iii) Integrated CAD-CAM;

(iv)   Automated materials handling;

(v)   Flexible manufacturing systems (FMS);

Industrial Robots. Basically, a robot replaces the actions of a human arm and consists of 3 main elements, a mechanical arm with 'wrist' joint, power unit and microprocessor or central controlling computer. To be called a robot, it must be able to react, albeit in a limited way, to external events and alter its course of action according to a stored program. Such sensitivity to the environment is provided by sensors, for example, to recognise stylised characters and differentiate between shapes. The main areas of use are in spot welding, paint spraying, die casting and to a lesser extent, assembly.

Computer Numerical Control (CNC). CNC operation of machine tools has been widespread for some years because the repetitive nature of machining tasks lends itself to simple programming. However, as is the case with robots, the use of microprocessors allows the machine tool to vary its actions according to external information. The actions of the machine can be compared with a design pattern held by the computer. Any significant variations from the pattern are signalled to the machine tool which, through the microprocessor, reacts appropriately (known as Computer Aided Quality Assessment - CAQ). Other information regarding tool wear or damage can be picked up by sensors and communicated to the human supervisor who takes remedial action.

Integrated CAD-CAM. In fully integrated CAD-CAM systems, the designs produced using CAD are fed straight through to the software which controls the CNC machine tools, which can then produce the design piece. The CAD software checks the compatibility of the design with a component specification already stored in the computer.

Automated Materials Handling. There are around 80 fully automated warehouses in Britain. A fully automated materials handling system consists of a number of sub-systems:

❑   stock control;

❑   part or pallet co-ordination;

❑   storage and retrieval;

❑   conveyor control.

Installation generally proceeds one sub-system at a time, each being fully tested before proceeding with the next sub-system. A materials handling system, controlled by a central computer, allocates storage locations in the warehouse, automatically re-orders when a predetermined minimum level is reached, retrieves parts as required by the factory and delivers them by conveyor belt to the waiting robots or CNC machines.

Flexible Manufacturing Systems (FMS). Such systems are beneficial where production batches are small and necessitate frequent changes in the sequence and types of processes. The aim of FMS is to remove, as far as possible, the need for human intervention (other than a supervisor or 'machine minder') in the production process. The main elements of FMS are, CNC machine tools (with diagnostic facilities), robots, conveyor belt and central computer and controlling software. In simple terms, the computer has information on parts, machine tools and operations required. The robots serve the CNC machines by presenting them with parts to be machined and loading the correct machine tools from racks. In Crewkerne, Somerset, a factory uses FMS to produce bomb release mechanisms for military aircraft but the system is flexible enough to produce thousands of other components with the minimum of human intervention.

Computers in science and medicine

Science

To predict weather conditions accurately requires vast amounts of data regarding past conditions. Large supercomputers allow such volumes of data to be stored, recalled, updated, and analysed on a national and sometimes international basis. Computer graphics and computer enhanced satellite pictures are also used to provide interesting and informative weather forecasts for television viewers. Computer simulations can allow testing of product designs without, at least in the initial stages, the expense of building the actual product. Airline pilots are trained in computerised flight simulators which can simulate almost any event a pilot is likely to encounter.

Medicine

Computer-controlled life support systems can monitor a patient's condition via a number of sensor devices checking on, for example, pulse rate, body temperature and blood pressure. This frees nursing staff for other duties and has the benefit of providing a continuous monitoring facility. Computer-assisted diagnosis systems make use of artificial intelligence to assist a physician in diagnosing a patient's condition. This raises the question of how much reliance should be placed on computers with artificial intelligence. It seems reasonable that a doctor should use an expert system as an aid to diagnosis, but less reasonable that a treatment decision should be made on the basis of computer diagnosis alone. A particularly exciting development involves the use of computers to assist the plastic surgeon in the repair of facial injuries or deformities. The patient's face is scanned by a camera and the image digitised for display on a computer screen in three-dimensional form. This image can be rotated or tilted on screen by the surgeon and experimental 'cuts' made, the results of which can then be viewed on screen from any angle. In this way, a plastic surgeon can study the results of a variety of strategies before making a single mark on the patient.

Artificial Intelligence (AI)

Artificial intelligence is an attempt to model human thought processes and systems are evolving in the following areas:

(i)   Expert or knowledge-based systems (which are examined in Chapter 17);

(ii)   Robotics (described earlier in this Chapter);

(iii)   Natural language processing.

Expert systems may, in the future, pose a threat to the autonomy at present held by doctors, lawyers and other professionals. It is not inconceivable that medical diagnosis and legal advice may be provided by machine. Such systems exist already but only provide limited support. The restraint, if any, on such developments may stem from ethical and moral forces, as well as the professions wish to protect their interests. It may be, of course, that humans will prefer to retain personal contact with their doctor or solicitor, even if a machine is making most of the decisions.

Computers and employment

The rapid advances in computer and micro-electronic technologies have occurred in a period of erratic change in the Western economies and it is difficult to quantify the extent to which computerisation has affected the levels of employment. Although computerisation is far from being wholly responsible for increased unemployment, it has undoubtedly been a contributory factor. No attempt is made in this text to relate numbers of employed or unemployed to computerisation. Instead, discussion will centre on the identifiable effects of computerisation on employment patterns and prospects. The following effects may result from computerisation:

(i)   Retraining

(ii)   Redeployment

(iii)   De-skilling

(iv)   Changes in working practices

(v)   Regrading and changes in career prospects

(vi)   Redundancy

(vii)   Changes in working conditions (Health and safety).

Each of the above effects can be identified in different types of job.

Office work

Computerisation is common in most areas of office work, for example, word processing, electronic messaging, and accounting systems. Additionally in some specialised areas such as banking, automatic tellers are replacing humans for routine banking transactions.

Re-training

Generally, an organisation will choose to make full use of their existing staff, rather than search for new staff who already have the skills required. Depending on the nature of the job, the retraining needed may be radical or quite minor. For example, a typist has keyboard skills which are quite readily transferable to the task of word processing. The retraining needed centres on the concept of text editing, mailing lists, the use of floppy disks and printers. The aim is to give the operator the knowledge, skill and understanding to make maximum use of the facilities provided by a word processor. Word processing is a general skill which can be applied in different ways in different organisations. Similarly, the use of a software package for sales accounting or stock control needs knowledge and skills, some of which are transferable to other packages. Familiarity with computers in general and expertise in the use of some packages, provides an individual with the confidence to quickly pick up skills for new applications as they arise.

Redeployment

Computerisation generally reduces manpower requirements but increases the opportunities for business expansion. Redeployment means moving staff from one area of work or responsibility to another, generally with retraining. Redeployment is a common result of computerisation in any area of work.

De-skilling

The judgement as to whether or not a job is de-skilled by computerisation is a rather subjective one. For example, does a wages clerk using manual methods require a higher level of skill than a data entry operator? The answer is probably yes, although a trade union may argue otherwise in the interests of improved job regrading. On the other hand it is generally accepted that higher level skills are required to use a word processor than a typewriter.

Changes in working practices

Staff may be required to carry out a wider range of tasks as a result of computerisation. For example, in smaller offices a clerk may be required to answer customer enquiries and carry out data entry at a terminal. Flexibility rather than specialisation is often the key to the introduction of new technology. The lines of demarcation in the newspaper industry had to disappear before computerisation could take place.

Regrading and career prospects

Sometimes, improvements in job gradings are introduced in order to encourage staff to accept computerisation. At the same time, career prospects in office work are generally diminished. In the banking industry, the prospects for managerial jobs have diminished drastically in the last two decades. Currently, few clerical staff who did not enter the job with a degree have prospects for managerial posts.

Redundancy

Computerisation of office work inevitably reduces the manpower requirements for the existing level of work, but redundancy does not always result. This is usually because computers are introduced in response to an expansion in the business of an organisation.

Health and safety

Anxiety and stress could cause problems. Many staff, particularly older members, may feel anxious about the security of their job or possible redeployment. They may become unhappy about personal contact being replaced by a computer screen.

Most people, as they get older, prefer continuity rather than constant change and computerisation usually means radical and frequent change. Anxiety can also result from a fear of 'falling behind'. This applies to many people working with computers, because the changes and advances are so rapid.

Ergonomics

Ergonomic design recognises certain health and safety problems which can result from computer usage and attempts to design equipment and working environments which minimise the hazards. A number of health and safety concerns are recognised in relation to VDU screens:

- exposure to radiation;

- induction of epileptic fits;

- mental and physical fatigue;

- eyestrain, eye damage and visual fatigue;

- muscular strain.

Suitable working practices and well-designed equipment can largely avoid such dangers, for example, gentle lighting, lack of screen flicker and hourly breaks for VDU operators. Other concerns relate to the design of office furniture and the general office environment, including temperature and noise levels.

Manufacturing industry

Most of the factors described in relation to office work apply equally in factory work, but the following additional points are worth mentioning.

Job satisfaction. Shop floor workers who supervise and service the machines have a cleaner, less dangerous job than traditional skilled machinists. It may be surmised that young people, without the experience of the old skills, will look more favourably on such supervisory jobs than the older workers.

New job opportunities. If automated systems such as Flexible Manufacturing Systems (FMS) are to be successful, then the number of jobs in factories using FMS must inevitably decrease. Opportunities lie in the creation of a new range of jobs. Many such jobs are in software engineering and in the design of automated systems. The Japanese experience is that new, highly-skilled jobs are created in the development and design fields in companies which manufacture automated equipment and commercial machinery, whereas both skilled and unskilled jobs are lost in the companies using this equipment. The Japanese experience is being mirrored in the UK.

Increased unemployment. Many older, skilled workers have been made redundant because of the loss or de-skilling of their jobs through automation. On the other hand, the redundancies may have occurred without automation because of loss of competitiveness.

Computers and society

There is general agreement that computers and related technologies will bring great social changes, but there are wide differences of opinion about what they will be, the rate at which they will occur and the extent to which they are beneficial. It must be emphasised that many of the following points are highly subjective and open to debate.

Benefits

The benefits include:

- Increased productivity;

- Higher standard of living;

- Cleaner and safer working conditions;

- Shorter working hours (experience has indicated the opposite);

- More leisure time (this is not the experience of those in work).

Costs

The costs include:

❑ Polarisation of people into two groups - the technologically advantaged and disadvantaged;

❑ Increasing crime and delinquency rates;

❑ The threat of a totalitarian state;

❑ Invasion of privacy.

The remainder of this section looks at two important areas of concern regarding the future impact of computers on society, namely *telecommuting* and *personal privacy*. Some of the effects are already apparent.

Teleworking - the office at home

At present, millions of office workers travel by car or public transport to their respective places of work. Nearly all organisations carry out their business from centralised offices because information needs to be exchanged, usually on paper documents and decisions need to be made, which requires consultation between individuals. Through the use of telecommunications, and centrally available computer databases, office staff of the future may work from home via a computer terminal. There are a number of advantages to be gained from home-based work:

❑ Savings in travel costs;

❑ No necessity to live within travelling distance;

❑ Flexible hours of work;

❑ Equality between men and women. Bringing up children can be a shared activity;

❑ Savings for the organisation in terms of expensive city-centre offices.

There are also several potential drawbacks:

❑ Loss of social contact;

❑ Need for quiet workroom at home. This can be difficult in a small flat;

❑ The difficulty of 'office' accommodation is compounded when two or three members of a family all work from home;

❑ Loss of visible status for senior staff in terms of a 'plush' office and other staff to command.

Computers and personal privacy

Since the 1960s, there has been growing public concern about the threat that computers pose to personal privacy. Most countries, including the UK, have introduced legislation to safe-guard the privacy of the individual. The Data Protection Act of 1984 was passed after a number of government commissioned reports on the subject. The Younger Report of 1972 identified ten principles which were intended as guidelines to computer users in the private sector. A government White Paper was published in 1975 in response to the Younger Report, but no legislation followed. The Lindop Report of 1978 was followed by a White Paper in 1982 and this resulted in the 1984 Data Protection Act. The principles detailed in the Younger Report formed the foundation for future reports and the Data Protection Act. They are listed below.

(i)   Information should be regarded as being held for a specific purpose and should not be used, without appropriate authorisation, for other purposes.

(ii)   Access to information should be confined to those authorised to have it for the purpose for which it was supplied.

(iii)   The amount of information collected and held should be the minimum necessary for the achievement of a specified purpose.

(iv)   In computerised systems handling information for statistical purposes, adequate provision should be made in their design and programs for sepa-rating identities from the rest of the data.

(v)   There should be arrangements whereby a subject could be told about the information held concerning him or her.

(vi)   The level of security to be achieved by a system should be specified in ad-vance by the user and should include precautions against the deliberate abuse or misuse of information.

(vii)   A monitoring system should be provided to facilitate the detection of any violation of the security system.

(viii) In the design of information systems, periods should be specified beyond which information should not be retained.

(ix)   Data held should be accurate. There should be machinery for the correc-tion of inaccuracy and updating of information.

(x)   Care should be taken in coding value judgements.

The White Paper which followed the Younger Report identified certain features of comput-erised information systems which could be a threat to personal privacy:

(i)   The facility for storing vast quantities of data;

(ii)   The speed and power of computers make it possible for data to be retrieved quickly and easily from many access points;

(iii)   Data can be rapidly transferred between interconnected systems;

(iv)   Computers make it possible for data to be combined in ways which might otherwise not be practicable;

(v)   Data is often transferred in a form not directly intelligible.

The 1984 Data Protection Act sets boundaries for the gathering and use of personal data. It requires all holders of computerised personal files to register with a Registrar appointed by the Home Secretary. The holder of personal data is required to keep to both the general terms of the Act, and to the specific purposes declared in the application for registration.

Data protection terminology

The Data Protection Act uses a number of terms which require some explanation:

Data. Information held in a form which can be processed automatically. By this definition, manual information systems are not covered by the Act.

Personal data. That which relates to a living individual who is identifiable from the information, including any which is based on fact or opinion.

Data subject. The living individual who is the subject of the data.

Data user. A person who processes or intends to process the data concerning a data subject.

Consequences of the Data Protection Act

The requirements of the Act have resulted in organisations having to pay more attention to the question of security against unauthorised access than would otherwise be the case. Appropriate education and training of employees are now a requirement, to ensure that they are aware of their responsibilities and are fully conversant with their roles in the security systems. The Act also provides the right of a data subject (with some exceptions) to obtain access to information concerning him or her. Normally, a data user must provide such information free of charge, or for a nominal charge of around £10. From the individual's point of view, the Act can be said to have a number of weaknesses:

❑   Penalties for infringement of the rules are thought to be weak and ineffective.

❑   There are a number of exemptions from the Act. Some holders do not need to register and there are exceptions to the right of access to one's own file. There are also limits to confidentiality.

❑   The Registrar is appointed by the Home Secretary and cannot therefore, be wholly independent.

Computer fraud

Computer fraud is invariably committed for financial gain but, unlike some forms of fraud, the perpetrator(s) will make considerable efforts to prevent discovery of any loss by the victim. The rewards for such efforts may be complete freedom from prosecution, or at least a delay in discovery of the fraud and a consequent chance of escape. Unless proper controls and checks are implemented, computer systems are particularly vulnerable to fraudulent activity, because much of the time processing and its results are hidden. The following section examines some methods for committing fraud and the measures which can be taken to foil them. To extract money from a financial accounting system requires its diversion into fictitious, but accessible accounts. To avoid detection, appropriate adjustments must be made to ensure that the accounts still balance. Sometimes, fraudulent activity may involve the misappropriation of goods rather than cash. Frequently, the collusion of several people is necessary to effect a fraud, because responsibility for different stages of the processing cycle is likely to be shared. Some common methods of fraud are given below.

Bogus data entry. This may involve entering additional, unauthorised data, modifying valid data or preventing its entry altogether. Such activity may take place during the data preparation or data entry stages.

Bogus output. Output may be destroyed or altered to prevent discovery of fraudulent data entry or processing.

Alteration of files. For example, an employee may alter his salary grading in the payroll file or adjust the amount owing in a colluding customer's account.

Program patching. This method requires access to program coding and a detailed knowledge of the functioning of the program in question, as well as the necessary programming skill. For example, using additional code, in the form of a conditional subroutine, funds may be channelled to a fictitious account.

Suspense accounts. Rejected and unreconciled transactions tend to be sent to suspense accounts until they can be dealt with; fraud may be effected by directing such transactions to the account of someone colluding in the crime. Transactions can be tampered with at the input stage to ensure their rejection and allocation to the suspense/personal account.

Fraud prevention and detection

An organisation can minimise the risk of computer fraud by:

❑   controlling access to computer hardware; in centralised systems with a limited number of specialist staff access can be readily controlled. On the other hand, if power is concentrated in the hands of few staff, then the opportunities for undetected fraud are increased. Distributed systems or centralised systems with remote access may increase the number of locations where fraud can be perpetrated;

❑   auditing of data and procedures; until hard copy is produced the contents of files remain invisible and a number of auditing techniques can be used to detect fraudulent entries or changes.

❑   careful monitoring of the programming function; program patching can be controlled by division of the programming task, so that an individual programmer does not have complete responsibility for one application program. Unauthorised alterations to existing software can be detected by auditing utilities, which compare the object code of an operational program with an original and authorised copy.

Computer copyright

A computer program can now obtain the status of literary work and as such, retains protection for 50 years from the first publishing date. Computer software is now covered by the Copyright Designs and Patents Act 1988 and infringements include:

❑   pirating of copyright protected software;

❑   running of pirated software, in that a copy is created in memory;

❑   transmission of software over telecommunications links, thereby producing a copy.

The major software producers have funded an organisation called FAST (Federation Against Software Theft) which successfully lobbied for the inclusion of computer software into the above-mentioned Act.

Exercises

1. List four key features of a *Management Information System* (MIS).

2. A sales manager uses a spreadsheet to identify sales patterns across each of the five areas for which he is responsible. The data will be used to identify one area which is to be targeted for a special sales drive. What is the *general term* for this type of information system?

3. Identify three systems which form part of the modern IT-based office.

4. (i)   Identify three elements of an *industrial robot*.

    (ii) Suggest two industrial robot applications which make use of sensors and state the sensor's function for each application.

5. Briefly describe the processes involved in producing a machine part, using an *integrated CAD-CAM* system.

6. Identify an application which uses *computer simulation* in:

    (i)   science;

    (ii) medicine.

7. (i)   Using a commercial bank as an example, suggest three negative effects of computerisation on its employees.

    (ii) Suggest two *health* and *safety* issues the bank has to consider, as a consequence of computerisation.

8. A former office worker has decided to work from home, which she shares with her husband and two children; they are both at secondary school. She is to work as a *teleworker,* for her present employer and her working hours will be from 9.00 to 5.00, Monday to Friday. She is to use a spare bedroom as a small office and this will accommodate the computer system, linked to the company offices. They are located in a city centre, 5 miles from her home. Identify three benefits and two drawbacks which she is likely to experience from the new arrangement.

9. Define the Data Protection Act terms: *Data*; *personal data*; *data subject*; *data user*.

Chapter 16
Software

Introduction

Software is the term used to describe the complete range of computer programs which will allow a general-purpose digital computer to perform many different functions. The term *software* implies its flexible, changeable nature, in contrast to the more permanent characteristics of the hardware or equipment which it controls.

The type of software controlling the computer system at any particular moment will determine the manner in which it functions. For example, a certain type of software might cause the computer to behave like a word processor; another might allow it to do accounting tasks; graphic design jobs might be performed by yet another type of software. In this chapter we explain what software is, how programming languages have evolved and how they are handled by a computer.

Computer programs

At the level at which the computer operates, a program is simply a sequence of numeric codes. Each of these codes can be directly converted by the hardware into some simple operation. Built into the processor, the heart of the computer, is a set of these simple operations, combinations of which are capable of directing the computer to perform complex tasks. Computer programs, in this fundamental form, are termed *machine code*, that is code which is directly 'understandable' by the machine.

The numeric codes of the program are in binary form, or at least the electrical equivalent of binary, and are stored in the *memory* of the computer. Because this memory is volatile (in other words, it is temporary and can be changed), it is possible to exchange the program currently held in the memory for another when the computer is required to perform a different function. For this reason the term *stored program* is often used to describe this fundamental characteristic of the modern digital computer.

The collection of numeric codes which directs the computer to perform such simple operations as those mentioned above is called the instruction set. The *instruction set* of a typical computer would normally contain the following types of instructions:

(a)   Data transfer. This allows data to be moved within the processor, between the processor and the memory of the computer system or between the processor and external devices such as printers, VDUs and keyboards.

(b)   Arithmetic operations. Such instructions direct the computer to perform arithmetic functions such as addition, subtraction, multiplication, division, increment, decrement, comparison and logical operations such as AND, OR, NOT and EXCLUSIVE OR.

(c)   Shift operations. These move data to the left or right within a *register* or memory location.

(d)   Transfer of control. This directs the machine to skip one or more instructions or repeat previously encountered instructions.

These different types of fundamental operations are described in Chapter 23.

Programming languages

A program, consisting of a combination of the types of instructions outlined above, is *executed* by retrieving each instruction in turn from the memory of the computer, decoding the operation required and then performing this operation under the direction of the processor. This sequence of events is termed the *fetch-execute cycle* (See Chapter 23). On completion of each current instruction, the next instruction in the program's logical sequence of execution will be fetched from store automatically. This process ends, under normal circumstances, when a halt instruction in the program is recognised by the computer.

The example in Table 16.1 illustrates the form of a machine code program. Suppose that a computer has currently in its main store memory a simple machine code program to load two numbers into internal registers from memory, add them and store the result in memory. It could be shown as follows.

Each instruction in turn, starting with that resident in memory location 1000, would be fetched from memory, decoded and executed. This process would continue until the halt instruction in location 1007 was decoded.

The particular binary code or combination of binary digits (0's or 1's) in the instruction (shown in hexadecimal notation in the example) causes the decoding circuitry of the CPU to transmit to other components of the hardware the sequence of control signals necessary to perform the required operation.

Memory location	Contents (Hex)	Comments
1000	220F	Load R0 from ..
1001	2000	..memory location 2000
1002	221F	Load R1 from ..
1003	2001	..memory location 2001
1004	0901	Add R1 to R0
1005	351F	Store R0 in ..
1006	2002	..memory location 2002
1007	FFFF	Halt execution

Table 16.1. *Example machine code program*

When it is considered that a typical program might contain tens of thousands of machine code instructions, it might seem that programming is a formidable task, well beyond the capabilities of all but the most determined and meticulous of computer professionals. Indeed, if machine code were the only computer language in use, it is extremely unlikely that society would today be experiencing such a widespread presence of computers in almost every aspect of industrial, commercial, domestic and social life.

Fortunately for the computer industry, programming techniques have evolved along with advances in hardware. There is now a proliferation of programming languages designed to allow the programmer to concentrate most of his attention on solving the problem rather than on the tedious task of converting the solution to machine code form.

The evolution of programming languages

Low-level languages

In the history of programming languages, one of the first significant innovations was the development of assembly languages. A program written in an assembly language is much more readable and understandable than its equivalent in machine code. For example, a program, in some typical assembly language, equivalent to that given in Table 16.1 for the addition of two numbers, might take the form shown in Table 16.2.

Instruction	Comments
LDR R0, N1	;LoaD Register R0 with the contents of location N1
LDR R1, N2	;LoaD Register R1 with the contents of location N2
ADD R0, R1	;ADD Ro and R1 and store sum in R0
STR R0, N3	;STore Register R0 in location N3
HLT	;HaLT execution of program

Table 16.2. *Assembly language program for the addition of two numbers*

Notice that the operation codes LDR, ADD, STR and HLT (representing LOAD, ADD, STORE and HALT respectively) are now easily recognisable and easy to remember; such memory aids, or *mnemonics*, are chosen for these reasons. The references, N1, N2 and N3, relate to memory locations and are called *symbolic addresses*, and in many assembly languages it is possible to use more meaningful names such as HRS or RATE to indicate the type of data stored there. The internal registers, R0, R1, may be two of several available within the computer for use by the programmer.

The processor is unable to decode instructions in this coded form, so they must first be converted into the equivalent machine code. An *assembler* is a machine code program which performs this function. It accepts an assembly language program as data, converts mnemonic operation codes to their numeric equivalents, assigns symbolic addresses to memory loca-tions and produces as output the required machine code program. The assembly language program is termed the *source program* and the final machine code program is the *object program*. Thus assemblers and assembly languages have removed the need to write machine code programs and a considerable burden has been removed from the programming task; the computer itself now does much of the work required to produce the object program.

Though assembly languages aid the programmer considerably, they are still closely related to machine code; there is a one-to-one correspondence between a machine code instruction and one in assembly language. In other words each machine code instruction must have a matching assembly language instruction. This fundamental correspondence has led to the term *low-level* being applied to this type of programming language.

High-level Languages

Though assembly languages made computer programming easier, it was still a formidable and time-consuming task. Computer scientists recognised, however, that most programs could be broken down into a collection of smaller identifiable tasks and that no matter what the program, such tasks were present in some recognisable form, though probably occurring in different logical sequences.

For instance, the majority of programs require the evaluation of arithmetic expressions such as $X + Y \times Z - P/Q$, in other words expressions involving combinations of the four arith-metic operators +, −, × and / (addition, subtraction, multiplication and division respectively). Furthermore, most programs will produce some form of visible output, whether printed on paper or displayed on a screen and most programs require data to be input for processing.

All of these tasks require lengthy, complicated sequences of instructions, but, significantly, they can all be stated in a generalised form, and can therefore be implemented using general-ised machine code programs. *High-level* languages make extensive use of this characteristic. A high-level language is almost entirely constructed of these generalised sets of instructions or *statements*. A single statement, for instance, in a high-level language can specify the evaluation of a complex arithmetic expression requiring many machine code instructions. The translator required for such a source language is therefore much more complex than an assembler since each source language statement will generally generate many machine code instructions.

Taking the simple addition program introduced earlier to its conclusion, the program in a high-level language might merely reduce to the single statement

$$N3 = N1 + N2$$

meaning that the symbolic address N3 is to store the sum of the contents of the memory locations represented by the symbolic addresses N1 and N2. Notice that the programmer no longer needs to concern himself over the precise mechanics of the addition since the translator takes care of that automatically.

Most of the early high-level languages to be implemented (Fortran and COBOL for example) are classed as *procedure-oriented* languages, languages which allow the programmer to concentrate on the method of solving a problem (the *algorithm*), rather than on how the solution is to be expressed in a form that the computer can use directly. High-level languages thus remove the need for the programmer to get involved in the tedious and error-prone task of translating an algorithm into a low-level language. Since those days, other, more specialised languages have emerged. Many of these later languages are classed as *problem-oriented* languages because of their particularly close correspondence to certain application areas. For example, a number of high-level languages are used to define the movements of industrial robots, others are used for creating *expert systems* (see the next chapter) and there are some languages which are used exclusively for civil and electrical engineering applications.

To further complicate matters, high-level languages may also be described as *imperative* (sometimes *procedural*) or *declarative*. Imperative is the term used to describe high-level languages which require the programmer to show explicitly the order in which program statements are to be executed, and precisely how the programming solution is to be reached. The sequence of commands in a program is a key feature of imperative languages such as Pascal, FORTRAN and COBOL, since they are based on a conventional computer model in which a stored program is executed by sequentially stepping through instructions stored in the memory of a computer. Store locations are modified as a direct result of the action of the program. Similarly, imperative languages achieve their objectives by modifying program variables using assignment statements, and by causing sequential execution of program statements. Because imperative languages are so closely related to the operation of conventional computers, they are relatively efficient. However, other computer architectures, such as those using *parallel processing*, give rise to different types of programming languages.

Declarative languages rely on a different mechanism for solving programming problems. In these languages the emphasis is on defining the problem to be solved, not on the detailed sequence of instructions that are required in order to achieve the desired solution. It can be argued that a language such as Pascal is less procedural, and therefore more declarative, than an assembly language because there is less need for the programmer to define precisely how to do standard processing tasks such as input/output or arithmetic operations. For example, in an assembly language, it would require quite a complex sequence of instructions to perform the Pascal floating point calculation

```
x := (-b + sqrt(det))/(2.0*a);
```

Yet in Pascal it is merely a matter of specifying the calculation to be performed and allowing the compiler to determine how to organise the instructions required to do it. Thus languages that are predominantly procedural have elements of non-procedural characteristics.

Declarative languages take this a stage further, allowing the language translator to do much more of the work, so that the programmer can concentrate on specifying what the problem is rather than how to solve it.

Because declarative languages do not rely on the programmer specifying precisely in which order instructions are to be executed, it is often possible to process a number of instructions in parallel if the mechanism exists to allow this. The logic programming language Prolog is generally regarded as a good example of a predominantly declarative language. LISP, also described later, is also essentially declarative. Both Prolog and LISP have features which allow them to take advantage of alternative computer architectures.

Though it is true that by far the majority of computer programming today is in high-level languages such as Pascal, C or COBOL, programming in assembly languages is still essential for certain tasks. The reason for this, despite continual improvements in compiler design, is simply that the programmer, having total control over the structure of the machine code generated by the assembler, is able to write much faster and efficient code than that produced by a compiler. The very nature of high-level languages, allowing us to deal with a greatly simplified, virtual machine, often prevents the programmer from being able to fine tune code according to particular circumstances. Particularly where speed of execution is of primary importance, assembly languages invariably will be used in preference to high-level languages.

High-level language generations

Like computer hardware, high-level computer languages can be categorised according to a number of generations, from the first to the latest, or fifth generation. The five generations may be summarised as follows.

First generation. Appearing in the 1960s, these languages were based on the architectures of the current computers. Control structures were very basic, closely related to the instruction set of machines such as the IBM 704. Data structures were similarly based on the internal representations used for numbers and characters. The rather rigid syntactic structure of first generation languages was influenced by the use of punched cards as the main input medium for programs. Fortran is typical of this generation of languages.

Second generation. These elaborated on the structure of first generation languages in a number of important ways. Firstly, the overall structure was organised to aid program design. Secondly, there was a move towards structured programming by the introduction of more structured control structures. Thirdly, the syntax of the languages became more flexible, allowing statements to be expressed in a freer format. Algol-60 is typical of this generation.

Third generation. User-defined data structures became available, allowing a more application oriented approach to programming to be adopted. Control structures were modified to make them simpler and more efficient than those of the previous generation, and new, application orientated control structures such as the case statement, were added. These changes resulted in third generation languages becoming much more independent of computer hardware. Pascal is a good example of third generation languages.

Fourth generation. Such languages continue the tradition of reducing the work of the user and increasing the load on the computer. The terms Fourth Generation Language, and its contraction, 4GL, are subject to a wide variety of interpretations and definitions, but they all have a number of characteristics in common: they are easier to use than existing high-level languages, particularly by non-specialists; they allow quick solutions to data processing tasks; they are more concise than previous generations of high-level languages; the syntax of a 4GL is usually closer to natural language; they are more user-friendly.

Fifth generation. These languages break away from the conventional language format in ways which facilitate implementation on alternative computer architectures. For example, the fifth generation language Prolog allows programs to be implemented using parallel processing techniques. Object-oriented languages such as Smalltalk and functional languages such as LISP also allow this possibility, while still usable on conventional computers.

Though all HLLs can be applied to a wide variety of programming tasks, and are in that sense general-purpose languages, most high-level languages have been designed specifically for particular application areas. For example, Fortran's syntax facilitates modelling mathematical problems, COBOL allows data processing and file handling applications to be coded in a convenient manner, and LOGO was written to encourage children to approach problem solving logically and to explore mathematical concepts.

Some high-level languages

In the following sections we give a brief introduction to a number of well-known high-level languages.

BASIC(Beginners All-purpose Symbolic Instruction Code)

BASIC was developed at Dartmouth College, in the USA, in 1963 and was intended to be easy to learn and appropriate for a wide variety of applications. Its popularity has been largely the result of its ease of implementation on microcomputers, and it is frequently supplied with them. There is a standard for BASIC, just as there are standards for Fortran and COBOL, and most versions of BASIC adhere to this standard, but each version usually has additional features, many of which are specific to the particular version. Fortunately, however, having learned one version makes it easy to adapt to a different one.

In the past, BASIC has been heavily criticised for its tendency to encourage bad programming habits. Initially, few versions of BASIC had control structures to encourage or facilitate the use of structured programming techniques, and consequently large programs tended to be difficult to understand and modify. Some recent versions, however, have rectified this deficiency to greater or lesser extents by incorporating Pascal-like facilities.

Originally BASIC was an interpreted language, a feature which contributed to its suitability for novices, but over the past few years, such has been its popularity that a significant number of software houses have produced BASIC compilers which allow programs to be run independently of an interpreter and with the usual speed and security benefits provided by compiled languages.

C

C is a programming language developed by Bell Laboratories of the USA around 1972. It was designed and written by Dennis Ritchie who was at the time working on the development of the UNIX operating system. UNIX was designed to be particularly useful to the software engineer by providing a wide variety of software tools. In fact, the UNIX operating system was written in C, and even the C compiler is now written in C.

It was designed to be easy to learn and use, powerful and reliable and it has many characteristics of structured languages such as Pascal. Its roots are based in the language Algol and C retains many of its features, but C's strength lies in its simplicity, the facility with which complex programs may be built from simple building blocks.

Because Dennis Ritchie worked in the field of systems software, C is oriented to such applications as operating systems, computer language development and text processing. Its suitability for these areas is largely attributable to the fact that it is a relatively low-level language which facilitates very efficient programming, yet at the same time it retains the advantage of high-level languages to hide the details of the computer's architecture.

COBOL (COmmon Business-Oriented Language)

COBOL was first specified in 1959 and was designed primarily as a language for data processing applications involving a great deal of input and output operations with a relatively minor amount of calculation in between. It was the first language to place equal importance on data and procedures, allowing the separate definition of each in special sections of the language called *divisions*. This aids programmers to deal with multiple complex file structures in a well-defined and disciplined manner. COBOL is available on practically every type of computer system, including personal computers but, because of the large number of different implementations of the standard definition of the language and the tendency for software developers to add their own extensions, it is not very portable between different computers.

The final chapter of this book provides an introduction to COBOL, describing the overall structure of COBOL programs, and giving a number of illustrative programs.

Java

Java is programming language for the Internet. It allows programs to be transferred over the Internet in the same way as web pages - Java programs are executed by browsers just as web pages are displayed by browsers. Programs downloaded and executed in this way are called 'applets', that is small applications. Java was developed by Sun Microsystems Inc in the USA.

The team of developers designed Java to be:

Simple. They designed it to look like a simplified form of C++, a widely used programming language. Although it looks very much like C++, it lacks a number of features which are rarely used, can lead to poor programming practices , or are prone to introducing program 'bugs'. As a result, Java is relatively easy to learn, particularly for experienced programmers.

Distributed, so that it could support applications on networks, and in particular the Internet. With Java it is just as easy for a program to access a file on a remote computer anywhere in the world as one on your own computer.

Portable. A Java compiler is initially used to produce program object code in the form of 'byte-codes', a neutral form of code that is later run by a Java interpreter. This means that any computer system, no matter whether it is a mainframe, IBM PC or Macintosh, can download and run a Java applet if the browser is 'Java enabled' (which all of the latest browsers are).

Secure. Because Internet users can download and run Java programs from random sites on the Internet, Java has safeguards against such things as computer viruses or other programs that attempt to alter files.

Fortran(Formula Translator)

Fortran was designed by John Backus of IBM in 1953 for the science and engineering field. A Fortran compiler first appeared in 1955 for an IBM machine, and since that time it has enjoyed widespread popularity as a powerful software tool. Since its introduction, Fortran has steadily evolved, giving rise to such versions as WATFOR (developed at the university of WATerloo, Canada) and WATFIV as well as Fortran IV.

Mainly orientated towards scientific /mathematical /engineering applications, many of its statements resemble and provide for numerical calculations. A Fortran program may be defined as a subroutine (subprogram) which may be 'called' by other programs in order to perform some standard or common operation. By forming libraries of these subroutines a programmer is able to reduce the amount of work required to write a new program; where possible, his program will make reference to these prewritten modules which will be combined with his code when the program is compiled. The language has many standard mathematical functions, such as SIN, COS, and SQRT, built in.

LISP (LISt Processing)

LISP, developed in the late 1950's and early 60's, was designed as a list processing language. Statements in LISP look like functions. For instance, the function which adds numbers in

LISP is called PLUS and is written

(PLUS 2 3)

The function PLUS operates on the 'arguments' 2 and 3. All statements are written in this way.

However, LISP is primarily a language for manipulating symbols rather than performing complex numeric calculations. It treats all forms of data as being elements of lists and has facilities for conveniently manipulating these lists in various ways. Moreover, the language is extensible in that the user is able to create his own functions to be used like any of those supplied.

Programs in LISP are developed interactively. Typing the name of a function, followed by its arguments, causes the function to be performed and the result displayed. In the addition example above, LISP would return the number 5 as soon as the function had been entered. This characteristic is one of the strengths of the language in that programs are written in small, easily testable steps, the effects of which can be seen immediately.

Though LISP is one of the oldest computer languages (nearly as old as Fortran) it is used extensively in one of the most innovative of today's research areas: artificial intelligence. As its popularity increases it is becoming available on more and more machines; most mainframes and an increasing number of micros support a version of the language.

Logo

Designed as a language to provide a very early and easy route into programming, Logo is probably best known as the first language to use 'turtle graphics'. When running Logo, the turtle appears as a graphics cursor which can be instructed to move across the screen using commands such as FORWARD 20 or RIGHT 30. Remotely controllable devices can also be connected to the computer and controlled by the same commands.

The 'turtle' commands have been designed to be appealing and to motivate children to write programs to make the turtle perform visually pleasing manoeuvres. Seymour Papert, the American mathematician who designed the language, was largely influenced by Piaget's well-known ideas on intellectual development in children. Consequently Logo is regarded as an important educational tool. Unlike much educational software currently available in which the computer is the teacher, and the child reacts to it, Logo offers a completely different approach to computer assisted learning. With Logo the roles are reversed, the child teaching the computer what to do.

In his book,'Mindstorms', Seymour Papert explains the philosophy of Logo, how it was developed and how it works. Logo, however, is more than a language just for children. It is based on LISP and shares many of its features. Like LISP it is extensible, based on list processing, and allows recursion. Because it is interpreted, it is easy to use and allows programs to be edited without difficulty. In fact it is a surprisingly powerful language, as well as being easy to learn. It is by no means a 'toy' language and is attracting much interest in all kinds of areas, including artificial intelligence applications.

Pascal

Devised by Professor Niklaus Wirth in 1970 and named after the gifted 17th century mathematician and philosopher Blaise Pascal, Pascal is a general-purpose language based on Algol-60.

Because Pascal, like BASIC, was designed as a teaching language, it is a very easy language to learn. Moreover, being orientated towards structured programming, it encourages the clear expression of the logical structure of the program. This makes Pascal a very easy language to write programs in, and is particularly suitable for the development of large programs. For these reasons it is widely used in teaching, and is being adopted by more and more establishments of further and higher education as the main programming language for computing courses.

Each Pascal program consists of a declarations section in which the structure of the data to be processed and produced is defined, a section for the definition of *functions* and *procedures* which are referenced in the program body section. The program body defines the operation of the program in a precise series of steps. Functions and procedures are subprograms which can be 'called' from the program body whenever required.

Prolog (Programming in Logic)

Invented by Alain Colmerauer in the early 1970's, Prolog was first implemented in Marseilles in 1972. It provided a means allowing the programmer to specify a problem in terms related to formal logic rather than procedures. It has been used extensively in the development of *expert systems* because it includes facilities ideal for this type of application.

Prolog is said to be *goal oriented*, that is to say the programmer specifies the problem to be solved in terms of a goal, and is not expected to provide detailed instructions regarding the achievement of the goal. A goal is defined in terms of subgoals, the achievement of which will lead to the final solution. A subgoal may be a simple statement which evaluates to logical true or false, or may depend on its own subgoals which Prolog will try to evaluate. Since there may be alternative sets of subgoals for a particular goal, Prolog may having failed to successfully resolve one combination, backtrack and try another combination. It will continue to try different combinations until either a solution is reached or there are no further combinations of subgoals to try. The power of Prolog lies in its built-in ability to select goal combinations and to backtrack; in other languages this would have to be programmed explicitly.

Language processors

The function of a *language processor*, or *translator*, is to convert a program written in a computer language (the *source code*) into a machine sensible form (the *object code*). An *assembler* is a language processor for assembly language programs and *compilers* and *interpreters* are required for translating high-level languages.

Assemblers

As we saw earlier, a program written in an assembly language is much more readable and understandable than its equivalent in machine code; the problem arises, however, that it is no longer directly executable by the computer. An assembler is a computer program which carries out the necessary translation. The assembly process is illustrated in Figure 16.1.

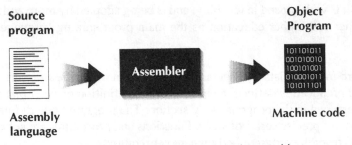

Figure 16.1. *Translation process with assembler*

The assembler accepts an assembly language program (the source code) as its data input, processes it and produces as output the required machine code program (the object code).

An assembler carries out a number of tasks during the process of assembly, including:

- ❑ Op-code translation. The mnemonic op-codes must be replaced by the numeric op-codes which the computer uses to identify its various instructions;

- ❑ Absolute address allocation. Each instruction or data word in the source program must be allocated an absolute machine address (its physical location). The assembler maintains a location counter (sometimes referred to as a load pointer) which, having been set to an initial base address, is incremented by the length of each data or instruction word as it is assembled.

- ❑ Symbolic operand conversion. This refers to the assembly process of replacing any symbolic operands with numeric machine addresses. A symbol table records each symbolic operand together with its corresponding absolute address; a similar table stores labels and their machine addresses.

The assembler must also convert any constant values to the machine's internal binary representation; this may involve conversion from decimal, hexadecimal or text. If the assembly language supports the use of *macro* instructions (a shorthand used by a programmer to express sequences of regularly used instructions by a macro name), they must be expanded by the assembler to their normal assembly language equivalents before any instructions are processed. Apart from sending the resulting object code to backing storage, an assembler will normally carry out a number of other tasks, including the generation of error messages and the output of source code listings.

The assembly process usually involves the assembler in executing several *passes* of the program's source code, each one carrying out certain of the tasks described above. The problem of forward referencing (an instruction uses a symbolic operand which is not defined until later in the program, so its address has not been allocated at that point and cannot be included in the instruction) means that assemblers carry out a minimum of two passes:

Pass 1   Any macro instructions are expanded as part of the pass or as a separate initial pass, making three in all. All instructions are examined and checked for syntactical correctness; any errors are recorded in an error table. After each instruction has been dealt with, the location counter is incremented, and a symbol table is constructed to link any symbolic operands and labels to their corresponding absolute addresses.

Pass 2   By reference to the symbol table, any instructions containing unresolved references are completed. If the second pass detects no errors, the assembler generates and outputs the object code, otherwise an error report is produced showing where errors were detected.

Compilers and interpreters

There are two main types of high-level language translators (or *language processors* as they are often known):

- ❑   compilers;

- ❑   interpreters.

Since the choice of translator has implications regarding program development time, debugging and testing, memory requirements, execution speed and program security, it is important from a programming point of view to be quite clear about the difference between the two types.

Somewhat like an assembler, a *compiler* accepts a source program, that is, a program written in some high-level language, Pascal for instance, checks that it is correctly formed and, if so, generates the equivalent object program in a low-level language. The translated program may be in the form of an assembly language, in which case it must first be assembled before it is executed, or it may be in machine code, allowing it to be executed directly without further modification. If any errors are detected during compilation, they will be reported and, if serious enough, may prevent the compiler from completing the translation process. Figure 16.2 illustrates the compilation process.

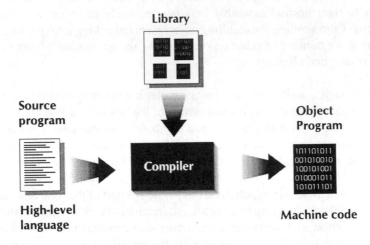

Figure 16.2. *Compilation process*

A compiler will often have access to one or more libraries of pre-compiled procedures for performing commonly used tasks. Included in these libraries of machine code subprograms will be routines for performing arithmetic operations, input/output operations, backing storage data transfers and other commonly used functions. Whenever the source code refers to one of these routines specifically, or needs one to perform the operation specified, the compiler will ensure that the routine is added to the object program.

Note that the final object code is independent of both the source code and the compiler itself. That is, neither of these two programs needs to be resident in main store when the object code is being executed. However, any alterations to the program subsequent to its compilation will necessitate modification and re-compilation of the source code prior to executing the program again.

An *interpreter* uses a different method to translate a source program into a machine-sensible form. An object program is not generated in this form of translation, rather the source program, or an intermediate form of it, is scanned statement by statement, each in turn immediately being converted into the actions specified. Figure 16.3 illustrates the interpreter process.

The source program statements are translated and executed separately, as they are encountered, while the source program is being processed by the interpreter. The object code actually executed is held within the interpreter; the latter merely identifies from the source statement which piece of object code (*subroutine*) is relevant and causes it to be performed. On completion of a statement, control returns to the interpreter which then processes the next logical statement in the program sequence.

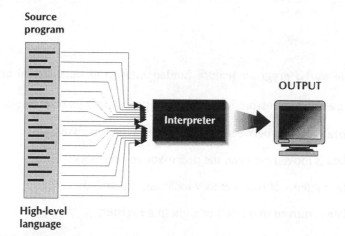

Source
program

High-level
language

Figure 16.3. *Interpreter translating high level language source program*

It might seem, therefore, that an interpreter has a big advantage over a compiler. In terms of the amount of effort required in obtaining an executable program, this is certainly true, but there are a number of other factors which favour the use of a compiler. For example, an interpreter must do a considerable amount of work before it can even begin to cause a source statement to be executed (error checking, for instance); on the other hand, a compiler has already done this work during compilation. Moreover, should a section of source code be repeated one or more times, an interpreter must re-interpret the section each time. Consequently, interpreted programs tend to run significantly slower than equivalent compiled programs, and for time-critical applications this might be a major concern. Furthermore, because the translation and execution phases are interwoven, the interpreter must be resident in memory at the same time as the source code. If memory space is at a premium, this can be a severe limitation of an interpreted language.

Languages designed for use by children or for teaching purposes are often interpreted. Logo, for example, originally designed as a language for children, is interpreted to facilitate its interactive nature. Similarly, BASIC is interpreted in order to simplify its use for programming novices.

A possible compromise is to provide both an interpreter and a compiler for the same language; this allows rapid development time using the interpreter, and fast execution obtained by compiling the code.

Exercises

1. Why is the *stored program* feature fundamental to modern digital computers?

2. Name the category of instruction in a typical processor's *instruction set* when:

    (i)   data is moved between registers within the processor;

    (ii)   data is moved between the processor and memory;

    (iii)   the contents of two memory locations are added;

    (iv)   data is moved to the left or right in a register;

    (v)   some program instructions are skipped to execute another set of instructions.

3. Why are many programming languages described as *problem-oriented*?

4. If a programming language emphasises facilities to define the problem to be solved, rather requiring the programmer to detail the precise steps needed for its solution, is it described as *procedural* or *declarative*?

5. Name the software used to translate:

    (i)   a *high-level*

    (ii)   an *assembly*

    language source program into machine code.

6. Create a table summarising major features of each of the following: *interpreter*; *compiler*; *assembler*.

7. List the stages involved in translating a program from *source* to *object* code.

8. Choose a modern operating system such as Windows 95 or NT and describe how the following functions are performed:

    (i)   running applications;   (ii) directory and file housekeeping;

    (iii)   finding files.

9. Define the term *virtual memory*

Chapter 17

Categories of Software

Introduction

The tree diagram shown in Figure 17.1 illustrates the different categories of software and, to some extent, their relationships to each other. This section begins by examining the distinction between *systems software* and *applications software*.

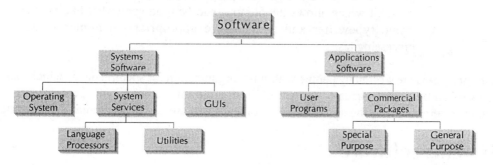

Figure 17.1. *Categories of software*

The term systems software covers the collection of programs usually supplied by the manufacturer of the computer. These programs protect the user from the enormous complexity of the computer system, and enable the computer to be used to maximum effect by a wide variety of people, many of whom will know very little about the inner workings of computers. Without systems software a modern digital computer would be virtually impossible to use; as computer hardware has evolved, so systems software has been forced to become more and more complex in order to make effective use of it. Broadly speaking, systems software consists of three elements:

❑ those programs concerned with the internal control and co-ordination of all aspects of the computer system, namely the *operating system;*

❑ a number of other programs providing various services to users. These services include *translators* for any languages supported by the system and *utility programs* such as program editors and other aids to programming;

❑ *graphical user interfaces* (GUIs) providing intuitive, easily learned methods for using microcomputer systems.

Applications software refers to programs which have some direct value to an organisation, and will normally include those programs for which the computer system was specifically purchased. For example, a mail order company might acquire a computer system initially for stock control and accounting purposes, when its volume of business begins to make these functions too difficult to cope with by manual means. Applications programs would be required to record and process customers' orders, update the stock file according to goods sent or received, make appropriate entries in the various accounts ledgers, etc. Commercially produced applications software falls into two main categories:

- ❑   *special-purpose* packages, such as a company payroll program used to store employee details and generate details of pay for each individual employee;

- ❑   *general-purpose* packages which may be used for a wide variety of purposes. An example of a general-purpose package is a *word processor*, a program which allows the computer to be used somewhat like an electronic typewriter and is therefore appropriate to numerous text processing tasks.

User programs are written by people within the organization for specific needs which cannot be satisfied by other sources of software. These program writers may be professional programmers employed by the organization, or other casual users with programming expertise.

Systems software

First generation computers are normally defined in hardware terms, in that they were constructed using valve technology, but another important characteristic of this generation of computers was the equally primitive software support provided for programmers and other users. Modern computers perform automatically many of the tasks that programmers in those days had to handle themselves: writing routines to control peripheral devices, allocating programs to main store, executing programs, checking peripheral devices for availability, as well as many other routine tasks.

In subsequent generations of computers, manufacturers started addressing themselves to the problem of improving the programming environment by providing standard programs for many routine tasks. Many of these routines became linked together under the control of a single program called the *executive, supervisor,* or *monitor*, whose function was to supervise the running of user programs and, in general, to control and co-ordinate the functioning of the whole computer system, both hardware and software. Early programs of this type have evolved into the sophisticated programs collectively known as *operating systems*.

Systems software has four important functions:

- ❑   to make it easier to run user programs;

❑   to improve the performance of the computer system;

❑   to provide assistance with program development;

❑   to simplify the use of the computer system for users other than computer specialists.

The operating system takes care of the first two requirements, system services provide assistance with program development and graphical user interfaces (GUIs) simplify the use of the computer system.

Operating systems

If a computer system is viewed as a set of resources, comprising elements of both hardware and software, then it is the job of the collection of programs known as the operating system to manage these resources as efficiently as possible. In so doing, the operating system acts as a buffer between the user and the complexities of the computer itself. One way of regarding the operating system is to think of it as a program which allows the user to deal with a simplified computer, but without losing any of the computational power of the machine. In this way the computer system becomes a virtual system, its enormous complexity hidden and controlled by the operating system and through which the user communicates with the real system.

The main functions of operating systems

Earlier it was stated that the function of an operating system is to manage the resources of the computer system. These resources generally fall into the following categories.

Central processing unit (CPU)

A *multi-user* computer system can be accessed by several users, simultaneously; since only one program can be executed at any one time, access to the CPU must be carefully controlled and monitored. In a *timesharing* multi-user system each user is given a small time-slice of processor time before passing on to the next user in a continuously repeating sequence. Another common scheme is to assign priorities to users so that the system is able to determine which user should next have control of the CPU.

Memory

Programs (or parts of programs) must be loaded into the memory before they can be executed, and moved out of the memory when no longer required there. Storage space must be provided for data generated by programs, and provision must be made for the temporary storage of data, caused by data transfer operations involving devices such as printers and disk drives.

Input/output (I/O) devices

Programs will request the use of these devices during the course of their execution and in a multi-user system conflicts are bound to arise, when a device being utilized by one program is requested by another. The operating system will control allocation of I/O devices and attempt to resolve any conflicts which arise. It will also monitor the state of each I/O device and signal any faults detected.

Backing store

Programs and data files will usually be held on mass storage devices such as magnetic disk and tape drives. The operating system will supervise data transfers between these devices and memory and deal with requests from programs for space on them.

Files

These may be regarded as a limited resource for multi-user systems, in the sense that several users may wish to share the same data file at the same time. The operating system facilitates access to files and ensures restricted access to one program at any one time for those files which are to be written to.

Resource allocation is closely linked to one part of the operating system called the *scheduler*. The term *scheduling* refers to the question of when, in a multi-user system, a new process should be introduced into the system and in which order the processes should be run.

The above is by no means a full list of the functions of an operating system. Other functions include:

❑   interpretation of the command language by which operators can communicate with the operating system;

❑   error handling. For example, detecting and reporting inoperative or malfunctioning peripherals;

❑   protection of data files and programs from corruption by other users;

❑   protection of data files and programs from unauthorized use;

❑   accounting and logging of the use of the computer resources.

Some current operating systems

OS/2

OS/2 Version 1.0 was announced by IBM and Microsoft in April 1987, as a multi-tasking operating system. Since then the collaboration between these two companies has broken down and Microsoft has produced its highly successful Windows GUI (see later).

Numerous improvements have been made to the original version of OS/2, but it is still failing to make any significant impression in the PC software market. In an effort to take an increased share of this market, IBM has ensured that OS/2 is able to run applications developed for MS-DOS and Windows, as well as OS/2 itself.

Workplace Shell - the OS/2 GUI

Workplace Shell has the main features of a conventional GUI, with windows that can be moved and re-sized, scroll bars (for viewing different areas of work within the available window), dialogue boxes, etc. Unlike the Windows GUI (see later), it does not allocate file management to a separate component. Instead, users are encouraged to view data files as the entry point for applications (rather than the other way around). Workplace Shell can be described as *object orientated*. An object can be a program, a data file, a folder (directory) or device (such as a printer). When an object is selected, a pop-up menu offers options appropriate to the object. For example, a program object menu includes a 'run' option. Similarly, a data file object provides options concerning, for example, the printing or copying of the file. When running Microsoft Windows applications, the desktop is presented accordingly, with the Program Manager window.

32-bit applications

For brevity, OS/2 Version 2.1 is referred to simply as OS/2. As a 32-bit operating system, OS/2 can take full advantage of the current 32-bit processors and 32-bit software. Handling data in 32-bit units, rather than 16 bits at a time, contributes to quicker system performance. To ensure its compatibility with a huge section of the PC software market, OS/2 can run 16-bit software; virtually all MS-DOS and a few Windows applications are designed to retain backward compatibility with the 16-bit 80286 processor. Windows 3.x also runs 32-bit applications (using an i386, or later, processor), when it is operating in *enhanced mode*.

Multi-tasking

OS/2 allocates a separate, private, area of memory to each application. It also provides facilities to protect one application from the activities of another. Device drivers (disk controllers, screen and printer drivers) operate at a higher level of privilege within memory, because they have to remain accessible to all current applications.

OS/2 uses *pre-emptive* multi-tasking. This means that the operating system controls the amount of processor time each application receives, before switching activity to one of the others. The amount of time received by a task, depends on its urgency (the user can specify priorities). OS/2 can *multi-thread* separate processes; for example, it can a initiate the printing of a document by a word processor and then immediately return to its previous task. The user can continue working on another task, while the document is being printed in the background.

File management

OS/2 offers two file management systems:

(i)   an enhanced File Allocation Table (FAT) system, which can be read by MS-DOS;

(ii)   a High Performance File System (HPFS).

Users have to choose which one to install. The choice depends largely on the capacity of the drive and whether or not MS-DOS applications are to be used.

The HPFS is completely different from the FAT system and is designed to manage, more effectively, the higher capacity (measured in gigabytes) hard drives. HPFS file names can be up to 254 characters in length (compared with the 8 permitted by MS-DOS). Both filing systems allow up to 64Kb of *attribute data* to be attached to each file; the data can comprise text and images. This permits extensive labelling of a file, describing its contents and perhaps associations with other files or applications. Effectively, this means that longer file names can also be used with the enhanced FAT system.

Both systems (like Windows) support *write caching*, which means that writing to disk can be delayed if the processor is busy. The mechanism can be disabled, as there is a small risk that data may be lost (while it waits in the cache memory) if there is a sudden power cut.

A short history of Microsoft Windows

Microsoft's Windows was initially developed as a front-end to DOS-based applications. It allowed novice computer users to use an IBM-compatible PC without having to learn the rather cryptic DOS commands. However, it was not really until 1990 that it became a serious alternative to DOS. The history of Windows is briefly traced here, from its rather inauspicious first appearance in 1985, to its huge popularity today.

Five releases preceded Windows 95, the latest version of the Microsoft Windows operating system. The first version, version 1.0 released in 1985, was beset with problems. The main reason for this was that the hardware generally available at the time did not lend itself to a graphical user interface. The combination of an under powered processor (the Intel 8086), low-resolution graphics and lack of internal memory conspired to produce a piece of software that was not very well received by the computer industry. Though it did make a PC easier to use for non-technical users, being text-based it was not what is recognised today as a true graphical user interface.

However, the success of Apple's Macintosh personal computer, with its intuitive, graphical user interface, encouraged Microsoft to continue in competition and the result was Windows 2.0. Still text-based, this version was not a great deal better than the previous one, though the Windows/386 version released in 1988 did offer multi-tasking as a direct result of the increased processing power that the Intel 80386 processor provided. It was not until 1990, when Windows 3.0 provided an attractive, user-friendly graphical interface and several other enhancements, that Windows was recognised as providing a real alternative to DOS-based application. Windows 3.0 offered improved memory management so that applications could do more; it made extensive use of icons and it provided the Program Manager utility which simplified the management of applications.

This version of Windows also allows several tasks to run at the same time. However, partly as a result of its attempt to make Windows 3.0 backwardly compatible with other versions and also with DOS applications, Microsoft introduced too much instability into the operating system. This manifested itself in system crashes, which announced themselves with the notorious 'Unrecoverable Application Error' message box. Version 3.1 addressed these problems by fixing known bugs in version 3.0 and, more importantly, by more carefully monitoring the behaviour of applications to trap possible problems before they caused the system to 'hang'. Moreover, in version 3.1 Microsoft introduced the facility to utilise disk space as *virtual* memory, thus releasing the user from having to be too careful about the amount of memory that was required by an application.

The next main development in the evolution of Windows was the release of Windows for Workgroups 3.11. This release represented Microsoft's efforts to support small organisations using small Local Area Networks. The new features included in Windows for Workgroups allowed a number of PCs to be linked by installing a network card and some cable. Network features such as meeting scheduling and e-mail were also provided. The reliability of Windows was further improved in this version.

Windows NT

The structure of Microsoft's Windows NT operating system is illustrated in Figure 17.2. It first became available in September 1993. It is a 32-bit multi-tasking operating system and competes directly with OS/2.Its hardware requirements are greater than those needed for the Windows 3.x GUI and it is not seen as a replacement for it. Windows NT needs a minimum of 12Mb of main memory and 75Mb of free disk space.

There are three main parts to Windows NT:

(i)   NT *executive*, which is the operating system and controls the hardware;

(ii)   Win32 sub-system, which the NT executive runs as an application. Win32 provides the Windows GUI;

(iii)   MS-DOS, OS/2 and Portable UNIX sub-systems, which allows the running of software written for these operating systems. Concerning OS/2, only applications written for the character-based interface are supported. Software written for Windows 3.x (see earlier) will also run under Windows NT. These sub-systems can only operate through the Win32 sub-system.

Figure 17.2 illustrates the main components in the structure and their relationship with one another and to the hardware.

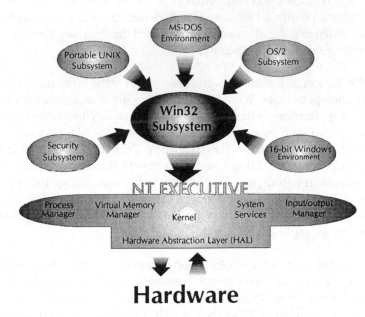

Figure 17.2. *Structure of Windows NT*

The Virtual Memory Manager controls the allocation of main memory to applications and ensures that each is protected from other processes. When there is insufficient main memory space, some memory contents are paged to disk (*virtual memory*) until room becomes available (when they are paged back in). This protection does not apply to Windows 3.x applications (run through the Windows sub-system) which can, at times, clash for memory space and crash.

The Process Manager controls the multi-tasking process. Windows NT (like OS/2) can carry out 'fine grained' multi-tasking. This enables the concurrent processing of tasks within the same application. For example, new records could be entered into a database, while a database sort is being executed in the background.

The Input/Output Manager handles file reading and writing operations, at the physical machine level. It provides a File Allocation Table (FAT) system, compatible with the MS-DOS system and a High Performance File System (HPFS) to handle OS/2 applications. NT's own file system (NTFS) allows the use of long file names and the storage of files of many gigabytes.

The *kernel* handles signals from the hardware, indicating conditions such as the completion of data transfer through a communications port.

Portability

The MS-DOS and OS/2 operating systems are designed to make particular use of the Intel series of processors. Apart from the kernel, the Windows NT operating system does not relate specifically to the architecture of any particular processor. To some extent it is 'processor independent' and can be used on non-Intel processor machines. This independence is achieved with the use of a Hardware Abstraction Layer (HAL), which comes between the hardware and the NT Executive.

Windows 95

Based on Windows NT, Windows 95 offers a PC operating system that also does not rely on DOS for its operation. Though it is not regarded as a replacement for the more powerful NT operating system, Windows 95 nevertheless has a number of major improvements over previous versions of Windows. These include:

❑   improved speed;

❑   improved reliability, though 'misbehaving' applications can still 'crash' a system.

❑   better user interface;

❑   better networking capabilities;

❑   'plug and play' capability;

❑   support for long file names.

The speed improvement results from the fact that Windows 95 uses 32-bit code to perform much of its work and that it uses *pre-emptive multitasking* to control applications. As mentioned earlier in this chapter, multi-tasking allows several applications, or *tasks*, to be running simultaneously, but with pre-emptive multi-tasking it is the operating system rather than the tasks, that controls the resources that are available. This ensures that each current task is allowed its fair share of the resources that it requests.

Improved reliability has resulted mainly from removing Window's dependence on DOS. Many of the instability problems experienced in previous versions of Windows were directly related to its use of DOS, which allowed applications to take complete control of the computer system. When more than one application is running in a multi-tasking environment, then each application must restrict itself to using only certain resources, especially memory, otherwise conflicts arise which cause the machine to crash. DOS applications can still run in Windows 95, but they are restricted to a virtual machine that emulates earlier processor architectures such as that of the 8086 family. This greatly reduces the possibility of a DOS application 'misbehaving'. Additional stability resulted from more 'bug fixes'. The new user interface is shown in Figure 17.3, in the section on the Graphical User Interface (GUI).

'Explorer' replaces in a single application the previous versions' Program Manager and File Manager utility programs. It provides a very flexible way of organising files and programs using 'folders' which are similar to directories. A *task bar* at the bottom of the screen has a 'Start' button which is used to activate pop up menus, and applications currently available, either running or idle, are shown as separate named buttons. By clicking on the name of an application on the task bar, that application's window becomes the current focus, thereby allowing access to the application's controls.

Note also the application shortcuts on the right, represented by icons and the shortcut bar on the left; both features add to the flexibility and ease of use of the system.

Windows 95 provides a form of networking called *peer-to-peer* support. This allows a network to be constructed simply by installing a network card in each workstation and connecting them together with cable. One or more workstations can be configured as servers, without the need to buy extra machines for this purpose. Peer-to-peer networking allows each user to have access to the files on every other machine, providing that they are granted the appropriate rights to do so.

Plug and Play (PNP) is the term given to a computer hardware standard which allows the operating system to detect and to deal with the installation and control of devices automatically. Windows 95 performs the following PNP facilities:

❑   identification of all of the PNP components attached to the system, thus greatly reducing the information that needs to be provided during installation;

❑   determination of the resource needs of each device;

❑   automatic creation of system configuration, thus removing the need for a user-controlled device manager;

❑   device driver loading and unloading as and when required;

❑   notification of configuration changes by displaying a dialogue box on-screen whenever a change in the number or type of devices has changed.

Because of their dependency on DOS, previous versions of Windows required the familiar 8.3 format (*filename.ext*) for file names. Windows 95 now allows filenames of almost any length to be used, including embedded spaces.

System services

Often a manufacturer will provide a number of programs designed specifically for program or application development. Some examples of such aids are as follow.

Language processors

These are computer programs designed to convert high-level language programs into machine code, that is, into a form directly usable by a computer. Common types of language processors are *compilers* and *interpreters*.

Utility programs

As part of the systems software provided with a computer system there are a number of utility programs specifically designed to aid program development and testing. These include the following.

Editors

These permit the creation and modification of source programs and data files. The facilities offered by these programs usually include such things as character, word and line insertion and deletion, automatic line numbering, line tabulation for languages which require program instructions to be spaced in a specific manner, the storage and retrieval of files from backing storage, and the printing of programs or other files.

Debugging aids

Programs in which the appropriate translator can find no fault will often contain errors in logic, known as bugs, which only become apparent when the program is run, producing results which are contrary to expectations, or even causing the computer to cease functioning. These bugs are often very difficult to detect and may lead to long delays in the implementation of the program. Debugging aids help programmers to isolate and identify the cause of bugs.

File managers

These simplify and facilitate a number of operations connected with program development and maintenance such as:

❑   keeping backup copies of important files;

❑   deleting files and creating space for new ones;

❑   merging files;

❑   providing details of current files held on backing storage;

❑   sorting file names into specified orders.

Without the help of such dedicated programs, operations such as these could be extremely time-consuming and consequently expensive.

Graphical user interfaces (GUIs)

The vast majority of microcomputer users are interested merely in using a computer as a tool, without any real interest in the technical details of its operation. A typical user will probably want to run one or more common general-purpose applications, organize files into directories, delete files and format disks. Though the operating system will provide these services, the user needs to have a certain amount of technical knowledge to perform these tasks. *Graphical user interfaces* (or GUI, pronounced *Gooey*) provide a more intuitive means of performing common tasks. They usually make use of a pointing device, typically a *mouse* (see Chapter 19), by means of which a *pointer* is moved around the monitor screen on which small pictures (or *icons*) are displayed. These icons represent, among other things, programs which can be run by moving the mouse pointer over the icon and then clicking one of the buttons on the mouse. Applications run in their own self-contained areas called *windows*. In addition, it is usually possible to activate *pull-down menus* which provide access to standard functions. When a GUI uses Windows, Icons, Mouse, Pointers and Pull-down menus, it is referred to as a *WIMP* environment.

Figure 17.3 shows the GUI for Microsoft's Windows 95 operating system.

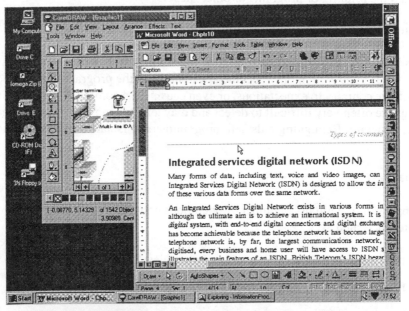

Figure 17.3. *Graphical user interface for Windows 95 operating system*

Two windows are shown Figure 17.3:

❑   one running CorelDraw, a graphic design program (see later);

❑   the other running the word processor, Microsoft's Word for Windows.

A file management utility, called explorer can be seen on the Task Bar at the bottom of the screen. This can be made the active window by clicking on its name on the Task Bar. All three programs are in memory, having already been loaded from disk. Only Microsoft Word, in the window with the black title bar, is active, that is, currently in use. Thus it is possible to be working on several applications at the same time, switching from one to the other very quickly and with minimum effort.

All such windows, no matter what the application, have a number of common features, including:

❑   a title bar with the name of the particular application and the name of the document being edited or created by that application;

❑   a menu bar containing the names of a number of pull-down menus;

❑   horizontal and vertical scroll bars providing access to parts of the document not shown in the window;

❑   a number of control icons for sizing, maximizing (making the current window occupy the whole screen), minimizing (reducing the window to an icon on the Task Bar in Figure 17.3) and closing the window;

❑   a tool bar containing icons which, when selected, perform frequently required tasks, such as saving documents to disk or printing documents as in the case of Word for Windows, or drawing tools in the case of CorelDraw;

❑   a help facility accessed from the menu bar and providing detailed information on the operation of all aspects of the application on the screen while the application is running.

The major advantage of applications having these common features is that, having learned how one application operates, it is possible to use much of the same knowledge with other windows applications, thus significantly reducing the time required to become proficient in the use of unfamiliar applications.

Applications software

An analysis of the uses to which companies and individuals put computers would reveal that the same types of tasks appear time and time again. Many organizations use computers for payroll calculations, others to perform stock control functions, accounting procedures, management information tasks and numerous other common functions. These types of programs are classed as *applications software*, software which is applied to practical tasks in order to make them more efficient or useful in other ways. Systems software is merely there to support the running, development and maintenance of applications software.

An organisation wishing to implement one of these tasks (or any other vital to its efficient operation) on a computer has several alternatives:

❑ Ask a software house, that is, a company specializing in the production of software, to take on the task of writing a specific program for the organization's needs.

❑ Use its own programming staff to produce the software in house.

❑ Buy a commercially available program off the shelf and hope that it already fulfils, or can be modified to fulfil, the organization's requirements.

❑ Buy a general purpose program, such as a database or spreadsheet package, that has the potential to perform the required functions.

The final choice will depend on such factors as the urgency of the requirements, financial constraints, size of the company and the equipment available. It is beyond the scope of this chapter to enter into a discussion regarding either the strategy for making such a decision or to investigate specific items of software available for specific applications; but, with the immense and growing, popularity of general-purpose packages, particularly for personal microcomputer systems, it is worth looking in more detail at this category of software.

General-purpose packages for microcomputers

Discussion of this class of software will be restricted here to the following headings, though they are not intended to represent an exhaustive list of all the categories of general purpose packages which are available:

❑ word processors;

❑ spreadsheets;

❑ databases;

❑ graphics packages, including desktop publishing (DTP), business graphics, graphic design and computer aided drawing (CAD);

❑ expert systems;

❑ hypertext systems and browsers.

What characterises these software types as belonging to the category of general-purpose packages is that they have been designed to be very flexible and applicable to a wide range of different tasks. For instance, a spreadsheet can be used as easily for simple accountancy procedures as for stock control; a database can be used with equal facility to store information on technical papers from journals, stock item details and personnel details for payroll purposes. In fact, particularly in respect of modern personal computer software, the trend is for general-purpose packages to do more and more. For example, recent word processors, such as Microsoft's Word for Windows and WordPerfect, include facilities, once only found in desktop publishing packages, for drawing diagrams and for producing graphs, in addition to the normal functions associated with a word processor; the graphic design package Corel-Draw, includes some word processing functions and graph drawing functions; the spreadsheet Excel has a number of facilities normally associated with database packages. Fierce market competition has resulted in the major software houses continually improving on their last version of a piece of software, attempting to outdo their competitors.

The suitability of a particular general-purpose package for a specific application will be largely dependent on the particular characteristics of the package. Though the general facilities afforded, for instance, by different database packages may be roughly equivalent, each manufacturer will adopt its own style of presentation and will provide certain services not offered by its competitors. A prospective buyer should have a clear idea of the main uses for which the package is to be purchased right at the outset, because some packages may be much more suitable than others.

Some advantages of general-purpose software compared to other forms of applications software are as follow:

□   Because large numbers of the package are sold, prices are relatively low;

□   They are appropriate to a wide variety of applications;

□   As they already have been thoroughly tested, they provide a great reduction in the time and costs necessary for development and testing;

□   They are suitable for people with little or no computing experience;

□   They are very easy to use;

□   Most packages of this type are provided with extensive documentation.

Some of the disadvantages are:

□   Sometimes the package will allow only a clumsy solution to the task in question;

□   In the case of a spreadsheet or database, for example, the user must still develop the application. This requires a thorough knowledge of the capabilities of the package, which are frequently extensive, and how to make the best use of them;

□   The user will need to provide his own documentation for the particular application for which the package has been tailored;

□   Unless the software is used regularly, it is easy to forget the correct command sequences to operate the package, particularly for people inexperienced in the use of computer software of this type;

❑   The user must take responsibility for security measures to ensure that vital data is not lost, or to prevent unauthorised personnel gaining access to the data.

Word processors

The word processor performs much the same function as a typewriter, but it offers a large number of very useful additional features. Basically, a word processor is a computer with a keyboard for entering text, a monitor for display purposes, one or more disk drives for storage of files produced by applications and a printer to provide the permanent output on paper. A word processor is really nothing more than a computer system with a special piece of software to make it perform the required word processing functions; some such systems have hardware configurations specifically for the purpose (such as special keyboards and letter-quality printers) but the majority are merely the result of obtaining an appropriate word processor package. Word processors can be used to produce:

❑   letters;

❑   legal documents;

❑   books;

❑   articles;

❑   mailing lists;

and in fact any type of textual material. Here are some of the advantages they have over ordinary typewriters:

❑   typing errors can be corrected before printing the final version;

❑   the availability of such automatic features as page numbering, the placing of page headers and footers and word/line counting;

❑   whole document editing, such as replacing every incidence of a certain combination of characters with another set of characters. For instance, replacing each occurrence of the name Mr. Smith by Mrs. Jones;

❑   printing multiple copies all to the same high quality;

❑   documents can be saved and printed out at some later date without any additional effort.

However, word processors do have some drawbacks. For instance, prolonged viewing of display monitors can produce eyestrain. They are generally considerably more expensive than good typewriters, and to be used properly, a certain amount of special training is required.

Typical word processor facilities

A typical word processing package will provide most of the following facilities:

Word wrap. As text is typed, a word is moved automatically to the start of a new line if there is insufficient room for it at the right-hand margin. With this facility, the only time that the Enter key needs to be pressed, to move the cursor to the beginning of a new line, is at the end of paragraphs or when a blank line is required.

Scrolling. Once the bottom of the screen is reached during text entry, the top of the text moves, line by line, up out of view as each new line of text is entered. This ensures that the line being entered is always visible on screen. The directional arrow keys on a standard keyboard allow scrolling to be carried out at will to view various parts of the document.

Deletion. This facility allows the deletion of characters, words, lines or complete blocks of text.

Insertion. This is concerned with the insertion of single letters or a block of text.

Block marking. A special function key, or more usually, by dragging the mouse pointer, allows the marking or highlighting of text to be dealt with separately from the rest of the document. The marked text may be moved, deleted, copied or displayed in a different style - in italics or bold print, for example.

Text movement or copying. The user may need to move or copy a marked block of text to a different part of the document.

Tabulation. Markers can be set to allow the cursor to be moved directly to column positions with the use of the TAB key. This is useful when text or figures are to be presented in columns.

Formatting. Text can be *aligned left*, with a straight left margin and a ragged right margin:

xxxx xxx xxxxx x xxxx xxxxxxxxxx xxx xxxxxxx xxxx xxxxxxx xxx xxxxxx xx
xxxxxxx x xxxxx xxxxxxx xx xxxx x xxx xxxxxxxxxxx xxx xxx xxxxxxx x xxxxxxx
xxx xxxxxx xxxxx x xxxx x xx xxxxxx x xxxx xxxxx xxx x xxxxxxxxxx xxxxxx xxx
xxxxxxxxx xx xxxxxxxxxxxxxx xxxx x.

or it can be *justified* so that it has a straight left and right margin:

xxxx xxx xxxxx x xxxx xxxxxxxxxx xxx xxxxxxx xxxx xxxxxxx xxx xxxxx xx xxxxxxx x
xxxxx xxxxxxx xx xxxx x xxx xxxxxxxxxxx xxxxxxxxxxxxxx xxx xxxxxxx xx xxxxxx xxx
xxxxxx xxxx xxxxxxxxx xxxx xxxxx xxx x xxxxxxxxxx xxxxxx xxx xxxxxxxxx xx
xxxxxxxxxxxxxx xxxx x.

or it can be *right aligned* with a straight right margin only:

XXXX XXX XXXXX X XXXX XXXXXXXXXX XXX XXXXXXX XXXX XXXXXXX XXX XXXXXX XX XXXXXXX
X XXXXX XXXXXXX XX XXXX X XXX XXXXXXXXXXXX XXX XXX XXXXXXX X XXXXXXX XXX XXXXXX
XXXXX X XXXX X XX XXXXXX X XXXXXXXXXXXXXX XXX XXXXXXX XX XXXXX XXX XXXXXX XXXX
XXXXXXXXX XXXX XXXXX XXX X XXXXXXXXXX XXXXX XXX XXXXXXXXX XX XXXXXXXXXXXXXX
XXXX.

or it can be *centred*:

XXXX XXX XXXXX X XXXX XXXXXXXXXX XXX XXXXXXX XXXX XXXXX XXX XX XXXXXXX X XXXXX
XXXXXXX XX XXXX X XXX XXXXXXXXXXXX XXX XXX XXXXXXX X XXXXXXX XXX XXXXXX XXXXX X
XXXX X XX XXXXXX X XXXXXXXXXXXXXX XXX XXXXXXX XX XXXXXX XXX XXXXXX XXXX
XXXXXXXXX XXXX XXXXX XXX X XXXXXXXXXX XXXXX XXX XXXXXXXXX XX XXXXXXXXXXXXXX
XXXX X.

Printing styles

Text can be printed in a variety of styles, including **boldface**, *italic,* ~~strike-through~~, under-scored ^{superscript} or _{subscript}. Most word processors allow these styles to be displayed on the screen as well as on the printer and are known as WYSIWYG (What You See Is What You Get) packages.

Various fonts and sizes of characters

Different character fonts, that is variations in the shapes of characters, and sizes of characters can be mixed in the same document:

This is called CG Omega 12 pt

This is Courier New 10 pt

This is Times New Roman 14 pt

THIS IS DESDEMONA 14 PT

Mailing lists

This allows a user to personalize standard letters. The mailing list is, in effect, a file of names and addresses, details from which can be inserted into marked points in a standard letter. The word processor prints multiple copies of the standard letter selected by the user and personal-ises each with data extracted from the mailing list.

Additional features

These include facilities for the checking of spelling (and sometimes its automatic correction as you type) in a document by reference to a dictionary held on disk, the import of text and figures from other packages such as spreadsheets, the incorporation of graphics and the export of text to other packages.

Windows-based word processors

Programs like Microsoft's Word for Windows and other windows-based word processors are have taken over from those that do not operate in a windows environment. These latest word processors allow the use of a mouse to move the cursor around documents quickly, to edit text and to provide easy access to commonly used functions such as saving and printing work, opening existing documents and creating tables. All the other advantages of windows-based programs also apply. Figure 17.3, earlier, shows part of a document produced using Word for Windows, to give you an idea of what can be achieved with this type of word processor.

Spreadsheets

Just as word processors are designed to manipulate text, spreadsheets are designed to do the equivalent with numerical information. A spreadsheet program presents the user with a blank grid of cells each of which is capable of containing one of three types of information:

- ❑ a label consisting of alphanumeric characters;

- ❑ a number;

- ❑ a formula, which usually will make reference to other cells. These allow calculations to be performed on data in other cells, or on the results from other formulae.

These three types of information are sufficient to allow a wide range of applications to be implemented in a very convenient and easily understandable way. For example, suppose that a small business, Acme Computers, dealing in the sale of personal computer systems wishes to use a spreadsheet to record on a monthly basis, the sales of its four salespersons. The spreadsheet might be set up as shown in Figure 17.4.

Column A contains labels describing the systems purchased. Columns C and D, E and F, G and H, I and J show respectively, the sales and commissions for each of the four salespersons. The commission is calculated automatically by means of a formula stored in the commission columns D, F, H and J.

Formulae are used to produce the calculated values. Thus John's sale of the 486DX costing £675 is entered in cell C8 and the commission is calculated using the formula '=C8*20/100'. This calculates 20% of the retail price. The actual value of the commission is displayed in cell D8.

The column totals, shown in cells C22 to J22, were calculated using a built-in function '=SUM(range)' which calculates the sum of a range of cells. For example, John's total commission, shown in cell D22, was calculated using the formula '=SUM(D8:D20)'. Note that empty cells are treated by formula as having a value of zero.

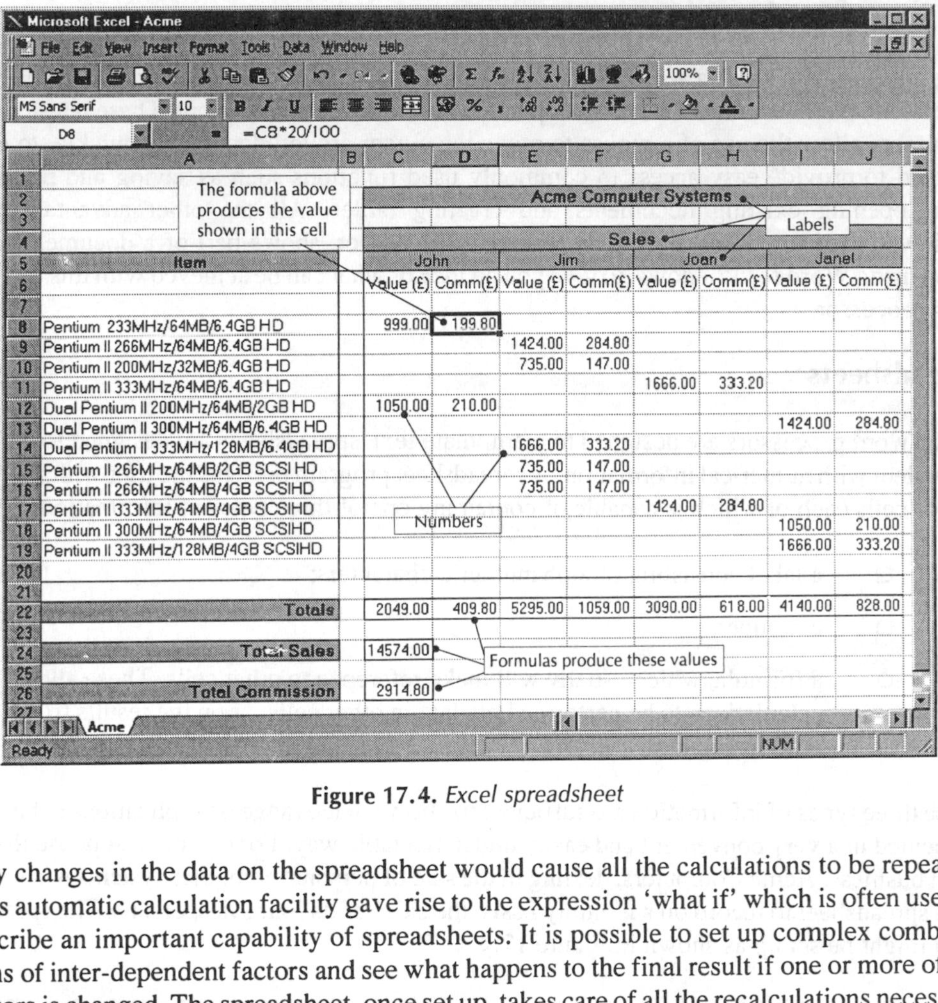

Figure 17.4. *Excel spreadsheet*

Any changes in the data on the spreadsheet would cause all the calculations to be repeated. This automatic calculation facility gave rise to the expression 'what if' which is often used to describe an important capability of spreadsheets. It is possible to set up complex combinations of inter-dependent factors and see what happens to the final result if one or more of the factors is changed. The spreadsheet, once set up, takes care of all the recalculations necessary for this type of exercise.

The earliest program of this form was called 'Visicalc' and it ran on an Apple microcomputer. Many such programs now exist, having capabilities far exceeding those of Visicalc, but they still closely resemble the original concept in appearance and operation.

Typical spreadsheet facilities

Apart from the entry of labels, numbers and formulae, a spreadsheet package normally allows the user to use various facilities from a menu to handle the data stored on the worksheet. Typically, spreadsheets offer the following facilities:

Copying. This allows the copying of fixed values or labels, or formulae which are logically the same in another part of the worksheet. Thus, for example, in the earlier worksheet sample, the formula '=SUM(C8:C20)', which totalled a group of values for John, could be copied to succeeding columns to the right as '=SUM(D8:D20)', '=SUM(E8:E20)', '=SUM(F8:F20)', and so on. The formula is logically the same but the column references change, according to the position of the formula.

Formatting. A cell entry can be centred, or left or right justified within a cell. Numeric values can be displayed in a variety of formats including fixed decimal, integer, percent and scientific or as money values prefixed by a $ or £ sign to 2 decimal places. Individual formats can be selected globally, that is throughout a worksheet or for selected ranges of cells.

Functions. These include =SUM(range) , which adds the contents of a specified range of cells, '=AVERAGE(range)', which calculates the average value in a specified range of cells, '=MIN(range)', which extracts the minimum value held in a specified range of cells, and '=SQRT(cell)', which returns the square root of a value in a specified cell. The full range of functions usually includes those used in mathematics, trigonometry, finance and statistics. These are examples of functions found in Excel.

Macros. Groups of regularly used key sequences can be stored and then executed by one key press in combination with the Alt key, for example, Alt C; alternatively, a macro can be assigned to a new button on the tool bar and executed by clicking it. Macros can be useful when the spreadsheet has been tailored for a particular application which may be used by inexperienced users. Without macros, each user would have to be completely familiar with the spreadsheet commands needed. With macros, one experienced user can tailor the spreadsheet so that training time for other staff is minimised.

Graphs. Numerical data can be displayed in a variety of graphical forms, including bar charts, line graphs, scatter diagrams and pie charts. All modern spreadsheet packages provide graphical output directly and also allow numerical data to be exported to another package for graph production. The range and quality of graphs vary greatly from one package to another. With the use of a colour printer, very attractive and presentable graphs can be produced to illustrate business reports.

Consolidation. This feature allows the merging of several worksheets into a summary sheet, whilst keeping the original worksheets intact. Consolidation adds together cells with the same co-ordinates in the various worksheets.

Other Facilities. These include, amongst others, cell protection facilities to prevent alteration of certain entries, the alteration of individual column widths and the display of cell contents as formulae instead of the results of their calculation.

Spreadsheets have a number of attractive features compared to traditional programming solutions to processing needs:

❑   designed for laypeople;

❑   easy to learn and use;

❑   wide range of uses;

❑   relatively cheap;

❑   easily modified;

❑   well tried and tested;

❑   provide quick development time.

On the debit side:

❑   they tend to be too general-purpose and therefore tend to provide satisfactory rather than ideal solutions;

❑   the problem must still be analysed and a solution method identified.

Database

At one time, database programs, or Database Management Systems (DBMS) as they are often called, were restricted to mainframe computers because of the large memory requirements demanded of such applications. Currently, however, even personal business microcomputers have sufficient internal memory to make such applications not only feasible but also extremely powerful. These programs allow files, comprising collections of records, to be created, modified, searched and printed.

Here are just a few examples of database applications:

❑   names and addresses of possible customers for a mail order firm;

❑   details of the books in a library giving author, title and subject covered by each book, to aid with locating books of a certain type;

❑   details of the items stored in a warehouse, giving location, cost, number currently in stock and supplier;

❑   lists of people on the electoral register for a certain region;

❑   details of the employees of a large firm.

Typical database facilities

A typical database program will offer, as a minimum, the following facilities:

❑   user-definable record format allowing the user to specify the fields within the record;

- ❏ user-definable input format to allow the user to define the way the data is to be entered into the computer;

- ❏ file searching capabilities for extracting records satisfying certain criteria from a file;

- ❏ file sorting capabilities so that records can be ordered according to the contents of a certain field;

- ❏ calculations on fields within records for inclusion in reports;

- ❏ user-definable report formats, so that different types of reports containing different combinations of record fields may be produced.

Database packages for microcomputers

These packages fall broadly into two groups, *card index* and *relational*. Generally, card index systems are simpler to set up and operate but they provide less sophisticated data manipulation and search facilities than do the relational type. Further, the relational type provide a programming language which allows the development of user friendly, tailored applications. Thus, a user can be protected from the complexities of package operation by being presented with, for example, a menu-driven system with options for record insertion, modification, deletion and retrieval and perhaps the production of summary reports. The card index type cannot be programmed in this way, so the user must have a more detailed knowledge of package operation. On the other hand, card index packages tend to be easier to use. The superior data management facilities provided by the relational type tend to be underused unless professional database designers and programmers are involved in the development of the database application. The business executive who plans to use the database as a personal tool without such professional help, will probably be well advised to purchase a card index package rather than a relational database package. Another factor to be considered when choosing a database, is disk space and access speed. In contrast with spreadsheet packages, database packages require frequent disk accesses when carrying out sorting and retrieval operations. Floppy disk access times tend to be too slow and their storage capacity inadequate for anything but the simplest application. A package should also allow sorting with the use of indexes, so that files do not have to be physically sorted. Indexed sorts are much quicker and a number of different indexes can be set up so that the database can be displayed in a variety of logical orders without reorganising the data on disk.

Graphics packages

Common types of graphics packages provide facilities for: business graphics; graphic design; desktop publishing; computer-aided design. Some graphics packages will to a greater or lesser degree cater for all of these applications, but many are designed specifically for one of them.

Business graphics

Business graphics packages allow the production of such things as bar charts, line graphs and pie diagrams, that is, diagrams of a statistical nature likely to be included in business reports. Examples of this type of diagram are shown in Figure 17.5.

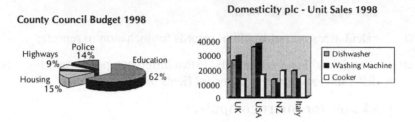

Figure 17.5. *Examples of business graphics*

Graphic design

Packages for *graphic design* consist of a collection of special functions aimed at aiding the graphic designer. The artist uses the screen as a canvas and a light-pen, mouse or equivalent device as a brush. Figure 17.6 shows a typical graphic design program with the user in the process of editing a picture.

Figure 17.6. *Editing a bit-map image with a 'paint' package*

They generally allow work of professional quality to be produced in a relatively short amount of time, and include such facilities as:

❑   large colour palette;

❑   geometric figure drawing, e.g. lines, rectangles, circles;

❑   filling areas with colour or patterns;

- undoing mistakes;

- moving/copying/deleting/saving areas of the screen display;

- choice of a variety of character fonts;

- printing the finished design;

- a large number of pre-drawn pictures for inclusion in designs. This is called 'clip-art'.

The drawing tools shown down the left-hand side are used to produce a variety of effects. They include tools for:

- cutting out rectangular or irregularly shaped areas of the drawing so that they may be moved or erased;

- spraying colour;

- producing text;

- erasing parts of the drawing using a variable size eraser;

- filling areas with colour;

- brushing colour onto the screen using brushes of different sizes and shapes;

- drawing filled or unfilled shapes, such as rectangles and circles.

Colours are selected by clicking with the mouse pointer on the colour palette along the bottom of the screen, and other functions can be chosen from the menus along the top of the screen. Drawings can be stored on disk or printed.

Desktop publishing

Desktop publishing programs are designed to produce such things as posters, illustrated articles, books and other documents which combine large amounts of text with illustrations. As such they tend to contain a number of facilities in common with graphic design packages, but emphasise layout and printing. These packages place a lot of emphasis on being able to experiment with arranging sections of the document and seeing its overall appearance. Text is also given more importance; a rudimentary word processor may be provided, or text may be imported from a prepared file, and the user is generally able to experiment with different type fonts on text already displayed on the screen. Typically, a DTP package will have facilities for:

- modifying text by means of using different fonts and type styles;

- importing text from word processors;

❑   displaying text in columns;

❑   importing pictures/diagrams from graphic design packages;

❑   re-sizing pictures;

❑   producing simple geometrical shapes such as lines, rectangles and circles;

❑   mixing text and graphics;

❑   automatically numbering pages;

❑   producing contents pages, lists of figures and indexes.

Figure 17.7 is an example of a poster produced with a DTP program. Notice that the poster contains a mixture of graphics objects and text of various sizes and fonts. All of these components can be repositioned, re-sized and modified very easily using a mouse.

Figure 17.7. *Poster produced with a DTP package*

Computer-aided design

Computer-aided design constitutes perhaps one of the most widely used commercial applications of computer graphics. Figure 17.8 shows two three-dimensional images, produced with a CAD package. The user simulates real-world geometrical objects using various software drawing tools. Often these tools are selected and used in a WIMP style environment. Sometimes a graphics tablet is used in conjunction with a pressure-operated stylus, or a light-pen might be used to draw electronically on the VDU screen. Whatever the physical method of using the system, the types of software tools and facilities available are fairly standard, providing tools for operations such as:

- ❑   drawing common objects (lines, curves, circles, ellipses, rectangles, polygons etc.);

- ❑   editing objects (modifying or deleting objects);

- ❑   filling shapes with patterns or colours; ·

- ❑   generating three-dimensional objects; Figure 17.8 shows some examples.

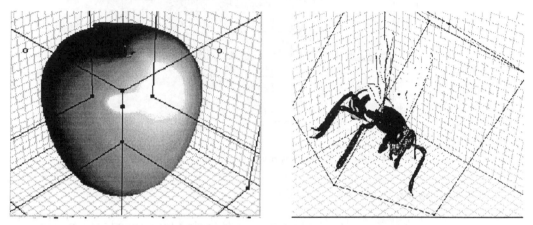

Figure 17.8. *Three-dimensional images from a CAD package*

- ❑   rotating two-dimensional and three-dimensional objects;

- ❑   viewing three-dimensional objects from different directions;

- ❑   displaying three-dimensional objects in wireframe or solid form;

- ❑   applying different texturing effects to solid objects.

Applications of CAD programs include:

- ❑   engineering drawing; Figure 17.9 shows an example.

- ❑   architectural design;

- ❑   interior design;

- ❑   printed-circuit and integrated circuit design;

- ❑   advertising material;

- ❑   computer animation for tv advertising;

- ❑   special effects in films.

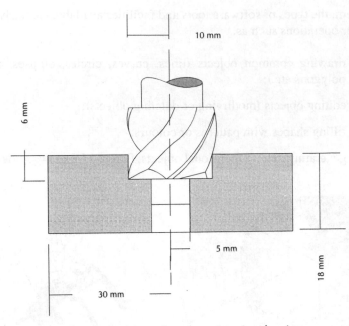

Figure 17.9. *Dimensioned, engineering drawing*

Knowledge-based systems

A knowledge-based system embodies human knowledge in a form suited to processing by a computer program. Such a system will store facts about a certain subject area, and relationships, often in the form of rules, which will allow conclusions to be drawn from the facts. A Prolog program is a good example of a knowledge base, and a Prolog translator executing such a program could be classed as a knowledge-based system.

The most common type of knowledge-based system is the expert system, and this is discussed in some detail in the following section.

Expert systems

Pure research in the field of artificial intelligence has had a number of practical spin-offs. One such spin-off has been the development of programs known as expert systems, or intelligent knowledge based systems. These are programs designed to be able to give the same sort of help or advice, or make decisions, as a human expert in some narrow field of expertise. For instance, a program called PROSPECTOR is capable of predicting the existence of mineral ores given various pieces of information gathered from physical locations. In the same way that, given certain evidence, an expert might say that a particular site looked favourable for containing ore, PROSPECTOR indicates the probability of the existence of the ore. PROSPECTOR is in fact attributed with the discovery of an extremely valuable quantity of molybdenum which had previously been overlooked by human experts.

Expert systems have been developed in numerous areas which traditionally have been the province of human experts. For example, several expert systems have been developed to aid medical diagnosis and treatment. However, decisions in areas such as this are often so critical that it would be foolish to blindly accept the pronouncement of a computer. For this reason, expert systems have the built-in ability to justify the chain of logical reasoning leading to any conclusion, so that it can be checked and verified (or rejected) by a human.

Another characteristic of many expert systems is the use of *fuzzy logic* which allows degrees of uncertainty to be built in to logical deduction processes. Such expert systems are able to state conclusions which are qualified by a probability value indicating the probability of the conclusion being correct.

Other successful expert systems include:

- ❏   MYCIN - diagnosis of infections

- ❏   HEURISTIC DENDRAL - identifies organic compounds

- ❏   XCON - for configuring (VAX) computer systems

- ❏   SACON - for advice on structural analysis

An expert system has three main components:

(i)   A *knowledge base* consisting of rules which use facts supplied by some external source, typically a user.

(ii)   An *inference engine* which processes the knowledge base.

(iii)   A *user interface* to facilitate communication with the user.

As an example, the following knowledge base is for a simple botanical expert system to identify whether a particular plant is a shrub, tree, herb or vine.

Four rules are to be used:

1.   IF STEM IS GREEN THEN TYPE IS HERB.

2.   IF STEM IS WOODY AND ATTITUDE IS CREEPING THEN TYPE IS VINE.

3.   IF STEM IS WOODY AND ATTITUDE IS UPRIGHT AND ONE MAIN TRUNK IS TRUE THEN TYPE IS TREE.

4.   IF STEM IS WOODY AND ATTITUDE IS UPRIGHT AND ONE MAIN TRUNK IS FALSE THEN TYPE IS SHRUB.

This forms the knowledge base.

The inference engine starts by attempting to satisfy a primary goal, in this instance to determine the TYPE of the plant. To this end, it searches its knowledge base for the goal by looking for a rule containing the word TYPE in the conclusion part of the rule (after the THEN part of a rule). This process of examining conclusions to rules while attempting to resolve goals is called backward chaining (or goal-driven inference).

Rule 1 satisfies this requirement, but in order to establish if the plant is a HERB, the system must obtain information regarding the STEM. Initially this information will not be available and must be supplied by the user. Consequently, obtaining the STEM information is added to a list of subgoals to be evaluated, along with rule 1, and the system looks for another rule containing the goal in its conclusion. The subgoal list also notes the rule which generated the subgoal in question.

After the remaining rules have been processed in a similar fashion, the system must then attempt to satisfy the subgoal list. Consequently, the user interface is invoked. This generates a question of the form

```
IS THE STEM OF THE PLANT GREEN?
```

Let us suppose that the plant is a SHRUB (which has a woody stem, grows upright, and has more than one main trunk). The user answers NO which is stored as a fact relating to the stem of the plant.

Having succeeded with a subgoal, the inference engine again searches for a rule conclusion containing TYPE. It can attempt to evaluate the first rule now that it has all the necessary information. The rule does not produce a conclusion since the STEM is not green. This rule is therefore discarded since it can never cause the primary goal to succeed in this particular consultation.

Examination of the second rule reveals to the inference engine that it cannot be resolved until the ATTITUDE of the plant is in its list of facts, so this is added to its list of subgoals.

Eventually, all the necessary facts are available and the inference engine is able to discard all rules except rule 4 which establishes that the plant is a SHRUB. In the course of a consultation the user might wish to know why the system is asking a certain question. The information required to answer this question is easy to find: the subgoal generating the question being asked was stored along with the rule from which it came, and this contains all the necessary information. For example, if the inference engine was attempting to resolve rule 4 by asking about the number of TRUNKS, the user interface might respond,

```
I am trying to determine the TYPE.
I know that the STEM is woody.
I know that the ATTITUDE is upright.
If ONE MAIN TRUNK is false then I will know that the TYPE is
SHRUB.
```

Expert system shells

The term shell is given to expert systems which have been given no specific knowledge base, only the inference engine and user interface; the knowledge base has to be provided by the user. A single expert system shell can thus be used to provide advice or help in a number of areas of expertise, providing it is given the appropriate knowledge base for each area. For example, an expert system shell could be used to give advice on the procedures and sequence of steps necessary for selling a house (what solicitors call 'conveyancing'), or to give advice about possible causes and cures of diseases in houseplants, or diagnosing faults in cars. Not only could these applications be of practical use, but they could also be instructive because the user could ask for and obtain the reasons behind any conclusions. One of the problems of using such shells is the determination of the rules which represent the wisdom of a human expert; many experts are not consciously aware of the precise reasoning processes they themselves use in order to come to some conclusion, yet in order to produce an expert program, these processes must be defined in a form that is usable. The process of determining the knowledge base rules is known as 'knowledge elicitation' or 'knowledge acquisition' and is performed by 'knowledge engineers'.

Hypertext

Hypertext, also called 'linked text' and 'extended text', systems are concerned with classifying and categorising text. Such systems allow blocks of text to be linked together in various ways for the purpose of establishing a chain of connected topics. Blocks of text may be established as a connected set of nodes or subsections of text nodes can be linked to other subsections or to other nodes. A hypertext system does not rearrange the text in its database; it merely allows a user to define a method of organising it. For example, in researching for a book an author may read many papers and reference books and in the course of doing so may make notes in a notebook to summarise their contents. A hypertext notebook would, for example, allow the author to link his own annotations to references, and link references to other references. Obviously this would greatly simplify the task of collecting together material relevant to writing about a particular topic. Hypertext systems usually allow the user to browse through a hypertext document, adding, deleting or modifying links between nodes and points. Software on-line help facilities are usually based on hypertext ideas. Current hypertext systems, which allow the inclusion graphical or even sound nodes in addition to text, are termed *hypermedia* systems. The World Wide Web, a major information source on Internet, offers globally distributed hypermedia pages. Internet users are able to obtain hypermedia pages on an enormous variety of subjects from all over the world.

Web browsers

These are graphical interface client programs to help users to navigate through the Web, to transmit and to receive information from other users or information providers. By using a browser, the user does not have to know the format and location of the information: he or she simply jumps from site to site by clicking on hypertext links. Examples of commercially available browsers are Netscape's *Navigator*, Microsoft's *Explorer* (Figure 17.10).

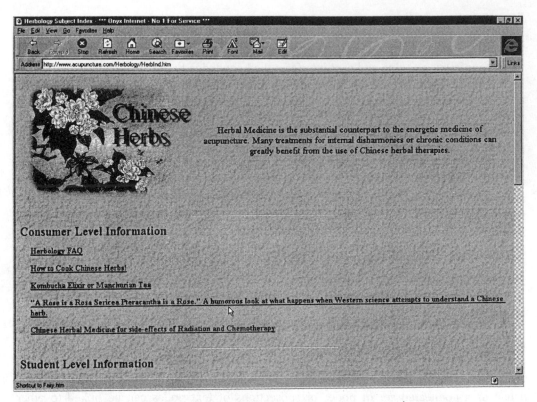

Figure 17.10. *Microsoft's Explorer browser displaying a Web page*

Although there are many different ways to represent a document on the screen, it is often called a *page*. Usually, those responsible for creating a given collection of interrelated documents also create a special document which is intended to be viewed first - one that contains introductory information and/or a master menu of documents within that collection. This type of document is called a *home page* and is generally associated with a particular site, person, or named collection. The example document has underlined hypertext phrases. These phrases are hyperlinks (or links) - typically, clicking on one of them with a mouse will cause another document to appear on the screen, which may hold more images and hyperlinks to other places. There is no single way to represent text which is linked to other things - some browsers underline, others use special colours, and many give the user a variety of options. Images which are part of the document and are displayed within the page are called *inline images*.

There is usually a toolbar at the top or bottom of the screen. This contains buttons which perform frequently used operations. For example, a set of navigation buttons is provided because a user might go to many different pages by selecting links in hypertext and there needs to be some method of retracing one's steps and reviewing the documents that have been explored.

Exercises

1. (i)   List the five computer system *resources* managed by an operating system.

    (ii) Which resource works on *time slices* in a multi-user system?

    (iii) Suggest a circumstance when device *conflicts* may arise in a multi-user system.

    (iv) Define the term *scheduling*.

2. Define the term *multi-tasking*.

3. What major advantage does the Windows NT *file system* provide over that of the older MS-DOS system?

4. If a device is *Plug 'n' Play* compatible, what does this mean?

5. List three features of a *graphical user interface* (GUI).

6. Briefly describe the components of a *mail merge* operation in a word processor.

7. What spreadsheet facility allows a user to tailor an application for others to use?

8. *Graphic design* and *computer-aided design* packages are aimed at different types of user. Suggest a typical application for each.

9. What term is used to describe a computer system which, through interaction with the user, can give specific advice on the procedures for buying a house?

10. What is the function of a *hyperlink* in a Web document?

Chapter 18
Computer Systems

Introduction

The components of a system and the ways they interrelate constitute its *architecture*. A computer system consists of a number of individual elements, working together, with the common aim of processing data to produce information. As computer processing is carried out electronically, a computer system may also be called an *electronic data processing system*.

Data can be distinguished from *information* by reference to a simple example. To produce a customer invoice (which notifies the customer of the amount owed in respect of an order), several separate items of data need to be accessed and processed, including the item descriptions, prices and quantities and the customer's name and address. It is only when the particular values of these data items are combined that they become the information represented by the invoice. To be described as information, a computer's output must be relevant and useful to the user receiving it.

Elements of a computer system

The major elements of a computer system are:

- ❑ hardware;
- ❑ software.

The system requires both, as neither can perform any useful function without the other.

Hardware components

The term *hardware* describes all the physical, electronic and mechanical components forming part of a computer system. The components can be grouped according to function, as follows.

Input

To allow the computer to process data it must be in a form which the machine can handle. Before processing, data is normally in a human-readable form, for example, as it appears on an employee's time sheet or a customer's order form. Such alphabetic and numeric (decimal) data cannot be handled directly by the internal circuitry of the computer. Firstly, it has to be translated into the binary format which makes the data machine-sensible. The function of an input device is to translate human-readable data into a machine-sensible form that the computer can handle. There is a wide variety of input devices, but the most common is a keyboard. Data are always transferred from the input device to main memory.

Main memory

This element, also commonly known as *RAM (random access memory)*, has two main functions:

1.   to temporarily store programs currently in use for processing data;

2.   to temporarily store data:

    (i)   entered through an input device and awaiting processing;

    (ii)   currently being processed;

    (iii) which results from processing and is waiting to be output.

Central processing unit (CPU)

Often referred to as the *processor*, the CPU handles program instructions and data and consists of two elements.

    (i)   *Arithmetic/logic unit (ALU)*. The ALU carries out arithmetic operations such as addition, multiplication, subtraction and division. It can also make logical comparisons between items of data. For example, it can determine whether one value is greater than another. Such logical operations can also be performed on non-numeric data.

    (ii)   *Control unit*. The control unit governs the operation of all hardware, including input and output devices and the CPU. It does this by fetching, interpreting and executing each instruction in turn, in an automatically controlled cycle; this fetch-execute cycle is described in detail in Chapter 23. For example, when an instruction to accept data through the keyboard is to be executed, the control unit sends the appropriate signals to the keyboard device. Instructions which involve arithmetic computation are signalled to the ALU, which carries out such functions.

Output

Output devices perform the opposite function of input devices by translating machine-sensible data into a human-readable form, for example, onto a printer or the screen of a visual display unit (VDU). Sometimes, the results of computer processing may be needed for further processing, in which case they are output to a storage medium (Chapters 4, 5 and 19) which retains it in machine-sensible form for subsequent input.

Backing storage

Backing, or auxiliary, storage performs a filing function within the computer system. In this context it is important to consider two important concepts.

Memory volatility. It is not practical to store data files and programs in main memory because of its volatility. This means that the contents of the main memory can be destroyed, either by being overwritten as new data is entered for processing and new programs used, or when the machine is switched off. Such volatile memory is termed random access memory (RAM).

Retrievable data. Backing storage media provide a more permanent store for programs (which may be used many times on different occasions) and data files (which are used for future reference or processing). When the results of processing are output to a printer or screen, the user is provided with visual information, which is not normally retrievable by the computer, unless it is also recorded on a backing storage medium. The following example illustrates some aspects of file storage. In a payroll operation, data on hours worked by employees, together with other relevant data for the current pay period are processed against the master (permanent) payroll file. The results of this processing update the details on the payroll master file and produce the payslips.

Peripherals

Those hardware devices which are external to the CPU (comprising the ALU and control unit) and main memory, namely those devices used for input, output and backing storage, are called peripherals. Figure 18.1 illustrates the *logical structure* of the computer and thereby, the relationships between various hardware components.

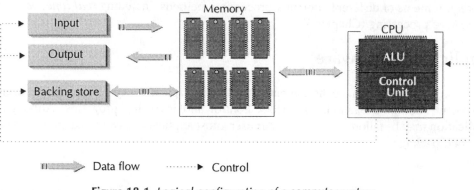

Figure 18.1. *Logical configuration of a computer system*

It shows the data flow through the system and the flow of control signals from the processor.

Software

This topic is examined in some detail in Chapters 16 and 17, but some basic ideas are introduced here to allow a simple understanding of computer systems. The role of software is to run the hardware. Software can be divided into two main groups:

(i)   systems software;

(ii)   applications software.

Systems software

Systems software is dedicated to the general organisation and running of a computer system. Standard tasks, such as handling files on backing storage and controlling programs in memory, are common to all applications and are managed by a particular group of systems programs known collectively as the operating system. Familiar examples include Windows 95, Windows NT, OS/2 and Unix.

Types of operating system

Different types of operating system are necessary to handle different computer configurations and the variety of processing modes in which they can operate. For example, a microcomputer with keyboard, mouse, screen, printer and disk drives requires a much less sophisticated operating system than a mainframe computer system, which has a large variety and number of input, output and storage devices. Computer systems which allow multi-user operation (where multiple users access shared files and programs at the same time) require a *multi-user* operating system, with facilities for controlling individual user access and security. Conversely, a microcomputer designed for single-user operation can be operated with a simpler, single-user operating system. There are a variety of operating systems which serve the requirements of different computer processing methods, including *real-time*, *batch* and *time-share* processing (Chapter 6).

Applications software

Applications programs make the computer function in a specific way, for a particular user requirement. Common examples are stock control and invoicing programs. Although an application may be tailored for a particular user, most applications can be catered for by off-the-shelf packages.

Computer systems classified

Computer systems can be classified according to the following characteristics: purpose; size and complexity; generation.

Purpose
General-purpose computers

As the term suggests, general-purpose machines can carry out processing tasks for a wide variety of applications and constitute what are normally recognised as computers.

Dedicated or special-purpose computers

In their logical structure, these machines are fundamentally the same as the general-purpose machine except that they have been programmed for a specific application. Dedicated word processors used to provide one example, though they are now virtually obsolete. The advent of cheap, microprocessor-based, special-purpose systems has led to an expansion of their use in controlling machines and many household products, such as washing machines and microwave ovens, are controlled by such systems. These are also described as *embedded* systems.

Size and complexity

It should be emphasised that the following categories are only broad guidelines and changes in technology are continually blurring the differences between them. For example, there are now powerful microcomputer systems (often referred to as super-micros) which far exceed the power and flexibility of earlier generation minicomputer systems. However, the generally accepted categories of computer system are as follow.

Mainframe computers

Such computers are commonly used by large national and multi-national organisations such as banks, airlines and oil companies. They usually support a large number and variety of peripherals and can process a number of applications concurrently (*multi-programming*). The mainframe's power stems from the phenomenal speeds of the processor and the large size of the main memory. Mainframes may also play a central role in wide area networks. Their huge capital cost invariably places them in centralised processing roles; for the same reason, about fifty per cent of the mainframes currently in use are rented or leased from specialist companies. Mainframe computers are generally accommodated in special-purpose, air-conditioned rooms to ensure trouble free operation.

Supercomputers with processing speeds many times those of mainframe systems are used for scientific and statistical work, being capable of completing such work in a small fraction of the time that a mainframe would require.

Minicomputers (or high-end workstations)

The term 'minicomputer' is falling out of use because of its association with rather slow and expensive systems, dependent on the hardware and software products of one manufacturer. A major feature of a minicomputer is its facility for *multiprogramming* and more recently its use of multiple processors for *parallel processing*. Digital Equipment Corporation (DEC) is manufacturer of the VAX, the most popular model of minicomputer. Prime, Data General and IBM also manufacture minicomputer systems. Because the distinction between mini-computer and *high-end workstation* is now blurred manufacturers now use the latter term when referring to their minicomputer range. Frequently they are aimed at computer-aided design (CAD) which needs the vast memory capacity and multiple processors to provide rapid response times. The manufacturers also provide systems based on different *platforms* (operating systems). DEC, for example, offers Unix, Windows NT and VMS alternatives.

The division still exists between these high-end workstations and the standard desktop microcomputer, so describing this separate category is still valid. To emphasise the division and to avoid confusion, we will continue to refer to the term minicomputer.

Minicomputers can support a number of applications concurrently and are often used with *time-sharing* (Chapter 6) operating systems and *intelligent terminals* to provide organisations with decentralised processing facilities. Used in this way, many applications such as word processing, invoicing and customer enquiry can be carried out by users in their own departments. Medium-sized organisations may use minicomputers for their main processing applications. Larger organisations may apply them to *front end processing* (FEP). Employed in this way, a minicomputer handles a mainframe's communications traffic (Chapter 24) with remote terminals or other computers, leaving the mainframe free to handle the organisation's information processing tasks.

Microcomputers

The microcomputer is the smallest in the range and was first developed when the Intel Corporation succeeded in incorporating the main functional parts of a computer on a single *chip* using *integrated circuits* (IC) on silicon. Subsequently, the technique of *large scale integration* (LSI) further increased the number of electronic circuits which could be packed onto one chip. LSI has been superseded by *very large scale integration* (VLSI) which packs even more circuitry onto a single chip thus further increasing the power and storage capacity of microcomputers and computers generally. This type of computer storage is known as *metal oxide semiconductor* (MOS) storage and has completely replaced the *core store* used in earlier mainframe computers.

Originally, microcomputers were only capable of supporting a single user and a single application at any one time. The increase in processor speed and memory capacity now permits their use for *multi-tasking* (the running of several tasks concurrently by one user). *Multi-user* operation is made possible through networking; it is now extremely popular to link micro-computers into a *local area network* (LAN), to allow resource-sharing (disk, printer, programs and data files), as well as electronic communications between users (*electronic mail*). Microcomputers can now support applications packages previously restricted to mini and mainframe systems, including, for example, those used for database and *computer aided design* (CAD) work.

The range of microcomputer software is now extremely wide and the quality generally very high. There are software packages available for most business applications. One area of recent rapid growth has been in the development of graphics-based applications and most popular applications software can now be operated via a *graphical user interface* (GUI) and a *mouse*.

The low cost of microcomputers and the increase in the range of software available, makes their use possible in almost any size and type of organisation. In the small firm, a microcomputer may be used for word processing, stock control, costing, and general accounting. In the larger organisation they may be used as intelligent terminals. Such systems provide the user with the processing facilities of a central mini or mainframe computer and at the same time, a degree of independent processing power through the use of the microcomputer's own processor and memory store.

Multi-media systems

The term 'multi-media' is used to describe systems which allow the integration of sound, video, graphics and text in a single software product. Thus, the user of a multi-media encyclopaedia, can not only read about the life of Martin Luther King, but also see video sequences and hear his voice. At present, much multi-media software still leaves the user relatively passive, but future developments are likely to give the user increased flexibility to alter the outputs from a package. The meaning of multi-media has to be frequently updated as advances in software and hardware enable the range of media to be increased. Thus, computer animation may be used to illustrate, for example, the movement of a horse when walking, trotting and galloping, without any interaction with the user, save for the selection of the initial type of movement. The multi-media experience can be enhanced by allowing the user to hear different sounds, by selecting the type of ground on which the horse is moving, for example, on a muddy field, on gravel, sand or in shallow water, or a sequence of different surfaces, perhaps over a route planned by the user. Future developments could allow the use of more senses than just sight and hearing, perhaps touch and smell.

At present, microcomputers configured to run multi-media software include a *sound card* (to process sound files), speakers, a microphone (for voice input) and CD-ROM drive. Memory and processor requirements are higher than for routine business machines because multi-media software has to handle complex graphics, animation and sound files in *real-time*.

It should be pointed out that a CD-ROM drive is now a standard component of all microcomputer systems, partly because most software packages are now available on CD-ROM, as well as floppy disk, but also because the storage requirements of packages require the capacity of CD-ROM.

Portable computers

The first portable computer was developed in the early 1980s, but was nicknamed a 'lugg-able', because of its size and considerable weight (more than 10 kilograms). It also used a CRT (cathode ray tube) screen, which added to its power requirements. Today's portables are worthy of the name. Apart from pen-based, personal digital assistants (PDAs - see later), the A4 size notebook computer is the main portable product. Features include:

❑   powerful processor;

❑   liquid crystal display (see earlier) screen. Sometimes, the screen is back-lit to improve definition. Colour displays are available, although the resolution cannot yet match that of conventional screens;

❑   memory is either static RAM (SRAM) or flash memory. SRAM is vola-tile and its contents need battery power to be maintained. Typical capacity is 8 Mb. Flash memory is cheaper and does not require battery power. Unfortunately, flash memory is slower and wears out after ap-proximately 10,000 erasures. Flash memory cards can be write protected and include a standard interface, which allows them to appear as hard disks to the rest of the system;

❑   integral hard disk, typically, with hundreds or thousands of megabytes capacity;

❑   ports for connection to external devices. These include serial connections for use with a modem and communications network; parallel printer port; mouse port; external VGA screen connection;

❑   keyboard, sometimes full layout (but no numeric keypad).

Smaller notebooks, often referred to as sub-notebooks and about half the size of the A4 vari-ety, are becoming increasingly popular. Many machines include a number of card slots for the connection of additional devices, such as a modem and network adapter. The most widely used standard for these card slots is PCMCIA (Personal Computer Memory Card Interna-tional Association). The display size is between 180 mm and 235 mm, across the diagonal. A typical sub-notebook weighs about 1.5 kilograms.

Pen-based computers

A pen can be used as an alternative to the mouse but is most effective for handwriting, in con-junction with a digitising tablet, which is either separate or integral to the screen. The latter option is chosen for personal digital assistants (PDAs), pocket-sized computers designed for use on the move; the inclusion of a keyboard would destroy its usefulness as a light, highly portable device. A pen is used to write directly onto the screen. Recognition software at-tempts to identify and then translate hand-written characters by reference to stored prototypes; some symbols may represent commands, called gestures, whilst others may be letters of the alphabet. Hand-written input can then be handled as if it had been keyed in. The system can be trained to recognise how any given user draws a particular shape, if the recognition software cannot read their writing. The pen is the only feasible technology because touch-screens and mice lack the necessary precision, and light pens only function with CRT (Chapter 19) displays.

Generations

Since the first electronic computers were built in the 1940s, a number of developments in electronics have led to computer hardware being categorised by generation, that is, its place in the history of the computer. These generations can be simply defined as follows.

First generation. During the 1940s, this first generation of computers used electronic components including vacuum tubes. The first computer to allow a program to be stored in memory (a stored-program computer) was EDSAC, developed at the University of Manchester. The vacuum tubes were fragile, subject to overheating and caused frequent breakdowns.

Second generation. The introduction of low-cost and reliable transistors allowed the computer industry to develop at a tremendous rate during the late 1950s. The cost and size of the machines were radically reduced so it became possible for large commercial organisations to make use of computers. Examples of such machines include LEO III, UNIVAC and ATLAS.

Third generation. The development of integrated circuit (IC) technology in the mid-1960s heralded the development of more powerful, reliable and compact computers, such as those of the IBM 360 series.

Fourth generation. This generation is typified by large-scale integration (LSI) of circuits, which allowed the development of the microprocessor, which in turn allowed the production of the microcomputer. All computers used today make use of such silicon chip technology.

Fifth generation. At present, most computers are still of the fourth generation variety. Developments are continuing towards expanding memory size, using very large scale integration (VLSI) techniques and increasing the speed of processors. This increasing power is allowing the pursuit of new lines of development in computer systems:

  ❑   more human orientated input/output devices using voice recognition and speech synthesis should allow communication between computers and humans to be more flexible and natural. In the future, the aim is to allow computers to be addressed in languages natural to the users. Current techniques on some microcomputers allow acceptance of some spoken commands. Others allow the selection of user options displayed as graphics on the screen via a hand-held mouse.

  ❑   parallel processing techniques (the use of multiple processors).

Exercises

1. Distinguish between *data* and *information*, using the payroll function to illustrate your answer.

2. Distinguish between the terms *hardware* and *software*.

3. Identify the two main components of the *central processing unit* and describe their functions.

4. Why is *backing storage* an essential component of a computer system?

5. How is the function of an *input* device the reverse of an *output* device's function?

6. In the context of *RAM*, explain the significance of *volatility*.

7. Distinguish between *systems* and *applications software*, illustrating your answer with a commercial example of each.

8. What additional components are needed to ensure that a microcomputer can perform as a *multi-media* machine?

9. Apart from cost and physical size, identify two features of a *mainframe computer* which distinguish it from a *microcomputer*.

10. (i)   What does PCMCIA stand for and to which type of computer does it particularly relate?

    (ii) Give an example of a PCMCIA product.

11. (i)   Apart from size, what is the main feature of a *PDA*?

    (ii) In the same context, what is a *gesture*?

12. Identify two features of *fifth generation computers* that did not form part of earlier generations.

Chapter 19
Peripherals

Introduction

As the name suggests, peripheral devices are the external elements of the computer system described in Chapter 18. They provide a means of communication between the central processor and its human operators, as shown in Figure 19.1.

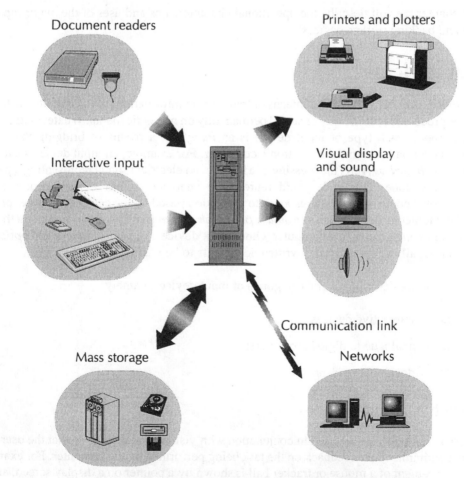

Document readers

Printers and plotters

Interactive input

Visual display and sound

Mass storage

Communication link

Networks

Figure 19.1. *Types of peripheral device*

Peripheral devices can be grouped according to their general function, as follows.

☐   Input. These include interactive input devices such as keyboards, light pens, mice and graphics tablets, and document readers, such as bar code readers, scanners/digitisers, optical character readers (OCR), and magnetic ink character readers (MICR).

☐   Output. These include devices such as visual display units (VDU), voice synthesisers and sound systems, and for hard copy, printers and plotters.

☐   Backing storage. There are mass storage devices such as microfiche, microfilm, floppy disk drives, hard disk drives, magnetic tape drives, streamers and CD-ROM drives.

☐   Communications devices, such as modems. These and the networks to which they give access are described in Chapter 24.

In this chapter we will describe the operational characteristics and uses of the major input, output and backing storage devices.

Input devices

Input devices provide a convenient means of transferring information into a computer so that it may be processed in some way or stored permanently on magnetic media. Whatever its particular purpose, each type of input device is an *interface*, a means of bridging the gap between the human user and the electronic computer. For example, an input device such as computer *keyboard* converts the pressing of a key into an electrical signal representing a particular binary code. This code could represent a character within a word processing document, or it could be part of a response to a question posed by the current computer program. An interactive device such as a *mouse* or a *touch screen* provides a convenient method of communicating actions to a computer. Other input devices, such as *scanners* and *optical mark readers*, allow typed or hand-written documents to be read into a computer.

In this section we describe several categories of input devices, namely:

☐   interactive devices;

☐   analogue to digital converters;

☐   document readers.

Interactive input devices

Interactive input devices are used in conjunction with visual display units so that the user is provided with immediate feedback on the task being performed by the computer. For example, the movement of a mouse or tracker ball is shown by a pointer on a display screen, and when a key is pressed on a keyboard, the appropriate character appears on the screen.

Computer keyboard

The main section of a computer keyboard is similar to a typewriter keyboard, with the usual alphabetic and punctuation characters. The *shift* keys are used to switch between upper case (capital) letters and lower case (small) letters. The *control* keys are sometimes used to change the operation of a normal key. For example, holding down one of the control keys while hitting the *F* key might activate a menu. The separate *numeric keypad* is useful when data includes a high proportion of numeric characters. Application programs use the *function keys* for special purposes, so the operation of a function key will often be different from one program to another. Quite frequently function key *F1* is used to gain access to a help facility if one is provided.

A keyboard is usually detachable, enabling the operator to position it to suit personal comfort, but it remains physically connected by a coiled cable. The desirable qualities of a keyboard are reliability, quietness and light operating pressure and in these terms keyboards vary considerably.

Concept keyboards

In specialist applications, the standard keyboard is not always the most convenient method of input. In a factory, for example, a limited number of functions may be necessary for the operation of a computerised lathe. These functions can be set out on a touch-sensitive pad and clearly marked. This is possible because all inputs are anticipated and the range is small. The operator is saved the trouble of typing in the individual characters which form instructions. Concept keyboards also have application in education, particularly for the mentally and physically handicapped. Interchangeable overlays, which indicate the functions of each area of the keyboard allow the user to design it according to particular specifications. For example, if the responses required by a user are limited to 'yes' and 'no', the overlay is simply divided into two parts, one for each response. The keyboard comprises a flat, aluminium box and a touch-sensitive membrane on the top surface. The membrane on which overlays are placed is divided into a matrix of cells, for instance 128 on a 16 x 8 format. The cells have to be programmed to conform to the desired overlay.

Mouse

A mouse is a small, hand-held device, which the user can move on a flat surface to direct a pointer on the computer screen. It has two or more buttons, which work in conjunction with software packages, allowing the user to draw, erase, select and format textual and graphical images. The most common type incorporates a ball which makes contact with the flat surface on which the mouse is moved and turns two rollers, one tracking vertical movements on screen, the other horizontal (Figure 19.2). The movement of the rollers is detected by sensors, which continually send electrical signals through the mouse cable to the computer, reporting the location of the mouse. The software then uses these signals to adjust the pointer's position on the computer screen so that the pointer follows the movement of the mouse. Another type of mouse detects movement purely by optical sensors which work in conjun ction with a special mouse pad, and some are cable-less, using infra-red to transfer signals to the computer in a way similar to the use of remote controls for televisions. Most computer systems are equipped with a mouse facility and many packages, including those for art, design, word processing and desktop publishing can only be operated effectively with a mouse. Graphical user interfaces (GUIs - see Chapter 17) such as Microsoft Windows also depend heavily on its use.

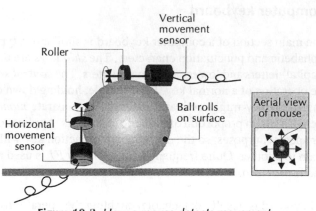

Figure 19.2. *How a mouse detects movement*

Tracker ball

A tracker ball is another variation of a mouse and is used for the same purposes. As shown in Figure 19.3, a tracker ball is a bit like an upside-down mouse, with the ball visible on the top of the base. To use a tracker ball you simply move the ball in the required direction using your fingers. Buttons are supplied just like on a mouse. Like joysticks, tracker balls have the advantage over mice that a flat surface is not

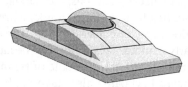

Figure 19.3. *Tracker ball*

required for its operation, and for this reason they are often used with portable computers.

Touch screen

A touch screen is a touch-sensitive display, used to read the position of a fingertip. The screen displays options, which a user can select, simply by touching them. The computer detects the position touched and performs the appropriate action. The range of input values available for selection will normally be small (a finger is not a very precise pointing device).

A touch screen might typically be used by a tourist agency, to allow visitors to request information on, for example, local accommodation, entertainment and tourist attractions, or by a bank to allow customers to view details of banking services. The main components of a touch screen are a special film coating on the surface of the screen and a controlling microprocessor which determines the co-ordinates of the finger's contact point and displays the required information.

Digitising tablet

A *digitising tablet* (shown in Figure 19.4) consists of a flat surface, containing an active area, typically 250mm square, which has a grid of very fine horizontal and vertical wires embedded into it. Attached to the tablet is a *stylus,* which produces a magnetic field at its tip. The grid of wires allows the position of the stylus on the tablet to be determined very accurately

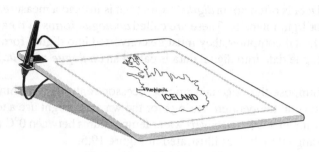

Figure 19.4. *Digitising tablet*

(the grid can contain up to 1000 points per inch), so that the computer can track and store the movement of the stylus. As the user 'draws' on the tablet the results appear on the computer screen. Drawings are stored in the computer's memory so that they can be manipulated or displayed.

Digitising tablets are useful for entering drawings consisting of lines - engineering drawings or maps for example - into the computer. The line drawing can be placed on the tablet and the stylus used to trace the outline or locate key points. Usually the tablet can also be used as a device for selecting options in a similar way to the touch screen described earlier, but with the capability of providing many more options. Computer-aided drawing programs often allow templates of pre-defined shapes - electrical circuit components for example - to be overlaid on the tablet so that the user can select a shape which will then appear on the screen ready to be used in a drawing.

Light pen

A light pen has an optical sensor in its tip and can only be used in conjunction with a *cathode ray tube* (CRT) display, which creates images on screen through the use of a scanning electron beam. As the beam creates the screen images, line by line (see the section on Visual Display Units), the light pen's optical sensor detects the exact moment when the beam passes beneath it and, from this, its position at any particular moment. By displaying functions at particular locations on the screen, the controlling program can allow the light pen to be used to make selections from several alternatives. It may also be used in conjunction with a drawing package to create, edit or manipulate images on screen. Though similar to the operation of a graphics tablet and stylus, a light pen is not capable of the same high accuracy, but it is generally cheaper. LCD (liquid crystal display) displays used in laptop, notebook and palmtop computers do not make use of electron beam scanning and cannot, therefore, support the use of light pens.

Analogue to digital converters (ADCs)

Data is often not in *digital* format but is instead a measurement of, for example, temperature or light intensity. These are called *analogue* forms of data and, before they can be used by a digital computer, they must be converted into digital format. A device which converts analogue data into digital data is called an *analogue to digital converter* (ADC).

Suppose that a certain microprocessor-controlled washing machine allowed you to select several temperature settings for the water. It might use a temperature sensor, in conjunction with an ADC, to convert water temperatures between $0°C$ and $100°C$ to a binary signal in the range 0 to 255, as illustrated in Figure 19.5.

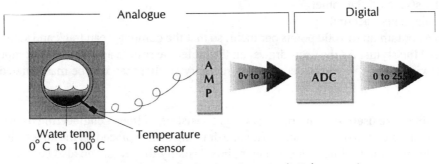

Figure 19.5. *Example of analogue to digital conversion*

The diagram shows a temperature sensor immersed in the water. This will produce a small electrical signal, proportional to the water temperature, which must be amplified so that it produces a voltage in the range 0 volts to 10 volts, for example. The ADC then converts this voltage to a binary signal in the range 0 to 255 (11111111 in binary), so that $0°C$ is represented by 0 and 100C is represented by 255. Thus a temperature of $25°C$ would produce about 2.5 volts from the amplifier and this would translate to binary 63 (00111111).

The term *digitiser* is usually reserved for more complex ADCs used for converting whole frames of photographic film into digital images which, with the aid of suitable software, can be displayed on a computer screen and edited. The output from a video camera, or medical scanning equipment can also be digitised for use in a computer. Digitisers designed for use with textual or graphical documents are usually termed *scanners*, which are described in the next section.

Document readers

There are a number of devices designed to capture information, in the form of pictures or text, already printed on paper. Examples of such devices are *scanners, optical character readers* (OCRs), *optical mark readers* (OMRs), *magnetic ink character readers* (MICRs) and *bar code readers*

Scanners

Scanners allow whole documents to be scanned optically and converted into digital images. These vary from small hand-held devices, which are manually moved slowly over the document as shown in Figure 19.6, to machines which allow whole sheets of paper to be fed in and scanned automatically (Figure 19.7). Versions of both of these types of scanners are capable of dealing with colour images as well as black and white, though colour scanners tend to be significantly more expensive. Special scanners are available to convert textual documents, typed or hand-written, into the sort of format used by word processors. These devices perform *optical character recognition* (OCR) and have special software which processes the images once they have been converted into a form which can be processed by computer. Software capable of dealing with handwriting tends to be distinct from that for typed text, and is now commonly available for pen-based portable computers as described in Chapter 18.

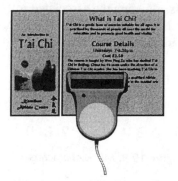

Figure 19.6. *Hand-held scanner*

Figure 19.7. *Flat-bed scanner*

Optical character reader

As described earlier, these devices perform *optical character recognition* (OCR), the process of converting images of printed or hand-written material into a format suitable for computer processing. Figure 19.8 shows the main components of an optical character reader designed for printed documents. The document is illuminated and scanned by a strong light source and the lens concentrates the document's image onto a detector. The detector passes the image data to the OCR software which processes each character of the image, individually matching each character against stored data of the character set. Non-text regions containing graphics, for example, are often separated out and saved separately from the text. The text is output in a format which can be processed by an application program such as a word processor. Most commercial general-purpose OCR devices read machine-written text, but a few can cope with hand-printed text. Special-purpose OCR readers are available for such tasks as reading data on pre-printed forms or processing gas and electricity meter readings.

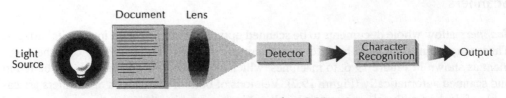

Figure 19.8. *Components of an OCR system*

Optical mark reader (OMR)

An OMR is designed to read simple marks placed in pre-set positions on a document. The document is pre-printed and the values which can be entered are usually limited to marks placed in specially placed boxes. Thus, a suitable application for OMR is a multi-choice examination paper, where the answer to each question has to be indicated by a pencil mark in one of several boxes located after the question number. The OMR scans the answer sheet for boxes containing pencil marks and thus identifies the answers, allowing the associated software to determine automatically the candidate's grade. National Lottery tickets are completed and checked in a similar fashion. Optical mark readers can read up to 10,000 A4 documents per hour.

Magnetic ink character reader (MICR)

This particular device is employed almost exclusively by the banking industry, where it is used for sorting and processing huge volumes of cheques. The millions of cheques, which pass through the London

0 1 2 3 4 5 6 7 8 9

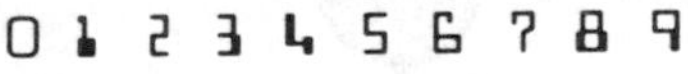

Figure 19.9. *MICR characters*

Clearing System each day, could not possibly be sorted and processed without the use of devices such as MICRs. Highly stylised characters, such as those illustrated in Figure 19.9, are printed along the bottom of the cheques by a special printer, using ink containing iron oxide.

The characters are first magnetised as the cheque passes through the MICR, which then electronically reads the magnetised characters. A high degree of reliability and accuracy is possible, partly because of the stylised font, but also because the characters are not affected by dirty marks. This is obviously important when cheques may pass through several hands before reaching their destination. Such marks could cause problems for an optical character reader.

Bar code readers

A *bar code* usually consists of a series of black bars of varying thickness with varying gaps between. These bars and gaps are used to represent data, which are often printed underneath in human-readable form. Using a laser scanner, the beam passes over the code, noting the occasions when a bar reflects light, and when the light is absorbed by a space. The feedback is then converted by the scanner to a computer-readable code. Several standard codes are in use, each having particular features which are appropriate to certain application areas. One very common code is the Universal Product Code (UPC), a purely numeric code which, as the name suggests, is associated with supermarkets and general product distribution; an example is shown in Figure 19.10.

Figure 19.10. *Universal Product Code*

Bar codes are commonly used to store a variety of data such as prices and stock codes relating to products in shops and supermarkets. A sticker with the relevant bar code (itself produced by computer) is attached to each product, or alternatively, the packaging may be pre-coded. By using the data from the code, the cash register can identify the item, look up its latest price and print the information on the customer's receipt. Another useful application is for the recording of library issues. A bar code sticker is placed inside the book cover and at the time of issue or return it can be scanned and the library stock record updated. By providing each library user with a bar-coded library card, the information relating to an individual borrower can be linked with the book's details at the time of borrowing.

Output devices

Just as input devices allow human beings to communicate with computers, so output devices allow computers to present electronically stored, binary coded data in a form which we can comprehend. In this section we describe *visual display units*, a number of different types of *printers*, and two types of *plotters*.

Visual display unit

The most commonly used device for communicating with a computer is the *visual display unit* (VDU). Input of text is usually by means of a full alphanumeric keyboard and output is displayed on a viewing screen similar to a television. The term VDU *terminal* is normally used to describe the screen and keyboard as a combined facility for input and output. On its own, the screen is called a *monitor* or *display*. So that an operator can see what is being typed in through the keyboard, input is also displayed on the screen. A square of light called a *cursor* indicates where the next character to be typed by the operator will be placed. Keyboards are described in the section on input devices.

Text and graphics modes

All modern display screens operate in either *text* or *graphics mode*. Text consists of letters (upper and lower case), numbers and special characters such as punctuation marks. Most applications require some text display, although it is safe to say that even basic word processors rely almost entirely on the graphics capability of modern screens to permit the use of various character styles or *fonts*. Despite this, the term *graphics* generally refers to picture images, such as maps, charts or drawings produced using graphic design programs, or even photographic images captured with an appropriate *digitising* device (see section earlier in this chapter).

Text mode dot matrix characters

In text mode (see preceding section), characters are formed using a matrix of *pixels* as shown in the example in Figure 19.11 and the clarity of individual characters is determined by the number of pixels used. Selected dots within the matrix are illuminated to display particular characters. A 9 x 16 matrix obviously gives greater clarity and definition than an 8 x 8 matrix. Although both upper and lower case can be accommodated in a particular size matrix, it is usual to add extra rows for the 'tails' of lower case letters, such as *g*, *p*, *y* and *j*. There are two main text modes, each defined as the number of characters which can be displayed on a single line and the number of rows accommodated within the screen's height. The two text modes are 40 characters x 25 rows and 80 characters x 25 rows. The highest *resolution* (see next section) display standard uses 132 characters by 25 or 43 rows,

Figure 19.11.
Dot matrix character

Screen resolution and size

A screen's *resolution* determines the clarity or sharpness of the displayed text or graphics characters. The achievement of high quality graphics generally requires a higher resolution or sharper image than is required for text display. Images are formed on the screen with pixels or tiny dots of light and the density with which they are packed determines the screen's resolution. A typical high-resolution screen provides a pixel density of 1024 columns by 768 rows, a total of 786,432 pixels.

Most microcomputer screens are 14-inch (across the diagonal), but larger screens are often used for applications such as computer-aided design (CAD). This is because the level of detail on some designs cannot be properly seen on a standard screen. An A4 screen, used in desktop publishing (DTP), allows a complete page to be displayed at one time, using characters of a readable size. Other typical screen sizes are 15, 17, 20 and 21-inch.

Graphics display with bit mapping

To provide maximum control over the screen display, each pixel can be individually controlled by the programmer. This gives maximum flexibility in the design of individual images. Several *bits* of memory are needed to store the colour information for each pixel on the screen. If more colours are to be displayed, then each pixel requires more bits. The total amount of memory needed for a complete screen depends on the screen resolution, that is, the number of pixels to be displayed. An image, built up in memory pixel by pixel, is used to automatically generate the screen display. This is termed *bit mapping*, which is illustrated in Figure 19.12. With black and white images, for example, only one bit per pixel is needed, with logic 0 to represent black and logic 1 for white. With four colours, black, red, yellow and white for instance, two bits are needed (00=black, 01=red, 10=yellow, 11=white); three bits are necessary for eight colours, and so on.

Where movement is required, for example in computer games, this is achieved in a similar manner to filmed cartoons - smooth movement is simulated by altering the contents of the appropriate memory locations to make small changes to the shape and location of the image. In addition to animation, bit mapping allows the drawing of extremely detailed and life-like pictures and is therefore used by many graphic design and drawing packages. Even word processors or other text-orientated packages make use of bit mapping to allow the display of different character styles and sizes as well as the *icon* images commonly used in WIMP-based *graphical user interfaces* or GUIs (see Chapter 17).

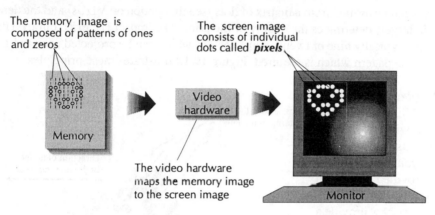

Figure 19.12. *How a bit mapped image is formed*

Monochrome and colour

A monochrome screen uses one colour for the foreground and another for the background. White on black is not generally used because of indications from various research studies that users suffer greater eye fatigue than is the case with combinations such as green on black or amber on black.

Colour displays require more memory than monochrome, and as we explained earlier, the greater the number of colours available for a particular screen resolution, the more memory that is needed. However, a greater range of colours can obtained by using a process called *dithering*. Close to one another, two different colours appear to merge into a new colour, so by carefully 'mixing' pixels of different colours on the screen, many new colours can be created from the true ones available. Though colour displays require a great deal of memory, over recent years the fall in memory costs and the improvements in screen resolution and quality are making them the norm rather than the exception.

Printers

Printers are classed as being either *impact* or *non-impact* devices, but within these two categories there are large variations in speed of operation and quality of print. Speed of operation is largely dependent on whether the printer produces a character, a line or a page at a time. Impact printing uses a print head to strike an inked ribbon, which is located between the print head and the paper. Individual characters can be printed, either by a *dot-matrix* mechanism, or by print heads which contain each character as a separate font (*solid font* type). Non-impact printers do not use mechanical hammers. Though non-impact *ink* and *bubble jet printers* use dot matrix heads similar to some impact printers, the method of transferring the ink to the paper is different, and *laser printers* work on a different principle entirely, a technology closely related to that used in photocopiers.

Dot matrix printers

Characters can be formed from a matrix of dots (see the section on VDUs) and the density of the matrix largely determines the quality of the print. The impact is carried out by a number of tiny pins (typically nine or twenty-four) each of which can be projected or withdrawn according to the pattern which is required. Figure 19.13 illustrates these principles.

A *ROM* (*Read Only Memory*) 'chip' inside the printer provides it with one or more character sets, and character styles, or *fonts*. Other fonts may be provided by plug-in cartridges or by software. Most printers now provide a range of print qualities and styles, which can be selected through a keypad on the casing. Increased density of printing is achieved by passing the print head over a line twice (*double-striking*). Because the individual pins of dot matrix printers can usually be controlled by software, such printers are capable of producing graphical images as well as text.

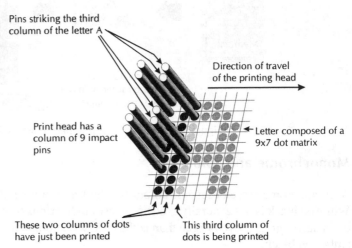

Pins striking the third
column of the letter A

Direction of travel
of the printing head

Print head has a
column of 9 impact
pins

Letter composed of a
9x7 dot matrix

These two columns of dots
have just been printed

This third column of
dots is being printed

Figure 19.13. *How a character is formed by a dot matrix printer*

Some matrix-dot printers have special mechanisms and ink ribbons, which enable them to produce colour images.

Barrel printer

The barrel printer has a band with a complete set of characters at each print position, of which there are usually 132. Each print position has a hammer to impact the print ribbon against the paper. The mechanism is illustrated in Figure 19.14.

One complete revolution of the barrel exposes all the characters to each print position, so a complete line can be printed in one revolution. The characters on the barrel are arranged so that all characters of the same type are in the same horizontal position. Thus, for example, any required *A*s can be printed, then *B*s and so on, until the complete line is printed. The barrel revolves continuously during printing, the paper being fed through and the process repeated for each line of print. Typical printing speeds are 100 to 400 lines per minute. Barrel printers are used for high volume text output.

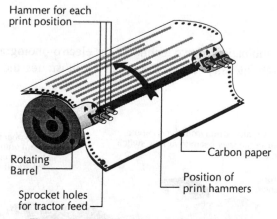

Hammer for each print position

Carbon paper

Rotating Barrel

Position of print hammers

Sprocket holes for tractor feed

Figure 19.14. *Operation of a barrel printer*

Line printers are expensive compared with character printers but may be necessary where large volume text output is required. Printing speeds of up to 3000 lines per minute are achieved with impact line printers. Even higher speeds are possible with non-impact printers.

Ink jet printers

Ink jet printers spray high-speed streams of ink droplets from individual nozzles in the print head onto the paper to form characters. There are two different approaches to propelling the ink onto the paper. In *thermal* ink jet printers (see Figure 19.15) electric heating elements are used to heat the ink and form vapour bubbles, which force the ink through fine nozzles onto the paper; the empty nozzles then refill.

The other main approach is to use the *piezo-electric effect*. Here, a small electrical signal causes a special type of crystal to alter in size, thus creating a pump-like action, which forces the ink through the nozzle. Otherwise, the action of this printer is essentially the same as for the thermal type. As for a impact dot matrix printer, characters are formed by the print head printing a number of columns of dots, but because the ink nozzles can be made so small, the separation of the individual dots is much smaller, thus

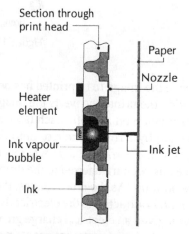

Section through print head

Paper

Nozzle

Heater element

Ink vapour bubble

Ink jet

Ink

Figure 19.15. *Part of the print head of an inkjet printer*

producing much higher quality output. (Typically, there are between 40 and 60 such nozzles). By a series of passes and adjustments to the head's position, graphical images can be produced. Ink jet printers produce output much more slowly than laser printers. However, printing quality is very high and they provide a relatively cheap alternative to the laser printer, particularly so when colour output is required.

Laser printers

Laser printers use a combination of two technologies: electro-photographic printing used in photocopying, and high-intensity lasers. Figure 19.16 illustrates the operation of a laser printer.

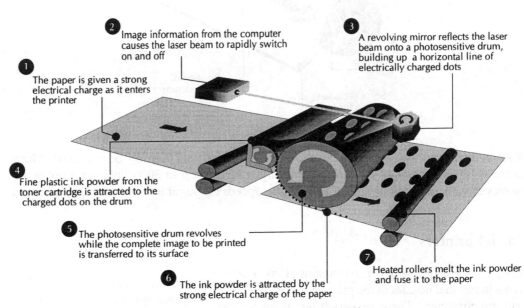

② Image information from the computer causes the laser beam to rapidly switch on and off

③ A revolving mirror reflects the laser beam onto a photosensitive drum, building up a horizontal line of electrically charged dots

① The paper is given a strong electrical charge as it enters the printer

④ Fine plastic ink powder from the toner cartridge is attracted to the charged dots on the drum

⑤ The photosensitive drum revolves while the complete image to be printed is transferred to its surface

⑥ The ink powder is attracted by the strong electrical charge of the paper

⑦ Heated rollers melt the ink powder and fuse it to the paper

Figure 19.16. *How a laser printer works*

Once the image to be printed has been transferred to the printer's memory, a microprocessor inside the printer converts the image, line by line, into a sequence of signals which switch a laser beam on and off. Each laser beam pulse, representing a single dot of the image, is reflected by a rotating mirror onto the surface of a drum. The special surface of the drum is given an electrical charge wherever the laser beam strikes. After a horizontal line of the image has been transferred to the drum in this manner, the drum rotates so that the next line can be built up. As the drum rotates, it comes into contact with plastic ink powder, called *toner*, which is attracted to the electrically charged areas of the drum. Because the printer paper has been given an electrical charge greater than that of the drum, the toner is transferred to the paper as the latter comes into contact with the drum. Finally, the toner is permanently bonded to the paper by means of heated rollers.

Achieving print speeds of 500 pages per minute (ppm), the most expensive laser printers are used in very large systems which require exceptionally high speed output. Effectively, complete pages are printed at one time.

Although more costly than dot matrix and ink jet printers, laser printers offer greater speed and quality. Typically, speeds range from 6 to 26 pages per minute. Printing definition, or *resolution*, is measured in *dots-per-inch* or *dpi*; until recently the norm has been 300 dpi but more expensive machines producing 600 dpi are becoming increasingly common. The high quality of the printed image makes the laser printer highly suitable for producing the camera-ready copy used in book and magazine publishing.

Other types of printers

Liquid crystal shutter printer

A liquid crystal shutter uses a very similar technology to that of a laser printer, but instead of a laser it contains a powerful halogen light source. In laser printers, the laser is fixed in one position, so to complete an image the width of a page, the beam is reflected from a rotating mirror which moves the laser beam horizontally across the drum (see previous section). This scanning action involves some complicated mechanical machinery which, together with the laser, form a major part of the component costs. Liquid crystal shutter printers, on the other hand, use a halogen light bulb as their light source. An array of liquid crystal shutters (the same technology used for liquid crystal displays (LCD) on watches and portable computer display screens) controls which positions on the photo-sensitive drum are exposed at any one time. Typically, the array contains 2400 shutters, sufficient to produce a full page-width line of ink dots at one time. In a liquid crystal shutter printer, moving parts are limited to the revolving drum and the paper and this makes the machine simpler and cheaper to service than its laser counterpart.

Chain printer

In a chain printer several complete sets of characters are held on a continuous chain which moves horizontally across the paper. The ribbon is situated between the chain and the paper and an individual hammer is located at each of the 132 print positions. A complete line can be printed as one complete set of characters passes across the paper. Thus, in one pass as many lines can be printed, as there are sets of characters in the chain. Printing speeds are therefore very high.

Thermal printers

Characters are burned onto heat-sensitive thermographic paper, which is white and develops colour when heated above a particular temperature. Rods in the dot-matrix print head generate the heat. By selective heating of the rods, individual characters can be formed from the matrix. Printing can be carried out serially, one character at a time or, by several heads, on a line-by-line basis. Serial thermal printing is slow but speeds of more than 1000 lines per minute are possible with line thermal printing.

Electro-sensitive printers

This type produces characters in a similar fashion to the thermal printer except that the paper used has a thin coating of aluminium, which covers a layer of black, blue or red dye. Low voltage electrical discharges in the matrix rods produce sparks which selectively remove the aluminium coating to reveal the layer of dye underneath. Operated as line printers with heads at each print position, printing speeds of more than 3000 lines per minute are achieved.

Plotters

A plotter is a device designed to produce charts, drawings, maps and other forms of graphical information on paper. The images may be produced by *pens*, *electro-statically* or with *ink jets* (see Printers section). Electrostatic plotters are quicker but the quality of the image is inferior to that produced with the pen type. Ink jet plotters, though expensive, produce the best quality drawings. Pen plotters use an ink pen or pens to create images on paper. There are two types, *flatbed* and *drum*.

Drum plotter

A drum plotter has a different drawing mechanism. Instead of the paper remaining still, it moves to produce one of the lateral movements whilst the pens move to execute the other movements. To control the paper, the drum plotter uses sprocket wheels to interlock with the paper. The main advantage of the drum plotter is its ability to handle large sheets of paper. The operation of a drum plotter is illustrated in Figure 19.17. Plotters are commonly used in conjunction with computer-aided design (CAD) systems for the production of engineering and architectural drawings.

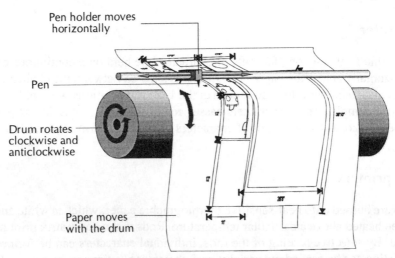

Figure 19.17. *Operation of a drum plotter*

Flatbed plotter

This type of plotter looks like a drafting board with pens mounted on a carriage which moves along guide tracks. The paper is placed on the 'bed'. The pens can be raised or lowered as the image being created requires and different coloured pens can be brought into use at various stages of the process. Drawing movements are executed by movement of the carriage along the tracks and by the pens along the carriage. Figure 19.18 illustrates these principles.The size of paper which can be accommodated is limited by the size of the plotter 'bed', but this can be extremely large.

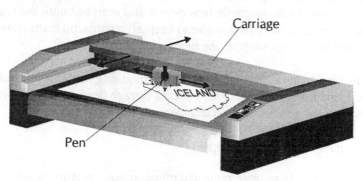

Figure 19.18. *Operation of a flatbed plotter*

Backing storage

All backing storage systems consist of two main components, a *device* and a *medium*. For example, a disk drive is a device and a magnetic disk is a storage medium. Under program control, data can be transferred between main memory and the storage medium by way of a storage device connected on-line to the CPU. Although conventional magnetic tape and magnetic disk systems still account for the majority of data storage, a number of new products are now available, particularly in the area of removable disk systems. This section of the chapter describes:

❑   magnetic tape, including reel-to-reel and streamer systems;

❑   fixed and removable magnetic disk systems;

❑   optical disk systems.

Magnetic tape

Despite the continued evolution of disk storage, magnetic tape is still used in most large-scale computer installations as a cheap and secure method of storing large volumes of data. The problem with using magnetic tape, however, is that the data stored on it can only be accessed *serially*, that is, in the order in which it was stored. This is similar to the way that a domestic music cassette tape is 'processed', because to hear a track in the middle of the cassette tape, you must either listen to, or wind the tape past, the preceding tracks - in general, you can't get instant access to a particular track. For many applications, for example, in the processing of an organisation's payroll where the data relating to each person must be used, serial processing is not a disadvantage. In applications such as this, the data items stored on the tape are simply processed from the first to the last in that order. Tape is also useful for the storage of historical or *archival* data where rapid access to data is not essential. The Police National Computer system for example, stores old, *inactive* criminal records in magnetic tape libraries, whilst millions of records of current criminal activities are kept *on-line* so that they are immediately available using fast magnetic disk devices (see the next section on magnetic disk). When an inactive record needs to be retrieved, the relevant tape is removed from the tape library, placed in the magnetic tape device and searched until the required data is found. It would be inefficient and expensive to keep all records, no matter how old, on-line (that is, connected to the computer) all the time.

However, there are a large number of applications, requiring fast, direct access to data, for which magnetic tape is not suitable. Other backing storage devices, such as those described later in this section, are used in such circumstances.

General features of magnetic tape

The type of tape used on large mainframe and minicomputer systems is stored on a detachable reel approximately 1 foot in diameter. A tape is a long ribbon of plastic film coated with a substance which can be magnetised. Typically, a tape is 2400 feet long and half an inch wide. Before a tape can be accessed by a computer system it must be loaded into an on-line *tape unit*, the main features of which are shown in Figure 19.19.

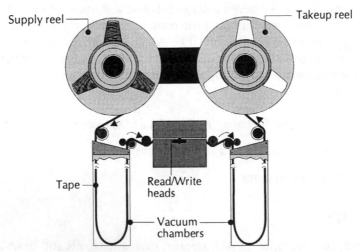

Figure 19.19. *Reel-to-reel magnetic tape system*

It can be seen from the figure that there are two reels, the *supply* reel containing the tape which is to be *read* from or *written* to by the computer system and the *take-up* reel which collects the tape as it is unwound from the supply reel. During processing, the tape is rapidly propelled past separate *read* and *write heads* at high speed and data is transferred between tape and main memory in units of data called *blocks*. A small gap (*inter-block gap*) is left between each block, so that following the transfer of a block, the tape can decelerate and stop and then accelerate again to the speed required for transfer of the next block, without any loss of data. To keep the tape at the proper tension, even during acceleration and deceleration, vacuum chambers are used to allow some slack in the tape beneath each reel. When processing is finished, the tape is re-wound onto the supply reel, which is then removed from the tape unit. The take-up reel remains in the unit.

Data storage on magnetic tape

Figure 19.20 shows how data are stored on magnetic tape. Each character is represented by a group of binary digits (nine for example), across the width of the tape. As the Figure shows, each 0-bit or 1-bit is stored as a magnetic 'dot' in a single *track* along the length of the tape and each group of bits representing one character occupies one *frame* across the tape. The binary coding system used is either ASCII or EBCDIC (the standard for IBM equipment), both of which are described in Chapter 21.

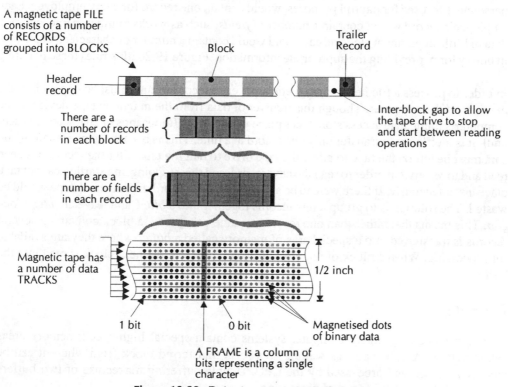

Figure 19.20. *Data storage on magnetic tape*

In the case of EBCDIC, each character is represented by a group of 8 binary digits (bits), either 0 or 1, plus a *parity* bit (for checking transmission errors), across the width of the tape. Chapter 21 deals with the topic of parity checking. As the figure shows, each 0-bit or 1-bit is accommodated in a single longitudinal track and each group of bits representing one character occupies one *frame* across the tape.

The particular method used to represent a 0 or 1 bit depends on the recording system in use but simplified examples are:

❑   the presence of a magnetic field to represent 1 and the lack of a magnetic field to represent 0;

❑   the 0 and 1 bits are represented by magnetic fields of opposite polarity, say north for 1 and south for 0.

The tape unit reads across the nine tracks in a frame to identify the character represented.

Blocking data on magnetic tape

Data stored on tape are frequently organised as a *file* of *records*. For example, a company's personnel file, used for payroll purposes, would contain one record for every employee. Each employee's record would contain a number of *fields*, such as works number, name, address, data of birth, department etc., and each field would contain a number of characters, or *frames*, in binary form, providing the appropriate information. Figure 19.20 illustrates these features.

In order to process a file held on magnetic tape, each record in turn must be copied into the memory of the computer. Though this transfer of data from the magnetic tape device to the computer's immediate access store takes place very quickly (thousands of characters per second), it is inefficient to transfer only one record at a time. This is because gaps containing no data must be left on the tape to allow the tape drive to halt the tape after the record has been read and to restart it in order to read the next record, and this stopping and starting cannot take place instantaneously. If there were to be a gap after every record, far too much tape would be wasted. The solution is to group a few records together into a *block* and leave an *inter-block gap*. This means that rather than one record at a time being read, a block containing several records is transferred into a special area of memory called a *buffer* where they are available for processing. When a block of records has been processed, the next block is read into the buffer.

Buffering

To speed processing, many computer systems contain special high-speed memory areas called *buffers*. A buffer acts as waiting area for a transferred block from where it can be quickly accessed and processed by the CPU. Double buffering makes use of two buffers which work 'in tandem' to speed processing.

So, the first block is transferred into *buffer 1* and the second into *buffer* 2. Read instructions from the applications program retrieve the data from these buffers; the CPU can retrieve logical records more quickly from the buffer than from tape. As soon as all logical records from *buffer 1* have been processed, the reading process transfers to the logical records in *buffer 2*. Meanwhile, the next block on tape is transferred into *buffer 1* and the cycle of events is repeated until the complete file is processed.

Streamer tapes

These look like audio cassette tapes, but are slightly larger, and are often used to *back-up* (copy for security purposes) hard disks on microcomputer systems. The tape back-up device may be built into the computer's system unit, but frequently it is purchased as a separate item. Streamer tapes have huge capacity, ranging from hundreds of megabytes to several gigabytes.

Several standards are in common use, including digital audio tape (DAT) and digital data storage (DDS). The DDS standard of tape has to meet strict international standards, has a lower *bit error rate* and is significantly more reliable than DAT. DDS tapes are certified as 'error free' and are preferred by most users.

Magnetic disks

Many computer applications require quick, *direct access* to data or programs, without the need to search through data not of immediate interest before a particular item is located. This is not the case when data are stored on magnetic tape - if the required item is in the middle of the tape, the computer must read all the preceding data first in order to locate it. The facility provided by magnetic disk, allowing an item to be located directly, is the main reason for it being the most important backing storage medium in use today.

General features

The disk is usually made of aluminium with a special coating, which allows data to be re-corded magnetically. Data are stored in concentric rings or *tracks*. The storage is fundamentally the same as that for tape, except that the magnetic states representing binary patterns are stored in single-file around the tracks.

Figure 19.21 illustrates these features. Each track is divided into a number of *sectors* and each sector has a certain storage capacity. Each track, and sector within the track, is identified by a number, known as an *address*, which can be used by software to locate a particular item stored on the disk. A common method of using these addresses is to use part of the disk for an index containing the names and track/sector addresses of every item stored on the remainder of the disk. So, whenever a particular item needs to be used by the computer, the item's address is first retrieved from the index so that the read-write head can be directly positioned over the track containing the item's sector address.

The number of tracks and sectors available on a disk's surface is known as its *format*. The sector size can either be fixed permanently by a physical marker on the surface of the disk, or it can be set by software. The former is known as *hard* sectoring and the latter as *soft* sectoring. All microcomputer systems use soft sectoring, so that a disk employed in such a system must always be *formatted* before it can be used. This involves writing track and sector information to the disk according to the requirements of the particular disk operating system concerned. A sector of a track, in a similar way to a block on magnetic tape, is the unit of data transferred between a disk drive and the computer.

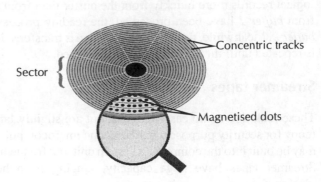

Figure 19.21. *How data are stored on magnetic disk*

Magnetic disk systems can be classified as follows:

□   integral hard disks;

□   removable disks.

Integral hard disks

Figure 19.22 shows the internal features of a microcomputer's hard disk drive. While the computer is switched on, the disk is rotating continuously. The read-write head does not touch the disk's surface as this would result in rapid wear of the surface and the head. Instead, the head flies just above the surface of the disk, so that information can be recorded onto or read from the concentric tracks. The head is specially shaped so that as the disk passes beneath it at high speed, a flow of air forces the head to rise a tiny distance above the surface.

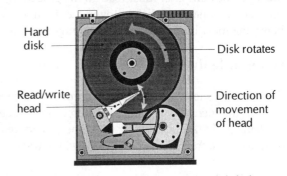

Figure 19.22. *A microcomputer's hard disk drive*

The most common approach to the design of the read-write head's access mechanism is by means of a single *movable* head per disk surface. To increase on-line storage capacity, a number of disks, or *platters*, may be mounted on the same spindle, each surface of the disk having its own read-write head.

Winchester disk technology

To begin with, Winchester disks were designed for use only in minicomputer systems. To-day, all microcomputer systems are equipped with a *hard drive* or *hard disk unit*, because its large storage capacity and quick data access times are essential for the use of modern soft-ware. The system consists of a *pack* of hard disks or *platters*, stacked as shown in Figure 19.23. The disks are not removable and are sealed inside the storage units together with the read-write mechanism. The hermetically sealed environment is free of contamination, per-mitting very high storage densities and spin speeds, typically 7200 or more revolutions a minute. Storage capacities are increasing and data access times (see Disk Access Time) are falling as technology advances. Commonly available systems for microcomputers have gigabytes (thousands of megabytes) of capacity and average access times of around 10 milli-seconds (ms).

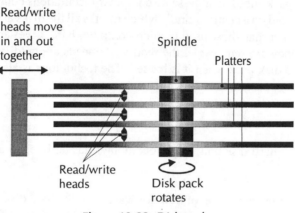

Read/write
heads move
in and out
together

Spindle

Platters

Read/write
heads

Disk pack
rotates

Figure 19.23. *Disk pack*

Disk access time

Access time is the interval between the moment the command is given to transfer a data block (sector) between disk and main memory and the moment the transfer is completed. Three stages in disk access time can be identified

(i)   seek time. This is the time taken for the read-write heads to move across the surface of the disk, to the required track.

(ii)   rotational delay. When a read or write instruction is issued, the head is not usually positioned over the sector where the required data are stored, so there is some rotational delay while the disk rotates into the proper posi-tion. On average, the time taken is half a revolution of the disk pack. This average time is known as the latency of the disk.

(iii)   data transfer time. This is the time taken to read the block of data into main memory.

Importance of access time

Access time is a vital consideration when choosing a storage system. For the retrieval of applications programs or the updating and retrieval of large data files, speed is vital. Waiting 2 or 3 seconds for a file to load can be frustrating and over a period, causes much wasted time. Winchester technology systems offer the quickest access times and some of the removable (or exchangeable) systems, described below, have access times which permit their use as an extension of the main hard drive storage. Other systems are too slow to be used in this way and are only suitable for backup and archiving purposes.

Removable magnetic disk systems

Exchangeable disk packs

Exchangeable disk packs used in large-scale computer installations contain six, eight, ten or twelve platters mounted on a central spindle which rotates all the disks at the same speed. The platters are much larger than those used in microcomputer hard drives and have much larger capacity. Because they are removable, the read-write heads are held in the drive unit, and only interface with a disk pack when it is loaded. The technology is also used in several removable disk systems, described later.

Floppy disk

Apart from a built-in hard disk unit, a microcomputer has an integral 3½-inch floppy disk drive to:

(i)   enable the installation of new software onto the hard disk (most commercial software packages can also be installed from CD-ROM;

(ii)   allow the copying of files for security purposes.

A floppy disk is a flexible plastic disk. The disk is protected with a square, protective casing. As with all magnetic disks, it is coated in a magnetisable material. The diskette revolves inside the casing at approximately 360 revolutions per minute (rpm), which is much slower than a hard disk. The casing is lined with a soft material, which helps to clean the diskette as it revolves. The read-write head makes contact with the diskette surface when data transfer is in progress and withdraws at other times to reduce wear. Unlike a hard disk, the diskette does not rotate continuously - it only rotates when data is being transferred to or from the computer. A diskette will eventually wear out after about 500 to 600 hours of contact. Figure 19.24 shows the component parts of a diskette.

The 3½-inch disk is stored in a rigid plastic casing. A metal sliding shutter, covering the slot which provides access to the recording surface, slides open when the disk is placed in the drive unit

A small hole with a sliding cover is located in one corner of the casing and acts as the write-protect slot. The drive unit uses an infra-red light source to determine whether the slot is open, indicating that the disk is *read only,* or closed allowing data to be both written to the disk or read from it. The figure shows the disk with the slot in the open, read-only, state. The huge increase in the size of integral hard drives has made the 3½ floppy disk inadequate to the task of backing up, except for small files. Its storage capacity of 1.44 MB is often insufficient for the storage of a single file, if it contains graphics images, which require larger amounts of storage than text. It is also extremely slow. There are numerous alternatives, all of which provide much greater storage capacity and much quicker access times and these are describe in the following sections.

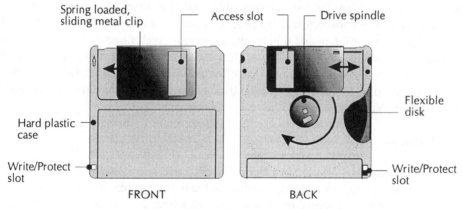

Figure 19.24. *3½-inch floppy disk*

Magneto-optical (MO) drives

Like conventional disk drives, magneto-optical devices use magnetism to write data onto the disk, but in combination with laser technology. The recording head does not come into contact with the disk surface, but flies above it. This reduces the risk of head crashes and the problem of wear and tear associated with conventional floppy disk systems, which require contact for both reading and writing. Briefly, a magneto-optical drive operates in the following way.

To write to the disk involves a two-stage process. First, the laser is used to heat the surface of the disk to a temperature of about 180°C and the write head is set to record bit-0s in the required location. Once the surface is heated the write head causes the magnetic polarity within the current disk location to change and when the surface cools (which it does quickly), the polarity condition is retained. A second recording pass reverses the polarity of those bit positions which are to represent 1s.

Read operations use the laser at a reduced intensity to detect the bit-1s and bit-0s. They are then translated into the equivalent electrical signals for transmission through the device to main memory. There is no magnetic read head involved in the process.

Disks used in magneto-optical drives require heating before the polarity of stored magnetic fields can be altered. This means that data cannot be corrupted by magnetic fields emanating from, for example, a telephone placed on top of the disks or from nearby electric cabling. Data stored on conventional floppy disks can be corrupted in such circumstances. Reading data only requires the detection of changes in polarised light reflected from the surface of the disk. The manufacturers claim that provided the surface is not scratched, then spilling coffee onto it, for example, would only require that the surface be wiped with a special cleaning kit before it is re-used. To avoid over-heating during the writing process, a small, electric fan is attached to the back of the drive; for the same reason most magneto-optical drives are designed to be attached externally.

Magneto-optical cartridges have storage capacities ranging from hundreds of megabytes to several gigabytes. The two-stage writing process means that two revolutions of the disk are required before it is complete and this results in average seek times (see earlier section on disk access time) which are much slower than those for a conventional hard disk drive. Magneto-optical drives could become a cost-effective way of increasing a system's backing storage capacity, but there are much quicker disk systems, which provide similar capacities and much quicker access times.

Bernoulli drives

The removable disk cartridge used in a Bernoulli drive uses air pressure caused by the disk's revolution to flex the disk towards the read/write head as it passes. It is named after Daniel Bernoulli, an eighteenth century mathematician who first documented the particular airstream effects, which are applied in this type of drive. In a conventional Winchester hard disk drive (see earlier section), the read/write heads fly over the surface of the revolving disk and when power is removed may crash onto it, causing severe damage to both and loss of data. Equally, jolting the unit may cause the heads to bounce onto the disk surface and result in similar damage. In the Bernoulli drive, the disk surface is pushed towards the heads, which are at a fixed height, so the risk of head crashes is virtually nil. The robustness of the cartridge makes it a popular choice for users wanting removable storage which can be sent through the post or be used for file backup. A single Bernoulli disk can store around 200 MB. The cost per megabyte of storage is relatively high when compared with, for example, magneto-optical drives.

Magnetic-cartridge drives

A magnetic-cartridge drive makes use of a magnetic disk or disks in a removable cartridge. The read/write heads are an integral part of the drive and move out over the disk surfaces when the cartridge is inserted. A standard hard drive is sealed and provides a clean operating environment, which permits the read/write heads to pass very close to the surface of the disk. This is not the case with a removable cartridge and the dustier environment requires the gap between heads and surface to be greater and this in turn reduces the possible recording density. The capacity of such devices, ranging from hundreds of megabytes to several gigabytes provides a true alternative to the streamer tape as a backup system, with the significant advantage of direct access. For example, an Iomega Zip™ disk uses a single platter approximately twice the thickness of a conventional floppy, which allows greater spin speeds and greater storage capacity, approximately 100Mb. An Iomega Jaz™ disk incorporates two Winchester technology platters, permitting gigabyte of storage capacity and access times comparable to an integral hard disk. These drives provide a realistic option for users wishing to expand their primary disk storage, without changing the integral hard drive.

Docking drives

Docking drives are, effectively, removable standard hard drive units and provide identical access times and storage capacities. However, they are equally delicate, which for a removable device is a significant disadvantage. If security is vital, then the ability to remove and lock up a file storage system is an obvious benefit. Docking drives are expensive and could be used as the primary backing storage facility in place of an integral hard disk system, if the security advantages justify the additional costs.

CD-ROM (compact disk-read only memory)

This type of optical disk uses laser beam technology to allow data to be recorded and read. Data is again recorded as bit-patterns represented by tiny holes in the surface of the disk produced by high-intensity laser beams. The data can then be read from the disk using a laser beam of reduced intensity.

The majority of CD-ROM drives, just like domestic CD music players, are capable only of reading CDs, but much more expensive machines exist which allow reading and writing, and it is likely that in the near future they will become as common as the current read-only drives.

Typically, a single CD-ROM disk can store approximately 600 Mb of data, sufficient space for storing video sequences and digitised sound such as speech. *Multimedia* systems, which use a microcomputer with sophisticated sound capabilities, a CD-ROM drive and a high resolution colour screen, are becoming increasingly popular as a result. These systems use computer programs which combine music and speech with full motion video. They are used for applications such as computer-based training (CBT) and interactive games. CD-ROM is also used for storing and providing access to reference material such as dictionaries, encyclopaedias and graphic images such as clip art. A number of manufacturers are marketing machines specially designed for multimedia applications.

Compared to magnetic disk, CD-ROM currently has two major drawbacks: it is significantly slower, and it is read-only. For these reasons magnetic disk drives are preferable in a great number of areas, but it is very likely that further technological advances will increase the popularity of CD-based backing storage in the very near future.

CD-R (recordable compact disk)

This is a CD which can be written to once, but which can be read as many times as required. The CD-R drive is an example of a WORM (write once, read many) drive. The large storage capacity of the CD means that the writing facility can be used for a considerable period before all the space is used. Provided the recorded data does not have to be updated, this can be a useful medium for *archiving* documentary and other material. The disks are extremely cheap, making cost per megabyte of storage very low. A major advantage, compared with magnetic storage is that the information cannot be erased, making it highly suitable for archiving.

CD-E (erasable compact disk)

When it is generally available, this form of optical storage then has the same facilities presently provided by magnetic media, except that capacities are much greater. Optical storage will then be a viable alternative to magnetic media as the primary form of information storage.

Exercises

1.   Give an example of an application of each of the following: *OMR*; *OCR*; *MICR*.

2.   List the names of *hand-held input devices* which provide alternatives to a keyboard and give an example when each device may be essential or desirable.

3.   Explain the value 1024×768 in the context of *screen resolution*.

4.   Explain why *colour* displays require more memory than *monochrome displays*.

5.   Identify and briefly describe, the process of converting a printed sheet of text into a form which can then be edited in a word processor.

6.   Using the example of greenhouse ventilation, briefly explain circumstances when an *analogue-to-digital converter* (ADC) may be used.

7.   Give two reasons why a publisher would need a *laser printer*, in preference to other types of printer.

8.   How does the arrangement of *magnetic dots* (representing binary digits) on disk differ from that on tape?

9.   Which factor is generally most important when choosing between *magnetic tape* and *disk*?

10.   (i)   Identify the processes which jointly determine *disk access time*.

       (ii)   Which process takes the longest and why?

11.   Suggest why the *floppy disk* is soon likely to be obsolete. What kind of devices may take its place?

Chapter 20

Number Systems

Although the denary number system has proved to be the simplest for people to use, it is more convenient for computers to use the binary number system. The electronic components used in computers can be in either one of two physical states, permitting the representation of 0 and 1, the two symbols of the binary number system. This chapter explains the basis of this and other number systems relevant to the subject of computing.

The base of a number system

First consider the denary system. There are ten symbols, 0, 1, 2, 3, 4, 5, 6, 7, 8 and 9; the *base* or *radix* of a number system is identified by the number of different symbols it uses. Thus, the denary number system has a radix or base of 10. To identify a number, for example 123, as a denary number, it can be written as 123_{10}.

Place value

Each symbol can be given a weight or place (or positional) value, according to its position within any given number. In the denary system, each place value is a power of ten. Remember that the base of the denary number system is ten. Thus, for denary integers each place value is ten raised to a power. Starting from the least significant digit on the right, there are units (10^0), tens (10^1), hundreds (10^2), thousands (10^3) and so on.

power	10^3	10^2	10^1	10^0
	thousands	hundreds	tens	units
	1	2	6	3

Table 20.1. *Place values example 1263_{10}*

The idea of place value can be illustrated with examples of integer (whole) numbers. Table 20.1 shows that 1263_{10} can be expressed as one thousand, plus two hundreds, plus six tens and three units, or $1 \times 1000 + 2 \times 100 + 6 \times 10 + 3 \times 1 = 1263_{10}$.

Similarly, Table 20.2 shows that 487_{10} is the same as zero thousands, plus four hundreds, plus eight tens and seven units, or $0 \times 1000 + 4 \times 100 + 8 \times 10 + 7 \times 1 = 487_{10}$. Note that any number ($n$) raised to the power of zero (n^0) is equal to 1. This can be seen from Tables 20.1 and 20.2 and from the place value tables shown

power	10^3	10^2	10^1	10^0
	thousands	hundreds	tens	units
	0	4	8	7

Table 20.2. *Place values example 487_{10}*

later, for each of the binary, octal and hexadecimal number systems. The *fractional* component of a number is also determined by position, except that the power is negative, as shown in Table 20.3.

	10^{-1}	10^{-2}	10^{-3}
decimal point	tenths	hundredths	thousandths
.	6	2	5

Table 20.3. *Place values example $0 \cdot 625_{10}$*

Table 20.3 shows that $0 \cdot 625_{10}$, can be seen as:

$$6 \times \tfrac{1}{10} + 2 \times \tfrac{1}{100} + 5 \times \tfrac{1}{1000} = {}^{625}\!/_{1000} = \tfrac{5}{8}$$

Binary system

The binary system uses only two symbols, 0 and 1. Each digit in a binary number is known as a binary digit or *bit*. An example binary number is 11001_2, which is equivalent to 25_{10}. The binary system has a base of 2, so each place value is a power of two. The next two tables each show a range of integer place values and an example binary number. Table 20.4 demonstrates that the binary number 11101_2 is equivalent to denary $1 \times 16 + 1 \times 8 + 1 \times 4 + 0 \times 2 + 1 \times 1$ or 29_{10}. Table 20.5 shows that the binary number 01100111_2 is equivalent to $0 \times 128 + 1 \times 64 + 1 \times 32 + 0 \times 16 + 0 \times 8 + 1 \times 4 + 1 \times 2 + 1 \times 1 = 103_{10}$.

2^4	2^3	2^2	2^1	2^0
16	8	4	2	1
1	1	1	0	1

Table 20.4. *11101_2 or 29_{10}*

2^7	2^6	2^5	2^4	2^3	2^2	2^1	2^0
128	64	32	16	8	4	2	1
0	1	1	0	0	1	1	1

Table 20.5. *01100111_2 or 103_{10}*

Binary *fractions* can also be represented and an example is shown in Table 20.6.

	2^{-1}	2^{-2}	2^{-3}	2^{-4}
binary point	half	quarter	eighth	sixteenth
.	0	1	1	1

Table 20.6. *Fraction 0.0111_2*

We can see from this that $0 \cdot 0111_2$ is equivalent to $0 \times \frac{1}{2} + 1 \times \frac{1}{4} + 1 \times \frac{1}{8} + 1 \times \frac{1}{16} = \frac{7}{16}$

Table 20.7 shows the binary equivalents of 0 to 9 in the denary system.

base$_{10}$	base$_2$	base$_{10}$	base$_2$	base$_{10}$	base$_2$	base$_{10}$	base$_2$	base$_{10}$	base$_2$
0	0000	1	0001	2	0010	3	0011	4	0100
5	0101	6	0110	7	0111	8	1000	9	1001

Table 20.7. *Denary symbols and their binary equivalents*

Using the place values for the binary system shown in Tables 20.4 and 20.5, it can be seen how each of the denary numbers in Table 20.7 equates with its binary representation.

Rules of binary arithmetic

Addition rules are given, together with example sums, in Table 20.8. The rules for binary addition are needed when studying computer arithmetic in Chapter 21.

addition rules	carry	example sum	example sum
$0 + 0 = 0$		011010	101100
$0 + 1 = 1$		$+\ 110100$	$+\ 000010$
$1 + 0 = 1$		$\overline{1001110}$	$\overline{101110}$
$1 + 1 = 0$	1		

Table 20.8. *Binary addition rules and examples*

Octal and hexadecimal numbers

These number systems are often used as a shorthand method for representing binary numbers. As can be seen from the binary numbers in the earlier tables, they are very confusing to the eye and it is sometimes difficult, even with small groupings, to distinguish one pattern from another. Where it is necessary for the computer's binary codes to be written or read by programmers, for example, it is invariably more convenient to use alternative coding methods. Octal and hexadecimal (*hex*) notations are used in preference to denary because they are more readily converted to or from binary. It must be emphasized that computers can only handle binary forms of coding. Therefore octal and hexadecimal codes must be converted to binary before they can be handled by the computer.

Octal coding

The octal number system has a base of 8, using 0, 1, 2, 3, 4, 5, 6 and 7 as its symbols. Each place value is a power of eight; some of the place values are shown in Table 20.9.

8^4	8^3	8^2	8^1	8^0	8^{-1}	8^{-2}	8^{-3}
4096	512	64	8	1	$\frac{1}{8}$	$\frac{1}{64}$	$\frac{1}{512}$

Table 20.9. *Some octal place values*

Octal coding uses three bits at a time, allowing 8 or 2^3 (see Table 20.10) different patterns of bits.

Binary	0 0 0	0 0 1	0 1 0	0 1 1	1 0 0	1 0 1	1 1 0	1 1 1
Octal	0	1	2	3	4	5	6	7

Table 20.10. *Octal symbols and binary equivalents*

To represent any given value, a binary number can be split into groups of 3 bits, starting from the right-hand side, as the two 16-bit examples in Table 20.11 show.

0111001101100110_2	0	1 1 1	0 0 1	1 0 1	1 0 0	1 1 0
Octal code	0	7	1	5	4	6
1101010100101011_2	1	1 0 1	0 1 0	1 0 0	1 0 1	0 1 1
Octal code	1	5	2	4	5	3

Table 20.11. *Octal coding symbols*

Because the 16 bits will not divide exactly into groups of 3, the left-most or *most significant bit* (MSB) can only take the values 0_8 or 1_8.

Hexadecimal coding

The hexadecimal number system has a base of 16, and uses the following symbols: 0, 1, 2, 3, 4, 5, 6, 7, 8, 9, A, B, C, D, E and F. The six letters, A to F, are used instead of the denary numbers 10, 11, 12, 13, 14 and 15, respectively. This brings the number of hexadecimal symbols to sixteen. Some place values, each being a power of 16, are shown in Table 20.12.

16^3	16^2	16^1	16^0	16^{-1}	16^{-2}	16^{-3}
4096	256	16	1	$\frac{1}{16}$	$\frac{1}{256}$	$\frac{1}{4096}$

Table 20.12. *Hexadecimal place values*

A group of 4 bits provides 16 unique binary patterns, the number required to represent all 16 symbols of the hexadecimal (hex) number system. The symbols and their binary equivalents are given in Table 20.13.

Binary	0000	0001	0010	0011	0100	0101	0110	0111
Hex	0	1	2	3	4	5	6	7
Binary	1000	1001	1010	1011	1100	1101	1110	1111
Hex	8	9	A	B	C	D	E	F

Table 20.13. *Hexadecimal symbols and binary equivalents*

Therefore, a binary number can be coded by grouping the bits into groups of four and using

110000111110110_2	1100	0011	1111	0110
Hexadecimal code	C	3	F	6
0101011010111101_2	0101	0110	1011	1101
Hexadecimal code	5	6	B	D

Table 20.14. *Hexadecimal coding examples*

the appropriate hexadecimal symbol for each group, as the examples in Table 20.14 show.

In practice, hexadecimal is used in preference to octal code because computers organise their internal memory in 8-bit groupings (*bytes*) or multiples of bytes. These groupings conveniently divide into 4-bit *nibbles* which can be coded in the shorthand of hexadecimal. A knowledge of hexadecimal is essential for the interpretation of computer manufacturers' manuals, which use the coding system extensively to specify memory and backing storage features. Programmers using low level languages (see Chapter 16), such as assembly code, also need to be familiar with this number system.

Exercises

1. Calculate the *denary* equivalents of the following binary numbers:

    (i)   11001110

    (ii)   10101011

    (iii)   01001100

    (iv)   11110000

    (v)   00001111

2. Using the conversion tables provided in this chapter, write down the *octal* and *hexadecimal* equivalents of the binary numbers in Exercise 1.

3. Why is hexadecimal notation used in preference to other number bases, as a short-hand for binary code?

Chapter 21

Data Representation

Data, in the context of this chapter, is a general term which covers any data or information which is capable of being handled by the computer's internal circuitry, or of being stored on backing storage media such as magnetic tape or disk. To be processed by computer, data must be in a form which the computer can handle; it must be *machine-sensible*.

Forms of coding

To be machine-sensible, data has to be in *binary* format. In Chapter 20, it is explained that the binary number system uses only two digits, 0 and 1. Both main memory and external storage media, such as magnetic disk and tape, use electrical/magnetic patterns representing the binary digits 0 and 1 to record and handle data and instructions.

Why binary? - bi-stable devices

Computer storage uses two-state or bi-stable devices to indicate the presence of a binary 0 or 1. The circuits inside a computer represent these two states by being either conducting or non-conducting, that is, current is either flowing or is not flowing through the circuit. A simple example of a bi-stable device is an electric light bulb. At any one time it must be in one of two states, on or off. Magnetic storage media use magnetic fields and the two possible polarities (north and south) are used as bi-stable devices to represent 0 and 1.

To understand the benefits of using binary representation, consider the electronic requirements which would be necessary if the denary system were used. To record the ten denary symbols 0 to 9, a computer's circuitry would have to use and accommodate ten clearly defined physical electronic states. Extremely reliable components would be needed to avoid the machine confusing one physical state with another. With bi-stable devices, slight changes in performance do not prevent differentiation between the two physical states which represent 0 and 1.

Character and numeric codes

Much of the data processed by computer and stored on backing storage are represented by *character* codes. The codes used inside the computer are referred to as *internal* codes, whereas those used by various peripherals are termed *external* codes. Data transferred between peripheral devices and the processor may use a variety of binary character codes, but when processing data the processor will tend to use a particular internal code, which will vary with machines of different manufacture. Sometimes, an external character code may continue to be used for storage of data in main memory; alphabetic data remains in character code form during computer processing. On the other hand, numeric data, presented by a peripheral in character code form, is converted to one of a number of numeric codes for processing purposes. Code conversion may be executed within a peripheral, within the *interface* device between a peripheral and the processor, or within the processor itself.

Characters may be grouped according to the following categories:

❑   alphabetic (upper and lower case);

❑   numeric (0 to 9);

❑   special characters (apostrophe, comma, etc.);

❑   control characters and codes.

Control characters are used in data transmission, perhaps to indicate the start or end of a *block* of data; *control codes* can be used to affect the display of data on a VDU screen and include those which cause, for example, carriage return, delete, highlight or blinking. Control characters and control codes do not form part of the data which are to be usefully processed, but are needed for control.The range of characters which can be represented by a computer system is known as its *character set*. The ASCII (American Standard Code for Information Interchange) code uses seven binary digits (*bits*) to represent a full range of characters; an extract is shown in Table 21.1.

character	ASCII	character	ASCII	character	ASCII	character	ASCII
0	0110000	9	0111001	I	1001001	R	1010010
1	0110001	A	1000001	J	1001010	S	1010011
2	0110010	B	1000010	K	1001011	T	1010100
3	0110011	C	1000011	L	1001100	U	1010101
4	0110100	D	1000100	M	1001101	V	1010110
5	0110101	E	1000101	N	1001110	W	1010111
6	0110110	F	1000110	O	1001111	X	1011000
7	0110111	G	1000111	P	1010000	Y	1011001
8	0111000	H	1001000	Q	1010001	Z	1011010

Table 21.1. *Extract from ASCII character set*

Data passing between a peripheral and the computer is usually in character code, typically ASCII or EBCDIC (Extended Binary Coded Decimal Interchange Code). This latter 8-bit character code has a 256 character set and is generally used with IBM and IBM-compatible equipment. An extract is shown in Table 21.2.

char	EBCDIC	char	EBCDIC	char	EBCDIC	char	EBCDIC
0	11110000	9	11111001	I	11001001	R	11011001
1	11110001	A	11000001	J	11010001	S	11100010
2	11110010	B	11000010	K	11010010	T	11100011
3	11110011	C	11000011	L	11010011	U	11100100
4	11110100	D	11000100	M	11010100	V	11100101
5	11110101	E	11000101	N	11010101	W	11100110
6	11110110	F	11000110	O	11010110	X	11100111
7	11110111	G	11000111	P	11010111	Y	11101000
8	11111000	H	11001000	Q	11011000	Z	11101001

Table 21.2. *Extract from EBCDIC character set*

Parity checking of codes

The ASCII code shown in Table 21.1 is a 7-bit code. An additional bit, known as the *parity bit* (in the left-most or most significant bit position), is used to detect *single bit* errors which may occur during data transfer. Such errors may result from a peripheral fault or from corruption of data on storage media.

The parity scheme used for detecting single bit errors is simple (the detection of multiple bit errors is more complex) . There are two types of parity, odd and even, though it is of little significance which is used. If odd parity is used, the parity bit is set to binary 1 or 0, such that there is an odd number of binary 1s in the group. Conversely, even parity requires that there is an even number of binary 1s in the group. Examples of these two forms of parity are provided in Table 21.3.

data - no parity	parity bit	data - odd parity	parity bit	data - even parity
1 0 0 1 0 1 0	0	1 0 0 1 0 1 0	1	1 0 0 1 0 1 0
0 1 0 1 1 0 1	1	0 1 0 1 1 0 1	0	0 1 0 1 1 0 1

Table 21.3. *Examples of data using odd and even parity*

If even parity is being used and main memory receives the grouping 10010100 then the presence of an odd number of binary 1s indicates an error in transmission. Provided that the number of bits corrupted is odd, all transmission errors will be detected. However, an even number of bits in error will not affect the parity condition and thus will not be revealed. Additional controls can be implemented to detect multiple bit errors; these controls make use of parity checks on blocks of characters; known *as block check characters* (BCC), they are used extensively in data transmission control.

Data storage in main memory

Character codes, such as the ASCII code (Table 21.1), are primarily of use during data transfer between a peripheral and the main memory. They are also generally used to represent non-numeric data inside the computer. Numeric data are usually converted to one of a number of *numeric codes*, including binary coded decimal (BCD) and floating point formats (see later).

Binary coded decimal (BCD)

As the name suggests, BCD uses a binary code to represent each of the decimal symbols. It is a 4-bit code, using the natural binary weightings of 8, 4, 2 and 1 and is only used for the representation of numeric values.

denary	0	1	2	3	4	5	6	7	8	9
BCD	0000	0001	0010	0011	0100	0101	0110	0111	1000	1001

Table 21.4. *BCD equivalents of denary symbols*

Each of the ten symbols used in the decimal system is coded with its 4-bit binary equivalent, as shown in Table 21.4. In this way, any decimal number can be represented by coding each digit separately. An example BCD number is shown in Table 21.5.

denary	6	2	4
BCD	0110	0010	0100

Table 21.5. *BCD representation of 624_{10}*

BCD arithmetic

Floating point arithmetic can introduce small inaccuracies which can be a problem in financial data processing applications. For example, an amount of $120 \cdot 50$ stored in floating point form may return a value of $120 \cdot 499999$; although the application of *rounding algorithms* (see later) can adjust the figure to the required number of significant figures, the rounding is being carried out on the binary representation, when it is the decimal form which should be rounded. For BCD numbers, each decimal character is separately coded and their addition cannot be accomplished with the normal ADD instruction (Chapter 23); more complex electronics are needed to carry out arithmetic on data in BCD form than are necessary for pure binary numbers. BCD numbers also take more memory space than pure binary numbers. For example, with a 16-bit word the maximum BCD number is 9999_{10}, while using binary it is 65535_{10}. Numbers with a fractional element (*real* numbers) are represented with an implied decimal point which can be located between any of the 4-bit groupings.

Internal parity checks

Most mini and mainframe computers use parity bits to detect and sometimes correct, data transfer errors within the computer, so the actual length of codes is extended to allow for this. Parity checking, built into the circuitry of the memory chips is a feature of many microcomputer systems. Memory chips can develop faults, so it is important that a user is made aware of parity errors (which may indicate the beginnings of major memory faults), before significant data loss occurs.

The structure of main memory

Main memory is divided into a number of cells or *locations*, each of which has a unique name or *address* and is capable of holding a unit or grouping of bits which may represent data or an instruction. More is said about instructions in Chapter 23. Memory locations are normally addressed using whole numbers from zero upwards. The *size* of memory location used varies from one make of computer to another and is related to the coding methods employed and the number of bits it is designed to handle as a unit.

Memory words and bytes

A *memory word* is a given number of bits in memory, addressable as a unit. The addresses of memory locations run consecutively, starting with address 0 and running up to the largest address. Each location contains a word which can be retrieved by specification of its address. Similarly, an instruction to write to a location results in the storage of a word into the quoted address. For example, the word 01100110 may be stored in location address 15 and the word 11000110 in location address 16. A memory word may represent data or an instruction. The topic of memory addressing is dealt with in Chapter 23.

The memory's *word length* equates with the number of bits which can be stored in a location. Thus, memory which handles words of 16 bits is known as 16-bit memory, whilst that which makes use of 32-bit words is known as 32-bit memory. In practice, a machine may use words of different lengths for different operations. Word length is one of the most important design characteristics of computers, in that it can be fundamental to the efficiency and speed of the computer. Generally, the larger and more powerful the computer, the greater the word length. Until recently, 32-bit and 64-bit words were largely used by mainframe and minicomputer systems exclusively. When first introduced, microcomputers were 4-bit or 8-bit machines, but advances in technology have made 32-bit and 64-bit microcomputers commonplace. Even if a machine normally handles words of 16 or 32 or 64 bits, reference sometimes needs to be made to a smaller unit, the *byte*, which is 8 bits. Programming in a low level language (Chapter 16) requires separate identification of bytes. Table 21.6 illustrates the formation of a 16-bit word, with byte subdivisions. The leftmost bit in a word is referred to as the most significant bit (MSB) and the rightmost as the least significant bit (LSB). The most significant *byte* in a 16-bit word is identified as the *high order byte*, the least significant byte as the *low order byte*. A 32-bit word would be divided into byte-1 (the lowest order byte), byte-2, byte-3 and byte-4 (the highest order byte). A number of different memory structures have been used, based on different word lengths, which have sufficient flexibility to accommodate the requirements of both numeric and non-numeric data.

high order byte								low order byte							
MSB															LSB
bit 15	bit 14	bit 13	bit 12	bit 11	bit 10	bit 9	bit 8	bit 7	bit 6	bit 5	bit 4	bit 3	bit 2	bit 1	bit 0

Table 21.6. *High and low order bytes*

Number representation inside the computer

To be of practical use, a computer must be able to store, manipulate and differentiate between positive and negative numbers. There are a number of different ways this can be done. The most common are: sign and magnitude; complementation.

Sign and magnitude

With this method, the MSB position is occupied by an explicit *sign bit*; binary 0 and binary 1 are used to indicate, respectively, a positive and a negative number. The remainder of the binary word holds the *absolute* (independent of the sign) *magnitude* of the number. The examples in Table 21.7 illustrate this method, using a 16-bit word. Note from the top row in Table 21.7, that the number zero uses a positive sign (0).

	MSB															LSB
$+0_{10}$	0	0	0	0	0	0	0	0	0	0	0	0	0	0	0	0
$+33_{10}$	0	0	0	0	0	0	0	0	0	0	1	0	0	0	0	1
-33_{10}	1	0	0	0	0	0	0	0	0	0	1	0	0	0	0	1
$+85_{10}$	0	0	0	0	0	0	0	0	0	1	0	1	0	1	0	1
-85_{10}	1	0	0	0	0	0	0	0	0	1	0	1	0	1	0	1
	bit-15	bit-14	bit-13	bit-12	bit-11	bit-10	bit-9	bit-8	bit-7	bit-6	bit-5	bit-4	bit-3	bit-2	bit-1	bit-0
	sign	<							m a g n i t u d e							>

Table 21.7. *Sign and magnitude format*

Complementation

Complementation enables a computer to carry out subtraction by addition of the complement, as we explain in the following sections.

Ten's complement

The ten's complement of a single denary digit is found by subtracting the digit from ten. Thus, the ten's complement of 4 is $10-4$, which is +6. In the denary system, subtracting a denary number is equivalent to adding the ten's complement of that number. Consider the following subtraction:

$$8 - 3 = 5$$

By switching the number 3 to its ten's complement ($10 - 3 = 7$), the calculation becomes $8 + 7 = 15$, which with the carry of ten being ignored, gives the answer 5.

A more detailed explanation of the process of number complementation is given in Chapter 26 on Arithmetic Operations. There is no benefit in using ten's complement for subtraction because the process of complementation itself involves subtraction. However, this is not the case with binary complementation.

Two's complement numbers

To follow the computer arithmetic examples in this chapter, you need to know the rules for binary addition, listed in Chapter 20.

Computers are able to perform both addition and subtraction by using two's complement arithmetic. The sign bit of a two's complement

	MSB	place values						LSB
	-128_{10}	64_{10}	32_{10}	16_{10}	8_{10}	4_{10}	2_{10}	1_{10}
$+33_{10}$	0	0	1	0	0	0	0	1
-33_{10}	1	1	0	1	1	1	1	1
$+85_{10}$	0	1	0	1	0	1	0	1
-85_{10}	1	0	1	0	1	0	1	1

Table 21.8. *Two's complement, positive and negative numbers*

number forms part of the number and therefore contributes to its magnitude. In other words, it has a place value which contributes to the magnitude of the number, as well as indicating its sign (positive or negative). A two's complement number thus has an *implicit sign bit*. Table 21.8 shows four 8-bit examples. Note that the positive numbers (+33 and +85) contain a binary 0 in the sign position, so the place value of -128 does not contribute to the magnitude of the numbers. The negative numbers (-33 and -85) contain a binary 1 in the sign bit position, so its place value of -128 forms part of each number's value. The negative value is calculated by adding the negative place value of the sign bit to the positive values of the remaining bits, which contain a binary 1.These points can be illustrated with the following analysis of the numbers already shown in Table 21.8.

$$+33_{10} = 00100001_2 = 0 + 0 + 32 + 0 + 0 + 0 + 0 + 1$$
$$-33_{10} = 11011111_2 = -128 + 64 + 0 + 16 + 8 + 4 + 2 + 1$$
$$+85_{10} = 01010101_2 = 0 + 64 + 0 + 16 + 0 + 4 + 0 + 1$$
$$-85_{10} = 10101011_2 = -128 + 0 + 32 + 0 + 8 + 0 + 2 + 1$$

Subtraction, using two's complement numbers uses the following method. The second number (the *subtrahend*) is negated and is added to the first (the *minuend*). This is equivalent to expressing in denary, for example, $(+55) - (+25)$ as $(+55) + (-25)$.

Conversion of binary to two's complement

Stage 1

The number is converted to its *one's complement* representation by inverting the values of all the bits in the number. Thus, all ones are flipped to zeroes and all zeroes are flipped to ones. The examples in Table 21.9 illustrate the one's complements of some binary numbers.

	Example (i) $+13_{10}$	Example (ii) $+36_{10}$	Example (iii) $+76_{10}$
binary number	00001101	00100100	01001100
one's complement	11110010	11011011	10110011

Table 21.9. *One's complement of binary numbers*

Stage 2

The one's complement of the binary numbers in Table 21.9 can then be converted to *two's complement* by adding 1, as shown in Table 21.10. The two's complement numbers in each example now represent the following denary values.

2's complement of 13_{10} is $-128 + 64 + 32 + 16 + 0 + 0 + 2 + 1 = -13_{10}$

2's complement of 36_{10} is $-128 + 64 + 0 + 16 + 8 + 4 + 0 + 0 = -36_{10}$

2's complement of 76_{10} is $-128 + 0 + 32 + 16 + 0 + 4 + 0 + 0 = -76_{10}$

	Example (i) $+13_{10}$	Example (ii) $+36_{10}$	Example (iii) $+76_{10}$
one's complement	1 1 1 1 0 0 1 0	1 1 0 1 1 0 1 1	1 0 1 1 0 0 1 1
+	1	1	1
two's complement	1 1 1 1 0 0 1 1	1 1 0 1 1 1 0 0	1 0 1 1 0 1 0 0

Table 21.10. *Converting from one's to two's complement*

Integer arithmetic using two's complement

Binary subtraction

Subtraction can be carried out by negating the second number (the *subtrahend*), in this case by conversion to two's complement form and adding it to the first number (the *minuend*). The ease with which binary numbers can be switched from positive to negative and vice-versa, by complementation, makes subtraction by addition suitable for computers. Consider the examples in Tables 21.11 and 21.12, assuming a 6-bit word length.

minuend	0 1 1 1 0 1		$+29_{10}$
subtrahend	0 0 0 1 1 1	–	$+7_{10}$
one's complement of subtrahend	1 1 1 0 0 0		
	1	+	
two's complement of subtrahend	1 1 1 0 0 1	=	-7_{10}
minuend	0 1 1 1 0 1	+	$+29_{10}$
result	1 0 1 0 1 1 0		
ignore carry (c)	0 1 0 1 1 0	=	$+22_{10}$

Table 21.11. *Two's complement arithmetic* $29_{10} - (+7_{10}) = 22_{10}$

The result shown in the final row of Table 21.11 can be proved as follows.

$$010110_2 = 0_{10} + 16_{10} + 0_{10} + 4_{10} + 2_{10} + 0_{10} = 22_{10}.$$

Now consider the example in Table 21.12, where the minuend is smaller than the subtrahend, resulting in a negative answer.

minuend	0 0 0 1 1 1			$+7_{10}$
subtrahend	0 0 1 0 0 1	$-$		$+9_{10}$
one's complement of subtrahend	1 1 0 1 1 0			
	1	$+$		
two's complement of subtrahend	1 1 0 1 1 1	$=$		-9_{10}
minuend	0 0 0 1 1 1	$+$		$+7_{10}$
result	1 1 1 1 1 0	$=$		-2_{10}

Table 21.12. *Two's complement arithmetic example* $+7_{10} - (+9_{10}) = -2_{10}$

The result in Table 21.12 can be proved as follows.

$$111110_2 = -32_{10} + 16_{10} + 8_{10} + 4_{10} + 2_{10} + 0_{10} = -2_{10}$$

The most significant bit (MSB) is the sign bit, which in two's complement is part of the number. As the examples in Tables 21.11 and 21.12 show, a positive value is indicated by a 0 and a negative value by a 1 in the MSB position. Thus, a 1 in the MSB position means its place value is negative (-32 in the 6-bit examples). The addition of lower significance place values which contain a bit 1, to a negative sign bit, still results in a negative value (in Table 21.12 the place values for the answer are $-32 + 16 + 8 + 4 + 2 + 0 = -2$).

Number range and arithmetic overflow

The *number range* for any given word is determined by the number of bits in the word and the fact that the MSB is needed to indicate the sign (unless, of course, the number is unsigned). This applies whatever method is used to indicate the sign of numbers. The number range which can be stored in any given word length can be readily calculated.

Thus, in an 8-bit word using *two's complement* (illustrated in Table 21.13), the maximum number which can be represented is either +127 ($2^{n-1} - 1$) or -128 (-2^{n-1}), where n = word length.

$01111111_2 =$	$0_{10} + 64_{10} + 32_{10} + 16_{10} + 8_{10} + 4_{10} + 2_{10} + 1_{10} = +127_{10}$
$10000000_2 =$	-128_{10}
	sign bit implicit (-128)

Table 21.13. *Two's complement number range in an 8-bit word*

For *sign and magnitude*, 8 bits gives a range of $\pm127_{10}$ ($\pm2^{n-1} - 1$), as shown in Table 21.14.

$01111111_2 =$	$+(64_{10} + 32_{10} + 16_{10} + 8_{10} + 4_{10} + 2_{10} + 1_{10}) = +127_{10}$
$11111111_2 =$	$-(64_{10} + 32_{10} + 16_{10} + 8_{10} + 4_{10} + 2_{10} + 1_{10}) = -127_{10}$
	sign bit explicit $(0 = +, 1 = -)$

Table 21.14. *Sign and magnitude number range in an 8-bit word*

Detection of overflow

If the result of an operation involving two numbers exceeds the maximum permitted by the word, then overflow occurs. For example, using 16-bit words and two's complement representation, overflow occurs if the result is outside of the range -32768_{10} (-2^{16-1}) to $+32767_{10}$ $(2^{16-1}-1)$. Similarly, a 24-bit word permits a range of -8388608_{10} (-2^{24-1}) to 8388607_{10} $(2^{24-1}-1)$.

Overflow needs to be detected by the computer so that an incorrect result is not overlooked. The hardware in the arithmetic logic unit (ALU) can detect an overflow condition by comparing the states of the *carry in* to, and the *carry out* from, the sign bit. If they are not equal, overflow has occurred and the answer is incorrect. Consider the two's complement examples in the next two tables, assuming an 8-bit word length. The sum in Table 21.15 shows a correct result,

	64_{10}	0 1 0 0 0 0 0 0
+	4_{10}	0 0 0 0 0 1 0 0
=	68_{10}	0 1 0 0 0 1 0 0
	carry	0 0

Table 21.15. *Sum without overflow*

but the example in Table 21.16 appears to result in a negative sum (-96); this incorrect result is a consequence of overflow, indicated by the conflicting *carry in* and *carry out* states. Overflow will also occur when two *negative* numbers are added to produce a sum beyond the range of the word.

	96_{10}	0 1 1 0 0 0 0 0	
+	64_{10}	0 1 0 0 0 0 0 0	
=	-96_{10}	1 0 1 0 0 0 0 0	incorrect answer
	carry	0 1	carries differ - overflow

Table 21.16. *Incorrect sum resulting from overflow*

An *overflow flag* (a single bit) in the *condition codes, status* or *flag register* is set as soon as an overflow occurs. Thus, following the execution of an arithmetic process, a low level programmer can include a single test on the overflow flag to determine whether or not incorrect results are due to arithmetic overflow. Other machines may use the flag to implement an *interrupt*, which interrupts the processor's operations, to suspend processing and display an error message.

The problem of limited number range and the need for accuracy can be overcome by the use of two or more words of memory to store a single number.

Real numbers

The first part of this section has concentrated on the storage and handling of *integers*. Although a programmer could choose to restrict numbers to integer format, all general-purpose computers must be able to deal with *real numbers*. Real numbers include all the integers and fractions of a number system, that is, all numbers above and below zero and including zero. Many computer applications require the use of numbers with a fractional element, that is, real numbers. Clearly, this can provide for a greater level of precision than is permitted by integer numbers, but at the cost of increased storage requirements. There are two basic methods of representing real numbers in computer storage:

❑   fixed-point representation;

❑   floating-point representation.

Fixed-point representation

Fixed-point numbers use what can be seen as a conventional format. The binary point is *assumed* to be immediately to the right of the integer part, which is where we would locate the decimal point if we were expressing real

integer part	.	fractional part

Table 21.17. *Fixed point format*

denary values. A programmer can require the binary point to be in any position within a memory word, according to the number of bits he or she wishes to assign to the integer and fractional parts. If more bits in a memory word are assigned to the fractional part, greater precision is possible; on the other hand fewer bits are then available for the integer part and this reduces the magnitude range. Conversely, increasing the proportion of a word given to the integer part increases the magnitude range, but reduces the possible level of precision. Table 21.17 illustrates fixed point format.

Of course, a programmer may equally assume a given memory word to be entirely integer, with no fractional part. The binary point is said to have an *assumed* position which gives meaning to a number. Using 8-bit words, the programmer may instruct that the binary points for two numbers, labelled (i) and (ii), are located as shown in Table 21.18.

If the programmer then relocates the binary points, the same binary groupings take on different values. Using the numbers from Table 21.18, the point for number (i) is shifted one place to the <u>left</u>, which *halves* its value; the point in number (ii) is shifted one place to the <u>right</u>, which *doubles* its value (for clarification of this, refer to Chapter 23). The results of the shifts are shown in Table 21.19. Therefore, a programmer using fixed point numbers must keep track of the point position in order to know their value. This problem is of particular concern to the programmer using low level languages.

If a programmer is using fixed point numbers, this simply means that the decisions on the degree of precision are made by the programmer. If no floating point facility is available, the programmer must use integer arithmetic (see earlier) and set the precision after each calculation. The practicalities of this are of concern to the low level programmer,

	integer part		fractional part
(i) 2.75_{10}	$0\ 0\ 0\ 0\ 1\ 0$	.	$1\ 1_2$
(ii) 28.25_{10}	$0\ 1\ 1\ 1\ 0\ 0$	.	$0\ 1_2$

Table 21.18. *Fixed point numbers*

	integer part		fractional part
(i) 1.375_{10}	$0\ 0\ 0\ 0\ 1$	.	$0\ 1\ 1_2$
(ii) 56.5_{10}	$0\ 1\ 1\ 1\ 0\ 0\ 0$	.	1_2

Table 21.19. *Fixed point numbers after moving binary point*

but briefly, involve the *scaling* of numbers to remove any fractional part, carrying out integer arithmetic and then re-scaling the result to the required number of fractional places. Today, all computers provide a floating point number facility, but there was a time when a programmer had to represent all real numbers in fixed point form. As explained later, floating point numbers require a longer word length than 8 bits, which was the norm, for example, for the first generation of microcomputers.

Number range and precision of fixed point numbers

Continuing with the topic of fixed point numbers, consider a 16-bit word with the binary point assumed to be between the bit-4 and bit-5 positions; sign and magnitude format is being used, so the sign bit (shown in bold) occupies the most significant bit position, which leaves 10 bits for the integral part and 5 bits for the fractional part of the number. The number range which can be represented is limited to that given in Table 21.20.

Positive 0_{10} to $+1023 \cdot 96875_{10}$	Negative 0_{10} to -1024_{10}
$0\ 0\ 0\ 0\ 0\ 0\ 0\ 0\ 0\ 0\ 0 \cdot 0\ 0\ 0\ 0\ 0_2$	$0\ 0\ 0\ 0\ 0\ 0\ 0\ 0\ 0\ 0\ 0 \cdot 0\ 0\ 0\ 0\ 0_2$
$0\ 1\ 1\ 1\ 1\ 1\ 1\ 1\ 1\ 1\ 1 \cdot 1\ 1\ 1\ 1\ 1_2$	$1\ 0\ 0\ 0\ 0\ 0\ 0\ 0\ 0\ 0\ 0 \cdot 0\ 0\ 0\ 0\ 0_2$

Table 21.20. *Example sign and magnitude range*

Precision is limited by the number of bits allocated to the fractional part of the number and no matter what word length is used, some loss of precision is, occasionally inevitable.

Arithmetic overflow

Consider the multiplication of two denary values in Table 21.21, where only 1 place is available for the integer part and 3 places for the fractional part. The maximum positive value the location can hold is $9 \cdot 999_{10}$. Although such a location is large enough to hold each of the two numbers to be multiplied, the product $11 \cdot 057$ (after rounding to 3 decimal places) results in an arithmetic overflow error.

$1 \cdot 363_{10} \times 8 \cdot 112_{10} = 11 \cdot 057_{10}$	**The 10s digit is lost**

Table 21.21. *Multiplication resulting in overflow*

Given a particular word length for *fixed point* numbers, the allocation of more bits to the fractional part improves precision but at the cost of reduced number range. Conversely, the result of the above multiplication could be accommodated if 2 places are given to the integer part, but this would leave one less bit for the fractional element and consequently, reduced precision.

Arithmetic underflow

This condition occurs when a number (a fraction or a negative number) is too small to fit into a given length word. The denary example in Table 21.22 illustrates underflow which results from the smallness of a fraction. Provision is made for a maximum of 3 decimal places. Multiplication of the two decimal fractions gives a product which underflows, giving an erroneous result of zero.

$0 \cdot 125_{10} \times 0 \cdot 005_{10} = 0 \cdot 000625_{10}$	**underflow error**

Table 21.22. *Arithmetic underflow*

Another example illustrates how a negative number can underflow and result in more serious error; given the provision of only two integer places, $-99_{10} \times 2_{10}$ gives a product of -198_{10}, which does not fit. The main drawback of fixed point form is the small range of numbers which can be represented. *Floating-point* number representation helps overcome this problem at the cost of slightly slower computation and some reduction in precision; this latter point is discussed later.

Floating-point representation

A *mantissa* and *exponent* (or *index*) can be used to represent a number. Denary numbers, written in *standard index* form, reveal a format similar to that used for the storage of binary floating point numbers. Examples of binary floating point and denary standard index numbers are given in Table 21.23. Note that the formats are not exactly the same.

binary	binary floating point		denary	denary standard index	
	mantissa	exponent		mantissa	exponent
101.0101_2	0.1010101_2	$\times 2^3$	$6{,}800{,}000_{10}$	6.8_{10}	$\times 10^6$
0.0011001_2	0.11001_2	$\times 2^{-2}$	0.00000564_{10}	5.64_{10}	$\times 10^{-5}$

Table 21.23. *Binary floating point and denary standard index examples*

In floating-point notation, the point is not fixed by the programmer. Instead it remains in a position at the left of the mantissa. Floating-point notation is based on the expression: $m \times r^e$, where m is positive or negative and e is positive or negative, m is the mantissa, r is the radix or base and e is the exponent (power). In binary, the radix is 2 (see Chapter 20).

Fixed-point numbers can be converted to floating-point numbers by a process of *normalisation*. As the first example (101.0101_2) in Table 21.23 shows, if the number is *greater than* 1_2 then the point floats to the left (actually achieved by shifting the mantissa to the right), to a position immediately before the most significant bit. This part becomes the mantissa (m). The point has moved 3 places to the left, the mantissa is now 0.1010101_2 and the exponent (e) is therefore, 3. The second example (0.0011001_2) in Table 21.23 shows that, if the number is a *fraction* and a binary 1 does not immediately follow the point, then the point floats to the right (actually achieved by shifting the mantissa to the left) of any leading zeros, until the first non-zero bit is reached; the mantissa becomes 0.11001_2. The point has moved 2 places to the right, so the exponent (e) is -2. Two more examples are given in Tables 21.24 and 21.25.

In Table 21.24, the point moves four places to the left, so the exponent is 4; in Table 21.25, the fraction is normalised by moving the point three places to the right, so the exponent is -3.

fixed point	binary floating point	
	mantissa	exponent
1110.001_2	0.1110001_2	$\times 2^4$

Table 21.24. *Fixed point > binary 1 converted to floating point*

fixed point	binary floating point	
	mantissa	exponent
0.0001111_2	0.111000_2	$\times 2^{-3}$

Table 21.25. *Fixed point < binary 1 converted to floating point*

The floating point format used in this text follows a number of rules.

❑   With normalised *positive* numbers the binary point must not be followed immediately by a binary 0. Only positive, floating point number examples have been provided so far.

❑   Conversely, normalised *negative* numbers require that the binary point is not followed immediately by a binary 1. The next section, on storage of floating point numbers, describes the format for negative numbers in more detail.

❑   Any normalised binary mantissa must be a fraction falling within the range $+0 \cdot 5$ to less than $+1$ for positive values and -1 to less than $-0 \cdot 5$ for negative values. The range of possible normalised mantissas, given a 4-bit allocation, is shown in Table 21.26.

positive mantissas	denary equivalent	negative mantissas	denary equivalent
0.100_2	$+\frac{1}{2}$	1.000_2	-1
0.101_2	$+\frac{5}{8}$	1.001_2	$-\frac{7}{8}$
0.110_2	$+\frac{3}{4}$	1.010_2	$-\frac{3}{4}$
0.111_2	$+\frac{7}{8}$	1.011_2	$-\frac{5}{8}$

Table 21.26. *Range of possible normalised, 4-bit mantissas, with zero exponent*

Storage of floating-point numbers

As already indicated, floating-point numbers are stored in two parts:

❑   The *mantissa*, the length of which is determined by the precision to which numbers are represented. Clearly, if fewer bits are allocated to the mantissa (which is always a left-justified fraction) then less precision is possible.

❑   The *exponent*, which is usually allocated one-third to one-half of the number of bits used for the mantissa.

Table 21.27 assumes the use of a 16-bit word for the storage of each floating-point number, in two's complement form, 12 bits being used for the mantissa and 4 bits for the exponent.

	sign	mantissa (fraction)										exponent (integer)			
bit	15	14	13	12	11	10	9	8	7	6	5	4	3	2	1	0

Table 21.27. *Example floating point format for a 16-bit word*

The binary point in the mantissa fraction is immediately to the right of the sign bit, which is 0 for a positive and 1 for a negative floating-point number (Table 21.28).

positive floating point form			negative floating point form	
12 bits	4 bits		12 bits	4 bits
0 · 1 * * * * * * * * * *	* * * *		1 · 0 * * * * * * * * * *	* * * * *
mantissa	exponent		mantissa	exponent

Table 21.28. *Positive and negative representation in floating point form*

In two's complement form, the most significant digit to the right of the binary point is 1 for a positive and 0 for a negative floating-point number. It should be noticed that the sign bit and the most significant non-sign bit differ in both cases. As explained earlier, any representation where they are the same indicates that the mantissa needs to be normalised. This may be necessary after any floating-point arithmetic operation.

Floating-point conversion

To obtain the denary equivalent of a number held in floating point form requires the mantissa to be multiplied by 2, raised to the *power* of *e*, which has the value stored in the exponent part of the number. For example, the floating point number in Table 21.29, which uses 8 bits for the mantissa and 4 bits for the exponent, converts to denary as follows.

8-bit mantissa		4-bit exponent
0.1 1 0 1 0 0 1	×	0 1 0 1 (2^5)

Table 21.29. *Floating point number*

$$0 \cdot 1101001_2 \times 2^5 = 11010 \cdot 01_2 \quad \text{(by moving the binary point 5 places to the right)}$$

$$= (16 + 8 + 2 + \tfrac{1}{4}) = 26\tfrac{1}{4}$$

So, the floating point number $0 \cdot 1101001_2 \times 2^5$ is equivalent to fixed point $11010 \cdot 01_2$.

If 4 bits are allocated to the exponent, *e* can have a value between +7 and −8 (assuming two's complement form). Alternatively, in a 16-bit machine, two words with a total of 32 bits may be used to store each floating-point number, the mantissa occupying 24 bits, and the exponent, 8 bits. In such a representation, the exponent *e* could have a value between +127 and −128 (assuming two's complement). The earlier section entitled Number Range and Arithmetic Overflow gives an explanation of these calculations.

Alternative floating-point forms

Different machines may use different methods for coding floating-point numbers. The mantissa may be coded in two's complement, as described previously, or it may be stored as sign and magnitude. The advantage for machine arithmetic of storing numbers in two's complement form has already been identified, but machines with the circuitry to handle floating-point numbers may also have the facility to carry out subtraction without two's complement representation. The above illustrations of floating-point numbers assume that the exponent is also stored in two's complement form. In practice, the exponent is often stored in sign and magnitude.

Floating-point arithmetic

The floating point addition and subtraction examples used in this section assume the use of a 6-bit mantissa and a 4-bit exponent. Both mantissa and exponent are expressed in two's complement form.

Addition

To add two floating-point numbers, they must both have the same value exponent. If they differ, the necessary *scaling* is achieved by *shifting*, to the right (equivalent to the binary point floating to the left), the mantissa of the number with the smaller exponent and *incrementing* the exponent at every shift until the exponents are equal. The shifting process follows the rules for arithmetic shifts, which are described in Chapter 23. The addition procedure consists of equalising the exponents by scaling, adding the mantissas and then, if necessary, normalising the result. Tables 21.31 to 21.32 illustrate the floating-point addition procedure with the example sum in Table 21.30.

	mantissa		exponent	
6.75_{10}	$0.1\,1\,0\,1\,1_2$	$\times$	$0\,0\,1\,1_2$	2^3
$+12.50_{10}$	$0.1\,1\,0\,0\,1_2$	$\times$	$0\,1\,0\,0_2$	2^4

Table 21.30. Binary floating point sum 6.75_{10} + 12.5_{10} = 19.25_{10}

☐   *Scaling*. In Table 21.31, the mantissa with the smaller exponent is shifted one place to the right and the exponent is incremented. As a result, a binary 1 is lost from the least significant bit position.

mantissa		exponent		mantissa		exponent
$0.1\,1\,0\,1\,1_2$	$\times$	$0\,0\,1\,1_2$	scales to	$0.0\,1\,1\,0\,1_2$	$\times$	$0\,1\,0\,0_2$
6.75_{10}		2^3		LSB (1) lost)		2^4

Table 21.31. Equalising the exponents by scaling

☐   *Add the mantissas*. Table 21.32 shows that this is clearly incorrect, because the sign bit is now 1, indicating a negative value, when the result should be positive. The method by which the computer detects this type of error is explained earlier in the section on Arithmetic Overflow.

❑ *Normalise the result* $(1 \cdot 00110_2)$ shown in Table 21.32, which is beyond the permitted range (see Table 21.26) for a positive number. Table 21.33 shows the result of shifting the mantissa one place to the right and incrementing the exponent.

	mantissa		exponent	
	$0.0\,1\,1\,0\,1_2$	×	$0\,1\,0\,0_2$	2^4
+	$0.1\,1\,0\,0\,1_2$	×	$0\,1\,0\,0_2$	2^4
=	$1.0\,0\,1\,1\,0_2$	×	$0\,1\,0\,0_2$	2^4

Table 21.32. *Mantissas added*

	mantissa		exponent	
	$0.1\,0\,0\,1\,1_2$	×	$0\,1\,0\,1_2$	2^5

Table 21.33. *Result normalised*

The floating-point result in Table 21.33 can be expressed as follows.

$$0 \cdot 10011_2 \times 2^5 = 10011_2 = (16 + 2 + 1) = 19_{10}$$

Some loss of accuracy has resulted (19_{10} instead of 19.25_{10}). The loss of accuracy results from the right-shift operation required to equalise the exponents (Table 21.31); a significant bit is lost when the binary value for $6 \cdot 75_{10}$, $(0 \cdot 11011_2 \times 2^3)$ becomes $6 \cdot 5_{10}$ $(0 \cdot 01101_2 \times 2^4)$. The decimal value of this discarded bit is its fractional value of 1/32, multiplied by the exponent (before scaling) of $2^3(8_{10})$, giving a result of $0 \cdot 25_{10}$. Although a further right-shift is needed to normalise the result (Table 21.33), the discarded bit is a 0 and does not produce any additional inaccuracy.

Subtraction

The procedures for subtraction are the same as for addition except that the mantissas are subtracted. This can be achieved by negating the subtrahend and then adding it to the minuend. Consider the example in Table 21.34. In denary, this is the same as saying $12 \cdot 5_{10} + (-6 \cdot 75_{10}) = 5 \cdot 75_{10}$. The subtraction process, using floating point arithmetic is illustrated in Tables 21.35 to 21.36.

	mantissa		exponent	
12.50_{10}	$0.1\,1\,0\,0\,1_2$	×	$0\,1\,0\,0_2$	2^4
6.75_{10}	$0.1\,1\,0\,1\,1_2$	×	$0\,0\,1\,1_2$	2^3

Table 21.34. $12.5_{10} - 6.75_{10} = 5.75_{10}$

❑ Scale the mantissa (Table 21.35) with the smaller exponent and increment the exponent, repeatedly if necessary, until the exponents of the two numbers are equalised. In this case, one right-shift is needed.

❑ Negate the subtrahend by finding the two's complement of its mantissa, as shown in Table 21.36.

mantissa		exponent		mantissa		exponent
0.110111_2	×	0011_2	scales to	0.011101_2	×	0100_2
		2^3		LSB (1) lost		2^4

Table 21.35. *Scale mantissa*

	mantissa
	0.01101_2
one's complement	1.10010_2
+	1_2
two's complement	1.10011_2

Table 21.36. *Convert subtrahand to two's complement*

	mantissa		exponent	
	0.110011_2	×	0100_2	2^4
+	1.100111_2	×	0100_2	2^4
=	10.011100_2	×	0100_2	2^4
carry ignored				

Table 21.37. *Add the mantissas*

❑   Add the mantissas, as shown in Table 21.37; the carry of binary 1 (in bold) is ignored.

❑   If necessary, normalise the result. In this case, the answer is not in normal form because the sign bit and the most significant bit to the right of the binary point, are the same. The result is normalised by carrying out a

	mantissa		exponent	
	0.11000_2	×	0011_2	2^3
zero inserted as least significant bit				

Table 21.38. *Normalise result*

left-shift of one on the mantissa and decrementing the exponent accordingly; the result is shown in Table 21.38.

The result in denary is as follows

$$0 \cdot 11000_2 \times 2^3 = 110 \cdot 00_2 = 6_{10}$$

Note that in Table 21.38 a zero (in bold) is inserted into the least significant bit position of the mantissa. This floating point example has resulted in some significant loss of accuracy (an answer of 6_{10} instead of $5 \cdot 75_{10}$). In reality, inaccuracies of this order would clearly be intolerable and techniques are used to ensure that floating point arithmetic operations produce the degree of precision needed for the most demanding applications. Some aspects of these techniques are introduced in the next section.

Fixed point versus floating point representation

Precision. As stated earlier, given a particular word length, fixed point representation allows greater precision than is possible with floating point form. Consider, for example, a word length of six bits, used to store wholly fractional numbers. In fixed point form, all the bit positions can be used by significant digits, but in floating point form, if two bits are reserved for the exponent, this leaves only four bits for the mantissa and thus a maximum of four figure precision.

Range. As is demonstrated in the previous section, a major advantage of floating point form is the facility for storing an increased number range.

Maintenance of floating point arithmetic precision

Floating-point arithmetic precision can be improved by: increasing the number of bits allocated to the mantissa; rounding; double precision numbers and arithmetic.

Mantissa length

Increasing the number of bits allocated to the *mantissa* will improve precision but inaccuracies can never be completely eliminated. In practice, memory words are much longer than those used for illustration here and where memory words are of insufficient length to ensure acceptable accuracy, two adjacent locations may be used. Machines which make use of this method are providing what is referred to as *double-precision floating-point* facilities.

Rounding

The subtraction example in Tables 21.34 to 21.38 demonstrates a loss of accuracy through *truncation*; a significant bit 1 is lost when the mantissa is shifted one place to the right, in order to equalise the exponents of the minuend and the subtrahend. If a computer process requires a series of calculations, each using the results of previous ones, repeated truncation may accrue considerable inaccuracy and this will be reflected in the final result. As can be seen from the example of floating-point addition in Tables 21.30 to 21.33, the process of normalising the result also requires the shifting or justification of the mantissa.

Consider the example in Table 21.39, which only shows the mantissas to illustrate the normalisation process. Normalisation has resulted in the loss of a binary 1 from the least significant bit position (a 0 is inserted into the sign bit position) and consequent loss of accuracy. Rounding dictates that, if during an arithmetic shift the last bit

	mantissa	
	$0.1\ 0\ 0\ 1_2$	
+	$0.1\ 1\ 0\ 0_2$	
=	$1.0\ 1\ 0\ 1_2$	sign bit now 1
	$0.1\ 0\ 1\ 0\ 1_2$	right shift of 1

Table 21.39. *Normalisation of mantissa*

to be discarded (the *most significant* of those which are lost) is a 1, then 1 is added to the *least significant* retained bit.

Consider an 8-bit mantissa, rounded as in Table 21.40. The accumulated errors caused by repeated truncation of values during a lengthy arithmetic process can partially, though not entirely, be avoided by rounding. In practice, rounding can sometimes result in greater inaccuracies than would result without rounding. Many rounding algorithms exist to try to overcome this problem and the type of inaccuracy which occasionally occurs will depend on the rounding algorithm.

	7 bits	$1 0 1 0 1 1 1_2$
$1 0 1 0 1 1 0 1_2$	6 bits	$1 0 1 0 1 1_2$
rounded to	5 bits	$1 0 1 1 0_2$
	4 bits	$1 0 1 1_2$

Table 21.40. *Rounding*

Floating-point multiplication and division

To multiply two floating-point numbers, the mantissas are multiplied and their exponents are added. Floating-point division is carried out by dividing the mantissas and subtracting their exponents. The details of these processes are beyond the scope of this chapter, but the principles of integer division and multiplication, used by computers, are described in Chapter 26.

Hardware and software control of computer arithmetic

The execution of computer arithmetic operations often involves a mixture of hardware and software control. Increasingly, to improve processing efficiency, many computers are equipped with additional circuitry to handle floating-point numbers directly.

Exercises

1. Why do digital computers rely on the use of *binary code* in preference to, say, the denary system?

2. Distinguish between *control codes* and *control characters*.

3. Examine the ASCII and EBCDIC character sets in Table 21.1 and 21.2, respectively. In what two ways do they differ?

4. (i) A binary code, 0110110, is sent from one computer to another, but the code is received as 0010110. Show how the error could have been detected by the inclusion of an extra bit.

   (ii) The same binary code, 0110110, arrives at the receiver as 1000111. Assuming use of the technique identified in (i), why would this error not be detected?

5. Convert the denary number 8432 to *binary coded decimal* (BCD) format.

6. How many *bytes* are there in a 32-bit *memory word*?

7. If a computer uses a 16-bit word to represent integers, how would it represent the values 32, -32, 72, -72, 473 and -473 in:

   (i) *sign and magnitude* format;

   (ii) *two's complement* format.

8. Using two's complement representation and an 8-bit word, calculate the following:

   (i) $42 + 74$;

   (ii) $74 - 42$;

   (iii) $35 - 46$.

9. Assuming byte storage, why would the addition $75 + 96$ result in *arithmetic overflow*?

10. What would be the denary equivalents of the two's complement *number range* for a 12-bit word?

11. A particular computer uses a 16-bit word to store floating-point numbers, allocating 10 bits to the mantissa and 6 bits to the exponent; both parts are stored in two's complement form. Positive numbers are normalised when the bit immediately to the right of the binary point has a value of 1. Negative numbers are normalised when the bit immediately to the right of the binary point has a value of 0.

    (i)   Calculate the denary values of:

        a.   0110100101000011;

        b.   1010010100100101;

        c.   0001010101001110.

    (ii)   Write down the bit patterns for the following numbers, in normalised form:

        a. $+5\cdot4$;

        b. $-0\cdot625$

    (iii)   Subtract $4\cdot25$ from $10\cdot75$, showing each stage detailed in the text.

12. How can the precision of floating point numbers be improved?

Chapter 22
Computer Logic

Introduction

In Chapter 21 it is explained that data and instructions in a digital computer are represented by the binary numbering system. Internal registers and locations within the memory of the computer must be able to 'remember' data and instructions as sequences of binary digits. The ALU must be able to perform arithmetic on numbers held in this form, and the decoding circuitry of the Control Unit must be able to recognise and interpret program instructions represented by binary numbers. All of these functions, and many more, are performed by logic circuits.

Computer logic is based on a branch of mathematical logic called Boolean Algebra (named after the English mathematician George Boole) which allows the symbolic manipulation of logical variables in a manner very similar to the manipulation of 'unknowns' in an ordinary algebraic expression of the form

$$x.(y+z) \text{ or } x.y + x.z$$

Just as laws are needed for ordinary algebraic expressions, fundamental laws exist for the manipulation of Boolean expressions. These laws permit complex logical expressions, representing logic circuits, to be analysed or designed.

This chapter introduces the foundations of Boolean Algebra, its relevance to computer circuitry, and the processes by which such circuitry may be designed and analysed.

Boolean variables

A Boolean variable has one of two values, normally represented by 1 and 0. In terms of computer circuitry, a Boolean variable represents a voltage on a line which may be an input to a logic circuit or an output from a logic circuit. For instance, a value of 1 might represent five volts and a value of 0, zero volts. Boolean variables are denoted by letters of the alphabet. Thus the variables X, Y, Z, P, Q, R are each able to represent a value of 1 or 0.

Gates

The term 'gate' is used to describe the members of a set of basic electronic components which, when combined with each other, are able to perform complex logical and arithmetic operations. These are the types of operations associated with the ALU (Arithmetic and Logic Unit) of the CPU. For present purposes, the physical construction of the gates is of no direct concern, and the discussion will be restricted to their functions only.

The 'Or' gate

Gates have one or more inputs but only a single output. The nature of the gate determines what the output should be given the current inputs. For example, the OR gate could be defined as in Table 22.1.

Inputs		Output
X	Y	X OR Y
0	0	0
0	1	1
1	0	1
1	1	1

X and Y are Boolean variables capable at any time of having the value 1 or 0. Thus at any instant X could have a value of 0 and Y a value of 1, or X could have a value of 1 and Y could have a value of 1; there are four such combinations of the values of X and Y as shown in the table above. With an OR gate, when there is at least one 1 in the input variables, the output is 1. The third column of the table shows the output produced by each combination of the two inputs. The complete table is known as a *truth table*

Table 22.1. *Truth table for 'OR' gate*

and completely defines the operation of the OR gate for every combination of inputs. As will be shown throughout this chapter, truth tables are extremely useful for describing logic circuits.

Symbolically, the combination of X and Y using an OR gate is written

X   OR   Y or X + Y (read as 'X or Y')

Both forms mean that X and Y are inputs to an OR gate. The second form is that required for Boolean Algebra and the '+' is known as the OR operator.

The symbol used when drawing an OR gate in a logic circuit is shown in Figure 22.1. It shows that

❑   the output is 1 if the X OR Y input is 1.

Gates are the physical realisations of simple Boolean expressions. The design of logic circuits is performed symbolically using Boolean Algebra. A Boolean algebraic expression can then be converted very easily into a logic circuit consisting of a combination of gates.

Figure 22.1. *OR gate symbol*

The OR gate is only one of several which are used to produce logic circuits. The other gates of interest are AND, NOT, EOR, NAND and NOR. The first two, in conjunction with the OR gate, are of the greatest importance since these three are directly related to the Boolean operators used in Boolean Algebra.

The 'And' gate

The AND gate is defined by the truth table in Table 22.2. It shows that

❑ the output is 1 when the X input AND the Y input are 1s.

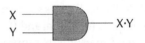

X	Y	X AND Y
0	0	0
0	1	0
1	0	0
1	1	1

Table 22.2. Truth table for AND gate

This time, the gate only produces an output of 1 when both inputs are 1s. The Boolean operator equivalent to the AND gate is the AND operator '.', and is written

❑ X.Y (read as 'X and Y')

The symbol for the AND gate is shown in Figure 22.2.

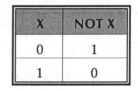

Figure 22.2. AND gate symbol

The 'Not' gate

The third important gate is the NOT gate which has the truth table shown in Table 22.3.

This gate only has a single input which is inverted at the output. A NOT gate is often called an 'inverter' for this reason and is written $\overline{X}$ or $\sim X$ in Boolean expressions.

The symbol for a NOT gate is shown in Figure 22.3.

X	NOT X
0	1
1	0

Table 22.3. Truth table for NOT gate

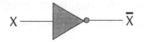

Figure 22.3. NOT gate symbol

Example of a useful logic circuit

At this point it is worth considering an example of a widely used logic circuit to illustrate the relevance of this chapter. The circuit, which is called a *half adder*, performs the addition of two binary digits to give a sum term, S and a carry term, C, both being Boolean variables. The inputs to the circuit are X and Y representing the two binary digits to be added. The rules for binary addition are shown in Table 22.4 and the equivalent truth table is shown in Table 22.5.

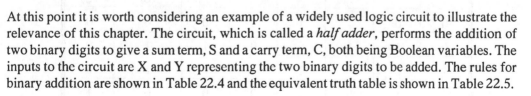

0 + 0 = 0 carry 0 (00)
0 + 1 = 1 carry 0 (01)
1 + 0 = 1 carry 0 (01)
1 + 1 = 0 carry 1 (10)

X	Y	S	C
0	0	0	0
0	1	1	0
1	0	1	0
1	1	0	1

Table 22.4. *Rules for binary addition*   **Table 22.5.** *Truth table for binary addition*

The requirement is for a combination of AND/OR/NOT gates to give two separate outputs for (S)um and (C)arry given any two binary digits represented by X and Y. The circuit is shown in Figure 22.4 (notice that the various gates have the same X and Y inputs) and the equivalent Boolean expressions for S and C are

$$S = X.\overline{Y} + \overline{X}.Y$$

$$C = X.Y$$

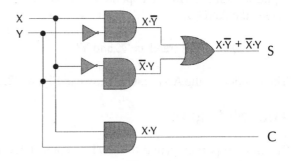

Figure 22.4. *Half adder circuit*

To prove that the circuit actually works a truth table (Table 22.6) is constructed showing the output from every component in the circuit from stage to stage, given the inputs to that stage.

X	Y	$\overline{X}$	$\overline{Y}$	$X.\overline{Y}$	$\overline{X}.Y$	$X.\overline{Y}+\overline{X}.Y$ (S)	$X.Y$ (C)
0	0	1	1	0	0	0	0
0	1	1	0	0	1	1	0
1	0	0	1	1	0	1	0
1	1	0	0	0	0	0	1

Table 22.6. *Truth table for half adder circuit*

Thus if X=0 and Y=0, $\overline{Y}$=1 and using the truth table for the AND gate, $X.\overline{Y} = 0.1 = 0$ and $\overline{X}.Y$ = 1.0 = 0. The rightmost OR gate in the diagram has inputs $X.\overline{Y}$ and $\overline{X}.Y$, that is, 0 and 0 , and using the truth table for the OR gate, it can be seen that this results in an output of 0 for S. Similarly, if X=0 and Y=0, the truth table for the AND gate shows that X.Y=0, that is C=0 for this combination of inputs.

Following this type of argument for the remaining rows in the truth table, it can be seen that the circuit produces exactly the right output for each combination of inputs to perform binary addition on the input bits. Thus a combination of a few elementary components has produced a most important circuit. A truth table allowed the operation of the circuit to be confirmed. Later it will be shown how the Boolean expressions representing the circuit can be derived directly from the first truth table defining the required operation of the circuit.

Deriving Boolean expressions from truth tables

Suppose that it is required to produce a suitable logic circuit from the following circuit specification.

❏   A circuit has two binary inputs, X and Y. The output from the circuit is 1 when the two inputs are the same; otherwise the output is 0.

X	Y	OUTPUT
0	0	1
0	1	0
1	0	0
1	1	1

Table 22.7. *Truth table for specified circuit*

The first step is to produce a truth table to define the circuit fully and this is shown in Table 22.7.
Each possible combination of X and Y has been listed. Where X and Y are the same, OUTPUT has been assigned a value of 1; where X and Y are different, OUTPUT has been assigned a value of 0.

The next step is to define, for each entry in the OUTPUT column having a value of 1, a Boolean expression involving X and Y which uniquely defines that value. So for the first row in the table, where X=0 and Y=0, the expression $\overline{X}.\overline{Y}$ has a value of 1; for any other combination of X and Y it has a value of 0. The expression therefore satisfies the requirement of uniquely defining this combination of values. The expression X.Y has a value of 1 only when X=1 and Y=1, otherwise it has a value of 0, and so it uniquely defines the last row in the truth table. Together the expressions $\overline{X}.\overline{Y}$ and X.Y will produce an output of 1 when X=0 and Y=0 or when X=1 and Y=1. Hence

X	Y	$\overline{X}$	$\overline{Y}$	$\overline{X}.\overline{Y}$	X.Y	$\overline{X}.\overline{Y}+X.Y$
0	0	1	1	1	0	1
0	1	1	0	0	0	0
1	0	0	1	0	0	0
1	1	0	0	0	1	1

Table 22.8

$$\text{OUTPUT} = \overline{X}.\overline{Y} + X.Y$$

The truth table in Table 22.8 confirms this result and the circuit is shown in Figure 22.5.

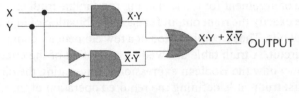

Figure 22.5.

The process of converting a truth table to a Boolean expression is summarised as follows:

(a)   Consider only the rows of the truth table for which the output is to be 1.

(b)   Take each of these rows in turn and write alongside the row an expression containing the input variables connected by the AND operator. If the value of an input variable is 0 then it will appear inverted in the expression.

(c)   Combine these expressions using the OR operator.

To provide another illustration of the process suppose that three binary signals A, B and C, are required to represent a number in the range 0 to 4. The variable A represents the most significant digit of the binary number ABC, B is the next significant digit, and C is the least significant digit. A circuit is required to detect an illegal combination (that is the numbers 5 to 7) by producing an output of 1. The truth table is shown in Table 22.9.

A	B	C		OUTPUT	
0	0	0	(0)	0	
0	0	1	(1)	0	
0	1	0	(2)	0	
0	1	1	(3)	0	
1	0	0	(4)	0	
1	0	1	(5)	1	A.$\overline{\text{B}}$.C
1	1	0	(6)	1	A.B.$\overline{\text{C}}$
1	1	1	(7)	1	A.B.C

Table 22.9.

Therefore

$$\text{OUTPUT} = \text{A}.\overline{\text{B}}.\text{C} + \text{A}.\text{B}.\overline{\text{C}} + \text{A}.\text{B}.\text{C}$$

and the required circuit is shown in Figure 22.6.

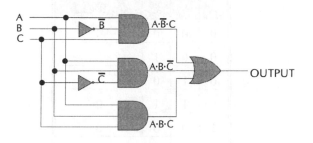

Figure 22.6.

As an exercise, use a truth table to prove that the Boolean expression above does indeed produce the required outputs.

The laws of Boolean algebra

Though the circuit above does perform as specified, it is very inefficient; it uses more gates than are absolutely necessary to produce the required outputs. In fact rather than six gates, only two are necessary because, as the truth tables in Tables 22.10 and 22.11 show,

$$A.\overline{B}.C + A.B.\overline{C} + A.B.C = A.(B + C)$$

A	B	C	$\overline{B}$	$\overline{C}$	A.$\overline{B}$.C	A.B.$\overline{C}$	A.B.C	(A.$\overline{B}$.C+A.B.$\overline{C}$+A.B.C)
0	0	0	1	1	0	0	0	0
0	0	1	1	0	0	0	0	0
0	1	0	0	1	0	0	0	0
0	1	1	0	0	0	0	0	0
1	0	0	1	1	0	0	0	0
1	0	1	1	0	1	0	0	1
1	1	0	0	1	0	1	0	1
1	1	1	0	0	0	0	1	1
								= OUTPUT

Table 22.10.

A	B	C	A.(B + C)
0	0	0	0
0	0	1	0
0	1	0	0
0	1	1	0
1	0	0	0
1	0	1	1
1	1	0	1
1	1	1	1

Table 22.11.

The circuit for the simplified expression is shown in Figure 22.7.

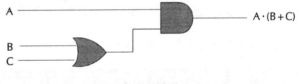

Figure 22.7.

The laws of Boolean algebra enable Boolean expressions such as that in the example to be transformed and, where possible, simplified. The most useful of these laws are as follows:

1. Commutative Laws.

    (a) X+Y=Y+X; (b) X.Y=Y.X

2. Associative Laws.

    (a) X+(Y+Z) = (X+Y)+Z; (b) X.(Y.Z) = (X.Y).Z

3. Distributive Laws.

    (a) X.(Y+Z) = X.Y + X.Z; (b) X + Y.Z = (X+Y).(X+Z)

4. De Morgan's Laws.

    (a) $\overline{(X + Y)} = \overline{X}.\overline{Y}$; (b) $\overline{(X.Y)} = \overline{X} + \overline{Y}$

5. Laws of Absorption.

    (a) X + X.Y = X; (b) X.(X + Y) = X

6. Laws of Tautology.

(a) $X + X = X$; (b) $X.X = X$

7.   Law of Complementation.

$\overline{\overline{X}} = X$

8.   Other useful identities.

(a) $X + \overline{X} = 1$; (b) $X.\overline{X} = 0$

(c) $X + 1 = 1$; (d) $X.1 = X$

(e) $X + 0 = X$; (f) $X.0 = 0$

Notice that with each of the first six laws, there is a connection between (a) and (b). Given one of these rules, the other may be derived by replacing the '+' operator with the '.' operator or vice-versa. Thus if it is known that $X + X.Y = X$, then the 'dual' of the rule, that $X.(X+Y)=X$, is also true. All identities in Boolean Algebra have this useful property.

To illustrate the use of these laws in the simplification of Boolean expressions, consider the expression derived earlier:

$$A.\overline{B}.C + A.B.\overline{C} + A.B.C$$

Simplification of this expression could proceed as follows:

(i) $A.\overline{B}.C + A.B.\overline{C} + A.B.C = A.\overline{B}.C + (A.B.\overline{C} + A.B.C)$

Rule 1 allows us to deal with terms in any order.

(ii)   Considering the bracketed pair of terms,

$A.B.\overline{C} + A.B.C = A.B.(\overline{C} + C)$ by rule 3(a)

Here A.B is treated as if it were a single variable, and the expression is therefore of the form

$X.\overline{C} + X.C = X.(\overline{C} + C)$ where X represents A.B

(iii)   Rule 8(a) shows that $\overline{C} + C = 1$, so that

$A.B.(\overline{C} + C) = A.B.1$

and by rule 8(d),

$A.B.1 = A.B$

(iv)   Hence,

$A.\overline{B}.C + (A.B.\overline{C} + A.B.C) = A.\overline{B}.C + A.B$

(v)   Again using rule 3(a),

$A.\overline{B}.C + A.B = A.(\overline{B}.C + B)$

This is of the form

$X.Y + X.Z = X.(Y + Z)$

(vi)   Now consider the term $\overline{B}.C + B$.

Using rule 1(a), this can be rewritten $B + \overline{B}.C$, and now using rule 3(b),

$B + \overline{B}.C = (B + \overline{B}).(B + C)$

As in step (iii), $(B + \overline{B}) = 1$ and $1.(B+C) = (B+C)$.

Hence $B + \overline{B}.C = (B + C)$ and therefore

$A.(B + \overline{B}.C) = A.(B+C)$

Thus the original expression has been considerably simplified and confirms the identity stated earlier.

Fortunately, the process of simplifying expressions involving AND terms separated by OR operators can be performed in a much simpler way using the Karnaugh Map method. This method, as well as being quicker and less prone to error, is also more likely to result in the best simplification possible, particularly where four variables are involved. In certain cases, however, a knowledge of the laws of Boolean Algebra are required. Examples of such instances will be provided later.

Karnaugh maps

A Karnaugh map consists of a two-dimensional grid which is used to represent a Boolean expression in such a way that it can be simplified with great ease. For example, consider the expression

$$\overline{X}.Y + X.\overline{Y} + X.Y$$

This expression involves two Boolean variables, X and Y. The number of different terms possible with two variable is four, and therefore the Karnaugh map for expressions involving two variables is a 2×2 grid, as shown in Figure 22.8.

Figure 22.8.

Each cell in the grid may be regarded as having a co-ordinate formed from a combination of X and Y. Thus the cell labelled (a) has the co-ordinate $\overline{X}.\overline{Y}$, (b) has the co-ordinate $\overline{X}.Y$, (c) has the co-ordinate $X.\overline{Y}$, and (d) has the co-ordinate $X.Y$. When entered onto the map, the expression quoted above translates to the map in Figure 22.9.

Figure 22.9.

Each '1' on the map indicates the presence of the term corresponding to its cell co-ordinate in the expression, and each '0' indicates its absence.

Using a further example, the expression $\overline{X}.Y + \overline{X}.\overline{Y}$ translates to the map shown in Figure 22.10.

	$\overline{Y}$	Y
$\overline{X}$	1	1
X	0	0

Figure 22.10.

Having drawn the appropriate Karnaugh map, the next stage is to attempt to identify a simplified expression. The procedure is as follows:

(i)   Identify all pairs of adjacent '1's on the map (horizontally and vertically).

(ii)   Draw loops around each pair.

(iii) Attempt to include every '1' on the map in at least one loop; it is allowable to have the same '1' in two different loops.

(iv)   The aim is to include each '1' in at least one loop, but using as few loops as possible.

Thus the expression $\overline{X}.Y + X.\overline{Y} + X.Y$ is mapped as shown in Figure 22.11.

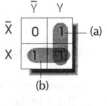

(v)   Take each loop in turn and write down the term represented: the loop labelled (a) in Figure 22.12 spans both X and $\overline{X}$, but Y remains constant. The loop is therefore given the value Y. In the loop labelled (b), both Y co-ordinates are covered but X remains constant. This loop has the value X.

Figure 22.11.

(vi)   The loop values are ORed together. In the example, the expression is therefore equivalent to X + Y.

Karnaugh maps take advantage of a small number of the laws of Boolean Algebra. The Distributive Law allows terms with common variables to be grouped together:

$$X.\overline{Y} + X.Y = X.(\overline{Y} + Y) \text{ (see rule 3(a))}$$

Another law, 8(a), gives the identity $\overline{Y} + Y = 1$.

And finally, law 8(d) says that X.1 = X.

The Karnaugh map allows this sequence of applications of laws to be performed in a single step:

the loop (b) representing $X.\overline{Y} + X.Y$ becomes X.

'1's may be included in more than one loop because of the Law of Tautology (Tautology is saying the same thing twice). Thus $X + X = X$, and conversely, $X = X + X$. In other words, any term in an expression may be duplicated as many times as desired without affecting the value of the expression. So, given the expression

$$\overline{X}.Y + X.\overline{Y} + X.Y,$$

the term $X.Y$ may be duplicated to give the equivalent expression

$$\overline{X}.Y + X.Y + X.\overline{Y} + X.Y,$$

where loop (a) is $\overline{X}.Y + X.Y$, and loop (b) is $X.\overline{Y} + X.Y$.

As a further example, the expression

$$\overline{X}.\overline{Y} + \overline{X}.Y + X.Y$$

gives the map in Figure 22.12 and the equivalent expression is

$$\overline{X} + Y$$

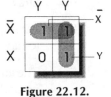

Figure 22.12.

Karnaugh maps for three variables

Expressions containing three variables can contain up to eight terms. The 3-variable map is drawn as shown in Figure 22.13.

This time a co-ordinate pair comprises an X variable and a YZ term.

For example, the cell (a) represents the term $\overline{X}.\overline{Y}.Z$, and (b) represents $X.Y.Z$.

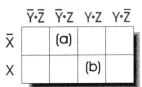

Figure 22.13.

The map in Figure 22.14 represents the expression $X.\overline{Y}.Z + X.Y.\overline{Z} + X.Y.Z$.

In loop (a), X and Z are common factors, but Y changes ($\overline{Y}.Z + Y.Z$). The loop has the value X.Z. In loop (b), X and Y are constant but Z changes ($Y.Z + Y.\overline{Z}$). Thus (b) has value X.Y. The expression therefore simplifies to

$$X.Y + X.Z$$

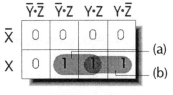

Figure 22.14.

and a further application of law 3(a) gives the final solution

$$X.\overline{Y}.Z + X.Y.\overline{Z} + X.Y.Z = X.(Y + Z)$$

With a 3-variable map, as well as looping pairs of '1's, it is necessary to look for groups of four '1's. For example, the map shown in Figure 22.15 could represent the expression

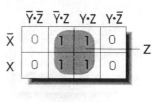

$$X.Y.Z + \overline{X}.\overline{Y}.Z + \overline{X}.Y.Z + X.\overline{Y}.Z$$

Figure 22.15.

The single loop spans the X co-ordinate completely, and so X can be removed from the simplified expression. In the YZ terms spanned, Y changes and Z is constant. The simplified expression is merely Z.

Two further examples of groups of four are shown in Figures 22.16 and 22.17.

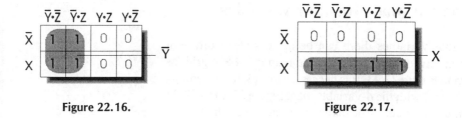

| **Figure 22.16.** | **Figure 22.17.** |

In Figure 22.18 the group of four is formed from opposite sides of the grid.

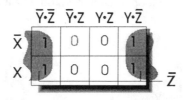

Figure 22.18.

Figure 22.19 to 22.22 provide some further examples with combinations of different types of loops illustrated.

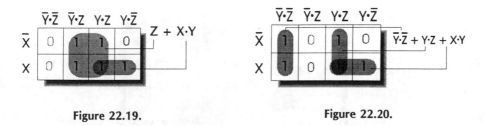

| **Figure 22.19.** | **Figure 22.20.** |

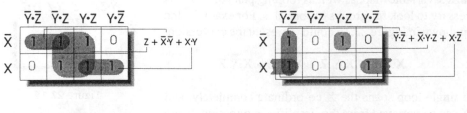

Figure 22.21.

Figure 22.22.

Note that the largest groups are identified first, and then sufficient smaller groups so that every '1' is in at least one loop.

Karnaugh maps for four variables

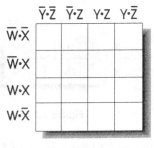

Figure 22.23.

With four variables there can be up to sixteen different terms involved, and the 4-variable map is a 4×4 grid, as shown in Figure 22.23. It is necessary to look for groupings of 8, 4 and 2 with the 4-variable map. Figure 22.24 to 22.27 illustrate a number of possible groupings, including some that occur on the edges of the maps and which are sometimes difficult to recognise. Again, to determine the term equivalent to the loop, look for the variables that remain common to the co-ordinates of the loop's range horizontally and vertically.

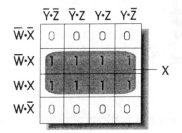

Figure 22.24.

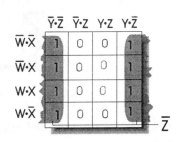

Figure 22.25.

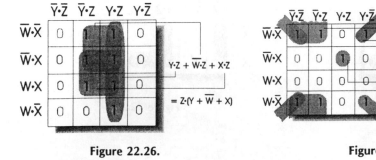

Figure 22.26.

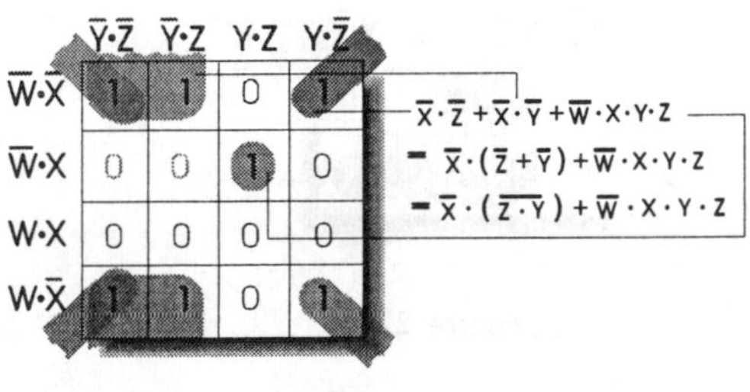

Figure 22.27.

The design of logic circuits

The complete process of designing a logic circuit may be summarised as follows:

(i) Identify Boolean variables equivalent to the inputs to the circuit required.

(ii) Identify the outputs from the circuit.

(iii) Draw a truth table to define the output required for each possible combination of the input variables.

(iv) Derive an expression from the truth table for the output in terms of the input variables.

(v) Simplify this expression using a Karnaugh map.

(vi) Examine the simplified expression for possible further simplifications using direct applications of the laws of Boolean Algebra.

(vii) Draw the circuit using the appropriate gate symbols.

The following problem illustrates the process.

Four binary signals A, B, C, D represent a single Binary Coded Decimal (BCD) digit. A logic circuit is required to output logic 1 on the occurrence of an invalid combination of the signals, that is, when they represent a number in the range 10 to 15.

(i) The inputs to the circuit are clearly defined and it is assumed that A is the most significant digit and D the least significant digit.

(ii) The single output is to be 1 when the binary number represented by ABCD is in the range 10 to 15, that is, 1010 to 1111 in binary.

A	B	C	D		OUTPUT	
0	0	0	0	(0)	0	
0	0	0	1	(1)	0	
0	0	1	0	(2)	0	
0	0	1	1	(3)	0	
0	1	0	0	(4)	0	
0	1	0	1	(5)	0	
0	1	1	0	(6)	0	
0	1	1	1	(7)	0	
1	0	0	0	(8)	0	
1	0	0	1	(9)	0	
1	0	1	0	(10)	1	$A.\bar{B}.C.\bar{D}$
1	0	1	1	(11)	1	$A.\bar{B}.C.D$
1	1	0	0	(12)	1	$A.B.\bar{C}.\bar{D}$
1	1	0	1	(13)	1	$A.B.\bar{C}.D$
1	1	1	0	(14)	1	$A.B.C.\bar{D}$
1	1	1	1	(15)	1	$A.B.C.D$

Table 22.12.

(iii) The truth table (Table 22.12) has 16 entries, representing the numbers 0 to 15.

(iv) The expression for the output is given by

$$\text{OUTPUT} = A.\overline{B}.\overline{C}.\overline{D} + A.\overline{B}.C.\underline{D} +$$
$$A.B.\overline{C}.\overline{D} + A.\overline{B}.C.\overline{D} + A.B.C.\overline{D} +$$
$$A.B.C.D$$

(v) The Karnaugh map is shown in Figure 22.28.

(vi) Using the Distributive law, 3(a), the expression A.B + A.C may be written A.(B + C).

(vii) This expression translates to the logic diagram in Figure 22.29.

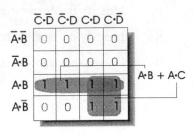

Figure 22.28

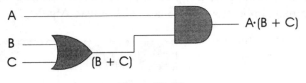

Figure 22.29.

More logic gates

The gates that have yet to be defined are the NOR(Not OR), NAND(Not AND) and XOR (eXclusive OR) gates.

The truth table for the NOR gate (Table 22.13) shows that its outputs are the inverse of those for the OR gate.

Algebraically, the NOR gate is written $\overline{(X+Y)}$. Thus the gate appears to be formed from one OR gate and one NOT gate inverting the output from the OR gate. In practice, however, the OR gate outputs are generated from a single simple circuit and not by the combination of an OR gate followed by a NOT gate. The symbol for the NOR gate is shown in Figure 22.30(a).

The truth table for the NAND gate (Table 22.14) shows that its outputs are the inverse of those for the AND gate.

In Boolean Algebra, the gate is written $\overline{(X.Y)}$. The comments above regarding the construction of the NOR gate similarly apply here: the NAND gate is not constructed from an AND gate followed by a NOT gate, but consists of a single circuit no more complex than the other gates.

X	Y	X NOR Y
0	0	1
0	1	0
1	0	0
1	1	0

Table 22.13. *NOR gate truth table*

X	Y	X NAND Y
0	0	1
0	1	1
1	0	1
1	1	0

Table 22.14. *Truth table for NAND gate*

The symbol for the NAND gate is shown in Figure 22.30(b).

(A) NOR gate

X
Y ———— $\overline{X+Y}$

(B) NAND gate

X
Y ———— $\overline{X \cdot Y}$

Figure 22.30.

The importance of the NAND gate and NOR gate

The importance of these gates may be attributed to two factors:

(i)   each may be manufactured cheaply and easily;

(ii) each can be used in the production of any circuit using AND/OR/NOT logical components. In other words, NOR gates and NAND gates can be used in the place of AND, OR or NOT gates.

These two properties mean that a logic circuit using, for instance, NOR gates only, can be produced more easily and cheaply than the same circuit using combinations of three different types of components (AND, OR and NOT gates). A unit using a number of the same component is much easier to manufacture than one using several different components.

The logic diagrams in Figure 22.31, (a), (b) and (c), show how NOR gates may be used to represent the functions of NOT, AND and OR gates.

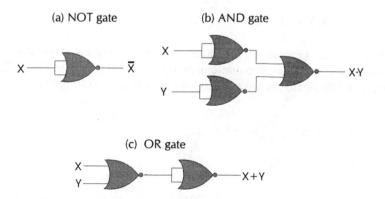

(a) NOT gate

X ———— $\overline{X}$

(b) AND gate

X
Y ———— X·Y

(c) OR gate

X
Y ———— X+Y

Figure 22.31. *NOR gates used to represent functions of NOT, AND and OR gates*

The logic diagrams in Figure 22.32, (a), (b) and (c), show how NAND gates may be used to represent the functions of NOT, AND and OR gates.

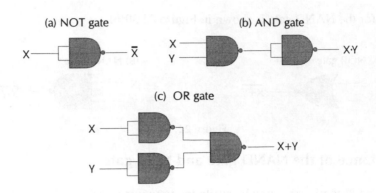

Figure 22.32. *NAND gates used to represent functions of NOT, AND and OR gates*

(As an exercise, write down Boolean expressions equivalent to the circuits shown above and prove their validity using truth tables). It may appear from the diagrams shown above that circuits using NAND or NOR gates will generally require more gates than when using AND/OR NOT components. This may be true on occasions, but at other times fewer gates may be required. The number of gates required often may be reduced by transforming the Boolean expression into a more suitable form. For example, the following expression, when implemented directly using NOR gates, uses more gates than the expression requires using AND/OR/NOT logic:

$$X.\overline{Y} + \overline{X}.Y \text{ (2 AND gates, 2 NOT gates, 1 OR gate} = 5 \text{ gates)}$$

However, it can be shown that the following identity is true:

$$X.\overline{Y} + \overline{X}.Y = \overline{\overline{(\overline{X} + \overline{Y})} + \overline{(X + Y)}}$$

which may not look very helpful but, in fact, shows that the original expression can be transformed into one much more suited to implementation by NOR gates. As Figure 22.33 shows, the circuit based on this transformed expression has only five NOR gates.

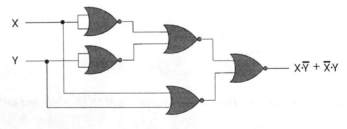

Figure 22.33.

The Exclusive OR gate

This is usually abbreviated to XOR or EOR. The truth table for the XOR gate is shown in Table 22.15.

The exclusive OR gate is so named because, of its output values, the case where both inputs are logic 1 is excluded; in the OR gate these inputs produce an output of 1. In effect, the XOR gate has an output of logic 1 when the inputs are different; when the inputs are the same, the output is logic 0.

Algebraically, the XOR gate is $X.\overline{Y} + \overline{X}.Y$ and the symbol that is frequently used is shown in Figure 22.34.

As an example of its use, suppose that it is required to generate an even parity bit (see Chapter 21) for a four bit word ABCD. The truth table for this problem is shown in Table 22.16.

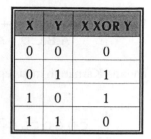

X	Y	X XOR Y
0	0	0
0	1	1
1	0	1
1	1	0

Table 22.15. *Truth table for XOR gate*

Figure 22.34. *Symbol for XOR gate*

A	B	C	D	parity bit	
0	0	0	0	0	
0	0	0	1	1	$\overline{A}.\overline{B}.\overline{C}.D$
0	0	1	0	1	$\overline{A}.\overline{B}.C.\overline{D}$
0	0	1	1	0	
0	1	0	0	1	$\overline{A}.B.\overline{C}.\overline{D}$
0	1	0	1	0	
0	1	1	0	0	
0	1	1	1	1	$\overline{A}.B.C.D$
1	0	0	0	1	$A.\overline{B}.\overline{C}.\overline{D}$
1	0	0	1	0	
1	0	1	0	0	
1	0	1	1	1	$A.\overline{B}.C.D$
1	1	0	0	0	
1	1	0	1	1	$A.B.\overline{C}.D$
1	1	1	0	1	$A.B.C.\overline{D}$
1	1	1	1	0	

Table 22.16.

The expression for even parity is thus

Parity bit = $\overline{A}.\overline{B}.\overline{C}.D + \overline{A}.\overline{B}.C.\overline{D} + \overline{A}.B.\overline{C}.\overline{D} + \overline{A}.B.C.D + A.\overline{B}.\overline{C}.\overline{D} + A.\overline{B}.C.D +$
             $A.B.\overline{C}.D + A.B.C.\overline{D}$

and the Karnaugh map representation is shown in Figure 22.35(a).

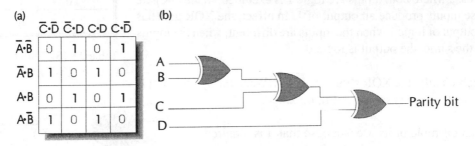

	$\overline{C}{\cdot}\overline{D}$	$\overline{C}{\cdot}D$	$C{\cdot}D$	$C{\cdot}\overline{D}$
$\overline{A}{\cdot}\overline{B}$	0	1	0	1
$\overline{A}{\cdot}B$	1	0	1	0
$A{\cdot}B$	0	1	0	1
$A{\cdot}\overline{B}$	1	0	1	0

Figure 22.35. *Karnaugh map and equivalent circuit*

As the map shows, there is no way of simplifying the expression. However, if the terms are grouped together as follows, a pattern begins to emerge. Parity bit =

$$\overline{A}.\overline{B}.(\overline{C}.D + C.\overline{D}) + \overline{A}.B.(C.D + \overline{C}.\overline{D}) + A.\overline{B}.(\overline{C}.\overline{D} + C.D) + A.B.(\overline{C}.D + C.\overline{D})$$

Rearranging the terms, parity bit =

$$\overline{A}.\overline{B}.(\overline{C}.D + C.\overline{D}) + A.B.(\overline{C}.D + C.\overline{D}) + \overline{A}.B.(C.D + \overline{C}.\overline{D}) + A.\overline{B}.(C.D + \overline{C}.\overline{D})$$

Again, using the Distributive law, the first two and the last two terms can be grouped together to give: parity bit =

$$(\overline{A}.\overline{B} + A.B).(\overline{C}.D + C.\overline{D}) + (\overline{A}.B + A.\overline{B}).(\overline{C}.\overline{D} + C.D)$$

Notice that two of the terms in brackets are immediately recognisable as XOR functions. In addition it can be shown that

$$\overline{X}.\overline{Y} + X.Y = \overline{(\overline{X}.Y + X.\overline{Y})}$$

Using this identity, the expression for parity becomes: parity bit =

$$(\overline{A}.B + A.\overline{B}).(\overline{C}.D + C.\overline{D}) + \overline{(\overline{A}.B + A.\overline{B})}.\overline{(\overline{C}.D + C.\overline{D})}$$

Now each bracketed term looks like an XOR gate and, treating each bracketed term as a unit, the complete expression has the form

$$\overline{X}.Y + X.\overline{Y}, \text{ where } X = (\overline{A}.B + A.\overline{B}) \text{ and } Y = (\overline{C}.D + C.\overline{D})$$

Thus the whole expression, and every term within it, represent XOR gates. The equivalent circuit is shown in Figure 22.35(b).

Logic circuits for binary addition

The logic circuits which perform the function of addition in the Arithmetic and Logic Unit of the Central Processing Unit are called *adders*. A unit which adds two binary digits is called a *half adder* and one which adds together three binary digits is called a *full adder*. In this section each of these units will be examined in detail, and it will be shown how such units are combined to add binary numbers.

Half adders

Earlier in this chapter, the function of a half adder was explained in order to illustrate the relevance of computer logic. Remember that the function of a half adder is to add two binary digits and produce as output the Sum term and Carry term. The operation of the half adder is defined by the truth table in Table 22.17.

X	Y	Sum		Carry	
0	0	0		0	
0	1	1	$\overline{X}.Y$	0	
1	0	1	$X.\overline{Y}$	0	
1	1	0		1	$X.Y$

Table 22.17.

Thus, the expressions for the Sum and Carry terms are given by:

$$Sum = \overline{X}.Y + X.\overline{Y}$$

$$Carry = X.Y$$

The circuit equivalent to these expressions was presented earlier in Figure 22.4.

The symbol in Figure 22.36 will henceforth be used for a half adder.

Figure 22.36.

Full adders

Table 22.18 shows the truth table for the addition of three binary digits.

Considering the Sum term first, the expression derived from the truth table is

$$Sum = \overline{X}.\overline{Y}.Z + \overline{X}.Y.\overline{Z} + X.\overline{Y}.\overline{Z} + X.Y.Z$$

Grouping together the first and third terms, and the middle two terms gives

$$Sum = \overline{Z}.(\overline{X}.Y + X.\overline{Y}) + Z.(\overline{X}.\overline{Y} + X.Y)$$

X	Y	Z	Sum		Carry	
0	0	0	0		0	
0	0	1	1	$\overline{X}.\overline{Y}.Z$	0	
0	1	0	1	$\overline{X}.Y.\overline{Z}$	0	
0	1	1	0		1	$\overline{X}.Y.Z$
1	0	0	1	$X.\overline{Y}.\overline{Z}$	0	
1	0	1	0		1	$X.\overline{Y}.Z$
1	1	0	0		1	$X.Y.\overline{Z}$
1	1	1	1	$X.Y.Z$	1	$X.Y.Z$

Table 22.18. *Truth table for addition of three binary digits*

Using the identity

$$\overline{\overline{X}.Y + X.\overline{Y}} = (\overline{X}.\overline{Y} + X.Y)$$ (the proof for this has been given earlier)

the Sum term can be written

$$Sum = \overline{Z}.(\overline{X}.Y + X.\overline{Y}) + Z.\overline{(\overline{X}.Y + X.\overline{Y})}$$

which is of the form

$$\overline{Z}.S + Z.\overline{S} \text{ where } S = \overline{X}.Y + X.\overline{Y}$$

In other words, S is the sum term from a half adder with inputs X and Y, and Sum is one of the outputs from a half adder with inputs Z and S. The Sum term can now be produced using two half adders, as shown in Figure 22.37.

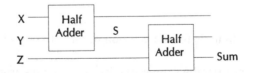

Figure 22.37. *Using two half adders to produce Sum term*

Returning to the Carry term, the expression derived from the truth table is

$$Carry = \overline{X}.Y.Z + X.\overline{Y}.Z + X.Y.\overline{Z} + X.Y.Z$$

Again gathering terms,

$$\text{Carry} = Z.(\overline{X}.Y + X.\overline{Y}) + X.Y.(\overline{Z} + Z)$$

$$= Z.(\overline{X}.Y + X.\overline{Y}) + X.Y \text{ since } \overline{Z} + Z = 1 \text{ and } X.Y.1 = X.Y$$

Substituting S for $\overline{X}.Y + X.\overline{Y}$ as before, the expression becomes

$$\text{Carry} = Z.S + X.Y$$

Both of these terms look like the carry term from a half adder: Z.S is the carry term from a half adder with inputs Z and S (the carry term from the second half adder in the diagram above); X.Y is the carry output from the first half adder in the diagram. The two carry outputs merely need to be ORed together, to give the final circuit in Figure 22.38.

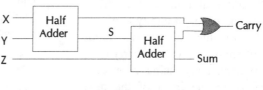

Figure 22.38.

Adding binary numbers

So far, the circuits for addition have only been capable of adding two or three binary digits; more complex schemes are necessary in order to add two binary numbers each comprising several digits. Two approaches will be considered. The first adds numbers bit by bit, one pair of bits after another and is termed *serial addition*; the other accepts as inputs all pairs of bits in the two numbers simultaneously and is called *parallel addition*.

Serial addition

Suppose that the numbers to be added have a four-bit wordlength, and the two numbers A and B have digits a3, a2, a1, a0, and b3, b2, b1, b0 respectively. The circuit for a four-bit serial adder is shown in Figure 22.39.

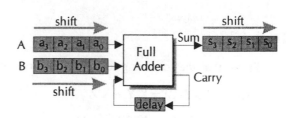

Figure 22.39. *Four-bit serial adder*

In this particular design, a single full adder is presented with pairs of bits from the two numbers in the sequence a0 b0 , a1 b1 , a2 b2 , a3 b3 . As each pair of bits is added, the sum term is transmitted to a shift register to hold the result, and the carry term is delayed so that it is added in to the next addition operation.

Though this method is cheap in terms of hardware requirements, it is not often (if at all) used in modern digital computers because of its slow operation. The degree to which hardware prices have dropped in recent years has resulted in the almost universal adoption of parallel addition.

Parallel addition

In parallel addition, a separate adder is used for the addition of each digit pair. Thus for the addition of two four-digit numbers, one half adder and three full adders would be used. In this type of circuit, all the digits are input simultaneously, with the carry term from each stage being connected directly to the input of the next stage. This is shown in Figure 22.40.

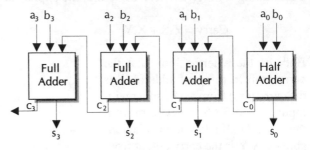

Figure 22.40. *Circuit for parallel addition*

Though faster than serial addition, one fault of the type of parallel adder shown above is the successive carry out to carry in connections which cause relatively long delays; more elaborate schemes are capable of overcoming this problem (at the expense of added circuitry).

The efficiency of the addition circuits is of particular importance in microprocessors where the functions of multiplication and division, as well as subtraction, often use these circuits. Most computers have special purpose circuitry for multiplication and division.

Exercises

Truth tables

1. Prove that the following identities are true using truth tables:

   (i) $X.(Y+Z) = X.Y + X.Z$

   (ii) $X+Y.Z) = (X+Y).(X+Z)$

   (iii) $\overline{(X+Y)} = \overline{X}.\overline{Y}$

   (iv) $\overline{(X.Y)} = \overline{X} + \overline{Y}$

   (v) $X + X.Y = X$

   (vi) $X.(X+Y) = X$

(vii) $\overline{A.B} + A.B = \overline{(A.\overline{B} + \overline{A}.B)}$

(viii) $A.\overline{B}.C + A.\overline{B}.\overline{C} + A.B.C + \overline{A}.\overline{B}.\overline{C} = A.(\overline{B}+C) + \overline{(B+C)}$

Karnaugh maps

2.   Simplify the expressions represented by the following Karnaugh maps:

(i)

	$\overline{Y}.\overline{Z}$	$\overline{Y}.Z$	$Y.Z$	$Y.\overline{Z}$
$\overline{X}$	1	0	1	1
X	1	0	0	0

(ii)

	$\overline{Y}.\overline{Z}$	$\overline{Y}.Z$	$Y.Z$	$Y.\overline{Z}$
$\overline{X}$	1	0	0	1
X	1	1	1	1

(iii)

	$\overline{Y}.\overline{Z}$	$\overline{Y}.Z$	$Y.Z$	$Y.\overline{Z}$
$\overline{X}$	0	1	1	0
X	1	1	1	0

(iv)

	$\overline{Y}.\overline{Z}$	$\overline{Y}.Z$	$Y.Z$	$Y.\overline{Z}$
$\overline{X}$	1	1	0	1
X	1	1	1	0

(v)

	$\overline{Y}.\overline{Z}$	$\overline{Y}.Z$	$Y.Z$	$Y.\overline{Z}$
$\overline{X}$	1	0	1	1
X	1	0	0	0

(vi)

	$\overline{Y}.\overline{Z}$	$\overline{Y}.Z$	$Y.Z$	$Y.\overline{Z}$
$\overline{X}$	1	1	1	1
X	0	0	1	1

(vii)

	$\overline{Y}.\overline{Z}$	$\overline{Y}.Z$	$Y.Z$	$Y.\overline{Z}$
$\overline{W}.\overline{X}$	1	0	1	1
$\overline{W}.X$	0	0	1	1
$W.X$	1	0	0	0
$W.\overline{X}$	1	0	0	0

(viii)

	$\overline{Y}.\overline{Z}$	$\overline{Y}.Z$	$Y.Z$	$Y.\overline{Z}$
$\overline{W}.\overline{X}$	0	0	1	0
$\overline{W}.X$	1	1	1	1
$W.X$	1	0	1	1
$W.\overline{X}$	0	0	1	0

(ix)

	$\bar{Y}.\bar{Z}$	$\bar{Y}.Z$	$Y.Z$	$Y.\bar{Z}$
$\bar{W}.\bar{X}$	1	1	0	1
$\bar{W}.X$	0	1	0	0
$W.X$	0	1	1	0
$W.\bar{X}$	1	1	1	1

(x)

	$\bar{Y}.\bar{Z}$	$\bar{Y}.Z$	$Y.Z$	$Y.\bar{Z}$
$\bar{W}.\bar{X}$	1	0	0	1
$\bar{W}.X$	1	1	1	1
$W.X$	0	1	1	1
$W.\bar{X}$	1	1	0	1

The design of logic circuits

3. Draw logic diagrams using AND/OR/NOT gates for the expressions derived in the questions on Karnaugh maps in the previous section.

4. For each of the following, simplify the expression using a Karnaugh map and draw a circuit of the simplified expression:

   (i) $X.Y.\bar{Z} + X.Y.Z + X.\bar{Y}.Z$

   (ii) $A.B.C + A.\bar{B}.C + A.B.\bar{C} + \bar{A}.\bar{B}.C + \bar{A}.B.C$

   (iii) $A.B.C.D + A.B.\bar{C}.D + A.B.C.\bar{D} + \bar{A}.B.\bar{C}.D + \bar{A}.B.C.\bar{D} + A.\bar{B}.C.\bar{D}$

   (iv) $\overline{W}.X + X.\bar{Y} + X.\bar{Y}.Z + \overline{W}.\bar{Y}.\bar{Z} + W.X.\bar{Y}.Z$

5. Use truth tables to prove the laws of Boolean algebra.

6. Given two binary signals, X and Y, produce a truth table to define the difference of the two digits for every combination. There will be two outputs representing the difference and a 'borrow'. Hence, draw the circuit for a 'half subtractor'.

7. Produce a truth table which defines the 4-bit product when two numbers are multiplied together (the largest number produced will be $3 \times 3 = 9$, which requires 4 bits). Simplify each of the four outputs, using Karnaugh maps and produce a circuit for hardware multiplication of 2-bit numbers.

Chapter 23
Computer Instructions

This chapter deals with activity of the Central Processing Unit (CPU) and the ways in which computer program instructions are stored, interpreted and executed in order that the computer can perform its tasks. The various methods for addressing memory are also examined. In Chapter 21 it is stated that data can take various forms when stored as a *memory word*, namely:

❑   pure binary;

❑   coded binary, for example, binary-coded decimal (BCD);

❑   character codes, for example, ASCII.

All the above are considered to be *data* and can be interpreted as such by the CPU, but in order to perform any tasks, it has to have access to computer *instructions*. During processing, data currently being processed and the instructions needed to process the data are stored in main memory. Thus, a memory word can also form an instruction, in which case, it is referred to as an *instruction word*; one formed from data is known as a *data word*.

The central processing unit (CPU)

The CPU has a number of *registers* which it can use to temporarily store a number of words read from memory. These registers are used to apply meaning to memory words. It should be noted that memory words cannot be determined as being data or instructions simply by examination of the code. The CPU differentiates between data and instructions by locating:

❑   instructions in an *instruction register*;

❑   data in *data registers*.

A computer program stored in main memory comprises a sequence of instructions, each of which is transferred, in turn, into the CPUs instruction register, thus identifying the next operation which the CPU is to perform. The instructions are retrieved from consecutive memory locations, unless the last instruction executed requires the next one to be fetched from a different location. Those dealing with the latter circumstance are called *branch* or *jump* instructions. The various types of instruction are described later. The process of fetching, interpreting and executing instructions is called the *fetch-execute cycle* but may also be referred to as the *instruction cycle* or *automatic sequence control*.

in Chapter 18, the *control unit* has the function of governing all hardware opera-
ng the activities of the CPU itself. To understand the fetch-execute cycle it is
be aware of the names and functions of the various CPU *registers* used.

The program counter (PC)

The PC keeps track of the locations where instructions are stored. At any one time during a
program's execution the PC holds the memory address of the next instruction to be executed.
Its operation is possible because, in all computer systems, the instructions forming a program
are stored in adjacent memory locations, so that the next instruction will normally (except
when a branch instruction is executed) be stored in an address a single increment more than
the address of the last instruction to be fetched. By incrementing the address in the PC each
time an instruction is received, the PC always has the address of the next instruction to be
retrieved.

The program counter is also known by a variety of other names, including the *Sequence Control Register* (SCR) and the *Instruction Address Register* (IAR).

Memory buffer register (MBR)

Whenever the contents of a memory word are to be transferred into or out of main memory,
they pass through the MBR. This applies to both data and instructions.

Memory address register (MAR)

The MAR provides the location address of the specific memory word (both instructions and
data) to be read from or written to memory via the MBR.

Current instruction register (CIR)

As the name suggests, the function of the CIR is to store the current instruction for decoding
and execution.

Accumulators and general-purpose registers

These registers are situated within the arithmetic/logic unit (ALU) and provide a working
area for data fetched from memory. Values about to be added or subtracted can be copied, via
the MBR, into the accumulators. The arithmetic result can be placed in one accumulator and
copied from there into a main memory location. All communications between the CPU and
the memory take place through the MBR, as Figure 23.1 illustrates.

In order to fetch an instruction from memory the CPU places the address of the instruction in
the MAR and then carries out a memory read; the instruction is then copied into the MBR and
from there, into the CIR. Similarly, an instruction which itself requires the reading of a

particular data word causes the address of the data word to be placed into the MAR. The execution of the memory read then results in the copying of the addressed data word into the MBR, from where it can be accessed by the processor. The MBR acts as the point of transfer for both data and instructions passing, in either direction, between the main memory and the CPU.

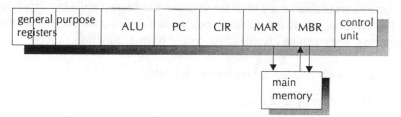

Figure 23.1. *CPU registers used in the fetch-execute cycle*

Fetch-execute cycle

The instruction fetch-execute cycle can be described as follows:

Fetch phase - common to all instructions.

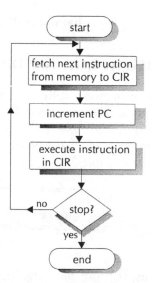

Figure 23.2. *Fetch-execute cycle*

(i)   the contents of the PC are copied into the MAR. The MAR now contains the location address of the next instruction and a memory read is initiated to copy the instruction word from memory into the MBR.

(ii)   the PC is incremented and now contains the address of the next instruction.

(iii)   the instruction word is then copied from the MBR into the CIR.

Execute phase - the action taken is unique to the instruction.

(iv)   the instruction in the CIR is decoded

(v)   the instruction in the CIR is executed.

(vi)   unless the instruction is a STOP instruction, then the cycle is repeated.

The cycle is illustrated in the flowchart in Figure 23.2. The fetch-execute cycle is carried out automatically by the hardware and the programmer cannot control its sequence of operation.

Of course, the programmer does have control over which instructions are stored in memory and the order in which they are executed.

Types of instruction

All the instructions available on a particular machine are known collectively as the *instruction set* of that machine. There are certain types of instruction commonly available in most computer systems. They can be classified according to their function as follow:

❑   arithmetic and logical operations on data;

❑   input and output of data;

❑   changing the sequence of program execution (branch instructions);

❑   transfer of data between memory and the CPU registers;

❑   transfer of data between registers within the CPU.

Instruction format

An instruction usually consists of two main components, the *function* or *operation code* (*opcode*) and the *operand*. The opcode part of the instruction defines the operation to be performed, for example to add or to move data and the operand defines the location address in memory of the data to be operated upon. The storage of a 16-bit instruction word is illustrated in Table 23.1.

bit-15															bit-0
opcode				operands											

Table 23.1. *Components of an instruction*

Thus, the four most significant bits determine the type of instruction and the remaining twelve bits specify the operand or operands to be used.

Three-address instruction

If an expression requiring the use of three memory variables is to be accommodated by one instruction, then the instruction word will need to contain the address of each variable, that is three operands. An addition instruction can be expressed symbolically as,

```
ADD Z,X,Y
```

that is, add the contents of X to the contents of Y and store the result in Z. The instruction word needs to be large enough to store the three addresses and the format is illustrated in Table 23.2. Because of the large number of bits required this format is not often used.

opcode	operand address	operand address	operand address

Table 23.2. *Three-address instruction format*

Two-address instruction

With this format, only two addresses are available in the instruction, so it is implicit that the result is to be stored in one of the operands (X or Y). This means that one of the original numbers is overwritten by the result. If only one instruction is used, then adding the contents of X and Y and placing the result in X is expressed symbolically as,

ADD X,Y

The instruction word format is shown in Table 23.3. In order to place the result in Z (as in the first expression) and to preserve the original contents of X, a preceding instruction could be used to copy the contents of X to Z. Assuming that a MOVE instruction has this effect, then the following two expressions will effect the addition.

opcode	operand address	operand address

Table 23.3. *Two-address instruction format*

MOVE Z,X
ADD   Z,Y

One-address instruction

It should be obvious that this format only allows an opcode to refer to one operand and that two assumptions regarding storage are implicit. Firstly, as with the two-address format, it must be assumed that the re-sult is to be stored in Z. Secondly, if only one operand can be referred to, the addition process must use another storage area for the second operand. Generally, a CPU general-purpose register, called the accumulator, is used. The single-address instruction is used where there is only a single accumulator, so the instruction does not need to refer to the address of the accumulator; it is implicit. The instruction word format is shown in Table 23.4.

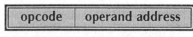

opcode	operand address

Table 23.4. *One-address instruction*

The processes needed to achieve the addition are described below.

(i)   Copy the contents of one operand, X, into the accumulator. This operation uses a LOAD (accumulator) instruction.

(ii) ADD the contents of operand Y, placing the result in the accumulator. At the time of the addition, the contents of operand Y are in the MBR, having been read from memory as part of the instruction. An ADD instruction usually has this effect.

(iii)   Copy the result from the accumulator into address Z using a STORE command.

An assembly language coding for the above process may be as follows:

```
LDA X          {copies the content of X, via the MBR into the}
               {accumulator}
ADD Y          {reads the contents of Y to the MBR, adds it to
               the} {accumulator and  leaves the result there}
STA Z          {copies the result from the accumulator into
               memory} {address Z, via the MBR}
```

One-and-a-half-address instruction

Where there is more than one accumulator, an instruction using the accumulator must indicate which one is to be used. Since the number of accumulators is generally small, the

opcode	ACC	operand address

Table 23.5. *One-and-a-half address instruction*

number of bits needed to refer to a single accumulator is usually less than the number needed for a memory location address. The processes for carrying out the example sum are the same as for the one-address format, except that a specified accumulator is used. Table 23.5 shows the instruction format.

Zero-address instruction

This type of instruction is particularly popular with small machines because of its economy in size. Many microcomputer systems operate with a combination of one-address and zero-address instructions. A zero-address instruction does not specify any operands within it and relies on the use of a memory-based data structure called a *stack*, to provide the operands.

A stack consists of a group of adjacent memory locations, the contents of which are addressed by a *stack pointer*, a register that contains the address of the current top of stack. Values can only be added (*pushed*) to or removed (*popped*) from the top of the stack, which is indicated by the current position of the stack pointer. The value of the stack pointer is incremented or decremented when an item is pushed or popped. A value located below the top item on the stack (as indicated by the stack pointer) cannot be removed until any values above it have been removed.

Consider, for example, an ADD instruction which requires the addition of two operands, X and Y. The operands X and then Y are pushed onto the stack; Y is thus at the top of the stack and is the first one which can be removed. The ADD instruction causes the popping of Y and X from the stack; they are added and the sum is pushed onto the top of the stack.

Although this instruction format is extremely short, additional instructions are needed in order to transfer operands from memory to the stack and from the stack to memory; obviously these instructions need to be longer in order to allow specification of memory addresses.

They are similar to single instruction words, except that operands are copied to and from the stack rather than to and from the accumulator.

Instruction format and memory size

Given a particular word length (the number of bit positions), single-address instructions can directly address (specify the actual memory address) a larger number of memory locations than one-and-a-half or multiple-address formats because all the address bits can be used for one address. Many computers allow a variable length instruction word so that the number of bits available for the address portion of the instruction can be increased, to allow a larger number of memory locations to be directly addressed. If, for example, there are 16 bits for the address, then the highest location which can be *directly* addressed is:

$$2^{16} - 1 = 65,535$$

Therefore, 65,536 locations can be addressed, numbered 0 to 65,535 (computer memory sizes are quoted in nK, K being 1024 and n being a variable) and this example illustrates a 64K memory, that is, 64 × 1024 which equals 65,536. Clearly, this is insufficient for modern computer systems and a number of approaches are used to extend addressable range.

By increasing the number of bits available for the address to, say 20, the number of locations which can be addressed is over a million, although in practice, not all memory words need to be addressed directly. For example, to enable the direct addressing of all locations in a 256K (256 × 1024 = 262,144) memory requires the use of 18 bits (2^{18} = 262,144). There are addressing techniques to reduce the number of bits needed for a memory address and some of these are described later in the chapter. An increase in word size also allows an increase in the number of bits available for the opcode and the possibility of an increase in the size of the instruction set. It has to be said, however, that a recent development in computer architecture, namely that of the RISC (Reduced Instruction Set Computer) processor, is making this latter benefit somewhat less relevant.

Instruction set

The range of instructions available for any particular machine depends on the machines architecture, in terms of word length and the number and types of registers used. For this reason it is only possible to list some typical types of instruction (the names LOAD etc are not actual mnemonic opcodes) some of which were used in the earlier example:

- ❏   *Load* - copies the contents of a specified location into a register.

- ❏   *Add* - adds the contents of a specified memory location to the contents of a register.

- ❏   *Subtract* - subtracts the contents of a specified memory location from the contents of a register.

❑   *Store* - copies the contents of a register into a specified memory location.

❑   *Branch* - switches control to another instruction address other than the next in sequence.

❑   *Register-register* - moves contents from one register to another.

❑   *Shift* - moves bits in a memory location to the left or to the right for arithmetic purposes or for pattern manipulation.

❑   *Input/output* - effects data transfers between peripherals and memory.

❑   *Logical operations* (AND, OR, NOT, NAND and so on) which combine the contents of a register and a specified memory location or register. These operations are described in Chapter 22 on Computer Logic. The first four instruction types in this list have already been explained in the earlier addition example, so the following sections deal with those remaining.

Branch instruction

These instructions cause the program to divert from the sequence which is dictated by that of contiguous memory locations containing program instructions. A branch instruction causes the value of the Program Counter (PC) to be altered, to direct the next instruction to be fetched from a location which is not physically adjacent to the current instruction. A branch may be *conditional* (dependent on some condition) or *unconditional*. In the latter case, the branch is always made, whereas in the former, the branch only occurs if a specified condition occurs. The conditions tested usually include tests on CPU register contents for zero, non-zero, negative and positive number values. The branch or jump may be to a specified address or simply to skip the next instruction (or several instructions). In either case the program counter must be altered accordingly to change its contents to the address specified by the branch instruction. Branching can be used to repeat a sequence of instructions in a *loop*. Usually this is conditional to avoid an infinite program iteration.

Subroutine or subprogram

As explained in the previous paragraph a branch instruction is used to jump or skip to a specified instruction address, so that the program sequence may continue from that address. On the other hand if the branch is to a subroutine, the original sequence can be restored after its execution. This requires a special form of branch instruction. It may be necessary, for example, to carry out a particular sequence of calculations at different points in a program. Instead of coding the instructions at each point where they are required, the coding can be written as a subroutine. Whenever a subroutine is used or *called*, there must be a mechanism for returning control to the original program sequence. One method is to save the current contents of the PC in the first location of the subroutine before the branch to the subroutine is made. Upon completion of the subroutine the contents of the first location can be loaded into the PC and control returned to the calling program. The process of branching to a subroutine and then returning to continue the instruction sequence is illustrated in Figure 23.3.

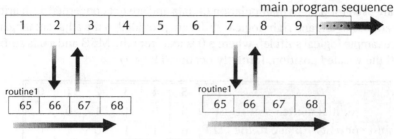

Figure 23.3. *Subroutine operation*

Alternatively, the return address may be placed on a *stack* (a memory facility described earlier in this chapter) and copied back into the PC to allow a resumption of the normal program sequence. The stack is particularly useful where subroutines are nested, which means that a subroutine may be called from within another subroutine. The return addresses are placed onto the stack and removed in reverse order so that the last return address is the first to be removed. The technique is described in detail in the chapter on Data Structures. Subroutines called in this way are referred to as *clos*ed, but where a subroutine is inserted, as and when required, as part of the main program, it is referred to as *open*.

Register-register instruction

As the name suggests, instructions of this type are used to transfer the contents of one register to another. Its format is similar to that of the two-address instruction described in the previous section, and is illustrated in Table 23.6.

opcode	reg 1	reg 2

Table 23.6. *Register-register instruction*

Although operands to address memory are not used, the instruction allows two operands to address the registers involved. The number of registers available will tend to be small, perhaps two or three, so that a single byte may be sufficient to contain the two operands. In an 8-bit machine, such instructions may be two bytes long, one for the opcode and one for the two register addresses.

Data transfers between registers within the CPU are carried out through a communications system which is a subdivision of the computer systems *architecture*.

Shift instruction

A shift operation moves the bits in a register to new positions in the register, either to the left or to the right and may be *logical* or *arithmetic*. A shift instruction format is given in Table 23.7.

opcode	register no	no. of shifts

Table 23.7. *Shift instruction format*

Logical shift

Logical shifts are used for pattern manipulation of data and are not concerned with arithmetic operations. Examples of left and right logical shifts are provided in the adjacent tables. Table 23.8 shows an example logical shift left where a 0 is lost from the MSB and a 0 is shifted into the LSB (to fill the vacated position, formerly occupied by a 1).

bit-	5	4	3	2	1	0
initial contents of register	0	0	1	1	0	1
shift contents 1 place to the LEFT	0	1	1	0	1	0
	0 dropped from MSB			0 moved into LSB		

Table 23.8. *Logical shift **left** of 1 place*

The example of a logical shift right in Table 23.9 starts with the same register contents as Table 23.8. This time the right shift of 1 moves each bit, one position to the right, causing the loss of a 1 from the LSB and the insertion of a 0 to fill the vacated MSB position. Another type of logical shift, referred to as *rotational* or *cyclic*, involves rotation of bits in a register or location.

bit-	5	4	3	2	1	0
initial contents of register	0	0	1	1	0	1
shift contents 1 place to the RIGHT	0	0	0	1	1	0
	0 moved into MSB			1 dropped from LSB		

Table 23.9. *Logical shift **right** of 1 place*

Rotational logical shift

A rotational shift can be either to the right or to the left, as shown in the next two tables. Table 23.10 shows that for a right shift the 1 in the LSB position is moved to the MSB position, as each bit moves one place to the right.

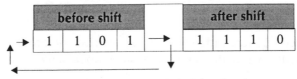

Table 23.10. *Rotational shift **right** of 1 place*

In the left shift example in Table 23.11, the 1 in the MSB position is moved to the LSB position as each bit moves one place to the left.

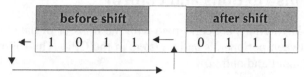

Table 23.11. *Rotational shift **left** of 1 place*

Arithmetic shift

Left and right shift operations are used for multiply and divide operations but arithmetic meaning must be maintained. A left shift of one doubles the number and a right shift of one halves the number. Computer multiplication can be carried out through a sequence of additions and shifts, and division by a sequence of subtractions and shifts. Some examples of arithmetic shifts using two's complement notation are provided in the adjacent tables. Table 23.12 illustrates an arithmetic shift left of 1 where zeros are inserted into the LSB position. Note that in the last example in Table 23.12, the sign has been changed from positive to negative by the shift left operation. In these circumstances an overflow signal would be set.

before shift						after shift				
sign						sign				
0	0	1	1	+3		0	1	1	0	+6
1	1	0	0	−4		1	0	0	0	−8
1	1	1	0	−2		1	1	0	0	−4
0	1	1	0	+6		1	1	0	0	−4
sign changed to negative, indicating overflow										

Table 23.12. *Arithmetic shift left examples*

Table 23.13 shows two shift right examples. In the second example, a 1 is shifted into the sign bit position to maintain the integrity of the sign.

before shift						after shift				
sign						sign				
0	1	1	0	+6		0	0	1	1	+3
1	1	0	0	−4		1	1	1	0	−2

Table 23.13. *Arithmetic shift right examples*

Input/output instructions and control

Input/output (I/O) instructions are concerned with the transfer of data between peripherals and memory or between peripherals and registers in the CPU. The following section deals with the control of input and output.

Figure 23.4 illustrates the *architecture* of the communication system which allows data transfers between the various elements of a computer system.

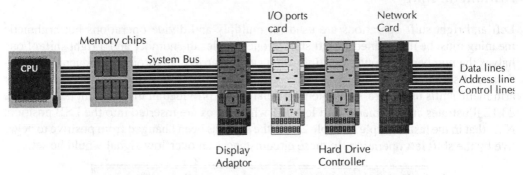

Figure 23.4. *Architecture of a typical microcomputer's communication system*

A number of components can be identified:

❏ *Bus* or *highway*. A bus consists of a number of wires, one for each bit making up the unit of data transfer. A common I/O bus connects all I/O peripherals to the processor, so only one peripheral can use the bus at a time. This is not normally a restriction because the processor can only handle one instruction at a time, but most computers have an I/O bus which is independent of that used for processor/main memory transfers. Those machines using a common bus for I/O and processor/memory data movements are referred to as single bus systems;

❏ *Interface*. This is a hardware device containing electronic components, which connects an I/O peripheral to the computer. The chapter on Data Representation describes the use of internal and external codes for internal computer and external peripheral operations respectively; one of the functions of an interface is to carry out the conversion process between the two codes, according to whether data is being transferred to or from the peripheral;

❏ *Device controller*. This device is fundamentally the same as the interface, except that it is associated with the control of data transfers to and from storage devices, such as magnetic disk and tape drives.

Methods of I/O control

The transfer of data to and from a peripheral device can take place either:

❑   under the control of the host machine's processor; this is *programmed input/output* or *PIO*;

❑   or, under the autonomous control of the device; most commonly, this is *direct memory access* or *DMA*.

Programmed input/output (PIO)

Some microcomputers still use PIO for the control of data transfers. This means, for example, that the computer's processor controls each stage of data transfer between the system's hard disk drive and itself. PIO can be effected in one of two ways: *software polling*; *hardware interrupts*.

Software polling

The operating system software regularly *polls* (checks) each device to see if it requires attention. To achieve I/O transfers by this method, instructions are needed:

❑   for *input* - to transfer data from peripheral to processor;

❑   for *output* - to transfer data from processor to peripheral;

❑   to *set* individual control flags in the I/O interface unit;

❑   to *test* individual flags in the I/O interface unit.

A peripheral device is attached to an interface unit by a cable. The interface unit (usually inside the computer) is connected to one of a number of I/O slots, each of which has a fixed address, by which a peripheral can be identified for input or output. There are 3 basic elements in an interface unit which is polled by software:

❑   a control bit or *busy* flag - used to signal a device to start input or output. This cannot be set by the device as it is under control of the processor;

❑   a flag bit or *done* flag - this is set by the device when the data transfer is complete and can be tested or cleared by program instructions;

❑   a *buffer register* for the storage of data transferred into (read by) or to be transferred from (written by) the device.

When a 'start read' instruction is given, one character is transferred between the interface buffer register and the device. A single character is transferred in the opposite direction if a 'start write' instruction is given. A processor instruction commands the device to operate by setting the busy flag and then repeatedly tests the done flag to discover when the transfer is complete. The major difficulty with software polling is that the repeated testing of the done flag is carried out at the same time as it continues with some other computation. This means that the program instructions currently being executed (probably the program that issued the I/O instruction) must be interleaved with the regular issue of instructions to test for completion of the transfer. The last operating system to use software polling was CP/M (Control Program/Microcomputer) which was used on some early microcomputer systems, but is now obsolete. An example instruction sequence for software polling may be as follows:

For *input* from a specific device:

- instruction to interface to set the busy flag for 'start transmit';

- send instruction to test done flag. If the flag indicates that the transfer is complete, skip next instruction;

- branch to previous instruction;

- issue instruction to transfer character from buffer register into processor accumulator;

- issue store instruction to transfer character from accumulator to main memory.

For *output* to a specific device:

- issue instruction to transfer character from processor accumulator into buffer register of interface device;

- issue instruction to set busy flag to start transfer;

- issue instruction to test done flag and if set, skip the next instruction;

- branch to previous instruction.

The repetitive flag-test loop is necessary to ensure that a character transfer is completed before the next one is transmitted. A more efficient method of PIO control is to use hardware interrupts.

I/O using hardware interrupts

An I/O interrupt is a signal from an I/O device to the processor to indicate that:

- data is waiting to be read;

- an I/O error has occurred;

- a previous I/O transfer is complete.

To enable I/O devices to initiate requests for service from the processor, an I/O bus includes interrupt request (IRQ) lines, typically 15. All the IRQ lines go to every expansion slot in the I/O bus, so when a device adapter card (for example, a disk drive controller) is plugged into a slot, the specific IRQ line it is to use can then be set, by configuring the card, either through utility software or by physical switches on the card. The device then uses that IRQ line to signal the processor that it requires service. A processor has only one interrupt pin, which is set when an I/O interrupt occurs, to indicate the presence of an interrupt, but not its source. An interrupt handler routine (part of the operating system software) is executed when an interrupt is detected, to establish its source. On a typical microcomputer, interrupts are used by the keyboard, mouse, disk and the COM ports.

Establishing the source of an interrupt

The source of the interrupt is determined by checking each IRQ line to see if it has been set. If more than one device has set its IRQ line, the handler routine will select the one with the highest priority. Once the source has been identified, the interrupt handler calls the relevant *interrupt service routine*. Following completion of the service, control of the processor must be returned to the original process. The checking of the processor's single I/O interrupt register is carried out at the start of each instruction, as part of the fetch-execute cycle.

Executing the interrupt

Before entry to the relevant interrupt service routine, the current state of the machine must be saved. This includes storing the state of the current process and the contents of the Program Counter (PC) in a separate location; the PC value is then replaced by the starting address of the interrupt service routine and the routine is executed. Once the interrupt has been serviced, control of the processor must be returned to the appropriate point in the original program by copying its stored continuation address back into the PC. An interrupt-on/off flag in the processor must be set to off prior to acceptance of an interrupt and then cleared to on as soon as control has been returned to the original program, in order to prevent an interrupt from another device being accepted until the original program has resumed control.

Interrupt priority

Interrupts may emanate from a variety of sources (I/O and others) and for a number of different reasons, such as error conditions or the completion of an input/output process; the operating system can be used to allocate different priority ratings to particular events and devices.

Direct memory access (DMA)

Not all data transfers between peripheral devices and the processor are carried out under continual program control (programmed input/output or PIO). Other schemes such as DMA allow data transfer to or from high speed storage devices such as tape or disk to be effected without continual processor control. Data is transferred in blocks, as opposed to character by character. DMA is possible because of the ability of peripheral devices to operate autonomously, that is, after the initial input or output instruction has been given by the processor, the peripheral is able to complete the data transfer independently. To allow the memory to be accessed directly by a peripheral, instead of via the processor, hardware known as a DMA controller is needed. For transfers from main memory to peripheral, the processor supplies the DMA controller with the start address in memory of the data block to be transferred and its length. A transfer from, for example, a disk pack to memory would require the processor to tell the DMA controller the relevant disk address and into which memory locations the data is to be copied. The DMA controller 'steals' memory cycles from the processor while the data transfer is taking place. Meanwhile, the processor can continue execution of its current program, although its operation is slowed slightly by the cycle stealing. Under these circumstances, DMA is not as quick as PIO, but is an essential component to any computer system working in multi-programming mode. Recently, the use of 'bus mastering' processors has removed the need for cycle stealing, thereby allowing the main processor to continue work at its normal rate. For this reason, DMA is now widely used.

Memory addressing methods

The physical memory addresses ultimately used by the hardware are the *absolute* addresses. As explained earlier, addressing memory locations directly restricts the size of usable memory and for this reason a comput-

| opcode | addressing mode | address |

Table 23.14. *Instruction with addressing mode*

ers instruction set will normally include facilities for addressing locations beyond those directly addressable with a given address length. Thus, absolute addresses may be referenced in a variety of ways and the addressing mode used is indicated in the operand of an instruction word. The format of an instruction word may be as shown in Table 23.14. The following addressing modes are common to most machines: *immediate*; *indirect*; *relative*; *indexed*.

Immediate addressing

With this method, the operand to be accessed by the instruction is stored in the instruction word or in the word immediately following it in memory. In the former case, the operand would be fetched with the instruction and no separate memory read would then be necessary. In the latter case, an ADD instruction which employed this method of addressing would indicate that the operand is to be found immediately after the opcode in memory. In a byte organized machine, the first byte would contain the opcode, the execution of which would involve the fetching of the next byte in memory which contained the required operand. Computers based on the Intel 8080 or Motorola 6800 processor series use this latter method for immediate addressing. The Intel 8080 provides the opcode ADI (add immediate) as part of its instruction set. Immediate addressing is useful when small constants or literals are required in a program, for example, a set value of 3 to be subtracted from the contents of a register at some stage in the program. It is inappropriate to use this method if there is any need for the value to be changed as this would require changing the program coding.

Direct addressing

As the name suggests, this addressing mode specifies the actual or effective memory address containing the required operand, in the address field of the instruction word. The addressed memory location specified must be accessed to obtain the operand.

Indirect addressing

With this method, the location address in the instruction word does not contain the operand. Instead, it contains the address of another location which itself contains the address of the data item. Thus, an indirect address is, in effect, a pointer to the address containing the operand. For example, IAD 156 (indirect add) indicates that the address 156 contains the address of the required operand.

If specific indirect addressing instructions are not provided, an instruction word may contain a flag bit to indicate whether or not an operand is an indirect or direct address; the flag bit may be set to 1 if the address is indirect and to 0 if it is direct. In this way, an LDA (load accumulator) instruction is able to refer to a direct or indirect address by the appropriate setting of the flag bit. Figure 23.5 illustrates the principle of indirect addressing.

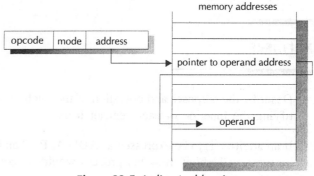

Figure 23.5. *Indirect addressing*

Indirect addressing is generally slower in execution than direct addressing as an extra *memory cycle* is needed each time the actual address is deferred. Indirect addressing is also known as *deferred* addressing and if the address is deferred more than once it is known as a *multi-level* address.

Relative addressing

With relative addressing, the instruction word contains an *offset* address which indicates the location of the operand relative to the position of the instruction in memory (sometimes known as *self-relative* addressing). Thus, if an instruction is stored in address N and the offset is 5, then the operand is in address N + 5. It is a useful technique for branching a program, in which case the offset address will indicate the relative address of the next instruction to be fetched, rather than a data item. The program counter (PC) is used to calculate the effective address in that it contains the address of the current instruction. By adding the offset to the PC, the address is determined. The instruction set usually contains instructions which allow such program jumps to be made. Absolute addresses may also be determined as being relative to a *base* address. By alteration of this base address, programs can be *relocated* rather than be tied to particular absolute addresses each time they are loaded. Multi-programming or multi-tasking techniques demand that programs are relocatable.

Indexed addressing

With this method, the effective address is calculated by the addition of an index value to the address given in the instruction. The index value is usually stored in either a general-purpose CPU register or a special *index* register. The method can be employed by a programmer when an ordered block of data is to be accessed and each data item is to be processed in the same way. If the value of the index is N and the address in the instruction is X, then the effective address for an operand is N + X. The register is set to an initial value and incremented as the instructions step through the memory locations. A branch instruction is used to create a program loop to repeat the same set of instructions needed for each item of data in the block.

Exercises

1. Describe the purposes and operation of the fetch-execute cycle, naming and identifying the function of each register it uses.

2. If an addition is to be expressed as ADD A, B, C and the values in A and B are to be preserved, show how the process would be completed using a *two-address instruction*.

3. An 8-bit word contains the binary pattern 10110010. How does the pattern (and in the case of (iii), its value) alter after:

    (i)   a logical left shift of 1 bit;

    (ii)   a rotational right shift of 2 bits;

    (iii)   a left shift of 2 bits, assuming it's a two's complement integer.

4. In respect of input-output control differentiate between a *software polling* and *hardware interrupt* system.

5. Referring to the opcode and the operand, distinguish between *immediate*, *direct* and *indirect* addressing.

6. If a *base address* is defined as B and an operand contains an *offset* of 15, what type of addressing is it?

7. Outline the processes needed to execute a subroutine instruction and return control to the instruction following the branch to the subroutine.

Chapter 24

Computer Networks and Distributed Systems

Introduction

This chapter deals with the network and data communications technologies and their facility for distributing the data processing function. A number of factors have encouraged organisations to adopt decentralised computer processing systems, in particular:

    (i)   the cost of computers has fallen dramatically, making it cost-effective to process and analyse data at a local level;

    (ii)   the expansion of local and wide area network technologies has made national and global communication between computer systems straightforward.

Networking computer systems has the effect of decentralising computer processing and improving communications within and between organisations and between organisations and individuals. Some computer networks use dedicated intelligent terminals or microcomputer systems to permit some independent processing power at sites remote from the *host* computer, to which they are connected. Other networks distribute even more processing power by linking microcomputer, minicomputer, mainframe and supercomputer systems. They are sometimes referred to as *distributed processing* systems.

Networks can be configured to suit almost any application, from the provision of a worldwide airline reservation system to home banking. *Nodes* (connection points in the network) may only be a few feet apart and limited to a single building, or they may be several thousand miles apart.

Local and wide area networks

Computer networks can be classified according to their geographical spread. A network confined to, say, one building, with microcomputer workstations distributed in different rooms, is known as a *local area network* (LAN). One particular type, known as a ring network can extend over a diameter of around five miles.

A computer network distributed nationally or even internationally makes use of telephone and sometimes, satellite links, and is referred to as a *wide area network* (WAN). In large organisations with several branches, it is common practice to maintain a LAN at each branch for local processing requirements and to link each LAN into a WAN covering the whole organisation. In this way, branches of an organisation can have control over their own processing and yet have access to the organisation's main database at headquarters. In addition, inter-branch communication is possible.

Network architecture

The architecture of any network includes definition of: its *components*, both hardware and software, identified by *name* and *function*; the ways the components are connected and communicate with one another. The topic of wide area networks (WANs) is dealt with later in this chapter and the following primarily relates to local area networks (LANs). However, the section on Network Topologies does relate, in part, to WANs.

LAN architecture

It is important that the components are combined in such a way that the LAN can be: *extended*. The LAN must be capable of providing for new users and new equipment, as the need arises; *upgraded* to take advantage of new technologies which can improve network performance; *connected* to other LANs, both local and remote and Wide Area Networks.

LAN architecture comprises hardware and software, both for the control of the LAN communications and as an interface between the LAN and its users. In order that all components are compatible and operate as a coherent system, it is important that they conform to agreed standards (see later). This means that LAN producers have to take account of generally agreed standards for equipment linking and data communications, so that as new products come onto the market, the user is not left with a system which cannot take advantage of them. Unfortunately, a number of different standards exist and this means that the decision on which type of LAN to purchase is not always straightforward.

Hardware components

Figure 24.1 shows a simple *client-server* LAN and identifies the main hardware components: *workstation*; *file server*; *printer server*; network *cabling*. The way in which they are connected defines its general *topology* or physical shape.

LAN Workstation

A *workstation* gives a user access to a LAN and its facilities. A workstation comprises a *microcomputer* with a *network card*, which fits into an *expansion slot* inside its system casing. The network card enables workstations to communicate across the network, and with the *file server* (see later). The network card converts computer-generated data into a form suitable for transmission over the LAN and as such is an *interface*. The card is operated with a network card *driver* (software).

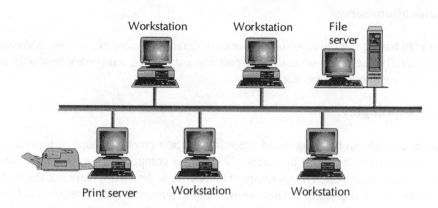

Figure 24.1. *Main components of a local area network*

Servers

The general function of servers is to allocate shared resources to other nodes on the network. There are a number of different types of server, which can be categorised according to the resources they control.

File server

The file server is usually a specially configured microcomputer, with a network card, more memory and disk storage, as well as a more powerful processor than is needed for a workstation. It has to control access to shared storage, directories and files. In addition, it controls the exchange of files between network users. Most network software provides *multiple device* support. This means that file servers can support several disks, allowing file storage capacity on the LAN to be increased beyond that of the file server's integral hard disk. A LAN can also consist of several file servers; indeed except for the smallest of networks, this is normally the case.

Print server

A print server (there may be several) accepts and queues jobs from workstations; the user may be informed when printing is complete. The print server may also provide certain print management functions, for example, to attach priorities to different print jobs so that certain jobs are printed before others, no matter what their positions in the queue. A print server will be configured to:

❏   support the use of particular printers;

❏   service particular printer *queues*; users with the right to use a particular print queue can then place their jobs in that queue.

Communications server

If a LAN is to have access to external networks or databases, a communications server is required. Generally, the communications server can establish a temporary link with remote computers or users on other networks.

Network topologies

Computer networks can be categorised according to their physical shape or topology. Each terminal in a network is known as a *node*. If a central computer controls the network it is known as the *host* computer. The topology of a network is the *arrangement* of the nodes and the ways they are interconnected. The communication system within a network is known as the *subnet*. Data can be transmitted around the subnet either on a *point-to-point* basis or through a *broadcast* channel. If point-to-point transmission is used, the data passes through each device in the network. Thus, if two devices wish to communicate, they must do it indirectly, via any intervening devices. Each device must have the facility to store the entire message and forward it when the output channel is free. If a broadcast channel is used, a common communication channel is shared by all devices in the network. This means that any message sent by a device is received by all devices. The message contains the address of the device intended to receive it, so that the other devices can ignore it. There are a number of recognised network topologies and some of the most common are described below.

Star network

A star topology means that each node is connected, by separate connections to a computer at the centre, known as the *hub*. Figure 24.2 shows a LAN in a star topology.

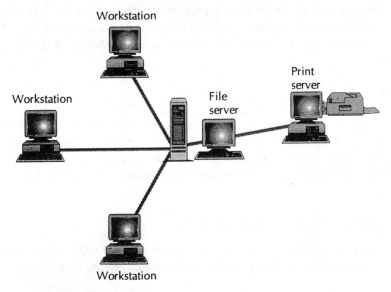

Figure 24.2. *Star topology*

The star is also a popular topology for a WAN. In this structure, all messages pass through the host (probably a mainframe or minicomputer) computer, which interconnects the different devices on the network. So, in this topology the host computer at the hub has a *message switching* function. Messages are transmitted point-to-point. The topology is particularly useful for intercommunications between pairs of users on the network (via the host). The network may consist of numerous computer systems (the nodes), connected to a larger host computer which switches data and programs between them.

The star computer network is by far the most popular for WANs, because most large organisations start with a central computer at the head office, from which branch computer facilities are provided through the telephone network. The main aim is to provide computer communication between the branches and head office. Most other network topologies aim to provide communication between all devices on a network.

The *advantages* of a star network topology are as follow:

- It is suitable for WANs where organisations rely on a central computer for the bulk of processing tasks, perhaps limiting the nodes to their local processing needs and the validation of data, prior to transmission to the central computer;

- Centralised control of message switching allows a high degree of security control;

- Each spoke in the star is independent of the rest and a fault in a link or device in one spoke, can be identified by the computer at the hub;

- The data transmission speeds used can vary from one *spoke* (a link from the hub to a node) to another. This is important if some spokes transmit using high speed devices, such as disk, whilst others transmit from low speed keyboard devices. The method of transmission may also vary. For example, one node may only require access to the network at the end of each day, in which case a *dial-up* connection may be sufficient. A dial-up connection uses the public telephone network and the user only pays for the time taken for transmission. Alternatively, other nodes may require the link for most of the working day, in which case a permanent *leased line* is appropriate. Leased lines provide a more reliable transmission medium and also allow higher speeds of data transmission.

The main *disadvantages* inherent in star networks are as follow:

- The network is vulnerable to hub failures which affect all users. As a distributed processing system, some processing is still possible at the nodes but inter-node communication is lost when the host computer fails;

- For a WAN, the control of communications in the network requires expensive technology at the hub, probably a mini or mainframe computer. Complex operating and communications software is needed to control the network.

Ring network

The ring topology is specifically designed for use with a LAN and is not suitable for a WAN. A ring network connects all the nodes in a ring, as illustrated in Figure 24.3. The *Cambridge Ring*, developed at Cambridge University, has no host computer and none of the nodes need have overall control of access to the network. In practice, a monitoring station is used for the control of data transmission in the network. Messages in a ring network flow in one direction, from node to node.

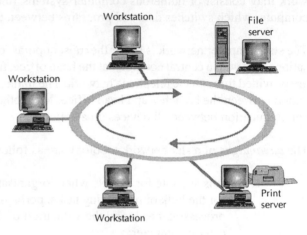

Figure 24.3. *Ring topology*

The ring consists of a series of repeaters, which are joined by the physical transmission medium (twisted pair, coaxial, or fibre-optic cable). The choice of medium depends on the distances to be covered and the desired transmission rates. Fibre-optic cable allows the greatest distances to be covered and the highest transmission rates. Repeaters are used to regenerate messages as they pass around the network. The use of repeaters allows a ring network to cover larger distances than is possible for other topologies. In fact, recent developments using fibre optic cable allow a ring with a range of about 100 kilometres, which makes it a *metropolitan area network* (MAN). The user devices are connected to the repeaters. A message from one node, addressed to another, is passed continually around the ring until the receiving node flags that it is ready to accept it. Acceptance of a message is determined by its *destination address*, which is examined by each node it passes. If the destination address matches the node's own address, the node takes the message; otherwise, the node repeater regenerates the signal to be passed to the next node in the ring. Data is transmitted in mini-packets of about 40 bits and contains the address of the sending node, the address of the destination node and some control bits. A variation on the Cambridge ring is the IBM ring, which uses a different protocol to allow better control of message flow on the network; the two protocols, *empty slot* and *token passing* are described in the section on Network Access Protocols. The ring network presents particular advantages:

❑   There is no dependence on a central host computer as data transmission around the network is supported by all the devices in the ring. Each node device has sufficient intelligence to control the transmission of data from and to its own node;

❑   Very high transmission rates are possible; 10 megabits/sec is typical;

❑   Routing between devices is relatively simple because messages normally travel in one direction only around the ring;

❑   The transmission facility is shared equally amongst the users.

The main disadvantages are as follow:

❑   The system depends on the reliability of the whole ring and the repeaters, although it can be designed to bypass any failed node;

❑   It may be difficult to extend the length of the ring because the physical installation of any new cable must ensure that the ring topology is preserved.

Star/ring network - IBM token ring

The *IBM Token Ring* Network is a star-based topology, with a hub or *multiple access unit* (MAU) to which all the workstations are connected. The movement of data is, however in a *logical ring*. All signals between workstations are through the MAU. The star/ring structure has a major advantage over the basic ring. If one workstation breaks down, or the connection with the MAU is broken, other workstations are not affected (except that they cannot communicate with the damaged workstation). Failure of the MAU will prevent operation of the network. The Cambridge ring structure, described earlier, is prone to complete failure if one workstation fails (the continuous ring is broken).

Bus network

The topology is illustrated in the Figure 24.4.

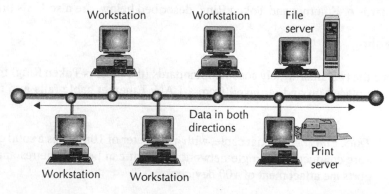

Figure 24.4. *Bus topology*

With a bus topology, the workstations are connected to a main cable (known as the *bus* or trunk), along which data travels. The ends of a bus are not connected, so that data has to travel in both directions to reach the various nodes on the network. The bus topology makes the addition of new devices straightforward, either by attachment to the existing cable or to cable which can be added at either end. The main bus standard is known as *Ethernet*. The term *station* tends to be used rather than node for this type of network. The communications subnet uses a *broadcast* channel, so all attached stations can hear every transmission. As is the case in the ring network, there is no host computer and all stations have equal priority in using the network to transmit. The maximum length of a single bus *segment* is 500 metres and 100 stations can be attached to it. Segments can be specially linked to form larger configurations, up to a maximum of about 12 kilometres. Transmission speeds of 100 megabits/second are obtainable. The bus network provides certain benefits:

❑   If a node malfunctions, it simply stops communicating; it doesn't prevent the rest of the network from working;

❑   The attachment of devices is straightforward and the cable can be extended, if necessary; additional *segments* can be linked to extend the network.

The main drawback is that:

❑   If a part of the Ethernet cabling develops a fault, the whole network (assuming it consists of a single segment) fails.

Network cabling - the transmission medium

In order to share resources on a network, servers, workstations and other devices must be connected; although wireless radio media are possible, most LANs use physical cabling, which acts as the *transmission medium*. The physical layout of the cabling should conform to one of the basic *topologies*: star, ring or bus. The type of cable used depends on the chosen topology and the rules governing the transmission of data through the cable (the *protocol*). The cabling standards of Ethernet and Token Ring, described below, are also LAN protocols.

Ethernet cabling

Ethernet is one the two most widely accepted standards (the other is Token Ring) for specifying how data is placed on and retrieved from a LAN. Ethernet cable falls into three main categories:

❑   *Thick Ethernet* coaxial cable, with a diameter of 10mm has a solid copper core conductor. A single network segment can be 500 metres and supports the attachment of 100 devices.

❑   *Thin Ethernet*, which is 10 millimetres in diameter, has a core of stranded cable. The maximum length of cable which can be used in a single network segment is around 180 metres and the maximum number of workstations is around 30.

- ❑ *10BaseT* Standard Ethernet. The T stands for *twisted pair*. This cable is much cheaper than the thick Ethernet cabling, but provides the same transmission rate of 10 Mb/s; being the same as most telephone cabling, it is easier to install.

Token ring cabling

Used in *IBM token ring* networks use twisted pair cabling, either two pairs or four, depending on data transmission requirements. A single IBM Token Ring network will support up to 260 network devices at rates of 4 Mb/s or 16 Mb/s. Up to eight rings can be connected using *bridges*.

Fibre-optic cabling

Cable of this type is available for use with any of the network types, but provides greater *bandwidth* and permits transmission over greater distances, without the use of *repeaters*.

Cable bandwidth

There are two different methods of utilising a LAN cable for the transmission of data; *base-band* and *broadband*. In a baseband network, a transmitting device uses the whole bandwidth (frequency range), so only one signal can be carried at any one time. This means that, for a brief moment, a transmitting device has exclusive use of the transmission medium. In general, broadband networks are suitable for networks which only transmit data signals.

Broadband networks provide a number of channels and thus allow simultaneous use by different devices on the network. Generally, one channel is dedicated to the user workstations, leaving others free for transmitting video pictures for the security system, voice communication, television pictures and so on.

Network access protocols

Empty slot technique

This system is appropriate for networks in the shape of rings or loops, where messages are passed point-to-point in one direction. One or more empty *slots* or *packets* circulate continuously around the ring. When a device has information to transmit, it loads it into the slot, which carries it to its destination. At the time of loading, the destination address is placed in the slot and a full-empty flag is set to full. As the slot is passed from one repeater to another, no attempt will be made to load the slot as long as the flag is set to full. When the slot reaches the destination device, the devices repeater reads the information without clearing the slot. Before passing it on, the repeater sets a received message flag in the slot. When the slot again reaches the sending device, the flag is set to empty. The destination device can check that the message was received by checking the received flag. If the message was not successfully received, perhaps because the destination device was not listening, the sender device can check the acknowledgement flag and re-transmit in the next slot.

Token passing technique

This technique is also used for ring networks. An imaginary *token* is passed continuously around the ring. The token is recognised as such by the devices, as a unique character sequence. If a device is waiting to transmit, it catches the token and with it, the authority to send data. As long as one device has the token, no other device can send data. A receiving device acknowledges the receipt of a message by inverting a 1-bit field. Token Ring (IEEE 802.5 Standard) employs this access method.

Carrier sense multiple access (CSMA)

This method of access control is used on broadcast systems such as the bus network. Each device is theoretically free to transmit data to any other device at any time. Before attempting to transmit, a device's network card polls the network path to ensure that the destination device is free to receive data and that the communications channel is free. A device wishing to transmit must wait until both conditions exist. Generally such delay will be no more than a few millionths of a second.

CSMA-CD (Collision Detection). Because of the possibility of collision through simultaneous transmission, a collision detection mechanism is used. When collision does occur, the devices involved cease transmission and try again some time later. In order to avoid the same collision, each device involved is made to wait a different time. If a number of retries prove unsuccessful, an error will be reported to the user. Ethernet networks use a form of CSMA/CD.

CSMA-CA (Collision Avoidance). This strategy attempts to improve on that of CSMA-CD, which allows a device to place a packet onto the network path as soon as its network card detects it as being free. In the time between the test (measured in fractions of a microsecond) and the placing of the packet onto the path, another device's network card may have detected the path as free and be about to place another packet onto it. CSMA-CA seeks to remedy this problem by requiring a device's network card to test the path *twice*, once to see if the path is free and a second time, after alerting the device that it may use the network, but before the packet is placed onto the path.

Client-server network

A *client-server* LAN aims to exploit the full processing power of each computer in the network, including the *file server* and the user workstations or *clients*. This is effected by dividing the processing tasks between a client and a server. The client, a microcomputer in its own right (as opposed to the *dumb* terminal found in older mainframe systems) provides the user with a completely separate facility for running applications. The file server which could be a microcomputer, minicomputer, or mainframe, enhances the client component by providing additional services. These services are traditionally offered by minicomputer and mainframe systems operating a *time-sharing* operating system; they include shared file management, data sharing between users, network administration and security. The major benefit of a client-server network is that the power of the client and server machines is used jointly to carry out the processing of an application. Interactive activities, for example, construction of a spreadsheet or the word processing of a report, are carried out by the client machine; having logged onto the network, the user can load the required applications software from the file server.

Matters of backup and file sharing security, relating to the application, can be handled by the server. Printing tasks can also be queued and handled as a shared printer becomes available. This task is handled by one or more *print servers*, which can be dedicated devices, or micro-computers assigned to the task. Except for very small LANs, most operate on the client-server principle.

Peer-to-peer network

With a peer-to-peer configuration, it is not necessary to have a file server; instead all the workstations on the network contribute to the control of the network. Thus, any workstation can supply or use resources of others, as required. Unfortunately, this has the effect of slow-ing performance; in addition it means that files are not held centrally and this complicates file management. *Novell Personal Netware* and *LANtastic 6.0* are popular examples of peer-to-peer networking products. The peer-to-peer approach is highly suitable for very small net-works, but both the products mentioned allow the system to be developed to introduce some file server control. Facilities are also included to allow users to share resources in groups; the name of another peer-to-peer networking product illustrates this feature: *Windows for Work-groups*; up to 10 users can be networked.

Data communications

The word *telecommunications* can be applied to any system capable of transmitting text, sounds, graphical images or indeed, data of any kind, in electronic form. The signals may travel along wires or they may be radio signals, which require no wires, but can travel through the atmosphere and space. Currently, not all aspects of telecommunications system are digital, so sometimes, data may be transmitted in *analogue* form. Computer data is repre-sented in *digital* form, so where the telecommunications systems support it, data is moved between remote computer systems as digitised signals. The topic of analogue and digital sig-nals is dealt with later. The combination of computer and telecommunications technologies has profoundly affected the way computer systems are used. To a computer, text, sounds and graphical images all constitute data, which it represents digitally, using the *binary* coding system. Although not all transmissions of digital data involve general-purpose computers, they are often generated and controlled by digital computer technology. Data generated by a computer is already in digital form, but other data (the term is used in its broadest sense), such as sounds of human speech, or a photograph, need to be digitally encoded before trans-mission over a digital network. The term *data communications* can be applied to systems that combine the use of telecommunications and computer technologies.

Standards authorities

The data communications industry has always had to deal with problems of *incompatible* standards. As explained later, standards have to do with all aspects of a communications system, including, for example, the *hardware devices*, the *encoding* of data and the forms of *signals* used. At first, the only computer systems available for use in data communications systems were mainframes and later, minicomputers. These computer systems were produced by a small number of very large manufacturers, the most important being IBM; they also produced the communications devices that worked with their computers. In competition with one another, each manufacturer set the standards for use with its equipment. These *closed* systems prevented a customer from using equipment, produced by different manufacturers, in the same data communications system.

The huge expansion in the uses of data communications, both nationally and internationally has been made possible through the adoption of some common standards. Common standards lead to *open* systems, which allow users to use components from more than one manufacturer. A number of bodies are concerned with the establishment of international standards and these are listed below. Frequently, a standard arises initially from the work of a particular manufacturer, and then, often because of the importance of the manufacturer, it is included in the recommendations of the standards authorities.

CCITT. This is an acronym for Comité Consultatif Internationale de Télégraphie et Téléphonie an organisation that has its headquarters in Geneva, Switzerland. It is part of the United Nations International Telecommunications Union (ITU). The CCITT makes recommendations on most aspects of data communications, for example, modems (see Data Circuit Termination Equipment), networks and facsimile transmission or FAX and publishes them every four years. These recommendations usually obtain world-wide acceptance. CCITT's 'V' series of standards cover equipment used on telephone lines and its X series relate to digital packet transmission standards.

ANSI is the acronym for American National Standards Institute. ANSI has long maintained a strong influence on standards in the computer and data communications industries. It is formed from industrial and business groups and is a member of the International Standards organisation (ISO). Examples of its influence can be found in the fields of computer hardware and programming languages. For example, by conforming to ANSI standards, the FORTRAN, COBOL and C languages enable the production of computer software, which is largely *portable*. In other words, because each language is more or less universal, a program written in, for example, COBOL can be readily translated for use on any make of computer. In the area of microcomputer hardware, the ANSI standards define the SCSI (an acronym for Small Computer System Interface) parallel interface, for the connection of peripherals, such as disk drives and printers. The institute is also responsible for the ANSI.SYS *device driver*, a program that provides facilities for greater control of a computer console (screen and keyboard), than is possible with the MS-DOS operating system.

IEEE is the acronym for the Institute of Electrical and Electronic Engineers. The organisation has set numerous standards for various aspects of telecommunications and computing. Notably, the IEEE has defined standards for local area network (LAN) protocols.

The **ISO** (International Standards organisation), has its headquarters in Geneva, Switzerland and is responsible for the definition of the Open Systems Interconnection (OSI) model. This model aims to ensure that any computer terminal is able to connect to any network and communicate with any other terminal, whether it is connected to the same or any other linked network. The OSI model is examined in greater detail later.

Public telecommunications authorities

The main telecommunications network in the United Kingdom is the public switched telephone network (*pstn*), which is owned by British Telecom (BT). Although BT owns the network, Mercury Communications (a competitor *public telecommunications operator* or PTO), is able to use the pstn to provide telephone and network services. Increasing competition is being provided from the independent providers of cellular telephone services.

Types of communications networks

Public switched telephone network (pstn)

The *pstn* is the main telecommunications network for the United Kingdom. It was originally designed for voice transmission, using analogue electrical signals; these electrical signals represent what is spoken and heard at each end of a link. A telephone mouthpiece contains a diaphragm, which vibrates when struck by sound waves. The vibrations are converted into electrical impulses and are sent over the network to the earpiece on the receiving telephone; a diaphragm in the earpiece converts the impulses back into sound. Much of the pstn is now digital, in particular the national trunk network and call switching exchanges; the analogue connections are mainly confined to the pstn's local links to homes and businesses. Digital voice transmission uses coded patterns of digital impulses, which are similar to those used to represent computer data. To transmit computer data over analogue sections of the pstn, requires use of a *modem* (see Data Circuit Termination Equipment or DCE). This device converts the computer's digital signal into an appropriate analogue form before transmission; a modem at the receiving end converts the analogue signal back to the digital form required by the computer.

Types of telecommunications lines

Dedicated lines

These can be leased from British Telecom and provide a permanent connection for devices in a network. They provide high transmission rates and are relatively error-free. They are only cost-effective for high volume data transmission, or when a permanent link is vital to the users. Charging is by a flat rate rather than when calls are made.

Dial-up or switched lines

These are cheaper, but support lower transmission rates than leased lines. They are more cost effective than leased lines for low-volume work and allow the operator to choose the destination of transmissions.

Digital network systems

Public switched data network (psdn) or switchstream

The psdn, owned by British Telecom (BT) and named *Switchstream*, is a *packet switching* (see later) network. Modems are not required and transmission performance is better than that achievable over the partially analogue pstn. Switchstream is one of four digital services, collectively known as X-Stream; the other services are Kilostream, Megastream and Sat-stream. Switchstream conforms to the CCITT (see Standards Authorities) standard known as the X.25 protocol; for this reason, the network is often referred to as the X.25 network. A major benefit of using this CCITT standard is that the network can be used for international communications.

Packet switching

The main components of a packet switching network are: high speed data lines; packet switching exchanges (PSEs); packet assembler/disassembler (PAD); packet terminal. With the use of a specialised computer, called a *packet terminal*, a customer can create the packets and connect directly to the network through a dedicated dataline. If the customer is not using a packet terminal, a dial-up connection is used and the data has to go through a *packet assembler/disassembler* (PAD). This device converts data to and from the networks protocol as it enters and leaves the network. Figure 24.5 illustrates these features.

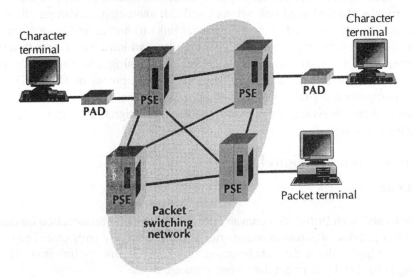

Figure 24.5. *Packet switching network*

The principles of packet switching are as follow. Messages are divided into data packets, which are then directed through the network to their destination under computer control. Besides a *message* portion, each packet contains data concerning:

❑   the destination address;

❑   the source identification;

❑   the sequence of the packet in the complete message;

❑   the detection and control of transmission errors.

The progress of a packet is monitored and controlled by *packet switching exchanges* (PSE) located at each *node* in the network. A node is a junction of network lines, which could be a computer or a computer terminal or other device. As a packet arrives at a node, the exchange checks the addressing instructions and unless it corresponds to its present location, forwards it on the most appropriate route. Each node has an *input queue*, into which all arriving packets are entered (even those which are addressed to the node itself) and a number of *output queues* (to allow for the possibility of network congestion). Figure 24.6 illustrates the operation of these queues.

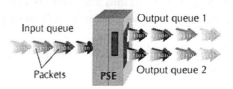

Figure 24.6. *Packest switching exchange (PSE) queues*

Network traffic information is continually transmitted between the various nodes, so that each switching computer has information to allow, for example, the avoidance of congested routes.

X.25 protocol

As already mentioned, the psdn uses a packet switching protocol, known as X.25. The CCITT (see Standards Authorities) provide the X.25 protocol for interfacing terminals with a psdn. The protocol provides users with the following facilities.

❑   Division of a message into packets.

❑   Error checking and re-transmission of any packet effected by an error.

❑   An addressing format that allows international transmission.

❑   The PSEs control the transmission of packets through the network.

Kilostream

An alternative to packet switching is to use *multiplexing*. The Kilostream service uses this technique for data transmission. The service provides a high speed direct link between two points. Data can pass in both directions at the same time; this is known as *full duplex* mode.

The main link can transmit data at a rate of 2·048 megabits per second (Mbits/s); this allows a number of low speed terminals to be connected to the high speed link through separate low speed links, each transmitting at either 128 kilobits per second (Kb/s) or 64 Kb/s. The signals from each terminal can then be merged for transmission along the high speed link, using a technique known as *time division multiplexing* (TDM). The process of multiplexing is carried out by a *terminal multiplexer*. At the receiving end of the link, the signals are separated out for transmission along low speed lines connected to their respective terminals. The terminal multiplexer at each end of the link can carry out the functions of multiplexing (combining signals) and demultiplexing (separating the signals). This is obviously necessary for full duplex operation.

Time division multiplexing, as the term suggests, provides a *time slice* on the higher-speed line for each terminal. The multiplexer has a number of registers, one per low-speed channel. Each register can store one character. The multiplexer scans each register in sequence, emptying the contents into a continuous stream of data to be transmitted. A multiplexer will send a null character whenever it finds an empty slot.

Figure 24.7 illustrates the multiplexing of signals from three terminals to a remote mainframe computer.

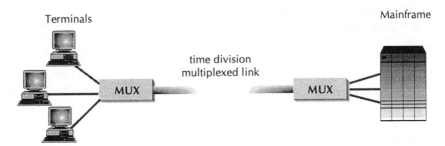

Figure 24.7. *Multiplexers to allow several terminals to use a single link*

Connecting to a remote mainframe

In organisations with mainframe computers, it is often desirable for staff with microcomputers on their desks to be able to communicate with the mainframe via those systems. With non-IBM systems, where the host computer uses asynchronous transmission, the connection can be made via the RS232C (this refers to a standard used in most serial communications) serial transmission port, located at the back of the microcomputer's system casing. However, the most common mainframe systems, IBM and ICL in particular, use synchronous communications, so special terminal emulation cards are required.

Thus, microcomputer workstations can be converted to mainframe terminals using a technique called emulation. A terminal emulation card is fitted into one of the expansion slots in the microcomputer's system casing. If there are a number of terminals to be connected, the microcomputer is then connected, via a coaxial cable, to a terminal cluster controller. The controller is linked to a front-end processor (usually a minicomputer, dedicated to handling incoming and outgoing communications for the mainframe), which is itself connected to the mainframe computer. In this way, a microcomputer can, for example, be converted into an emulation of an IBM 3270 terminal.

The advantage of using a microcomputer as a mainframe terminal is that it can also be used on a stand-alone basis for local processing tasks, such as word processing or spreadsheet work. The terminal emulation package ensures that the mainframe responds in the same way as it would to a dedicated terminal. Security mechanisms, such as passwords, prevent users of emulated terminals from carrying out processes which are forbidden to users of dedicated terminals. However, the microcomputer's facility for local storage and processing can present serious security problems for the mainframes data and various mechanisms have to be included to prevent unauthorised updates.

Where emulated terminals are to be linked to a mainframe via a wide area network, adapter cards are available which combine the terminal emulation with the gateway software, to access the intervening network.

Megastream

This service is similar to Kilostream, except that no terminal multiplexing equipment is provided. Data can be transmitted at $2 \cdot 048$, 8, 34 or 140 Mbits/s. A user can choose to use the high speed circuit directly or multiplex the circuit, such that a number of low speed channels are made available across the link. Each separate lower speed channel can then be used to carry data or some may be left for the transmission of digitised speech.

Satstream

This digital data service provides customers with a small dish aerial to allow radio transmission of data, through a communications satellite. Customers are thus able to connect with networks in Western Europe.

Integrated services digital network (ISDN)

Many forms of data, including text, voice and video images, can be digitised and an Integrated Services Digital Network (ISDN) is designed to allow the *integrated* transmission of these various data forms over the same network. An Integrated Services Digital Network exists in various forms in different countries, although the ultimate aim is to achieve an international system. It is defined as a wholly *digital* system, with end-to-end digital connections and digital exchanges throughout. ISDN has become achievable because the telephone network has become largely digital. The public telephone network is, by far, the largest communications network, so once it is fully digitised, every business and home user will have access to ISDN services. British Telecom's ISDN began with a pilot scheme in 1985, which was extended in 1986 and has continued to develop since.

Modes of data communication

Direction of transmission

The following standards are generally accepted:

- *Simplex* mode allows communication in one direction only.

- *Half-duplex* supports communications in both directions, but not at the same time; in other words there is only a single channel and the direction is switched after completion of transmission in the other direction.

- *Duplex* mode allows communication in both directions at the same time, as there are two channels permanently available. In interactive systems, where two way communication is continuously required, duplex is the only suitable mode.

- *Asymmetric duplex* is the same as duplex, except that the transmission speed in one direction is different from that of the other.

Devices differ in the ways they communicate or talk with each other. One such difference is in the number of *conductors* or lines they use to transmit data.

Serial transmission

With serial transmission, the binary signals representing the data are transmitted one after another in a serial fashion. Serial data transmission is normally used, except for very short connections between a peripheral and a computer, where parallel techniques are employed. The technique is illustrated in Figure 24.8.

Figure 24.8. *Serial transmission between two devices*

Parallel transmission

As the term makes obvious, data bits are transmitted as groups in parallel; Figure 24.9 illustrates this form. This is obviously quicker than sending them serially, but it is only practicable over short distances. Communication between a computer and its nearby peripherals can be carried out using parallel transmission, which is particularly important where high-speed devices, such as disk or tape units, are concerned. Microcomputer systems often use parallel transmission to communicate with a nearby printer. The number of lines needed for a parallel connection defines its *bus width*.

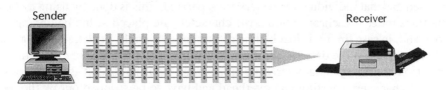

Figure 24.9. *Parallel transmission between a computer and a local printer*

Asynchronous serial transmission

When a sending device transmits characters at irregular intervals, as does for example, a keyboard device, it is said to be transmitting *asynchronously*. Although the characters are not sent at regular intervals, the bits within each character must be sent at regularly timed intervals. An example of asynchronous character format is shown in Figure 24.10. It can be seen that the line has two electrical states, representing 1

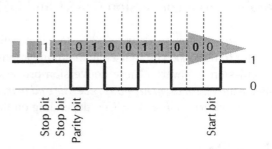

Figure 24.10. *Asynchronous character format*

and 0. Between characters, the line is in the *idle* state, a 1 or *mark* condition. The first or *start bit*, set to 0, indicates the start of a character, whilst a *stop bit* marks the end. The receiving machine listens to the line for a start bit. When it senses this it counts off the regularly timed bits that form the character. When a stop bit is reached, the receiver switches back to its listening state. The presence of start and stop bits for each character permits the time interval between characters to be irregular, or asynchronous.

Synchronous serial transmission

The start and stop bits used in asynchronous transmission are wasteful, in that they do not contain information. With higher speed devices or *buffered* low-speed devices, data can be transmitted in more efficient, timed, or *synchronous* blocks (Figure 24.11).

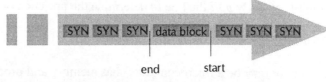

Figure 24.11. *Synchronous character format*

A variety of formats may be used, each having their operating rules or protocol. Communications protocols are dealt with later in this chapter. In synchronous transmission, a data stream may be very long, so it is vital that the timing between transmitter and receiver is synchronised and that individual characters are separated. This is done by using a *clock lead* from the transmitter. Synchronisation (*syn*) characters are placed at the beginning of each data block and, in case timing is lost by line disturbance, several syn characters may be situated at intervals within the data block. Thus if timing is lost, the receiver can re-time its bit groupings from the last syn character. Like the start and stop bits used in asynchronous transmission, syn characters constitute an overhead and have to be stripped out by the receiver. Synchronous transmission is generally used for data speeds of 2400 bps or more. Some VDU terminals are designed for high speed data transmission and use synchronous transmission; many others use asynchronous transmission.

Parallel-serial conversion (UART and USRT)

As data moves around a computer system in parallel form, it needs to be converted to serial form for transmission though a telecommunications link and from serial to parallel, when the transmission is inward. These conversion processes are carried out by a hardware device called a *universal asynchronous receiver and transmitter* (UART) or *universal synchronous receiver and transmitter* (USRT), depending on the type of computer being used.

Devices

Data terminal equipment (DTE)

All the external devices attached to a network may be referred to collectively as data terminal equipment (DTE). Examples of DTE equipment are: computer terminals, including microcomputers used for that function; minicomputers; bank cash dispensers; printers.

Dumb terminal

The DTE may be a *dumb* terminal, that is, one which has no processing power of its own, possibly no storage, and is entirely dependent on a controlling computer. As soon as each character is entered by the operator, it is transmitted over the communications link, to the controlling computer; this makes editing extremely difficult and slow. The remote computer, to which the terminal is connected, has to use an *input buffer* (small amount of memory assigned to that purpose) to store characters as they arrive. Because the terminal is dumb, the remote computer must regularly *poll* the line to determine the presence of data.

Intelligent terminal

An *intelligent* terminal (it may be a microcomputer) has memory and processing power, so an operator can use it to store, edit and manipulate data, independently of any other connected computer. For example, a document could be retrieved from a remote computer, be edited within the intelligent terminal and then, in its updated form, be transmitted back to the remote computer. The intelligent terminal's processing facility is provided by an internal processor, usually a microprocessor; its internal memory allows data to be held and manipulated before transmission. The facility may also include local backing storage and a printer. Intelligent terminals can use either EBCDIC or ASCII code (see Standards for Data Representation), but a dumb terminal can only use ASCII. Two points need to be made concerning the methods used to transmit data and the type of terminal used.

1. Dumb terminals, having no processing power and no buffer memory have to use a *point-to-point* connection with the remote, controlling computer. Such terminals transmit data asynchronously. The characters are not evenly separated, because the transmission of characters is determined by the typing speed of the operator and the characters will obviously not be transmitted at precise, regular intervals.

2. Intelligent terminals, having a buffer store, can accumulate the keyed characters and send them in blocks or streams. The remote computer signals when transmission of a data stream can begin, thus allowing line sharing by numerous communicating devices. Such line sharing is carried out by multiplexing, a technique described in the earlier section on Packet Switching Networks.

Data circuit termination equipment (DCE)

The intervening connections of a network are leased from the main telecommunications provider, which in the UK is British Telecom. The equipment that allows the DTE to be connected to and interfaced with the network is known as *data circuit termination equipment* (DCE). The CCITT (see Standards Authorities) use the term *data communication equipment* (also DCE). An example of DCE is a *modem*, which allows computer data to be transmitted over sections of the pstn (usually local connections to homes and businesses) which still use analogue signalling.

Modem

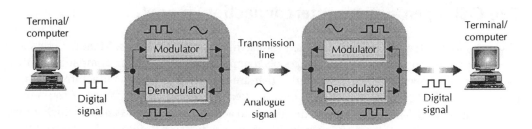

Figure 24.12. *Modems in a data communcations link*

Figure 24.12 illustrates the role of the modem in a data telecommunications link. Even though much of the public switched telephone network (pstn) uses digital transmission techniques, local connections to homes and businesses still use analogue signals. To allow transmission of computer data (which is digital) over these analogue links, a device called a *modem* is needed to *modulate* and *demodulate* the computers signals. The modem for the transmitter device has to modulate the digital signal into the corresponding analogue form for transmission along the telephone line. The modem at the receiver device has to carry out the reverse operation. Modems are capable of both functions, so that two way communications are supported.

Telephone-modem connections. To allow computer communication through a telephone line, the user must obtain a modem, of which there are two main types:

❑   asynchronous serial modems. Each character requires *start* and *stop bits* to separate one character from another.

❑   synchronous serial modems. Start and stop bits are not required, because the transmitting and receiving modems are synchronised.

Modem speeds. *Baud rate* indicates the number of signal changes or pulses per second supported by a communication link. The term used to be synonymous with *bits per second* (bps), but improved data encoding (compression) techniques mean, for example, that a 28,800 baud link can support data transfer rates up to 115,200 bps. Different modems provide different data transmission rates, measured in bits per second (bps). The data compression and error correction standards are set by standards bodies (see earlier).

Computer-modem connection. To make use of a modem, the microcomputer should have a serial communication (RS232) port. However, there are two possible alternatives; an adapter card with a serial port capability; a communications board (this fits in an expansion slot, located inside the computer's system casing), which combines the functions of the serial port and the modem.

Data communications standards

The OSI (open systems interconnection) model

Many computer devices are now designed for use in networked systems. Manufacturers are now tending to conform to standard protocols that make their equipment compatible with a variety of user networks. *Closed* networks, that are restricted to one manufacturer's equipment and standards, are not attractive to the user, because it restricts the choice of equipment which can be used. The aim of standardisation is to achieve more open systems which allow users to select from a wider range of manufacturers' products. A Reference Model for Open Systems Interconnection (OSI) has been under development by the International Standards organisation (ISO) since 1977. Other standards, including SNA (IBM's System Network Architecture) and Ethernet, are largely incompatible with one another. Certain standards in the OSI model have been set by manufacturers as their commercial products have gained in popularity. The OSI reference model for communications protocol identifies a hierarchy of seven layers. The layers and their functions are briefly described below.

Application layer. This is the highest layer in that it is closest to the user. It supports the transfer of information between end-users, applications programs and devices. Several types of protocol exist in this layer, including those for specific applications and those for more generalised applications, such as accounting, entry control and user identification. The applications layer hides the physical network from the user, presenting a user-orientated view instead. For example, the user need not know that several physical computers are involved when accessing a database.

Presentation layer. This layer covers standards on how data is presented to the end-user devices. The aim is to ensure that different devices, which may be using data in different formats, can communicate with one another. The presentation layer can, for example, handle conversions between ASCII and EBCDIC character codes. It may also carry out encryption to ensure data security during transmission over vulnerable telecommunication links. The presentation layer also attempts to deal with conversions between terminals which use different line and screen lengths and different character sets.

Session layer. The session layer is concerned with the exchange of information between different applications and users; it is the users' interface into the network. When a user requests a particular service from the network, the session layer handles the dialogue.

Transport layer. The data transmission system on any network will have its own peculiarities and the function of the transport layer is to mask out any undesirable features which may prevent a high quality transmission for the network.

Network layer. The function of the network layer is to perform the routing of information around the network and also to connect one network to another. The software can also carry out accounting functions to enable the network owner to charge users.

Data link layer. The physical data transmission media used in a network are subject to interference which can corrupt data and other signals. The data link layer handles data transmission errors and thus improves the quality of the network. The techniques used, for example, for the receipt and acknowledgement of data by a receiver device, are determined by the data link layer. The CCITT V42bis protocol, with its error detection and correction facilities falls into this level.

Physical layer The physical layer provides the means to connect the physical medium and is concerned with the transmission of binary data within the communication channel. Standards are set regarding the mechanical, electrical and procedural aspects of interface devices. For example, standards are set for the number of pins a network connector should have and the function and position of each pin. The RS232 and V24 protocols are within this level.

Exercises

1. List the main *hardware components* of a local area network.

2. (i) Name the *network topology* which features a central computer for message switching between the attached nodes.

    (ii) What is the topology's main weakness?

3. (i) Which weakness of the *Cambridge ring* topology is the *IBM Token Ring* network designed to overcome?

    (ii) Name the device used to overcome the weakness.

4. (i) Name the topology for which *Ethernet* is the main standard.

    (ii) Distinguish between *thick* and *thin* Ethernet, in terms of the number of devices which can be attached and the data transmission rates each supports.

5. A *baseband* network will support the transmission of only one signal at a time. What sort of network is needed to allow the simultaneous transmission of, say, computer data and video communications?

6. (i) What does CSMA-CA stand for?

    (ii) What is CSMA-CA?

    (iii) Which network topology uses CSMA?

7. (i) What is the main role of *standards organisations* in the technologies of networking and data communications?

    (ii) Why are they important?

8. List the typical contents of a *packet* used in a packet-switching network.

9. Kilostream is a *multiplexed* service. What does multiplexed mean?

10. Distinguish between *synchronous* and *asynchronous* serial transmission.

Chapter 25
The Internet

Introduction

The Internet is a world-wide network composed of thousands of smaller regional networks scattered throughout the globe. A common set of communication protocols enables every computer connected to the Internet to interchange information with every other computer so connected. On any given day it connects roughly 20 million users in over 50 countries. Over the last 25 years, the Internet has grown to include government and educational institutions, and, more recently, commercial organisations.

Figure 25.1 shows the estimated coverage of the Internet in 1995. The countries in black have facilities to connect to the Internet, though the number of people with Internet access in these countries varies widely. Countries in white may have access to e-mail, local isolated networks, or no facilities for connection to networks at all. No single person or organisation owns the Internet. There are companies which help manage different parts of the networks which tie everything together, but there is no

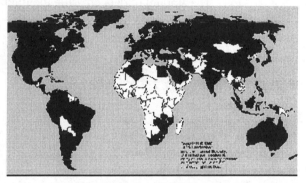

Figure 25.1. *Internet world coverage*

single governing body which controls what happens on the Internet. The networks within different countries are funded and managed locally according to local policies. The Internet began in early 1969 under the experimental project ARPAnet. ARPA (Advanced Research Projects Agency, later known as the Defence Advanced Research Projects Agency) wanted to demonstrate the feasibility of building computer networks over a wide area such that the loss of a number of hosts on that network did not disrupt it. So ARPA initially interconnected four computers and linked them with Internet Protocol (IP), and the Internet grew from there. In the 70s and 80s US universities began to link with DARPAnet so that it could be used for academic research and in 1991 the U.S. government lifted its ban on commercial use of the Internet. The considerable business opportunities provided by the Internet ensure that it will continue to grow.

Today the Internet is a huge collection of different, intercommunicating networks funded by commercial, government and educational organisations. It has developed to handle larger volumes of data, software has become more powerful and user-friendly, and the types of services available have grown. The Internet now links more than 150 countries. All types of computers make up the hardware connected on the Internet. They vary from PCs, Macintoshes and UNIX workstations to minicomputers, mainframes and supercomputers. Anyone who wants to have access to the enormous amount of information available regionally or around the world can use the Internet. They can access electronic libraries, receive periodicals, exchange ideas, read the news, post questions with newsgroups, examine the weather (from reports or satellite photos), obtain the latest stock market prices and currency exchange rates, and access public government information on trade, laws, research and other subjects. It is likely that in the very near future, every school will be connected to the Internet, an Internet connection in your house will be no more unusual than a telephone line and, if you run a business, the Internet will be a vital tool. Here are some interesting facts concerning the Internet.

- ☐   It is estimated that the Internet now connects over 3.5 million computers.

- ☐   On average, more than 1000 computers are added to the Internet daily.

- ☐   The amount of data crossing the Internet grows by 10% each month.

- ☐   Each day world-wide over 10 million people directly (and 25 million indirectly) use the Internet to send and receive electronic mail.

Connecting to the Internet

Figure 25.2 shows a PC connected to the Internet via a remote service provider which is itself a LAN (Local Area Network). The PC connects to the service provider using a modem and the telephone system. The service provider is directly connected to the Internet by means of a *router,* a computer which provides the link to special data transmission lines required to access the Internet. A large organisation might have its own direct link to the Internet, but many private users rely on commercial service providers for the connection, for which they must pay a subscription.

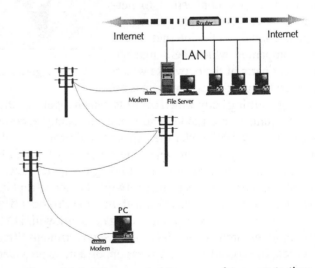

Figure 25.2. *PC connected to a server for access to the Internet*

Uses of the Internet

The Internet is essentially a tool for transferring information between computers. This can be achieved in numerous ways and for various purposes. For example, *E-mail* is a convenient, quick and cheap alternative to the postal system for business and personal correspondence; *File Transfer Protocol (FTP)* allows large amounts of information to be transferred between two computers very conveniently; *Usenet,* the world-wide collection of interest groups, or *Newsgroups*, allows groups of people with similar interests to exchange views and information. Another important use of the Internet is the remote control of computer systems via *Telnet*. The *World-Wide Web* provides a uniform means of accessing and transferring information in the form of hypermedia documents. Accessing these documents does not require any particular machine or operating system. These and other Internet services are discussed in the following sections.

Note that programs used on the Internet can be classified as being either *server* or *client*. Server programs operate at Internet sites where the particular Internet service being used is provided; the program which is used to access a site, on a home PC for example, is the client program. For instance, a Web server at a Web site processes requests made by client programs called Web *browsers*.

The World-Wide Web

Abbreviated to the Web and WWW, this is the fastest growing Internet service. Though the World-Wide Web is mostly used on the Internet, the two terms do not mean the same thing. The Web refers to a world-wide collection of knowledge, while the Internet refers to the physical side of the global network, an enormous collection of cables and computers. The World-Wide Web uses the Internet for the transmission of hypermedia documents between computer users connected to the Internet. As with the Internet, nobody actually owns the World-Wide Web. People are responsible for the documents they author and make available publicly on the Web. Via the Internet, hundreds of thousands of people around the world are making information available from their homes, schools, colleges and workplaces. The aim of WWW is to make all on-line knowledge part of one interconnected web of documents and services.

The World-Wide Web began in March 1989, when Tim Berners-Lee of the European Particle Physics Laboratory (known as CERN, a collective of European high-energy physics researchers) proposed the project as a means of distributing research results and ideas effectively throughout the organisation. The initial project proposal outlined a simple system of using networked hypertext to transmit to members of the high-energy physics community. By the end of 1990, the first piece of Web software had been introduced on a NeXT machine. It had the capability to view and transmit hypertext documents to other people on the Internet, and came with the capability to edit hypertext documents on the screen. Since then hundreds of people throughout the world have contributed their time writing Web software and documents, or telling others about the Web. Given that many sites are private (hidden behind corporate firewalls or not connected to the public Internet), it can be safely stated that there are at least 4,500 hypertext Web servers in use throughout the world and in excess of a quarter of a million active Web users.

The World-Wide Web is officially described as a wide-area hypermedia information retrieval initiative aiming to give universal access to a large universe of documents. What the World-Wide Web (WWW, W3) project has done is provide users on computer networks with a consistent means to access a variety of media in a simplified fashion. With the aid of a popular software interface to the Web, called a *browser* (described later), the WWW has changed the way people view and create information. The first true global hypermedia network, it is revolutionising many elements of society, including commerce, politics, and literature.

Hypertext and hypermedia

The operation of the Web relies mainly on *hypertext* as its means of interacting with users. Hypertext is basically the same as ordinary text - it can be stored, read, searched, or edited -with an important exception: hypertext contains links to other places within the same document or to other documents. A Web browser indicates text links by the use of colour or by underlining. For example, Figure 25.3 shows part of a document called Writing Java Programs which contains three underlying links to other documents, the second one being The Anatomy of a Java Application.

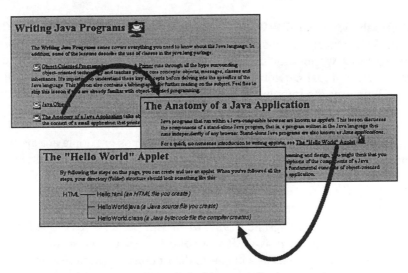

Figure 25.3. *Three linked hypermedia documents*

This latter document in turn contains a link to a third document called The Hello World Applet. The first document would be retrieved from the WWW using a browser and the user, by pointing and clicking with a mouse on a link, will cause the browser to retrieve the appropriate document automatically, no matter where it is located.

Hypermedia is hypertext with a difference - hypermedia documents contain links not only to other pieces of text, but also to other forms of media, namely sounds, images, and movies. Images themselves can be selected to link to sounds or documents. Hypermedia simply combines hypertext and multimedia. Figure 25.4 shows a browser displaying a hypermedia document with three buttons which, when clicked with a mouse, would demonstrate sound, graphics and video files.

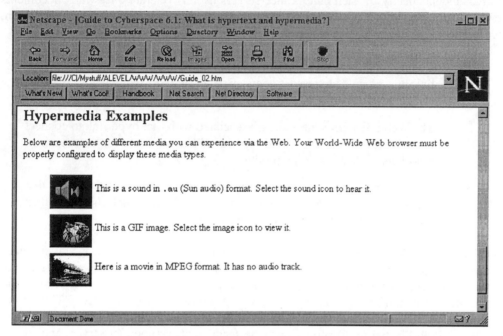

Figure 25.4. *A hypermedia document being displayed by a Netscape browser*

The appearance of a hypermedia document when it is displayed by a browser is determined partly by the browser which provides a certain amount of control over such things as text fonts and colours, but mainly by the language used to encode the document. This language is *HyperText Mark-up Language* (HTML). HTML is described in more detail in a later section of this chapter.

Web browsers

These are graphical interface client programs to help users to navigate through the Web, to transmit and to receive information from other users or information providers. Chapter 17 describes their typical features and uses.

How the Web works

Web software is designed around a distributed client-server architecture. A Web client (called a Web browser if it is intended for interactive use) is a program which can send requests for documents to any Web server. A Web server is a program which, upon receipt of a request, sends the document requested (or an error message if appropriate) back to the requesting client. Using a distributed architecture means that a client program may be running on a completely separate machine from that of the server, possibly in another room or even in another country. Because the task of document storage is left to the server and the task of document presentation is left to the client, each program can concentrate on those duties and progress independently of each other. Since servers usually operate only when documents are requested, they put a minimal amount of workload on the computers on which they run. Here is an example of how the process works:

1.   Running a Web client program, such as a browser, the user selects a hyperlink in a piece of hypertext connecting to another document - Java Programming for example.

2.   The Web client uses the address associated with that hyperlink to connect to the Web server at a specified network address and asks for the document associated with Java Programming.

3.   The server responds by sending the text and any other media within that text (pictures, sounds, or video clips) to the client, which the client then renders for presentation on the user's screen.

The World-Wide Web is composed of thousands of these virtual transactions taking place per hour throughout the world, creating a web of information flow. Web servers are now beginning to include encryption and client authentication abilities, allowing them to send and receive secure data and be more selective as to which clients receive information. This allows freer communications among Web users and ensures that sensitive data is kept private. In the near future, it will be harder to compromise the security of commercial servers and educational servers which want to keep information local.

The language which Web clients and servers use to communicate with each other is called the *HyperText Transfer Protocol* (HTTP). All Web clients and servers must be able to 'speak' HTTP in order to send and receive hypermedia documents. For this reason, Web servers are often called HTTP servers.

HTML - The Hypertext Markup Language

The standard language the Web uses for creating and recognising hypermedia documents is the Hypertext Mark-up Language (HTML). Figure 25.5 shows part of the underlying HTML document which produces the page being displayed by the browser shown in Chapter 17.

An important characteristic of HTML is its ease of use. Web documents are typically written in HTML and are usually named with the suffix *.html* or *.htm*. HTML documents are nothing more than standard 7-bit ASCII files with formatting codes which contain information about layout (text styles, document titles, paragraphs, lists) and hyperlinks.

```
<HTML>
<HEAD>
  <TITLE>Herbology Subject Index</TITLE>
</HEAD>
<BODY BACKGROUND="Back.gif"

<CENTER><TABLE WIDTH="100%">
<TR>
<TD ALIGN=CENTER><IMG SRC="Herb.gif" HEIGHT=233 WIDTH=340
</TD>

<TD><FONT SIZE=+1>Herbal Medicine is the substantial counterpart
to the energetic medicine of acupuncture. Many treatments for
internal disharmonies or chronic conditions can greatly benefit
from the use of Chinese herbal therapies. </FONT></TD>
</TR>
</TABLE></CENTER>

<CENTER><P>
<HR SIZE=2 WIDTH=30%></P></CENTER>

<H2>Consumer Level Information</H2>
<UL>
<H4><A HREF="Herbology.htm">Herbology FAQ</A> </ H4>

<H4>A HREF="Cook.htm">How to Cook Chinese Herbs!</A> </H4>

<H4><A HREF="Man.htm">Kombucha Elixir or Manchurian Tea</A> </ H4>

<H4><A HREF="Fairy.htm">&quot;A Rose is a Rosa Sericea Pteracantha
is a Rose.&quot; A humorous look at what happens when Western
science attempts to understand a Chinese herb.</A></H4>
<H4><A HREF="Chemo.htm"Chinese Herbal Medicine for side-effects of
Radiation and Chemotherapy</A></H4>
</UL>
<CENTER><P>
<HR SIZE=2 WIDTH=30%></P></CENTER>
<H2Student Level Information</H2>
<UL>

.........
```

Figure 25.5. *An HTML document*

Note the *tags* indicated by keywords enclosed between < and >. Most tags are of the form
`<tagname>`........ `</tagname>`, with the text being controlled by the tag appearing between the two parts. For example, text enclosed between `<H2>` and `</H2>` is shown as a

type 2 heading by the browser, and text between <B> and </B> is shown as bold type. Hypertext links are indicated by <A....>and </A>. An example of a hypertext link is

```
<A HREF="Cook.htm"How to Cook Chinese Herbs!</A>
```

This tag causes the browser to show 'How to Cook Chinese Herbs!' as a hypertext link by displaying it in a different colour from ordinary text, and the page to be loaded from the same web site directory as the current document has the file name 'Cook.htm'

Images, such as the picture in the top left-hand corner of the displayed page shown in Figure 8.5, use the <IMG...> tag. The tag

```
<IMG SRC="Herb.gif" HEIGHT=233 WIDTH=340>
```

indicates, among other things, that the source of the image to be displayed is to be found in the same directory as the parent document under the filename, 'Herb.gif'. The file extension '.gif' is the standard format for Web page inline graphics.

One of the major attractions of using HTML is that every WWW browser can 'understand' it, no matter what machine the browser is being run on. This means that Web page developers do not need to worry about producing different versions for different computer platforms.

Uniform Resource Locators

The World-Wide Web uses what are called Uniform Resource Locators (URLs) to represent hypermedia links and links to network services within HTML documents. It is possible to represent nearly any file or service on the Internet with a URL. The first part of the URL (before the two slashes) specifies the method of access. The second is typically the address of the computer which the data or service is located on. Further parts may specify the names of files, the port to connect to, or the text to search for in a database. A URL is always a single unbroken line with no spaces.

Sites which run World-Wide Web servers are typically named with a "www" at the beginning of the network address.

Here are some examples of URLs:

```
http://www.nc.edu/nw/book.html
```

Connects to an HTTP server and retrieves an HTML document called 'book.html' in a directory called 'nw'

```
file://www.nc.edu/sound.au
```

Retrieves a sound file called 'sound.au' and plays it.

```
file://www.abc.com/picture.gif
```

Retrieves a picture and displays it, either in a separate program or within a hypermedia document.

```
file://www.bcd.org/dd/
```

Displays the contents of directory 'dd'.

```
ftp://www.wer.uk.co/pub/file.txt
```

Opens an FTP connection to www.uk.co and retrieves a text file.

```
gopher://www.hcc.hawaii.edu
```

Connects to the Gopher at www.hcc.hawaii.edu.

```
telnet://www.nc.edu:1234
```

Telnets to www.nc.edu at port 1234.

```
news:alt.hypertext
```

Reads the latest Usenet news by connecting to a news host and returns the articles in the "alt.hypertext" newsgroup in hypermedia format.

Most Web browsers allow the user to specify a URL and connect to that document or service. When selecting hypertext in an HTML document, the user is actually sending a request to open a URL. In this way, hyperlinks can be made not only to other texts and media, but also to other network services. Web browsers are not simply Web clients, but are also full-featured FTP, Gopher, and telnet clients (see later for a discussion of these Internet services).

WWW search engines

The WWW is a vast, distributed repository of information, and more is being added to the Web each day. However, the only consistent characteristics of the information available are the manner in which it is coded, that is, in HTML, and the way in which it can be located, that is, by using URLs. To access this huge bank of information, dispersed over the entire world, and locate specific information on a certain subject, there are numerous information retrieval utilities which provide access to databases of Web page details. These *search engines* allow Web users to enter search criteria in the form of keywords or phrases and they retrieve summaries of all database entries satisfying the search criteria. Of the many information retrieval services available, some of the most well known include *InfoSeek*, *Magellan*, *Lycos* and *Yahoo*.

Figure 25.6 shows the Magellan search engine being used to find information on shiatsu.

Figure 25.6. *A keyword entered in the Magellan search engine*

The search produced short summaries of over 100 Web pages containing the keyword shiatsu, the first few of which are shown in Figure 25.7. Clicking on any of the links shown as underlined headings would cause the browser to retrieve the appropriate page which might also have links to further pages containing related information.

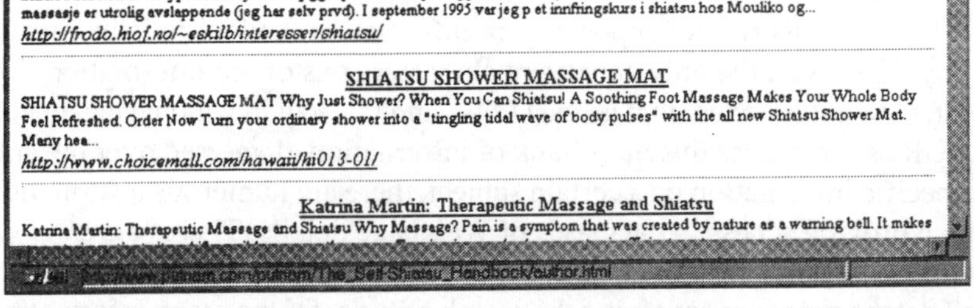

Figure 25.7. *A partial list of the result of searching for the keyword 'shiatsu'*

Gopher

Gopher is an Internet-wide tool used to search for and retrieve text-based information stored at Gopher sites throughout the world. One way to picture Gopherspace is to think of each Gopher site as a page in an extremely large index of information. Gopher resources include research results (both governmental and commercial), special-interest groups and databases of almost any kind of documented information.

A Gopher *client* is a software package which allows you to search this master index for information which meets your criteria. There are Gopher clients available for most computers. With its user-friendly menu-based interface, Gopher spares the user the need to learn many computer commands. In effect, Gopher presents the Internet as if it were all part of a single directory system. There are numerous programs specifically designed to access Gopher sites, but general purpose Web browsers, such as Netscape, will also handle Gopher. Figure 25.8 shows Netscape displaying a Gopher menu at the University of Minnesota in the USA where Gopher was created.

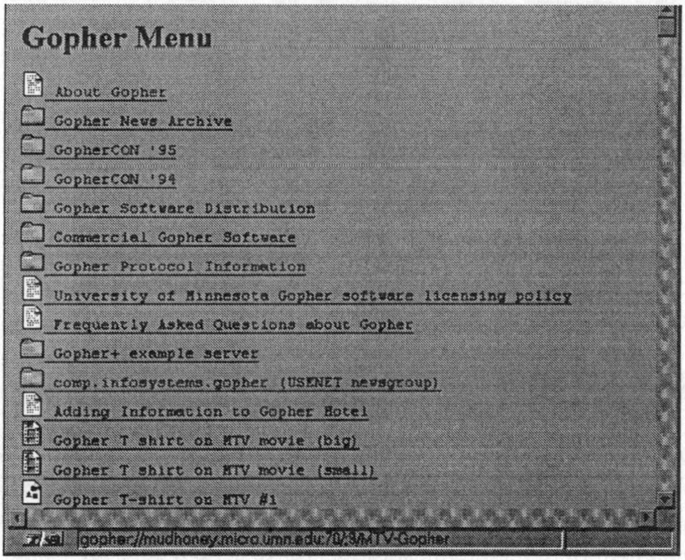

Figure 25.8. *A Gopher menu displayed by the browser*

As can be seen, the menu contains a mixture of different types of files, including text documents (for example, 'About Gopher'), further directories of files (for example, 'Gopher News Archive'), video clips (for example, 'Gopher T shirt on MTV movie') and pictures (for example, 'Gopher t shirt on MTV #1').

Figure 25.9 shows the information received by the browser when the link to the first document, 'About Gopher', was selected.

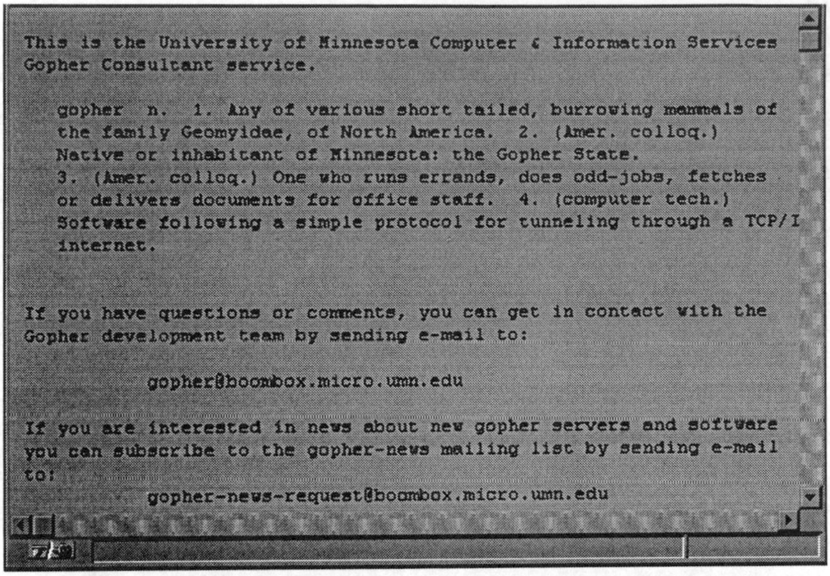

This is the University of Minnesota Computer & Information Services
Gopher Consultant service.

gopher n. 1. Any of various short tailed, burrowing mammals of
the family Geomyidae, of North America. 2. (Amer. colloq.)
Native or inhabitant of Minnesota: the Gopher State.
3. (Amer. colloq.) One who runs errands, does odd-jobs, fetches
or delivers documents for office staff. 4. (computer tech.)
Software following a simple protocol for tunneling through a TCP/I
internet.

If you have questions or comments, you can get in contact with the
Gopher development team by sending e-mail to:

gopher@boombox.micro.umn.edu

If you are interested in news about new gopher servers and software
you can subscribe to the gopher-news mailing list by sending e-mail
to:

gopher-news-request@boombox.micro.umn.edu

Figure 25.9. *A text document retrieved from the Gopher menu*

Because information held on Gopher servers is accessed through menu hierarchies, which is time consuming if many levels of menus have to be negotiated, a widely available tool called *Veronica* is used to search 'Gopherspace' for keywords. Veronica uses a database which has been compiled from Gopher servers - almost every item offered by a Gopher server is indexed by Veronica. Veronica uses Gopher client programs to act as user interfaces, allowing searches to be performed and presenting the results of searches, in much the same way as search engines available through Web browsers function.

WAIS (Wide Area Information Servers)

WAIS is a networked information retrieval system. Client applications are able to retrieve text or multimedia documents stored on the servers. and request documents using keywords. Servers search a full text index for the documents and return a list of documents containing the keyword. The client may then request the server to send a copy of any of the documents found. Although the name Wide Area implies the use of the large networks such as the Internet to connect clients to servers distributed around the network, WAIS can be used between a client and server on the same machine or a client and server on the same LAN.

Currently, there are a large number of servers running and topics range from recipes and movies to bibliographies, technical documents, and newsgroup archives.

The information which is provided by WAIS is not limited to ASCII text only. With WAIS you can also get multimedia information like pictures, graphics, sounds and even video. WAIS uses natural language queries to find relevant documents. The result of the query is a set of documents which contain the words of the query. The documents which provided the most hits with the given query are placed at the top of the list of documents. WAIS databases can be accessed using specific WAIS client programs, or alternatively Gopher, Telnet and Web browser client programs.

E-mail

The most used application of the Internet is electronic mail, or *e-mail* as it is widely known. E-mail is primarily used to send and receive text-based messages such as personal or business letters, orders, reports and statements.

To use Internet e-mail, access to a computer which is connected to the Internet and has e-mail software is required. Most commercial Internet service providers include e-mail facilities in their subscriber services. Subscribers are given an identifying code called an e-mail *address*. The service provider collects and forwards mail sent from that address and holds mail to be received by that address until able to deliver it. The service provider thus acts like a post office, and in fact there is a close analogy between the way which e-mail is implemented and the traditional manual postal system (which is disparagingly termed snail mail by e-mail devotees). The same principles apply to e-mail users who do not rely on commercial service providers - messages are automatically forwarded from users to their destinations and incoming mail is stored on their service provider's computer until the user is able to accept it.

The process of composing and sending an e-mail message is as follows:

1.   The message to be sent is composed (usually off-line) using some form of text editor.

2.   A *mailer* program is used to connect to the Internet and transmit the message to its destination computer. The mailer examines the code containing the address to which the message is to be sent and makes a decision regarding how the message should be routed to the destination before sending it on its way.

3.   The message is automatically passed from computer to computer until it arrives at the recipient's *mailbox* which is generally a special directory used for storing messages which are waiting to be read.

4.   The recipient accesses his/her mailbox and removes any messages which have arrived.

Because e-mail is delivered by electronic means, it is much faster than the manual system, taking minutes or seconds rather than days to arrive at practically any destination in the world. Though the technology which makes e-mail possible is complex, from a user's viewpoint e-mail is simple to use and extremely useful.

FTP

File Transfer Protocol (FTP) provides the facility to transfer files between two computers on the Internet. There are thousands of FTP sites all over the Internet with data files, software, and information for almost any interest. Figure 25.10 shows an FTP program being used to provide a link between a PC and a remote computer.

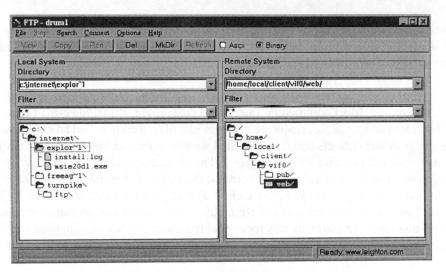

Figure 25.10. *An FTP program being used to link to computers*

The file directory structures of both machines are being displayed in adjacent windows, allowing files to be selected and transferred between the two machines.

Some FTP programs require typed commands to accomplish file-handling operations, but modern programs usually provide convenient graphical user interfaces such as the one illustrated.

Though there are other methods of transferring files between computers on the Internet, FTP allows such tasks to be performed quickly and easily. It is worth noting, however, that in order to access a remote host computer in this way, you need to have:

The host name, that is, the Internet name of the computer system to which you hope to connect. This will be used by your FTP software to establish a link to the host. A typical host name might be of the form *www.layton.com.*

A valid login name and a password which will allow you to access the host. These are obviously for security purposes - many computer systems on the Internet contain confidential information which only authorised personnel should be able to access. However, unrestricted files which are available on host computers can often be accessed by using the special visitor password *anonymous*.

In Figure 25.10, the user has already provided an acceptable login name and password, through the FTP software, and consequently has been given access to the host system.

Closely associated with FTP, *Archie* is a program which periodically searches all FTP sites on its master list, and stores the filenames it finds in a central database. This information is then made available to users to retrieve via FTP. This, in common with other types of search engines found on the Internet, provides a convenient method of locating items of information which could be in an FTP site anywhere in the world.

Telnet

Telnet allows you to use a remote computer system from your local system. For example, an employee of an organisation which is on the Internet and supports Telnet working, could use the firm's computer system from home. The employee would simply Telnet the employer's computer system using his/her home PC and, once connected, could run programs available on the remote system. The Telnet software provides an interface window through which commands can be issued and results displayed.

This *virtual terminal* allows the remote computer to be controlled as if it were the local computer. Any task which can be performed on a workstation connected directly to the remote computer can also be done using a Telnet connection.

Usenet

Usenet is a large collection of newsgroups, of which there are many thousands. Newsgroups allow people with common interests to exchange views, ask questions and provide information using the Internet. Almost anything you care to find can be found as a newsgroup, which acts like a community bulletin board spread across millions of computer systems world wide. Anyone can participate in these groups, and moderation ranges from strict to none. Everything imaginable is discussed, from selling and trading goods and services, to discussing the latest episode of a popular TV show. Subscribers can read news articles, and reply to them - either by posting their own news articles, or by sending E-mail to the authors.

Since Usenet news is not limited to any political or geographic boundaries, it provides the possibility of being able to interact with an enormous number of individuals.

A program called a *newsreader* allows access to a newsgroup and the articles available for reading, retrieval of articles of interest and the posting of articles for others to read. Each article has a header which summarises the contents of the article, and the newsreader can be configured either to read all available article headers or those which meet certain criteria.

Figure 25.11 shows a Microsoft Windows newsreader displaying a selection of headers for a newsgroup devoted to the Internet language Java.

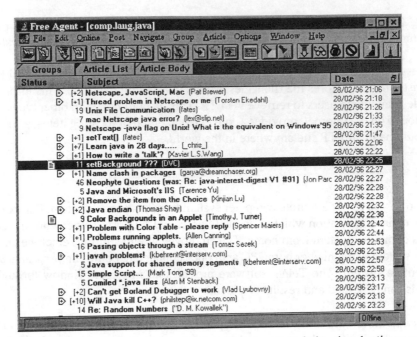

Figure 25.11. *A Newsreader program showing a selection of article headers for the newsgroup comp.lang.java*

The shaded item with the document symbol to the left has been retrieved so that the complete article (shown in Figure 25.12) could be read. The author of the article is posing the question 'setBackground???' in the hope that someone with a similar interest in Java will know the answer to the full question shown below and post it to the newsgroup.

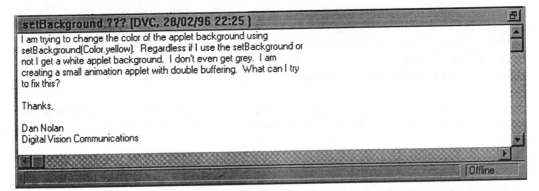

Figure 25.12. *The body of the article corresponding to the shaded header in Figure 25.11*

As mentioned earlier, there are now well over 13,000 different newsgroups with many new ones adding to the list every day. To give you an idea of the range of interests represented, Figure 25.13 shows a number of recent additions.

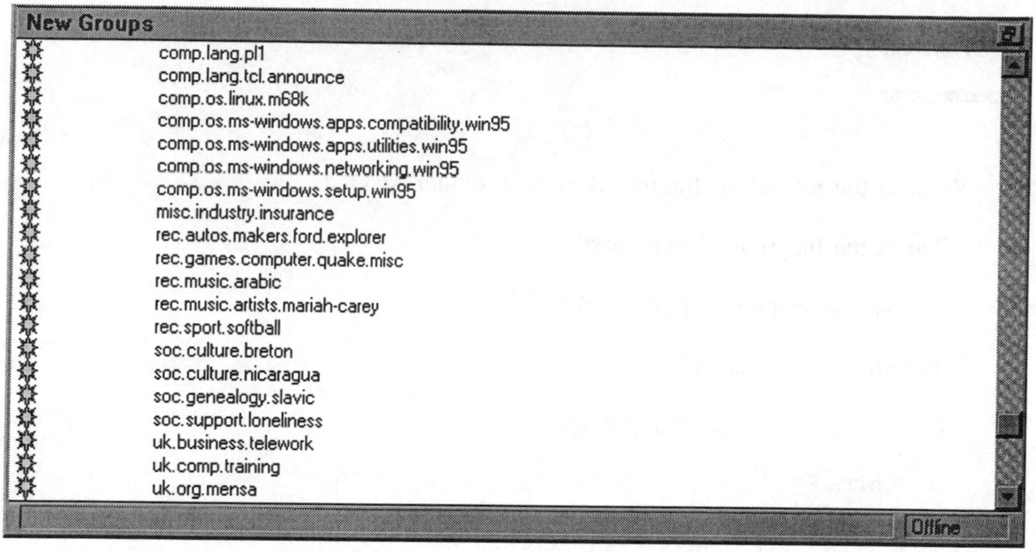

New Groups

```
comp.lang.pl1
comp.lang.tcl.announce
comp.os.linux.m68k
comp.os.ms-windows.apps.compatibility.win95
comp.os.ms-windows.apps.utilities.win95
comp.os.ms-windows.networking.win95
comp.os.ms-windows.setup.win95
misc.industry.insurance
rec.autos.makers.ford.explorer
rec.games.computer.quake.misc
rec.music.arabic
rec.music.artists.mariah-carey
rec.sport.softball
soc.culture.breton
soc.culture.nicaragua
soc.genealogy.slavic
soc.support.loneliness
uk.business.telework
uk.comp.training
uk.org.mensa
```

Offline

Figure 25.13. *A selection of newsgroups*

IRC

IRC, or *Internet Relay Chat*, is a multi-user talk program. IRC allows several people to simultaneously participate in a discussion over a particular channel, or even multiple channels. There is no restriction to the number of people who can participate in a given discussion, or the number of channels which can be formed over IRC.

All conversations take place in real time and IRC has been used extensively for live coverage of such things as world events, news and sports commentary. It is also an extremely inexpensive substitute for long distance calling.

Exercises

1. What is the role of an Internet Service Provider?

2. What is the function of hypertext?

3. Give three examples of hypermedia objects.

4. What are in-line images?

5. (i)   What is this an example of?

```
<html>
<head>
<meta http-equiv="Content-Type"
content="text/html; charset=iso-8859-1">
```

   (ii)   What software package is normally used to view it?

6. What are search engines used for?

7. How does a Gopher tool differ from a search engine?

8. Which Internet service is designed for the transfer of files between two, temporarily connected, computers?

9. Which Internet service is designed to allow members of common interest groups to exchange views and ask questions?

10. Which Internet service allows simultaneous communication between several users?

Chapter 26

Arithmetic Operations

Introduction

The four fundamental processes of arithmetic are addition (+), subtraction (−), multiplication (×) and division (÷), and these are termed *arithmetic operations*. Arithmetic operations are performed on numbers which may be presented and described in different forms:

(a)   *Integers* are whole numbers, such as 1, 2, 6, 25 and −7, −12, for example;

(b)   *Common fractions* (or *vulgar fractions*) are numbers like $\frac{1}{2}$, $\frac{6}{8}$, $\frac{3}{5}$, $\frac{9}{10}$, each representing a part of a whole number;

(c)   *Decimal fractions*, where the fractional part of the number is separated from the whole part by a dot called a *decimal point* as in $1\cdot237$, $2\cdot2$, $13\cdot986$;

(d)   *Directed* (or *signed*) *numbers* are preceded by a (+) or a (−) to indicate a positive quantity or a negative quantity respectively: +13, −21, +13, $-\frac{1}{3}$, −23568. The + sign is usually omitted for positive numbers;

(e)   *Indexed numbers* are shown as a number raised to a power. For example, the indexed number 3^3 represents $3 \times 3 \times 3$, and 10^2 represents 10×10;

(f)   *Standard form* occurs frequently in computing (see floating point) and is a representation which combines decimal numbers with indexed numbers:

$$7\cdot5 \times 10^5, 3\cdot98 \times 10^{-5}$$

(g)   *Real numbers*. In computer studies, sets of numbers are often given an overall classification depending on whether they are exclusively integer values or may contain fractional numbers. The latter are called *real* numbers. Thus the following numbers are all classed as *real* even though the list contains some integer values:

$$13\cdot62, -175\cdot3, 9\cdot0, 63\cdot01, -202\cdot00, 0\cdot1472$$

The following sections in this chapter will examine the ways in which arithmetic operations are performed on numbers represented in these various forms. It will be assumed that the reader is familiar with arithmetic operations on signed integers and fractions, so these will be given only a cursory treatment. Particular emphasis will be placed on those representations and operations relevant to computer studies and therefore most likely to be unfamiliar. However, it is important to understand the basis of the numbering system that we normally use and its relation to other numbering systems, and this will be discussed first.

The denary numbering system

The numbering system with which we are most familiar is the *denary* system which is based on the number ten. In common with other positional notations for representing numbers, the denary system uses only a small set of symbols for representing a number of any size; the positions of the symbols within the number determine their precise value. In the denary system, ten different symbols are used: 0, 1, 2, 3, 4, 5, 6, 7, 8, and 9. Thus a number such as 4293_{10} (the subscript$_{10}$ indicates denary) is an abbreviated way of representing the values, expressed in three different ways, in Table 26.1.

The number 10^3 is in *index notation* and represents 10 $\times$ 10 $\times$ 10 or 1000; the number 10 is called the base and 3 is the *index*. This nota-

4 thousands	+	2 hundreds	+	9 tens	+	3 units
4×10^3	+	2×10^2	+	9×10^1	+	3×10^0
4000	+	200	+	90	+	3

Table 26.1. *4293_{10} expressed in different ways*

tion will be given further treatment later. Using index notation, Table 26.2 shows how the value of a digit is related to its position within the number.

millions	hundred thousands	ten thousands	thousands	hundreds	tens	units
10^6	10^5	10^4	10^3	10^2	10^1	10^0
			4	2	9	3

Table 26.2. *Index notation to represent positional or place value*

(Note that any number raised to the power 0 is 1: $10^0=1$, $2^0=1$, $8^0=1$.)

A numbering system such as binary is based on the same principles except the base is 2 and the only symbols used are 0 and 1 (The binary and octal (base 8) numbering systems are explained in Chapter 20). Thus the binary number 1011_2 represents:

$$1 \times 2^3 + 0 \times 2^2 + 1 \times 2^1 + 1 \times 2^0 = 11_{10}$$

Multiplication by the base results in the number being shifted one place to the left, with a zero filling the rightmost digit position. Table 26.3 illustrates this with three examples.

4293_{10}	$\times$	10_{10}	$=$	42930_{10}	denary
1011_2	$\times$	10_2 (i.e. 2_{10})	$=$	10110_2	binary
453_8	$\times$	10_8 (i.e. 8_{10})	$=$	4530_8	octal

Table 26.3. *Multiplication by the bases 10, 2 and 8*

Division by the base shifts the number to the right, as the examples in Table 26.4 show.

430_{10}	$\div$	10_{10}	$=$	43_{10}	denary
1100_2	$\div$	10_2	$=$	110_2	binary
330_8	$\div$	10_8	$=$	33_8	octal

Table 26.4. *Division by the bases 10, 2 and 8*

Addition and subtraction of signed integers

When two or more numbers are added together, the result is called the *sum* of the numbers; the *difference* of two numbers results when one is subtracted from the other. A list of numbers to be added are written one above the other with every digit in its correct column: 1234 + 567 + 82 + 307 is written as

```
      1 2 3 4
        5 6 7
          8 2
  +     3 0 7
      2 1 9 0
```

The sum of the numbers is 2190. The addition is performed by first adding the digits in the units column, followed by the tens column and so on.

Another way of performing the same addition is by splitting the addition into a number of stages as indicated by the brackets:

$$(((1234 + 567) + 82) + 307)$$

In other words, find the sum of the first two numbers, add it to the third number and then add the last number to this sum, as shown on the right.

```
      1 2 3 4
  +     5 6 7
      1 8 0 1
  +       8 2
      1 8 8 3
  +     3 0 7
      2 1 9 0
```

Though this might seem like a rather laborious method for performing such a simple task, this is the way a computer would perform the calculation; it is easier for a computer to add complete numbers in pairs rather than adding the separate digits of several numbers as we do when performing such calculations manually. (This is explained in Chapter 22 on Computer Logic).

To find the difference of two numbers, again the numbers are written with the digits in each number aligned correctly. Starting at the units column, each pair of digits is subtracted. Thus the subtraction 397 − 245 is written as

The difference of the numbers is 152.

Where a digit in the second number exceeds the corresponding digit in the first number, as in 356 − 64, then the method used is to 'borrow' 10 from the adjacent digit to the left, thus

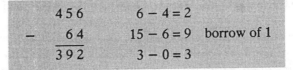

Another way of considering a subtraction is by regarding it as the addition of a negative quantity:

$$456 - 64 = 456 + (- 64)$$

This has the merit of dispensing with the need to perform subtraction at all, but what is needed is a method of representing negative numbers which takes advantage of this. Such a representation exists and is called the *complement* of a positive number. Suppose that the magnitude of the numbers being considered is less than 1000 (this is called the *modulus*). To calculate the complement of a number in this range, it is subtracted from 1000, the modulus. For example, the complement of 420 is (1000 − 420) = 580. Thus in ten's complement form, modulus 1000, the number −420 is represented as 580. Similarly, the number − 64 would be represented as (1000 − 64) = 936.

Now suppose that the same subtraction, 456 − 64, is to be performed using complement arithmetic. The subtraction now requires the addition of the complement of 64 (936) thus

$$
\begin{array}{r}
456 \\
+ \quad 936 \\
\hline
1392
\end{array}
$$

The final answer is given by neglecting the leading 1 (representing 1000) from the answer. Thus, once negative numbers have been converted into their complement forms, arithmetic operations involving combinations of addition and subtraction need only use addition. For manual arithmetic this is not too much of an advantage, but for computer arithmetic it is very important for two reasons:

(i)   It reduces the amount of circuitry required in the ALU and control unit; not only does it mean that a single type of circuit is required for addition and subtraction, but also, as will be shown shortly, the functions of multiplication and division often use addition circuits.

(ii)   Calculation of the complement of a binary number is much simpler than that for a denary number. For example, to find the complement of the number 6 in binary (0110_2), assuming a 4-bit wordlength (in other words, the modulus is $2^4 = 16$), only two simple steps are required:

(a)   invert each bit;

(b)   add 1_2.

Thus the complement of 0110_2 is $1001_2 + 1_2 = 1010_2$. This is now the two's complement of 6 and represents -6. Two's complement arithmetic is explained in Chapter 21.

Multiplication and division of signed integers

The *product* of two numbers results when they are multiplied together. For example, the product of 432 and 102 would be calculated as shown below

	4 3 2	multiplicand	
×	1 0 2	multiplier	
	8 6 4	(2 × 432)	1st partial product
	0 0 0 0	(0 × 4320)	2nd partial product
+	4 3 2 0 0	(1 × 43200)	3rd partial product
	4 4 0 6 4		Complete product

Note that the multiplication does not take place in one step. Instead the process is broken down into a series of simpler procedures. Starting with the rightmost digit of the multiplier, the multiplicand is multiplied by each digit of the multiplier. Each multiplication results in a partial product. Successive partial products are written one place further to the left than the previous one to allow for the magnitude of the multiplying digit. Note that multiplication by 0 gives 0000 for the second partial product, and normally this would not be written down. The final product is the sum of the partial products.

Computers frequently perform the calculation in much the same way. The main difference between the scheme shown above and the way a computer might manage the same calculation is that the partial products would be accumulated as the calculation progressed, rather than leaving the addition of the partial products until they had all been calculated. Another difference lies in the nature of the binary system that the computer would be using for the calculation: since both numbers would be in binary form, consisting only of 1's and 0's, calculation of partial products is tremendously simplified. The example above illustrates this point. Where the multiplying digit is 0, the partial product is 0; where the digit is 1, the partial product is merely the multiplicand shifted the appropriate number of places left. Using the example above (remembering that the computer would be working in binary, of course) a computer's multiplication procedure might be:

(i)   Determine the first partial product, p1.

$$p1 = 2 \times 432 = 864$$

(ii)   Add the first partial product to a register, A (initially containing 0) to be used for accumulating the partial products.

$$A = 0 + p1 = 864$$

(iii) Shift the multiplicand, M, left.

$$M = 4320$$

(iv)   Determine the second partial product, p2.

$$p2 = 0 \times 4320 = 0000$$

(v)   Add this to the accumulator register.

$$A = 864 + p2 = 864$$

(vi)   Shift the multiplicand left.

$$M = 43200$$

(vii) Determine the third partial product, p3.

$$p3 = 1 \times 43200 = 43200$$

(viii) Add this to the accumulator register.

$$A = 864 + 43200 = 44064$$

(ix)   Stop

Using this type of process, there is no necessity for using multiplication at all: the only processes required are shifting and adding. Though many microprocessors still use this scheme, most modern computers have special circuitry specifically for multiplication to improve processing speed.

A problem in division, such as $195 \div 15$, is usually tackled as shown below.

$$
\begin{array}{r}
13 \\
15\overline{)195} \\
\underline{150} \\
45 \\
\underline{45} \\
00
\end{array}
$$

$19(5) \div 15(0)$ =	1 remainder 4	...(1)
150×1 =	150	...(2)
45 =	$195 - 150$	...(3)
$45 \div 15$ =	3 remainder 0	...(4)

195 is called the *dividend*, 15 is the *divisor* and the result, 13, is called the *quotient*.

The process involves the following steps:

(1)   The leftmost digit of the divisor is aligned with the leftmost digit of the dividend. Thus the divisor in this case is being treated as if it were a factor of ten greater, that is, 150.

(2)   Comparison of the dividend, 195, with the divisor, 150 gives the first quotient digit of 1, representing ten 15's.

(3)   The previous two steps have established that there are at least ten 15's in 195. The process is now repeated with the remainder after 150 has been subtracted from the dividend. This remainder is 45.

(4)   Since there are exactly three 15's in 45, and there are no more digits of the dividend to consider, the final quotient has been determined.

This familiar process is the basis for a method used by many computers for performing integer division. This process is summarised as follows:

(i)   Align the leftmost digits of the divisor and dividend.

(ii)   Subtract the divisor from the dividend: $195 - 150$.

(iii) If the result is not negative, continue to subtract the divisor from the remainder. The current quotient digit is the number of successful subtractions performed. For the example in Figure 26.7, the second subtraction, $45 - 150$, would terminate this stage with a quotient digit of 1.

(iv)   Shift the divisor right and use the remainder as the new dividend.

(v)   Repeat stages (ii) - (iv) until all digits in the dividend have been used. In the example, 45 would be shifted left to give 450; three successful subtractions of 150 are possible, giving a second quotient digit of 3; all digits of the dividend will then have been used.

To illustrate the process further, suppose that a computer is required to perform the division $138 \div 6$. The annotated Table 26.5 shows the steps involved.

Action	Dividend	Divisor	Remainder	Quotient digit
	138	6	138	—
Align leftmost digits	138	600		
Subtract			−462	0
Restore remainder	138	600	138	
Shift divisor right	138	060	138	
Subtract divisor	138	060	78	
Subtract divisor	138	060	18	
Subtract divisor	138	060	−42	2
Restore remainder	138	060	18	
Shif divisor right	138	006	18	
Subtract divisor	138	006	12	
Subtract divisor	138	006	6	
Subtract divisor	138	006	0	
Subtract divisor	138	006	−6	3
Stop				

Table 26.5. *Stages in computer division $138 \div 6$*

Note that the only operations required are those of subtraction and shifting. The multiple subtractions shown are not necessary when working in binary. Each subtraction will give either a quotient digit of 1 or 0, and the remainder will either be positive or negative respectively. Remember also that since subtraction may be performed by addition of the complement, division can also be performed by adding and shifting operations exclusively.

Thus all the basic arithmetic operations of addition, subtraction, multiplication and division are possible using only adding and shifting functions.

Numbers in standard index form

When a decimal number, whether an integer or a fraction, is represented as the product of a number between 1 and 10 and a power of 10, it is said to be in standard index form. Numbers in standard index form having a magnitude greater than or equal to 1 have a positive integer index. For example, 7×10^2 and $3 \cdot 34 \times 10^3$ are both greater than 1. Fractions, that is numbers with magnitude less than 1, have a negative integer index. Thus $2 \cdot 35 \times 10^{-1}$ and 463×10^{-5} represent fractions.

To convert a decimal number into standard index form:

(i)   move the decimal point so that it is immediately to the right of the first non-zero digit;

(ii)   count the number of places the decimal point has been moved;

(iii) use this number as the index, with the sign determined as follows: if the point was moved left, the index is positive; if the point was moved right, the sign is negative; if the point was not moved at all, then the index is zero.

The following examples illustrate the process.

$289 \cdot 7$	$=$	$2 \cdot 897 \times 10^2$	point moved 2 places left
$0 \cdot 00567$	$=$	$5 \cdot 67 \times 10^{-3}$	point moved 3 places right
$8 \cdot 44$	$=$	$8 \cdot 44 \times 10^0$	point moved 0 places

To convert a number from standard form into normal decimal representation:

(i)   move the decimal point the number of places indicated by the index of the number in standard index form;

(ii)   if the index is positive, move the point right; if the index is negative, move the point left; if the index is zero, the point is not moved.

The following examples illustrate the process.

$3 \cdot 67 \times 10^1$	$=$	$36 \cdot 7$	point moved 1 place right
$7 \cdot 025 \times 10^{-3}$	$=$	$0 \cdot 007025$	point moved 3 places left
$9 \cdot 5 \times 10^0$	$=$	$9 \cdot 5$	point not moved

Numbers output from computers are frequently presented in standard index form, but using the letter 'E' to separate the decimal part of the number (usually called the *mantissa*) from the index (usually called the *exponent*). For instance, a computer might display the result of a calculation as

$$-4 \cdot 365982E+07$$

which means

$$-4 \cdot 365982 \times 10^7 = -43659820$$

This form of representation is used extensively in computers for the internal representation of numbers, usually when arithmetic operations are required to be performed on real numbers. (This is explained in the section on 'floating point' in Chapter 21).

The procedures for performing arithmetic operations on standard index numbers are explained in the following sections.

Addition and subtraction

To add two numbers expressed in mantissa and exponent form, the following steps are required:

(i)   Adjust the position of the decimal point in the mantissa of one of the numbers(usually the smaller of the two) to make its exponent the same as that of the other number.

(ii)   Add the mantissas of the two numbers.

(iii) If necessary, adjust the result to put it into standard index form.

As an illustration, consider the addition of $2 \cdot 365 \times 10^1$ and $9 \cdot 978 \times 10^2$.

(i)   To make the exponent of $2 \cdot 365 \times 10^1$ the same as that of the other number, move the point one place to the left in the mantissa and add 1 to the exponent, thus

$$2 \cdot 365 \times 10^1 = 0 \cdot 2365 \times 10^2$$

(ii)   Add the mantissa of the numbers, as shown below.

$$
\begin{array}{r}
9 \cdot 978 \\
+ \quad 0 \cdot 2365 \\
\hline
10 \cdot 2145 \\
\end{array}
$$

The answer is $10 \cdot 2145 \times 10^2$

(iii)   The answer is no longer in standard index form. The answer in the required form is therefore

$1 \cdot 02145 \times 10^3$

The process of subtraction is identical to that of addition except for step (ii) in which the mantissas of the numbers are subtracted.

Multiplication and division

The procedure for the multiplication of two numbers in standard index form is:

(i)   multiply the mantissas;

(ii)   add the exponents;

(iii)   if necessary, put the result into standard form.

Thus, for the numbers $1 \cdot 42 \times 10^2$ and $8 \cdot 92 \times 10^3$ the product would be given as

$$(1 \cdot 42 \times 8 \cdot 92) \times 10^{(2+3)} \quad = \quad 12 \cdot 6664 \times 10^5$$
$$= \quad 1 \cdot 26664 \times 10^6$$

Where the signs of the mantissas and/or the exponents of the numbers are mixed, the same rules apply, as the next example shows.

$$(-1 \cdot 42 \times 10^2) \times (8 \cdot 92 \times 10^{-3}) \quad = \quad (-1 \cdot 42 \times 8 \cdot 92) \times 10^{(2-3)}$$
$$= \quad -12 \cdot 6664 \times 10^{-1}$$
$$= \quad -1 \cdot 26664 \times 10^0$$

With division, the mantissas are divided and the exponents are subtracted, as shown below.

$$(3 \cdot 74 \times 10^4) \div (8 \cdot 32 \times 10^2) \quad = \quad (3 \cdot 74 \div 8 \cdot 32) \times 10^{(4-2)}$$
$$= \quad 0 \cdot 4495 \times 10^2$$
$$= \quad 4 \cdot 495 \times 10^1$$

A further example is provided below.

$$(5 \cdot 62 \times 10^{-3} \div (1 \cdot 45 \times 10^{-2}) \quad = \quad (5 \cdot 62 \div -1 \cdot 45) \times 10^{(-3-(-2))}$$
$$= \quad -3 \cdot 876 \times 10^{-1}$$

Errors in calculations

In real life the numbers that we deal with are always approximate to some degree. Any physical measurement depends on the accuracy of the measuring instrument, and it is important to be aware of the limitations of the measuring device being used. For example, the accuracy of a measurement obtained from a ruler is dependent on the accuracy with which the ruler was constructed and how accurately it can be read. A measurement of 234 millimetres implies that the measurement could have been anywhere between $233 \cdot 5$ and $234 \cdot 5$ millimetres, assuming that the millimetre scale itself is accurate.

Where calculations using approximate figures are cumulative, as in $23 \cdot 6 + 556 \cdot 25 - 99 \cdot 7$, errors in the individual numbers could conceivably accumulate to give an answer with an unacceptably large error component. In order to exercise control over the accuracy of calculations, and to have confidence in the answers produced, it is necessary to know something about the errors implicit in individual numbers and how these errors combine during arithmetical operations.

This is particularly relevant to computer arithmetic where it is not always possible to represent numbers exactly. The following sections show how the effects of errors in numbers used in computations can be analysed, and in particular how this is related to arithmetic operations in computers.

Absolute errors

The absolute error in a number is the exact value of the error. For example, if the cost of a litre of petrol is 37p and a customer puts $16 \cdot 3$ litres into his car, the total cost should be $603 \cdot 1$ p. If customer is charged £$6 \cdot 03$, the absolute error is $0 \cdot 1$ p. In general, however, the absolute error is not known; instead the maximum value of the absolute error modulus is given or can be deduced. The absolute error modulus is the magnitude of the absolute error in a number. For example, given that the number $24 \cdot 63$ is correct to four significant digits (or two decimal places in this case) the exact number could have been anywhere in the range $24 \cdot 625$ to $24 \cdot 635$.

The maximum absolute error modulus is therefore $\pm 0 \cdot 005$ or $\pm 0 \cdot 5 \times 10^{-2}$.

Suppose that a certain computer is only capable of storing numbers to an accuracy equivalent (in binary) to seven places. It must be assumed when performing calculations that the maximum absolute error modulus for any number stored in this computer is $\pm 0 \cdot 5 \times 10^{-7}$. Absolute error, a, may be defined mathematically as follows:

$$a = A* - A$$

where $A*$ represents the exact value of a number, and A represents the approximate value of the number.

The absolute error modulus is shown as $|a|$, where the vertical bars indicate the magnitude of the enclosed symbol.

Relative errors

Sometimes it is convenient to express the magnitude of an error in an approximate value as the ratio between the absolute error modulus and the magnitude of the number itself. This is called a relative error and is calculated by dividing the absolute error modulus by the magnitude of the exact value:

$$r = \left| \frac{a}{A*} \right|$$

However, it frequently happens that the exact value is not known, only the approximate value, and so quite often the relative error is given by

$$r = \left| \frac{a}{A} \right| \text{ which is generally accurate enough for most purposes.}$$

For example, the maximum relative error in the number 239·27 , assuming that the number is correct to two decimal places, is given by

$$r = \frac{0 \cdot 005}{239 \cdot 27} = 0 \cdot 0000208 \text{ or } 2 \times 10^{-5} \text{ approximately.}$$

Relative errors are useful in determining absolute errors in calculations involving multiplication and division.

Errors in addition and subtraction

When a number of numbers are added, the maximum absolute error modulus in the sum is found by adding the individual errors in the numbers. The same rule also applies when numbers are subtracted. If the absolute errors associated with numbers A, B, C, D are a, b, c, d respectively, then the maximum error in the sum of these numbers is a + b + c + d.

Example 1

Suppose that the internal representation of numbers in a certain computer allows a maximum accuracy of the equivalent of four decimal places. The following calculation is to be performed on four numbers, A, B, C, D stored in memory: $A + B + C - D$. No matter what the value of these numbers, the absolute errors associated with each of them will have a maximum value of $0 \cdot 5 \times 10^{-4}$. Thus, when the calculation is performed, the maximum absolute error in the result will be the sum of the individual errors in the numbers, that is,

$$0 \cdot 5 \times 10^{-4} + 0 \cdot 5 \times 10^{-4} + 0 \cdot 5 \times 10^{-4} + 0 \cdot 5 \times 10^{-4}$$

$$= 4 \times (0 \cdot 5 \times 10^{-4}) = 2 \times 10^{-4}$$

Example 2

Suppose that the answer to a calculation involving the addition of 1000 numbers must be accurate to two decimal places. Given this condition, it is possible to determine the minimum accuracy required for each number used in the calculation. The reasoning is as follows:

(i)   The absolute error modulus in the individual numbers will be magnified by a factor of 1000 in the answer.

(ii)   If the numbers were accurate to four decimal places, then the error in the answer would be

$$1000 \times (0 \cdot 5 \times 10^{-4}) = \frac{1000 \times 0 \cdot 5}{10000} = \frac{0 \cdot 5}{10} = 0 \cdot 5 \times 10^{-1}$$

Thus the maximum error modulus could be $0 \cdot 05$, and therefore unacceptably large.

(iii) Numbers accurate to 5 decimal places could combine to give a maximum error of

$$1000 \times (0 \cdot 5 \times 10^{-5}) = 0 \cdot 5 \times 10^{-2} = 0 \cdot 005 \text{ in the answer.}$$

This satisfies the accuracy requirements for the calculation.

Errors in multiplication and division

The relative error in the product of two approximate numbers is the sum of the relative errors in the numbers. For example, if $12 \cdot 36$ and $52 \cdot 2$ are to be multiplied, the accuracy of the product could be specified as follows:

$$\text{Relative error in } 12 \cdot 36 = \frac{0 \cdot 5 \times 10^{-2}}{12 \cdot 36} = 0 \cdot 4 \times 10^{-3}$$

$$\text{Relative error in } 52 \cdot 2 = \frac{0 \cdot 5 \times 10^{-1}}{52 \cdot 2} = 0 \cdot 95 \times 10^{-3}$$

$$\text{Relative error in product} = 0 \cdot 4 \times 10^{-3} + 0 \cdot 95 \times 10^{-3} = 1 \cdot 35 \times 10^{-3}$$

Using $r = \left| \dfrac{a}{A} \right|$ for the relative error, where $r = 1 \cdot 35 \times 10^{-3}$ and $A = 12 \cdot 6 \times 52 \cdot 2$,

Absolute error in product is then as shown below.

$$= (1 \cdot 35 \times 10^{-3}) \times (12 \cdot 36 \times 52 \cdot 2)$$
$$= 1 \cdot 35 \times 10^{-3} \times 645 \cdot 192$$
$$= 0 \cdot 871$$

Thus the answer could be expressed as $645 \cdot 192 \pm 0 \cdot 871$ or, keeping the answer to 2 decimal places,

$$645 \cdot 19 \pm 0 \cdot 88.$$

This is equivalent to saying that the exact answer could be anywhere between $644 \cdot 31$ and $646 \cdot 07$. The relative error in a quotient is the sum of the relative errors in the numerator and denominator.

With this final relationship it is now possible to determine the accuracy of any arithmetical process involving combinations of addition, subtraction, multiplication and division.

Example 3

The following calculation is to be performed on numbers which are accurate to 3 decimal places:

$$\frac{(2 \cdot 603 + 19 \cdot 255)}{0 \cdot 376 \times 5 \cdot 123}$$

The accuracy of the answer is to be determined. The calculation is performed as follows.

Maximum absolute error in numerator		$(2 \cdot 603 + 19 \cdot 255)$
	$=$	$0 \cdot 5 \times 10^{-3} + 0 \cdot 5 \times 10^{-3}$
	$=$	1×10^{-3}
Relative error in numerator	$=$	$\dfrac{1 \times 10^{-3}}{(2 \cdot 603 + 19 \cdot 255)}$
	$=$	$\dfrac{1 \times 10^{-3}}{21 \cdot 858}$
	$=$	$0 \cdot 000045$
Relative error in denominator	$=$	$\dfrac{0 \cdot 5 \times 10^{-3}}{0 \cdot 376} + \dfrac{0 \cdot 5 \times 10^{-3}}{5 \cdot 123}$
	$=$	$0 \cdot 0014$
Relative error in quotient	$=$	$0 \cdot 000045 + 0 \cdot 0014$
	$=$	$0 \cdot 001445$
Approximate answer	$=$	$\dfrac{21 \cdot 858}{1 \cdot 9262} = 11 \cdot 3477$

Hence the answer is $11 \cdot 3477 \pm 0 \cdot 001445$

Exercises

Addition and subtraction

1. Perform the following additions as they would be performed by a computer, that is, in stages adding only two numbers at each stage:

    (a) $13 + 279 + 67$

    (b) $32 \cdot 7 + 169 \cdot 0 + 72 \cdot 350 + 0 \cdot 732$

    (c) $73 \cdot 88 + 96 \cdot 2312 + 3 \cdot 142 + 7 \cdot 79$

2. Convert the following numbers into ten's complement form:

    $$12, 127, 3, 99, 100$$

3. Perform the subtractions listed below using addition of the complement. Check your answers by performing the calculations in the normal way.

    (a) $65 - 37$

    (b) $72 - 6$

    (c) $-19 + 123$

    (d) $35 - 74$

    (e) $-17 - 425$

(Note that if the answer is a negative number, its magnitude may be checked by taking its complement).

Multiplication and division

1. Find the products of the pairs of denary numbers listed below by means of a sequence of shifting and adding operations. At each step in the calculations show the value of the partial product and the multiplicand.

    (a)   318 and 72

    (b)   763 and 101

    (c)   11,011 and 110

(Notice that the last example does not require any multiplications at all, because the only digits used are 1's and 0's: this is the basis of binary multiplication).

2. Perform the following divisions using shifting and subtracting operations. Set each calculation out in the form of a table such as that shown in the text to illustrate the process.

    (a) $144 \div 24$

    (b) $72 \div 18$

    (c) $255 \div 15$

    (d) $197 \div 37$

Standard index form

1. Convert the following numbers into standard index form.

    $$123, 733 \cdot 5, -33 \cdot 34, 0 \cdot 0012, 5 \cdot 34, -0 \cdot 2234$$

2. Convert the following indexed numbers to standard index form. (Remember that the E in the numbers is read as "ten to the power".)

    $$0 \cdot 2301E+03 \quad -22 \cdot 312E+05 \quad 123 \cdot 340E-02 \quad -0 \cdot 3124E-05$$

3. Perform the following additions and subtractions using the numbers converted to standard index form. The answers should also be converted to standard index form.

    (a) $234 + 1234$

    (b) $0 \cdot 0035 + 0 \cdot 1203$

    (c) $34 \cdot 22 + 0 \cdot 014$

    (d) $166 - 17 \cdot 2$

    (e) $-0 \cdot 0157 + 0 \cdot 349$

4. Perform the following multiplications and divisions using the numbers converted to standard index form. Convert the answers to standard index form where necessary.

    (a) $32 \cdot 7 \times 5 \cdot 91$

    (b) $176 \times 15 \cdot 3$

    (c) $0 \cdot 003 \times 45 \cdot 2$

    (d) $0 \cdot 123 \times 0 \cdot 00566$

    (e) $67 \div 2 \cdot 2$

(f) $243 \div 19$

(g) $5 \cdot 03 \div 0 \cdot 12$

(h) $0 \cdot 04 \div 0 \cdot 00017$

Errors in calculations

1. State the maximum absolute error modulus for each of the numbers below. Assume that the numbers are accurate to the number of decimal places shown.

$$23 \cdot 34, 678 \cdot 1, 778, -0 \cdot 0023, 0 \cdot 112, -0 \cdot 3$$

2. Determine the relative error for the numbers listed above and express the answer in standard index form.

3. Find the maximum absolute errors in the following calculations:

(a) $13 \cdot 2 + 177 \cdot 33 + 67 \cdot 41$

(b) $193 \cdot 97 - 46 \cdot 66$

(c) $220 \cdot 3 - 1089 \cdot 22 + 338 \cdot 4 - 18 \cdot 67$

4. Determine the accuracy with which the calculations below may be performed.

(a) $321 \cdot 712 \times 63 \cdot 101$

(b) $10 \cdot 22 - 18 \cdot 9 \times 0 \cdot 15$

(c) $568 \cdot 44 \div 18 \cdot 9$

(d) $90 \cdot 8 + \dfrac{123 \cdot 5 \times 3}{32} - 32$

Chapter 27
Algebra

Introduction

In algebra the processes of arithmetic are described in general terms using letters to represent numbers. Algebra is invaluable in a great number of scientific disciplines, including physics, chemistry, electronics and computer science. Many computer languages contain instructions closely resembling algebraic expressions, and a knowledge of algebra is an essential prerequisite to understanding and constructing computer programs.

Algebraic notation

An algebraic *expression* is a generalisation of an arithmetic expression such as

$$15 \cdot 3 \times 6 \times (13 - 10) + \frac{17 \cdot 3}{9}$$

Letters are used in place of some or all of the numbers in the expression, but the normal rules of arithmetic still apply. An algebraic expression equivalent to the arithmetic expression above might be

$$pq(13 - b) + \frac{c}{d}$$

This algebraic expression has the same form as the arithmetic expression, but the letters represent any set of numbers rather than specific values. The letters used are often termed *variables*. By *substituting* values for the variables, the expression can be *evaluated*, that is, its numeric equivalent can be determined.

An algebraic expression consists of a number of *terms* separated by addition or subtraction operators, and each term contains a number of *factors* containing numbers and letters connected by multiplication and division operators. For example, the expression

$$a + bc - \frac{e}{f} + 16$$

has four terms, $a, bc, \dfrac{e}{f}$ and 16.

The first term contains only the single factor, a; the second term contains factor b and c connected by a multiplication operator (not usually shown but assumed to be there); the third term has factor e divided by factor f; the final term consists of the *constant* 16. Variables and constants are particular instances of factors.

Most, if not all, high level computer languages use variables to represent the contents of memory locations. In Pascal for instance, the statement x:=a+3; uses the variables x and a. The statement requires the value represented by a to be added to the constant 3 and the result transferred to the memory location represented by x.

Indexed variables such as p^3 or c^{-2} with constants as indices, also appear in algebraic expressions. In addition, however, the index itself may be a variable, term or expression:

$$x^i, \quad p^{xy}, \quad c^{j+3k}$$

Operator precedence

When numbers are assigned to the variables in an algebraic expression, so that it might be evaluated, there are rules of arithmetic operator precedence which determine how the evaluation should proceed. For example, in the expression $x + yz$ the multiplication of y and z must precede the addition operation. If the requirement was for the sum of x and y to be multiplied by z then the expression would be written $(x + y)z$ or $z(x+y)$.

The brackets indicate that the addition operation is to precede the multiplication. The order of operator precedence is as follows:

1.   Brackets.

2.   Exponentiation (raising to a power).

3.   Negation (e.g. -3)

4.   Multiplication and division

5.   Addition and subtraction

To illustrate these rules, consider the expression: $x(y + 3z)^{-3} - \dfrac{p}{qr}$

Given values for all of the variables, the expression would be evaluated as follows:

(i)   Evaluate $(y + 3z)$. The term $x(y + 3z)^{-3}$ contains an expression in brackets which must be evaluated first. Within this bracketed expression are two terms, y and $3z$; the latter term involves a multiplication and so $3z$ would be calculated first. The product of 3 and z would then be added to y.

(ii)   Evaluate $(y + 3z)^{-3}$. Since exponentiation has a higher precedence than multiplication, the value of the bracketed expression would be raised to the power -3.

(iii)   Evaluate $x(y + 3z)^{-3}$. Multiply result of last step by x to give the value of the first term.

(iv)

The second term, $\dfrac{p}{qr}$, could be regarded in two different ways, both giving the same answer but requiring different arithmetic operations. The term could be written in the following two equivalent forms:

$$\frac{p}{(qr)} \quad \text{or} \quad \left(\frac{\left(\frac{p}{q}\right)}{r}\right)$$

In the first form the multiplication in the brackets would be performed before the division; the second form would involve the division of p by q first and this quotient would then be divided by r. Both methods would result in the same answer. The ambiguity results from the equal precedence of multiplication and division in algebra.

(v)   Evaluate

$$x(y + 3z)^{-3} - \frac{p}{qr}$$

Now that the two terms have been evaluated, the second can be subtracted from the first to give the final answer.

It is worth noting at this point that the order of operator precedence explained above generally applies also to arithmetic expressions in high level computer languages, but great care must be taken when writing such expressions. For instance, in Pascal statement such as

A:=P/Q*R   (/ is used for divide and * for multiply)

the expression on the right hand side of the := sign would be interpreted as

$$\frac{P}{Q} \times R \quad \text{and not} \quad \frac{P}{Q \times R}$$

This is because the expression is evaluated from left to right, causing the division to be performed before the multiplication. However, to ensure that the order of evaluation goes as expected, it is wise to include brackets; if the required expression was

$$\frac{P}{Q \times R}$$

the Pascal statement would be written

$$A := P/(Q*R) \text{ or } A := (P/Q)/R$$

Subscripts in algebra

The Greek letter $\sum$ (pronounced sigma) is frequently used in algebraic notation to represent the sum of a number of numbers. Thus the notation

$$\sum_{i=1}^{i=5} x_i$$

represents the sum of the five variables

$$x_1, x_2, x_3, x_4, \text{ and } x_5$$

In other words, it is the sum of any five numbers represented by these five variables. The integer 'subscripts' attached to the variables indicate that the variables have some link with each other, but apart from that they are like any other variables. A variable with a subscript that is itself a variable, such as x_i represents a range of variables, as illustrated above. The number of variables so represented is determined by the consecutive integer values which can be taken by the subscript; these subscript values are 1 to 5 in the example above.

Thus, for the numbers $12, 3 \cdot 3, -7, -9 \cdot 2, 21$, the notation

$$\sum_{i=1}^{i=5} x_i$$

represent $12 + 3 \cdot 3 + (-7) + (-9 \cdot 2) + 21$ and the variables x_1, x_2, x_3, x_4, x_5 would have, in this case, the values $12, 3 \cdot 3, -7, -9 \cdot 2, 21$ respectively.

Subscript notation is often used to define certain types of repetitive processes suited to computer processing. For example, the following algorithm (method of solution) uses subscript notation to define how to convert an 8-bit binary integer number to an equivalent denary integer. If the binary number is represented by the variables

$$a_7, \quad a_6, \quad a_5, \quad a_4, \quad a_3, \quad a_2, \quad a_1, \quad a_0,$$

then the denary number, N, is built up using an *iterative* (repetitive) process based on the relationship

$$N = a_i + 2N \quad \text{where } i = 6, 5, \ldots\ldots, 0 \text{ and } N = a_7 \text{ initially}$$

Note that this relationship is not to be viewed as an equation; it merely represents that successive values of N are calculated, each new value depending on the previous one. The process is best explained by means of an example. Suppose that the binary number to be converted to denary is 01010010_2 (82_{10}). Then

$$a_7 = 0; \; a_6 = 1; \; a_5 = 0; \; a_4 = 1; \; a_3 = 0; \; a_2 = 0; \; a_1 = 1; \; a_0 = 0;$$

To start the process, N is set to the value of $a_7 = 0$. A new value of N is then calculated using its current value:

$$N = a_6 + 2N = 1 + 2 \times 0 = 1$$

The process is repeated until all of the binary digits have been processed. The complete process is shown below.

N	$=$	a_7			$=$	0
N	$=$	$a_6 + 2N$	$=$	$1 + 0 \times 2$	$=$	1
N	$=$	$a_5 + 2N$	$=$	$0 + 2 \times 1$	$=$	2
N	$=$	$a_4 + 2N$	$=$	$1 + 2 \times 2$	$=$	5
N	$=$	$a_3 + 2N$	$=$	$0 + 2 \times 5$	$=$	10
N	$=$	$a_2 + 2N$	$=$	$0 + 2 \times 10$	$=$	20
N	$=$	$a_1 + 2N$	$=$	$1 + 2 \times 20$	$=$	41
N	$=$	$a_0 + 2N$	$=$	$0 + 2 \times 41$	$=$	82

Thus the final answer is 82.

Subscript notation occurs frequently in high level programming languages. In Pascal, for instance, the statement

X:=A[1] + 1

contains the subscripted variable A with subscript 1. This indicates that A represents a number of memory locations containing numbers, and these locations are called A[1], A[2], A[3], and so on. The statement makes reference to the first of these locations, A[1], the content of which is to be added to the constant 1 and the result stored in the location called X. The variable, A, is called an array and such variables are extremely useful in allowing reference to be made to a number of variables in a general manner.

Again the subscript may itself be a variable having a (previously assigned) integer value. Thus the statement

$$A[I]:=B*3 + D$$

refers to the particular element of the array, A, defined by the value of the subscript, I. Arrays are described in more detail in the Chapter 28.

Algebraic equations

Placing an equals sign between two algebraic expressions indicates that they have the same numeric value:

$$5x - 6 = 3 \quad \text{and} \quad 3y + 5 = y - 3$$

are both equations involving a single unknown variable. In each case the value or values of the variable for which the equation holds true may be determined by making the unknown the subject of the equation. This is achieved by applying a sequence of arithmetic operations to both sides of the equation until the variable alone is on the left hand side of the equals sign. For example, to solve the first equation ($5x - 6 = 3$) the steps would be as shown below

(i) add 6 to both sides:	$5x - 6 + 6 = 3 + 6$
	that is, $5x = 9$
(ii) divide both sides by 5:	$\dfrac{5x}{5} = \dfrac{9}{5}$
and the solution is	$x = 1 \cdot 8$

The solution to the second example ($3y + 5 = y - 3$) might proceed as follows.

(i) subtract 5 from both sides:	$3y + 5 - 5 = y - 3 - 5$
	that is, $3y = y - 8$
(ii) subtract y from both sides:	$3y - y = y - y - 8$
	that is, $2y = -8$
(iii) divide both sides by 2:	$y = -4$

The three examples which follow illustrate the procedures required for solving a variety of different equations with a single unknown.

Example 1: Solve $3(p - 3) = p + 2$

(i) Expand the brackets	$3p - 9$	$= p + 2$
(ii) Add 9	$3p$	$= p + 11$
(iii) Subtract p	$2p$	$= 11$
(iv) Divide by 2	p	$= 5 \cdot 5$

Example 2: Solve $\dfrac{2t}{6} + 7 = \dfrac{t}{4}$

(i) Subtract 7	$\dfrac{2t}{6}$	$= \dfrac{t}{4} - 7$
(ii) Subtract $\dfrac{t}{4}$	$\dfrac{2t}{6} - \dfrac{t}{4}$	$= -7$
(iii) Multiply by 6	$2t - \dfrac{6t}{4}$	$= -42$
(iv) Multiply by 4	$8t - 6t$	$= -168$
	$2t$	$= -168$
The solution is	t	$= -84$

Example 3: Solve for x, $3x + c = k(1 - 2x)$

(i) Remove the brackets	$3x + c = k - 2kx$
(ii) Add $2kx$ to get all terms containing x to one side	$3x + 2kx + c = k$
(iii) Subtract c	$3x + 2kx = k - c$
x is common to the terms $3x$ and $2kx$	$x(3 + 2k) = k - c$
(iv) Divide by terms in brackets	$x = \dfrac{k - c}{(3 + 2k)}$

In the final example, without knowing the value of k and c, it is impossible to determine a numeric value for x. However, when values for these are known, the value of x can be determined.

Transposition of formulae

As illustrated above, the subject of a formula is the single variable on one side of the equation. Transposing a formula means rearranging it so that a different variable is the subject of the formula. For example, in the equation of motion

$$s = \frac{1}{2} ft^2$$

the distance travelled, s, by an object is related to its acceleration, f, and the time duration, t. By making t its subject, the equation can be used to find how long it takes for an object to travel the distance s :

$$2s = ft^2$$

$$\frac{2s}{f} = t^2$$

Thus $t = \pm \sqrt{\dfrac{2s}{f}}$ and now t is the subject of the formula.

In general, the following guidelines will enable the subject of a formula to be changed:

1. Remove any roots by raising to the appropriate power.

2. Remove any fractions by multiplying each term by the common denominator.

3. Remove any brackets by multiplying out.

4. Bring all terms containing the subject variable to one side.

5. Where the subject occurs in more than one term, take it out as a common factor.

6. Isolate the subject by multiplying or dividing by factors.

7. Take a root if necessary.

The following three examples illustrate the process. The number of the rule being applied is given in brackets.

Example 1: Make x the subject of the formula $y = a - bx^2$

$$y = a - bx^2$$

$$-bx^2 = y - a \qquad (4)$$

$$x^2 = \frac{y-a}{-b} = \frac{a-y}{b} \qquad (6)$$

$$x = \pm\sqrt{\frac{a-y}{b}} \qquad (7)$$

Example 2: Make E the subject of the formula $V = \sqrt{\dfrac{2E}{M}}$

$$V = \sqrt{\frac{2E}{M}}$$

$$V^2 = \frac{2E}{M} \qquad (1)$$

$$V^2 M = 2E \qquad (6)$$

$$E = \frac{V^2 M}{2} \qquad (6)$$

Example 3: Make x the subject of the formula $y = (x + a)(x - a)$

$$y = (x + a)(x - a)$$

$$y = x^2 - xa + xa - a^2 = x^2 - a^2 \qquad (3)$$

$$x^2 = y + a^2 \qquad (4)$$

$$x = \pm\sqrt{\left(y + a^2\right)} \qquad (7)$$

Exercises

Algebraic equations

1. Solve the following equations.

(i) $3x + 5 = 2$ (iv) $p - 3p/2 = 1/2$

(ii) $10s - 7 = 2s + 9$ (v) $3/x + 2/x = 1/4$

(iii) $6x/3 = 9$ (vi) $0 \cdot 3(3x + 2) = 0 \cdot 1(5 - x)$

2. Make the variable in brackets the subject of the equation.

(i) $v = u + at$ (t)

(ii) $1/u + 1/v = 1/f$ (f)

(iii) $y = (x - a)(x + a)$ (x)

(iv) $z = x - 3y$ (y)

(v) $c = \sqrt{\dfrac{E}{M}}$ (E)

Subscripts

1. Use subscripts and the summation (sigma) notation to represent the following:

(i)   The sum of 100 numbers.

(ii) The sum of the first 20 integers.

(iii) The sum of the squares of 25 numbers.

(iv) The sum of the squares of the integers from 25 to 35 inclusive.

2. Use the algorithm for binary to denary conversion to find the denary equivalents of the following binary numbers (denary value in brackets):

(i)   01101010   (106)

(ii) 00010101   (21)

(iii) 01000111   (71)

(iv) 11001101   (205)

Chapter 28
Tabular Data

Introduction

The idea of an *array* of data was introduced in the previous chapter, and it was shown that such a data structure is an important tool in computer programming. This chapter develops further the concept of an array and its relevance to data processing by computer.

Arrays

A data structure comprising a list of data items, such as numbers, is called an *array*. Algebraically, an array is usually defined as follows:

$$L_i \qquad i = 1,......,N$$

The array has the name, L, in this instance and the i subscript takes values from 1 to N, where N is an integer representing the number of values in the array. Thus, for the six values, 3,4,2,0,1,9, N=6 and

$$L_1 = 3; \quad L_2 = 4; \quad L_3 = 2; \quad L_4 = 0; \quad L_5 = 1; \quad L_6 = 9$$

This is called a one-dimensional array because it is a simple list of numbers in which any particular number can be referenced by a single subscript.

One-dimensional arrays

A one-dimensional array could be used to represent a list of student marks in a number of subjects, prices of a number of articles, heights of children, or in fact any collection of numbers which can be conveniently grouped together. For this reason, arrays are frequently used to represent data which are to be analysed statistically.

Arrays used in computer languages represent a set of consecutive memory locations. Array notation allows this area of memory to be referred to by a single variable. In a Pascal program, for instance, the declaration

```
ListNums    :array[1..20] of integer;
```

reserves 20 storage locations (or areas of memory capable of storing a single number) which are collectively know as ListNums. A subscript in brackets is used to specify which one of these 20 is being referenced at any time. Thus the notation ListNums[5] refers to the fifth element of the array, ListNums, in memory. In programs, a variable used for the subscript greatly facilitates processing operations on arrays. For example, in order to add 20 numbers held in the array, ListNums, in memory, the following Pascal code could be used:

```
for i:= 1 to 20 do S:= S + ListNums[i];
```

Here S is being used to accumulate the contents of the array elements and would initially be set to zero. The for statement sets the subscript i to an initial value of 1, and every time the statement following do is executed, increments i by 1 and again executes the statement; S:= S + ListNums[i] adds the specified array element to the running total, S, and stores the result back to S.

The sequence of processing is therefore

S = 0 + ListNums[1]
S = ListNums[1] + ListNums[2]
S = (ListNums[1] + ListNums[2]) + ListNums[3]
S = (ListNums[1] + ListNums[2] + ListNums[3]) + ListNums[4]

and so on until ListNums(20) is finally referenced.

If arrays were not implemented in the language then the addition would be effected by writing

S:= Num1 + Num2 + Num3 + Num4 + ... + Num20

where each number now has its own individual variable name and the numbers must be treated as individuals. This is obviously very unwieldy, and unworkable for large numbers (say 100 or more) of values.

Other languages such as C and COBOL have similar facilities for allowing the use of arrays.

Two-dimensional arrays

A table of information is an example of a two-dimensional array. A particular item in a table is referenced by its row and position within the row (or column). For example, Table 28.1 details features of four makes of removable media.

Media	Syquest	Olympus	Panasonic	Iomega
1 Price (£)	105	229	229	359
2 Price (£) per disk	17	7	20	15
3 Capacity (Mb)	230	230	650	1,000
4 Buffer size (k)	32	256	512	256
5 Seek time (ms)	13.5	27	92	12

Table 28.1. *Two-dimensional 5 × 4 array*

The Mb capacity figure (230) for the Olympus requires two 'co-ordinates': the row for capacity and the column for Olympus. If the table contained only a single column for Olympus then it would be an example of a one-dimensional array. Thus a two-dimensional array may be viewed as a set of one-dimensional arrays.

In array notation, the table could be represented by a single variable, M, with two subscripts, i (for the rows) and j (for the columns):

$$M_{i,j} \qquad i = 1,...,5$$
$$j = 1,...,4$$

The array is of size 5 by 4 (written 5 × 4), the size of arrays being defined as row × column. Thus, in Figure 28.1

$$M_{2,1} = 17, \ M_{4,1} = 32, \ M_{5,4} = 12$$

High level programming languages which allow one-dimensional arrays will almost invariably cater for two-dimensional arrays too. Again using Pascal as an example, the same two-dimensional array could be declared before use with the declaration

```
M    :array[1..5, 1..4] of integer;
```

which allocates storage space sufficient for the 20 elements (5 × 4) of array, M. Program statements which make reference to this array must use two subscripts to refer to a particular element. Thus M(3,2) makes reference to the second element in the third row.

Performing calculations on arrays

Suppose that a certain computer program for producing graphics on a monitor stores information about simple geometrical shapes in tabular form. Each point of a figure to be drawn is

stored in a table of *x-y*
co-ordinates.   These
co-ordinates give the
displacement of the
next point to be drawn
from the current posi-
tion of the cursor (not
just its absolute posi-
tion).   For example,
the rectangle in Figure
28.1 might be stored as detailed in Table 28.2.

Point	x	y
1	100	0
2	0	200
3	−100	0
4	0	−200

Table 28.2. *Co-ordinates for drawing rectangle*

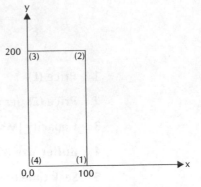

Figure 28.1. *Rectangle drawn from co-ordinates in Table 28.2*

A positive value indicates cursor movement right for
x and up for *y*; negative values mean move left for *x*
and down for *y*. By performing various calculations
on the co-ordinates, the original rectangle in Figure
28.1 can be transformed in a number of different
ways.

The following examples assume that the original rectangle's co-ordinate values are stored in the
two-dimensional array, A, of dimension 4 × 2,
shown in Table 28.3. The transformed co-ordinates
will be stored in the array B, also 4 × 2.

i \ j	1	2
1	100	0
2	0	200
3	−100	0
4	0	−200

Table 28.3. *Co-ordinates in array A*

Each of the transformation illustrations shows the original rectangle filled grey, for
comparison.

Scaling

In this transformation, Figure 28.2 (on the next page) retains the
original shape but is drawn either larger or smaller depending on
a *scaling factor*. The new co-ordinate values are calculated by
multiplying each of them by a constant scaling factor. For example, to double the dimensions of the figure, each co-ordinate
value in array A (Table 28.3) would be multiplied by a scaling
factor of 2,

$$B_{i,j} = 2 \times A_{i,j}$$
$$i = 1,..4$$
$$j = 1,2$$

i \ j	1	2
1	200	0
2	0	400
3	−200	0
4	0	−400

Table 28.4. *Array B with scaling factor of 2*

and storing the resulting co-ordinates in array B (Table 28.4).

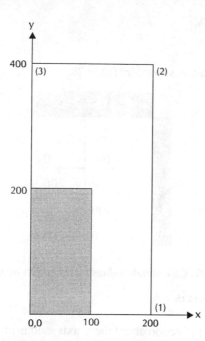

Figure 28.2. *Original rectangle scaled by a factor of 2*

Multiplication by a value smaller than 1 would reduce the size of the rectangle.

Reflection about the x-axis

As Figure 28.3 shows, when the rectangle is reflected about the x-axis the size and shape of the figure remain exactly the same but it is a mirror image of the original.

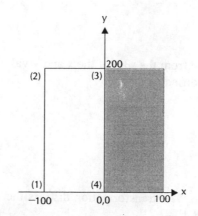

Figure 28.3. *Original rectangle reflected about the x-axis*

This transformation is effected by multiplying each x-ordinate by −1 as follows.

$$B_{i,j} = (-1) \times A_{i,j}$$
$$i = 1,..4$$

Array B then contains the values shown in Table 28.5.

j	1	2
i		
1	-100	0
2	0	200
3	100	0
4	0	-200

Table 28.5. *Co-ordinate values for reflection about x-axis*

Reflection about the y-axis

This has a similar effect to a reflection about the x-axis, and is produced by multiplying each y-ordinate by -1:

$$B_{i,2} = (-1) \times A_{i,2}$$
$$i = 1,..4$$

The x-ordinate is left as it is:

$$B_{i,1} = A_{i,1}$$
$$i = 1,..4$$

x-shear

Here the x-ordinate is formed from the sum of the x and y values, and the y value is unmodified:

$$B_{i,1} = A_{i,1} + A_{i,2}$$
$$i = 1,..4$$
$$B_{i,2} = A_{i,2}$$
$$i = 1,..4$$

The results are in Table 28.6. The transformation distorts the shape, as shown in Figure 28.4.

j	1	2
i		
1	100	0
2	200	200
3	-100	0
4	-200	-200

Table 28.6. *Co-ordinate values for x-shear*

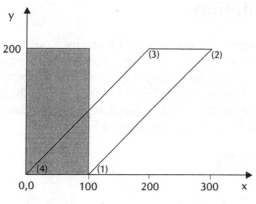

Figure 28.4. *x-shear on original rectangle*

y-shear

Similar to x-shear :

$$B_{i,2} = A_{i,1} + A_{i,2}$$
$$i = 1,...,5$$
$$B_{i,1} = A_{i,1}$$
$$i = 1,...,5$$

B now contains the values in Table 28.7, giving the shape shown in Figure 28.5.

i \ j	1	2
1	100	100
2	0	200
3	−100	−200
4	0	−200

Table 28.7. *Co-ordinate values for y-shear*

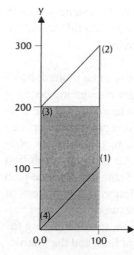

Figure 28.5. *Y-shear on original rectangle*

Linear interpolation

Graphics animation effects on computers are frequently produced by plotting sequences of picture 'frames' in rapid succession. As a very simple example, suppose that a program is required to 'animate' a single dot by making it appear to follow a curved path. An array is to be used to store a number of co-ordinates of points on the path, but the amount of memory available for this purpose is severely restricted. The table of co-ordinates to be plotted are in Table 28.8 and the plotting of the points is illustrated in Figure 28.6.

Position	x	y
1	200	100
2	400	225
3	600	400
4	800	625
5	1000	900

Table 28.8. *Moving dot co-ordinates*

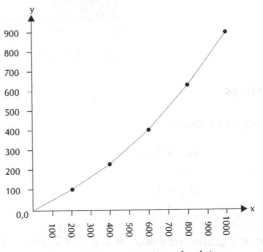

Figure 28.6. *Animation of a dot*

The animation effect would be achieved by displaying the dot at the first point, pausing briefly, erasing it, displaying it at the second point, pausing briefly, erasing it, and so on until the dot had been displayed at every co-ordinate in turn. This same principle could be used to animate any figure by using this repetitive process of drawing, erasing and moving.

With so few points at which the dot is to be plotted, however, the movement would not be very convincing because the gaps between the points are too large to give the illusion of a smooth movement. The effect could be improved by defining more points on the path, but memory constraints may make this impossible. An alternative solution is to calculate intermediate points (Table 28.9) on the path using *linear interpolation*. Interpolation is the process of calculating an intermediate value between two given values on a curve. In *linear* interpolation, the line joining the two points is assumed to be a straight line, and the interpolated point lies on this line.

Position	x	y
1	200	100
1a	300	163
2	400	225
2a	500	313
3	600	400
3a	700	513
4	800	625
4a	900	763
5	1000	900

Table 28.9. *Dot co-ordinates plus interpolated positions*

Suppose that we decided to calculate a single intermediate point mid-way between each of the values given on the curve, the new values would become those in Table 28.9. Figure 28.7 shows the plotted result.

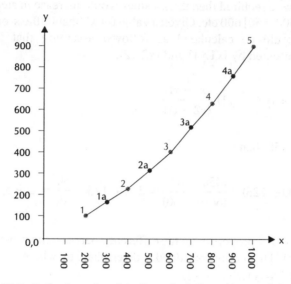

Figure 28.7. *Path of moving dot after calculation of interpolated points*

Positions 1a, 2a, 3a, 4a, are the calculated values and are marked on the graph. Each of these interpolated points has been calculated as follows:

    (i)   Take the two x-ordinate values between which the intermediate point is to be found.

    (ii)   Subtract these two values.

    (iii)   Halve the difference.

    (iv)   Add the difference to the first x value.

    (v)   Do the same with the y-ordinates.

So, to interpolate linearly between two points where $x2 = 400$, $y2 = 225$ and $x3 = 600$, $y3 = 400$, the calculation would be:

$$x' = 400 + (600 - 400)/2 = 400 + 100 = 500$$
$$y' = 225 + (400 - 225)/2 = 225 + 87 \cdot 5 = 313 \text{ approx.}$$

where x' and y' represent the co-ordinates of the calculated point between the points (400, 225) and (600, 400).

The interpolated point need not be mid-way between the other two. Perhaps it may be necessary to calculate several intermediate points in order to make the movement sufficiently smooth. Generally, with linear interpolation, one of the ordinates (the x-ordinate, for instance) is known, and the other ordinate is to be calculated. In our example, if three intermediate points were required then the x values would increase in steps of 50: 200 [250, 300, 350] 400 [450, 500, 550] 600 etc. Given a value for x′ (that is, the x-ordinate of the intermediate point) y′ could be calculated as follows, assuming that the two enclosing co-ordinates are represented by (x1,y1) and (x2,y2):

$$y' = y1 + (y2 - y1)\frac{(x' - x1)}{(x2 - x1)}$$

For example, if x′ = 450 then

$$y' = 225 + (400 - 225) \times \frac{(450 - 400)}{(600 - 400)} = 225 + 175 \times \frac{50}{200} = 269 \text{ approx.}$$

The formula merely adds a proportion of the difference between the y-ordinates (y2 − y1) to the lower y-value (y1). The proportion added is determined by where x′ is located relative to x1 , that is the ratio (x′ − x1)/(x2 − x1).

If we represent (x′ − x1)/(x2 − x1) as the *interpolating factor*, *p*, then the formula becomes

$$y' = y1 + p(y2 - y1)$$

This is the standard formula for *linear interpolation*. Notice that *p* is always a value between 0 and 1. Though the concept of linear interpolation has been illustrated with a simple problem in computer graphics programming, it is not limited to this type of application. For example, given any table of information such as Table 28.10 for logarithms, it is possible to determine (approximately) any intermediate value.

For example, linear interpolation could be used to determine approximately the value of log 81·25, as follows.

x	log x
80	1·9031
81	1·9085
82	1·9138
83	1·9191
84	1·9243
85	1·9294

Table 28.10.
Logarithmic values

log 81·25   = log 81   + 0·25(1·9138 − 1·9085)

            = 1·9085   + 0·25(0·0153)

            = 1·9113 approx.

Exercises

Two-dimensional arrays

1. With reference to the following two dimensional array, T, answer the questions below:

i	j 0	1	2	3	4
0	10	13	6	−2	0
1	33	17	−21	16	39
2	45	−9	40	39	22
3	49	71	12	88	−45

(i) What are the values of the following elements of T?

$T_{3,4}$ $T_{0,1}$ $T_{2,1}$ $T_{1,3}$

(ii) What elements of T contain the following values?

−9   12   45   6   33   0

Performing calculations on arrays

2. The following table represents the x-y coordinates of a simple geometrical figure.

x	0	1	3	1	0	−1	0	−1
y	3	1	0	−1	−3	−1	−3	1

(i) Plot the figure on graph paper.

(ii) Apply the following scaling factors to the figure and plot the new shape:

2   5   ·5   3·5

(iii) Perform an x-shear and y-shear on the original figure and plot the new shapes.

Linear interpolation

3.   Use the following table of sine values for the exercises which follow.

Angle(deg)	Sine
0	0
10	0·173648
20	0·34202
30	0·5
40	0·642788
50	0·766044
60	0·866025
70	0·939693
80	0·984808
90	1

(i)   Find approximations to the following angles using linear interpolation:

sin(45)   sin(65)   sin(75)   sin(12)   sin(66)

(ii)   Complete the table below by finding approximate values for the sines of angle 0° - 10°:

angle	0	1	2	3	4	5	6	7	8	9	10
sine											

Chapter 29

Geometry and Graphics

Introduction

In Chapter 17, Categories of Software, a number of types of graphics packages were discussed. The main purpose of this chapter is to provide a basic grounding in the types of facilities offered by such graphics packages, and in particular those which facilitate the drawing of simple two and three-dimensional geometrical figures.

Software packages for *computer-aided design* (CAD) and *graphic design* in particular assume fundamental familiarity with simple geometrical principles and terminology. These too will be examined in this chapter.

Common geometrical figures

In this section a number of common geometrical figures will be described. Each will be defined, a guide to sketching the figure will be provided where necessary, and formulae will be given for calculating perimeters, areas and volumes where relevant. Symbols quoted in formulae or referred to in explanations are related to the diagrams provided for each figure.

2-dimensional figures

Triangle

Definition: A triangle is a closed figure having three sides and three included angles. Certain triangles have special names:

(i)   A right-angled triangle - one of the enclosed angles is 90 degrees (that is, a right-angle).

(ii)   An isosceles triangle - two sides and two angles are the same.

(iii)   An equilateral triangle - all sides and angles are equal.

(iv)   A scalene triangle - all its sides and angles unequal and does not contain a right-angle.

Figure 29.1 shows an example of each.

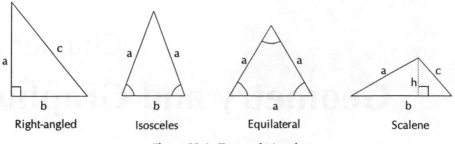

Figure 29.1. *Types of triangle*

Perimeter of triangle: This is the sum of the sides, that is,

$$perimeter = a+b+c$$

Area of triangle: The area is given by the formula

$$area = \frac{b \times h}{2}$$

Rectangle

Definition: A rectangle is a quadrilateral (four sided figure) in which opposite sides are equal and parallel and adjacent sides are at right-angles to each other. A square is a special case of a rectangle in which all of the sides are of equal length. Both are illustrated in Figure 29.2.

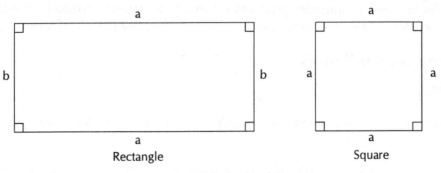

Figure 29.2. *Rectangles*

Perimeter of rectangle: This is twice the sum of two adjacent sides, that is,

$$perimeter = 2(a+b) \text{ and for a square } = 4a$$

Area of rectangle: The area is the product of two adjacent sides:

$$area = a \times b \text{ and for a square } = a \times a = a^2$$

Parallelogram

Definition: Parallelograms are quadrilaterals with opposite sides equal and parallel, but the included angles are not right-angles. A parallelogram with adjacent sides of different lengths is called a rhomboid, and when all four sides are of equal length, it is called a rhombus. An example of each is provided in Figure 29.3.

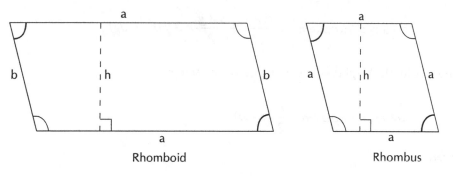

Figure 29.3. *Parallelograms*

Perimeter of parallelogram: Calculated the same way as for a rectangle, that is by finding the sum of all the sides.

$$perimeter = 2(a+b) \text{ and for a rhombus} = 4a$$

Area of parallelogram: Choose one side and draw a perpendicular from it to the opposite side. The area is a product of the length of the side and the perpendicular.

$$area = a \times h$$

Trapezium

Definition: A trapezium is a quadrilateral with no parallel sides. A trapezoid has two parallel sides. Figure 29.4 illustrates various trapezia.

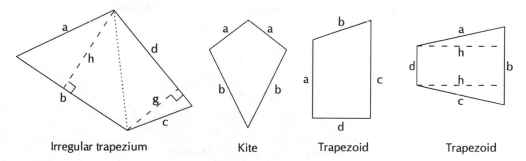

Figure 29.4 *Trapezia*

Perimeter of trapezium: The sum of the sides:

$$perimeter = a+b+c+d$$

Area of trapezium: In general, this is found by splitting the shape into two triangles (in Figure 29.4, a dotted line shows the division of the trapezium) and adding their areas together. Thus

$$area\ of\ a\ trapezium\ =\ \frac{b \times h}{2} + \frac{d \times g}{2} = \frac{1}{2}\ (bh + dg)$$

For a trapezoid, the heights of the triangles are the same:

$$area\ of\ a\ trapezoid = \frac{h}{2}\ (b + d)$$

Polygon

Definition: Strictly speaking, polygons are figures having three or more sides. However, a polygon is usually regarded as a figure with more than four sides. If the sides are all the same length the figures are classed as regular polygons; irregular polygons have sides of unequal lengths. Regular polygons are named according to the number of sides they have:

5 sides: *pentagon* 6 sides: *hexagon* 7 sides: *heptagon* 8 sides: *octagon* 9 sides: *nonagon*

An example of each is shown in Figure 29.5.

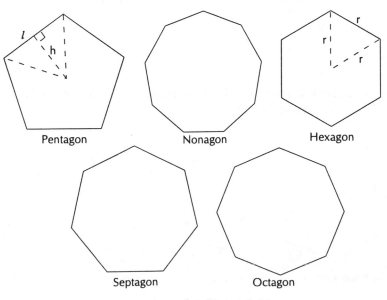

Pentagon   Nonagon   Hexagon

Septagon   Octagon

Figure 29.5. *Regular polygons*

The accurate construction of a regular polygon can be quite difficult and depends on the particular polygon required, but for sketching purposes the easiest method, which will work for any polygon, is as follows:

(i) draw a circle;

(ii) using dividers or a compass, divide the circumference of the circle into an equal number of parts by trial and error;

(iii) join the divisions with straight lines.

Perimeter of polygon: The sum of the sides. For a regular polygon having n sides of length, l, the perimeter is given by

$$perimeter = nl$$

Area of polygon: The area of an irregular polygon is found by dividing it into triangles and calculating the sum of the areas.

For a regular polygon of n sides each of length, l, the area is given by

$$area\ of\ regular\ polygon = \tfrac{1}{2}\,(lh) \times n$$

where h is the perpendicular distance from one of the sides to the centre of the figure.

Circle

Definition: A circle is the path of a point passing round a given point (the centre of the circle) and keeping the same distance from it (the *radius*).

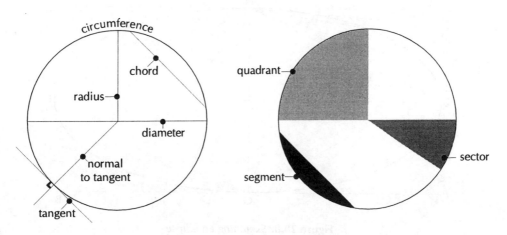

Figure 29.6. *Circle characteristics*

Figure 29.6 shows the characteristics of the circle in terms of lines and areas created by the lines.

Circumference of circle: This is given by

$$circumference = 2 \times \pi \times radius, \text{ or } \pi \times diameter$$

Area of circle: If *r* is the radius of the circle,

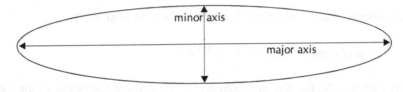

$$area = \pi r^2$$ where $\pi = 3 \cdot 142$ approximately.

Ellipse

Definition: An ellipse is rather like a flattened circle. It has a major axis, which is the longest line that can be drawn through the centre of the ellipse, and a minor axis, which is the shortest line through its centre (Figure 29.7).

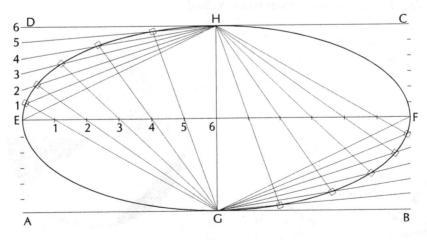

Figure 29.7. *Ellipse*

To sketch an ellipse, the following method (illustrated in Figure 29.8), called the intersecting lines method, can be used.

Figure 29.8. *Sketching an ellipse*

(i)   Draw the rectangle ABCD and the major and minor axis.

(ii)   Divide EO into a number of equal parts, say 6.

(iii)   Divide ED into the same number of equal parts.

(iv)   Join the points on ED to H and draw lines from G through the points on EO.

(v)   The points of intersection marked with the small square give points on the curve.

3-Dimensional figures

Prism

Definition: A prism has a base which is a three or more sided figure and a uniform cross section. In right prisms the plane of the base is perpendicular to the height of the prism. Figure 29.9 provides examples of various prisms.

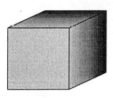

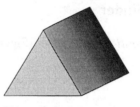

Cube   Cuboid   Triangular prism

Figure 29.9. *Various prisms*

A cube, or regular hexahedron, is a square prism with six square faces. A cuboid is a rectangular right prism.

Surface area of prism: This is the sum of the areas of the faces of the prism. The general formula for the surface area of a right prism of height h is given by

$$Surface\ area\ of\ right\ prism = Ph + 2A$$

where P is the perimeter and A the area of the base.

Volume of right prism, with cross sectional area A, is given by

$$Volume\ of\ right\ prism = Ah$$

where h is the height of the prism.

Sphere

Definition: A sphere (Figure 29.10) is formed when a circle is rotated through 180 degrees about its diameter. Every point on the surface of the sphere is the same distance from its centre.

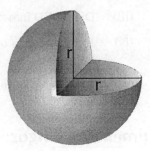

Surface area of sphere: If r is the radius of the sphere then

$$surface\ area\ of\ sphere = 4\pi r^2$$

Figure 29.10. *Sphere with segment removed to show relationship with circle rotation*

Volume of sphere: This is given by

$$volume\ of\ sphere = \tfrac{4}{3}\pi r^3$$

Cylinder

Definition: A cylinder (Figure 29.11) is a prism with a circular base.

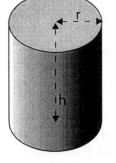

Figure 29.11. *Cylinder*

Surface area of cylinder: Given radius r and height h,

$$surface\ area\ of\ cylinder = 2\pi rh + 2\pi r^2 = 2\pi r(h + r)$$

Volume of cylinder: This is the area of the base times the height:

$$volume\ of\ cylinder = \pi r^2 h$$

Right pyramid

Definition: In a right pyramid, the perpendicular from the apex to the base (the height of the pyramid) passes through the centre of the base. A rectangular pyramid has a rectangular base and a triangular pyramid has a triangular base (both are shown in Figure 29.12). A triangular pyramid in which all four faces are equilateral triangles is called a tetrahedron.

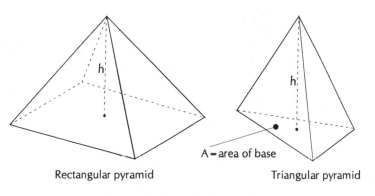

Rectangular pyramid   Triangular pyramid

Figure 29.12. *Right pyramids*

Surface area of pyramid: This is the sum of the areas of the faces.

Volume of right pyramid: The general formula is given by

$$volume\ of\ right\ pyramid = \tfrac{1}{3}Ah$$

where A is the area of the base and h is the height perpendicular to the base.

Cone

Definition: A cone is a right pyramid with a circular base, as shown in Figure 29.13.

Surface area of cone: The curved surface of a cone has area $\pi r l$, where l is the slant height of the cone, and the base is a circle.

Thus, *surface area of* $cone = \pi r^2 + 2\pi r l = \pi r(r + 2l)$

Volume of cone: is given by

$$volume\ of\ cone = \tfrac{1}{3}\pi r^2 h$$

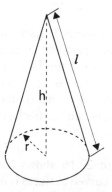

Figure 29.13. *Cone*

Pictorial drawings

There are various ways of presenting 3-dimensional objects pictorially, the commonest and most important of which is the *isometric projection*. This, and three other types of presentation are illustrated in Figure 29.14.

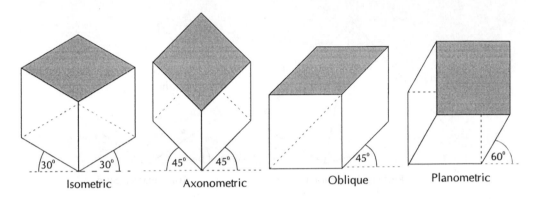

Isometric   Axonometric   Oblique   Planometric

Figure 29.14. *Isometric projections of 3-dimensional objects*

Isometric projections

In an isometric drawing all horizontal lines are drawn at 30 degrees and all vertical lines remain vertical. The only slight difficulty with isometric projections is in dealing with curves such as circles. The technique for doing so is illustrated in Figure 29.15.

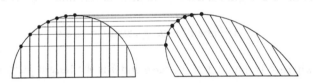

Figure 29.15. *Isometric view of a semicircle*

A base line is divided into a number of equal parts, and vertical lines are drawn from the base to the curve. These lines are transferred to the equivalent points on the isometric drawing and a freehand curve is drawn to join the ends.

Figure 29.16 shows how a block with curved surfaces is drawn as an isometric projection.

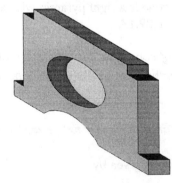

Figure 29.16. *Isometric drawing of block with curved surfaces*

Orthographic projections

An orthographic projection is a representation of a solid object by showing it viewed from three different viewpoints, or *elevations*. The three elevations are:

(i)   Front elevation - the object viewed from the front.

(ii)   Side elevation - the object viewed from the side.

(iii)   Plan - the object viewed from directly above.

In each case, the view that an observer would have is translated as a 2-dimensional representation on the drawing paper.

Figure 29.17 illustrates the process for an orthographic projection of a rectangular prism placed on one edge.

Where the plan is shown below the front elevation, as in the previous figure, the projection is termed a *1st angle projection*. A *3rd angle projection* shows the plan view above the front elevation, as in Figure 29.18.

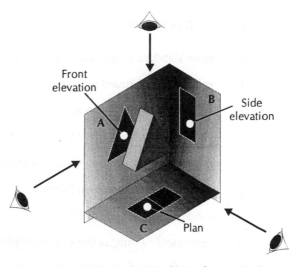

Figure 29.17. *Principle of orthographic projection*

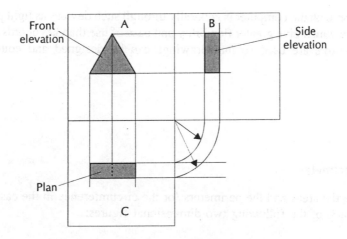

Figure 29.18. *Process of orthographic projection*

Computer-aided design (CAD)

In computer-aided design, interactive graphics (where the user has control over the operation of the graphics software) is used to design components and systems of mechanical, electrical and electronic devices. These applications include designing buildings, car body shapes, hulls of ships, machine components and electronic circuits.

The emphasis is frequently on producing precise drawings for manufacturing or architectural purposes. Such graphics packages offer facilities for drawing and manipulating 2-dimensional or 3-dimensional geometrical figures.

Typical facilities allow the user to:

❑   draw standard shapes such as rectangles, triangles and circles;

❑   move shapes around the screen;

❑   enlarge or reduce figures;

❑   pattern fill areas of the screen;

❑   position text of various sizes at different angles;

❑   automatically dimension lines;

❑   rotate figures about specified axes;

❑   generate 3-D images from orthographic projections;

❑   magnify specified areas of the screen to allow fine detail editing;

❑   transfer the work to output devices such as plotters.

Communication with the computer is generally through such devices as light pens, mice and graphics tablets which give greater flexibility and ease of use than keyboards. Special high-resolution monitors are used so that drawings can be designed and edited with great accuracy.

Exercises

Areas and perimeters

1.   Calculate the areas and the perimeters (or the circumference in the case of a circle) of each of the following two-dimensional figures:

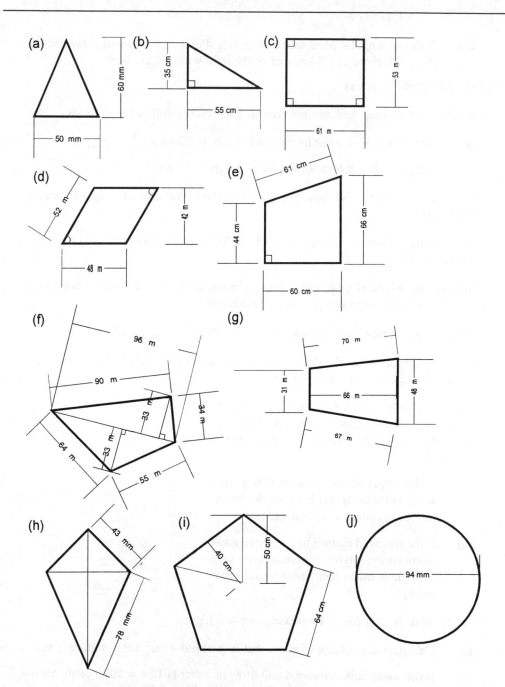

2. A rectangular field covers an area of 500 square metres.

    i)   If its length is 25 metres, what is its width?

    ii)   The field is to be divided into rectangular plots of 5 metre by 10 metres. How many such plots will there be?

iii)   If the rectangular plots are to be of size 4 metres by 6 metres, how many plots will there be? What area of the field will be left over?

Volumes and surface areas

1.   Calculate the volume and surface area of each of the following cuboids:

    i)   Length = 1.5 m; breadth = 0.7 m; height = 2.3 m

    ii)   Length = 8 cm; breadth = 4.7 cm; height = 3.3 cm

2.   A cube has a volume of 50 cubic cm. Calculate the length of each side correct to 2 decimal places.

3.   Calculate the volume and surface area of a cylinder having a radius of 0.8 m and a height of 5.5 m.

4.   Calculate the height of a cylinder having a radius of 5 cm and a volume of 1,963 cm^3. Give your answer to the nearest centimetre.

5.   Calculate the volume and surface area of a sphere having a radius 12 cm.

6.   The triangular face of a triangular prism has an area of 45 cm^2. If the prism has a volume of 315 cm^3, how long is it?

7.   A tunnel is to be made through a hillside. The cross-section of the tunnel is shown in the diagram. The curved part of the cross-section is semicircular.

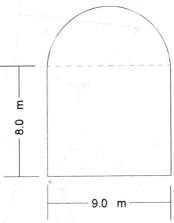

    (i)   If the length of the tunnel is 550 metres, what volume of earth needs to be removed in order to make the tunnel?

    (ii)   If the removed earth is to be carried away in containers having dimensions 6m x 4m x 3m, how many containers would be required?

8.   A water tank is 6m long, 4.5m wide and 4m high.

    (i)   Calculate the volume of water that it can hold when it is completely full.

    (ii)   If the water tank contained 800 litres of water (1 litre = 1000 cubic centimetres), what would be the water level in the tank?

9.   How much material would be required to manufacture a 2m long copper pipe having an outside diameter of 10mm and an inner diameter of 8mm?

Chapter 30
Graphs

Introduction

This chapter deals with Cartesian graphs of simple algebraic functions. An equation of the form $y = 3x + 2$ is called a Cartesian equation, and a graph of the equation is called a Cartesian graph. The *dependent* variable, y (the value of y depends on x), is said to be a *function* of the *independent* variable, x, or $y = f(x)$. When y is used as the vertical scale of a graph, and x is used for the horizontal scale, every point on the resulting grid can be represented by a pair of values, (x,y), called the Cartesian coordinates of the point. Cartesian coordinates are also referred to as *rectangular coordinates*. Henceforth, they will be referred to as just coordinates. The point at which the two axes meet is called the *origin* and has coordinates (0,0). Figure 30.1 shows the coordinates of a number of points on a graph.

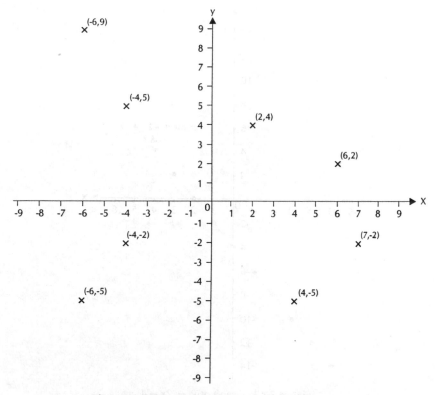

Figure 30.1. *Examples of rectangular coordinates*

In each case, the coordinates have been derived by counting the number of units the point is horizontally displaced from the origin for the x-ordinate, and the displacement vertically for the y-ordinate. The x-ordinate is negative for points to the left of the origin and the y-ordinate is negative for points below the origin.

Graphs of linear functions

A function of the form $y = mx + c$, where m and c are constants (values which do not change), is called a *linear* function of x, since it defines a straight line with *slope* or *gradient*, m, and *intercept*, c. Table 30.1 shows a number of coordinates on the line when $m = 2$ and $c = -4$.

x		−5	−4	−3	−2	−1	0	1	2	3	4	5
$y = 2x - 4$		−14	−12	−10	−8	−6	−4	−2	0	2	4	6

Table 30.1. *Co-ordinates for y = 2x – 4*

Figure 30.2 shows the corresponding graph of the straight line. Notice that the line intersects the y-axis at the point y = −4; this is called the intercept and is the value of c.

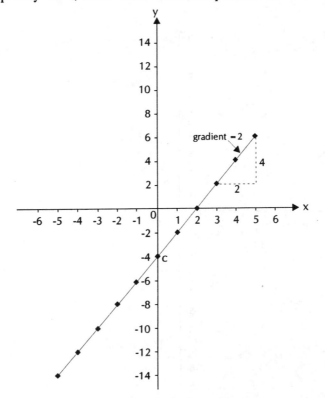

Figure 30.2. *Graph of y = 2x – 4*

Though eleven points are given in the table above, in fact only two are absolutely necessary in order to draw the graph. However, it is best to use three points as a check that no mistake has been made in calculating the points.

Determination of the equation of a straight line

Given that a line can be drawn knowing only two coordinates on the line, it should be possible to find the equation of the line from these two coordinates.

First it is necessary to define what is meant by the slope or gradient of a line. Given two points on the line, the gradient is the ratio between the change in y to the change in x. So for the points (3,2) and (5,6) the gradient is given by

$$gradient = \frac{change\ in\ y}{change\ in\ x} = \frac{6-2}{5-3} = \frac{4}{2} = 2$$

In order to define a line, it is necessary to determine its gradient and intercept. Suppose it is required to find the equation of a line between the points (0,2) and (4,14). This is the type of problem which programs for graphic design must solve frequently. First the gradient of the line is determined:

$$gradient = \frac{14-2}{4-0} = 3$$

The equation of the line is therefore

$$y = 3x + c$$

Now the value of c, the intercept, is determined by substituting one pair of coordinates into the equation:

$$14 = 3(4) + c, \ or \ 2 = 3(0) + c$$

Therefore $c = 2$.

The equation of the line is

$$y = 3x + 2$$

Graphs of non-linear functions

Quadratic functions

Functions of the form

$$f(x) = x^2 - 2 \quad \text{or} \quad f(x) = x^2 - 3x + 2$$

are called *quadratic* functions and when plotted as graphs they produce curves called *parabolas*. In general, functions involving powers of the independent variable of greater than one are called *non-linear* functions. The quadratic functions

$$y = x^2 - 3x + 2, \quad y = x^2 - 2x + 1 \quad \text{and} \quad y = x^2 + x + 1$$

are shown in Figure 30.3. The points where the curves cross the x-axis are called solutions or *roots* of the equations $x^2 - 3x + 2 = 0$, $x^2 - 2x + 1 = 0$ and $x^2 + x + 1 = 0$, respectively.

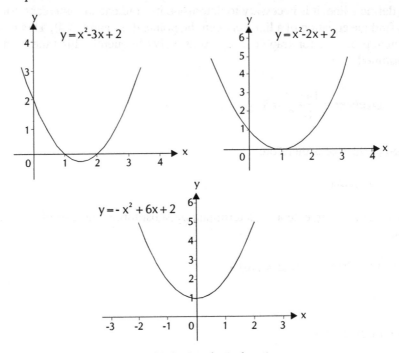

Figure 30.3. *Quadratic functions*

Notice that the graphs show three different possibilities for the number of roots of a quadratic equation:

(i)   Two different roots where the curve crosses the x-axis.

(ii)   A double root where the curve just touches the x-axis.

(iii)   No roots because the curve never crosses the x-axis.

Another point to note is that if the coefficient of the x^2 term is negative then the curve will have a single maximum point and if the coefficient of the x^2 term is positive the curve will have a single minimum point. These two cases are illustrated in the Figure 30.4.

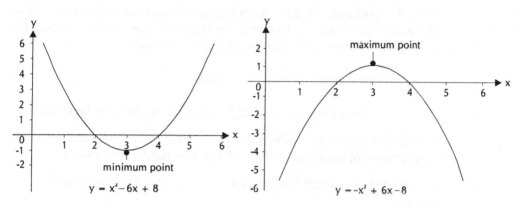

Figure 30.4. *Minimum and maximum of quadratic*

Drawing quadratics

A quadratic function has the general form

$$y = ax^2 + bx + c$$

The values that the coefficients a, b and c have determine the form of the quadratic curve. The effect of the sign of the coefficient, a, has been noted already; more useful observations for drawing quadratics are listed below and are illustrated in Figure 30.5.

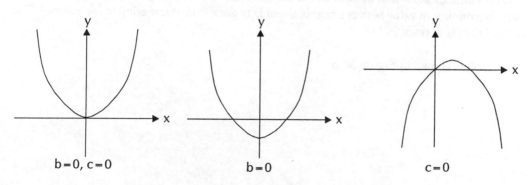

Figure 30.5. *Various graphs of quadratic functions*

(i)   When $b=0$ and $c=0$, the curve is symmetrical about the y-axis and the roots of the function are both at the origin.

(ii)   When $b=0$, the curve is symmetrical about the y-axis, and the roots, if they exist, symmetrically straddle the origin.

(iii) When $c=0$, the curve passes through the origin.

To sketch the graph of a quadratic, use the observations above in conjunction with a table of at least six evenly spaced coordinates on the curve. The range of these coordinates should be such that it covers the roots of the function and the maximum or minimum point.

The locations of these points may be identified as follows:

(a)   Roots occur where the y values change sign for consecutive values of x.

(b)   A maximum point occurs where, for consecutive increasing values of x, the magnitude of the y values change from increasing to decreasing.

(c)   A minimum point occurs where the y values change from decreasing to increasing.

Table 30.2 shows the coordinates for the function $y = 2x^2 - x - 6$

x	−4	−3	−2	−1	0	1	2	3	4
y	30	25	4	−3	−6	−5	−0	9	22
			A	B	C	D	E		

Table 30.2. Coordinates for $y = 2x^2 - x - 6$

The coordinates show that there is a root between points A and B (y changes sign), and that there is a minimum value between points C and D (y goes from decreasing to increasing). The second root is at point E.

The graph is shown in Figure 30.6.

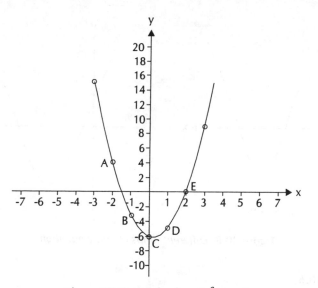

Figure 30.6. *Graph of* $y = 2x^2 - x - 6$

Cubic Functions

Functions of x of the form

$$f(x) = ax^3 + bx^2 + cx + d$$

are called *cubic* functions and, like quadratic functions, have characteristic curves. The cubic function

$$y = x^3 - 6x^2 + 11x - 6$$

is shown in Figure 30.7.

The graph of a cubic function has one maximum point and one minimum point, and the curve crosses the x-axis at a maximum of three places. Thus a cubic equation of the form

$$ax^3 + bx^2 + cx + d = 0$$

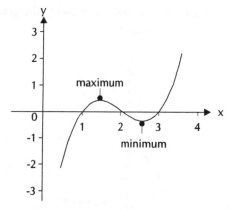

Figure 30.7. *Cubic function of* $y = x^3 - 6x^2 + 11x - 6$

has at most three roots. The orientation of the curve depends on the sign of the coefficient, a. Figure 30.8 illustrates the two possible cases.

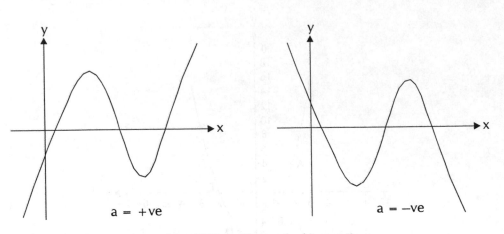

Figure 30.8. *Different forms of cubic equations*

Drawing cubics

The procedure for sketching graphs of cubic functions is similar to that for quadratics, that is, once the location of the roots and the maximum and minimum points have been identified from a table of xy values, drawing the graph is quite straightforward. Figure 30.9 illustrates a number of examples.

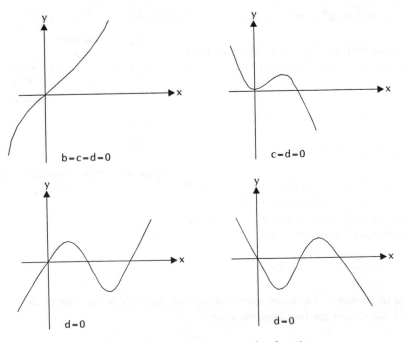

Figure 30.9. *Various graphs of cubic functions*

Once more, the coefficients give a good indication of the character of the curve. Some consequences of the values of the coefficients are given below:

(i)   When b, c and d are all zero, the curve passes through the origin which is the only root of the curve, that is, the only place at which $x = 0$.

(ii) When c and d are both zero, the curve has two roots, one of which is zero.

(iii) When d is zero, there will be at least one root at the origin, and a possibility of a further two roots elsewhere.

Using graphs

The types of graphs considered in this chapter, namely Cartesian graphs, are very convenient sources of reference. Other types of graphs, such as those considered in the next chapter, provide useful means of conveying statistical information in a visual manner but, unlike graphs in this chapter, they are not too useful for analytical purposes. A good example of the usefulness of Cartesian graphs is their application in kinematics, the study of the motions of bodies as a function of time.

Time and distance graphs

If the velocity of a moving object is constant, the graph of the distance it has travelled after a number of seconds is a straight line, the gradient of which is its velocity. Figure 30.10 provides an example of a time and distance graph.

If we wished to know, from the graph, how far the object had travelled after, say, 10 seconds, we would merely read off the distance corresponding to 10 seconds, that is 50 metres. Similarly, we could easily determine from the graph that it would take the object 2 seconds to travel 10 metres.

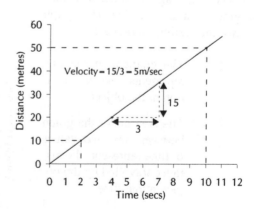

Figure 30.10. *Time and distance graph*

Moreover, suppose that the graph had been determined by direct observation, for example by measuring the distance travelled by the object at fixed times (as indicated by the 5 points on the graph). Plotting these points shows that the object must have been travelling at a constant velocity (because the graph is a straight line) and consequently the graph could be used to interpolate between these fixed points to give us information about any time/distance combination, not just those marked. The graph could also be used to extrapolate values beyond the current limits of the graph's axes.

Another example of a time and distance graph is the graph of the motion of an object, such as a ball, thrown vertically into the air. The object initially has a certain velocity which gradually diminishes to zero at its highest point and then increases again under the influence of gravity until it collides with the ground. The graph of height against time, in Figure 30.11, is parabolic. The velocity of the object is constantly changing but, at any point in time, it can be determined by measuring the gradient of the tangent to the curve at that time.

Again the graph can be used to determine the height of the object after any time period, or the time taken to reach any height.

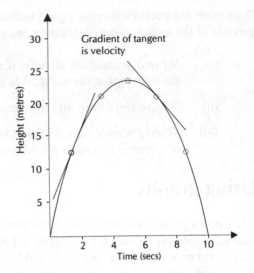

Figure 30.11. *Parabolic time and distance graph*

Time and velocity graph

When the velocity of an accelerating object is plotted against time, the resulting graph is a straight line. This graph has two interesting properties:

(i)   The gradient of the line represents the acceleration of the object.

(ii)   The area under the graph between any two values of time represents the distance travelled by the object in that time.

For an object starting at rest and accelerating at 3 metres/second^2, the graph would appear as shown in Figure 30.12. Thus the distance travelled in 4 seconds from rest is shown by the shaded area in the figure. The area, which is triangular, is calculated by applying the formula

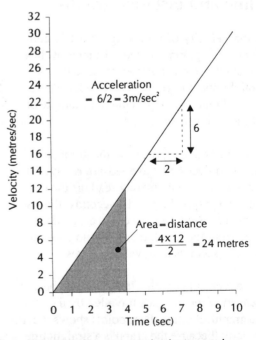

Figure 30.12. *Time and velocity graph*

$$area = \frac{base \times height}{2} = \frac{4 \times 12}{2} = 24\ metres$$

The average speed of the object could be calculated by determining the total distance travelled (that is the total area under the graph) and dividing this by the total time taken.

Finding the distance travelled from a time and velocity graph is rather more difficult when the acceleration of the object is not constant; the resulting graph is no longer a single straight line, and may in fact be a curve as illustrated in Figure 30.13. Here the curve is a quadratic, representing a constant rate of change of acceleration. The simplest method for determining the area under a curve is to plot the curve on squared graph paper and count the number of squares covered. Complete squares are counted first; part squares greater than a half are counted as whole squares; part squares less than a half are ignored. The final count is multiplied by the number of distance units represented by a single square. Figure 30.13 illustrates the process.

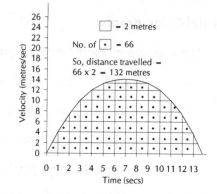

Figure 30.13. *Counting squares method to calculate distance travelled*

Another method, which is more amenable to computer analysis, is called the *trapezoidal rule*. The area under the curve is considered to be a number of thin trapezoids, the area of each of which is found by applying the following formula:

$$area\ of\ strip = \frac{1}{2}d(y_i + y_{i+1})$$

where d is the width of the strip, and y_i and y_{i+1} are consecutive values of the function at a distance d apart. (See Figure 30.14). The total area is the sum of all of the trapezoids:

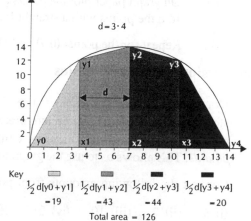

Figure 30.14. *Trapezoidal rule*

$$A = \frac{1}{2}d(y_0 + y_1) + \frac{1}{2}d(y_1 + y_2) + \ldots + \frac{1}{2}d(y_{n-1} + y_n)$$

or
$$A = \frac{1}{2}d[(y_0 + y_n) + 2(y_1 + y_2 + \ldots + y_{n-1})]$$

Where there are assumed to be x_0 to x_n points on the horizontal axis. The more trapezoidal strips used, the more accurate is the estimation of the area.

Exercises

Straight line graphs

1. Draw graphs of the following equations:

    (i) $y = x + 3$ (ii) $y = 2x - 2$ (iii) $y = 3 - 2x$

    (iv) $y = 3x - 1$ (v) $y = x/2$ (vi) $y = -3 \cdot 5x - 4 \cdot 4$

2. Write down the slope and the intercept of each of the graphs in Q 1.

3. On the same axes draw the graphs of the lines

    $$y = 3x + 1 \quad \text{and} \quad y = 5 - x$$

    Write down the co-ordinates of the point of intersection.

4. (i)   On graph paper plot the points given by the co-ordinates (2, 1) and (4, 5).
           Join the points with a straight line. What is the equation of this line?

    (ii)   Repeat for the points (0,7) and (1,2).

Conversion graphs and tables

1. Draw a graph of the equation $y = 1 \cdot 5x$ for values of x ranging from 0 to 10. The
    slope of the line $(1 \cdot 5)$ can be interpreted as a conversion factor for converting
    pounds to dollars. In this case we could write the equation as *dollars* $= 1 \cdot 5$
    pounds. This allows us to use the graph to convert between pounds and dollars.

    Convert the following amounts from pounds to dollars:

    (i) 5   (ii) 7   (iii) 10   (iv) 0·5   (v) 5·5

    Convert the following amounts from dollars to pounds:

    (i) 8   (ii) 6   (iii) 14   (iv) 13   (v) 11.5

2. Devise a method for converting larger amounts of pound/dollars, say for amounts
    up to £100.

3. There are 2·2 pounds (lbs) to the kilogram (kg). Draw the conversion graph of
    pounds/kilograms. Choose axes to allow values up to 20lbs to be converted into
    kilograms.

4. Sometimes it is preferable to use a conversion table rather than a graph. Construct
    a table that shows the total cost of goods assuming a VAT rate of 17·5%. The

equation that links the cost to the total cost is

$$TotalCost = 1.175 \times Cost$$

Contruct the table as shown alongside.

Use the table to find the total price of the following amounts:

(i) £7   (ii) £12   (iii) £38   (iv) £157

How could you also allow for amounts less than £1?

Cost	Cost + VAT
£1·00	£1·18
£2·00	£2·35
.....etc......	.....etc......
£10·00	£11·75
£20·00	£23·50
£30·00	£35·25
....etc.....	....etc......
£100·00	£117·50

5. What are the advantages and disadvantages of using a table rather than a graph for conversion purposes?

Quadratic equations

1. The following table shows selected values for the quadratic equation

$$y = 0 \cdot 5x^2 - x - 12$$

x	-5·0	-4·0	-3·0	-2.0	-1·0	0·0	1·0	2·0	3·0	4·0	5·0	6·0	7·0
y	5·5	0·0	-4·5	-8·0	10·5	-12·0	-12·5	-12·0	-10·5	-8·0	-4·5	0·0	5·5

    (i)   Between what two pairs of values of x do the roots of the equation occur?

    (ii)   Does the curve have a maximum or a minimum point?

    (iii)   Between which two x values does the maximum or minimum point lie?

    (iv)   Draw the curve.

Check your answers using a spreadsheet.

2. Repeat the exercises in 1. for the following tables and equations:

    (i) $y = 8 - 6 \cdot 5x - 2x^2$

x	-6·0	-5·0	-4·0	-3·0	-2·0	-1·0	0·0	1·0	2·0
y	-25·0	-9·5	2·0	9·5	13·0	12·5	8·0	-0·5	-13·0

    (ii) $y = x^2 - 10x + 10$

x	-1·0	0·0	1·0	2·0	3·0	4·0	5·0	6·0	7·0	8·0	9·0	10·0
y	21·0	10·0	1·0	-6·0	-11·0	-14·0	-15·0	-14·0	-11·0	-6·0	1·0	10·0

    (iii) $y = x^2 - 6x + 9$

x	-1·0	0·0	1·0	2·0	3·0	4·0	5·0	6·0	7·0
y	16·0	9·0	4·0	1·0	0·0	1·0	4·0	9·0	16·0

Cubic equations

1. For the following cubic equation, produce a table of x and y values, state where the roots of the equation lie and draw the curve:

$$y = x^3 + 5x^2 - 11x - 6$$

(Use x values between -2 and $+5$ in steps of ·5)

Check your results with a spreadsheet.

2. Investigate the effects of changing the coefficients of the x terms on a cubic equation of the form

$$y = ax^3 + bx^2 + cx + d$$

by setting:

$d = 0$ (e.g. $y = x^3 + 5x^2 - 11x$)

$c = d = 0$ (e.g. $y = x^3 + 5x^2$)

$b = c = d$ (e.g. $y = x^3$)

$a = -a$ (e.g. $y = -x^3 + 5x^2 - 11x - 6$)

Using graphs

1. Draw a time and distance graph for an object travelling at a constant speed of 10 metres per second for 5 seconds, assuming that it starts from rest.

Use the graph to determine the distance it travelled in

(i) 0·5 seconds   (ii) 2·5 seconds   (iii) 4·5 seconds.

2. Draw a time and velocity graph for an object accelerating at $9·81$ m/sec^2. (This is the acceleration due to gravity). Use the graph to determine the distance fallen by an object dropped from a high tower after the following lengths of time:

(i) 1 second   (ii) 2·9 seconds   (iii) 5·3 seconds

Chapter 31

Statistics

Types of statistics

The term *statistics* refers to the processing of numerical data in order to make it more comprehensible. The figures derived from statistical analysis are also known as 'statistics'. The word 'statistics' derives from 'state', since it was governments that first recognised the urgent need for coherent information relating to population densities, distribution of wealth, political trends, and so on. Broadly speaking, the subject can be divided into two areas:

❑   *descriptive* statistics. These deal with methods of describing large amounts of data. Such data is summarised in a wide variety of different forms: as single numbers representing central values or measures of dispersion; as tables of figures; as pictorial representations; as graphs. Whatever the method employed, its function is to make a mass of figures easier to understand by organising it in a way which emphasises any trends within the figures.

❑   *analytical* statistics. These deal with methods enabling conclusions to be drawn from the data.

This chapter will consider only descriptive statistics since analytical statistics generally involves mathematical techniques beyond the scope of this book. Statistics are quoted in all manners of ways in everyday life:

> "Megadent can reduce tooth decay by up to 30%"
> "Smoking causes 200 deaths per day"
> "Profits rose by 50% last year"
> "The average salary of teachers is £19563·79"

The student of statistics must be able to consider critically, statements such as those above by asking such questions as:

> "What is the source of this information?"
> "What (if anything) is being left unsaid?"
> "How has the data been obtained?"
> "What evidence is there for making this statement?"
> "Is it intended to be misleading?"
> "What does it actually mean?"

Hopefully, this chapter provides a framework for producing and evaluating simple statistical quantities, so that they can be viewed intelligently and produced without ambiguity.

Pictorial representations

Suppose that a certain college is divided into four faculties and it is necessary to show pictorially the relative number of students in each faculty for particular academic years. Table 31.1 shows the figures to be used.

Faculty	Number of students			
	1992	1993	1994	1995
Business Studies	889	913	1076	1253
Humanities	501	626	715	836
Science	416	481	263	352
Technology	387	412	448	479
Total	2193	2432	2502	2920

Table 31.1. *Student numbers from 1992 to 1995, arranged by faculty*

This data could be represented diagrammatically in a number of forms:

❏   pictogram;

❏   pie chart;

❏   bar chart;

❏   graph.

Spreadsheet, word processing and graphics packages are available to take the hard work out of producing the last three types of diagrams.

Pictograms

This form of presentation involves the use of pictures to represent a set of figures. For example, the student numbers in the four faculties for 1992 could be shown as Figure 31.1.

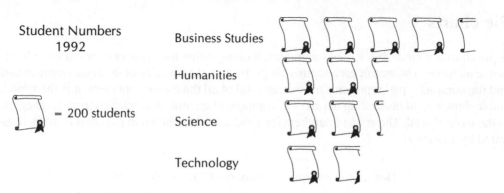

Figure 31.1. *Pictogram representing student numbers from Table 31.1*

Here the same picture, representing a number of students, is shown repeatedly; the values of the figure for each faculty is indicated by the number of pictures shown.

An alternative method, illustrated in Figure 31.2, is sometimes employed to represent a number by the size of the picture used.

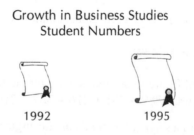

Figure 31.2. *Using picture size to represent number*

This second type of representation, however, can easily be very misleading. If the height of the picture is made approximately proportional to the quantity being represented, then the width of the picture will probably be increased by a corresponding amount to make it look right. However, this produces an increase in area and gives a false impression to the eye. For example, if the figure being represented doubles, then the area will look disproportionately large. Even if great care is taken in making the area of the pictures relatively accurate representations of the quantities, it is still quite difficult to interpret such diagrams, and they are best avoided altogether.

Pictograms which are drawn well and which are not misleading can be very effective in presenting data in a non-technical way. The pictures immediately arrest the attention of the observer and at the same time impart the required information.

Pie charts

A pie chart is a circle divided into segments, looking rather like a pie or cake cut into slices - hence its name. The area of each segment is proportional to the size of the figure represented, and the complete 'pie' represents the overall total of all the component parts. It is therefore a convenient way of illustrating the sizes of component quantities in relation to each other and to the overall total. The student numbers for 1992 could be shown in pie chart form as illustrated by Figure 31.3.

Distribution of Student Numbers 1992   *(Total 2193)*

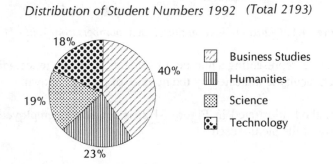

Figure 31.3. *Pie chart for student numbers in 1992*

The pie chart is constructed as follows:

(i)   Find the overall figure to be represented by the full circle by totalling the component figures: $889 + 501 + 416 + 387 = 2193$.

(ii)   Since the area of a segment depends on the angle that it makes at the centre of the circle, each figure is used to determine the angle required for its segment of the chart:

889 *requires an angle of* $\dfrac{889}{2193} \times 360 = 146°$ *approximately.*

501 *requires an angle of* $\dfrac{501}{2193} \times 360 = 82°$ *approximately.*

416 *requires an angle of* $\dfrac{416}{2193} \times 360 = 68°$ *approximately.*

387 *requires an angle of* $\dfrac{387}{2193} \times 360 = 64°$ *approximately.*

$$Total = 360°$$

(iii)   Draw a circle and use a protractor to divide the circle into the appropriately sized segments.

(iv)   Indicate the percentage contribution that each segment makes to the whole 'pie', label each sector and give the whole diagram a title.

(v)   Where appropriate, state the source of the data.

In order to compare the student figures for the two years, 1992 and 1995 for instance, the relative size of the circles can be used to reflect the growth in numbers, as a comparison of Figure 31.4 with Figure 31.3 shows.

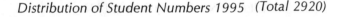

Distribution of Student Numbers 1995   *(Total 2920)*

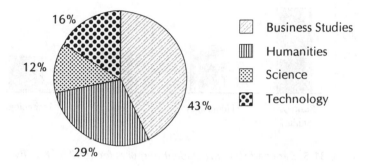

Figure 31.4. *Pie chart for student numbers in 1995*

However, great care must be taken to ensure that the *areas* of the circles represent the total figures and not their radii or diameters. The two circles should be correctly proportioned. If $r1$ represents the radius of the circle used for representing the student numbers for 1992, and $r2$ is used for the radius of the circle for 1995, then the relationship between $r1$ and $r2$ is given by

$$\frac{\pi r1^2}{\pi r2^2} = \frac{2193}{2920}$$

In other words, the ratio between the areas of the first circle of radius $r1$ and the second circle of radius $r2$ is the same as the ratio between student numbers for 1992 and 1995.

When $r2$ is made the subject of the formula, we have

$$r2 = r1 \sqrt{\frac{2920}{2193}}$$

Thus, for $r1 = 4$ units,

$$r2 = 4 \times \sqrt{\frac{2920}{2193}} = 4 \times \sqrt{1 \cdot 33} = 4 \times 1 \cdot 15 = 4 \cdot 62 \text{ units}$$

Bar charts

A basic bar chart, such as that shown in Figure 31.5 for 1992 student numbers, consists of a series of bars with lengths proportional to the quantities they represent. The scale of the vertical axis in the diagram is in units of number of students and the horizontal axis is labelled with the names of the four faculties.

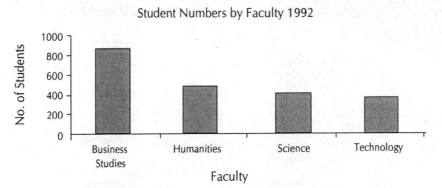

Figure 31.5. *Bar chart showing student numbers for 1992 by Faculty*

There are numerous variations of the basic bar chart, the commonest of which is the *multiple bar chart* shown in Figure 31.6. Here, the figures for two years are represented side by side for each faculty.

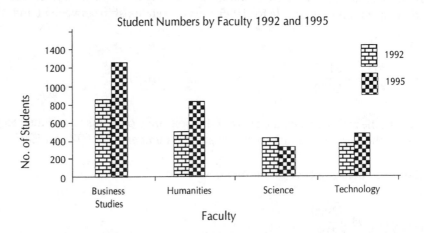

Figure 31.6. *Multiple bar chart showing student numbers for 1992 and 1995, by Faculty*

Bar charts are very useful for depicting a series of changes in the figures of interest. They are generally preferable to pictograms because they are easier to construct and they can represent data more accurately. Multiple bar charts are not recommended for more than four sets of

figures. More than this number of adjacent components detracts from the clarity and usefulness of the diagram.

Graphs

Again referring to the student numbers given earlier, suppose it was required to compare the
way that student numbers changed over the four years, for the faculties of Business Studies
and Science. One possible way to do this would be to use a multiple bar chart with the horizontal axis labelled with the four years 1992-95. Two adjacent bars could be used for the
faculty figures for each year and the diagram would look much the same as in Figure 31.6.

However, the figures could be illustrated in a more striking manner by means of a graph such
as that shown in Figure 31.7.

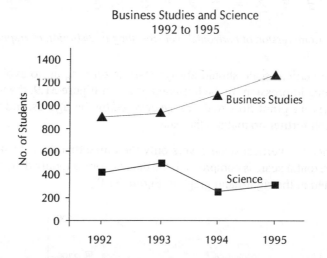

Figure 31.7. *Line graph emphasising trends in student numbers for Business Studies and Science*

The lines joining the points marked with the square and triangle symbols help to emphasise
trends, so that it is quite easy to see that Business Studies student numbers are increasing
whereas those of Science are declining. It should be noted, however, with this particular type
of diagram, that using the connecting lines to interpolate intermediate values is not possible:
the horizontal scale does not represent a continuous quantity with meaningful values between those marked.

The construction and use of graphs in general have already been discussed in Chapter 30, but
it is appropriate at this point to make some observations about the presentation of the type of
graph used in this current context.

(i)   The choice of horizontal scale can greatly affect the visual impression that
        is given. Though the two graphs in Figure 31.8 represent the same data, by

compressing the horizontal scale in the right hand graph the profit trend appears more dramatic. The left hand graph conveys an accurate impression of the data whereas the right hand graph distorts it.

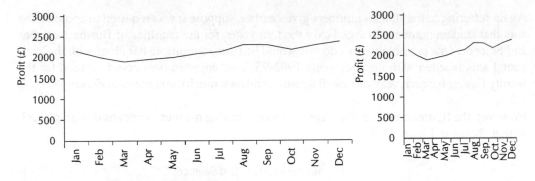

Figure 31.8. *Compression of horizontal scale resulting in distortion of graphed figures*

(ii)   The vertical scale should always start at zero, again to avoid giving the wrong impression. In the left-hand graph in Figure 31.9, the vertical scale starts at a point close to the range covered by the figures, and the resulting graph further dramatises the data.

When the vertical scale covers only the range that the data spans and the horizontal scale is compressed, the data becomes totally distorted, as illustrated in the right-hand graph in Figure 31.9.

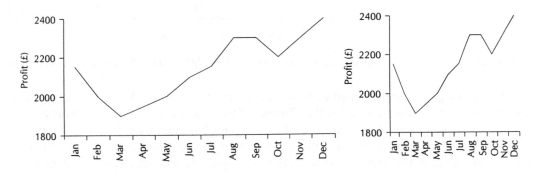

Figure 31.9. *Distortion through restricted data range and compression of horizontal scale*

It is difficult to believe that all four graphs in Figures 31.8 and 31.9 are based on exactly the same data.

(iii)   Quote the source of the data so that the actual figures used can be checked if required.

Frequency distributions

Table 31.2 shows the mileages recorded by a number of refuse disposal vehicles in one week.

Mileages recorded by refuse disposal vehicles											
482	502	466	408	486	440	470	447	413	451	410	430
469	438	452	459	455	473	423	436	412	403	493	436
471	498	450	421	482	440	442	474	407	448	444	485
505	515	500	462	460	476	472	454	451	438	457	446
453	453	508	475	418	465	450	447	477	436	464	453
415	511	430	457	490	447	433	416	419	460	428	434
420	443	456	432	425	497	459	449	439	509	483	502
424	421	413	441	458	438	444	445	435	468	430	442
455	452	479	481	468	435	462	478	463	498	494	489
495	407	462	432	424	451	426	433	474	431	471	488

Table 31.2. *Unsorted, raw data*

A casual examination of this set of figures is unlikely to reveal anything other than the fact that most of the figures are in the 400's with an occasional one in the 500's. From a table in this form it would be very difficult to determine any patterns present in the data. For instance, are the numbers evenly distributed, or is there a certain small range containing a preponderance of figures compared to other similar ranges?

The statistical techniques considered in this part of the chapter allow raw data such as that in the above table to be summarised and presented in a form which facilitates identification of trends and allows the significance of the figures to be grasped. It should be noted, however, that as the crude data is converted into more convenient forms of representation, the fine details within the data begin to be lost.

Ungrouped frequency distributions

A first step in the analysis of the data in the table could be to sort the figures into ascending order of magnitude and at the same time to note the number of times any figures are repeated. Table 31.3 has been produced in this manner and it is termed an *ungrouped frequency distribution*. The table consists of a list of every unique mileage with its *frequency* of occurrence, that is, the number of times it occurred in Table 31.2.

mileage	freq	mileage	freq	mileage	freq	mileage	freq
403	1	434	1	456	1	479	1
407	2	435	2	457	2	481	1
408	1	436	3	458	1	482	2
410	1	438	3	459	2	483	1
412	1	439	1	460	2	485	1
413	2	440	2	462	3	486	1
415	1	441	1	463	1	488	1
416	1	442	2	464	1	489	1
418	1	443	1	465	1	490	1
419	1	444	2	466	1	493	1
420	1	445	1	468	2	494	1
421	2	446	1	469	1	495	1
423	1	447	3	470	1	497	1
424	2	448	1	471	2	498	2
425	1	449	1	472	1	500	1
426	1	450	2	473	1	502	2
428	1	451	3	474	2	505	1
430	3	452	2	475	1	508	1
431	1	453	3	476	1	509	1
432	2	454	1	477	1	511	1
433	2	455	2	478	1	515	1

Table 31.3. *Ungrouped frequency distribution*

Notice that the sum of the frequencies is equal to the number of items in the original table, that is,

$$\sum f = 120$$

Grouped frequency distribution

Though the data has now been organised, there are still too many numbers for the mind to be able to grasp the information hidden within them. Therefore the next step is to simplify the presentation of the data even further. At this stage, in the production of a *grouped frequency distribution*, the crude data is replaced by a set of groups which split the mileages into a number of small ranges called *classes*. Table 31.4 is an example of a grouped frequency distribution based on the ungrouped frequency distribution shown earlier in Table 31.3.

Mileages	Frequency
400 to under 420	12
420 to under 440	27
440 to under 460	34
460 to under 480	24
480 to under 500	15
500 to under 520	8
Total	**120**

Table 31.4. *Grouped frequency distribution*

The overall range of mileages, 403 to 515, has been split into six classes each covering an equal subrange of the total range of values. Notice that the class limits, that is the boundary values of the classes, do not overlap, nor are there any gaps between them; these are important characteristics of grouped frequency distributions.

The effect of grouping data in this way is to allow patterns to be detected more easily. For instance, it is now clear that most of the figures cluster in and around the '440 to under 460' class. The cost of being able to extract this piece of information is loss of the exact details of the raw data; a grouped frequency distribution summarises the crude data. Thus any further information deduced or calculated from this grouped frequency distribution can only be approximate.

Choice of classes

The construction of a grouped frequency distribution will always involve making decisions regarding the number and size of classes to be used. Though these choices will depend on individual circumstances to a large extent, the following guidelines should be noted:

(i)   Class intervals should be equal wherever possible.

(ii)   Restrict the number of classes to between ten and twenty; too many or too few classes will obscure information.

(iii)   Classes should be chosen such that occurrences within the intervals are mainly grouped about the mid-point of the classes in order that calculations based on the distribution can be made as accurately as possible. Examination of the ungrouped frequency distribution should highlight any tendencies of figures to cluster at regular intervals over the range of values considered.

(iv)   Class intervals of 5, 10 or multiples of 10 are easier to work with than intervals such as 7 or 11 (manually, that is: it is not a problem when using a computer package for statistical analysis).

Cumulative frequency distributions

Table 31.5 contains an additional two columns to the data in Table 31.4. The entries in the column labelled 'Cumulative Frequency' have been calculated by keeping a running total of the frequencies given in the adjacent column. As expected, the final entry shows that the sum of all the frequencies is 120. The final column shows the same accumulated figures as percentages of the total number of figures.

This new table allows further observations to be made regarding the data being examined. For example, the table now shows that $80 \cdot 8\%$ of the vehicles travelled less than 480 miles; $6 \cdot 7\%$ $(100 - 93 \cdot 3)$ of the vehicles travelled more than 500 miles; 20% $(80 \cdot 8 - 60 \cdot 8)$ of the vehicles travelled between 440 and 480 miles.

Mileages	Frequency	Cumulative frequency	Cumulative percentage
400 to under 420	12	12	$10 \cdot 0$
420 to under 440	27	39	$32 \cdot 5$
440 to under 460	34	73	$60 \cdot 8$
460 to under 480	24	97	$80 \cdot 8$
480 to under 500	15	112	$93 \cdot 3$
500 to under 520	8	120	$100 \cdot 0$
Total	120		

Table 31.5. *'Less than' cumulative frequency distribution*

Because the figures have been accumulated from the lowest class to the highest, Table 31.5 is called a 'less than' cumulative frequency distribution.

Table 31.6 shows a 'more than' cumulative frequency distribution in which the frequencies have been accumulated in reverse order.

Hence, Table 31.6 shows directly that 90% of the vehicles travelled more than 420 miles and $6 \cdot 7\%$ travelled more than 500 miles. Simple calculations also allow 'less than' figures to be derived, just as 'more than' figures can be calculated from the 'less than' cumulative frequency distribution.

Mileages	Frequency	Cumulative frequency	Cumulative percentage
400 to under 420	12	120	100·0
420 to under 440	27	108	90·0
440 to under 460	34	81	67·5
460 to under 480	24	47	39·2
480 to under 500	15	23	19·2
500 to under 520	8	8	6·7
Total	120		

Table 31.6. *'More than' cumulative frequency distribution*

Histograms

When the data in a grouped frequency distribution is presented diagrammatically, the resulting representation is called a *histogram*. The class groupings are used to label the horizontal axis, and the frequency (either as an actual figure or as a percentage of the total number of figures) is used for the vertical axis. Figure 31.10 shows the grouped frequency distribution.

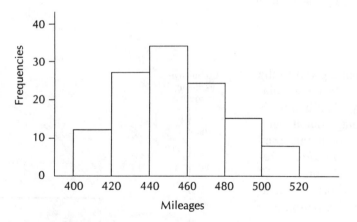

Figure 31.10. *Histogram of grouped frequency distribution*

A histogram essentially consists of vertically aligned rectangles in which:

(i)   the widths represent the class intervals;

(ii)   the heights represent the frequencies.

The area of a rectangle in a histogram is directly proportional to the quantity that it represents. This is the distinction between a histogram and a bar chart which looks somewhat similar. Where a histogram has unequal class intervals, as illustrated in the Figure 31.11, great care must be taken to ensure that the areas under the rectangles are still proportioned correctly.

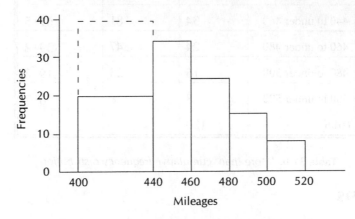

Figure 31.11. *Histogram with unequal class intervals*

Notice that the first class, representing 39 occurrences, being twice as wide as the other class intervals, is drawn half height. The dotted line shows the result of drawing it incorrectly: the diagram would be seriously in error.

Ogives

Ogive is the name given to the graph obtained when a cumulative frequency distribution is represented diagrammatically. Another name commonly used for an ogive is a *cumulative frequency curve*. Figure 31.12 shows one 'less than' cumulative frequency distribution as a 'less than' ogive.

Note that ogives start at zero on the vertical scale and end at the outside class limit of the last class. The vertical axis on the right of the diagram gives the cumulative frequency as a

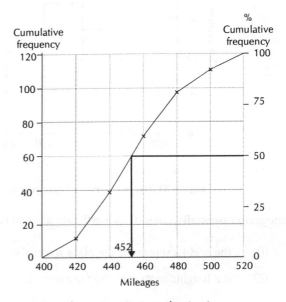

Figure 31.12. *'Less than' ogive*

percentage, so that either scale may be used. The graph may be used in the same way as Table 31.5, on which it is based. Thus, approximately 50% of the mileages are less than 452 miles. This is an approximate figure because the 50% point does not correspond exactly with a class boundary; it is not clear whether the mileages in the interval 440 to under 460 are evenly distributed over the interval.

Ogives may also be of the 'more than' variety when they are based on the corresponding cumulative frequency distribution. An ogive curve provides a useful and efficient method of determining *percentiles*. Percentiles are points in the distribution below which a given percentage of the total lies. A percentile divides a set of observations into two groups. For example, using a 'less than' ogive, 25% of the mileages are below the 25 percentile (that is below 434 miles approximately). Commonly used percentiles are known as *quartiles*:

- ❑ the 25th percentile is the first quartile;
- ❑ the 50th percentile is the second quartile (also known as the *median*);
- ❑ the 75th percentile is the third quartile.

Percentiles are a very useful way of expressing such statistics as "50% of the individual wealth of the U.K. is in the hands of 5% of the population".

Measures of location

Measures of location, or measures of central value, are average values. The most common types of averages are

(i)   The *arithmetic mean* (or just *mean*).

(ii)   The *median*.

(iii)   The *mode*.

Each one of these measures attempts to represent a collection of figures with one single figure, though in fact each really is only representative of one aspect of the figures. They all may be determined exactly from ungrouped data, or approximately from grouped data. The following sections summarise the methods of calculation and the significance of each average. In the following pages reference will be made to the data in the ungrouped frequency distribution shown in Table 31.7.

House number	1	2	3	4	5	6	7	8	9	10	11	12	13	14	15	16	17	18	19
Number of children	0	0	0	0	0	0	1	1	1	1	2	2	2	2	3	3	4	5	6

Table 31.7. *Children in Mean Street*

The following notation will be used:

$$\Sigma = \text{sum of}$$
$$\bar{x} = \text{mean value}$$
$$x_i = \text{single value}$$
$$n = \text{number of values}$$
$$f = \text{frequency}$$

Mean

Calculation of the mean

(a) Ungrouped data:

    (i)   add together all the values;

    (ii)   divide by the number of values.

         The mathematical notation for the calculation is

$$\bar{x} = \frac{\sum x_i}{n} \qquad i = 1, ..., n$$

         Using the values in Table 31.7, this gives

$$\bar{x} = \frac{33}{19} = 1 \cdot 74 \text{ approx}$$

(b) Grouped frequency distribution

    (i)   multiply each class mid point by the class frequency;

    (ii)   add these values together;

    (iii)   divide by the sum of the frequencies.

         The mathematical notation for the calculation is

$$\bar{x} = \frac{\sum (f \times ClassMid)}{\sum f}$$

         Using the values in Table 31.7 this gives

$$\bar{x} = \frac{12 \times 410 + 27 \times 430 + 34 \times 450 + 24 \times 470 + 15 \times 490 + 8 \times 510}{120}$$

$$\bar{x} = 454 \cdot 5$$

Significance of the mean

The arithmetic mean indicates what value each item would have if the total of all values were shared out equally. To discover the result which would follow from an equal distribution of something (consumption of beer per head, say) the mean is the most suitable measure.

Features of the mean

The mean:

- ❑   makes use of every value in the distribution;

- ❑   can be distorted by extreme values;

- ❑   can be used for further mathematical processing;

- ❑   may result in an impossible figure (1·74 children);

- ❑   best known of all the averages.

Median

Calculation of the median

(a)   Ungrouped data

   (i)   arrange the data into ascending order of magnitude;

   (ii)   locate the middle term - this is the median. (If there are an even number of numbers and there is no middle term then the nearest to the mid-point on either side will do)

   The median item in the Mean Street example is the 10th one and the value of the median is therefore 1. In the mileages example, from Table 31.3 the middle item is the 60th and the median value is 452 miles.

(b)   Grouped frequency distribution

   (i)   produce the equivalent ogive;

   (ii)   read off the value of the 2nd quartile - this gives the median value. (See the 'less than' ogive in Figure 31.12)

Significance of the median

The median is merely the value of the middle term when the data is arranged into ascending order of magnitude. Consequently there will be as many terms above it as below it. If a person interested in a job with a firm wanted some idea of the salary to expect, he or she might use the median salary as a guide.

Features of the median

The median:

- ❑ uses only one value in the distribution;

- ❑ cannot be used for further mathematical processing;

- ❑ it is always an actual value occurring in the distribution;

- ❑ it can be computed from incomplete data.

Mode

Calculation of the mode

The mode is usually derived from an ungrouped frequency distribution by determining the value which occurs most frequently. In Mean Street, the value occurring most frequently is 0 children. In Table 31.3, which shows an ungrouped frequency distribution, there are several modes: each mileage which occurs three times is a mode of the distribution of mileages.

Significance of the mode

As the mode is the value that occurs most frequently, it represents the typical item. It is this form of average that is implied by such expressions as 'the average person' or 'the average holiday'.

Features of the mode

The mode:

- ❑ is an actual value;

- ❑ cannot be used for further mathematical processing.

Dispersion

Quoting an average value, such as the mean, is an attempt to describe a distribution figure by a single representative number. Such averages, however, suffer from the disadvantage that they give no indication of the spread, or dispersion, of the figures represented. For example, the following two sets of numbers have identical means but the range of values is much greater in the first case than the second:

$$10 \ 20 \ 30 \quad \text{mean value} = 20$$
$$18 \ 20 \ 22 \quad \text{mean value} = 20$$

Figure 31.13 further illustrates how two distributions with the same mean value can have greatly different distributions.

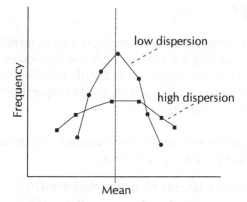

Figure 31.13. *Two widely differing distributions of the same mean value*

It is therefore also desirable to be able to describe the dispersion of data in a distribution with just a single figure.

Four such measures will be described. They are:

(a)   the *range*;

(b)   the *interquartile range*;

(c)   the *mean deviation*;

(d)   the *standard deviation*.

Range

The *range* is merely the difference between the highest and the lowest values:

range = highest value – lowest value

The range of the distribution of mileages given in the ungrouped frequency distribution in Table 31.3 is given by:

range = 515 – 403 = 112 miles

Unfortunately the range, like the mean, is influenced by extreme values. If the majority of the figures in the distribution cluster around a certain value, but there are a small number having extreme values, then the range does not provide a very accurate measure of the dispersion of the majority of the distribution. For example, if in the ungrouped frequency distribution in

Table 31.3, one of the mileages had been 112 miles, then the range would be $515 - 112 = 403$ miles, more than three times the previous figure, even though only one figure had changed.

Interquartile range

The disadvantage with the range as a measure of dispersion, as identified above, can be overcome to some degree by ignoring the extreme high and low values so that the measure of dispersion is representative of the majority of the distribution. One method of doing this is to use the values at the lower limit of the 3rd quartile and the upper limit of the 1st quartile as the values from which the range is calculated.

These figures give the *interquartile range*. For example, with reference to the 'less than' ogive in Figure 31.12, these figures are as follows:

> lower limit of 3rd quartile (75th percentile) = 476
> upper limit of 1st quartile (25th percentile) = 434
> interquartile range = 476 – 434 = 42 miles

Another measure of dispersion which is sometimes useful is the *semi-interquartile range* which is found by dividing the interquartile range by two. Another name for this latter measure of dispersion is the *quartile deviation*.

The chief disadvantages of these measures of dispersion are that they still are unable to take into account any degree of clustering in the distribution, and they do not use all of the values in the distribution.

Mean deviation

Another method of measuring dispersion is to find the deviations of all the items from the average, ignore their signs, and find the arithmetic mean of their magnitude. This is known as the *mean deviation*.

For example, to find the mean deviation of the following set of numbers,

> 27   33   36   37   39   39   40   44   50   55

the mean deviation can be calculated as follows.

(i) Sum of numbers	$= 400$
(ii) Mean value	$= \dfrac{400}{10} = 40$
(iii) Deviation from mean:	$-13 \quad -7 \quad -4 \quad -3 \quad -1 \quad -1 \quad 0 \quad 4 \quad 10 \quad 15$
(iv) Sum of deviations (ignoring sign)	$= 58$
(v) Mean deviation	$= \dfrac{58}{10} = 5 \cdot 8$

The mean deviation of the numbers is $5 \cdot 8$.

Standard deviation

The Greek letter σ is universally adopted to represent standard deviation. The formula for standard deviation is as follows:

Standard deviation $(\sigma) = \sqrt{\dfrac{\Sigma\left(x - \bar{x}\right)^2}{n}}$

or, where the figures come from an ungrouped frequency distribution,

$$\sigma = \sqrt{\dfrac{\Sigma f\left(x - \bar{x}\right)^2}{\Sigma f}}$$

Setting out the calculation in the form of a table, and using the figures above for the mean deviation calculation, the calculation may be performed as shown on the right.

Note that by squaring the difference between the mean and a value, the minus signs disappear.

x	$(x - \bar{x})$	$(x - \bar{x})^2$
27	-13	169
33	-7	49
36	-4	16
37	-3	9
39	-1	1
39	-1	1
40	0	0
44	4	16
50	10	100
55	15	225
$\Sigma x = 400$		$\Sigma(x - \bar{x})^2 = 586$

Standard deviation $(\sigma) = \sqrt{\dfrac{(x - \bar{x})^2}{n}} = \sqrt{\dfrac{586}{10}} = 7 \cdot 655$

To summarise, the steps involved in calculating the standard deviation of a distribution are as follows:

(i)   Calculate the arithmetic mean.

(ii)   Subtract the mean from each value.

(iii) Square each value in (ii).

(iv)   find the sum of all the values in (iii).

(v)   Divide by the number of numbers.

(vi)   Take the square root of the result of (v).

Where the standard deviation is to be calculated from an ungrouped frequency distribution, in step (ii) the result would be multiplied by the frequency of the value, and in step (v) the sum of the frequencies would be used as the divisor.

Reference is frequently made to the *variance* of a distribution. This is the square of the standard deviation. In the previous example, the variance of the distribution is given by

$$\text{Variance} = (\text{standard deviation})^2 = 58 \cdot 6$$

and conversely,

$$\text{Standard deviation} = \sqrt{\text{variance}} = \sqrt{58 \cdot 6} = 7 \cdot 655$$

Comparison of measures of dispersion

Of the measures of dispersion considered in this section, the *standard deviation* is the most important, but also the most difficult to comprehend. Basically, the standard deviation provides a measure of the likelihood of any random value from the distribution being close to the arithmetic mean of the distribution. The greater the measure of deviation, the less likely it is that any value chosen at random will be the mean value. Its importance lies chiefly in the considerable use made of it in analytical statistics, and a familiarity with it is crucial to making progress in more advanced statistical techniques.

The *range* is very easy to calculate but is sensitive to extreme values, and it does not take into account all of the figures or give any indication of the clustering of data. It is not generally a very reliable or accurate measure of dispersion.

The *interquartile range* also has the disadvantage that only two values from the distribution are used in its calculation, but it is less affected by extreme values. It is useful when the distribution is evenly distributed except for a number of extreme values.

The *mean deviation* has the advantage of using all of the figures in the distribution and is a measure of how far, on average, the values in the distribution are dispersed from the mean value. Its chief disadvantage is that it is not particularly well suited to algebraic treatment.

If the distribution of values is fairly symmetrical about the mean, bell shaped and the number of items is large, (that is, it is more or less what is known as a *normal distribution* as shown in Figure 31.14), then the following relations are approximately true:

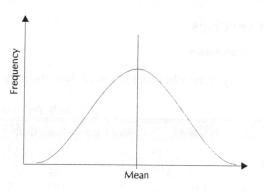

Figure 31.14. *Normal distribution*

$$\text{Quartile deviation} = \frac{2}{3} \text{ standard deviation, and}$$

$$\text{Mean deviation} = \frac{4}{5} \text{ standard deviation.}$$

Thus, for approximately normal distributions (which are of great importance in analytical statistics), the quartile and mean deviations may be used to approximate the standard deviation.

Statistics packages

Because of the usefulness of statistical analysis in such a wide variety of disciplines - in business, medicine, social sciences and many others - there are now a great number of computer programs available to ease the amount of laborious (and error-prone) work involved in statistical analysis. Many of these packages are subject orientated (for example, SPSS - Statistical Package for Social Sciences) offering facilities relevant to the subject, while others are purely general purpose. Many statistics packages will generate diagrams such as pie charts and bar charts automatically. Most of the well known integrated packages and spreadsheets contain functions to calculate means and standard deviations and also to produce statistical diagrams from data entered.

When using such packages, however, it is vital that the user is aware of the theory on which the package operates, particularly when the package is being used for analytical statistics. When considering the use or purchase of a program for statistical analysis, a vital factor is the quality and detail of the documentation provided; with good documentation the user can be confident about the interpretation of the statistical analysis undertaken.

Exercises

A dairy farmer has decided to analyse the milk yields of his cows for 1997, shown below.

Milk Yields (pints) 1997

Mth	Bessie	Maisie	Cowslip	Dandelion	Dolly	Ermintrude	Ruth	Bob	Gretchen	Polly
Jan	177	186	194	178	153	116	186	186	100	204
Feb	179	192	212	182	154	116	178	198	112	194
Mar	186	184	210	181	155	113	184	190	113	206
Apr	176	195	194	177	148	93	186	199	102	206
May	182	191	205	183	146	113	185	200	122	205
Jun	186	186	209	180	148	93	178	183	110	203
Jul	178	194	201	182	152	102	179	210	107	207
Aug	185	187	189	182	149	100	186	195	106	200
Sep	175	187	195	179	148	119	176	204	99	200
Oct	178	194	196	182	153	108	176	171	97	196
Nov	182	192	204	182	154	95	177	193	104	205
Dec	178	190	197	179	156	82	179	188	113	199

Using the table for milk yields calculate the following statistics:

(i)   Overall range of milk yields.

(ii)   Range of yields for each cow.

(iii)   Mean yields of each cow for 1997.

(iv) Modal yields of each cow for 1997.

(v)   Median yields of each cow for 1997.

(vi) Mean overall yield.

(vii)   Produce a grouped frequency distribution for the milk yields for all the cows for 1997.

(viii) Draw a histogram using the frequency distribution.

(ix)   Draw a pictogram of the total monthly milk yields. (i.e. total milk yield for each month)

(x)   Use a bar chart to compare the total monthly yields

(xi) Draw a line graph showing Polly's milk yields for 1997.

(xii) Use a line graph to compare the milk yields of Cowslip and Ermintrude for 1997.

(xiii) Use a bar chart to compare the mean yields of the cows for 1997.

(xiv) Calculate the standard deviation of Dandelion's milk yields.

Chapter 32
Financial Accounts Software

This chapter describes the various financial accounting systems of a typical business and the packaged software available to support them. Intuit's QuickBooks© is used to illustrate various features of accounting packages.

The ledgers

Business accounts are needed to record:

- debtor transactions; debtors are people or organisations who owe money to the business for goods or services provided (credit sales);

- creditor transactions; creditors are people or organisations to whom the business owes money, for the supply of goods (credit purchases).

These transactions are recorded in the *sales ledger* (or *accounts receivable*) and the *purchases ledger* (or *accounts payable*) respectively. A third ledger, the *general* (or nominal) *ledger* is used to record the overall income and expenditure of the business, with each transaction classified according to its purpose.

Sales ledger or accounts receivable

General description

The purpose of the sales ledger is to keep a record of amounts owed to a business by its trading customers or clients. It contains a record for each customer with a credit arrangement. Most businesses permit their customers to buy goods on credit. The goods are usually supplied on the understanding that, once payment has been requested, the debt will be paid for within a specified period of, for example, 14 or 30 days. Payment is requested with the use of an *invoice* addressed to the customer and containing details of goods supplied, the amount owing and credit days given. Once a customer order has been accepted and processed, the total amount due for the order is recorded in the relevant customer's account in the sales ledger and the balance owing is increased accordingly. When a payment is received from the customer, the amount is entered to the customer's account and the balance owing is decreased by the appropriate amount. There are two main approaches to sales ledger maintenance, *balance forward* and *open item*.

(i) Balance forward. This method provides: an opening balance (the amount owing at the beginning of the month); the transactions for that month, giving the date, type (for example, goods sold or payment received); the amount of each transaction; a closing balance. The closing balance at the end of the month is carried forward as the opening balance for the next month. A statement of account, detailing all the transactions for the month will normally be sent to the customer and a copy filed away for business records. The customer's account in the sales ledger will not then contain details of the previous month's transactions so any query will require reference to the filed statements of account.

(ii) Open item. The open item method is more complicated in that each invoice is identified by a code and requires payments from customers to be matched against the relevant invoices. All payments received and relating to a particular invoice are recorded against it until it is completely paid off. This method can make control difficult as some customers may make part payments, which cannot be tied to a particular invoice. If a customer does not specify to which invoice a particular payment relates it is normally assigned to the oldest invoice(s). Once an invoice has been completely settled it is cleared from the ledger and any subsequent statements of account.

Package requirements and facilities

Customer master file

When setting up the Sales Ledger system, one of the first tasks is to open an account for each customer. These accounts are maintained in a sales ledger *master file*, which is updated by sales and account settlement transactions.

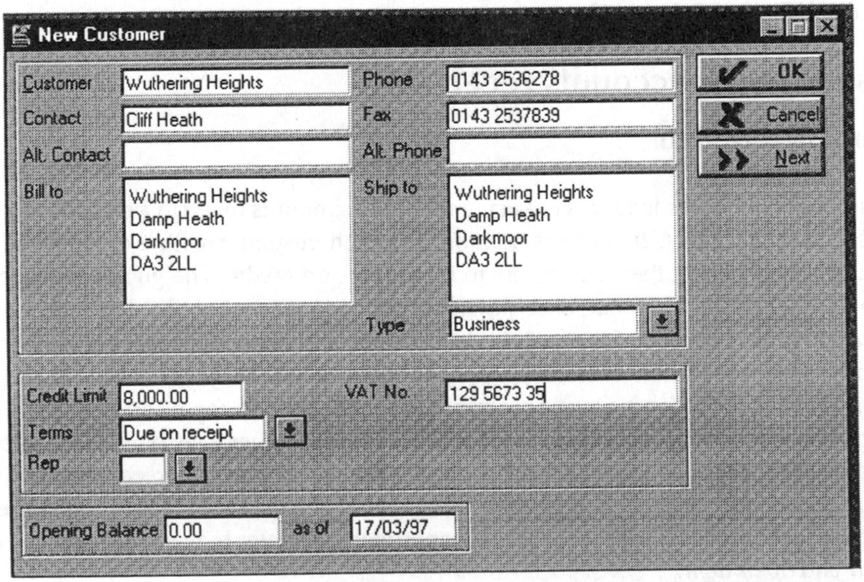

Figure 32.1. *New customer entry form*

A typical package should provide as a minimum, the following data item types for each customer record:

❑   account number - used to identify uniquely a customer record;

❑   name and address - this will normally be the customer's address to which statements of account and invoices are sent;

❑   credit limit - the maximum amount of credit to be allowed.

❑   balance - this is the balance of the customer's account.

Sometimes, when the file is first created, a zero balance is recorded and outstanding transactions are entered to produce a current balance. An open item system stores details of any unpaid invoices, so that each can be associated with a particular customer account. Figure 32.1 on the previous page provides an example of a form for entry of a new customer record.

Transaction entries

Transactions may be applied directly to customer accounts in the sales ledger (*transaction processing*) or they may be initially stored as a transaction file for a *batch* updating run. Whichever method the package uses, it should allow for the entry of the following:

❑   invoice - this is sent to the customer requesting payment concerning a particular order. The amount of the invoice is debited to the customer's account in the sales ledger, thus increasing the amount owing. Figure 32.2 illustrates the process for creating an invoice.

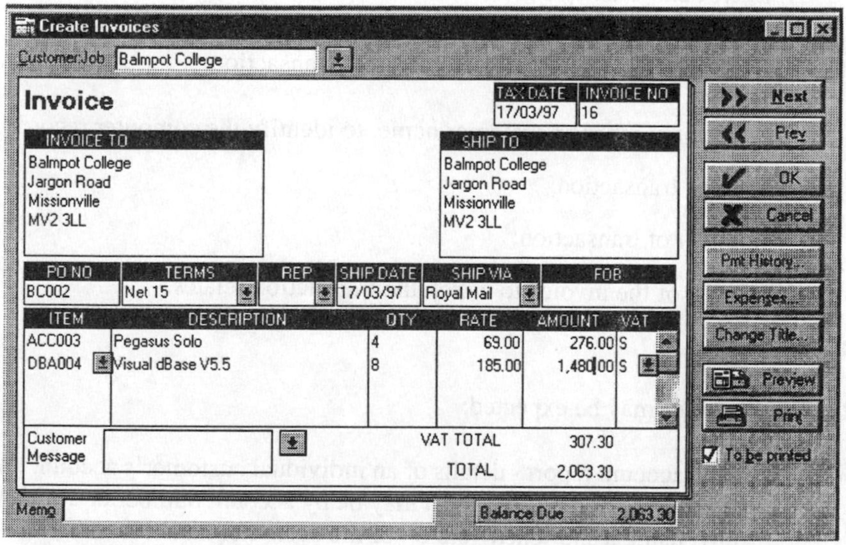

Figure 32.2. *Form for creating new invoices*

    ❑   credit note. If, for example, goods are returned by a customer or there is a dispute concerning the goods, a credit note is issued by the business to the customer. The amount of the credit note will be credited to the customer's account in the sales ledger, thus reducing the balance owing. Credit notes are often printed in red to distinguish them from invoices;

    ❑   receipt of payment - this is any payment or remittance received from a customer in whole or partial settlement of an invoice. Such an entry will be credited to the customer's account and reduce the balance owing accordingly. Figure 32.3 shows such a payment being recorded.

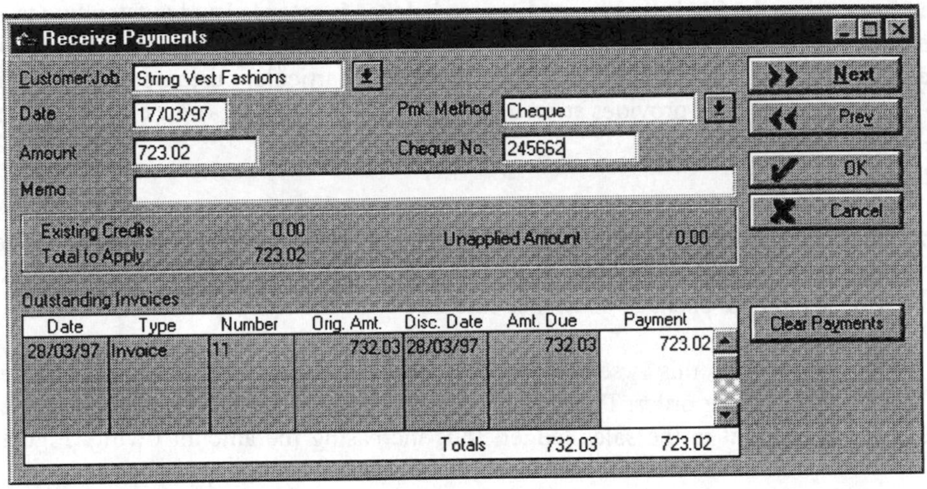

Figure 32.3. *Entering a payment received in settlement of an invoice*

The following data may be entered with each type of transaction:

    ❑   account number or customer name, to identify the computer record;

    ❑   date of transaction;

    ❑   amount of transaction;

    ❑   details of the invoice to which the transaction relates.

Outputs

The following facilities may be expected:

    ❑   single account report - details of an individual customer's account can be displayed on screen. Retrieval may be by account number or a search facility, using a shortened version of the customer name. If more than one record is retrieved by this method they may be scanned through on screen until the required record is found. Figure 32.4 shows an example.

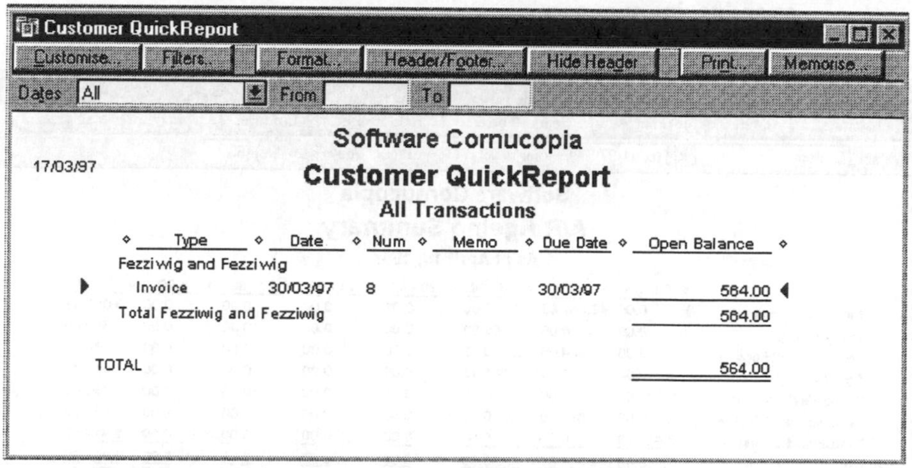

Figure 32.4. *Viewing a customer account*

- customer statement printing - it is essential that the system can produce monthly statements for sending to customers;

- status of invoices (accounts receivable), indicating whether paid or unpaid and due dates. Figure 32.5 shows an extract of such a report.

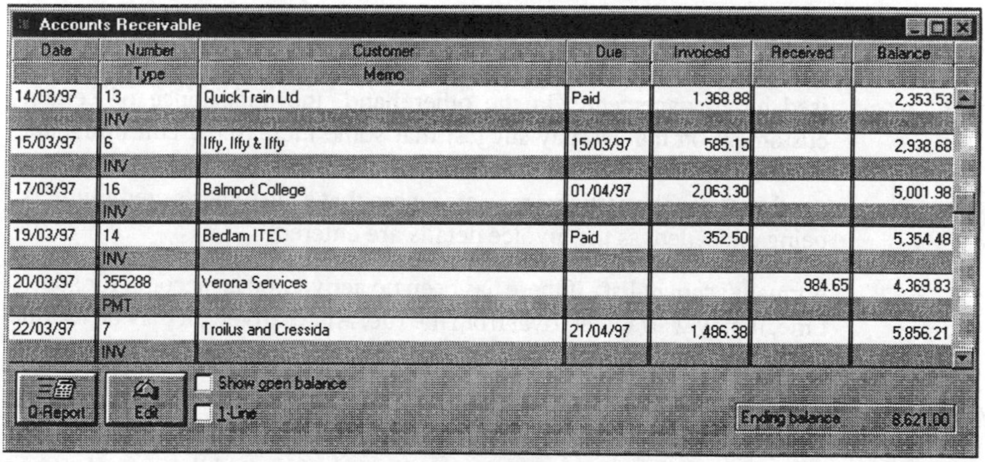

Date	Number / Type	Customer / Memo	Due	Invoiced	Received	Balance
14/03/97	13 INV	QuickTrain Ltd	Paid	1,368.88		2,353.53
15/03/97	6 INV	Iffy, Iffy & Iffy	15/03/97	585.15		2,938.68
17/03/97	16 INV	Balmpot College	01/04/97	2,063.30		5,001.98
19/03/97	14 INV	Bedlam ITEC	Paid	352.50		5,354.48
20/03/97	355288 PMT	Verona Services			984.65	4,369.83
22/03/97	7 INV	Troilus and Cressida	21/04/97	1,486.38		5,856.21

Figure 32.5. *Debtors*

- debtors' age analysis - this provides a schedule of the total amounts owing by customers, categorised according to the time various portions of the total debt have been outstanding (unpaid). It is important for a business to make financial provision for the possibility of *bad debts*. These are debts which are unlikely to be settled and may have to be taken out of business profits. Figure 32.6 shows a debtors analysis report, referred to as an 'ageing summary'.

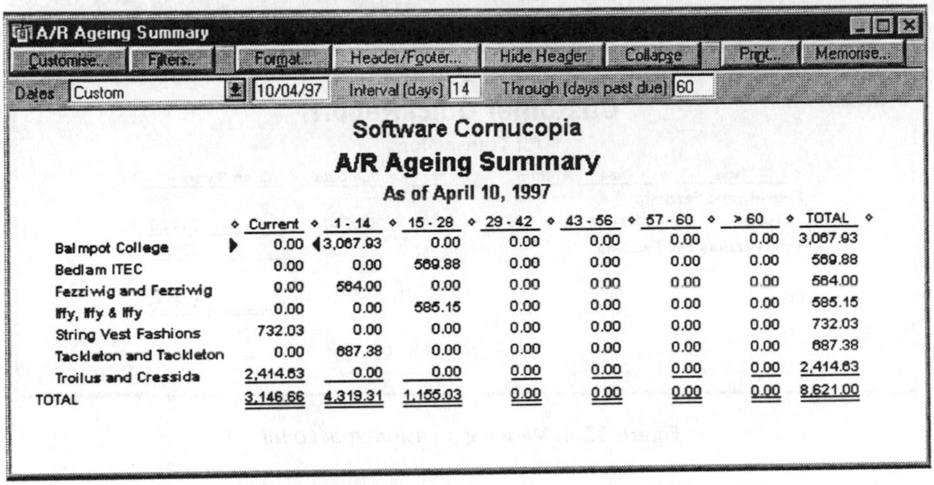

Software Cornucopia

A/R Ageing Summary

As of April 10, 1997

	Current	1 - 14	15 - 28	29 - 42	43 - 56	57 - 60	> 60	TOTAL
Balmpot College	0.00	3,067.93	0.00	0.00	0.00	0.00	0.00	3,067.93
Bedlam ITEC	0.00	0.00	569.88	0.00	0.00	0.00	0.00	569.88
Fezziwig and Fezziwig	0.00	564.00	0.00	0.00	0.00	0.00	0.00	564.00
Iffy, Iffy & Iffy	0.00	0.00	585.15	0.00	0.00	0.00	0.00	585.15
String Vest Fashions	732.03	0.00	0.00	0.00	0.00	0.00	0.00	732.03
Tackleton and Tackleton	0.00	687.38	0.00	0.00	0.00	0.00	0.00	687.38
Troilus and Cressida	2,414.63	0.00	0.00	0.00	0.00	0.00	0.00	2,414.63
TOTAL	3,146.66	4,319.31	1,155.03	0.00	0.00	0.00	0.00	8,621.00

Figure 32.6. *Debtors' age analysis*

From his or her own experience of the trade, the proprietor of business should be able to estimate the percentage of each debt that is likely to become bad. Generally, the longer the debt has been outstanding, the greater the likelihood that it will remain unpaid.

- ❑ customers over credit limit - this may form the basis of a 'black list' of customers. Any new order from one of these customers has to be authorised by management. On the other hand, the appearance of certain customers on the list may suggest that some increased credit limits are needed. When a business is successful, it often needs more credit to expand further. The software may also warn that a customer's credit limit is being exceeded, as the invoice details are entered.
- ❑ dormant account list - if there has been no activity on an account for some time, it may warrant removal from the file. Alternatively, it may be useful to contact the customer to see if further business may be forthcoming.

Validation and control

The package should provide for careful validation of transactions and the protection of records from unauthorised access or amendment. Generally, for example, a customer record cannot be removed from the sales ledger while the account is still 'live' (there is a balance outstanding). More details of validation and control are given in Chapter 13 on System Controls.

Purchase ledger or accounts payable

General description

The purchase ledger function mirrors that of the sales ledger, except that it contains an account for each *supplier*, from whom the business buys goods. When trading with a supplier, it is usually through credit arrangements similar to those provided by the business for its own customers. Thus, the business receives an invoice requesting payment, within a certain period, for goods purchased. The amount of the invoice is credited to the supplier's account and the balance owing to the supplier is increased accordingly. When payment is made to a supplier, in full or part settlement of an invoice, the supplier's account is debited by the appropriate amount and the balance is decreased. Most purchase ledger systems operate on an open item basis. Each supplier invoice is given a reference number and when payment is made to a supplier, the reference number can be used to allocate the payment to a particular invoice.

Package requirements and facilities

Supplier master file

The supplier master file contains the suppliers' (*creditors*) accounts. It is updated by supplier invoices and payments to suppliers. Figure 32.7 shows the process of entering a new supplier's details.

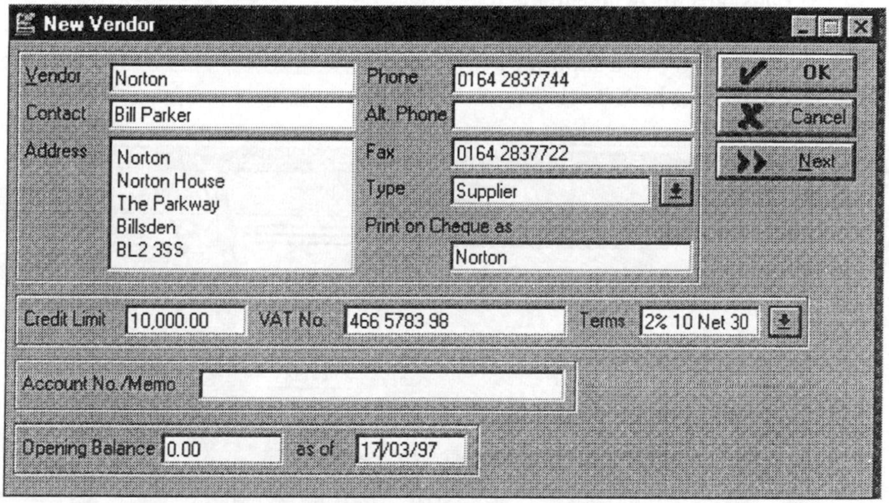

Figure 32.7. *Entering details for a new supplier*

A typical package should provide, as a minimum, the following data item types for each supplier record:

❏   account number or name, to identify a supplier record;

□   name and address - the name and address of the supplier business;

□   credit limit - the maximum amount of credit allowed to the business by the supplier at any one time. A check should be kept on this to avoid rejection of orders;

□   credit terms - this may include an amount of discount, if an invoice is settled within a specified discount period.

□   balance - the current balance on the account.

A choice is usually provided to select the form of purchase ledger required (either open item or balance forward).

Transactions

Transactions may update the supplier accounts directly (transaction processing) or they may be initially stored as a transaction file for a later updating run. A purchase ledger package should allow for the following transactions:

□   supplier invoices or bills. Before entry, each invoice must be checked against the appropriate order and then against the relevant delivery note, for actual receipt of goods. The balance on a supplier's account (the amount owed to the supplier) is increased by an invoice entry. Some packages allow unsatisfactory (there may be doubt about the delivery of the goods) invoices to be held in abeyance until cleared. Figure 32.8 shows entry of a supplier's invoice, together with details of the purchase orders to which it relates.

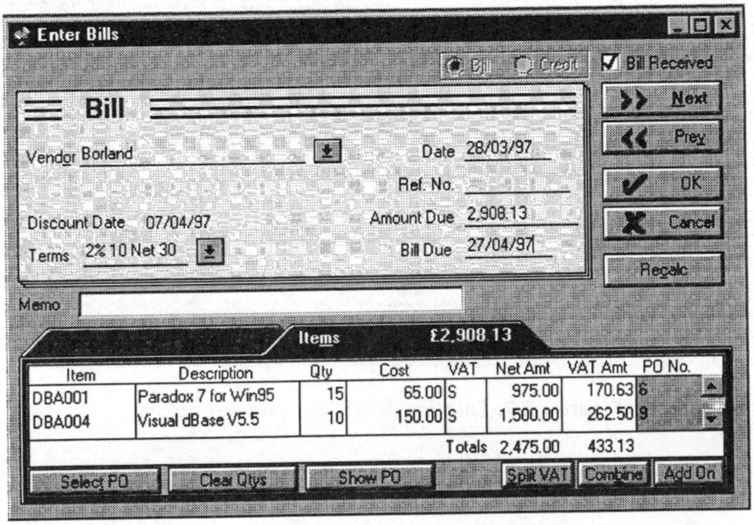

Figure 32.8. *Entering a bill (invoice) received from a supplier*

❑ approved payments - once an invoice has been cleared for payment, a voucher may be raised to ensure payment, on or before a due date, and discount for prompt payment. The entry of the payment value decreases the balance of a supplier's account and thus the amount owed by the business to the supplier. Cheques may be produced automatically on the due date, but there should be some checking procedure to ensure that payments are properly authorised. Figure 32.9 shows one outstanding invoice (bill) being paid.

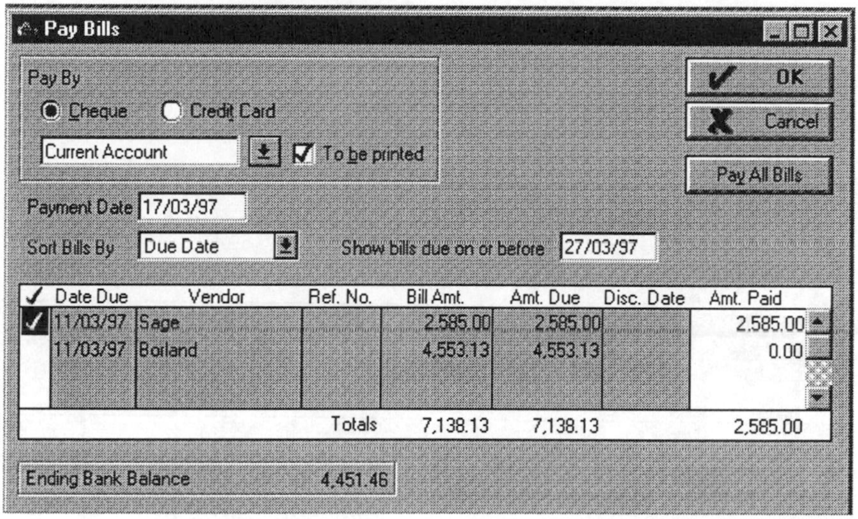

Figure 32.9. *Paying an outstanding bill or invoice*

❑ adjustments - to reverse entries made in error.

Outputs

The following output facilities may be expected:

❑ single account enquiries - details of an individual supplier's account can be displayed on screen. Retrieval may be through a supplier code or name. Figure 32.10 shows a screen report of Autocad's account.

❑ payment advice slip - this may be produced to accompany a payment to a supplier. Each payment slip details the invoice reference, the amount due and the value of the payment remitted. Payment advice slips help the supplier, who may be using an open item sales ledger system;

❑ status of invoices - a list of all paid and outstanding invoices (accounts payable), together with details of supplier, amount owing and due date. Figure 32.11 shows an extract of such a report;

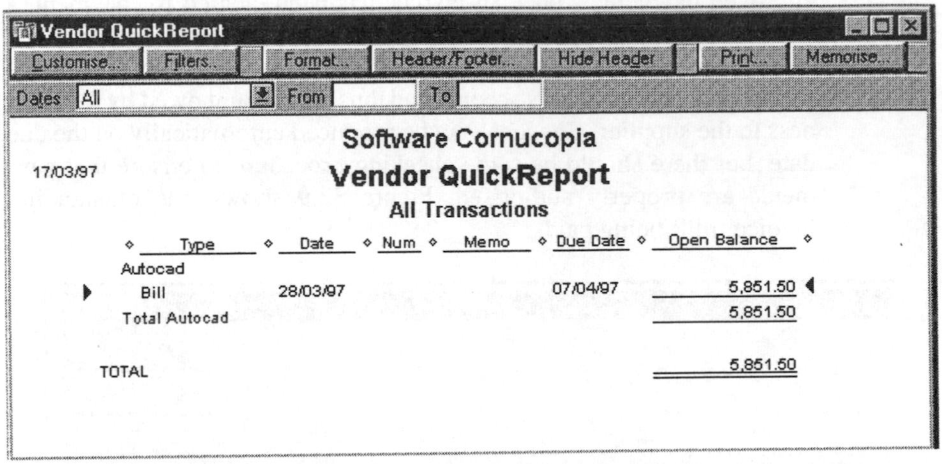

Figure 32.10. *Screen report on a supplier's account*

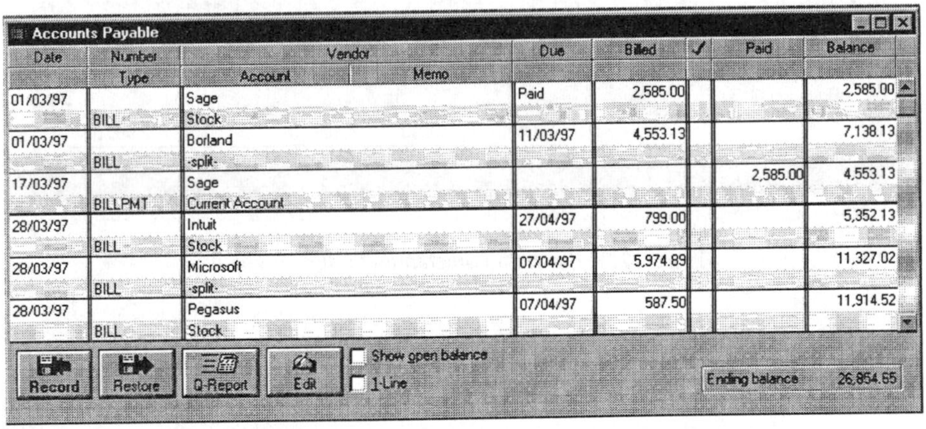

Figure 32.11. *Supplier invoice details (accounts payable)*

❑   creditors' age analysis - this is the supplier equivalent of debtors' age analysis. The report provides a schedule of total balances owing to suppliers, analysed according to the time the debt has been outstanding. The report may be used to determine which payments should be given priority over others. Figure 32.12 shows an example, referred to as an 'ageing summary'.

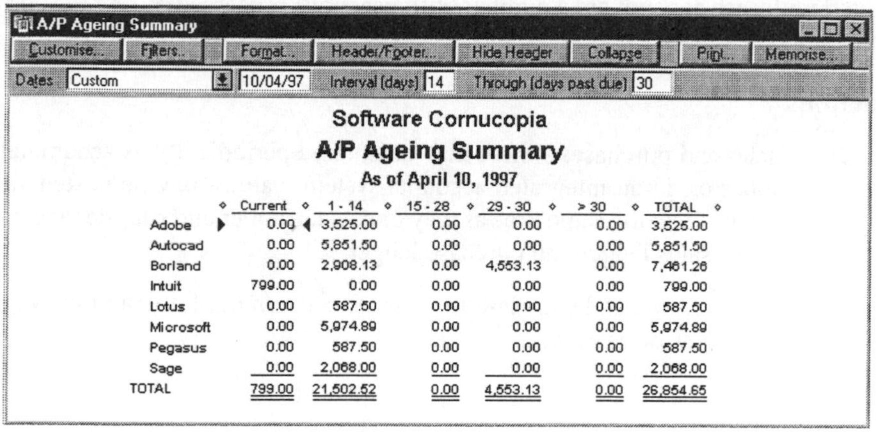

Software Cornucopia

A/P Ageing Summary

As of April 10, 1997

	Current	1 - 14	15 - 28	29 - 30	> 30	TOTAL
Adobe	0.00	3,525.00	0.00	0.00	0.00	3,525.00
Autocad	0.00	5,851.50	0.00	0.00	0.00	5,851.50
Borland	0.00	2,908.13	0.00	4,553.13	0.00	7,461.26
Intuit	799.00	0.00	0.00	0.00	0.00	799.00
Lotus	0.00	587.50	0.00	0.00	0.00	587.50
Microsoft	0.00	5,974.89	0.00	0.00	0.00	5,974.89
Pegasus	0.00	587.50	0.00	0.00	0.00	587.50
Sage	0.00	2,068.00	0.00	0.00	0.00	2,068.00
TOTAL	799.00	21,502.52	0.00	4,553.13	0.00	26,854.65

Figure 32.12. *Creditors' age analysis*

General ledger

General description

The general ledger is used to record the income and expenditure of a business, classified according to purpose. Thus, for example, it contains an account for *sales*; sales totals are entered on a daily basis. The sales ledger analyses sales by customer, whereas the *sales account* provides a cumulative total for sales as the accounting year progresses. The *purchases account* in the general ledger fulfils a similar purpose for purchases by the business. Other income and expenditure accounts recorded in the general ledger may include, for example, *rent*, *heating* and *wages*. If some items of income and expenditure are too small to warrant separate analysis, there may also be *sundry income* and *sundry expenditure* accounts. The information held in the general ledger accounts is used to draw up a *profit and loss account*. This account provides information on the trading performance of the business over the year. A *balance sheet* can then be produced to give a 'snapshot' view of the business's assets and liabilities, on a particular date.

Package requirements and facilities

General ledger accounts master file

When an account is opened in the general ledger, the following data item types should be available:

- ❑ account name - each account is given a name, to allow the allocation of transactions. For example, an entry for a gas bill payment may be directed to the Heating account;
- ❑ balance.

Associated with each account are a number of transactions processed during the current accounting period.

Transactions

- ❑ sales and purchases - these may be entered periodically as accumulated totals or, in an integrated accounts system, values may be posted automatically at the same time as they update customer and supplier accounts in the sales ledger and purchase ledger;
- ❑ other income and expenditure - entries concerning, for example, wages, rent, rates or heating.

Outputs

Typical output facilities include:

- ❑ trial balance - this is a list of debit and credit balances categorised by account. The balances are taken from the general ledger and the total of debit balances should agree with the total of credit balances. Figure 32.13 provides an example.

Software Cornucopia

Trial Balance

As of April 10, 1997

	Apr 10, '97 Debit	Apr 10, '97 Credit
Current Account	19,322.80	
Deposit Account	40,000.00	
Owner's Equity		40,000.00
Accounts Receivable		425.34
Undeposited Funds	0.00	
Stock	45,744.00	
Motor Vehicles:Van	7,031.91	
Accounts Payable		26,854.65
Lloyds business loan		20,000.00
VAT Control	3,061.70	
Opening Bal Equity		31,774.00
Retained Earnings	3,393.58	
Owner's Drawings	500.00	
TOTAL	119,053.99	119,053.99

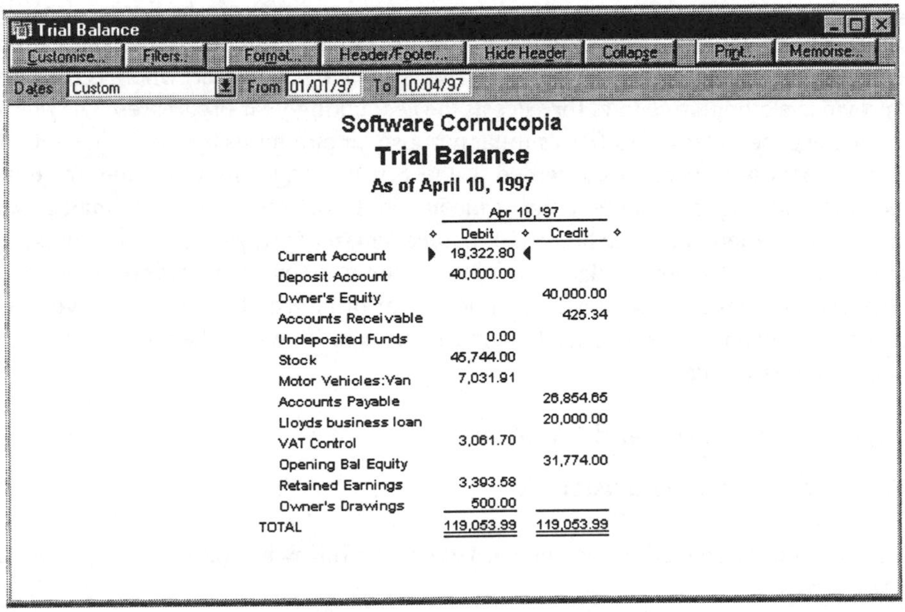

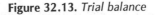

Figure 32.13. *Trial balance*

- ❑ audit trail - a full list of transactions which may be used for error checking purposes and to allow the validity of transactions to be checked by an external auditor. An extract of an audit trail is shown in Figure 32.14.

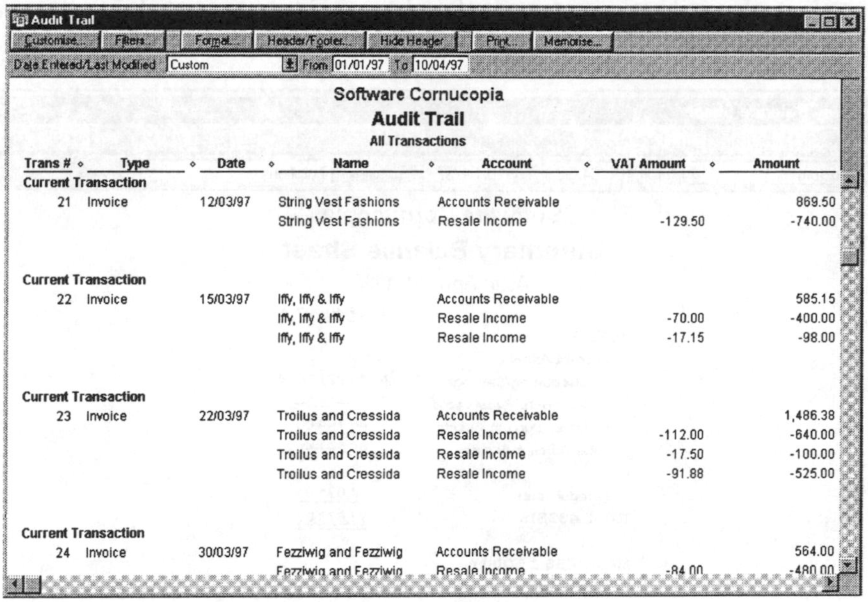

Software Cornucopia
Audit Trail
All Transactions

Trans #	Type	Date	Name	Account	VAT Amount	Amount
Current Transaction						
21	Invoice	12/03/97	String Vest Fashions	Accounts Receivable		869.50
			String Vest Fashions	Resale Income	-129.50	-740.00
Current Transaction						
22	Invoice	15/03/97	Iffy, Iffy & Iffy	Accounts Receivable		585.15
			Iffy, Iffy & Iffy	Resale Income	-70.00	-400.00
			Iffy, Iffy & Iffy	Resale Income	-17.15	-98.00
Current Transaction						
23	Invoice	22/03/97	Troilus and Cressida	Accounts Receivable		1,486.38
			Troilus and Cressida	Resale Income	-112.00	-640.00
			Troilus and Cressida	Resale Income	-17.50	-100.00
			Troilus and Cressida	Resale Income	-91.88	-525.00
Current Transaction						
24	Invoice	30/03/97	Fezziwig and Fezziwig	Accounts Receivable		564.00
			Fezziwig and Fezziwig	Resale Income	-84.00	-480.00

Figure 32.14. *Extract from an audit trail*

- trading and profit and loss account - a statement of the trading performance of the business over a given period. An example is shown in Figure 32.15;

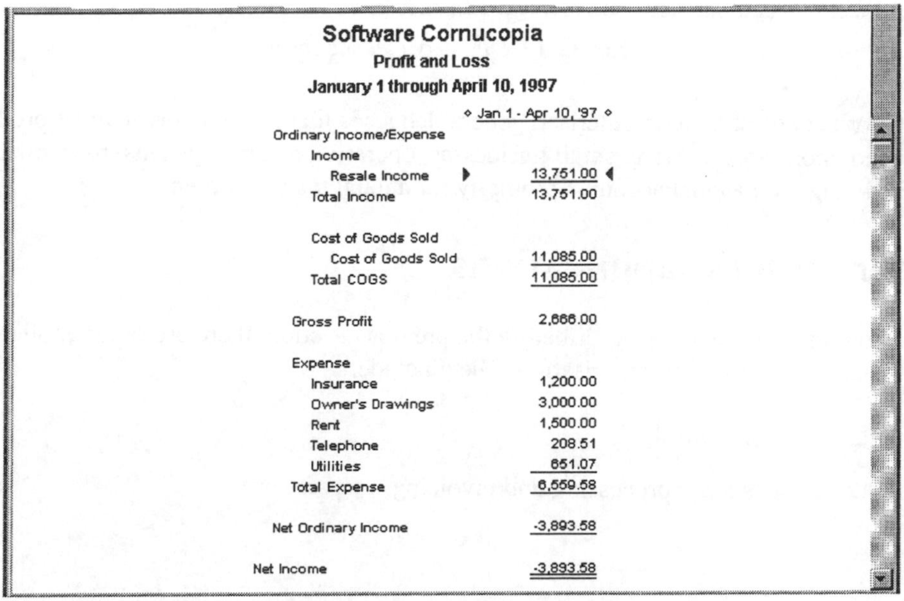

Software Cornucopia
Profit and Loss
January 1 through April 10, 1997

	Jan 1 - Apr 10, '97
Ordinary Income/Expense	
Income	
Resale Income	13,751.00
Total Income	13,751.00
Cost of Goods Sold	
Cost of Goods Sold	11,085.00
Total COGS	11,085.00
Gross Profit	2,666.00
Expense	
Insurance	1,200.00
Owner's Drawings	3,000.00
Rent	1,500.00
Telephone	208.51
Utilities	651.07
Total Expense	6,559.58
Net Ordinary Income	-3,893.58
Net Income	-3,893.58

Figure 32.15. *Profit and loss account*

❑   balance sheet - a statement of the business's assets and liabilities at a particular date. An example is shown in Figure 32.16;

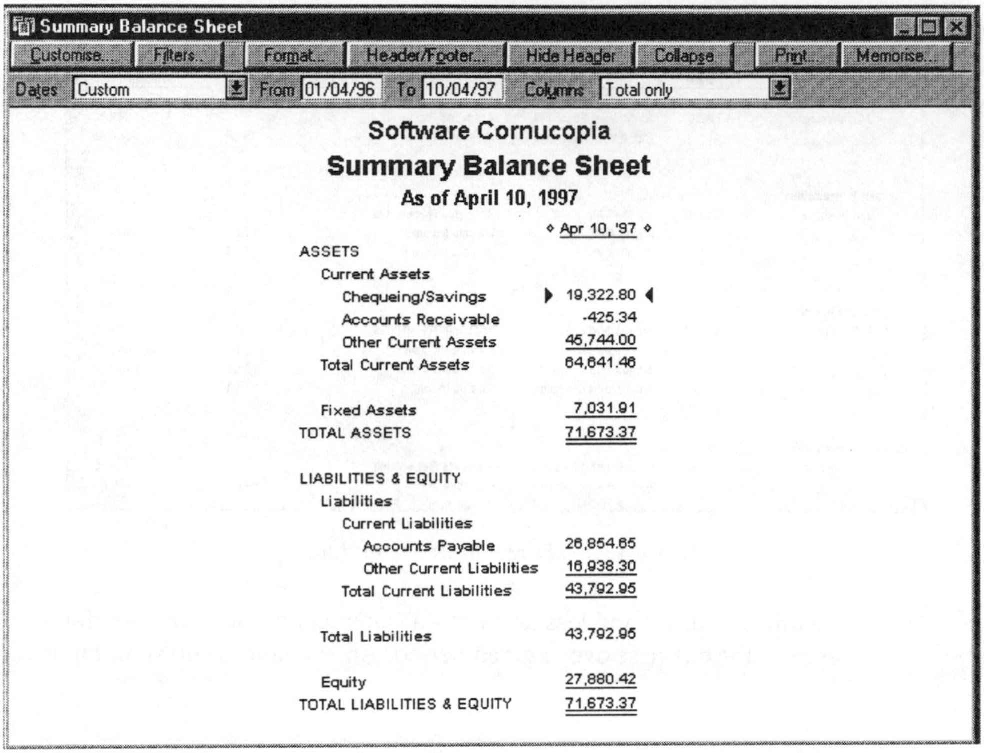

Figure 32.16. *Summary balance sheet*

The major benefit of the computerised general ledger is that these reports can be produced easily and upon request. Many small businesses, operating manual systems, have difficulty in completing their annual accounts promptly for annual tax assessment.

Other business applications

Apart from the basic ledgers described in the previous section, there are other applications which can benefit from computerisation. They include:

❑   stock control;

❑   sales order processing and invoicing.

Stock control

General description

Different businesses hold different kinds of stock. For example, a grocer holds some perishable and some non-perishable stocks of food and a clothing manufacturer holds stocks of materials and finished articles of clothing. Any trader's stock needs to be controlled, but the reasons for control may vary from one business to another. For example, a grocer wants to keep the full range of food items that customers expect, but does not want to be left with stocks of unsold items, especially if they are perishable. A clothing manufacturer's stocks will not perish if they are unsold, but space occupied by unwanted goods could be occupied by more popular items. On the other hand, if the manufacturer runs out of raw materials the production process can be slowed or even halted. Apart from such differences, there are some common reasons for wanting efficient stock control:

- excessive stock levels tie up valuable cash resources and increase business costs. The cash could be used to finance further business;

- inability to satisfy customer orders promptly because of insufficient stocks can often lead to loss of custom.

It is possible to identify some typical objectives of a stock control system and these can be used to measure the usefulness of facilities commonly offered by computer packages:

- to maintain levels of stock which will be sufficient to meet customer demand promptly;

- to provide a mechanism which removes the need for excessively high safety margins of stock to cover customer demand. This is usually effected by setting minimum stock levels which the computer can use to report variations outside these levels;

- to provide automatic re-ordering of stock items which fall below minimum levels;

- to provide management with up-to-date information on stock levels and values of stock held. Stock valuation is needed for accounting purposes.

Stock control requires that an individual record is maintained for each type of stock item held. Apart from details concerning the description and price of the stock item, each record should have a balance indicating the number of units held. A unit may be, for example, a box, 500 grams or a tonne. The balance is adjusted whenever units of that particular stock item are sold or purchased. Manual or computerised records can only give recorded levels of stock. Physical stock checks need to be carried out to determine the actual levels. If there is a difference between the recorded stock level of an item and the actual stock of that item, it could be because of pilferage or damage. Alternatively, some transactions for the item may not have been applied to the stock file.

Package requirements and facilities

Stock master file

The stock master file contains records for each item of stock and each record may usefully contain the following data item types:

❑   Stock code or reference - each stock item type should have a unique reference, for example, A0035. The code should be designed so that it is useful to the user. For example, an initial alphabetic character may be used to differentiate between raw materials (R) and finished goods (F) and the remaining digits may have ranges, which indicate particular product groupings. The stock file may also be used to record any consumable items used by a business, for example, stationery and printer ribbons. The initial character of the stock code could be used to identify such a grouping. The number and type of characters in a code, as well as its format, are usually limited by the package because the code is also used by the software to determine a record's location within the file;

❑   Description - although users may become used to referring to individual products by their codes or references, a description is needed for the production of, for example, purchase orders or customer invoices. Figure 32.17 shows a new item of stock being entered.

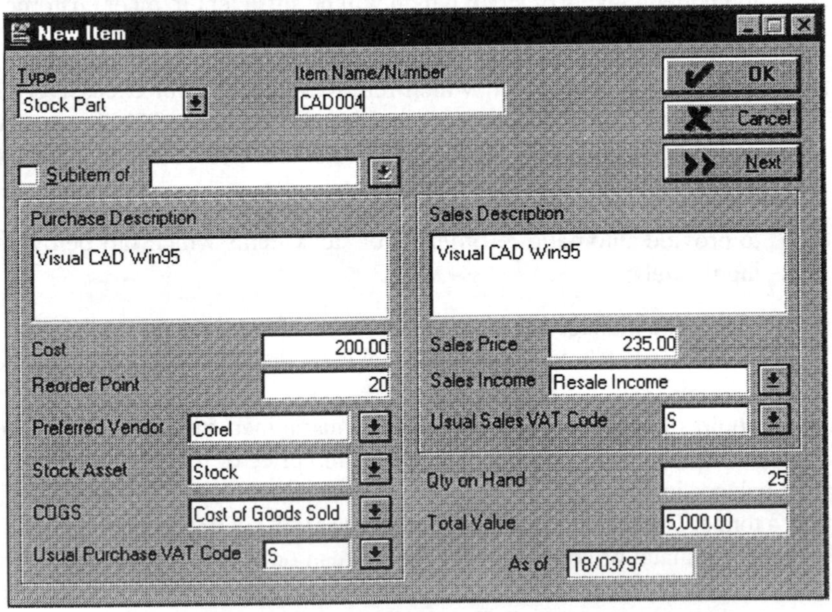

Figure 32.17. *Entering a new item of stock*

❑   Analysis code - this may be used in conjunction with sales orders so that they can be analysed by product group.

❑   Unit size - for example, box, metre, tonne, kilo;

❑   Re-order point - this is the stock level at which an item is to be re-ordered, for example, 30 boxes. Reaching this level may trigger an automatic re-order when the appropriate program option is run. Alternatively it may be necessary to request a summary report which highlights all items at or below their re-order level. The decision on what the re-order level should be for any particular item will depend on the sales turnover (the number of units sold per day or week) and the lead time (the time taken for delivery after a purchase order is placed with a supplier). Seasonal changes in sales figures will require that re-order levels for individual items are changed for time to time;

❑   Re-order quantity - this is the number of item units to be re-ordered from a supplier when new stock is required;

❑   Bin reference - this may be used to indicate the physical location of stock items within, for example, a warehouse;

❑   Cost price - the price paid by the business for the stock item;

❑   Sale price - the price charged to the customer. The package may allow the storage of more than one sale price to differentiate between, for example, retail and wholesale customers;

❑   VAT code - items may attract different rates of Value Added Tax (VAT);

❑   Supplier (vendor) - if orders can be produced automatically, then the supplier code may be used to access a supplier file, for the address and other details needed to produce an order;

❑   Quantity on hand - the current recorded level of stock. This will change whenever an issue, receipt or adjustment transaction is entered.

Transactions

❑   Entry of items received and bill (invoice) from supplier. Figure 32.18 shows the entry of a bill and a receipt of items.

❑   Goods returned - for example, stock returned by a customer or unused raw materials returned from the factory. Figure 32.19 illustrates the recording of returned itmes and the issue of a credit note to the customer.

❑   Goods issued - this may result from a customer order or from a factory requisition, if the business has a manufacturing process. In QuickBooks, the stock issue for a customer is recorded through entry of an invoice for the relevant items;

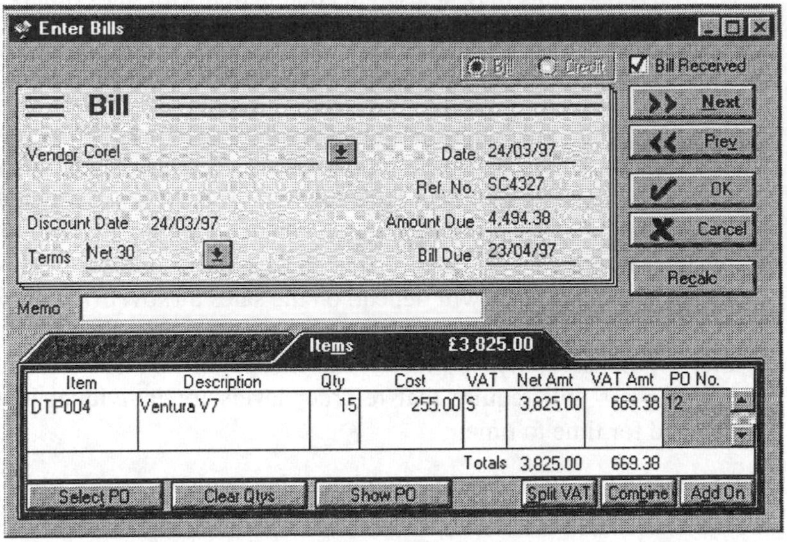

Figure 32.18. *Recording receipt of items and bill from supplier*

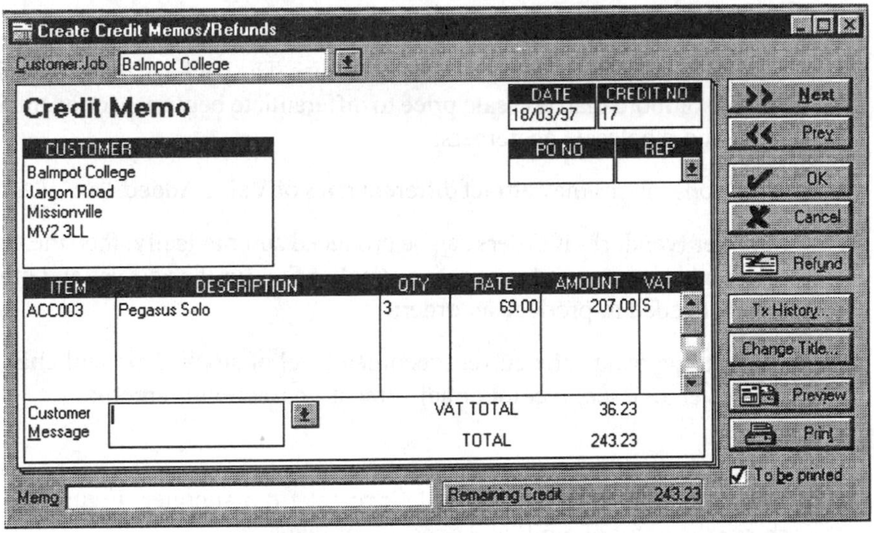

Figure 32.19. *Recording returned items and issue of credit to to customer*

❑   Stock allocated - this will not reduce the quantity in stock figure but the amount allocated should be used to offset the quantity in stock when judging what is available;

❑   Amendments - for, example, there may be amendments to price, re-order level or supplier code.

The method used to update the stock master file will depend on how up-to-date the figures need to be (this will depend on how 'tight' stock levels are) and how often the data entry operator can get at the computer. To keep the file up-to-date throughout the day, physical stock changes have to be notified immediately to stock control and the transactions have to be entered as they occur. Unfortunately, this means that a single-user system would be unavailable to any other users, such as sales staff, who needed to know quantities in stock. A networked system with central file storage, would allow continual updating and enquiry access. If the stock levels are sufficiently high to allow differences to arise between physical and 'book' totals without risking shortages, then daily batch updating may be acceptable. In such a situation, an enquiry on a stock item may reveal, for example, a 'book' stock of 200 units, when the physical stock is only 120 units (80 having been issued since the last update at the end of the preceding day).

Outputs

Typical outputs from a stock control package include:

❑   Stock enquiry - details concerning a stock item may be displayed on screen, or printed;

❑   Stock status report (Figure 32.20) - a list of stock items, reorder points, on hand, on order and delivery dates;

	Software Cornucopia								
	Stock Status by Item								
	◊ Item Description ◊	Pref Vendor ◊	Reorder Pt ◊	On Hand ◊	On Order ◊	Next Deliv ◊	Order ◊	Sales/Week ◊	
ACC001	QuickBooksV3	Intuit	12	20	0			0	◄
ACC002	MS Money97	Microsoft	10	15	0			0	
ACC003	Pegasus Solo	Pegasus	20	24	0			0	
ACC004	Sage Instant Aco	Sage	15	48	0			0	
ACC005	Sage Instant Pay	Sage	10	17	0			0	
CAD001	Autocad LT2	Autocad	10	19	0			0	
CAD002	Autocad LT95	Autocad	5	13	0			0	
CAD003	Autocad 3	Autocad	20	26	0			0	
DBA001	Paradox 7 for Win	Borland	15	42	0			0	
DBA002	MS Access V2	Microsoft	25	33	0			0	
DBA003	Lotus Approach 3	Lotus	10	15	0			0	
DBA004	Visual dBase V5.	Borland	5	17	0			0	
DTP001	Adobe Pagemak	Adobe	10	16	0			0	
DTP002	MS Publisher 97	Microsoft	20	35	0			0	
DTP003	Quark Express V3	Quark	8	8	10	30/03/97		0	
DTP004	Ventura V7	Corel	12	11	15	30/03/97		0	

Figure 32.20. *Stock status report*

❑   Stock valuation summary (Figure 32.21) - a full or limited (for example, within a certain stock code range) list of stock items, giving details of quantities held and their value. The value may be calculated using the cost or sale price, depending on the costing method used by the business;

◇ Item Description ◇	On Hand ◇	Avg Cost ◇	Asset Value ◇	% of Tot Asset ◇	Sales Price ◇	Retail Value ◇	% of Tot Retail ◇
Software Cornucopia							
Stock Valuation Summary							
ACC001 QuickBooksV3	20	68.00	1,360.00	3.0%	88.00	1,760.00	3.1%
ACC002 MS Money97	15	19.00	285.00	0.6%	23.00	345.00	0.6%
ACC003 Pegasus Solo	24	50.00	1,200.00	2.6%	69.00	1,656.00	2.9%
ACC004 Sage Instant Aco	48	88.00	4,224.00	9.2%	120.00	5,760.00	10.2%
ACC005 Sage Instant Pay	17	76.00	1,292.00	2.8%	100.00	1,700.00	3.0%
CAD001 Autocad LT2	19	285.00	5,415.00	11.8%	335.00	6,365.00	11.2%
CAD002 Autocad LT95	13	135.00	1,755.00	3.8%	175.00	2,275.00	4.0%
CAD003 Autocad 3	26	78.00	2,028.00	4.4%	98.00	2,548.00	4.5%
DBA001 Paradox 7 for Wi:	42	65.00	2,730.00	6.0%	80.00	3,360.00	5.9%
DBA002 MS Access V2	33	265.00	8,745.00	19.1%	320.00	10,560.00	18.6%
DBA003 Lotus Approach 3	15	50.00	750.00	1.6%	70.00	1,050.00	1.9%
DBA004 Visual dBase V5.	17	150.00	2,550.00	5.6%	185.00	3,145.00	5.5%
DTP001 Adobe Pagemak:	16	300.00	4,800.00	10.5%	378.00	6,048.00	10.7%
DTP002 MS Publisher 97	35	55.00	1,925.00	4.2%	75.00	2,625.00	4.6%
DTP003 Quark Express V3	8	485.00	3,880.00	8.5%	525.00	4,200.00	7.4%
DTP004 Ventura V7	11	255.00	2,805.00	6.1%	300.00	3,300.00	5.8%

Figure 32.21. *Stock valuation summary*

This is not an exhaustive list and package users can customise other analytical reports, according to their particular needs. This can help a business to maintain an efficient customer service and plan future production and purchasing more effectively.

Sales order processing and invoicing

Sales order processing

Sales order processing is concerned with the handling of customers' sales orders. It has three main functions:

1. Validation of orders. This means checking, for example, that the goods ordered are supplied by the business or that the customer's credit status warrants the order's completion.

2. To identify quantities of individual items ordered. A customer may request several different items on the same order form. An item will probably appear on many different order forms and the quantities for each need to be totalled to provide lists (picking lists) for warehouse staff to retrieve the goods.

3. To monitor back orders. If an order cannot be fulfilled it may be held in abeyance until new stocks arrive. The system should be able to report all outstanding back orders on request.

The efficient processing of customer orders is of obvious importance to the success of a business and in whatever form an order is received, the details should be immediately recorded. Preferably, the details should be recorded on a pre-designed order form, which ensures that all relevant details are taken. The order details should include:

- [ ]   the date the order is received;

- [ ]   the customer's order number;

- [ ]   a description of each item required including any necessary stock references or codes;

- [ ]   the quantity of each item ordered;

- [ ]   the price per item excluding VAT;

- [ ]   the total order value excluding VAT;

- [ ]   any discount which is offered to the customer;

- [ ]   the VAT amount which is to be added to the total price;

- [ ]   the total order value including VAT;

- [ ]   the delivery date required.

Invoicing

The invoice is the bill to the customer, requesting payment for goods or services supplied by the business. The following section describes typical package facilities which allow the integration of the sales order processing and invoicing systems. QuickBooks is a fully integrated package and the invoicing processes are described in the Sales Ledger section, earlier in this chapter.

Package requirements and facilities

To be effective, the sales order processing system needs to have access to the customer file (sales ledger) for customer details and to the stock file, so that prices can be extracted according to stock item codes entered with the order. This latter facility means that the system may also be integrated with invoicing.

Files

- [ ]   Customer file - when a customer account number or name is keyed in with an order, the package usually accesses the customer file and displays the address details, so that the operator can confirm the delivery address or type in an alternative address if this is required. The process also ensures that all orders are processed for registered customers

- [ ]   Stock file - as stock item codes are entered from an order form, the system accesses the price and displays it on the screen for confirmation by the operator. Access to the stock file also ensures that only valid stock codes are used

- [ ]   Completed order file - this is used for the generation of invoices after an order's completion;

❑   Back order file - this is needed to ensure that orders which cannot be fulfilled immediately are kept on file and processed as soon as goods become available.

Transactions

Sales order - details concerning an individual order, including customer number, items required (by item code), quantity of each item, delivery date, discount allowed and the date of the order.

Outputs

❑   Invoice - an invoice can be generated by using the details of customer number, stock codes and quantities from the order, together with information retrieved from the customer and stock files.

❑   Back order report - a report can be requested detailing all unsatisfied orders. This is useful for planning production schedules or generating special purchase orders.

❑   Picking list - a summary of the quantities required of each item ordered. These are used by warehouse staff to extract the goods needed to make up orders for delivery.

❑   Sales data - details of each customer's order need to be extended to include the financial ledgers (sales, purchase and general ledger).

Payroll

The task of calculating wages for a large company having hundreds or even thousands of employees is an enormous task. It involves taking into account some or all of the following factors:

❑   number of hours worked;

❑   amount of overtime;

❑   bonus payment;

❑   sickness leave;

❑   type of employee (for example, weekly or monthly paid, shop floor or management);

❑   deductions (for example, national insurance contributions and union fees);

❑   holidays;

❑   tax code;

❑   tax rate;

❑   cash analysis.

The gross pay is calculated from the hours worked and hourly pay rate for weekly paid employees, and is a standard sum for salaried employees. Added to this gross payment are any allowances from overtime or bonuses, for example. Tax is then calculated and subtracted from the total earnings and other deductions such as National Insurance, union fees and pension contribution are also taken from it. Thus the total calculation is quite complicated, and it will probably be different for each employee.

Producing payslips manually is therefore very time consuming and prone to error, so computers are particularly well suited to the task. Most computerised payroll systems use batch processing in which long-term employee information held on a master file is used in conjunction with a transaction file containing recent information such as hours worked and overtime details. The transaction file changes from week to week or month to month but most of the information on the master file either doesn't change at all or it changes only occasionally.

Exercises

1.   Which *ledger* would a business use to record:

  (i)   balances owing by customers for goods bought on credit?

  (ii)   expenditure on heating, light and wages?

  (iii)   balances owing to suppliers for goods bought on credit.?

2.   Name the type of document which is sent to a customer:

  (i)   requesting payment for goods bought on credit;

  (ii)   to show a refund on their account to the value of goods returned.

3.   Which accounting package report would be useful for identifying potential *bad debts*?

4.   Which report details the assets and liabilities of a business on a particular date?

5.   Which report shows the profit made by a business over a specified period?

6. Which fields in a stock record are concerned with maintaining optimum levels of stock?

7. List three transaction types which may be entered into a stock control system.

8.   (i)   Assuming a fully integrated financial accounting system, identify the files which would need to be accessed to produce an invoice.

    (ii)   What data would be extracted from each file identified in (i), to produce the invoice?

Chapter 33
Financial Modelling and Simulation

Introduction

The term *modelling* is used in information technology for computer applications which, for example, are used to investigate, analyse or plan a complex activity, or to *simulate* a complex process. Some models are concerned with investigating financial systems using a software tool such as a *spreadsheet* program. For example, a manufacturing company might use a spreadsheet-based model to determine the minimum number of items the company must produce in order to make a profit.

Modelling and simulation using spreadsheets

In this section we look at the use of spreadsheet for performing a break-even analysis to investigate a manufacturing business and to simulate a stock control system. We limit explanations to special functions that are required for simulation purposes and to the formulae that are required for the various calculations involved.

Financial planning - break-even analysis

The prime objective of most organisations is the achievement of profit. In order to make a profit the organisation must earn sufficient revenue from the sale of its products to exceed the costs that it has incurred in operating and producing. It is usually a relatively simple task to calculate revenue: simply determine the number of goods which have been sold and multiply this quantity by the price per item. The calculation of cost is slightly more complicated owing to the fact that the organisation incurs a variety of different costs in producing its products. *Fixed costs* remain constant irrespective of the number of items produced. Examples include rent on the premises or local council rates. Therefore, as production rises the fixed cost per item reduces. Other costs, however, increase with production. These are called *variable costs*. Raw materials are an example of variable costs since as more items are produced, more raw materials are required. Combining fixed and variable costs gives the organisation its total costs, and it is only when its total revenue exceeds these that it can make a profit. Clearly then, an organisation may make a loss if its output is low, but as it produces and sells more it will eventually move through a *break-even point* into profit. As the name suggests, the break-even point is where the organisation neither makes a loss nor a profit - it simply breaks even. Management are obviously very interested to know the level of production required to exceed the break-even point and make a profit. Combining the revenue and cost figures in order to determine the break-even point is called *break-even analysis*, and a graphical representation of the figures is termed a *break-even chart*. An example of a break-even analysis and its equivalent chart are shown in Figure 33.1.

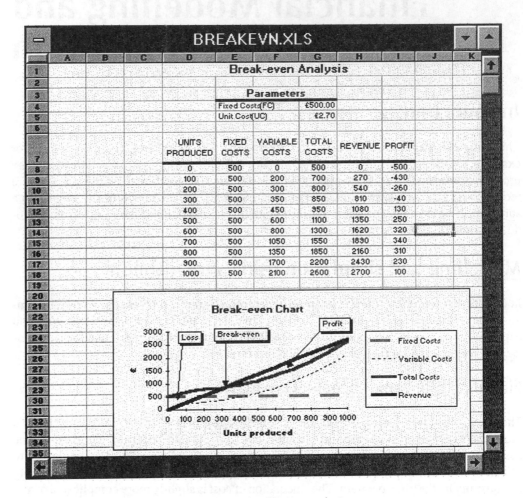

Figure 33.1. *Break-even analysis*

The UNITS PRODUCED and VARIABLE COSTS columns of the spreadsheet are constant values. FIXED COSTS are copied from the Fixed Costs (FC) parameter cell. The TOTAL COSTS column is the sum of FIXED COSTS and VARIABLE COSTS. The REVENUE is calculated by multiplying the units produced by the Unit Cost (UC) parameter. Finally, the profit is found by subtracting the TOTAL COSTS from the REVENUE.

The break-even chart, shown below the spreadsheet, graphs the three costs and the revenue figures; the break-even point is where the TOTAL COSTS curve crosses the REVENUE line. Profit occurs to the right of the break-even point, and you can see that in this case, when the fixed costs are at £500 and the selling price is £2.70, the break-even point occurs when just over 300 items are produced. Interestingly, the graph also shows that maximum profit occurs when between 600 and 700 items are produced and that at about 1000 items the company again breaks even.

Stock control simulation

Suppose that Agros is a large retail outlet which sells a wide range of household materials. It has a computerised stock control, or *inventory*, system which deals with obtaining, storing and supplying the goods it offers to the general public. Agros provides free catalogues containing descriptions of items which customers can obtain by visiting one of their outlets. The items shown in the catalogue are kept in a warehouse attached to the outlet. It is of vital importance to Agros to ensure that it has a full range of items in stock, so that customers can immediately obtain those that they require.

If an item is out of stock, the potential customer might decide to shop elsewhere thus causing Agros to lose the sale, and possibly future sales too. Agros attempts to prevent this situation by ordering quantities of those items that are in danger of being sold out. However, the time taken for the items to arrive from the suppliers may be several days, by which time the goods still could have sold out. Moreover, if the demand for an item is overestimated, and there are a large number of the item in the warehouse, Agros again loses money because each item incurs a warehouse storage cost.

Agros must try to achieve a balance between over-ordering and under-ordering goods. This would be an easy problem to solve if Agros knew exactly what the demand for a particular item is likely to be at any one time, but unfortunately this is never the case. Possibly the best prediction of demand will still involve a large amount of uncertainty. For example, past experience might provide an estimate of the average demand per day for an item, but the actual demand on a particular day will probably fluctuate fairly randomly. A possible means of investigating this type of system is therefore a simulation (often termed a Monte Carlo simulation) in which demand is simulated using a random number generator such as that described in the previous example. Before we show how a spreadsheet can be used for such a simulation, we define a number of terms commonly used to describe stock control systems.

- ❑ Demand - the quantity of a product that customers are willing to purchase.

- ❑ Opening stock - the number of items of stock immediately available for purchase at the start of trading on any day.

- ❑ Closing stock - the number of items of stock that remain in the outlet at the close of trading on any particular day.

- ❑ Re-order quantity - the number of items of stock ordered from a supplier at any one time.

❑   Re-order level - the minimum number of items held in stock before the item is re-ordered. As soon as the level of stock reaches this level, or drops below it, the re-order quantity is ordered from the supplier.

❑   Carrying costs - the cost of storing an item waiting to be sold.

❑   Stock out costs - the financial loss incurred when the demand for an item exceeds the stock level. In other words, a company loses money when it cannot supply an item to a customer because that item is out of stock. The term loss of goodwill also applies to this type of loss, because the disappointed customer might not use the outlet in the future.

❑   Order costs - the cost to the company of making an order a re-order quantity of a product. This in addition to the actual cost of buying the items from the supplier. Each time an order is generated, there is an order cost.

❑   Lead time - this is the time it takes to receive an item from the supplier once the order has been generated.

The simulation shown in Figure 33.2 illustrates the effects of the stock control parameters, shown at the top of the spreadsheet, over a period of fourteen days.

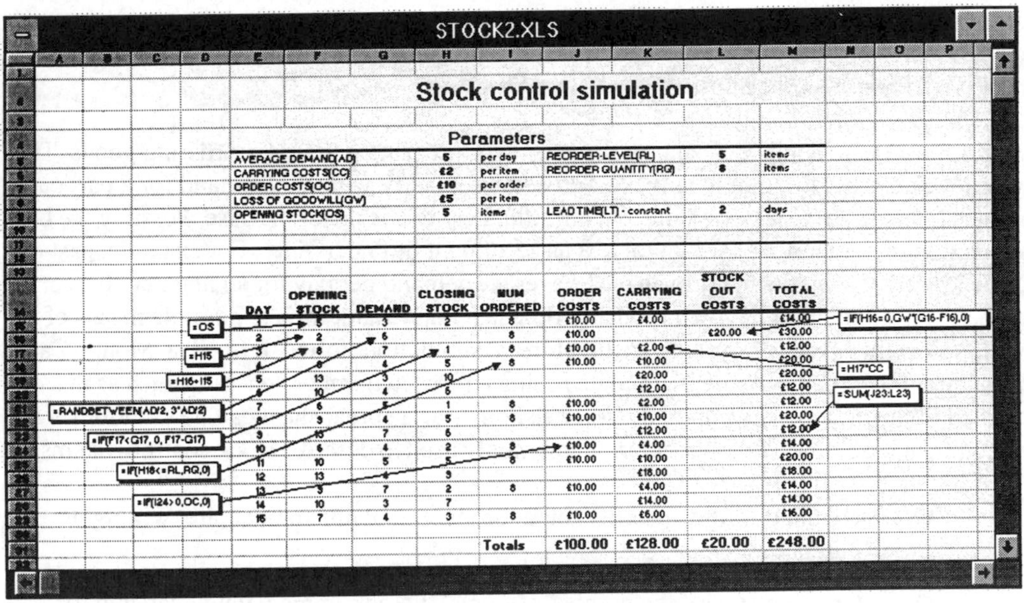

Figure 33.2. *Stock control simulation*

The columns in the table have been calculated as follows:

OPENING STOCK - On the first day of the simulation period this is the value OS which appears in the parameter table. On the second day it is the closing stock value for the first day, that is, the number of stock items left after close of business the previous day. On the third and subsequent days its is the closing value for the previous day plus any stock that was ordered two days previously. Thus, for day four, the opening stock (10) is the sum of the third day's closing stock (2) and the quantity ordered on the second day (8).

DEMAND - This is produced using a random number generator which produces a random number between half the average demand and one and a half times the average demand. For example, if the average demand is 6 items per day, a random number between 3 and 9 is generated. This represents the actual demand for the item on a particular day, and this is where the uncertainty factor is introduced.

CLOSING STOCK - the number of items remaining in the warehouse/storeroom at close of trading on that day.

NUM ORDERED - the number of items ordered that day. This will be either the re-order quantity, if the closing stock level is equal to or below the re-order level, or zero if the CLOSING STOCK level is greater than the re-order level.

ORDER COSTS - each time the item is re-ordered, there is an order cost incurred.

CARRYING COSTS - there is a charge for each item in stock at the close of trading on each day. Thus, on day 5, CLOSING STOCK was 9 and the order costs at £2 per item means that the CARRYING COSTS amount to £18.

STOCK OUT COSTS - a fixed cost is incurred for each item out of stock that a customer was willing to buy. This is calculated by subtracting OPENING STOCK from DEMAND and multiplying the result by the LOSS OF GOODWILL cost shown in the parameter table.

TOTAL COSTS - calculated by summing ORDER COSTS, CARRYING COSTS and STOCK OUT COSTS.

The column totals for the four costs calculated are shown below the appropriate columns. Examples of the spreadsheet formulae used for these calculations are shown in the shadowed formula boxes on the spreadsheet.

Note that the OPENING STOCK parameter is a constant value that can be changed in this particular simulation only by changing the formulae in the OPEN STOCK column. Each time the spreadsheet is recalculated (by pressing F9 in Excel) new DEMAND random numbers are generated for each day, and the resulting costs are displayed. This allows you to investigate the effects of changing the various parameters. You could, for example, investigate the effect on the total costs of increasing the re-order level, or of reducing the re-order quantity, or the effect of changing both of these parameters together.

Exercises

1. Study the image in Figure 33.1 (or reproduce it using a spreadsheet package) and answer the following questions.

    (i)   How are the Total Costs calculated?

    (ii)   How is the Revenue calculated?

    (iii)   How is the Profit calculated?

    (iv)   How many units need to be produced to make a profit?

    (v)   How much profit would be made on 1100 units if Fixed Costs did not change and Variable Costs amounted to £2300?

    (vi)   If the Fixed Costs are changed to £700, how many units need to be sold to break into profit?

2. Study the stock control simulation in Figure 33.2 (or reproduce it using a spreadsheet package) and answer the following questions.

    (i)   What is the relationship between Opening Stock and Closing Stock?

    (ii)   Which is the 'uncertainty factor' in the simulation?

    (iii)   What are the relationships between Re-order Quantity, Re-order Level and either the Closing or Opening Stock Levels?

    (iv)   What is the significance of lead time?

Chapter 34
Data Structures

Introduction

A sound knowledge of basic data structures is essential for any computer programmer. A programming task will almost invariably involve the manipulation of a set of data which normally will be organised according to some coherent structure. It could be that the data is to be read in and processed, in which case a detailed knowledge of its structure is obviously essential. Furthermore, processing the data might involve organising it in a way that facilitates its subsequent retrieval, as in information retrieval applications. Output from the program might require that the data is presented in yet another form. So a single program might be required to handle a number of data structures; only by having a thorough knowledge of basic data structures can the programmer choose, or design, the structures most appropriate to the problems being addressed.

From a programming viewpoint, the study of data structures involves two aspects, namely, the theoretical principles upon which the structures are founded, and the practicalities of implementing them using a computer. This chapter addresses both of these considerations by describing a number of important data structures and their applications to programming tasks.

A data structure is essentially a number of data items, also called elements or nodes, with some relationship linking them together. Each item consists of one or more named parts called fields occupying one or more memory locations in the computer. In its simplest form, an element can be a single field located in a single word of memory. A list of numbers occupying consecutive memory locations in a computer is a simple data structure called an *array* and an example is shown in Table 34.1.

memory location	contents
1000	56
1001	34
1002	123
1003	11
1004	77

Table 34.1. *Array data structure*

The relationship linking the individual elements is merely the order in which they are stored in memory. In order to access the next element in the list (that is, an element's successor) it is necessary only to increment the memory address; the previous element at any point in the list (that is an elements predecessor) is found by decrementing the current memory address. This simple structural relationship allows the list to be accessed in sequential order.

Data structures such as *linked lists* provide pointers linking elements together. So, for example, to access the above numeric list in ascending order of magnitude, an extra field could be added to each element to point to the next element in the sequence, as shown in Table 34.2.

memory location	link field	value
1000	1004	56
1001	1000	34
1002	0000	123
1003	1001	11
1004	1002	77

Table 34.2. *Linked list*

Now, starting with location 1003 and following the links, the list can be accessed in ascending order: the link contained in location 1003 indicates that the number succeeding 11 is in location 1001; location 1001 contains the number 34 plus a pointer showing that the next number in the sequence is to be found at location 1000; the list terminates at location 1002 which contains the final number, 123, and a zero link indicating that there are no more elements in the list. Linked lists make it easier to insert or delete elements at any position in the sequence of items, at the cost of increased complexity and increased memory demands. Other data structures such as *stacks* and *queues* restrict access to elements to certain points of a sequential data structure, normally the start or end. With stacks, elements may only be added or deleted at one end of the list; queues allow items to be added at one end and deleted at the other.

The attraction of using a simple array data structure is that a data item may be accessed by means of a simple key which specifies its position within the array. So, for example, if we used an array to store details of a collection of 30 videos, and we assigned to each of them a different code number in the range 1 to 30, searching the array for the details of a particular video would merely entail entering the code number; the required details would be obtained in a fixed length of time by using the code number as an index value.

However, if for a video hire shop we also wanted to use an array to store its videos, so that any one could be accessed in the shortest possible time, the amount of storage space required would be prohibitive. For instance, using a six-digit key would require 1,000,000 digits to be stored for the keys alone, and then the video details would be in addition. If the key was to be used to encode information concerning the video - how many duplicates, children's or adult's for example - then we would expect that out of these 1,000,000 possible keys only a relatively small proportion of them would be used. Suppose that this proportion is 10%, that is, the system is only intended to cope with a maximum of 1,000 videos. Then 90% of the space allocated to the storage of video details would be wasted. What is required is a method of mapping the 1,000,000 keys to a table containing only 1,000 keys. Hashing allows us to do this by applying a *hash function* to the key to produce an integer, in a much smaller range, which is used as the actual index to the table containing the records. The chief disadvantage of this scheme is that the hashing function will most probably generate non-unique index values, that is, two different keys could easily produce exactly the same index. This is termed a *collision*, and any hashing process must allow for this occurrence and cope with it using a *collision resolution strategy*.

Where a data structure is to be searched using an alphabetic key such as a surname, which could be incorrectly spelled, a useful method of coping with this problem is to use *Soundex Coding*. This allows words which sound alike, though spelled differently, to be given an identical code.

Arrays

Storage of arrays

High-level procedural languages such as BASIC, COBOL and Pascal allow programmers to manipulate tabular data stored in *arrays*. The programmer merely declares the name, size and dimension of the array and the language processor takes care of allocating memory for it. The immediate access store (memory) of a computer consists of a large number of memory locations, each with its own unique address (see Chapter 23). Memory locations have addresses ranging from 0 to $n1$, where n represents the total number of memory locations available in the computer. For example, in a computer which has 640K bytes of user memory, byte addresses will range from 0 to $(640 \times 1024)1$, that is, 0 to 655359. If a programmer defines a one-dimensional array of, say, twenty integers each occupying a single word, then the language processor must assign sufficient storage space for the array in user RAM and be able to find any array element as quickly as possible. Locating an array element requires a small calculation involving the starting address of the array, which is termed the *base address*, and the number of bytes per array element. For example, suppose we have a one-dimensional array A_k of single byte words, where k is over the range 0 to 20, with base address b. Then element A_0 will have address $b + 0 = b$. Element A_1 will have address $b + 1$ and, in general, element A_k will have address $b + k$.

Figure 34.1 shows the relationship between array elements and memory locations.

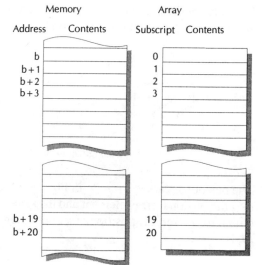

Figure 34.1. *Array-memory relationship*

Because the memory of a computer is essentially a one-dimensional array of memory locations, when it is required to represent a two-dimensional table, a slightly more complicated calculation is necessary: the language processor must convert the subscripts of two-dimensional array element into a one-dimensional physical memory address. Consider the storage requirements of a two-dimensional array, $T_{j,k}$ single word integers and size 10×6 that is, a table with 10 rows (j=0 to 9) and 6 columns (k=0 to 5) as shown in Figure 34.2.

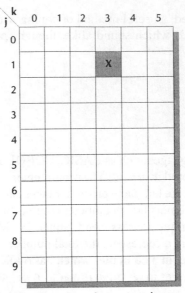

Figure 34.2. *Two-dimensional array*

If the base address is at location b, and the array is stored row by row, then the elements of the array might be stored in memory as shown in Figure 34.3.

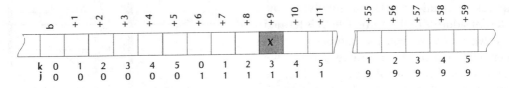

Figure 34.3. *Storage of array in memory*

The positions marked by an ✕ in Figures 34.2 and 34.3 show the correspondence between a two-dimensional array element and the same element's memory address. The calculation required to convert the position of a two-dimensional array element $T_{j,k}$ to a memory location, M, is

$$M = b + j \times 6 + k$$

For example, element $T_{0,3}$ would occupy the location

$$M = b + 0 \times 6 + 3 = b + 3,$$

and element $T_{3,2}$ would be at location

$$M = b + 3 \times 6 + 2 = b + 20$$

The calculations above assume that the array is of size 10 × 6. In general, if the array is of size m × n, then an element Tj,k would translate to the location

$$M = b + j \times n + k$$

This is called a *mapping function*, a formula which uses the array size and the element subscripts to calculate the memory address at which that element is located. Note that if the array is stored column by column rather than row by row, the mapping function becomes

$$M = b + k \times m + j$$

Extending this scheme to an array, $D_{i,j,k}$, of three dimensions and size $l \times m \times n$, the conversion calculation becomes,

$$M = b + i \times m \times n + j \times n + k$$

Figure 34.4 illustrates the correspondence between array elements and memory locations for a three-dimensional table of size 3 × 5 × 6.

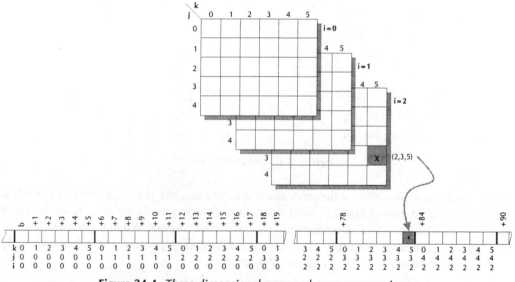

Figure 34.4. *Three-dimensional array and memory mappings*

Here, *i* can be considered to be the subscript which specifies a number of tables, each of size j × k. Thus, $D_{2,3,5}$ references element (3,5) of the third table (for which *i*=2). This corresponds to the location

$$M = b + 2 \times 5 \times 6 + 3 \times 6 + 5 = b + 83$$

Further application of the principles explained above allow arrays of any number of dimensions to be handled.

Iliffe vectors

When speed has a higher priority than memory requirements, a *table look-up* scheme is sometimes adopted for accessing array elements. The main drawback of using a mapping function is the time taken to perform the address calculation, which will generally involve one or more relatively slow multiplication operations. The number of calculations can be significantly reduced by pre-calculating row or column addresses and storing them in another table. For example, suppose that we have a 3×5 array as illustrated in Figure 34.5. We first calcu-

k j	0	1	2	3	4
0	b	b+1	b+2	b+3	b+4
1	b+5	b+6	b+7	b+8	b+9
2	b+10	b+11	b+12	b+13	b+14

Figure 34.5. 3×5 array

late, and then store in three consecutive memory locations, the starting address for each of the three rows. This is called an Iliffe vector (see Figure 34.6).

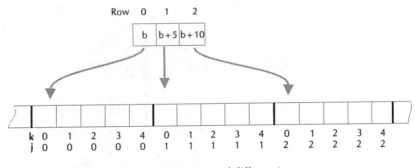

Figure 34.6. *Use of Iliffe vector*

So, given the row subscript for the array element to be accessed, the Iliffe vector is consulted for the starting address of that row, and the location of the required element is found by using the column subscript as an offset to be added to this row address. When implemented in assembly language or machine code using appropriate addressing modes, this scheme virtually eliminates the necessity for any address calculations.

Access tables

The principle of using a table containing the starting addresses of data items is particularly useful for accessing elements of string arrays. Figure 34.7 shows how an access table is used to point to the starting locations of string array elements stored in memory.

The array S_k ($k = 0$ to 4) to be represented consists of a number of string elements of variable sizes, each terminated by a special character indicating the end of the string. In this instance, the strings, with their subscripts, are:

```
0 CPU
1 Disk Drive
2 Printer
3 Random Access Memory
4 Monitor
```

The access table contains entries which point to the starting locations of each of the strings in order. For example, if the element S_3 was to be accessed, the entry in the access table corresponding to this element (that is, the element with subscript 3) provides the starting address for S_3 which has a value Random Access Memory.

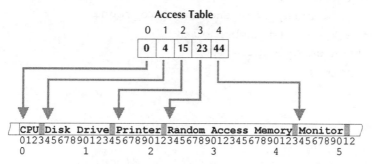

Figure 34.7. *Access table for string arrays*

Sometimes, rather than indicating the end of a string element by means of a special character, such as an ASCII carriage return code, the access table is used in conjunction with another table giving the length of the string (Figure 34.8).

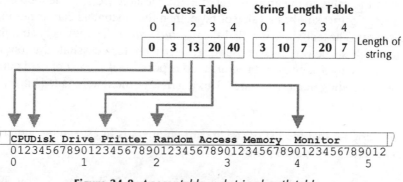

Figure 34.8. *Access table and string length table*

This scheme improves access speed but at the expense of additional storage requirements.

Search strategies

Having stored a number of data items in an array, it is more than likely that it will be necessary at some time to search the data structure for the occurrence of specific items of data. For example, suppose that an array A_k ($k=0$ to 9999) is being used to store stolen credit card numbers, and it is to be searched in order to ascertain whether a shop customer is using a stolen credit card. The search algorithm might be as shown in Listing 34.1.

Listing 34.1.   Sequential search

```
{search_array}
k:= 0
pos:= -1
card_found: = FALSE
while k < array_size and not card_found
  if S(k) = Card_number
    then card_found:= TRUE;
    pos:= k
  endif
k:= k+1
endwhile
if card_found
  then card number is located in S(pos)
      else card number is not in stolen cards list
endif
```

Each element in the list is compared with the number of the customers card; if a match is found, the iteration is terminated by setting the boolean variable `card_found` to true, and the position of the value in the array is stored in the variable `pos`; if the loop ends and the variable `card_found` still has a value of false, then the customers card is not in the list of stolen credit cards. The technique is called a *sequential search*. Though very straightforward, a sequential search can be very time consuming, since it could necessitate the complete list of 10,000 elements being searched. A faster method is possible if the list of card numbers is in ascending or descending numerical order. This alternative method is called binary search, or sometimes binary chop.

For example, suppose that the list of stolen card numbers is in ascending numerical order, then a binary search proceeds as follows:

1.   Set the array subscript to `mid`, middle value. In this case `mid` is 9999/2, which is 5000 to the nearest integer.

2.   Compare required `card_number` with `S(mid)`.

3.   (a) If `card_number` < `S(mid)` then `card_number` can only be in the

first half of the array.

(b) If `card_number>S(mid)` then card_number can only be somewhere in the latter half of the array.

(c) If `card_number = S(mid)` then the card number has been found.

4. If the card number has not yet been found, repeat from step 1 using `mid` as the size of the array.

The procedure successively reduces the size of the array to be searched by a factor of two. For an array of size 10,000, this means that only a maximum of 14 elements need to be examined in order to determine whether a particular element is a member of the list. Thus, for 10,000 elements, the search size reduces as shown in Table 34.3.

number of comparisons	array size to be searched
0	10,000
1	5,000
2	2,500
3	1,250
4	625
5	313
6	157
7	79
8	40
9	20
10	10
11	5
12	3
13	2
14	1

Table 34.3. *Array sizes and number of comparisons in binary chop*

Notice that 2^{14} is the smallest power of 2 which exceeds the maximum array size of 10,000:

$2^{13} = 8,192$ which is less than 10,000;

$2^{14} = 16,384$ which is greater than 10,000.

This is how the maximum figure of 14 comparisons has been derived. A more formal version of the binary search algorithm can be stated as in Listing 34.2.

Listing 34.2.   Binary chop

```
{binary}
low:= 0
high:= array_size - 1
pos:= -1
card_found:= FALSE
while low < high and not card_found
  mid:= int((low + high))/2
  select
    when S(mid) = card_number
      card_found:= TRUE
      pos:= mid
    when S(mid) > card_number
      high:= mid - 1
    when S(mid) < card_number
      low:= mid + 1
  endselect
endwhile
if card_found
  then stolen card number is located in S(pos)
      else card number is not in list
endif
```

In order to select the appropriate part of the array to be searched, the algorithm uses two variables, `low` and `high`, to store the lower and upper bounds of that part of the array. They are used to calculate the mid point, `mid`, (rounded to the nearest integer value), so that the value stored there can be compared with the value required (the card number, in this example). Each time the comparison fails, the lower or upper bound is adjusted and the procedure is repeated. The process continues until either the value is located or the lower and upper bounds coincide, in which case the value does not exist in the array. The variable `pos` is used to store the position of the value if it exists in the array; a negative value for `pos` indicates that the search was unsuccessful. The binary search method will usually be employed when the array size is large, otherwise the processing overheads caused by the algorithm's increased complexity make it unsuitable.

The stack

A *stack* is a data structure characterised by the expression Last In First Out (LIFO), meaning that the most recent item added to the stack is the first one which can be removed from the stack. A *stack pointer* is used to keep track of the last item added to the stack, that is, the current top of the stack. Suppose that we wish to implement a stack using a one-dimensional array, S_i where $i=1$ to 5. A special register, *sp*, must be reserved as the stack pointer, and this will have an initial value of 0 indicating that the stack is empty. To add, or *push*, an item to the stack, the following steps are required:

1. Check that there is room in the stack to add another item. In this case, the stack is full when *sp* has a value of 5, that is, when all of the elements in the array S_i have been used to store items. When the stack pointer is at its maximum value, and another item is required to be stored on the stack, a *stack overflow* condition has occurred, and it will not be possible to push the item onto the stack.

2. If an overflow condition does not exist, the stack pointer is incremented and the item is transferred to the array element pointed to by the stack pointer.

For example, suppose that the number 15 is to be pushed to the stack. After completing the operation the state of the stack will be as shown in Table 34.4, *sp* having a value of 1.

i	S_i	
1	15	⇦*sp*=1
2	-	
3	-	
4	-	
5		

Table 34.4. *One item pushed to stack*

i	S_i	
1	15	
2	6	
3	21	⇦*sp*=3
4	-	
5		

Table 34.5. *Stack with three items*

After adding two more numbers the stack will contain three elements and the stack pointer will have a value of 3, as shown in Table 34.5. The algorithm for pushing a value to a stack can be summarised as follows:

```
algorithm push              {add item to top of stack}
if sp < maximum stack size  {test for overflow}
   then sp := sp + 1;       {increment stack ptr}
      S(sp) := item          {push item}
   else Stack overflow
endif
end
```

To remove an item from the stack, often called *pulling* or *popping* a value, requires the reverse procedure:

1. Check that the stack is not empty, that is, sp is greater than zero. If the stack is empty, an attempt to pull a non-existent value causes a *stack underflow* condition to arise.

2. If the stack is not empty, the item on the top of the stack, as shown by the stack pointer, is transferred to its destination and the stack pointer is decremented.

Thus, after pulling a value from the stack S_i, it would be in the state shown in Table 34.6. Notice that the value pulled from the stack, 21 in this instance, still exists in the stack; it is not necessary to actually remove a value from the stack since, by decrementing the stack pointer, this is effectively what has happened. Pulling a value from a stack is effected by copying the value to its destination before decrementing the stack pointer. The top of the stack is now the second element of the array which contains the value 6.

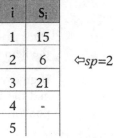

i	S_i	
1	15	
2	6	⇦sp=2
3	21	
4	-	
5		

Table 34.6. *One item pulled from the stack*

To summarise, the algorithm for pulling a value from a stack is:

```
algorithm pop            {remove item from top of stack }
   if sp > 0             {that is, stack is not empty    }
      then item := S(sp); {transfer item to destination   }
         sp := sp - 1    {decrement stack pointer         }
      else stack underflow
   endif
end
```

Application of stacks

The stack is used frequently in programming languages for control structures. In some versions of BASIC, for example, GOSUB, FOR...NEXT, REPEAT...UNTIL and procedure /function calls all use stacks in their implementation.

The GOSUB instruction causes control to be transferred to the line specified in the instruction. Subroutine instructions are executed as normal until a RETURN instruction is encountered, whereupon control returns to the instruction following the last GOSUB instruction executed. Thus, with the fragments of BASIC code illustrated in Listing 34.3, the subroutine starting at line 1000 is called at line 100 by the GOSUB 1000 instruction.

The BASIC interpreter must store its current position in the program so that after executing the subroutine it can return control to this same position when a RETURN instruction is encountered. This is accomplished by pushing the return address to a stack prior to jumping to the start of the subroutine.

Listing 34.3.

```
10 REM *** Mainline program ***
.............
.............
90 REM Call subroutine at line 1000
100 GOSUB 1000
105 REM Program contines here after completing subroutine
110 LET a = x + 1
120
990 STOP
999 REM *** End of Mainline program
REM *** Subroutine code goes here
1010
.............
etc
.............
1490 RETURN
```

When a RETURN instruction is executed, the top of the stack is pulled and the interpreter continues from that address. In this way the same subroutine can be called from different parts of the program and control will always return to the instruction following the GOSUB instruction. Another reason for using a stack is that it facilitates the use of nested control structures. In the example shown in Listing 34.3 it is possible to have another GOSUB instruction in the subroutine at line 1100. (See Listing 34.4).

Listing 34.4.

```
10 REM *** Mainline program ***
.............
.............
90 REM Call subroutine at line 1000
100 GOSUB 1000
105 REM Program continues here after completing subroutine
110 LET a = x + 1
120
.............
etc
.............
990 STOP
999 REM *** End of Mainline program ***
1000 REM *** Subroutine code goes here ***
1010
.............
1100 GOSUB 2000
1200
```

```
. . . . . . . . . . . .
1490 RETURN
2000 REM *** Code for second subroutine goes here ***
2010
. . . . . . . . . . .
etc
2490 RETURN
```

In this instance the stack is used twice: the return address appropriate to the subroutine call at line 100 is pushed to the stack, then the return address for the second, nested, subroutine call is pushed to the stack during execution of the first subroutine at line 1100.

When the RETURN statement at line 2490 is executed, BASIC pulls the top of the GOSUB stack causing control to return to line 1200, the line following the most recent GOSUB instruction. The RETURN statement at line 1490 causes BASIC to pull the new top of the stack which provides the return address for the first GOSUB call at line 100. This technique allows subroutines to be nested to any depth, subject to the size of the GOSUB stack.

The same principle applies to the management of FOR..NEXT loops in BASIC. A separate stack is used to store information regarding the FOR..NEXT control variables. The BASIC interpreter stores on the stack five pieces of information when it encounters a FOR statement: (i) the address of the control variable; (ii) the type of the control variable; (iii) STEP size; (iv) TO limit; (v) the address of the next statement following FOR.

The stack pointer is incremented by the number of words occupied by this information, and then the statement following the FOR instruction is executed. A NEXT instruction will cause BASIC to use the information on the top of the stack to either repeat the statements between the FOR and F"Courier New"NEXT instructions, or to exit the loop if the control variable has exceeded its maximum value. If the latter is the case, the FOR..NEXT stack pointer will be decremented to remove the top of the stack thus terminating this loop. The use of a stack again allows nesting of FOR..NEXT loops, subject to a depth governed by the size of the FOR..NEXT stack. A REPEAT..UNTIL stack is used in a similar way to that of the FOR..NEXT stack, though the procedures for managing REPEAT..UNTIL loops are simpler. Procedures and functions in BASIC are handled in a similar manner to the GOSUB structure, but the BASIC interpreter has to cope with additional problems associated with passing parameters and saving the values of local variables so that they can subsequently be restored. These extra problems are once again overcome by the use of stacks.

The queue

The data structure known as a *queue* has the same characteristics as the queues we encounter in everyday life. For instance, a queue at the checkout counter of a supermarket increases at its rear as customers join the queue to have their purchases totalled, and only reduces in size when a customer is served at the head of the queue, the checkout counter. A queue of cars at traffic lights behaves in a similar manner, with cars exiting the queue only at its head and joining the queue only at its rear. A *queue* is a data structure in which elements are added only at the rear of a linear list and removed only from the front, or head, of the list. A queue is often given the name FIFO list, from the initial letters of the words in the phrase First In First Out which describes the order of processing the elements of the list.

Suppose that an array, Q_k (k=0 to 31), is to be used as a queue. Head will be used to keep track of the front of the queue and Rear, the end of the queue as shown in Figure 34.9.

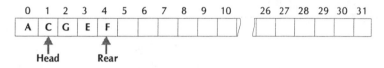

Figure 34.9. *Queue*

Initially, the queue is empty so that Head = Rear = 0. When an item is added to the queue, Rear is incremented; when an item is removed from the list, Head is incremented. Assuming that the queue is simply storing single alphabetic characters, Table 34.7 illustrates the operation of the queue for ten queue operations.

operation	item	Head	Rear	state of queue
		0	0	empty
1. Add item	A	0	1	A
2. Add item	C	0	2	AC
3. Add item	G	0	3	ACG
4. Add item	E	0	4	ACGE
5. Remove item	A	1	4	CGE
6. Add item	F	1	5	CGEF
7. Remove item	C	2	5	GEF
8. Remove item	G	3	5	EF
9. Remove item	E	4	5	F
10. Remove item	F	5	5	empty

Table 34.7. *Queue operations*

The following algorithms show how items are added to a queue and removed from a queue, assuming array_size is the maximum size of the array Q used for storing the queue.

```
algorithm queue {Add item to queue}
  if Rear <= array_size - 1
    then Q(Rear):= item
      Rear := Rear + 1
    else Queue is full
  endif
end
algorithm dequeue {Remove item from queue}
  if Rear <> Head
    then item := Q(Head)
      Head := Head + 1
    else Queue is empty
  endif
end
```

Notice that the queue is empty when the head pointer has the same value as the rear pointer. Notice also that, unlike a queue in real life, as items are added and removed, the queue moves through the array since both the head and rear pointers are incremented. This means that eventually the queue will run out of space, at which time an overflow condition will occur. One solution to this problem is to implement a circular queue which reuses array elements that are empty.

Circular queues

Figure 34.10 illustrates the principles of a circular queue. The circular arrangement of the array elements is merely a means of illustrating the principles of operation of a circular queue; the data structure used to store the queue is physically the same as before, that is, a one-dimensional array. Head and Rear are again used, but this time when either of them reach a value equal to m, the upper bound of the array, they start again at the beginning, using up elements which previously have been removed from the queue. The diagram shows the queue in a state where ten items have been added to the queue and three items have been removed. Figure 34.11 shows that the queue has completely traversed the array such that Rear is equal to m, and there are five items in the queue. The next item to be added to the queue will be inserted at position 1, so that Rear has a value of 0 rather than m + 1. In other words, when Rear exceeds the upper bound reserved for the queue, it takes the value of the lower bound. The same thing applies to the Head of the queue.

Figure 34.12 shows the queue, having traversed all the elements of the array, starting to reuse unoccupied positions at the beginning of the array.

A slight difficulty with a circular queue is being able to differentiate between an empty queue and a full queue; the condition for a non-empty queue can no longer be that Rear < Head since, depending how many items have been added and removed, it is possible for a non-empty queue to be such that Rear has larger value than Head. Figures 34.11 and 34.12 illustrate both queue states, the first where Head < Rear and the second where Head > Rear.

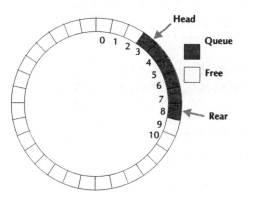

Figure 34.10. *Principles of circular queue*

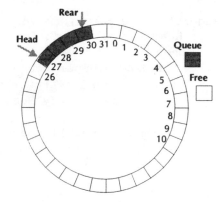

Figure 34.11. *Circular queue with Rear at upper bound*

One solution to this problem is to adopt the convention that Head always points to the array element immediately preceding the first item in the queue rather pointing to the first item itself; since Rear points to the last item in the queue, the condition that Head = Rear indicates an empty queue. Head and Rear are initialised to be equal to the arrays upper bound rather than zero. Thus, initially, the queue is empty.

The queue becomes full only when the rear pointer catches up with the head pointer.

The algorithms shown in Listing 34.5 define the processes of adding an item to a circular queue and removing an item from a circular queue.

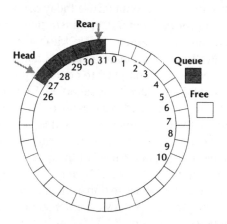
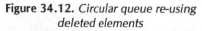

Figure 34.12. *Circular queue re-using deleted elements*

Listing 34.5.   Algorithms for adding and deleting queue items

```
algorithm c_queue {Add item to circular queue}
temp:= Rear {Copy Rear Pointer}
  if Rear = Upper_bound {check for upper limit}
    then Rear := Lower_bound {start at beginning or..
      else Rear := Rear + 1  .. increment rear pointer}
  endif
  if Rear <> Head {check for queue full}
    then Q(Rear) := item {add item to queue}
      else Queue is full{overflow condition}
        Rear := temp{restore Rear pointer}
  endif
end
```

```
algorithm c_dequeue{Remove item from circular queue}
  if Head <> Rear{check for queue not empty}
    then
      if Head = Upper_bound    {check for upper limit}
         then Head := Lower_bound{start at beginning or..
           else Head := Head + 1.. increment head pointer}
      endif
      item := Q(Head){remove item from queue}
    else Queue is empty{underflow condition}
  endif
end
```

Applications of queues

Most printers in common use today contain a quantity of RAM for the purpose of temporarily storing (or *buffering*) data transmitted from a computer. The buffer allows the computer to transmit, for example, a few kilobytes of data to the printer very quickly and allows the printer to print it autonomously, (that is, without further intervention from the computer). This allows the computer to continue processing other tasks while the relatively slow printer deals with the data it has received. The printer buffer must operate as a queue, because the data must be printed in the same order as it was transmitted from the computer. As data is received by the printer, it is added to the buffer queue until either the computer stops transmitting data or the queue is full. The printer then commences to process the data in the queue, starting at the head of the queue and ending when the queue is empty. This process of filling up the buffer quickly and then emptying it at the speed of the printer, continues until the computer ceases to transmit data. Buffers may range in size from a few kilobytes to several megabytes of RAM. A microprocessor in the printer itself deals with the way the data queue is processed.

Circular queues are frequently used by operating systems for spooling operations. For example, in a multi-user system in which a printer is shared between a number of users, print jobs may be spooled to a disk drive. The queue thus formed on the disk will be processed by the printer in the order the jobs were received (unless a priority system is in operation). As one job is printed, room will be available on the disk area allocated to the printer for another job; the circular queue principle applied to spooling will allow optimum use of the disk area allocated to print jobs. The operating system keeps track of the appropriate queue head and rear pointers required to operate the circular queue.

Linked lists

Suppose that we are using an array to store a number of alphabetic items in alphabetical order as shown in Table 34.8. Adding a new item such as Gregory, while maintaining the alphabetic ordering, is easy, as Table 34.9 shows. The item is merely added to the end of the list. However, to insert Crawford requires rather more effort: all of those entries after Craddock must be moved down the array so that Crawford may be inserted immediately after Craddock. The list is then as shown in Table 34.10.

element	data	element	data	element	data
0	Aaron	0	Aaron	0	Aaron
1	Abelson	1	Abelson	1	Abelson
2	Bateman	2	Bateman	2	Bateman
3	Craddock	3	Craddock	3	Craddock
4	Dunfy	4	Dunfy	4	Crawford
5	Eastman	5	Eastman	5	Dunfy
6		6	Gregory	6	Eastman
7		7		7	Gregory
8		8		8	
9		9		9	

Table 34.8. *Array with items in alphabetical order*   **Table 34.9.** *Adding an item to the end*   **Table 34.10.** *Inserting an item to maintain alphabetical order*

For a list containing hundreds or thousands of entries, this process could be considerably time-consuming.

An alternative approach is to introduce a second array containing pointers which link the elements together in the required order. Now an element, or *node*, contains a pointer in addition to the data. So, returning to the original list in Table 34.8, it would be represented as follows in Table 34.11. The original list is now in *linked list* form. Given the start position of the list, stored in `Start`, the pointers link the items together in the correct alphabetical order. The end of the list is indicated by a *null pointer*, in this case 1. Another pointer, `Free`, keeps track of the next free location for storing new items, and it is incremented whenever a new item is inserted or added to the list.

	node	data	pointer
start	0	Aaron	1
	1	Abelson	2
	2	Bateman	3
	3	Craddock	4
	4	Dunfy	5
	5	Eastman	−1
free	6		
	7		
	8		
	9		

Table 34.11. *Linked list*

Adding Gregory to the list would entail changing the Eastman pointer from 1 to 6 (that is, the value currently given by Free) and putting Gregory at the position indicated by Free (Table 34.12).

	node	data	pointer
start	0	Aaron	1
	1	Abelson	2
	2	Bateman	3
	3	Craddock	4
	4	Dunfy	5
	5	Eastman	6
	6	Gregory	−1
free	7		
	8		
	9		

Table 34.12. *Adding Gregory to the linked list*

Gregory is given a null pointer (-1) to indicate that it is the last item in the list, and Free is incremented.

In pseudocode form, the steps illustrated above to add an item to the end of a linked list are as shown in Listing 34.6.

Listing 34.6.   Adding a node to a linked list

```
algorithm add_node
  i := Start;              {copy start pointer                        }
  while ptr(i)<> null   {follow pointers until null pointer found}
    i := ptr(i)
  endwhile
  ptr(i) := Free          {link new item to current last node        }
  data(Free) := item      {store new data in next free node          }
  ptr(Free) := null       {store null pointer in next free node      }
  Free := Free + 1        {increment next free ptr                   }
end
```

The notation ptr(i) is used for the pointer located at node i, and data(i) represents the data at node i. For example, in the alphabetical list above, ptr(2) = 3 and data(2) = Bateman.

Now, to add Crawford only one pointer is altered, rather than rearranging the items in the array, and the new node is added to the end of the list (Table 34.13).

	node	data	pointer	
start	0	Aaron	1	
	1	Abelson	2	
	2	Bateman	3	
	3	Craddock	7	
	4	Dunfy	5	
	5	Eastman	6	
	6	Gregory	−1	
	7	Crawford	4	inserted node
free	8			
	9			

Table 34.13. *Inserting a node into the linked list*

Thus, the order of accessing the array in alphabetical order is 0 - 1 - 2 - 3 - 7 - 4 - 5 - 6.

In pseudocode, the algorithm for inserting a node to maintain the alphabetic ordering, is shown in Listing 34.7.

Listing 34.7.   Algorithm for insertion of node into linked list

```
algorithm insert_node
  i := Start {copy start pointer}
  found := FALSE
    repeat
      if data(i) > item{ie alphabetically}
          or Start = null {allow for empty list}
        then found := TRUE{insertion position found}
        else p := i {save current node}
          i := ptr(p) {next node in list}
      endif
    until found {insertion position located}
          or i = null {reached end of list}
    if i = start
      then data(Free) := item {insert at head of list}
        ptr(Free) := Start
        Start := Free
      else ptr(p) = Free; {insert in body of list}
        data(Free) := item
        ptr(Free) := i
    endif
    Free := Free + 1 {increment next-free pointer}
  end
```

The increased complexity of this algorithm arises partially from the necessity to allow for the list being initially empty, this state being recognised by Start containing a null pointer. If the list is empty initially, then Start is set equal to Free which contains a pointer to the first available node, and the new data together with a null pointer are stored in this node. To delete a node merely entails ensuring that its predecessors pointer links the node following it. For example, to delete Bateman, the pointers would be adjusted as shown in Table 34.14.

	node	data	pointer	
start	0	Aaron	1	
	1	Abelson	3	
	2	**Bateman**	3	deleted node
	3	Craddock	7	
	4	Dunfy	5	
	5	Eastman	6	
	6	Gregory	−1	
	7	Crawford	4	
free	8			
	9			

Table 34.14. *Adjustment of pointers after deletion of node*

The pointer order is now 0 - 1 - 3 - 7 - 4 - 5 - 6, which misses out the third item in the array containing Bateman. The pseudocode algorithm is shown in Listing 34.8.

Listing 34.8.   Algorithm for deleting node from list

```
algorithm delete_node
  i := Start                      {copy start pointer}
  found := FALSE
  repeat
    if data(i) = item or Start = null {found node or empty list}

      then found := TRUE          {deletion position found}
      else p := i                 {save current node}
        i := ptr(p)               {next node in list}
    endif
  until found or i = null         {deletion position located
                                  or reached end of list}

  if Start = null or i = null     {ie empty list or reached
                                  end of list without
                                  finding node}

    then node does not exist!     {impossible to delete node}
    else if i = start
           then Start := ptr(i)   {delete head of list}
           else ptr(p) := ptr(i)  {skip node in body of list}
         endif
  endif
end
```

The algorithm allows for three special cases:

(i)   the list is empty - this means that it is not possible to delete an element;

(ii)   the item to be deleted is not in the list - it is impossible to delete this item;

(iii)   the item to be deleted is the first one in the list - this requires that `Start` must be set to point to the second node in the linked list.

With a linked list it is possible to locate any element by following the pointers, irrespective of the physical location of the item. Rather than storing the list in consecutive elements of an array, confined to a certain range of memory locations, it is perfectly feasible to store the elements of the linked list anywhere in the memory space allocated to a user program. For this reason, an alternative, and more general, diagrammatic form is often used for linked lists, in which each node contains one or more pointers and one or more words of data. For example, the linked list immediately above might be represented as shown in Figure 34.13.

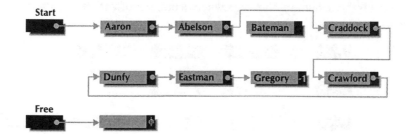

Figure 34.13. *Representation of linked list*

Arrowed lines are used to show the order in which nodes are linked together, and special nodes indicate the start point of the list and the next free node.

Linked lists have a number of advantages over arrays :

❑   Greater flexibility for the location of nodes in memory (it is even possible for nodes to be located on auxiliary storage, such as magnetic disks, rather than in main memory).

❑   The ease with which nodes may be added or deleted from the list.

❑   By adding more pointers, the list may be traversed in a number of different orders.

On the debit side for linked lists:

❑   Locating specific items necessitates searching the list from the start node, whereas arrays allow direct access to elements.

- ☐   Linked lists require more memory because of the need for pointers.

- ☐   Linked lists involve more housekeeping operations because of the necessity to change pointers when adding or deleting nodes.

Applications of linked lists

With an interpreted language such as BASIC, variables must be accessed as quickly as possible so that program processing speed is acceptably fast. One method of ensuring this is by the use of linked lists.

In one such scheme, used by Acorn BASIC, variables starting with the same character are given their own linked list, so that there is a linked list for each possible starting character. Though the lists are quite separate, each with its own start pointer, they occupy a common area of memory and link around each other. Each node in the linked lists contains the name and value of the variable, plus a pointer to the next variable with the same starting letter. Figure 34.14 illustrates this scheme at the stage where a number of variables with starting letters A, B or C have been created.

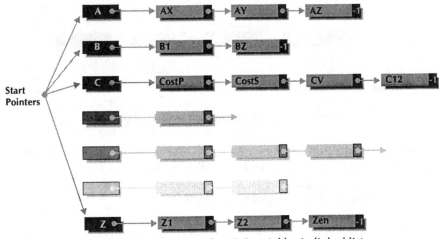

Figure 34.14. *Creation of BASIC variables in linked list*

The start pointers for the linked lists are stored in a table in a specific area of memory. The first pointer in the table contains the address of the node for the first variable starting with the letter A to be created in the current program, in this case AX. This node contains a pointer to the second variable created, AY, and its node contains a pointer to AZ, the last variable created starting with the letter A. Similar lists occur for the variables starting with B (B1 and B2) and C *(CostP, CostS, CV* and *C12).* Because the lists link around each other, there is a common free-space pointer for all the lists.

To find a particular variable's node, the starting letter of the variable is converted into an address giving the start pointer for its linked list, and the nodes of this list are traversed in pointer order until the variable is located. For example, suppose that the table of start pointers was at memory location 1000, and the variable *BZ* is to be accessed. The letter *B* is first converted into a number indicating its position in the alphabet, that is 2, and this is added to the start address of the table.

Thus, $1000 + 2 = 1002$ is the location of the start pointer for the linked list of variables beginning with B. The first node in the list is for variable B1, which is not the one required, so its pointer is used to access the next node in the list. This time the variable found is *BZ* as required.

For a program containing many variables, this scheme can dramatically reduce the time required to locate a certain variable, provided variable names are chosen with different starting letters. It is worth noting that in this instance, a knowledge of the internal organisation of an interpreter can help the programmer to write more efficient programs.

Linked lists are also used for procedures and functions so that they can be located as quickly as possible no matter where in the program they are referenced. Otherwise, a program would have to be searched sequentially from the beginning every time a procedure or function was invoked.

The tree

The term *tree* refers to a non-linear data structure in which nodes have two or more pointers to other nodes, forming a hierarchical structure as illustrated in Figure 34.15.

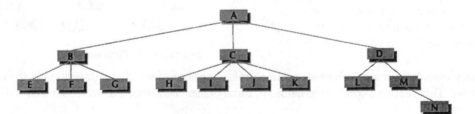

Figure 34.15. *Tree structure*

Node A is the *root* node of the entire tree with pointers to three *subtrees*. B, C and D are known as *children* of the *parent* node *A*. Similarly, *E*, *F* and *G* are children of *B*. Nodes *B* to *N* are all descendants of *A*, just as nodes *L* to *N* are all descendants of *D*. Nodes such as *H*, *I* and *L*, which have no children, are known as leaves or terminal nodes.

Trees are useful for representing hierarchical relationships between data items, such as those found in databases. For example, a record in an employee file might have the structure shown in Figure 34.16.

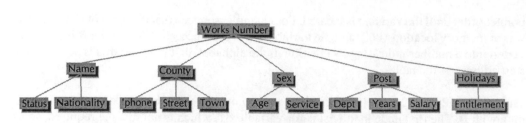

Figure 34.16. *Tree showing hierarchical structure of fields in an employee record*

Stored as a tree, the data can be accessed in a number of ways. For example, extracting the first level of the tree provides a summary of the employee, giving Name, Home county, Sex, Post and Holidays taken; accessing only the fourth subtree provides details of the employees current position; accessing the tree in order of the five subtrees provides all the employees details.

A binary tree is a particular type of tree which has more uses than a general tree as described above, and is also much easier to implement. Binary trees are described in the following two sections.

Binary trees

A binary tree is a special type of tree in which each parent has a maximum of two children which are linked to the parent node using a left pointer and a right pointer. The general form of a binary tree is shown in Figure 34.17.

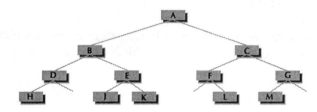

Figure 34.17. *Binary tree*

Binary trees have many important applications, a number of which are described in the next section. This section explores the nature of binary trees, how they are created, modified and accessed.

In the previous section we saw that in order to locate a specific node in a linked list it is necessary to search the list from the beginning, following the pointers linking the nodes together in the appropriate order. For a list containing a large number of elements, this process could be very time consuming. The solution to the same problem with an array structure was to use the binary search technique (see section on Search Strategies); the same principle can be applied to a linked list if the list is in the form of a *binary tree*. Consider the alphabetically ordered linked list described earlier in the section on linked lists and shown in Figure 34.18.

Figure 34.18. *Alphabetically ordered linked list*

Now suppose that the same list is represented as a binary tree with two pointers in each node, one pointing to an element alphabetically less than the node data (a *left pointer*) and the other pointing to an element alphabetically greater than the node data (a *right pointer*). (See Figure 34.19).

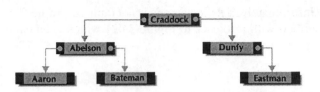

Figure 34.19. .*Alphabetic list as binary tree*

If we were looking for *Eastman*, the procedure would be as follows:

(i)   Compare *Eastman* with the *root* node, *Craddock.*

(ii)   Because *Craddock* is alphabetically less than *Eastman*, follow the right pointer to *Dunfy.*

(iii) Compare *Eastman* with *Dunfy.*

(iv)   *Dunfy* is alphabetically less than *Eastman* so again follow the right pointer to *Eastman.*

(v)   The next comparison shows that the required node has been located.

Each comparison confines the search to either the upper or lower part of the alphabetic list, thus significantly reducing the number of comparisons needed to locate the element required.

To add an element, *Crawford* for example, to the configuration shown above, whilst retaining the alphabetic ordering, is merely a matter of searching for the new item until a null pointer is encountered. In this example, a null pointer occurs when attempting to go left at *Dunfy.* *Crawford* is installed in the next free node and *Dunfy's* left pointer points to it.

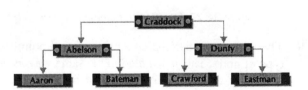

The new tree is shown in Figure 34.20.

Figure 34.20. *Adding the node, Crawford*

Unfortunately, deleting a node is not quite so simple. Three cases can arise, and these are described with reference to Figure 34.21 which is an extended form of the binary tree shown above.

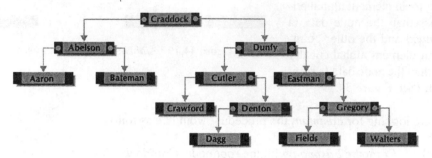

Figure 34.21. *Extended form of binary tree shown in Figure 34.19*

(i)   The node to be deleted is a terminal node, or leaf, having null left and right pointers. *Bateman* is an example of such a node. Deleting it is simply a matter of setting *Abelson's* right pointer to the null pointer (Figure 34.22).

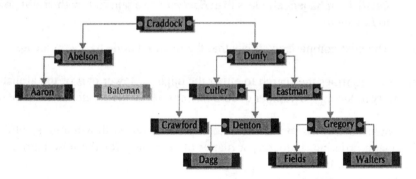

Figure 34.22. *Deletion of Bateman node which has null left and right pointers*

(ii)   The node to be deleted contains one null pointer. *Eastman* is an example of this type of node. This is handled in the same way as deleting a node from a linked list - *Dunfy's* right pointer is replaced by *Eastman's* right pointer (Figure 34.23).

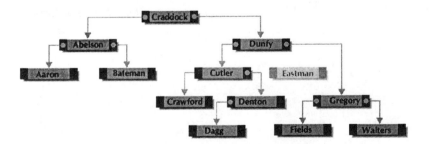

Figure 34.23. *Deletion of Eastman node which contains one null pointer*

(iii)   The node to be deleted contains no null pointers. There are two possibilities here: replace the deleted entry with an entry from its right subtree, or an entry from its left subtree. We will consider both of these using Dunfy as the item to be deleted from the original tree.

Taking the left subtree first, the procedure is to search the left subtree for the alphabetically largest entry by following the right pointers at each node until a null pointer is found. The left subtree of *Dunfy* is shown in Figure 34.24 and the largest value is *Denton*.

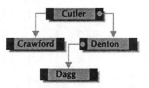

Figure 34.24. *Left subtree*

In order that *Dunfy* can be deleted whilst still retaining the correct ordering, it is replaced by *Denton* and a number of pointers are adjusted as shown in Figure 34.25.

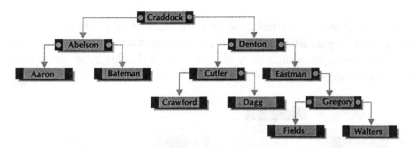

Figure 34.25. *Adjustment of pointers to delete Dunfy*

Denton's pointers are replaced by *Dunfy's* pointers; *Craddock's* pointer now points to *Denton*; *Cutler's* right pointer now points to *Dagg*.

Note that for clarity Figure 34.25 above gives the impression that nodes have been moved around, but all that occurs in practice is that pointers are changed to alter the nodes that are to be linked together or deleted; the *Dunfy* node still exists in the tree but is effectively deleted because no node pointers reference it.

This is made clear when the tree is represented in tabular form. Table 34.15 shows the structure of the original tree. With the node *Dunfy* deleted, the result is as shown in Table 34.16.

node	left	data	right
0	1	Craddock	4
1	2	Abelson	3
2	−1	Aaron	−1
3	−1	Bateman	−1
4	5	Dunfy	9
5	6	Cutler	7
6	−1	Crawford	−1
7	8	Denton	−1
8	−1	Dagg	−1
9	−1	Eastman	10
10	11	Gregory	12
11	−1	Fields	−1
12	−1	Walters	−1

Table 34.15. *Structure of original tree*

node	left	data	right	
0	1	Craddock	7	
1	2	Abelson	3	
2	−1	Aaron	−1	
3	−1	Bateman	−1	
4	5	Dunfy	9	deleted
5	6	Cutler	8	
6	−1	Crawford	−1	
7	5	Denton	−1	
8	−1	Dagg	−1	
9	−1	Eastman	10	
10	11	Gregory	12	
11	−1	Fields	−1	
12	−1	Walters	−1	

Table 34.16. *Tree with Dunfy deleted*

If the right subtree of *Dunfy* is selected rather than the left subtree to search for a replacement, then the procedure is very similar; this time the left pointers are followed in order to find the alphabetically smallest item, which then replaces *Dunfy*. In this case the smallest item is *Eastman* and the tree becomes as shown in Figure 34.26.

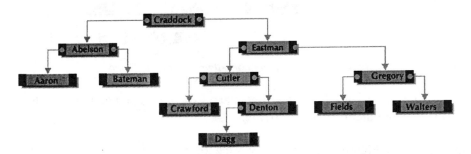

Figure 34.26. *Use of Dunfy's right subtree to find a replacement*

Methods of tree traversal

Having created a binary tree, it is likely that it will need to be accessed in some particular order, alphabetically for example. The algorithm for visiting the data items of a binary tree in alphabetical order is an example of *in-order* traversal and can be stated quite simply:

```
In-order traversal:
   visit the left subtree in in-order then
```

```
visit the root node then
visit the right subtree in in-order.
```

Notice that the algorithm makes reference to itself. In other words, the algorithm for visiting a subtree is exactly the same as that for visiting a tree. The seemingly endless process of visiting trees within trees within trees etc. continues until a null pointer is encountered, allowing the process to terminate, or *bottom out*. The operation of the algorithm is best illustrated by means of an example. Consider the tree shown in Figure 34.27.

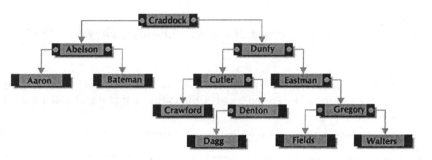

Figure 34.27.

Suppose that this tree is to be printed in alphabetical order, that is, an in-order traversal is to be performed. Then the procedure would be as follows. The left subtree of the *root node*, *Craddock* is shown in Figure 34.28.

Figure 34.28. *Left subtree of Craddock*

To print this subtree, we must first print its left subtree, which is just the entry *Aaron* which has no descendants. We therefore print Aaron. Now we can print the node data, Abelson and turn to the right subtree of *Abelson*. This right subtree is simply *Bateman*, which is then printed.

This completes the printing of the left subtree of *Craddock*, so now Craddock can be printed. Now the right subtree of *Craddock* is to be printed. The right subtree of *Craddock* has as its root node *Dunfy* (Figure 34.29).

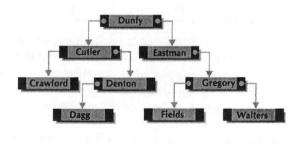

Figure 34.29. *Right subtree of Craddock*

We must first print *Dunfy's* left subtree, which is shown in Figure 34.30. *Cutler's* left subtree is *Crawford* which is a terminal node and is therefore printed. Cutler is then printed, followed by Dagg then Denton. This completes the printing of *Dunfy's* left subtree, so Dunfy is printed followed by its right subtree (shown in Figure 34.31).

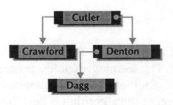

Figure 34.30. *Dunfy's left subtree*

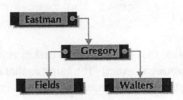

Figure 34.31. *Dunfy's right subtree*

In order, this subtree would be printed: 'Eastman'- ' Fields'- 'Gregory'- 'Walters', which completes the process.

The simplicity of this method is also reflected in the pseudocode version of the algorithm. We begin by defining a procedure called `Tree` which prints a tree starting at a specified node (Listing 34.9).

Listing 34.9.

```
define procedure Tree(node)
   l := lptr(node)          {get this node's left pointer}
   if l <> null             {if left subtree exists,
      then Tree(l)             print it}
   endif
   print(node)              {print the data at this node}
   r := rptr(node)          {get this node's right pointer}
   if r <> null             {if right subtree exists,
      then Tree(r)             print it}
   endif
endprocedure Tree
```

Notice that this procedure calls itself; this is termed *recursion*, a very useful programming device. The procedure `Tree` is invoked to print the left subtree at a particular node by passing the left pointer as a procedure *parameter*, or to print the right subtree by passing the right pointer as a procedure parameter. A procedure parameter allows values to be transmitted to the procedure which are local to the procedure, having no existence outside the procedure.

In Listing 34.9, `node` is a parameter which initially points to the root node. By making the procedure call, `Tree(root)`, the procedure is invoked with the value of `root` passed to the parameter `node`. In the procedure, `node` is used to get the value of the left pointer using `l = lptr(node)`. If it is not a null pointer, `l` is now passed to the procedure recursively using `Tree(l)`, and now `node` has the value of the pointer for the left subtree. In this way, the procedure `Tree` is used recursively to process subtrees, only printing a node and going on to the right subtree when a null pointer is encountered.

To illustrate the operation of the pseudocode, consider the binary tree shown in Figure 34.32 which is to be processed in alphabetical order.

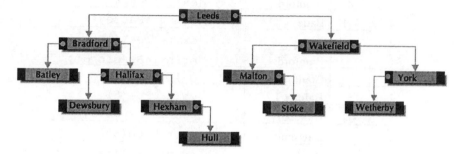

Figure 34.32. *Binary tree to be processed in alphabetical order*

The equivalent table is Table 34.17.

node	left	data	right
0	1	Leeds	6
1	4	Bradford	2
2	5	Halifax	3
3	−1	Hexham	9
4	−1	Batley	−1
5	−1	Dewsbury	−1
6	10	Wakefield	7
7	8	York	−1
8	−1	Wetherby	−1
9	−1	Hull	−1
10	−1	Malton	11
11	−1	Stoke	−1

Table 34.17. *Table representation of binary tree in Figure 34.32*

Table 34.18 traces the pseudocode in Listing 34.9, indicating the action taken at each invocation of Tree. Only the pointer currently relevant is indicated in the two pointer columns. The process is started by the call Tree(0).

node	left	data	right	action
0	1	Leeds		`call Tree(1)`
1	4	Bradford		`call Tree(4)`
4	−1	Batley		`print 'Batley'`
4		Batley	−1	`exit Tree(4)`
1		Bradford		`print 'Bradford'`
1		Bradford	2	`call Tree(2)`
2	5	Halifax		`call Tree(5)`
5	−1	Dewsbury		`print 'Dewsbury'`
5		Dewsbury	−1	`exit Tree(5)`
2		Halifax		`print 'Halifax'`
2		Halifax	3	`call Tree(3)`
3	−1	Hexham		`print 'Hexham'`
3		Hexham	9	`call Tree(9)`
9	−1	Hull		`print 'Hull'`
9		Hull	−1	`exit Tree(9)`
3		Hexham		`exit Tree(3)`
2		Halifax		`exit Tree(2)`
1		Bradford		`exit Tree(1)`
0		Leeds	6	`call Tree(6)`
6	10	Wakefield		`call Tree(10)`
10	−1	Malton		`call Tree(11)`
10		Malton	11	`print 'Stoke'`
11	−1	Stoke		`exit Tree(11)`
11		Stoke	−1	`exit Tree(10)`
10		Malton		`print 'Wakefield'`
6		Wakefield		`call Tree(7)`
6		Wakefield	7	`call Tree(8)`
7	8	York		`print 'Wetherby'`
8	−1	Wetherby		`exit Tree(8)`
8		Wetherby	−1	`print 'York'`
7		York		`exit Tree(7)`
7		York	−1	`exit Tree(6)`
6		Wakefield		`exit Tree(0)`
0		Leeds		

Table 34.18. *Tracing action of Listing 34.9 in printing an alphabetically ordered list*

As each invocation of `Tree` is completed, control is returned to the point where the procedure was called. For example, if currently the root node of a subtree is node 7, *York*, then exit Tree(7) returns control to the instruction following call Tree(7) which happens to be the end of Tree(6), *Wakefield*; similarly, exit Tree(6) returns control to the point where Tree(6) was called, the end of Tree(0). Successively returning to parent nodes is the bottoming out process referred to above, and it relies heavily on the use of a stack (see the earlier section on applications of stacks).

Using the recursive procedure, Tree, hides the use of the stack because of the way that procedure parameters are handled. On entering a procedure, the current values of its parameters are pushed to a stack and are replaced by the values passed to the procedure; the original values of the parameters are restored only when the procedure is exited. For example, the procedure call Tree(2) passes the value 2 to the parameter node. At this point, Tree(1) is being processed with node having a value of 1. So before node takes the value 2, its current value, that is 1, is pushed onto the stack. Then node is given the value 2 and the procedure is executed. When control returns to the point following the call Tree(2), the top of the stack, the value 1, is pulled and copied to node thus restoring it to its local value.

The tree traversal algorithm given above is called in-order tree traversal, one of three main methods of accessing trees. The other two methods are called *pre-order* and *post-order traversal*. These are defined as follow:

```
Pre-order traversal:
visit the root node, then
visit all the nodes in the left subtree in pre-order, then
visit all the nodes in the right subtree in pre-order
```

With reference to the tree above, pre-order traversal would produce the list:

Leeds Bradford Batley Halifax Dewsbury Hexham Hull Wakefield Malton Stoke York Wetherby

```
Post-order traversal:
visit all the nodes of the left subtree in post-order, then
visit all the nodes in the right subtree in post-order, then
visit the root node
```

This would produce the list:

Batley Dewsbury Hull Hexham Halifax Bradford Stoke Malton Wetherby York Wakefield Leeds

Notice that the definitions of pre-order and post-order traversals again are recursive, allowing them to be handled in the same way as the in-order traversal.

Applications of binary trees

Sorting

A binary tree can be used to order a set of integers using the algorithm given in Listing 34.10.

Listing 34.10.

```
algorithm tree_sort
  repeat
    read num                              {get next number}
    addnode(0)                            {call procedure}
  until no_more_numbers                   {continue until all
                                          numbers read}

end

define procedure addnode(node)
  if data(node) > num
    then if lptr(node) = null
            then createnode(num)
            else addnode(lptr(node))      {recurse using lptr}
         endif
    else if rptr(node) = null
            then createnode(num)
            else addnode(rptr(node))      {recurse using rptr}
         endif
  endif
endprocedure addnode
```

Initially, the first number in the list is stored in the root node. Then, in turn, each of the remaining numbers is compared with the current root node (that is, data(node)) to determine whether the number should be in the left subtree or the right subtree. If the number is greater, then it must go somewhere in the right subtree, otherwise it must go somewhere in the left subtree. If the appropriate subtree pointer is null, a new node is created containing the number and the subtree pointer links it to the tree; when the subtree pointer is not null, the process calls itself (recurses) using the pointer as the new root node. The procedure createnode(num), referred to in the algorithm merely allocates space for new nodes, stores the number in the new node and links it to the tree by adjusting the parents left or right pointer.

As an example, suppose the following list of numbers is to be used to created an ordered tree as described above: 57 10 26 13 85 2 30 63 120

The tree would assume the form shown in Figure 34.33.

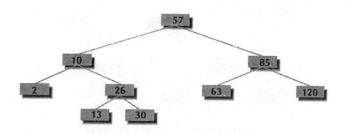

Figure 34.33. *Ordered tree of number list*

The numbers could be visited in ascending order using in-order traversal, as described in the previous section, to give the list

$$2 \quad 10 \quad 13 \quad 26 \quad 30 \quad 57 \quad 63 \quad 85 \quad 120$$

Representing arithmetic expressions

Compilers often transform arithmetic expressions into more manageable forms prior to generating object code. A binary tree representation of an arithmetic expression is one such transformation. Consider the expression B + C*D. The equivalent binary tree representation is shown in Figure 34.34.

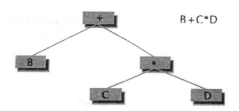

Figure 34.34. *Tree representation of B + C*D*

An in-order traversal of the tree produces the original expression. This type of representation is relatively easy to handle by a compiler: if a node contains an operator, the left subtree is evaluated, the right subtree is evaluated and the two values obtained are the operands for the operator at that node. If a subtree also contains an operator node, the same procedure is used recursively to produce the intermediate result. In the example above, + at the root node causes the left subtree to be evaluated, resulting in the value assigned to *B*; however, the right subtree contains the operator node * (multiplication) causing a recursive call to its left and right subtrees before the multiplication, *C*D*, can be evaluated.

Figures 34.35 to 34.37 provide further examples of expressions represented as binary trees. All of these expressions are in *infix notation*, that is, with the arithmetic operators positioned between the operands. Thus, to add two numbers, *A* and *B*, using infix notation we would write *A* + *B*. There are two other standard notations for arithmetic expressions, namely, *postfix* and *prefix* notations. In postfix notation, *A* + *B* is written *AB*+ and in prefix, +*AB*. By traversing the binary tree in in-order we saw that the infix expression resulted. Perhaps unsurprisingly, traversing the tree in post-order gives the postfix expression, and traversing the tree in pre-order gives the prefix expression.

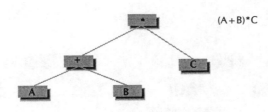

Figure 34.35. *Tree of A + B − C/2*

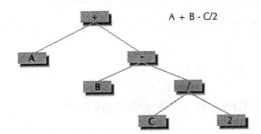

Figure 34.36. *Tree of (A + B)*C*

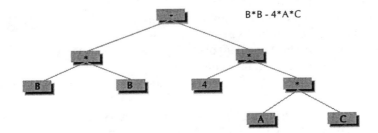

Figure 34.37. *Tree of B*B − 4*A*C*

Table 34.19 shows the same expressions in the three different forms.

Infix	Postfix	Prefix
B+C*D	BCD*+	+B*CD
(A+B)*C	AB+C*	*+ABC
A+BC/2	ABC2/+	+AB/C2
B*B4*A*C	BB*4AC**	*BB*4AC

Table 34.19. *Expressions in three different forms*

Postfix notation is also known by the name Reverse Polish notation, extensively used in the programming language Forth and of general importance in computing.

Exercises

1. Explain the purpose of:

   (i)   Iliffe vectors;

   (ii)   access tables.

   Illustrate your answer with examples.

2. Calculate the number of comparisons required to find a particular item using binary search for the following lists:

   (i)   1000 numbers;

   (ii)   2542 numbers;

   (iii)   20,333 numbers.

3. With the aid of an example show how a new number would be inserted into an array containing numbers that are stored in ascending order of magnitude. Write a pseudocode algorithm for the procedure.

4. State the main characteristics of the following types of data structures:

   (i)   stack;

   (ii)   queue;

   (iii)   circular queue;

   (iv)   linked list;

   (v)   binary tree.

   Illustrate your answer with examples to show how items are added and removed from them.

5. For each of the following situations described below suggest an appropriate data structure to use. Justify your choice of data structure in each case.

   (i)   A simulation of the flow of traffic at a set of traffic lights.

   (ii)   The storage of the names and values of variables used by a program written in an interpreted language such as BASIC.

   (iii)   Storing return addresses in a programming language that permits the use of subroutines.

(iv)   A college enrolment system which records the names of people who apply in advance for places on evening classes. Places are allocated on a 'first come, first served basis'.

(v)   A list of names which must be maintained in alphabetical order. New names are frequently added to the list and existing names are frequently deleted from the list.

(vi)   A train arrivals and departures system that provides information for passengers. The information is displayed on monitors which show (in separate lists) the next ten train arrivals and departures.

6.   Draw a binary tree which would allow the following list of numbers to be visited using in-order traversal:

55   23   78   13   122   61   3   321   8   43

7.   Draw a binary tree for each of the following arithmetic expressions:

(i)   (A+B)*(A-B)

(ii)   B*(C+D) - C*D

(iii)   A*(B-C/D) + E

(iv)   (X+N/X)/2

(v)   2*X*X - 5*X + 7

Use the trees to convert the expressions into postfix and prefix notation.

Chapter 35
Sorting Techniques

Introduction

For computing purposes, a distinction has to be made between *internal* and *external* sorting. Where large volumes of data have to be sorted, such as entire files held on magnetic tape or disk, an external sort is used; this involves repeated transfers of data between memory and backing storage media. Internal sorting, which is the subject of study in this section, involves the sorting of items entirely within memory into a strict ascending or descending order. For programming purposes, the items to be sorted are held in a one-dimensional array. The purpose of the data items will vary according to the application, but they may serve, for example, as keys to logical records. Direct access files frequently make use of indexes to identify the locations of individual records on a storage medium. Searching such an index for a particular record key value is often more efficient if the index is sorted into a particular sequence.

The study of sorting algorithms is a long standing area of research in computer science and many highly efficient but complex methods have been developed. In order that the main principles of sorting can be understood, this text provides a detailed description of three relatively simple sorting techniques, namely the:

❑   exchange or 'bubble' sort;

❑   selection sort;

❑   insertion sort.

Each narrative description is followed by:

❑   an outline of the main programming requirements needed to implement the sort in a high level language;

❑   a pseudocode algorithm with detailed annotation of the main processes;

❑   annotated sample programs implemented in Turbo Pascal.

Exchange sort

If it is assumed, for example, that items are to be sorted into ascending sequence, then the idea of the exchange sort is that, firstly the largest value moves to the end of the list, followed by the second largest before that, the third largest before that and so on. The process can best be illustrated by a practical example as follows.

Consider a one-dimensional array of 5 elements, each containing an integer value. The array is known by the symbol M and each element in the array is identified by its subscript. The array elements and their contents are shown in Table 35.1.

The exchange sort requires that the array of values be scanned repeatedly and that with each scan, or more properly, *pass*, adjacent pairs of numbers are compared to see if they are in the required order; if necessary they exchange positions. In the above example, the first pair, 3 and 6, are compared and found to be in the correct order; no exchange is necessary. Then the second and third items, 6 and 2, are compared, found to be in the incorrect order and are exchanged. The array now appears as in Table 35.2.

Array elements	M[1]	M[2]	M[3]	M[4]	M[5]
Contents	3	6	2	1	5

Table 35.1. Original, unsorted list

Array elements	M[1]	M[2]	M[3]	M[4]	M[5]
Contents	3	2	6	1	5

Table 35.2. Swap of M(2) and M(3)

The first pass continues with the comparison of the third and fourth items, 6 and 1; these require exchanging and the list is as shown in Table 35.3.

Array elements	M[1]	M[2]	M[3]	M[4]	M[5]
Contents	3	2	1	6	5

Table 35.3. Swap of M(3) and M(4)

The first pass ends with a comparison of the fourth and fifth items, now 6 and 5 respectively; again, an exchange is required. At the end of this first pass, the sequence appears as in Table 35.4.

Array elements	M[1]	M[2]	M[3]	M[4]	M[5]
Contents	3	2	1	5	6

Table 35.4. Swap of M(5) and M(6)

The sort is not yet complete and further passes are needed. The complete process is illustrated in Table35.5. Shading indicates those values currently being compared and, if necessary, exchanged.

array elements	swap	M[1]	M[2]	M[3]	M[4]	M[5]
begin Pass 1	no	3	6	2	1	5
	yes	3	6	2	1	5
	yes	3	2	6	1	5
	yes	3	2	1	6	5
end of Pass 1		3	2	1	5	6
begin Pass 2	yes	3	2	1	5	6
	yes	2	3	1	5	6
	no	2	1	3	5	6
	no	2	1	3	5	6
end Pass 2		2	1	3	5	6
begin Pass 3	yes	2	1	3	5	6
	no	1	2	3	5	6
	no	1	2	3	5	6
	no	1	2	3	5	6
end Pass 3		1	2	3	5	6
begin Pass 4	no	1	2	3	5	6
	no	1	2	3	5	6
	no	1	2	3	5	6
	no	1	2	3	5	6
end Pass 4		1	2	3	5	6

Table 35.5. *State of list at each stage of the sort.*

A number of features can be identified in the process.

- ❑ With each pass, the smallest value moves one position towards the beginning (the left) of the array.

- ❑ After the first pass, the largest value is at the end of the array. At the end of each subsequent pass, the next largest number moves to its correct position.

- ❑ The sort has been completed before the final pass.

Referring to this last feature, the sort is complete by the end of Pass 3. Why then is a further pass necessary? The answer is that the first comparison in Pass 3 results in an exchange between the values 2 and 1. If it is assumed that the occurrence of an exchange indicates that the sort is not complete, then a further pass is needed to determine that the array is sorted; that is, there have been no exchanges. The maximum number of passes required is always $n-1$, n being the number of items in the array. Frequently, the sort is complete well before this maximum is reached and any further passes are wasted. Consider the sequence in Table 35.6.

array elements	swap	M[1]	M[2]	M[3]	M[4]	M[5]	M[6]
initial contents		3	1	2	6	7	9
begin Pass 1	yes	3	1	2	6	7	9
	yes	1	3	2	6	7	9
	no	1	2	3	6	7	9
	no	1	2	3	6	7	9
end of Pass 1		1	2	3	6	7	9
begin Pass 2	no	1	2	3	6	7	9
	no	1	2	3	6	7	9
	no	1	2	3	6	7	9
	no	1	2	3	6	7	9
end of Pass 2		1	2	3	6	7	9

Table 35.6. *Sort completed in one Pass, with additional Pass needed to confirm*

The maximum number of passes necessary should be $n-1$, that is, 5. Instead, the sort is completed by the end of the first pass and confirmed by the lack of exchanges in the second pass.

Program requirements

(i)   Comparison of adjacent values in an array. Assuming that the values are held in a one-dimensional array, reference is made to elements within the array by subscript. For example, the 4th element in an array called *list*, is addressed by *list*[4]. To carry out a pass of all the elements in an array requires the use of a program loop to increment the subscript from 1 to n, the variable being the size of the array. This can reduce by 1 after each complete pass, because the largest number moves to the end of the list and therefore need not be considered in subsequent passes; the efficiency of the algorithm is thus improved. For the sake of simplicity, this particular feature is not used in the illustrative algorithm or programs.

(ii) Exchanging the positions of adjacent values. Assuming that the programming language in use does not provide an 'exchange' or 'swap' instruction, then a temporary store is required to allow the exchange to take place, For example, to exchange the contents of two variables, *First* and *Second*, using a temporary store, *Hold*, requires the following processes:

location	First	Second	Hold
initial contents	6	3	
after process 1	6	3	6
after process 2	3	3	6
after process 3	3	6	6

Table 35.7. *Exchanging contents of two variables, using a temporary, third variable*

1.   Copy contents of *First* into *Hold*;

2.   Copy contents of *Second* into *First*;

3.   Copy contents of *Hold* into *Second*.

This is illustrated, with some example values, in Table 35.7.

(iii) Detecting completion of the sort. A *flag* or *sentinel* variable, initialised for example, to 0 at the beginning of each pass and set to 1 if any exchanges take place during a pass, can be used to detect the completion of the sort before the maximum number of passes has been completed. For simplicity, the following algorithm does not include this feature, although it is used in the sample Pascal programs;

Listing 35.1.   Exchange sort pseudocode

```
{Exchange sort}
Number:= N                              {number of values and
                                        subscript    of last item}
Passes:= 1                              {initialise passes}
while Passes <= Number — 1 do           {control number of passes}
  Item:= 1                              {set array subscript}
  while Item <= Number — 1 do           {loop for one pass}
    if M[Item] > M[Item + 1] then
      swap                              {exchange if necessary}
    endif
    Item:= Item + 1                     {increment subscript}
  endwhile                              {end of single pass}
  Passes:= Passes + 1                   {increment passes}
endwhile                                {end of all passes
```

Listing 35.2.   Exchange sort in Turbo Pascal

```
program Exchange(input, output);
const
NUMBER = 20;

var
  M   :array[1..NUMBER] of integer;
  Exchange :boolean;
  Item, Passes, Spare :integer;

begin
  for Item:= 1 to NUMBER do
    begin
        write('Number :');
        readln(M[Item]);
    end;
  Passes:= 1;
  Exchange:= true;
  while (Passes <= Number - 1) and(Exchange) do
    begin
        Item:= 1;
        Exchange:= false
        while Item <= Number - 1 do
          begin
              if M[Item]> M[Item+1] then
                begin
                  Spare:= M[Item];
                  M[Item]:= M[Item+1];
                  M[Item+1]:= Spare;
                  Exchange:= true;
                end;
              Item:= Item+1;
          end;
          Passes:= Passes+1;
    end;
    for Item:= 1 to Number do
        begin
            writeln(M[Item]);
        end;
  end.
```

Selection sort

This method also requires the comparison and exchange of elements in a list. It is based on the principal that the item with the lowest value is exchanged with the item at the beginning or *head* of the list and that the process is repeated with $n-1$ items, $n-2$ items and so on, until only the largest item is left. Table 35.8 shows array M containing six, unsorted, integer values.

M[1]	M[2]	M[3]	M[4]	M[5]	M[6]
15	8	−3	62	24	12

Table 35.8. *Unsorted list*

M[1]	M[2]	M[3]	M[4]	M[5]	M[6]
−3	8	12	15	24	62

Table 35.9. *Sorted list*

The list is to be sorted into strict ascending sequence, as shown in Table 35.9

Table 35.10 shows the scanning process, the shaded values indicating the length of the list to be examined in each scan.

M[1]	M[2]	M[3]	M[4]	M[5]	M[6]	Action
15	8	−3	62	24	12	Starting sequence
−3	8	15	62	24	12	−3 swapped with 15 at head of list
−3	8	15	62	24	12	No swap needed
−3	8	12	62	24	15	12 swapped with 15 at head of list
−3	8	12	15	24	62	15 swapped with 62 at head of list
−3	8	12	15	24	62	No swap needed

Table 35.10. *Scanning process in selection sort*

The first pass of n items returns the value of −3 as being the smallest value in the list; this value moves to the head of the list and the previous head, 15, is moved to the position formerly occupied by −3. The list to be scanned is now $n-1$ items and has the value 8 at its head. The next pass reveals 8 as the smallest value, but no exchange is made because it already heads the shortened list. The next pass examines $n-2$ items and returns 12 as the lowest value, which is exchanged with 15 at the head of the shortened list. The process continues until only two items remain, 24 at the head and 62 at the rear; no exchange is needed and the list is sorted.

Program requirements

Certain features are similar to those of the exchange sort described earlier.

(i)   Comparison of values in different locations in an array.

(ii)   Exchange of values in different, although not necessarily adjacent, positions in the array.

(iii)   The use of a pointer to allow element positions to be stored and incremented and also to be used as a subscript to refer to the contents of an individual location.

(iv)   The use of a temporary store to enable an exchange of element positions.

Listing 35.3 illustrates a selection sort algorithm.

Listing 35.3.   Selection sort pseudocode

```
{Selection}
Number:= N                               {Values to sort            }
for Head:= 1 to N - 1                    {Increment Head            }
  PresentValue:= M[Head]                 {Value of current Head     }
  PresentPtr:= Head                      {Position of current Head  }
  for Next:= PresentPtr+1 to N           {Increment search pointer  }
    if M(Next) < PresentValue then
        PresentValue:= M[Next]           {Store smaller value and   }
        PresentPtr:= Next                {its position in the list  }
    endif
  endfor
  if PresentPtr <> Head then             {Check smallest not at head}
    Temp:= M[Head]                       {Temporary store for swap  }
    M[Head]:= M[PresentPtr];             {Swap smallest/head values }
    M[PresentPtr]:= Temp
  endif
endfor
```

The use of a temporary location `Temp` in the above algorithm is not strictly necessary, since the smallest value is assigned to `PresentValue` at the end of a scan and as the following program implementation illustrates, the swap could be implemented with:

```
M(PresentPtr) := M(Head);
M(Head)    := PresentValue;
```

Listing 35.4.   Selection sort in Turbo Pascal

```pascal
program Selection(input, output);
const
  NUMBER = 20;
var
  M :array[1..NUMBER] of integer;
  Head, Next, PresentValue, PresentPtr :integer;
begin
  for Next:= 1 to NUMBER do
    begin
      write('Number');
      readln(M[Next]);
    end;
  for Head:= 1 to NUMBER - 1 do
    begin
      PresentValue:= M[Head];
      PresentPtr:= Head;
      for Next:= PresentPtr + 1 to NUMBER do
        begin
          if M[Next] < PresentValue then
            begin
              PresentValue:= M[Next];
              PresentPtr:= Next;
            end;
        end;
      if PresentPtr <> Head then
          begin
            M[PresentPtr]:= M[Head];
            M[Head]:= PresentValue;
          end;
    end;
  for Next:= 1 to NUMBER do
    begin
      writeln(M[Next]);
    end;
end.
```

Insertion sort

This method can best be illustrated with the example of an unsorted pack of playing cards. Assuming that the cards are to be put into a row of ascending sequence (the least value on the left), the procedure may be as follows:

(i)   take the first card from the *source* pile and begin the *destination* row;

(ii)   continuing with the rest of the source pile, pick one card at a time and place it in the correct sequence in the destination row.

The process of finding the correct point of insertion requires repeated comparisons and where an insertion requires it, movement of cards to make space in the sequence. Thus, the card to be inserted, x, is compared with successive cards in the destination row (beginning from the largest value at the right hand end of the destination row) and where x is less than the card under comparison, the latter is moved to the right; otherwise x is inserted in the next position to the right.

Program requirements

The procedures are fairly simple, although a practical exercise with a pack of cards should help to clarify them.

(i)   As with previous sorts, reference to array subscripts is required to allow comparison with different elements in the array;

(ii)   Nested loops are needed; the outer one for selecting successive values to be inserted into a destination sequence and the inner for allowing the insertion value to be compared with those already in sequence;

(iii) Control of the outer loop does not present a problem as it simply ensures that all values are inserted, starting with the second; the first obviously needs no comparison as it is the first to be inserted.

(iv)   The inner loop controls the movement of values through the destination list to allow insertion of new values at the appropriate points. This loop may be terminated under two distinct conditions:

  (a)   a value in the destination sequence is less than the value to be inserted;

  (b)   there are no further items to the left in the destination sequence.

To ensure termination under these conditions, a *flag* or *sentinel* is used. In the algorithm and the program implementations, array element (0) is used to store the value to be inserted, thus ensuring that when the left hand end is reached, no further comparisons are made. The algorithm in Listing 35.5 illustrates the procedure; the analogy of a pack of cards is continued.

Listing 35.5. Insertion sort pseudocode

```
{Insertion}
for Pick:= 2 to NumInPack  {Pick card, starting with second      }
   InHand:= M[Pick]         {Store value of card to insert        }
   M[0]:= InHand            {Stop insertion beyond left end of list}
   J:= Pick - 1             {Ensure comparison with first card     }
   while InHand < M[J] do   {Card to insert < card to left in list }
     M[J+1]:= M[J]          {Move card > card to insert, to right  }
     J:= J - 1              {Move pointer to next card to compare  }
   endwhile
   M[J+1]:= InHand          {Insert card into destination sequence }
endfor
```

Listing 35.6. Insertion sort in Turbo Pascal

```
program Insertion(input, output);
const
  PACK = 20;
var
  M :array[0..PACK] of integer;
  Card, Pick, InHand, J :integer;
begin
  for Card:= 1 to PACK do
    begin
      write('Number');
      readln(M[Card]);
    end;
  for Pick:= 2 to PACK do
    begin
      InHand:= M[Pick];
      M[0]:= InHand;
      J:= Pick - 1;
      while InHand < M[J] do
        begin
          M[J+1]:= M[J];
          J:= J - 1;
        end;
      M[J+1]:= InHand;
    end;
  for Card:= 1 to PACK do
    begin
      writeln(M[Card]);
    end;
end.
```

Comparative efficiency of sorting methods

The sorts described so far are not the most sophisticated, and in many cases, are not very quick. They are, however, relatively simple to understand and they have been chosen for this reason. More efficient, and consequently more complex, sorting algorithms include the Shell and Quick sorts.

Shell sort

Named after its designer, D.L. Shell in 1959, it is a refinement of the insertion sort and divides the list into groups which are sorted separately. For example, with an array of eight items, those which are four positions apart are sorted first; the four groups will each contain two items. A second pass groups and sorts afresh the items which are two positions apart; this involves two groups, each with 4 items. Finally, all items (only one position apart) are sorted in a final pass. With each pass, the *distance* between the keys is *halved*, effectively changing the contents of each group. Successive passes continue until the distance between the elements in a group is one. The idea of the Shell sort is that the early passes compare items which are widely separated and thus remove the main disorders in the array. Later passes may then require fewer movements of items.

Quicksort

This *partition* sort was invented by C.A.R Hoare, who called it 'Quicksort' because of its remarkable speed. It is based on the exchange principle used in the bubble sort described earlier and is one of the fastest array sorting techniques, for large numbers of items, currently available. Quicksort is based on the general principle that exchanges should preferably be made between items which are located a large *distance* apart in an array. Initially, the array is divided into two *partitions*, using the mid-point. Beginning at the left-most position in the array, the item in this position is compared with the item at the mid-point position. If the former is less than the latter, the next item in the partition is compared with the mid-point element. The comparisons with the mid-point item are repeated with successive items in the partition until one is found which is greater than or equal to the mid-point item. The same process is used on the right-hand partition until an item is found which is less than or equal to that at the mid-point position. Once items are found in both partitions which satisfy these respective conditions, they are swapped. Successive comparisons and swaps are carried out until each item in each partition has been compared with the mid-point item. The whole process continues *recursively* (it calls itself repeatedly), further sub-dividing the partitions, until each sub-partition contains only one item, when the array is sorted. The topic of recursion is dealt with in Chapter 34 on Data Structures.

Quicksort's speed stems from the fact that the early passes bring items close to their final sequence, leaving the last few passes to make only minor changes.

Tree sort

This is a *selection* sort and is described in the chapter on Data Structures. Like Quicksort, the binary tree sort uses the technique of recursion.

Comparing the efficiency of various sorting algorithms with one another requires careful use of 'bench test' data to ensure that comparisons are fair and specialists in the subject of sorting have spent a great deal of time analysing the various methods. It is beyond the scope of this text to pursue such analysis in detail, but some broad comparisons can be made of the relative efficiency of the simple sorts described so far. It must be said that where only a few items are to be sorted, little tangible benefit will be gained from using a sophisticated sort, as opposed to a simple one. With a larger number of items, the limitations of simple sorting algorithms, such as the exchange sort, soon become apparent. Another factor which may affect a sort's performance is the degree to which items are out of order before the sort begins.

The *exchange* sort is probably the least efficient and is rarely used by experienced programmers. It is, however, a simple sort to understand and provides a good introduction to any programmer wishing to develop their skill in this area. The *selection sort* generally performs better than the *insertion sort*, except when the items are already almost in order.

Exercises

1. (i)   Study Table 35.5 which illustrates the *exchange sort* and prepare a similar table to show the processes needed to sort the following numbers.

    18 5 9 3 19 7

    (ii)   If there are 50 numbers to be sorted, what will be the maximum number of *passes* needed to complete the sort?

    (iii) In Listing 35.2, what is the function of the Boolean variable `Exchange`?

    (iv)   Why is it necessary to complete an additional pass after the sort has been completed?

2. (i)   Study Table 35.10 which illustrates the *selection sort* and prepare a similar table to show the processes needed to sort the numbers in Exercise 1(i).

    (ii)   What is the main difference between the selection and exchange sort processes?

3. Sort an unsorted pack of cards by following the instructions for the *insertion sort*.

4.   (i)   What is meant by *recursion*?

      (ii)   Which of the sorts described in the Chapter uses recursion?

5.   Distinguish between *internal* and *external* sorts.

6.   How can sorting assist access to *indexed* files?

Chapter 36
Program Design

Introduction

The single most important requirement of a computer program is that it runs without error at all times, since a program that either produces erroneous results or hangs up under certain circumstances is almost useless. Because of this stringent requirement, computer program design and production is a very skilled activity demanding meticulous attention to detail. It is not sufficient to address only the relatively easy problem of designing and implementing a program which produces the correct output when provided with ideal data. Rather, the program must be able to cope with non-ideal data such as that provided by a user who may be unfamiliar with its operation or data input requirements. Such a user might supply inappropriate input by, for example, entering alphabetic instead of numeric characters, and even experienced operators of the program might accidentally enter invalid data on occasions.

In fact there are many ways that a program could be presented with exceptional - that is, invalid or unreasonable - data and it is the responsibility of the program designer to allow for such. Consequently, the program design stage of program production, in which possible problems - and their solutions - are identified, is of vital importance. As a result, there are now a number of established program design methodologies to aid the program designer to produce well-crafted, error-free programs. The design method described here is a form of *structured programming* using *top-down, stepwise refinement*. Two forms of notation that we will use to express solutions to design problems are *pseudocode* and *structure charts*; these are called *program design languages* (PDLs). Structure charts provide a graphical representation of a program, allowing its logical structure to be easily appreciated, whereas pseudocode, having a form similar to program instructions, aids program writing and testing.

The three sequential file handling programs, designed later in this chapter, have been converted to COBOL and the listings included in the chapter of that title.

Problem solving

Whether a problem is computer-related or otherwise, the strategy for solving it has essentially the same three main stages:(1) *understand the problem*, (2) *devise a solution*, and (3) *test the solution*. In addition, for program design tasks there is a further stage which is to (4) *document the solution*.

1. Understand the problem

This first stage requires a *thorough* understanding of the problem being addressed so that you can identify what assumptions can be made and what can't in order to test your solution in the correct context.

Some problems are apparently straightforward but, when analysed with a view to producing a program design, become much more complex. As an example, consider the following outline program specification:

> *Write a program to read in a date and convert it to the number of days from the start of the calendar year.*

It sounds simple enough until you start to consider what the problem implies. For example, what format is to be used for the date? - 15th January, 1995 or 15 Jan 95, or 15/1/95, or 15-01-95 or 150195, or 950115, and so on. Is a particular format to be adopted and incorrectly formatted dates to be rejected, or is the program to attempt to interpret different formats? Are leap years to be considered when calculating the day number? Do you assume that the date is for the current year or can the date be for a different year? You may be able to think of more problems that could arise.

2. Design a solution

The method adopted here to design the solution involves tackling the problem in a number of steps. An outline program is designed first, showing the main modules of the program, and the order in which they are to be executed. Each main module is then reduced to a number of smaller, simpler, and more manageable components, and this process of refinement continues until the program designer judges that there is sufficient detail in the design for a programmer to be able to convert the design directly into a programming language. The process of reducing components into sequences of smaller components in stages is often termed *stepwise refinement*. Top-down, stepwise refinement encourages program design to be tackled methodically in a number of stages of increasing detail. Although structure charts and pseudocode are both suitable program design languages, we recommend that you adopt our approach of first using structure charts to produce your program designs in outline form and then translating them into detailed pseudocode prior to testing and subsequent conversion to program code.

An example of a simple structure chart and the equivalent pseudocode for the addition of two real numbers are shown in Figure 36.1. (Note that a *real* number is a number with a fractional part

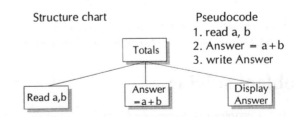

Figure 36.1. *Simple program design for addition of two real numbers*

such as 23·456, whereas an *integer* is a whole number such as 32). Answer, a and b are called variables which serve a similar function to the symbols used in algebra - they are general, symbolic representations of data that is to be processed. Thus, the pseudocode statement 1 in Figure 36.1 means 'read two values from the input device (such as a keyboard) and call them a and b respectively'. Statement 2 adds the two values and calls the result Answer. Statement 3 displays Answer on the output device (such as a display screen). By using variables rather than actual numbers, this sequence of statements defines how a computer is to deal with the addition of *any* two numbers. In addition to the problem solution itself, another part of the design is a *data table* which defines the purpose and type of the variables used in the solution. The data table (Table 36.1) would identify whether these variables were integers or real numbers and their purpose.

name	description	type
Answer	Holds the sum of the two numbers	real variable
a	First number entered	real variable
b	Second number entered	real variable

Table 36.1.

3. Test the solution

This involves using test data to manually step through the solution statements so that the computed output can be compared with the expected output. For instance, the date example mentioned above should give an answer of 69 for 10th March 1995, assuming that the days are calculated from 1st January, 1995. This value would be compared with that provided by the design - if the answer was different then the apparent design fault would need to be investigated and corrected before continuing with further testing. The design of test data is considered in Chapter 37.

4. Document the solution

The documentation contains the following: (i) the problem statement; (ii) the top-level program design; (iii) the final detailed program design; (iv) the data table. These are produced during the course of the first three stages of program design. The examples in later sections show the form of this documentation.

Structured programming

Most current program design methodologies are based on *structured programming* concepts. Structured programming is generally associated with certain basic principles:

1.   **Restricted use of control structures**. These are limited to three types: *sequence* consisting of instructions which are performed one after the other in the order that they appear in the program; *selection* of one set of instructions from several possible sets of instructions so that the program is able

to deal with a number of different circumstances; *repetition*, or *iteration*, of a set of instructions using some kind of program loop. Restricting design to using only these three constructs does not necessarily produce error-free code, but it does help to produce a program which is clear and relatively easy to test.

2.   **Modularity.** This is the subdivision of a program into easily identifiable and manageable segments, or *modules*. Each module should require no more than about one page of code. A module may be realised in the final program as one or more small subprograms. Using modules helps to clarify the logical structure of a program for human readers and, by incorporating subprograms, aids its construction.

3.   **Top-down, stepwise refinement.** This program design method was described in the earlier section *Problem Solving*.

4.   **Clear program format.** This is concerned with the layout of the program instructions. Each page of coding should contain clearly identifiable control structures and blocks of code. One main method of achieving this clarity of structure is by the consistent use of indentation showing the limits of loops, selections and blocks of instructions. Formatting standards apply both to pseudocode and actual program code.

5.   **Comments.** The thorough use of comments within the pseudocode design and the actual program in order to explain the purpose of each variable and each few lines of logically related code.

6.   **Simplicity.** Where there is a choice between a simple solution to a problem and a slightly more efficient solution which perhaps uses less code, then the simple solution is to be preferred. Straightforward, simple code is easier to test, modify and understand than obscure, 'clever' code.

Basic control structures

As explained earlier, structured programs are constructed using the three control structures sequence, selection and iteration. In order to illustrate how each of these is expressed and used in program design, consider the following programming problem:

> *Read a set of ten positive and negative numbers entered from a keyboard and find the separate totals of the positive numbers and the negative numbers. Print the two totals.*

It is assumed that only valid real numbers such as $1 \cdot 2, -7 \cdot 3, 25, -6$ will be entered. The program can be considered to be a *sequence* of three simple modules:

1.   **Initialise variables.** Two variables will be required: one for the total of the positive numbers and the other for the total of the negative numbers.

2. **Process the numbers.** This involves a loop to read numbers typed in from the keyboard until ten values have been entered. A count will be incremented every time a number is read in.

3. **Display the results.** This will involve writing out the two totals.

This top-level design is illustrated by the structure chart shown in Figure 36.2.

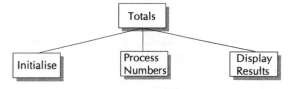

Figure 36.2. *Top level design as sequence of three modules*

The equivalent pseudocode for the top-level design is shown in Listing 36.1.

Listing 36.1.

```
{Totals}
1    Initialise
2    Process numbers
3    Display results
```

The first refinement of the design results in the structure chart shown in Figure 36.3.

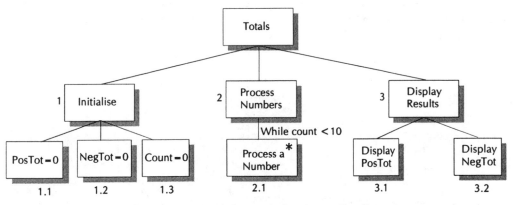

Figure 36.3. *First refinement showing an iteration*

The loop that reads the ten numbers, in other words the *iteration*, is indicated in the structure chart by an asterisk in the top right-hand corner of the component that is to be repeated.

The condition governing the loop is written above this component; in this case the loop continues while the count variable has a value less than ten. The equivalent pseudocode is shown in Listing 36.2.

Listing 36.2.

```
{Totals}
1.1   PosTot=0
1.2   NegTot=0
1.3   Count=0
2     while Count < 10
2.1      Process Number
2     endwhile
3.1   write PosTot
3.2   write NegTot
```

Each of the Listing 36.1 statements, numbered *1*, *2* and *3*, have all been refined in Listing 36.2; statement *1* (initialise) has been replaced by three detailed instruction, *1.1*, *1.2* and *1.3*. Similarly, statements *2* and *3* in Listing 36.1 have also been refined in Listing 36.2. (These statement level numbers reflect the depth of the structure diagram; a single statement level such as *1* indicates a top-level module, a statement number such as *1.2* indicate the second step of a refinement of level *1*. Number *2.3.1* indicates the first step of a refinement of statement *2.3*, and so on. A refinement of a statement is denoted by adding another level to the statement number.) Notice that the end of the loop is indicated by endwhile and the instruction inside the loop, Process Number, is indented. A loop thus translates into three pseudocode statements: one statement for the type of loop and the condition that governs it, another for the item that is to be repeated, and the third for the end of the loop. The final refinement is to expand Process Number, since this is the only statement that has not yet been fully defined: we need to show *how* a number is to be processed. The full design is shown in Figure 36.4.

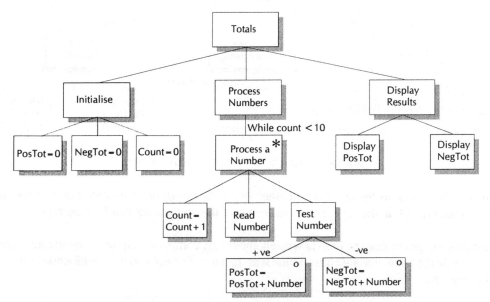

Figure 36.4. *Final refinement showing a selection*

The structure chart shows that the repeated component Process Number involves three steps: increment the count, read a number, and test the number to determine its sign. Positive numbers are to be accumulated in PosTot and negative numbers are to be accumulated in NegTot. The test involves a *selection*, each independent choice being indicated by a small circle in the top right-hand corner of the box. The condition governing each choice is written above the appropriate box as shown.

This version of the design needs no further refinement since it is now in a suitable form for conversion to pseudocode and subsequently to a programming language such as COBOL, Pascal or C.

The pseudocode in Listing 36.3 uses a select statement for the selection. If the condition following the first select is true, the statement or statements following are obeyed, otherwise the next select is considered. The endselect statement must be used to terminate the select statement. Note that the number of alternative sets of statements is not limited to two - as many as necessary can be chained together in this way. If some action is necessary when none of the select statements is true then the select when otherwise statement can be included before endselect.

Listing 36.3.   Totalling positive and negative numbers

```
      {Totals}
      1.1       PosTot = 0
      1.2       NegTot = 0
      1.3       Count = 0
      2         while Count < 10
      2.1          Count = Count + 1
      2.2          Read Number
      2.3          select
      2.3.1a          when Number > 0
      2.3.1b             PosTot = PosTot + Number
      2.3.2a          when Number < 0
      2.3.2b             NegTot = NegTot + Number
      2.3          endselect
      2         endwhile
      3.1       write PosTot
      3.2       write NegTot
```

The numbering follows the refinement levels of the structure charts. Thus if the first module is refined as a sequence of two statements, these statements are labelled *1.1* and *1.2*. In the case of an iteration, the start and end statements are given the same number. Thus in Listing 36.3, the while and endwhile both are labelled *2* showing that the iteration is the second top-level module in the program. The start and end statements of a selection are similarly labelled, but each option, which might involve a number of steps, has a small letter added to indicate that it is a step within the option. (For example, *2.3.1a* and *2.3.1b*). In addition, in the examples that follow, where a structure chart step has been expanded in the pseudocode, each part of the expansion is also designated with a lower case letter. This frequently occurs when the structure chart shows that a value is to be entered by a user through a keyboard; the pseudocode might be expanded thus: *5.1* `read Number` becomes

> *5.1a* `write 'Enter a number'`
> *5.1b* `read Number`

This helps to prevent the structure chart from becoming too detailed and thus unclear. To complete the design, the three variables must be defined in a data table (see Table 36.2).

name	description	type
`Count`	Counts how many numbers have been entered	integer variable
`PosTot`	The sum of the positive value numbers	real variable
`NegTot`	The sum of the negative value numbers	real variable

Table 36.2. *Definition of variables*

Summary

Figure 36.5 summarises the structure chart and pseudocode notation used for the three basic control structures, sequence, selection and iteration. Iteration is shown in a commonly used alternative form in which the condition is expressed as `repeat..until <condition>`. In this form the condition is tested at the end of the loop rather than at the beginning; this means that the statements within the loop will be repeated at least once. The `repeat..until` loop is illustrated in the worked examples.

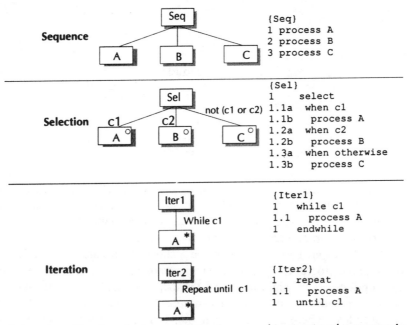

Figure 36.5. *The three basic control structures used in structured programming*

Worked examples

The worked examples presented in the next sections use a combination of structure charts and pseudocode to arrive at the final program design. Structure charts are used for the design refinements in order to express the overall logic in a clear, easily understandable form. The design is then presented in pseudocode, a form more suitable for testing and subsequent conversion to a programming language. At this stage some fine detail may also be added to the design. Some designs have been converted into COBOL code in the chapter of that title. Note, however, that the program design technique presented here, rather than being targeted at a particular programming language such as COBOL, is in a form suitable for conversion to any one of a number of quite different high-level languages.

Each of the following worked examples is in the format:

    (i)   the problem statement;

    (ii)   any assumptions that have been made;

    (iii)   structure charts showing the top-level design and any further refinement stages;

    (iv)   pseudocode for the final design;

    (v)   the data table for the complete design;

    (vi)   comments.

Reading and displaying information

Problem statement

Design a program which will accept from the keyboard a value representing a number of inches and display the equivalent number of centimetres.

Assumptions

1.   The input is a valid real number.

2.   There is no preferred format for the output.

Top-level design

The top-level design, shown on the right, now requires only minor refinements concerned with the precise form that the output is to take.

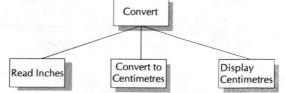

This can be accomplished conveniently in pseudocode without the need to draw another structure chart.

Pseudocode

Listing 36.4.   Converting inches to centimetres

```
{Convert}
1a   write 'Enter the length in inches: ', <newline>
1b   read Inches
2    Centimetres = Inches*2.54
3a   write <newline>
3b   write 'A length of ', Inches, ' inches is equivalent to ',
                     centimetres, ' centimetres', <newline>
```

Data table

name	description	type
Inches	Value entered at the keyboard and converted to centimetres	real variable
Centimetres	The value to be output	real variable

Comments

`<newline>` indicates that the cursor is to move to the beginning of the next line.

Loops - Running totals

One very frequent programming task is to keep a running total when a number of values are read within an iteration (that is, *loop*). This next example illustrates the technique usually adopted to accumulate a total in a variable.

Problem statement

Design a program to read ten numbers from a keyboard and display their sum.

Assumptions

1.   Exactly ten valid real numbers will be entered using a keyboard.

2.   The sum of the numbers is to be accumulated as the numbers are entered, and thus there is no requirement to store them.

Top-level design

The top-level design is a simple sequence of three modules. The second module, `Process Numbers`, involves a loop which is to repeat a known number of times (namely 10). It can therefore be implemented using a count variable as shown in refinement #1.

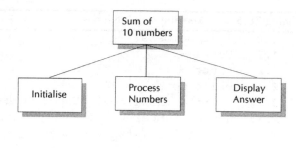

Refinement #1

The variable `Total` is to be used to accumulate the sum of the ten numbers and therefore must start with an initial value of zero. `Count` is to start at 1 because it must be increased by one each time a new number is read. Each time through the loop a new number is read into the variable `Number` and then added to `Total` which accumulates the numbers. When `Count` reaches 10, the loop terminates.

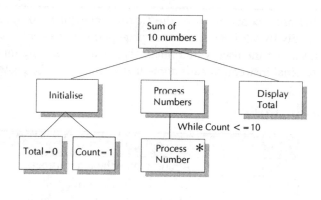

Refinement #2

The statements required for processing a number and incrementing the loop control variable have been added; this represents the final structure chart form of the design.

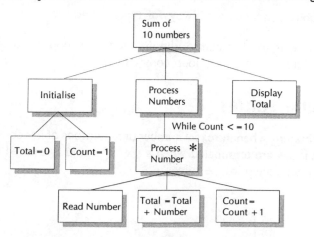

Pseudocode

Listing 36.5.   Keeping running totals

```
{Sum of 10 numbers}
1.1    Total = 0
1.2    Count = 1
2      while Count <= 10
2.1a     write <newline>, 'Enter number #', Count
2.1b     read Number
2.2       Total = Total + Number
2.3      Count = Count + 1
2      endwhile
3      write <newline> , 'The sum of the 10 numbers is: ', Total
```

This pseudocode form of the final refinement is to make the program a little more user friendly by adding some text to prompt the user to enter a number - this is much better than presenting the user with a blank screen and expecting him/her to know exactly what to do. The final instruction adds some text to announce the answer.

Data table

name	description	type
Total	Accumulates the ten numbers	real variable
Number	Stores the latest number input	real variable
Count	The control variable for the loop	integer variable

Comments

1.   Variables that are used as running totals and counts must always be initialised before a loop commences.

2.   Control variables for loops are always of type `integer`.

3.   A count variable is used to control the duration of a loop when the number of repetitions is known before the loop commences.

Loops - Rogue values

There are many occasions when the exact number of repetitions of a loop is not known in advance. Frequently loops are terminated when a special value is entered by the user. Such special values are often called 'rogue values'.

Problem statement

Design a program to read a set of numbers representing the cost of some purchased items. The end of the list is to be indicated by entering 0 for the cost. Display how many items were purchased and the total cost of the items.

Assumptions

1.   The values entered will be valid real numbers

2.   No negative numbers will be entered

Top-level design

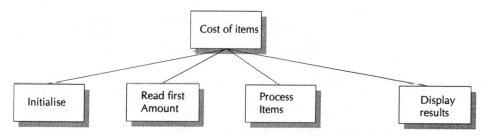

The strategy used in this instance is to read a value before the loop represented by the module, `Process Items`, is commenced. The condition governing the continuation of the loop will be `While Amount > 0` and this means that `Amount` needs to have been assigned a value before the loop starts. (This is called *reading ahead* and is a common method used for reading files, as we will see later in this chapter).

Refinement #1

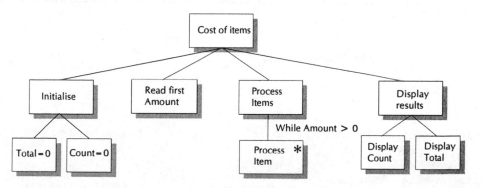

This refinement now shows that if the user initially enters zero for the amount, the loop is not executed at all because the condition, `Amount > 0`, is false. This is a very important characteristic of the `while` loop and a reason for not using the `repeat..until` loop construct in this instance.

Refinement #2

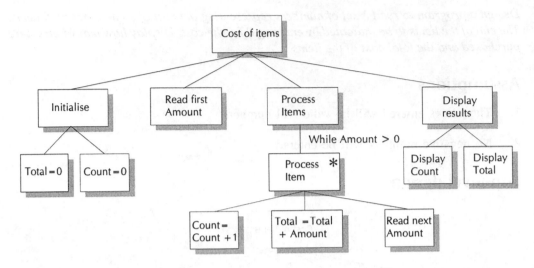

Processing an item requires a sequence comprising incrementing a count for the number of items, adding the current item's cost to the running total and finally obtaining another item cost. Again, if this latter amount is zero, the condition for continuing the loop becomes false and the loop is terminated. The results are then displayed.

Notice that the last statement executed in the loop is a read statement which obtains the data to be processed next. Since no further detail is required for the structure chart, this is the final refinement before writing the pseudocode.

Pseudocode

Listing 36.6.   Entering and totalling costs

```
{Sum of 10 numbers}
1.1    Total = 0
1.2    Count = 0
2a     write 'Enter the cost of the first item, or 0 to end'
2b     read Amount
3      while Amount > 0
3.1       Count = Count + 1
3.2       Total = Total + Amount
3.3a      write <newline>, 'Enter cost of next item, or zero to end'
3.3b      read Amount
3      endwhile
4.1a   write  <newline>,
4.1b   write  <newline>, Count, 'items were purchased'
4.2a   write <newline>
4.2b   write 'The total cost was: £', Total
```

The detail added to the pseudocode is again to improve communication with the user by displaying prompts such as that in statement *2.1* and by using blank lines (that is, `write <newline>`) to improve the clarity of the output.

Data table

name	description	type
Total	Accumulates the cost of the items	real variable
Amount	Stores the current item's cost	real variable
Count	Counts the number of items	integer variable

Comments

Try to avoid using a `while` condition such as `Amount <> 0` (not equal to zero) instead of `Amount > 0` because real numbers may not be represented exactly within a computer; the representation of zero might not be **exactly** zero and the condition `Amount <> 0` may still be true even when zero is entered for `Amount`.

Making decisions - the select statement

This example introduces the idea of taking one of several courses of action depending on the value of a variable read in from the keyboard. A loop is again terminated by testing for a rogue value, this time a negative value.

Problem statement

Design a program to accept a number of values representing student examination marks. Each mark is to be displayed as a grade as follows:

Mark	Grade
80 or over	Distinction
60 or over	Merit
40 or over	Pass
less than 40	Fail

A negative value is to be used to indicate the end of the set of marks.

Assumptions

The marks are entered as valid integers.

Top-level design

The third module in this sequence is an iteration which repeatedly reads and grades a mark until a negative mark is entered.

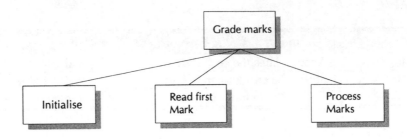

Refinement #1

The threshold values for the grades are assigned to integer constants. Any negative value entered will be regarded as the signal to terminate the program.

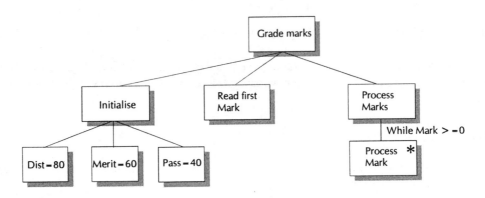

Refinement #2

The four actions comprising the selection statement, Grade, which determine the message to be displayed should not be considered as a sequence of tests; the selection notation simply shows which action is to be taken depending on the one condition which is true, and as such the four actions could have been drawn in any order.

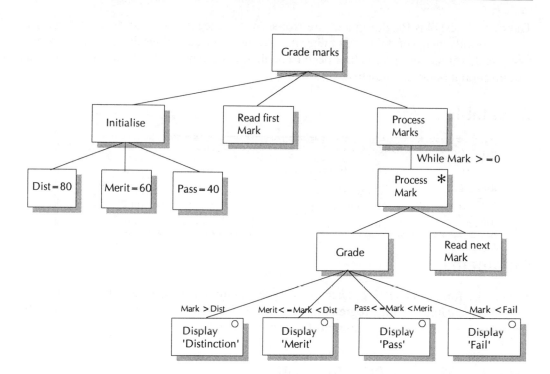

Pseudocode

Listing 36.7.   Using selection to convert marks to grades

```
        {Grade marks}
1.1       Dist = 80
1.2       Merit = 60
1.3       Pass = 40
2.1a      write 'Enter the first mark(-1 to end):'
2.1b      read Mark
3         while Mark >= 0
3.1         select
3.1.1a        when Mark >= Dist
3.1.1b          write 'Distinction', <newline>
3.1.2a        when Mark >= Merit and Mark < Dist
3.1.2b          write 'Merit', <newline>
3.1.3a        when Mark >= Pass and Mark < Merit
3.1.3b          write 'Pass', <newline>
3.1.4a        when Mark < Pass
3.1.4b          write 'Fail', <newline>
3.1         endselect
3.2a        write 'Enter the next mark(−1 to end):'
3.2b        read Mark
3         endwhile
```

The three thresholds for the grades are stored in the integer constants `Dist`, `Merit` and `Pass`. The advantage of doing this rather than using the actual values 80, 60 and 40 respectively is that if any of these values need to be modified, they need only be changed in the initialisation module and nowhere else.

Data table

name	description	type
Dist	The distinction mark	integer constant = 80
Merit	The merit mark	integer constant = 60
Pass	The pass mark	integer constant = 40
Mark	The student's exam mark	integer variable

Comments

The precise form of a selection statement in a programming language can vary considerably; it is the responsibility of the programmer to choose the most appropriate form available in the target language that exactly represents the required logic.

Decisions - A menu program

Where a program offers a user a number of different options, a menu-based program structure is often employed. The options are displayed and the user is invited to choose one of them by, for example entering its first letter. The program then performs the requested operation and re-displays the menu after it is completed. One of the options always allows the user to exit the program. This example illustrates the structure of a program which presents the user with four options concerned with currency conversion.

Problem statement

Design a menu-based program to allow a user to choose between converting pounds sterling to German marks, American dollars or French francs. The program will ask the user to enter the number of pounds and it will display the equivalent amount in the chosen currency before returning to the menu. The menu is to appear at the top of a blank screen and have the following appearance:

```
Currency conversion program

(M)arks
(D)ollars
(F)rancs
e(X)it

Which currency do you want to convert to Pounds?
```

Assumptions

1. Invalid choices (that is entering a letter other than M, D, F or X) will produce an error message and an invitation to try again.

2. Upper and lower case letters will be allowed.

3. The amount in pounds entered by the user will be a valid real number.

4. A single statement, ClearScreen, is available to blank the display screen.

Top-level design

The top-level design in this instance is very simple: the initialisation module sets the values for the three currency conversion factors and the remaining module, Main, repeatedly displays the user options and executes the one chosen.

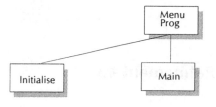

Refinement #1

Three constants used for the currency conversion calculations are defined at this point (don't rely on these figures for holiday plans!). Further, the iteration is defined as a repeat..until loop with condition c1. Logical conditions governing loops and selections can be coded in this way so that defining their precise form can be deferred until

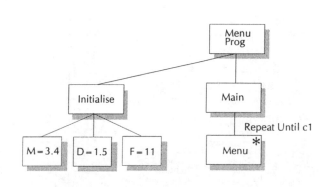

the design has been completed. We will see later in refinement #3 that c1 is the condition that indicates the user has chosen the exit option. Remember that the repeat loop causes the statements within the loop to be repeated at least once, and that the test for continuing to repeat the statements is made at the end of the loop.

Refinement #2

This refinement now shows that the loop controls a sequence of two modules. The first, Display menu, repeatedly clears the display screen, shows the menu of options and then reads the user's choice. The second module is a selection statement which processes the option chosen. The final refinement defines the operation of each of the options and under what circumstances each is chosen.

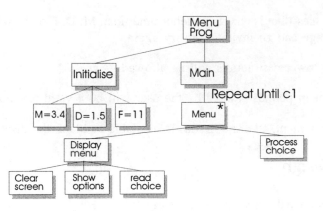

Refinement #3

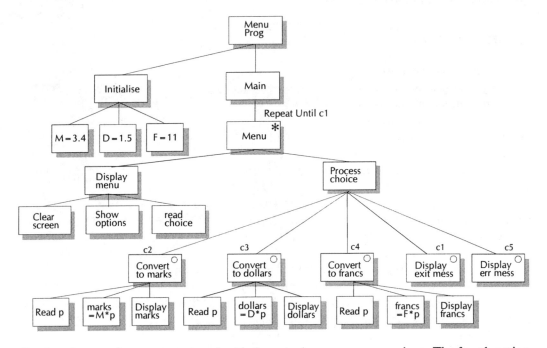

The first three options are concerned with the actual currency conversions. The fourth option displays a message to confirm that the user has chosen to exit the program. The final `select` statement is only invoked if the user has entered an invalid choice, that is, the letter entered is not 'M', 'D', 'F' or 'X'. The condition codes $c_1 - c_5$ are defined in the next table.

```
c1    choice = ('X' or 'x')
c2    choice = ('M' or 'm')
c3    choice = ('D' or 'd')
c4    choice = ('F' or 'f')
c5    choice <>  ('X' or 'x')or
                 ('M' or 'm')or
                 ('D' or 'd')or
                 ('F' or 'f')
```

Pseudocode

Listing 36.8.   Menu for Currency conversion

```
{Menu program}
1.1       M = 3.4
1.2       D = 1.5
1.3       F = 11
2         repeat
2.1.1        ClearScreen
2.1.2a       write 'Currency conversion program', <newline>
2.1.2b       write <newline>
2.1.2c       write '(M)arks'
2.1.2d       write '(D)ollars'
2.1.2e       write '(F)rancs'
2.1.2f       write <newline>
2.1.2g       write 'Which currency do you want to convert to pounds?'
2.1.3        read Choice
2.2          select
2.2.1a         when Choice = ('M' or 'm')
2.2.1b            write <newline>, 'Enter amount'
2.2.1c            read p
2.2.1d            Currency = M*p
2.2.1e            write ' = ', Currency, ' Marks'
2.2.1f            write <newline> 'Press <Enter> to return to menu'
2.2.1g            read key
2.2.2a         when Choice = ('D' or 'd')
2.2.2b            write <newline>, 'Enter amount'
2.2.2c            read p
2.2.2d            Currency = D*p
2.2.2e            write ' = ', Currency, ' Dollars'
2.2.2f            write <newline> 'Press <Enter> to return to menu'
2.2.2g            read key
2.2.2a         when Choice = ('F' or 'f')
2.2.3b            write <newline>, 'Enter amount'
2.2.3c            read p
2.2.3d            Currency = F*p
2.2.3e            write ' = ', Currency, ' Francs'
2.2.3f            write <newline> 'Press <Enter> to return to menu'
2.2.3g            read key
2.2.4a         when Choice = ('X' or 'x')
```

```
2.2.4b          write 'Exiting program..'
2.2.5a        when otherwise
2.2.5b          write 'Invalid option. Please try again'
2.2.5c          write <newline> 'Press <Enter> to return to menu'
2.2.5d          read key
2.2         endselect
2.3      until Choice = ('X' or 'x')
```

Data table

name	description	type
M	Conversion factor for pounds to marks	real constant = 3.4
D	Conversion factor for pounds to dollars	real constant = 1.5
F	Conversion factor for pounds to francs	real constant = 11
p	The number of pounds to convert	real variable
Choice	The user's menu choice	character variable
Currency	The equivalent value in the currency chosen	real variable
key	Dummy variable to accept the <Return> key	character variable

Comments

1. This is a good model for constructing menu-driven programs.

2. The manner of implementing the `select` statement can vary considerably with the target programming language. COBOL provides `if` and `evaluate` statements which each have their particular advantages and disadvantages. The programmer is responsible for choosing the most appropriate selection construct from those available.

File handling

The term *file* can be used to describe a number of different forms of storing data on backing storage. Here are some examples of different types of files:

❑   *Program source file* - the source code for a program written in a high-level language such as COBOL or C. This is usually a text file such as that produced by an editor or word processor.

❑   *Executable, or binary, file* - a file, containing compiled program code, which is in a form suitable for running. It could be a word processor or spreadsheet program or a scientific program, for example.

❑   *Picture file* - a collection of data representing a coloured or black and white picture which can be displayed on a computer screen with the aid of suitable software, such as a graphic design program.

❑   *Data file* - a file organised as a collection of *records*, each record comprising a number of fields. Such files are commonly used in data processing applications such as payroll, stock control and accounting.

We will be concerned with this last type of file. Most general-purpose high-level programming languages are able to create, read and modify files organised as collections of records; they provide single program instructions to transfer a complete record as a unit from backing storage into memory, at the same time splitting the record into separate data items called *fields*. The data in the fields are automatically allocated to variables declared for this purpose. This is the process of *reading a record* from a file. Another instruction allows the programmer to transfer a single, complete record as a unit from memory to a backing storage medium. This is the process of *writing a record*. Two other important file-handling operations are (1) *opening a file* in an appropriate mode and (2) *closing a file* which previously has been opened. The open file statement usually involves naming the file to be opened and specifying whether it is to be opened for input (that is, for reading records) or output (that is, for writing records).

The program designs which follow are concerned only with reading and writing sequential files, that is, where the records can be read only in a fixed sequence. Simple examples illustrate the logic required to create, read and search sequential files.

Creating a sequential file

Problem statement

Design a program to create a sequential file of car details. Each car record will contain the following data:

Make	*: maximum of 10 characters*
Model	*: maximum of 10 characters*
Insurance group	*: an integer value*
Cost	*: a real value*

Assumptions

1.   The data will be stored in the form that it is entered - no validation checks will be performed.

2.   A backing storage device such as a hard disk drive or a floppy disk drive is available to store the records of the file.

Top-level design

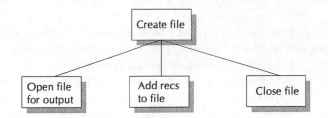

The top-level design is a sequence of a statement to prepare the file for output, followed by an iteration which allows the user to keep adding records to the file, and finally a statement which closes the file.

Refinement #1

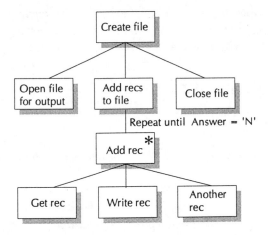

The iteration is implemented as a `repeat` loop which terminates when the user answers 'no' to the opportunity to add another record to the file. The loop repeatedly (1) requests the user to enter a set of car details (that is, a car record), (2) stores the record if the user consents to it, and (3) then asks if another record is to be entered. The character variable, `Answer`, will contain 'N' if the user wishes to discontinue adding records to the file and this will cause the `repeat` loop to terminate.

Refinement #2

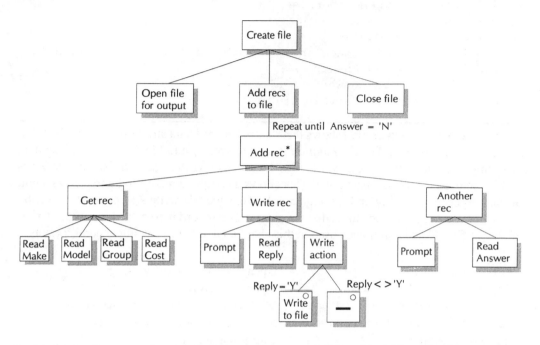

In this final refinement, the detail of the `Add rec` module is added. The selection statement, `Write action`, shows that we are interested only in `Reply` containing the character 'Y' indicating that the car record is to be stored; any other character simply results in no action being taken, which is indicated by the dash in the box.

Pseudocode

Listing 36.9.	Creating a sequential file

```
{Create file}
1              fopen output, Carfile
2              repeat
2.1.1a           write <newline>, 'Make (eg Ford):'
2.1.1b           read Car.Make
2.1.2a           write <newline>, 'Model (eg Escort):'
2.1.2b           read Car.Model
2.2.3a           write <newline>, 'Insurance group (eg 7):'
2.1.3b           read Car.InsGp
2.1.4a           write <newline>, 'Cost (eg 8450.50):'
2.1.4b           read Car.Cost
2.2.1            write <newline>, 'OK to save this record(Y/N) '
2.2.2            read Reply
2.2.3            select
2.2.3.1a           when Reply = ('Y' or 'y')
```

```
2.2.3.1b              fwrite CarFile, Car
2.2.3.2a          when otherwise
2.2.3.2b              next statement
2.2.3          endselect
2.3.1          write <newline>, 'Another record to file?(Y/N)'
2.3.2          read Answer
2           until Answer = ('N' or 'n')
3           fclose CarFile
```

The data table in the next section shows that Car is a record data structure with fields Make, Model, InsGp and Cost. The *dot notation* is used to specify a field within a record, so that, for example, the insurance group variable is designated Car.InsGp. This same notation is used in the pseudocode in Listing 36.9. This allows a complete record to be treated as a unit for the purposes of reading and writing records. Thus the file write statement, *2.2.3.1b* fwrite CarFile, Car specifies that the current Car record is to be written to CarFile. The list of file-related commands used in this chapter have the following general formats:

fopen output, FileName	Opens named file for writing
fopen input, FileName	Opens named file for reading
fwrite FileName, RecordName	Writes named record to the named file
fread FileName, RecordName	Reads named record from named file
fclose FileName	Closes named file

Finally, note that following statement from Listing 36.9, *2.2.3.2b* next statement means, in effect, that no action is to take place at this point and control passes to the next available statement. It is included to make the logic of the selection statement clear and consistent with the structure chart component that it represents.

Data table

name	description	type
Car	A car record	record
Car.Make	The manufacturer of the car	string field
Car.Model	The model of the car	string field
Car.InsGp	The insurance group of the car	integer field
Car.Cost	The price of the car	real field
CarFile	Sequential file of car records	file of Car record
Reply	Holds the user's answer (Y or N) regarding whether a record is to be written to the file	character variable
Answer	Holds the user's answer (Y or N) regarding whether another record is to be entered	character variable

Comments

This program creates the car file; each time that it is used, the car file would be re-created.

Reading sequential files

The design assumes that a programming language will detect the end of a file when an attempt is made to read a record after the last one in the file. The read file statement in this instance has an at end clause which allows some action (in our case setting a flag called EOF to boolean true) if an end-of-file condition has arisen.

Problem statement

Print in tabular form the contents of the car file created in the previous progam.

Assumptions

1.   The file is to be printed in the same order in which it was created.

Top-level design

This shows that the first record is read outside the loop, and the final operation within the loop is to read the next record (see refinement #1).

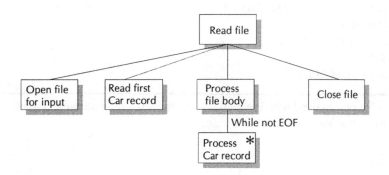

Refinement #1

Processing a record requires the current record to be printed before an attempt is made to read the next record. If no more records remain to be read, EOF is true and the loop is terminated.

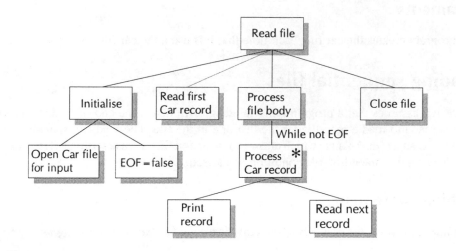

Pseudocode

Listing 36.10   Reading a sequential file

```
{Read file}
1.1    fopen input, Carfile
1.2    EOF = false
2a     fread CarFile, Car
2b       at end set EOF = true
3      while not EOF
3.1      write <newline>, Car.Make, Car.Model, Car.InsGp, Car.Cost
3.2a     fread CarFile, Car
3.2b       at end set EOF = true
3      endwhile
4      fclose CarFile
```

Note the `at end` option used with the read file statements - if an attempt is made to read past the last record in the file, `EOF` is set to `true`.

Data table

name	description	type
Car	A car record	record
Car.Make	The manufacturer of the car	string field
Car.Model	The model of the car	string field
Car.InsGp	The insurance group of the car	integer field
Car.Cost	The price of the car	real field
CarFile	Sequential file of car records	file of Car record
EOF	Boolean variable used to detect the end of the file	boolean variable

Searching sequential files

This example extracts details from all records in a file that satisfy some criterion. In this instance we want to find all the cars that are within a certain price range, but the logic would be the same if we were searching for any other characteristic of the data held in the car records. The structure of the design is very similar to that for reading a sequential file.

Problem statement

Produce a report of all cars which are within £1000 of a price which the user enters.

Assumptions

The complete record of cars matching the criterion will be printed.

Top-level design

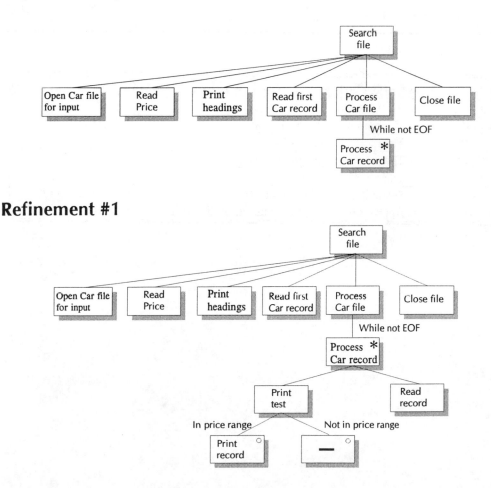

Refinement #1

Pseudocode

Listing 36.11.	Sequential file search

```
{Search file}
1        fopen input, Carfile
2a       write <newline>, 'Enter approximate price of cars to list'
2b       read Price
3        write <newline>,'Cars within £1000 of £', Price,':'
4        fread CarFile, Car
5        while not EOF(CarFile)
5.1        select
5.1.1a     when Price-1000 <= Car.Cost <= Price+1000
5.1.1b       write <newline>,Car.Make, Car.Model, Car.InsGp,Car.Cost
5.1.2a     when otherwise
5.1.2b       next statement
5.1        endselect
5.2        fread CarFile, Car
5        endwhile
6        fclose CarFile
```

Data table

name	description	type
Car	A car record	record
Car.Make	The manufacturer of the car	string field
Car.Model	The model of the car	string field
Car.InsGp	The insurance group of the car	integer field
Car.Cost	The price of the car	real field
CarFile	Sequential file of car records	file of Car record
Price	Approximate car price entered by the user	real variable

Exercises

Program design, programming and program testing

For each of the following problems, design and implement a program. Also create test classes and test cases as detailed in Chapter 37 and test each program accordingly.

Decisions

1. Read a number and display a message which states whether the number is positive, negative or zero.

2. Read a number and print it only if it is between 10 and 20.

3. Read a number followed by a single letter code. The number represents the price of an item and the code indicates whether tax is to be added to the price. If the code is 'V' then the tax is 20% of the item's cost. If the code is 'X' then the item is not taxed. Print out the total cost of the item.

4. Read three positive, non-zero integers which may represent the sides of a triangle. The numbers are in ascending order of size. Determine whether or not the numbers do represent the sides of a triangle.

5. Extend the previous question to determine the type of triangle if one is possible with the values provided. Assume that the only types of triangles to consider are: *scalene* - no equal sides; *isosceles* - two equal sides; *equilateral* - three equal sides.

6. Read in a single character and print a message indicating whether or not it is a vowel.

Loops

7. Write separate programs to produce conversion tables for:

    (i) Inches to centimetres (1 to 20 inches, 1 inch = $2 \cdot 54$ centimetres);

    (ii) Pounds to kilograms (1 to 10 pounds, 2.2 pounds per kilogram);

    (iii) Square yards to square metres: 10, 20 , 30,..., 100 sq yds (1yd = $\cdot 91$ m)

8. The cost and discount code of a number of items are to be entered by a user. The program must print out each item's cost, discount and cost less discount. The discount codes are as follows:

Code	Discount
A	5%
B	10%
C	15%

The program will terminate when the user enters 0 for the cost of the item. The program must then print the total cost of all the items entered.

9. Write a program to repeatedly display a menu containing a number of options for converting between different units, plus one option to exit the program. The user must enter a number or letter corresponding to a menu item. Valid entries are to accept a numeric value from the user and apply and display the appropriate conversion, invalid entries are reported and the user is reminded about what choices are valid, and the exit option terminates the program. An example is given below.

```
                      Menu

        1     Inches to centimetres
        2     Centimetres to inches
        3     Pounds to Kilograms
       etc
        4     Exit

              Please enter option number :
```

10. A program reads an integer representing the number of gas bills to be processed, followed by that number of customer details. Each set of customer details consists of a customer number, a single character code representing the type of customer and the number of units used. Customers are of type 'D' (domestic) or 'B' (business). Domestic customers are charged 8p per unit and business customers are charged 10p per unit. For each customer print the customer number, the number of units used and the cost of the gas used. Print the total number of units used for this batch of customers and the total amount charged.

11. Repeat the previous question assuming that all the domestic users are first and that separate totals are required for domestic and business users.

Chapter 37

Program Testing, Debugging and Documenting

Introduction

Once a program has been written, it must go through two stages in order to remove errors which almost inevitably will be present. No matter how much care has been taken in the design and coding of a program, it is still very likely to contain *syntax* errors, that is incorrectly formed statements, and probably errors in *logic* as well. *Debugging* is the term given to the process of detecting and correcting these errors or *bugs*.

The first stage in the removal of errors is the correction of syntax errors. Fortunately for the programmer, modern interpreters and compilers will provide a large amount of assistance in the detection of syntax errors in the source code. Badly formed statements will be reported by a compiler after it has attempted to compile the source code; an interpreter will report illegal statements as it attempts to execute them.

Logic errors, however, are largely undetectable by the translating program. These are errors which cause the program to behave in a manner contrary to expectations. The individual statements in the program are correctly formed, but when executed it does not operate correctly; it may give incorrect answers, or terminate prematurely, or not terminate at all. Hopefully, even the most puzzling logic errors, having been detected, eventually can be removed. But how can the programmer be confident that the program will continue to behave properly when it is in use? The answer is that the programmer never can be absolutely certain that the program will not fail. However, by the careful choice of test data in the second stage of the debugging process, the programmer can test the program under the conditions that are most likely to occur in practice. Test data is designed to determine the robustness of the program: how well it can cope with unexpected or spurious inputs, as well as those for which it has been designed specifically to process.

The purpose of *documentation* is to provide the user with all the information necessary to fully understand the purpose of the program and how that purpose has been achieved. The precise form that the documentation takes will be determined by a number of factors:

- The type of program.
- Who is likely to use the program.

❑   Whether it will be necessary to modify the program coding after it has
       been finally tested and accepted.

General guidelines for the contents and a complete example of program documentation are
given at the end of this chapter.

Detecting logic errors

If after examining program code for a reasonable amount of time the cause of an error remains a mystery, there are a number of courses of action which probably will be much more
productive than continuing to pore over the listing:

1.   Ask a fellow programmer to listen while you explain the operation of the program
      and the way it is behaving. Quite often you will see the cause of the error as you
      are making the explanation. Alternatively, your helper might recognise the type of
      error and its probable cause from his/her own experience, or might ask a question
      which makes you reconsider some aspect of the program which you have as-
      sumed to be correct or had no direct bearing on the problem. It is surprising how
      often this simple approach works.

2.   Examine the values of key variables while the program is running by inserting
      temporary lines of code throughout the program to display the values of key vari-
      ables. Comparison of the values actually displayed with expected values will nor-
      mally identify the likely source of the error.

3.   Use debugging utilities provided in the language itself or separately in the system
      software. Most high-level language development systems provide debugging
      aids. These allow the programmer to do such things as step through the program
      line by line and display the value of variables, or to insert break-points to interrupt
      the execution of the program so that the state of variables can be examined. It is
      the responsibility of the programmer to investigate the debugging aids available
      and make good use of them.

Test data

When the programmer feels that the more obvious program errors have been detected and removed, the next stage is to test the program using carefully selected data. The nature of the
test data should be such that:

❑   every statement in the program is executed at least once;

❑   the effectiveness of every section of coding devoted to detecting invalid
       input is verified;

❑   every route through the program is tried at least once;

❑   the accuracy of the processing is verified;

❑   the program operates according to its original design specification.

In order to achieve these aims, the programmer must be inventive in the design of the test data. Each test case must check something not tested by previous runs; there is no point in proving that a program which can add successfully a certain set of numbers can also add another similar set of numbers. The goal is to strain the program to its limit, and this is particularly important when the program is to be used frequently by a number of different people. There are three general categories of test data:

1. *Normal data*. This includes the most general data for which the program was designed to handle.

2. *Extreme values*. These test the behaviour of the program when valid data at the upper and lower limits of acceptability are used. The process of using extreme values is called 'boundary testing' and is often a fruitful place to look for errors. For numeric data this could be the use of very large or very small values. Text could be the shortest or longest sequence of characters permitted. A program for file processing could be tested with a file containing no records, or just a single record. The cases where zero or null values are used are very important test cases, frequently highlighting programming oversights.

3. *Exceptional data*. Programs are usually designed to accept a certain range or class of inputs. If invalid data is used, that is data which the program is not designed to handle, the program should be capable of rejecting it rather than attempting to process it. This is particularly important when the program is to be used by people other than the programmer, since they may be unaware of what constitutes invalid data. A programmer should from the outset assume that incorrect data will be used with the program; this may save a great deal of time looking for program errors which may actually be data errors.

Two commonly used approaches to the generation of good test data, namely *black box testing* and *white box testing*, are described in the following sections. Note, however, that good program testing will use a combination of testing techniques to generate test data, since no single method is sufficient to test a program thoroughly.

Black box testing

In *black box testing*, test data is created from a knowledge only of the function of the program module in terms of its inputs and outputs. In other words, only a knowledge of what it is supposed to do is required, not how it has been written. This approach allows people with no knowledge of the actual program code or of programming languages to be able to derive test data. A frequently used form of black box testing is *boundary value analysis*, but before describing this technique in more detail it is necessary to consider the concept of *equivalence classes*.

Equivalence classes

Suppose that a program accepts an input in the range 1 to 10. Suppose also that we use the values 2, 6, 7 and 8 to test the program. The test cases 2, 6, 7 and 8 are all values from a single equivalence class, that is, the class of numbers within the range 1 to 10. Each of these test cases is equivalent to all of the other test cases and so there is little point in using more than one or two such values, since if the program functions correctly with one of them, it most probably will work for the others. (Note, however, that this is never absolutely certain, which is why it is impossible to be sure that a program is completely error-free). Two types of equivalence classes are always considered, namely those that are *valid* and those that are *invalid*; it is essential that the program is executed with both good and bad data. To be clear about valid and invalid equivalence classes, Table 37.1 shows a number of examples of programs which require simple inputs. For each input we can identify both valid and invalid equivalence classes.

Input	Class	Description	Type
Integer in range 0 to 99	1	All values between 0 and 99 inclusive	Valid
	2	Values less than 0	Invalid
	3	Values greater than 99	Invalid
	4	Non-integer	Invalid
	5	Non-numeric	Invalid
Between 2 to 8	1	2 to 8 characters	Valid
characters	2	Less than 2 characters	Invalid
	3	More than 8 characters	Invalid
Between 2 to 6 values	1	Between 2 and 6 values	Valid
	2	Less than 2 values	Invalid
	3	More than 6 values	Invalid

Table 37.1. *Examples of programs requiring simple inputs*

Test cases

Having established the classes of test data, the next stage is to identify suitable test cases according to the following rules:

1. Create as many test cases as necessary in order to cover all the *valid* classes of test. This means that a single test case may cover more than one valid class.

2.   Create a *separate* test case for each *invalid* class of test.

The following example illustrates the procedure for deriving test cases.

Example

A program requires the following three inputs to be entered:

`Quantity`	Integer in the range 1 to 99
`Item Code`	Single letter followed by any three numeric digits
`Payment Code`	Single letter code: 'P', 'C' or 'D'

The valid and invalid equivalence classes for the three inputs are shown in Table 37.2.

Input condition	Valid	Class No	Invalid	Class No
`Quantity`				
Value	1-99	*1*	<1	*8*
			>99	*9*
			non-numeric	*10*
			non-integer	*11*
`Item code`				
1st character	Alphabetic	*2*	non-alphabetic	*12*
Size	4 chars	*3*	< 4 chars	*13*
			> 4 chars	*14*
Last 3 chars	Numeric	*4*	non-numeric	*15*
`Payment code`				
Value	'P'	*5*	not 'P', 'C' or 'D'	*16*
	'C'	*6*		
	'D'	*7*		

Table 37.2. *Equivalence classes for three inputs*

The next stage is to devise test cases according to the two rules given earlier for valid and invalid classes. The test cases are shown in Table 37.3.

Twelve test cases have been created. Notice that the first three test cases for valid inputs test several equivalence classes at once. The remaining test cases for invalid data only test a single equivalence class as required by the rules described earlier.

Test case	Inputs			Classes covered	Type
	Quantity	Item	Payment		
1	25	r123	'P'	*1,2,3,4,5*	Valid
2	33	X345	'C'	*1,2,3,4,6*	Valid
3	44	G786	'D'	*1,2,3,4,7*	Valid
4	0	h123	'D'	*8*	Invalid
5	123	D123	'C'	*9*	Invalid
6	1ab	S123	'P'	*10*	Invalid
7	1.26	f123	'P'	*11*	Invalid
8	25	0123	'P'	*12*	Invalid
9	36	e1	'P'	*13*	Invalid
10	65	a12345	'C'	*14*	Invalid
11	33	abcd	'D'	*15*	Invalid
12	10	v123	'B'	*16*	Invalid

Table 37.3. *Test cases for valid and invalid classes*

Note that this set of test cases represents the *minimum* set of values required to test the program; additional test cases could be easily justified. For example, in order to test Invalid class 16, that is, a Payment code other than 'P', 'C' or 'D', we have entered the letter 'B'. It would be advisable also to try entering numeric characters and other special characters such as '!' or '%' found on keyboards.

Boundary value analysis

Observation has revealed that many programs fail when data are at the extreme edges, that is *boundaries*, of expected input. For example, if a program is designed to accept a single numeric input in the range 1 to 10, what happens when values at the boundaries of these values are entered, that is, such values as 0 and 1 around the lower boundary and 10 and 11 around the higher boundary? Such test data are more likely to reveal problems than several values such as 2, 6, 7, 8 which are all within the expected input range. *Boundary value analysis* is the name given to a commonly used black box testing procedure for the identification of classes of test data at the boundaries of expected inputs and from which test cases can be created. Boundary value analysis extends the idea of equivalence classes by concentrating on the values at the boundaries of equivalence classes rather than those within them. For example, with a test class for a numeric value in a certain range, values at both ends of the range and just below and above the range would be selected for test cases. Where a number of values are to be entered, test cases would be chosen for the minimum number of values, the maximum number of values, one less than the minimum and one more than the maximum.

The rules for applying boundary value analysis are:

1.   Identify the valid and invalid equivalence classes.

2.   Identify boundary values for the valid and invalid equivalence classes.

3.   Produce test cases using the rules for equivalence classes.

The procedure for determining test cases using boundary value analysis is illustrated in Table 37.4, using the same example provided earlier for equivalence classes. Note that sometimes a boundary value for a class does not exist; where this occurs there is no entry in the table below.

Input condition	Valid		BV	Class No	Invalid		BV	Class No
Quantity								
Value	1-99		1	*1*	< 1		0	*13*
			99	*2*	> 99		100	*14*
					Non-numeric			
					Non-integer			
Item								
1st character	Alphabetic		'a' 'A' 'z' 'Z'	*3* *4* *5* *6*	non-alphabetic			*17*
Size	4 chars		4 chars	*7*	< 4 chars		3 chars	*18*
					> 4 chars		5 chars	*19*
Last 3 chars	Numeric		'000' '999'	*8* *9*	Non-numeric			*20*
Payment								
Value	'P', 'C' or 'D'		'P' 'C' 'D'	*10* *11* *12*	Not 'P', 'C' or 'D'			*21*

Table 37.4. *Determining test cases for boundary analysis*

Since the first character of Item can be either upper or lower case, there are in effect two lower boundaries, 'a' and 'A', and two upper boundaries, 'z' and 'Z', for the valid equivalence class. However, there are no boundary values for the invalid equivalence class; we can simply choose a non-alphabetic character as an invalid test case.

These boundary values lead to test cases such as those shown in Table 37.5.

Test case	Inputs			Classes covered	Type
	Quantity	Item	Payment		
1	1	a000	'P'	*1,3,7,8,10*	Valid
2	99	A999	'C'	*2,4,7,9,11*	Valid
3	44	z678	'D'	*5,12*	Valid
4	7	Z123	'D'	*6,12*	Valid
5	0	D123	'C'	*13*	Invalid
6	100	s345	'P'	*14*	Invalid
7	1ab	S123	'P'	*15*	Invalid
8	1·26	f123	'P'	*16*	Invalid
9	25	0123	'P'	*17*	Invalid
10	36	el	'P'	*18*	Invalid
11	65	a1234	'C'	*19*	Invalid
12	33	abcd	'D'	*20*	Invalid
13	10	v123	'B'	*21*	Invalid

Table 37.5. *Test cases for boundary values*

White box testing

Here the program code is examined in order to determine the various routes that can be followed through the program. This approach requires a knowledge of the language being used, and in particular being able to recognise and understand conditional and looping instructions. The following example illustrates the process for dealing with conditional instructions within a program.

Covering multiple conditions in a program

Suppose that a mail order firm supplies goods to locations all over the world. An order from a customer is given a code, and if this code is of type A, B or C a discount on the total cost of the order is given. In addition, providing the order exceeds a minimum value, postage is free for customers within the UK.

The pseudo-code in Listing 37.1 illustrates typical instructions which might be used to determine the total charge to the customer. It is assumed that the variables Quantity and UnitCost have already been assigned values.

Listing 37.1   Calculate total customer charge for order

```
1    {Calculate the order value}
2    TotalCost = Quantity * UnitCost
3
4    {Determine whether any discount can be allowed}
5    select
6      when OrderCode = 'A' or OrderCode = 'B' or OrderCode = 'C'
7         Discount  = TotalCost * DISCOUNT_RATE
8      when otherwise
9           Discount = 0
10   endselect
11
12   {Adjust the order value to allow for discount}
13   TotalCost = TotalCost - Discount
14
15   {Determine whether postage and packing needs to be charged}
16   select
17     when TotalCost > MIN_ORDER-VALUE and Country = 'GB'
18        Postage - 0
19     when otherwise
20          Postage = PP_RATE
21   endselect
22
23   {Adjust the order value to allow for postage and packing}
24   TotalCost = TotalCost + Postage
```

The code shows how the discount and the postage might be calculated given the three constants DISCOUNT_RATE, PP_RATE and MIN_ORDER_VALUE (assumed to be £100).

We need to ensure that the compound conditional instructions on lines *6* and *17* are fully tested. This is accomplished by identifying test classes which cause each part of the conditional instruction to be true and false. For instance, on line *6* we must use test data such that the order code is of type 'A' (so that the condition OrderCode = 'A' is true), and also such that the order code is not of type 'A' (so that the condition OrderCode = 'A' is false). The same applies to the other two order codes, 'B' and 'C'. A *truth table* of the type shown in Table 37.6 is a convenient way to organise these requirements.

Class no.	Order type		
	'A'	'B'	'C'
1	T	F	F
2	F	T	F
3	F	F	T
4	F	F	F

Table 37.6. *Truth table for OrderCode types*

The entries under the column headings 'A', 'B' and 'C' show that for the first class, the order will be type 'A', in the second class test the order type will be 'B' and in the third class, the order will be of type 'C'. In addition, we must also use a fourth test for the case where the order type is other than these three types in the table.

The same procedure needs to be used for the second conditional statement on line *17*. The truth table is shown in Table 37.7.

Class No.	Condition	
	TotalCost > MinOrderValue	Country = 'GB'
5	T	T
6	T	F
7	F	T
8	F	F

Table 37.7. Truth table for second conditional statement on Line 17

Again, all of the possible combinations of the two conditions are covered, adding a further four test classes.

Having identified all of the paths through the program, we must now devise test cases using data which ensures that all of the paths are covered.

Table 37.8 shows the data for four test cases which accomplish this requirement.

Test case	OrderCode	TotalCost	Country	Classes covered
1	'A'	123	'GB'	1, 5
2	'B'	720.45	'USA'	2, 6
3	'C'	62	'GB'	3, 7
4	'D'	27.34	'XXX'	4, 8

Table 37.8. Data for four test cases

Notice that this table illustrates that we can cover more than one test class with a single set of test data as long as all of the classes are covered by the total set of tests.

Covering loops within a program

We need to create test data, where possible, to cover the following situations:

❑   Going through the loop the minimum number of times (which may mean skipping the loop entirely).

❑   Executing the loop once (if not covered above).

❑   Executing the loop the maximum number of times.

❑   Executing the loop one less than the maximum number of times.

❑   Executing the loop several times (between the maximum and minimum number).

For example, consider the pseudocode program fragment in Listing 37.2 (the complete program, described in Chapter 36, counts items and accumulates their total cost).

Listing 37.2	Pseudocode program fragment to illustrate testing of loops

```
Total = 0
Count = 0
write 'Enter the cost of the first item, or 0 to end'
read Amount
while Amount > 0
   Count = Count + 1
   Total = Total + Amount
   write <newline>, 'Enter the cost of the next item, or 0 to end'
   read Amount
endwhile
write <newline>
write   <newline>, Count, 'Items were purchased'
write  <newline>
write 'The total cost was: £', Total
```

Suitable test data for the program fragment may be as shown in Table 37.9.

Test case	Test data (Amount followed by 0)	Comment
1	0	Minimum number of times through loop, i.e. none
2	12·23, 0	Once only through loop
3	25·67, 17·99, 222·05, 123·45, 6·91, 0	Several times through loop

Table 37.9. *Test data for program fragment*

In this instance, because there is no maximum limit to the number of amounts that can be entered, we cannot devise test data for the maximum repetitions or for one less than the maximum, but in the case of the next example this is possible. In this example the loop is set to repeat a fixed number of times determined by the constant, LoopLimit. To change the number of times the loop is repeated, we simply alter this constant in the program as shown below.

```
LoopLimit = 10
Count = 0
while Count < LoopLimit
    {Instructions to be repeated are here}
    . . . . . . .
    . . . . . . .
    Count = Count + 1
endwhile
```

The test cases for `LoopLimit` are shown in Table 37.10.

Test case	LoopLimit value	Comment
1	0	Minimum number of times through loop, i.e. none
2	1	Once only through loop
3	5	Several times through loop
4	9	One less than maximum
5	10	Maximum

Table 37.10. *Test cases for* `LoopLimit`

Test logs

Once the test cases have been devised, the program must be executed using the test data. The effect of using the test data is recorded in a *test log*. Since the point of program testing is to find errors, the log will indicate a <u>successful</u> test <u>if an error is found</u>, and an unsuccessful test otherwise. The test log will form part of the documentation of the program so that if the program is subsequently modified, the same test data can be re-applied to ensure that no program errors have been accidentally introduced by the modifications. For each set of test data, the expected output must be determined before running the program so that it can be compared with the actual output produced by the program. The test log could be set out in tabular form as follows.

TEST LOG

Date:

Program name:

Version:

Author:

Tested by:

Test case	Expected output	Observed output	Result	Comments
1				
2				
3				
4				
etc				

Validation

At some point the programmer must decide that the program has had sufficient testing. He or she will be confident that the program will operate according to specification and without 'crashing' or 'hanging up' under extreme or unexpected circumstances; the reputation of a professional programmer relies on this. Prior to release, the final testing is then performed by the user for whom the program was developed. The programmer may have overlooked areas of difficulty because it is often hard to consider a problem objectively or entirely from the viewpoint of the user. If this is the case, that the operation of the program is not entirely satisfactory, the program will be modified and re-tested until all user requirements are met.

Program documentation requirements

The documentation produced for a program will depend on a number of factors. For instance, a program which validates a temporary file prior to creating it permanently will probably require a minimum of user interaction and only a small number of user instructions. However, at some later date, it might be necessary for the author of the program, or a different programmer, to modify it. This possibility means that the structure of the program will have to be explained in great detail, and test procedures to ensure its correct operation will need to be provided.

A general purpose program such as a spreadsheet, designed for people who just want to use the computer as a tool, will require extremely detailed instructions regarding its function and use. Such programs are generally accompanied by detailed user manuals and tutorials. On the other hand, users would not be expected (and definitely not encouraged) to modify the program coding; thus no details would be provided regarding the way the program has been written. This latter type of documentation would only be required for the people responsible for producing the program. In addition to the documentation requirements of users and programmers, there is a third category of person to be considered. These are people such as managers who are neither likely to use programs extensively nor want to attempt to modify them. They merely need to have an overview of the program - its function, capabilities, hardware requirements etc.

Thus there are many factors governing the coverage of documentation, and for this reason in the next section it is only possible to provide a checklist of items which might reasonably be included.

Documentation checklist

The documentation for a simple program generally falls into four sections:

- Identification.
- General specification.
- User information.
- Program specification.

Most users will need access to the first three sections; in general the fourth section will only be needed if the program is to be modified. The amount of detail in each section will depend entirely on the particular application and, to some extent, the implementation language. COBOL, for example, is largely self-documenting: it contains an Identification Division containing all the information listed in the first section below; the Data Division of a COBOL program contains precise details regarding all of the files used by the program and which devices are required; the Procedure Division is written in 'English-like' sentences which are generally easy to understand, even by a non-programmer. Consequently, a program written in COBOL will generally require less documentation than one written in Pascal or C, languages which are not self-documenting. The following checklist is a guide to what might reasonably be included in the documentation for a program.

1. Identification.

- Title of program.
- Short statement of its function.
- Author.
- Date written.
- Language used and version if relevant.
- Hardware requirements.

2. General specification.

- Description of the main action(s) of the program under normal circumstances.
- File specifications.

    ❑   Restrictions and/or limitations of the program.

    ❑   Equations used or references to texts explaining any complex procedures /techniques involved.

3. Program specification.

    ❑   Structure charts/flowcharts/decision tables.

    ❑   Annotated listing.

    ❑   Testing procedure including test classes and test data with expected output and a test log.

4. User Guide.

    ❑   Installation instructions

    ❑   Detailed explanation of the operation of the program

    ❑   Tutorial

    ❑   Screen shots

    ❑   Troubleshooting guide

Documentation example

Identification

Program ID : StockFileUpdate

Author : Nick Waites.

Purpose : To update a master stock file with a transaction file containing details of sales and receipts of stock items.

Date written : April 1998.

Language: Microfocus COBOL

Hardware: PC

General specification

Operation of program

The purpose of the program is to read a sequential transaction file held on disk and use it to update a sequential file containing records of stock items. The transaction file comprises a set of records containing details of stock items received from suppliers, and records containing details of stock items sold. Each record in the transaction file will be used to modify a corresponding record on the master file. There may be several transaction records for each record on the master file. Where the transaction is a sale, the number sold will be subtracted from the current stock level; receipts will be added to the current stock level. The transaction file is assumed to have been pre-sorted such that all orders relating to a particular record are grouped together.

Once all transactions for a record have been processed, the updated record is written to a new stock file, again sequentially organised.

Systems flowchart

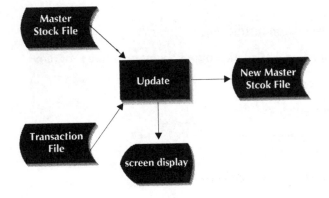

Data structures

(i)   Master stock file.

    (a)   Structure diagram

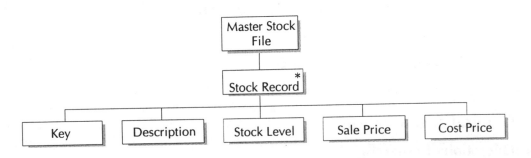

(b) File Definition:

File Name: master-file

Field	Program name	Type	Size (char)
Key	master-rec-key	numeric integer	
Description	description	alphabetic	30
Stock Level	stock	numeric integer	
Cost Price	cost-price	numeric real	
Sale Price	sale-price	numeric real	

(ii) Transaction File

(a) Structure Diagram

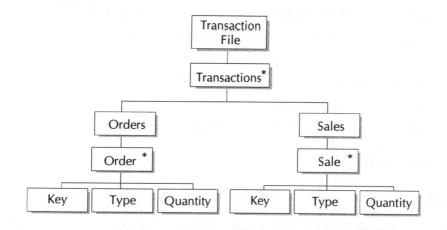

(b) File Definition:

File Name : transaction-file

Field	Program name	Type	Size (char)
Key	trans-rec-key	numeric integer	
Type	trans-type	character	4
Quantity	num-units	numeric integer	

(iii) New stock file

    (a)   Structure diagram:

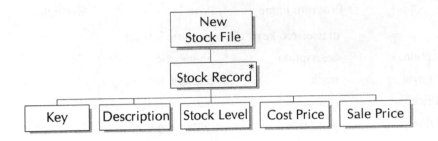

    (b)   File Definition:

        File Name: new-master-file

Field	Program name	Type	Size (char)
Key	n-mast-rec-key	numeric integer	
Description	n-description	alphabetic	30
Stock Level	n-stock	numeric integer	
Cost Price	n-cost-price	numeric real	
Sale Price	n-sale-price	numeric real	

Restriction/limitations

The program operates under two important assumptions:

    (i)   The transaction file has been thoroughly validated.

    (ii)   The transaction file has been sorted into the same sequential order as the records in the master stock file, namely, ascending order of key field.

User information

This program constitutes one element of a suite of programs forming a simple stock control system. Before running the update program, ensure that the transaction and master files have been created and that both are sorted into ascending, key field order. The operating system paths and filenames in the program source code must match the locations of the master and transaction files (the program was tested using "c:\work\mast.dat" and "c:\work\trans.dat"). The path and filename for the new master file must also be appropriate for your system. The program runs without user intervention.

Program specification

Program structure diagram

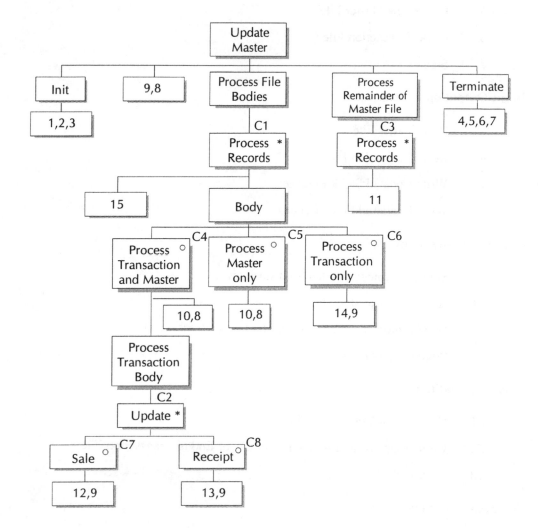

Operations

Initialisation operations

1. Open Master File for Input

2. Open New Master File for Output

3. Open Transaction File for Input

Program Termination operations

4.   Close Master File

5.   Close New Master File

6.   Close Transaction File

7.   Stop

Input/Output operations

8.   Read Master File

9.   Read Transaction File

10.   Write Updated Stock Record

11.   Write Unaltered Stock Record

Processing operations

12.   Subtract number of sales from stock level

13.   Add receipts to stock level

14.   Display error message: "No master for this transaction"

15.   Store transaction record key

Iteration conditions

C1.   Until End of Transaction File

C2.   Until change of transaction record key or End of Transaction File

C3   Until End of Master File

Selection conditions

C4.   Transaction record key matches stock record key

C5.   Transaction record key > stock record key

C6.   Transaction record key < stock record key

C7.   Transaction type = Sale

C8.   Transaction type = Receipt

Pseudocode

```
{Update master}
  fopen input, TransactionFile
  fopen output, MasterFile
  fopen output, NewMasterFile
  TransEOF = false
  MasterEOF = false
  fread TransactionFile, TransactionRec
    at end set TransEOF = true
  fread MasterFile, MasterRec
    at end set MasterEOF = true
  while not TransEOF
    TempKey = TransRecKey
    select
      when TransRecKey = MasterRecKey
        while not TransEOF or TransRecKey not equal to TempKey
          select
            when Type = 'SALE'
              StockLevel = StockLevel - NoOfUnits
              fread TransactionFile, TransactionRec
                at end set TransEOF = true
            when Type = 'ORDR'
              StockLevel = StockLevel + NoOfUnits
              fread TransactionFile, TransactionRec
                at end set TransEOF = true
          endselect
        endwhile
        fwrite NewMasterFile, NewMasterRec
        fread MasterFile, MasterRec
          at end set MasterEOF = true
      when TransRecKey > MasterRecKey
        fwrite NewMasterFile, NewMasterRec
        fread MasterFile, MasterRec
          at end set MasterEOF = true
      when TransRecKey < MasterRecKey
        write <newline>, 'No record for transaction:' TransRecKey
        fread TransactionFile, TransactionRec
          at end set TransEOF = true
    endselect
  endwhile
  while not MasterEOF
    fwrite NewMasterFile, NewMasterRec
    fread MasterFile, MasterRec
      at end set MasterEOF = true
  fclose TransactionFile, MasterFile, NewMasterFile
```

Program listing

```
000001  identification division.
000002  program-id. update-master.
000003  author. Nick Waites.
000004  date-written. April 1998.
000005* remarks. Updates existing master stock file with
000006*          transactions to create new master file.
000007
000008  environment division.
000009    configuration section.
000010      source-computer. ibm-pc.
000011      object-computer. ibm-pc.
000012    input-output section.
000013    file-control.
000014      select transaction-file assign to disk,
000015          organization is line sequential.
000016      select master-file assign to disk
000017          organization is line sequential.
000018      select new-master-file assign to disk
000019          organization is line sequential.
000020
000021  data division.
000022  file section.
000023
000024  fd transaction-file
000025      label records are standard
000026      value of file-id is "c:\work\trans.dat".
000027  01 transaction-rec.
000028      03 trans-rec-key      pic 9(6).
000029      03 trans-type         pic a(4).
000030      03 num-units          pic 99.
000031
000032  fd master-file
000033      label records are standard
000034      value of file-id is "c:\work\mast.dat".
000035  01 master-rec.
000036      03 master-rec-key     pic 9(6).
000037      03 description        pic a(40).
000038      03 stock              pic 99.
000039      03 cost-price         pic 9v99.
000040      03 sale-price         pic 9v99.
000041
000042  fd new-master-file
000043      label records are standard
000044      value of file-id is "c:\work\newmast.dat".
000045  01 new-master-rec.
000046      03 n-mast-rec-key     pic 9(6).
```

```
000047        03 n-description      pic a(40).
000048        03 n-stock            pic 99.
000049        03 n-cost-price       pic 9v99.
000050        03 n-sale-price       pic 9v99.
000051
000052 working-storage section.
000053 01 temp-key                  pic 9(6) value zero.
000054
000055 01 end-trans                 pic a value is "n".
000056        88 trans-eof           value is "y".
000057 01 end-master                pic a value is "n".
000058        88 master-eof          value is "y".
000059
000060 procedure division.
000061 para-1.
000062
000063*— Open files ————————————————
000064     open input transaction-file, master-file,
000065          output new-master-file
000066
000067*— Read first transaction and first-master file record —
000068     read transaction-file
000069        at end set trans-eof to true
000070     end-read
000071     read master-file
000072        at end set master-eof to true
000073     end-read
000074
000075*— Process transactions until end of transaction file —
000076     perform test before until trans-eof
000077        move trans-rec-key to temp-key
000078        evaluate true
000079
000080*— Transaction key matches master key ————————
000081           when trans-rec-key = master-rec-key
000082
000083*— Apply transactions to current master until end of ——
000084*— transaction file or change of transaction key    ——
000085              perform test before until trans-eof or
000086                  trans-rec-key not equal to temp-key
000087                 evaluate true
000088                    when trans-type = "SALE"
000089                       compute stock = stock - num-units
000090                       read transaction-file
000091                          at end set trans-eof to true
000092                       end-read
000093                    when trans-type = "ORDR"
000094                       compute stock = stock + num-units
```

```
000095                    read transaction-file
000096                       at end set trans-eof to true
000097                    end-read
000098                 end-evaluate
000099             end-perform
000100             write new-master-rec from master-rec
000101             read master-file
000102                at end set master-eof to true
000103             end-read
000104
000105*— Indicates no transaction for this master, so it is —
000106*— written to the new master file unaltered        —
000107             when trans-rec-key > master-rec-key
000108                write new-master-rec from master-rec
000109                read master-file
000110                   at end set master-eof to true
000111                end-read
000112
000113*— Indicates there is no record for the transaction ——
000114*— so an error message is displayed              ——
000115             when trans-rec-key < master-rec-key
000116                display "No master for transaction"
000117                read transaction-file
000118                   at end set trans-eof to true
000119                end-read
000120          end-evaluate
000121       end-perform
000122
000123*— All transactions have been processed, so remainder ——
000124*— of master records are written to new master unaltered -
000125       perform test before until master-eof
000126          write new-master-rec from master-rec
000127          read master-file
000128             at end set master-eof to true
000129          end-read
000130       end-perform
000131
000132*— Close all files and terminated program ————
000133       close transaction-file, master-file, new-master-file
000134       stop run
000135 end program update-master.
```

Testing procedure

Test classes

Class	Description	Type
1	1st Transaction key = 1st Master File key	valid
2	1st Transaction key 1st Master File key	valid
3	Last Transaction key = Last Master File key	valid
4	Last Transaction key Last Master File key	valid
5	No transactions for a Master File record	valid
6	No Order transactions for a Master File record	valid
7	No Sale transactions for a Master File record	valid
8	More than one Order for a Master File record	valid
9	More than one Sale for a Master File record	valid
10	At least one Order and one Sale for a Master File record	valid
11	At least one transaction for every Master File record	valid
12	No Master File record for a transaction	invalid

Table 37.11.

Test cases

Two transaction files of test cases are required to apply the test classes defined in Table 37.11. The Master File shown in Table 37.12. is not restored to its original state before processing Transaction File #2.

Key Field	Description	Level	Cost	Sale
100011	Apple juice	36	1·30	1·60
100027	Honey comb	20	0·35	0·50
100039	Long grain brown rice (organic)	44	0·32	0·41
100122	Sultanas (Australian)	22	0·55	0·69
100343	Shoyu (Japanese)	10	1·23	1·57

Table 37.12. *Master file*

Transaction File #1

Trans Key	Type	Quant	Test Classes Covered
100011	ORDR	12	1, 7
100011	ORDR	5	1, 8
100027	SALE	3	6
100027	SALE	2	9
100027	SALE	5	
100039	ORDR	10	10
100039	SALE	2	
100039	SALE	3	

Table 37.13. *Transaction File #1*

New Master File after processing Transaction File #1

Key Field	Description	Level	Cost	Sale Price
100011	Apple Juice	51	1.30	1.60
100027	Honey comb	15	0.35	0.50
100039	Long grain rice	44	0.32	0.41
100122	Sultanas	16	0.55	0.69
100343	Shoyu	15	1.23	1.57

Table 37.14. *New Master File using Transaction File #1*

Transaction File #2

Trans Key	Type	Quant	Test Classes Covered
100027	SALE	3	2, 5, 6
100027	ORDR	10	
100034	ORDR	4	12
100122	SALE	6	4, 5, 6

Table 37.15. *Transaction File #2*

New Master File after processing Transaction File #2

Key Field	Description	Level	Cost	Sale Price
100011	Apple Juice	51	1.30	1.60
100027	Honey comb	22	0.35	0.50
100039	Long grain rice	44	0.32	0.41
100122	Sultanas	10	0.55	0.69
100343	Shoyu	15	1.23	1.57

Table 37.16. *New Master File after processing Transaction File #2*

Exercises

1. Explain the difference between white box and black box testing.

2. What valid and invalid equivalence classes would you define for programs which accept the following inputs:

    (i)   a single integer value in the range 1 to 99;

    (ii)   a single name containing only alphabetic characters;

    (iii)   a single numeric digit;

    (iv)   an integer representing the number of units of a certain item sold, followed by the unit cost of the item;

    (v)   three names separated by commas;

    (vi)   a post code of the form *AA99 9AA*, where *A* represents any alphabetic character and *9* represents any numeric digit;

    (vii)   a telephone number which starts with an area code followed by a space.

   Devise test cases for your test classes.

3.   Use white box testing methods to devise test classes and test cases for the following fragments of pseudocode:

(i)

```
if (Letter = `a') or
   (Letter = `e') or
   (Letter = `i') or
   (Letter = `o') or
   (Letter = `u')
then
  VowelCount:= VowelCount + 1
endif
```

(ii)

```
if a > b then
    Temp:= a
    a:= b
    b:= Temp
endif
if b > c then
    Temp:= b
    b:= c
    c:= Temp
endif
```

(iii)

```
Count:= 0;
if a = b then
    Count:= Count + 1
endif
if b = c then
    Count:= Count + 1
endif
if c = a then
    Count:= Count + 1
endif
select
  when Count = 0
    TriangleType:= 0
  when Count = 1
    TriangleType:= 2
  when Count = 2
    {not possible}
  when Count = 3
    TriangleType:= 3
endselect
```

(iv)

```
repeat
  {get character from keyboard using}
  {readkey function               }
  key:= readkey

  {check that character is a numeric}
  {digit                          }
  if (key >= `0') and (key <= `9')
    then
       write(key)  {echo to screen}
  endif

until key = ` `{exit loop only when }
              {spacebar pressed    }
```

Chapter 38

COBOL

Introduction

COBOL is a very complex language intended to facilitate the development and implementation of full scale data processing applications in the business environment. Consequently, mastering COBOL in its entirety takes a great deal of time and effort, even with the help of one of the dozens of books aimed at facilitating this process. Our intention is merely to provide a sound basis for further study. To this end, the material presented covers a small subset of the full language, enough to be able to understand and construct fairly simple application programs.

The chapter is divided into four main sections.

❑   The first section provides an overview of the COBOL language, including a complete program described in detail to give you a 'feel' for the language.

❑   The second section describes the function and structure of COBOL more thoroughly, giving numerous examples of COBOL code.

❑   The third section contains a number of complete example programs based on a common theme, with suggestions for programming exercises.

❑   The final section contains ideas for programming projects.

If you work through the example programs provided, and spend time on the exercises, you should be in a strong position to undertake a more thorough study of COBOL. It cannot be emphasised strongly enough, however, that learning a programming language requires *practice* in writing programs and learning from mistakes; reading about COBOL will never make you a COBOL programmer.

There are many COBOL compilers on the market, each with its own minor variations and extensions aimed at getting the best out of the computer on which the programs are to be run. Though the programs provided in this book were written using Micro Focus COBOL on a PC, every attempt has been made to avoid the use of non-standard program constructs so that the programs are as transportable as possible to other machines/compilers. The only exception to this is the use of a `screen section` for coding of a screen mask in program Example #1. The alternative `display` and `accept` keywords are used in other programs to show how a screen mask can be coded without the use of this non-standard feature.

Concerning the compilation of the programs, it is not possible to provide detailed instructions since this is a compiler-dependent process; you must consult the reference manual provided with the COBOL compiler which you are using for the precise manner in which this is accomplished.

The structure of a COBOL program

The four divisions

A COBOL program is divided into four areas termed `divisions` which appear in the order:

```
identification division

environment division

data division

procedure division
```

The contents of each of these `divisions` is dependent on the requirements of the program, but generally a `division` will contain a number of `sections` subdivided into `paragraphs`. Within each paragraph there will be a number of `sentences` containing `clauses`. This structure deliberately follows the organisation of ordinary English text such as that found in a report. Many of the possible entries are optional; the program below contains just about the absolute minimum for a COBOL program:

```
000001 identification division.
000002 program-id. minprog.

000003 environment division.

000004 data division.

000005 procedure division.
000006 para-1.
000007 display "This is all I do!"
000008 stop run.
000009 end program minprog.
```

A COBOL program must have its name declared in the `identification division`, but both the `environment` and `data divisions` have no compulsory entries. The `procedure division` contains a single paragraph, 'para-1', containing just two statements. This program merely displays the message 'This is all I do!' on the monitor screen and then terminates. The final line of the program marks the physical end of the program, though not all COBOL compilers have this requirement.

Identification division

The identification division allows the programmer to describe the whole program in general terms by supplying, under appropriate headings, such information as the name of the program, its author, when it was written and what it does. Some of this information is optional and none of it has a direct effect on the program's operation.

Environment division

In the configuration section of the environment division are details of the computers on which the program was developed and is intended to be run, and the input-output section specifies the peripheral devices to be used for reading or writing the files which will be defined later in the program.

Data division

The data division contains a file section in which each file named in the input-output section is given a file description (FD). The FD contains the file name and one or more record names. The structure of a record is defined hierarchically using level numbers starting at 01 and getting progressively bigger (03, 05 and so on) for finer definitions.

The working-storage section of the data division contains definitions of other data items specifically referenced in the procedure division of the program but which are not part of any file.

Procedure division

Finally, the procedure division defines precisely how the processing is to be performed. The programmer may give paragraph names to groups of sentences to which reference may be made from other parts of the program, and these paragraphs may be grouped together into sections.

Each sentence defines one or more operations to be performed; although some compilers require that each sentence is terminated with a full stop COBOL-85 compilers do not. In keeping with the general philosophy of making a COBOL program easily readable, the instructions often read like ordinary English sentences. As an example, the sentence

```
read title-file into details
   at end
      set end-of-file to true
   end-read
```

specifies that a record from the file named title-file (defined at the FD level) is read into memory and stored in a record definition (defined at the 01 level) called details; if the end of `title-file` has been reached, the boolean variable `end-of-file` is set to 'true'.

Example program

Program specification

The program has been provided to give you an idea of the form of a COBOL program and the purpose of each of its main constituent parts. It is described in great detail so that you can use it for reference purposes when writing your own programs.

The program is designed to search a file of book titles and print those which deal with a certain subject. Each record in the file contains the title of the book, its author and three numeric codes related to its subject matter. The user enters one such subject code and the program prints out a list of books dealing with that subject.

Here is a sample of typical subject codes:

Subject	Code
Artificial Intelligence	10
BASIC	11
Boolean Algebra	12
C	13
COBOL	14
Computer Science	15
Data Structures	16
Databases	17
Fortran	18
Graphics	19
Hardware	20
Information Technology	21
Pascal	22
Program design	23
Programming	24
Robotics	25
Software	26
Spreadsheets	27
Wordprocessing	28

The category codes

A book such as 'Pascal' by Findlay and Watt would be stored in the file as the record

```
Pascal Findlay & Watt 222415
```

with the numeric code indicating that the book concerns Pascal (22), Programming (24) and Computer Science (15). This record would be selected if the file was being searched for any one of these three codes.

The program first asks the user to enter the code to be used for the search, and then searches the file printing out records that contain the code as they are located. The program structure diagram is shown in Figure 38.1.

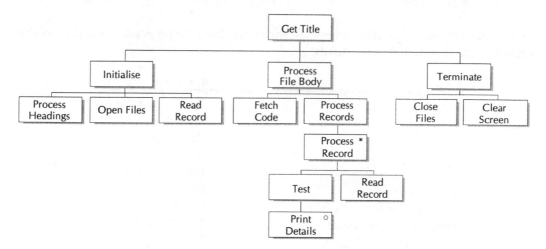

Figure 38.1. *Structure for Titles program*

The data file accessed by the program contains the following records:

Title	Author(s)	Categories
Artificial Intelligence	Charniak	001510
Computer Architecture	Wilks & Kerridge	001520
Computer Graphics	Hearn & Baker	152619
Educational Computing	Scanlon & O'Shea	152624
Foundations of Robotics	Siegler	102520
High Resolution Graphics	Angel & Griffith	152619
Hitch-hikers Guide to AI	Forsyth & Naylor	261024
Information Technology	Zorkoczy	212024
Introduction to Robotics	Critchlow	102520
Logo Programming	IBM	262410
Mastering Computers	Wright	152026
Microcomputer Graphics	McGregor & Watt	152619
Microcomputer Primer	Waite	152619
Pascal	Findlay & Watt	222423
Pascal for Students	Kemp	222423
Principles of Program Design	Jackson	232616
Problem Solving with Prolog	Conlon	241017
Programming for Poets	Conway & Archer	242618
Programming in C	Kochan	132426
Structured Programming in COBOL	Boettcher	142426

The AI Business	Winston & Prendergast	102615
The Intelligent Micro	Williams	102511
Turbo C	Borland	132426
Microfocus COBOL	Ellis Computing	142426

For a category code of 24 (Programming), the output from the program is a listing on the printer containing the following details:

Title	Author(s)
Educational Computing	Scanlon & O'Shea
Hitch-hikers Guide to AI	Forsyth & Naylor
Information Technology	Zorkoczy
Logo Programming	IBM
Pascal	Findlay & Watt
Pascal for Students	Kemp
Problem Solving with Prolog	Conlon
Programming for Poets	Conway & Archer
Programming in C	Kochan
Structured Programming in COBOL	Boettcher
Turbo C	Borland
Microfocus COBOL	Ellis Computing

Program listing

```
000001  identification division.
000002    program-id.    get-title.
000003    author.        Nick Waites.
000004    date-written.  April 1998.
000005*   remarks.       A program to extract titles and authors
000006*                  of books corresponding to a particular
000007*                  category code.
000008
000009
000010  environment division.
000011    input-output section.
000012    file-control.
000013        select title-file assign to disk
000014          access is sequential
000015          organization is line sequential.
000016        select print-file assign to printer.
000017
000018  data division.
000019  file section.
000020  fd title-file
000021        label records are standard
000022        value of file-id "c:\work\titles.txt".
```

```
000023   01 details.
000024      03 book-title        pic x(30).
000025      03 authors           pic a(20).
000026      03 categories.
000027         05 cat1        pic 99.
000028         05 cat2        pic 99.
000029         05 cat3        pic 99.
000030
000031   fd print-file
000032         label record is omitted.
000033   01 print-rec           pic x(80).
000034
000035   working-storage section.
000036   01 page-heading.
000037      03 filler           pic a(27) value spaces.
000038      03 filler           pic a(26) value
000039         "Titles for chosen category".
000040      03 filler           pic a(27) value spaces.
000041   01 column-headings.
000042      03 filler           pic a(12) value spaces.
000043      03 filler           pic a(5)  value "Title".
000044      03 filler           pic a(30) value spaces.
000045      03 filler           pic a(9)  value "Author(s)".
000046      03 filler           pic a(24) value spaces.
000047   01 title-line.
000048      03 filler           pic a(6) value spaces.
000049      03 book-title1      pic x(35).
000050      03 filler           pic a(6) value spaces.
000051      03 authors1         pic a(20).
000052      03 filler           pic a(13) value spaces.
000053   01 end-flag            pic x.
000054      88 end-of-file      value is "y".
000055   01 sub-code            pic 99.
000056
000057   screen section.
000058   01 code-request highlight.
000059      03 blank screen foreground-color is 6
000060                      background-color is 1.
000061      03 line 9 column 20 value
000062         "Enter category code  :".
000063      03 line 9 column 42 pic 99 using sub-code.
000064      03 line 11 column 20 value
000065         "A 2-digit number please".
000066
000067   01 wait-message highlight.
000068      03 blank screen foreground-color is 6
000069                      background-color is 1.
000070      03 line 9 column 24 value
```

```
000071              "Processing records - please wait".
000072
000073  procedure division.
000074  para-1.
000075
000076* —— Open book and printer files ————
000077      open input title-file
000078      output print-file
000079
000080* —— Print report headings ——————————
000081      write print-rec from page-heading
000082      write print-rec from column-headings
000083          after advancing 4 lines
000084      move spaces to print-rec
000085      write print-rec
000086          after advancing 1 line
000087
000088* —— First read of book file ————————
000089      read title-file into details
000090          at end
000091              set end-of-file to true
000092      end-read
000093
000094* —— Initialise and fetch category code ——
000095      move zeroes to sub-code
000096      display code-request
000097      accept code-request
000098      display wait-message
000099
000100* —— Identify books which match entered code —
000101      perform test before until end-of-file
000102          evaluate
000103              cat1 equal to sub-code
000104          or  cat2 equal to sub-code
000105          or  cat3 equal to sub-code
000106
000107* ————— Print book details ——————————
000108              when true
000109                  move book-title to book-title1
000110                  move authors to authors1
000111                  write print-rec from title-line
000112                      after advancing 1 line
000113          end-evaluate
000114
000115* ————— Read next record ——————————
000116          read title-file into details
000117              at end
000118                  set end-of-file to true
```

```
000119             end-read
000120        end-perform
000121
000122*  ──── Close files and clear screen ────
000123        close title-file,
000124              print-file
000125        display erase
000126        stop run.
000127
000128   end program get-title.
```

Description of program

Lines 1-7

This is the identification division in which the program is identified in terms of its name, get-title, its author, when it was written and a brief description of its function. The remarks declaration is preceded by the '*' in column 7 to identify it as a comment; some compilers accept the word remarks as a valid entry in the identification division. The program-id entry is the only compulsory entry in this division.

Lines 10-16

The environment division contains the input-output section in which the programmer defines the peripheral devices associated with any files accessed in the program. In this instance, two files are used: title-file which is the data file stored on disk, and print-file which is a file used for transferring output to the printer.

Line 18

This is the start of the data division in which each file and identifier referenced in the procedure division is specified in terms of structure and format. The data division comprises three sections in this program, namely: the file section in which the files named in the input-output section are defined; the working-storage section containing declarations of all the other identifiers used in the program; the screen section (not standard to COBOL-85) which defines screen layouts by reference to variables declared in either of the other two sections. An explanation of the screen section is provided later, in the section on the data division

Line 19

This is the start of the file section.

Lines 20-29

This block of lines contains the FD (File Description) of title-file. The sentence label records are standard is required for some compilers when defining disk files; label records are special internally generated records which provide information about the file.

Line 22 tells the compiler that this file is to be located on drive C:, in the directory cobprog, under the name titles.txt.

The *level number* 01 is used to identify the name assigned to the records of the file, in this case details. Other level numbers, from 02 to 49 are used to define the hierarchical structure of the records. Each field within the record is assigned a name and, providing it is not followed by a higher level number, its size and character is specified by means of a pic (picture) clause. For example, title has a picture of x(30) which means that the field will contain exactly 30 alphanumeric (x) characters. A 9 in the picture clause indicates a numeric field and an a means an alphabetic field.

The field called categories is termed a *group item* because it is a name given to a group of sub-fields. Only *elementary items*, that is fields not further subdivided, are given pictures. The structure of a group item is defined by the pictures of its constituent items, so categories comprises six numeric characters since each of its three sub-fields contains two numeric characters. Lines 31 to 33 define the structure of the file assigned to the printer. Again, the sentence label record is omitted is required by some compilers when specifying files that are assigned to a printer. This time the record definition indicates that the record merely contains 80 alphanumeric characters, the width of a line on an 80-column printer; this program will be transferring data to the printer a line at a time.

Lines 35-55

This is the working-storage section of the data division in which identifiers not directly associated with files are defined. Lines 36-40, for example, define a group item called page-heading which will be used to print a heading for the printout. The word filler is recognised by the compiler as an elementary item having no function other than to reserve an area of memory. Fillers can be used as frequently as required in the data division but may only be given values using the value clause in the working-storage section, not in the file section. Though a filler has the form of an identifier, it cannot be referenced in the procedure division. The three fillers constituting page-heading together define a line of text having the form

◄────────── 27 spaces ──────────► Titles for chosen category ◄────────── 27 spaces ──────────►

Similarly, the fillers in column-headings define a line of text of the form

◄─ 12 spaces ─► Title ◄────────── 30 spaces ──────────► Author(s) ◄────────── 24 spaces ──────────►

In the procedure division, page-heading and column-headings are transferred to print-rec, the record description associated with the file assigned to the printer. By this means, a variety of different lines of text can be printed without the need to define many different files, each with a different record description, all assigned to the printer.

The group item `title-line` contains the identifiers `book-title1` and `authors1`. In the `procedure division`, when a record is to be printed, the book title and authors given in the record will be transferred to these two fields prior to `title-line` being printed. This would not be possible if `title-line` consisted entirely of `filler`s. Note also that using the identifier names `book-title` and `authors` rather than `book-title1` and `authors1` here would cause ambiguity because the former two identifier names are used as field names within the record description `details` in the `file section`.

`Lines 53 and 54`

The level number `88` is reserved for the definition of *condition names*. A condition name is used in place of a condition to make it more readable. Thus, at line `101`, where the statement reads

        perform test before until end-of-file

without the use of the condition name `end-of-file` the statement would be of the form

        perform test before until end-flag equal to "y".

The first form of the statement is much more readable than that of the latter. Condition names are discussed further in the description of the operation of the `procedure division` below.

`Line 55`

The identifier `sub-code` is used to store the subject code of interest.

`Lines 73-126`

This constitutes the `procedure division` which specifies all the processing tasks to be performed by the program and closely corresponds to the program structure diagram. The very last instruction is required to be the `end program` statement in some COBOL compilers.

`Line 74`

`Para-1` is a *paragraph name* which, in this case, labels all the statements in the program. A number of paragraph names may be used to clarify the structure of a program, but the brevity of this program makes it unnecessary. Instead, comment lines are included to section the sentences into the logical groups reflected in the program structure diagram.

Lines 77 and 78

This first sentence, using the `open` statement, causes channels to the two files `title-file` and `print-file` to be opened. This is necessary before any records can be accessed. The statement tells the compiler that records are to be read sequentially from `title-file` and written sequentially to `print-file`.

Lines 81 to 86

These sentences deal with producing the page and column headings on the printer by writing a sequence of records to the file `printer-file` which is assigned to the printer.

The `write` verb is followed by a record name, `print-rec` in this instance, and two optional clauses. The first clause, starting with the word `from` allows data to be transferred from an identifier to the record before the record is written to the appropriate file. On line `81`, the data stored in `page-heading` is copied to `print-rec` before being transmitted to the printer. A second optional clause, `after advancing page`, could have been used to send a form feed character to the printer prior to printing the data held in `print-rec`. The same format allows a number of line feed characters to be sent to the printer before printing a line of text; this is illustrated in the next sentence starting on line `82`. Here the data in `column-headings` is transferred to `print-rec` and the printer is caused to skip four lines before printing the line of column headings.

In line `84`, blanks or `spaces` are transferred to the record `print-rec` (the `move` verb is used for data transfer in COBOL) prior to the record being printed, and has the effect of printing a blank line after the heading. This instruction is necessary because COBOL does not allow you merely to say 'advance 1 line'; the `after advancing` clause must accompany a `write` statement.

Lines 89-92

This statement reads the first record in the data file into the record definition `details`; if the read encounters an empty file, the condition-name `end-of-file` is set to `true`.

Lines 95-98

Here, the identifier `sub-code` is initialised to zero with the `move` statement. The `display` and `accept` statements use the `code-request` screen mask, as defined in the `screen section`, to prompt the user and accept the entry of the required category code. The user must type a two-digit, numeric category code, which is to be the focus of the data file search.

Lines 101-120

The `perform test before until` construct on line `101` repeatedly processes all the following statements up to the `end-perform` on line `120`.

The repetition is ended when `end-of-file` is `true`. Note that `test before` allows the relevant statements to be executed zero times, if the file is empty, because the file has already been read (lines `89-92`) before the `perform` statement. Note that the data file is read again, immediately before the `end-perform` statement, to allow the next record to be be examined and to test for the end-of-file condition which ends the repetition.

`Lines 102-113`

These statements search the category codes (`cat1`, `cat2` and `cat3`) of the current record for the presence of the code entered by the user (held in `sub-code`) and print the details of title and author if a match is found. The function of the `evaluate` statement should be quite clear: If one of the codes in the record matches the code stored in `sub-code` then the statement evaluates as `true`, in which case the statements following `when true` (lines `109-112`) are executed. These statements cause the title and author(s) of the current record to be printed; otherwise, if a match has not been found, control merely passes to the next sentence in line `116`. The two `move` statements cause the title and author(s) stored in the data record to be copied to the corresponding fields in `title-line` in `working-storage` section. This allows the output sent to the printer to be presented in a clearly and aligned with the appropriate column headings. The formatted line is then transferred to `print-rec` and then printed.

`Lines 116-119`

This statement, exactly the same as that on lines `89-92`, reads the next record in the data file if the end of file has not been reached, so that it is ready for comparison through the `evaluate` statement starting on line `102`. If a read is attempted after the last record in the file, the `end-of-file` condition is set to `true`. When the condition is found to be `true` at line `101`, the statements which follow are skipped and control passes straight to line `123`.

`Lines 123-126`

This is the final part of the program. The two active files are closed using the `close` statement, the monitor screen is cleared with `display erase`, and the program's execution is terminated with `stop run`. Note that the `display` verb, which is used exclusively for controlling output to the VDU, can be used in a variety of ways to display literal text or the value of variables as well as performing such functions as clearing the screen or producing inverse characters. The `display` verb is further described later.

Fundamental concepts

Though the preceding section described an example COBOL program at some length, a number of important details were either omitted or mentioned only briefly. This section will cover these points more thoroughly and prepare you for the task of writing your own programs.

Punctuation

Punctuation marks in COBOL serve much the same function as those in ordinary English prose. Commas and semicolons are interchangeably used to separate words and phrases so that statements are clearly presented. Full stops in COBOL indicate the end of sentences just as they do in English. COBOL-85 compilers do not require full stops at the end of sentences in the `procedure division`, except after paragraph names, `stop run` and `end program`. Certain things, like division declarations such as `data division` and section headings, such as `file section`, must be terminated with a full stop, but commas and semicolons are entirely optional. A sentence may span more than one line.

Here are some rules governing the use of punctuation characters in COBOL:

    (i)   Full stops, commas and semicolons must immediately follow the last letter of a word and be followed by a space.

        Example:

```
move 0 to total, count
```

    (ii)   The left parenthesis, '(', must not be followed by a space and the right parenthesis, ')', must not be preceded by a space.

        Example:

```
03 filler pic a(27) value spaces
```

Coding format

Each line of a COBOL program contains 80 columns split into 5 regions:

    (i)   a sequence (line) number occupying columns 1-6;

    (ii)   an indicator (typically a '-' or '*') occupying column 7;

    (iii)   area A occupying columns 8-11;

    (iv)   area B occupying columns 12-72;

    (v)   an identification code occupying columns 72-80.

The use of the identification code dates back to the days when programs were punched onto cards (which could be easily mixed up with those of other programs); the identification code is usually left blank these days.

The '-' indicator is used to continue a broken word or literal from one line to the next, otherwise there is no need to show that a line spans more than one line. For example, a literal requiring a continuation indicator would be written as shown in Figure 38.2.

```
        1         2         3         4         5         6         7
1234567890123456789012345678901234567890123456789012345678901234567 89012
     A...B.........................................................
     01 column-headings          pic x(80)  value
          "       Name               Number      District      Item Co
     -    "de     No.Sold    Value".
```

Figure 38.2. *Using a continuation indicator to split a literal onto a second line*

Notice that the literal stops at column 72 on the first line and continues on the next line after the quotation marks in column 12.

Generally speaking, it is not good programming style to split a word or a clause; the readability of a COBOL program is very important, so choose convenient places to break sentences. Figure 38.3 shows an example of poor programming style.

```
        1         2         3         4         5         6         7
1234567890123456789012345678901234567890123456789012345678901234567 89012
     A...B.........................................................
            write print-line from column-headings after advancing 2
            lines
```

Figure 38.3. *Poorly chosen continuation line split*

Instead, split the line at the beginning of the last clause and indent the second line:

```
        1         2         3         4         5         6         7
1234567890123456789012345678901234567890123456789012345678901234567 89012
     A...B.........................................................
            write print-line from column-headings
              after advancing 2 lines
```

Figure 38.4. *Line split between clauses*

A '*' indicator in column 7 causes the compiler to completely ignore the whole of the line, allowing the programmer to add comments to the program. Another good way to make a program readable is to insert blank lines at suitable places; the compiler will just ignore them. Area A is used to identify *headers*. Headers are division names, section names and paragraph names and must start somewhere in area A, though they are allowed to extend as far as necessary into area B. Examples of headers are

```
        procedure division.
        input-output section.
        program-id.
        process-record-para.
```

In addition, file descriptions (FD) and 01 levels must start in area A. Anything else is confined to area B.

Data item descriptions

Entries in the data division to describe data items have the following general format:

(i)   Level number

(ii) Item name

} must be present for all data items

(iii) picture clause -   must be present for all elementary items

(iv) value clause

(v)   occurs clause

(vi) redefines clause

} optional entries (note that there a number of others which are not discussed here).

Here is an example of a simple data division entry:

```
          1         2         3         4         5         6         7
 1234567890123456789012345678901234567890123456789012345678901234567890123456789012
 A...B...........................................................................
       05  surname              picture is a(20).
        |      |                    |
     level   item                picture
    number   name                clause
```

Figure 38.5. *Simple* data division *entry*

The picture clause is usually abbreviated to pic. In the remainder of this chapter, and where relevant, statements will be defined by format specifications showing their general structures using a standard form of notation. For example, the format of the move statement is given as

```
          { literal-1  }
    move {identifier-1} to identifier-2 [identifier-3] .....
```

and it is interpreted as follows:

1.   The underlined words must be present.

2.   One of the items in the curly brackets must be present.

3.   Items in square brackets may or may not be present.

Here are a number of possible move statements together with the appropriate format statements (shown in grey italics).

```
move account-num-a  to    account-num-b
move identifier-1    to    identifier-2
move "non-numeric value" to   error-message
move literal-1             to    identifier-2
move 0            to count      total      flag
move literal-1  to identifier-2 identifier-3 identifier-4
```

Some statements, such as the display statement, have a number of different formats; in such cases each format is listed.

The identification division

The function of the identification division is to identify the source program for documentation purposes. It has the following format.

```
identification division.
program-id. program-name.
[author. comment entry.]
installation. comment entry.]
[date-written. comment entry.]
[date-compiled. comment entry.]
[security. comment entry.]
```

Although entries in the identification division are treated as comments by the compiler, any reserved words present are checked and must therefore be correctly spelled and follow COBOL rules.

Here is an example using all of the possible entries.

```
000001   identification division.
000002   program-id. Example-prog.
000003   author.  Nick Waites.
000004   installation. own PC.
000005   date-written.  January 25th, 1998.
000006   date-compiled. January 25th, 1998.
000007   security. copyright F.N. Waites, 1998.
000008*  comment lines have an asterisk in column 7.
```

The environment division

The general format of the environment division is as shown in Figure 38.6.

```
          1         2         3         4         5         6         7
1234567890123456789012345678901234567890123456789012345678901234567890 12
A...B..................................................................

   environment division.

      [configuration section.
        source-computer. comment [with debugging mode].
        object-computer. comment.]

      [input-output section.
        file-control.
          select .........
          select .......
          ..............
          select ........ ]
```

Figure 38.6. *General format of* environment division

Both of the sections within the environment division considered here are optional; it is permissible to have the environment division header by itself with no other entries in this division.

The configuration section allows you to identify the computer on which the source code was compiled and on which the compiled program is to be executed; the two are often exactly the same. These entries are treated as comments by the compiler but when the with debugging mode clause is included, lines with 'd' in column 7 are compiled; otherwise, when this clause is omitted, lines with 'd' in column 7 are ignored. This allows you to include code solely for the purpose of debugging the program and which can be treated as comments when the program has been fully tested and the final version is compiled. The input-output section is used to link the names of files used in the program with physical devices such as disk drives and printers, and to specify the type of each file defined. Each such entry in this section is included under a select statement of which there may be several, as illustrated above. Every selected file must be described in the file section of the data division. (See "File descriptions" in the section on the data division). The next section deals with the different ways that files may be organised and accessed.

Types of files in COBOL

COBOL provides three types of file organisation:

(i)   sequential;

(ii)   relative;

(iii)   indexed.

Sequential files must be processed in a fixed order but relative and indexed files allow random file processing independently of the physical order in which the records are stored in the file. Sequential files are always provided by COBOL compilers but the latter two types, which both allow random file processing, may or may not be supported. Not all COBOL compilers directly support indexed organisation and since relative file organisation is a little simpler to use, it is this form of file organisation which is used where relevant here. However, for completeness, the principles governing the use of indexed files are also discussed in this section.

The later section on the `procedure division` contains details concerning the use and format of file-handling statements for each type of file discussed here.

Sequential files

The records of a sequential file must be processed in a fixed sequence which is determined by the order in which the records were initially created. So, to process a particular record of a sequential file, a program must start at the beginning of the file and read each record in turn into memory until the required record is located. Unlike a record within a random file, there is no means by which a certain record within a sequential file can be directly located and read into memory independently of the preceding records in the file.

File organisation and method of access is defined for each file used in the program in the `file-control` paragraph of the `input-output section`. For sequential files, the format in Figure 38.7 is used.

```
          1         2         3         4         5         6         7
123456789012345678901234567890123456789012345678901234567890123456789012
    A...B.......................................................................

        environment division.
        input-output section.
        file control.
                                        {printer}
            select file-name-1 assign to {disk    }

                                    {line sequential}
            {, organization is {sequential      }

            {, access mode is sequential}.
```

Figure 38.7. *Format of* `file control` *paragraph for sequential files*

Although 's' is now accepted as an alternative to the traditional 'z' in many words in UK English (for example, 'specialise', instead of 'specialize'), a COBOL compiler demands the spelling `organization`, **not** `organisation`. This is a common source of error and sometimes difficult to detect. Examples of `select` statements for sequential files, and how they relate to the general format of the `select` statement, are provided below.

Example 1

```
select customers   assign to disk.
select file-name-1 assign to disk.
```

This is the simplest form of a `select` clause. If, as illustrated here, the `organization` and `access` clauses are omitted, sequential organisation and access are assumed. Thus the select statement

```
select customers assign to disk,
   organization is sequential,
   access mode is sequential.
```

is exactly equivalent to example 1.

Example 2

```
select data-file assign to disk,
   organization is line sequential.
```

The `line sequential` option is used for text files, that is, files of records which have been produced using a text editor and which are separated from one another by a line feed and carriage return character.

Example 3

```
select report-1   assign to printer.
select file-name-1 assign to printer.
```

Relative files

The general format for the `select` statement of a relative file is shown in Figure 38.8. When a *relative* file is created, the relative position of each record within the file must be specified before the record is written to the file. This is achieved by storing the required position in a *relative key* field associated with the file prior to storing the record. The relative key is a numeric item defined in the `working-storage` section of the `data division`.

Each record must have a unique integer value, or *key*, which is used to identify its position in the file. For example, in a stock file consisting of stock item records, each item of stock will have a code to identify it uniquely, and part of this stock code might specify a record's position within the file: the four numeric digits of the code GRA0105 could be used to specify that this item occupies position 105 in the file.Thus, if the relative key was called "Stocknumber" the value 105 would be transferred to it prior to reading or writing the record. (See Example 1, which follows Figure 38.8, for the format of the appropriate `select` statement).

```
          1         2         3         4         5         6         7
12345678901234567890123456789012345678901234567890123456789012345678 9012
  A...B.....................................................................
        environment division.
        input-output section.
        file control.
            select file-name-1 assign to disk
                organization is relative

                            {dynamic   }
                            {sequential}
                access mode is {random    }

                relative key is data-name-1.
```

Figure 38.8. *General format for* select *statement of a relative file*

Examples of select statements for relative files are provided below.

Example 1

```
        select stock-file assign to disk
            organization is relative
            access mode is random
            relative key is stock-number.
```

Using the access mode is random clause allows you to read or write the file randomly and requires that in the procedure division you open the file for i-o (input-output) and read/write/rewrite/delete statements must use the invalid key format. (See 'File handling' in the section on the procedure division). The field containing the relative position of a record to be read or written is Stock-number which must be defined in the working-storage section as a numeric field of no more than seven digits.

Example 2

```
        select customer-file assign to disk
            organization is relative
            access mode is sequential.
```

Relative files may be accessed sequentially as well as randomly if the access mode is sequential clause is used. This is useful when all the records of a randomly organised file are to be processed, for printing out for instance. In this instance, the relative key is not used and the records are accessed as if the file was sequential. In this instance, in the procedure division the file can be opened for input, output or i-o and read/write/rewrite statements use the end format. (See 'File handling' in the section on the procedure division).

Example 3

```
select customer-file assign to disk
   organization is relative
   access is dynamic
   relative.key is cust-acc-no.
```

The `access is dynamic` clause allows the file to be accessed randomly and/or sequentially in the same program. Thus, for a relative file opened for `i-o` in the `procedure division`, the sequential file access statements or random file access statements may both be used. (See 'File handling' in the section on the `procedure division`).

Indexed files

Indexed files are associated with indexes which store the positions of records according to designated key fields. When a record within an indexed file is to be accessed, the index is first searched for the location of the required record and then the record is accessed. This allows the use of non-numeric keys. The general format of the `select` statement for an indexed file is shown in Figure 38.9.

```
          1         2         3         4         5         6         7
1234567890123456789012345678901234567890123456789012345678901234567 89012
   A...B.....................................................................
       environment division.
       input-output section.
       file control.
           select file-name-1 assign to disk
               organization is indexed

                                 {dynamic    }
                                 {sequential}
               access mode is {random     }

               record key is data-name-1.
```

Figure 38.9. *General format for* select *statement for an indexed file*

This time, *data-name-1* must be an alphanumeric field within the record definition of *file-name-1*. It is the *prime record key* which must have a unique value for each record in the file. As with relative files, when a record is to be accessed, the key value must be moved to the record key field before a `read/write/rewrite/delete` instruction is issued. Indexed files, like relative files, may be processed either sequentially or randomly. (See previous section on relative files). Some versions of COBOL allow alternate record keys to be specified so that files may be processed more flexibly. The examples for relative file `select` statements are applicable to indexed files, the only difference being the use of the `record key is ...` instead of `relative key is ...` clause.

The data division

The data division comprises a number of sections, including the file section, working-storage section and screen section (not standard to COBOL-85) to be considered here. You must define the structure of all the files used by the program in the file section, and all other identifiers referenced in the procedure division must be defined in the working-storage section. The screen section is used to define screen mask layouts. What follows is a simplified explanation of the structure and function of the data division, but it is perfectly adequate for the purpose of presenting an easy introduction to COBOL.

The file section contains complete descriptions of all the files included under the heading file-control in the input-output section of the environment division. Each file is described in terms of its record structure. COBOL allows you to define this record structure very flexibly using a number of useful language facilities, and the example file description in Figure 38.10 will be used to illustrate a number of these facilities.

```
          1         2         3         4         5         6         7
123456789012345678901234567890123456789012345678901234567890123456789012
     A...B.............................................................
     FD employee-file
          label records are standard
          value of file-id is "a:payroll.dat"
          data record is employee.
     01 employee.
          03 full-name.
               05 first-names          pic a(20).
               05 surname              pic a(15).
          03 sex                       pic a.
               88 male                  value IS "M".
          03 categories               pic a.
               88 valid-employee-type values are "C", "H", "S", "D"
          03 hourly-rates.
               05 normal-rate          pic 9(3)v99.
               05 overtime-rate        pic 9(3)v99.
          03 salary1 redefines hourly-rates.
               05 salary               pic 9(6)v99.
               05 filler               pic 99.
          03 tax occurs 12 times      pic 9(4)v99.
          03 rest-of-info             piv x(60).
```

Figure 38.10. *A sample file description* (FD)

Level numbers

01   indicates that the item is a *record*;

02 through 49   indicates that this item is a *field*, that is, part of a record;

77   indicates that this item is independent of any other item, a *non-contiguous* item;

88   used to define a *condition name*.

Items which are followed by one or more items with higher level numbers (in the range 02 to 49) are called *group items* and allow a number of items to be grouped together under one name.

Elementary items are not further subdivided. Below, for instance, the group item full-name is subdivided into the two elementary items surname and initials.

```
03 full-name.
     05 surname       picture is a(15).
     05 initials      picture is a(4).
```

Elementary items are always followed by a picture clause; group items are never followed by a picture clause.

Item names

An identifier (field) name, such as title or end-of-file must be formed according to the following rules:

(i)   it must not contain more than 30 characters;

(ii)   it must not contain any characters other than the letters (upper and/or lower case) a-z, the numeric characters 0-9 and the hyphen ('-');

(iii)   it must not start or end with a hyphen.

(iv)   it must not be a *reserved word*, that is, a word such as write or move or display, which is part of the COBOL language. A list of COBOL reserved words is given at the end of this chapter.

(v)   the word filler may be used to define a field name which is not required to be referenced in the procedure division.

Examples of valid identifier names are

```
cost-price, eof, running-total-1
```

Invalid identifiers are

`running-tot.`	because of the '.'
`end-flag-`	ends with a '-'
`date`	reserved word

Picture clause

The `picture is` clause (often abbreviated to `pic`) is used in the `data division` to define the format of elementary items. Certain characters are used to indicate the type of field being defined, the three most important being:

9	`numeric`
a	`alphabetic`
x	`alphanumeric`

The length of a field, that is the maximum number of characters it contains, may be defined by the repeated occurrence of one of these symbols or by the use of a number enclosed in parentheses. For instance,

`pic xxxxxx` is the same as `pic x(6)`

and means that the field being defined is composed of a combination of six alphabetic, numeric or special characters (such as ?, *, or &).

In addition, the symbol 'v' is used to indicate the position of the decimal point in a numeric field and the symbol 's' means that the number is signed (that is, it can be positive or negative). Here are some examples of `pictures` containing these symbols:

`a(20)`	an alphabetic field containing a maximum of 20 letters or spaces.
`999v99`	a number with three figures before the decimal point and two figures after.
`x(15)`	an alphanumeric field of 15 characters.
`99`	a two-digit integer number.
`s9(6)v99`	a signed number with six figures to the left of the decimal point and two figures after.

All of these types of field definitions may be used anywhere in the `data division`. Another set of characters is reserved for data items defined in the `working-storage section`. They are used for items which are to be output and are called *editing characters* and are of two forms: *insertion characters* and *floating characters*.

Insertion characters, such as '.' and ',' are used to insert the relevant symbol into a numeric field which is to be printed. For instance, to show a decimal point in a field you might write

```
picture is  9999.99
```

Floating characters like +, − and $ are used to display the relevant sign and at the same time suppress the printing of zeroes. The two characters * and z also suppress zeroes but leave the overall size of the field the same. The examples in Table 38.1 should clarify the effects of these editing characters. The examples assume that data is being transferred from a sending field to a receiving field, the second containing editing characters. The result is how the data would appear when printed.

Sending picture	Sending data	Receiving picture	Result
9(5)	12345	zzz99	12345
9(5)	00123	zzz99	123
9(5)	04000	zzz99	4000
9(3)	123	$999	$123
9(3)	012	$999	$012
9(3)	123	$$99	$123
9(3)	012	$$99	$12
s99	−12	−99	−12
s99	−12	+99	−12
s99	12	+99	+12
s99	12	−99	12
s99	−12	99	12
9(5)	12345	***99	12345
9(5)	00123	***99	**123
9(5)	12345	$zz,zz9.99	$12,345.00
9(5)	00123	$zz,zz9.99	$ 123.00
9(5)	12345	$$$,$$9.99	$12,345.00
9(5)	00123	$$$,$$9.99	$123.00
9999v9	12345	$$$,$$9.99	$1,234.50
999v99	12345	$**,**9.99	$***123.45
99v999	12345	$**,**9.99	$****12.34

Table 38.1. *Examples of use of editing characters*

Value clauses

In the working-storage section, the picture clause may be followed by an optional value clause which allows a value to be assigned to a field at the time the program is compiled. Fields cannot be given values in the file section. Figure 38.11 shows some typical examples of fields which have been assigned initial values:

```
          1         2         3         4         5         6         7
1234567890123456789012345678901234567890123456789012345678901234567 9012
    A...B........................................................
    working-storage section.
    01 valid-codes            pic x(26)    value is
          "ABCDEFGHIJKLMNOPQRSTUVWXYZ".
    01 total-1                pic 9(5)v99  value 0.
    01 total-2                pic 9(5)v99  value zero.
    01 Number-one             pic 9 value 1.
          03 answer           pic aaa      value "YES".
             05 empty-string  pic x(20) value spaces.
          03 filler           pic a(10) all "-"
```

Figure 38.11. *Use of* value *clause to assign initial values to fields*

Values such as 1, 2.6, −3 are called *numeric literals*, or *constants*. *Non-numeric literals* are such values as 'YES' or '-'. The words zero and spaces are called *figurative constants* and may also be used in the procedure division in conjunction with the move statement. The reserved word all can be used in front of literals to construct figurative literals.

File descriptions

Referring again to Figure 38.10, the file name is employee-file and the three clauses in the file description (FD) state that it is a disk file, to be found on drive A under the name payroll.dat, and the records within the file are called employee.

The clause, label records are standard, is always used for a file assigned to a disk drive. If a file is assigned to a printer rather than to a disk in the input-output section, then the clause label record is omitted is used instead.

The clause, value of file-id, is always used to connect the logical file name used in the program with the actual file on the disk; there is no necessity for the two names to be the same.

Records

A record description in the file section is indicated by an 01 level entry after the file description (FD). When a read-file instruction is encountered in the procedure division, a single record is transferred into a section of memory which has been allocated to the file. The contents of this section of memory are referenced according to a record description. This means that record descriptions must be devised to make it easy to extract data from a record. The example given previously shows a record called `employee` which has been defined using a variety of data structures.

Group items

The first `03` level, the group item `03 full-name`, has two components. In the `procedure division`, you could use either the group item or the elementary items `first-names` and `surname`. For instance, the complete name could be moved using a statement such as

```
move full-name to name-field.
```

or the surname alone could be transferred using

```
move surname to surname-field.
```

Notice that a group item does not have a `picture` clause; only elementary items are given `picture`s.

Group items are always regarded by the COBOL compiler as having an alphanumeric `picture`. The implication of this is that in the `procedure division` you cannot perform arithmetic operations on group items, though it is permissible to transfer group items. Thus, in the example record description provided earlier, an error would be generated if you tried to use the group item `salary1` in a calculation even though its two components are entirely numeric. However, the elementary item `salary` could be used in a calculation.

Condition names

A condition name is used either to simplify a conditional statement used in the `procedure division`, or to make such a statement more readable. In the example, it is used in two instances, both to simplify and to clarify the use of codes. The lines

```
03 sex                    pic a.
   88 male                value is "M".
```

are used to associate the code 'M' with the identifier `male`, allowing a `procedure division` statement such as

```
evaluate male
   when true
       move "Mr" to title
end-evaluate
```

to be written in preference to

```
evaluate sex = "M"
   when true
      move "Mr" to title
end-evaluate
```

The first conditional statement is easier to read than the second though they both perform exactly the same function: to move "Mr" to title if the employee is male.

The second example of the use of a condition name associates four possible values with the condition name employee-type. This considerably simplifies a code validation check. To check that the code in the field category is only one of the four possible, namely C, H, S, or D, we could write

```
evaluate
      category <> "C"
   or category <> "H"
   or category <> "S"
   or category <> "D"
      when true
         move "Y" to invalid-type-code
end-evaluate
```

This would move "Y" to invalid-type-code if the field category did not contain one of the permissible codes; otherwise it would skip to the next sentence.

Compare this with the same test using the condition name Employee-type:

```
evaluate invalid-employee-type
   when true
      move "Y" to invalid-type-code
end-evaluate
```

The second form is much easier to understand and to maintain if more categories are to be included at some later date.

The redefines clause

There are occasions when it is useful to store data with different formats in the same storage area. This is the case in the example record description in Figure 38.10, where the same storage locations are used to store the rates of pay for hourly paid employees or, if the record is for a salaried employee, the monthly salary. The redefines clause is used for this purpose, as illustrated in Figure 38.12.

```
        1         2         3         4         5         6         7
1234567890123456789012345678901234567890123456789012345678901234567890 12
    A...B..............................................................
            03 hourly-rates.
                05 normal-rate        pic 9(3)v99.
                05 overtime-rate      pic 9(3)v99.
            03 salary1 redefines hourly-rates.
                05 salary             pic 9(6)v99.
                05 filler             pic 99.
```

Figure 38.12. *Example use of* redefines *clause*

The group item, hourly-rates, consists of two elementary items each comprising five numeric digits (the v in 9(3)v99 is an *implied decimal point* which does not occupy a character position in the number - see the section on picture clauses). The group item, salary1, redefines hourly-rates, so they both occupy the same storage area, but their component items are different; this allows the programmer to reduce very easily the amount of storage space required for data, whilst still retaining the convenience of being able to use an appropriate data structure.

The redefines clause is often used in conjunction with the occurs clause described in the next section.

Defining arrays using the occurs clause

The OCCURS clause is used to define arrays of one or more dimensions. In the example record description in Figure 38.13, it is used to reserve space for twelve numeric fields, each containing six numeric digits.

```
        1         2         3         4         5         6         7
1234567890123456789012345678901234567890123456789012345678901234567890 12
    A...B.......................................................
            03 tax occurs 12 times    pic 9(4)v99.
```

Figure 38.13. *Definition of a one-dimensional array*

The twelve elements of the array thus defined are referenced in the procedure division with the aid of a subscript. For example, the first element is tax(1), the second is tax(2), and so on to tax(12).

As to be expected, a suitably defined variable can be used as the subscript, as in tax(k), where k would be defined as a two-digit integer in the working-storage section:

```
    01 k         pic 99.
```

Here is another example of the occurs clause, this time used in conjunction with the redefines clause:

```
01 days-of-week          pic a(21) value
   "MonTueWedThuFriSatSun".
01 day-table redefines days-of-week.
   03 week-day occurs 7 times    pic a(3).
```

Now, because the elements of the array day-table occupy the same storage area as days-of-week, week-day(1) contains "Mon", week-day(2) contains "Tue", and so on.

Though the examples of the occurs clause provided so far have involved the repeated occurrence of elementary items, this is not a restriction of the language, as illustrated by the next example:

```
01 item-details occurs 100 times.
   03 item-code      pic 9(6).
   03 in-stock       pic 9(5).
   03 unit-cost      pic 9(5)v99.
```

In this instance, item-details is a group item occurring 100 times. It can be subscripted in the usual manner, in which case it can only be treated as an alphanumeric field, or its components can be subscripted and treated as elementary items.

Thus it is allowable in the procedure division to use the following notations:

```
Item-details (i); item-code (i); in-stock (i); unit-cost (i)
```

where the elementary item, i, has been defined as an integer in the working-storage section.

Note that, when using subscripts in COBOL, the left parenthesis, '(', is always preceded by a space.

The screen section

This feature is not standard to COBOL-85. It enables the definition of a screen mask, which can then be used with the display and accept statements in the procedure division. This is illustrated in the example Titles program at the start of this chapter and in Example program #1 at the end of the chapter.

Screen layouts can be implemented without the use of a screen section and in some cases the program requirements do not enable its use.

Consider the following screen definition.

```
000008 screen section.
000009 01 employee-screen.
000010    03 blank screen foreground-color is 6
000011                      background-color is 1.
000012    03 line  6 column 25 value "PERSONNEL".
000013    03 line  9 column 20 value "Employee ID :".
000014    03 line  9 column 35 pic 9(4) using emp-id.
000015    03 line 11 column 20 value "Surname     :".
000016    03 line 11 column 35 pic a(20) using sname.
000017    03 line 13 column 20 value "Salary      :".
000018    03 line 13 column 35 pic 9(5) using salary.
```

Line 9 identifies this particular screen definition. The following statements would be used in the procedure division to call it.

```
display employee-screen
accept employee-screen
```

Lines 10 and 11 set the background colour and the colour of the text (blue and yellow respectively, in this case). Upon execution of the display employee-screen statement, lines 12, 13, 15 and 17 cause the specified literals to be displayed at the specified line and column positions.

Upon execution of the accept employee-screen statement, lines 14, 16 and 18 allow the acceptance of the relevant inputs into the specified data items (using identifier) The data items emp-id, sname and salary must all be separately defined in the file section or the working-storage section.

The picture clause used in the screen section need not be the same as that in the other definition and can be set to enable validation of numeric and textual data.

The procedure division

The procedure division is used to specify the processing that is to be performed by the program. The processing instructions are written in a form closely resembling ordinary English, in a deliberate attempt to make a COBOL program easy to understand by non-specialists.

A typical procedure division is composed of a number of sentences, the basic unit of the procedure division. Sentences may be combined to form paragraphs which in turn can be grouped into sections. Paragraphs and sections, being headers, must be given names.

The following sections describe some of the most commonly used COBOL statements.

Data transfer (move)

One of the most common tasks performed in the procedure division is the transfer of data from one memory location to another. In such a process the source of the transfer is often called the *sending field* or sender, and the destination is called the *receiving field* or receiver. A move statement is used to perform this type of operation. Its format is shown below:

```
         { literal-1  }
move {identifier-1} to identifier-2 [identifier-3] .....
```

A move statement is frequently used to transfer data from one field to another in preparation for producing output on a printer. The receiving field will often contain editing characters to improve the quality of the printout. Whatever the reason for the transfer, there are a number of rules which govern it:

(i)   The data is copied from the sending field to the receiving field(s), so that the data is still intact in the sending field.

(ii)   When the receiving field is alphanumeric or alphabetic, it is filled from left to right. If the sending field width is smaller than that of the receiving field, vacant character positions in the receiving field are filled with spaces (Δ):

      sender   **receiver**
      [abcdef]   [abcdef$\Delta\Delta\Delta$]
        x(6)   x(9)

If the sending field is wider than the receiving field, the receiving field is filled from left to right, truncation of the data occurring at the right-hand side:

      sender   **receiver**
      [abcdefghi]   [abcde]
        x(9)   x(5)

(iii)   With numeric moves the positions of the decimal points (implied or otherwise) in the sending and receiving fields determine the effect of the move on the receiving field:

      sender   **receiver**
      [123.45]   [0123.450]
      999.99   9999.999
      [123v45]   [0123v4500]
      999v99   9999v9999
      [1234.56]   [34.5]
      9999.99   99.9
      [1234]   [34.0]
      9(4)   99.9

In each case the decimal points are aligned first, and then the transfer of the digits from the sending field to the receiving field is effected. Any vacant positions are filled with zeroes.

(iv)   All group moves are treated as alphanumeric.

(v)   Figurative constants are allowed in move statements:

```
move spaces to blank-line
move all "-" to underline
move zeros to total, tax
```

Screen handling (`display, accept`)

See also earlier explanation of the `screen section`, available in Micro Focus COBOL. The `display` statement allows information to be displayed on the screen of the computer system.

Two formats are commonly used:

```
                    {literal-1 }    {literal-2   }
 (1) display {identifier-1} [{identifier-2}] ...

                    {literal-1   }   {literal-2   }
 (2) display {identifier-1} [{identifier-2}] ...
             at line {integer} col {integer}
```

Format (1) will cause the specified literals and/or contents of identifiers to be displayed at the current cursor position. Examples of `display` statements and their general formats are shown below:

```
display "the account number is: " cust-ac-no
display {literal-1}                      {identifier-2}

display   stock-num,      current-level, min-level
display {identifier-1} {identifier-2} {identifier-3}
```

Format (2) is similar to the other format except that the cursor position at which the data is to be displayed may be specified in terms of line and column. The line and column may be numeric literals or numeric data items:

```
display "reading file ....." at line 10 col 20
display item(i, j) at line i col j
```

Often used in conjunction with `display`, the `accept` statement allows data to be entered at the system keyboard during program execution and stored in a data item. Three formats are commonly employed:

```
(1)   accept identifier
(2)   accept identifier at line {integer} col {integer}
(3)   accept identifier from date
```

The first two formats are equivalent to the display statement formats; the cursor position can be specified, or not, prior to capturing data from the keyboard and transferring it to the designated identifier, as the following examples show.

```
accept yes-no-answer
accept number-of-sales at line 20 col 8
```

The third format allows the program to access data, in the form of the current date, already available in the system. The date is usually provided in the form YYMMDD, that is, the year of the century, the month of the year, and the day of the month. For example, 15th January 1999 would be represented as 990115. This six-digit, unsigned, numeric elementary item would be transferred to the named identifier, for example:

```
accept todays-date from date
```

Arithmetic operations (add, subtract, multiply, divide, compute)

Most business calculations can be performed using the arithmetic operations of addition, subtraction, multiplication and division. In COBOL these four operations are available in the form of the add, subtract, multiply, divide and compute statements. The compute statement provides a more concise alternative for all but the simplest of arithmetic expressions. Formats of the add, subtract, multiply and divide statements are similar.

Add

```
      {literal-1   }        {literal-2 }
add {identifier-1} [to] {identifier-2} [giving identifier-3]
```

Examples

```
add 3 to line-counter
add tax to cost giving total-price
```

Subtract

```
            {literal-1   }        {literal-2   }
subtract {identifier-1} from {identifier-2}
            [giving identifier-3]
```

Examples

```
subtract 1 from counter-down
subtract discounter from price giving selling-price
```

Multiply

```
             {literal-1   }     {literal-2   }
   multiply {identifier-1} by {identifier-2}
             [giving identifier-3]
```

Examples

```
   multiply 1.5 by ot-hours
   multiply hours by rate giving pay
```

Divide

```
           {literal-1   } {by  } {literal-2   }
   divide {identifier-1} {into} {identifier-2}
             [giving identifier-3]
```

Examples

```
   divide 11 into stock-num
   divide stock-num by 11 giving int-result
```

The following remarks apply to all four arithmetic statements defined above:

(i)   `Identifier-1` and `identifier-2` must be elementary numeric items.

(ii) If the optional `giving` clause is used, the result of the calculation is stored in `identifier-3`, otherwise the result of the calculation replaces `identifier-2`. For example, the statement

```
   add 1 to counter
```

is equivalent to

```
   counter = counter + 1
```

that is, the value stored in `counter` is increased by 1. However, the statement

```
   add 1 to counter giving new-counter
```

leaves `counter` unchanged and gives `new-counter` the value `counter` + 1.

(iii) `Identifier-3` may be a numeric item containing editing characters such as *, + and z.

Compute

```
compute {identifier-1} = arithmetic expression
```

Examples

```
compute gross-pay = hours * rate
compute tax = (hours * rate - tax-free) * tax-rate
```

Control structures (`evaluate`, `if`, `perform`)

These statements allow you to alter the order in which the program instructions are performed.

The `go to` statement is an unconditional branch instruction causing program control to transfer to a specified position in the program (normally a paragraph header). For example,

```
go to process-error
```

would cause the computer immediately to commence processing the statements following the paragraph header `process-error`. The use of the `go to` statement is discouraged in structured programming because of its tendency to produce programs which are difficult to understand and maintain. Its use can almost invariably be avoided, as is illustrated by the complete lack of `go to` statements in the example programs presented in this chapter.

Evaluate

The `evaluate` statement allows a selection to be made between alternative courses of action. Although the `if` statement is briefly explained later, the `evaluate` statement is used in this text and is generally preferred as a more powerful and flexible construct. There are a number of different forms, but a particularly useful one has the following format.

```
         {condition    }
evaluate {condition-name}
   when true  {statement-1} [statement-2]..
   [when false {statement-3} [statement-4]..]
end-evaluate
```

Examples

```
evaluate hours > 40
  when true
     compute ot-hours = hours - 40
     compute ot-pay = ot-hours * basic-rate * 1.5
  end-evaluate
```

```
evaluate invalid-input
  when true
      move pay-details to invalid-pay
      write invalid-pay
  when false
      move pay-details to valid-pay
      write valid-pay
end-evaluate
```

The first example tests the condition hours > 40 and if true, calculates and stores the overtime hours and pay. No alternative action is required, so the when false part of the statement is not required. The second example is checking a condition name which is set according to whether the input is invalid. If the condition name is true, the details are copied to invalid-pay (a record defined in the file section) and the record is then written to a file for invalid records. If the condition name is false the details are transferred valid-pay and written to a file for valid records.

The condition can take the two forms shown below.

```
                        {equal to  }
                        {less than } {literal    }
    identifier-1 [not] {greater than} {identifier-2}

                        {numeric   }
    identifier-3 [not] {alphabetic}
```

The symbols =, < and > may be used in place of equal, less than and greater than respectively.

The alphabetic and numeric *class tests* are often used in conjunction with evaluate to carry out validation checks, to ensure that fields are of the required format. The following examples illustrate.

```
evaluate surname not alphabetic
  when true
      move "y" to invalid-flag
end-evaluate
```

If the condition is true, that is, the class test surname not alphabetic is true, move "y" to invalid-flag is executed before control passes to the next sentence; otherwise control passes to the next sentence following the end-evaluate statement.

If an elementary item number-sold has been defined as x(6), then a statement such as

```
accept number-sold
```

will allow the user to enter any sequence of alphanumeric characters, not just numeric characters. Before the contents of this item could be processed numerically, it would be necessary to confirm that only numeric characters had been entered, otherwise a runtime error might occur; a statement such as

```
evaluate number-sold not numeric
   when true
        move number-sold to inv-number-sold
        set invalid flag to true
end-evaluate
```

could be used to prevent this from happening.

A condition may be a compound condition connected by the and and or logical operators. for example, the following statement checks that a code is one of a set of four.

```
evaluate
      dept-code = "RD"
  or dept code = "AC"
  or dept-code = "PU"
  or dept-code = "SA"
      when true
         move dept-details to print-line
         write printer-rec from print-line
end-evaluate
```

The evaluate statement is also used to select from several alternative actions. This form of the statement is as follows.

```
evaluate true
        {condition      }
   when {condition-name}
       {statement-1} [statement-2]..
        {condition      }
   when {condition-name}
       {statement-1} [statement-2]..
        {condition      }
   when {condition-name}
       {statement-1} [statement-2]..
            .
            .
   when other
       {statement-1} [statement-2]..
end-evaluate
```

Example

```
evaluate true
  when book-type = 1
     add 1 to adventure
  when book-type = 2
     add 1 to romance
  when book-type = 3
     add 1 to mystery
  when other
     move details to error-line
     write printer-rec from error-line
end-evaluate
```

The example checks a field book-type for three valid codes, 1, 2 or 3 and that which evaluates as true causes the following statement-1, statement-2 .. to be executed. If none of the codes match then when other is true and its following statements are executed. This form of the statement means that other will always be true if none of the preceding conditions is satisfied.

If

```
     {condition      } {statement-1  }          {statement-2  }
  if {condition-name} {next sentence} [else {next sentence}]
  end-if
```

Examples

```
if pay-rate is less than 3.50 perform err-rtn
end-if

if lines = 60 move 0 to lines else add 1 to lines
end-if
```

In the first example, if the condition is true, statement-1 is executed, otherwise statement-1 is ignored and control passes to the next sentence. In the second example, if the condition is true, statement-1 is executed, otherwise statement-2 is executed before control passes to the next sentence.

Perform

The forms of the perform statement which follow are part of the COBOL language and are included for that reason, but are not essential to the development of well-structured programs. The preferred forms, perform..test..before and perform..test..after are used in all the sample programs in this book, and are explained in the section after this.

The `perform` statement can be used for two main purposes:

1. To allow one or more sentences within a program to be executed out of sequence by transferring control to a part of the program labelled with a paragraph name. For instance, the statement

    ```
    perform check-digit-calc
    ```

    would cause the computer to branch to the paragraph called `check-digit-calc` and execute all the statements within this paragraph before returning to the statement immediately following the `perform`. There are two forms of the statement for this purpose.

    (i) <u>perform</u> `paragraph-1`

    This is the simplest form of the `perform` statement as described above. It is also possible to specify a range of paragraphs to be `performed` by using the word `through` or `thru`:

    (ii) <u>perform</u> `paragraph-1` <u>through</u> `paragraph-2`

    Here `paragraph-1` is the start of the range of paragraphs and `paragraph-2` is the last paragraph in the range to be performed.

    Example

    ```
    perform validation-check-1 thru validation-check-5
    ```

2. The paragraph, or range of paragraphs, named are executed a specified number of times or until a condition is satisfied. If *identifier-1* initially has a negative or zero value, the control will pass immediately to the next statement after the `perform`.

    ```
                               {integer-1  }
    (i) perform paragraph-1 {identifier-1} times
    ```

    This form of the statement can also be used with `through` or `thru` to execute several paragraphs repeatedly.

    Examples

    ```
    perform process-table 10        times
    perform paragraph-1 integer-1 times


    perform print-rtn    i             times
    perform paragraph-1 identifier-1 times


    perform p1           thru p3           j           times
    perform paragraph-1 thru paragraph-2 identifer-1 times
    ```

    The named paragraph or range of paragraphs can be executed until a specified condition is true. The condition may also be a compound condition using `and` and or operators. If the condition is initially true, control will pass immediately to the next statement after the `perform`.

```
                                {condition-name-1)
    (ii) perform paragraph-1 until {condition-1      }
```

Examples

```
    perform process-file until end-of-file
    perform paragraph-1  until condition-name-1

    perform p6          thru p8          until flag = 1
    perform paragraph-1 thru paragraph-2 until condition-1

    perform proc-list    until no-swaps or counter > list-length
    perform paragraph-1  until condition-name-1
```

In this last example, *condition*-1 is a compound condition consisting of a condition name, `no-swaps`, connected by the `or` operator to the condition `counter > list-length`.

Perform (with test before and test after)

`Perform` is used to execute statements interatively (repeatedly) and the scope of the *loop* extends from the `perform` statement to its associated `end-perform`. The statement form is:

```
                      {after }        {condition-name)
    perform [with] test {before} until {condition       }
        statement-1
        [statement-2]..
    end-perform
```

The use of `before` enables the controlled statements to be executed <u>zero</u> or more times; the condition or condition name is checked for its truth before the loop is entered. This form is used, for example, to enable the avoidance of statements to process a record when the file is empty and there is no record to process. The use of `after` ensures that the loop is executed at least once and is useful for the control of a menu system, which must be displayed at least once, even if the user chooses the exit option immediately afterwards. The following example should help to clarify the uses of `perform`..

Example

```
    move 1 to emp-no
    perform test before until counter > 5
      display pay-rate (emp-no)
      add 1 to emp-no
    end-perform
```

Here, the rates of pay for 5 employees are assumed to be held in an array pay-rate. The subscript for the array (defined in working-storage as pic 9) is the employee number emp-no and incrementing its value from 1 to 5 enables loop to be executed 5 times. Within the loop, the display statement outputs the contents of the array, in a vertical list. The condition counter > 5 is false for values in the range 0 to 5 and true for values 6 to 9. Note that emp-no is initialised to 1 in the statement preceding the loop, thus removing one of the true values and restricting the iteration to 5 times.

```
000100     read book-file into details
000101       at end
000102         set end-of-file to true
000103       end-read
000104
000105     perform test before until end-of-file
000106       move book-title to book-title1
000107       move authors to authors1
000108       write print-rec from title-line
000109           after advancing 1 line
000110       read title-file into details
000111         at end
000112           set end-of-file to true
000113       end-read
000114     end-perform
```

The initial read of the book-file in lines 100 to 103 prepares a record for printing and also allows the condition-name end-of-file to be tested for the case of an empty file, in which case the loop will not be performed and control passes to the statement following end-perform.

If the condition end-of-file is false, that is a record has been found, the record details are printed and another read is carried out on lines 110 to 113, to prepare another record for printing and to determine if the end of file has been reached. Otherwise, once entered, the loop would never be terminated.

File handling (open, close, read, write, delete, rewrite)

Sequential files

Statements that are appropriate to the processing of sequential files are:

```
open
read
write
rewrite
close
```

open - initialises file input and output operations. The open statement must precede any file processing statements. Sequential files may be opened according to the following format:

```
            {extend}
            {i-o  }
            {input }
open {output} file-name-1 [,filename-2] ...
```

Example

```
    open output son-payroll-file
```

The opening of a file for output prepares the computer system for transferring records to a backing storage medium (a disk, for example) or a printer from the memory of the computer. If the file has been assigned to a disk drive, a new file will be created or, if it already exists, it will be overwritten. This statement would precede the issuing of a write instruction.

```
    open input father-payroll-file
```

This prepares the computer for transferring records from a backing storage device to the area of memory reserved for the file. This statement would precede the issuing of a read instruction.

```
    open i-o updated-customer-file
```

This allows records to be read and then rewritten (usually after being modified) to the file. This allows a sequential file to be updated without the necessity of creating a new file. This statement would normally precede the issuing of read and rewrite instructions.

```
    open extend transaction-file
```

This prepares the computer for outputting records to the end of a file, that is, extending the number of records in the file without destroying existing records. This statement would precede the issuing of a write instruction.

write - transfers a record from memory to an output device. The general format of the write statement contains clauses relevant to vertical positioning for files assigned to a printer:

```
    write record-name [from identifier-1]

    {before}              {identifier-2}
    [{after } advancing {integer      } lines ]
                          {page          }
```

Example

```
    write customer-rec
```

This transfers the data currently contained in the specified record area to the output device (for example, disk file, printer) assigned to the relevant file.

```
write validated-rec from ws-rec
```

The from clause is the equivalent of executing a move statement prior to writing the record. Thus the statement above is equivalent to the two statements:

```
move ws-rec to validated-rec
write validated-rec
```

```
write detail-line after advancing 2 lines
```

This is appropriate to printer output, causing two carriage returns and line-feeds to be sent to the printer prior to printing the contents of the specified record (detail-line in this instance). The before option causes the control characters to be sent to the printer after the record has been printed.

```
write page-heading after advancing page
```

This causes a form feed control character to be sent to the printer before printing the contents of the specified record.

read - transfers the next available record from the assigned backing storage device to the area of memory allocated to the relevant file. The general format is shown below:

```
read file-name record [into identifier-1]
  [at end imperative-statement-1]
  [not at end imperative-statement-2]
end-read
```

Examples

```
read club-members record at end move 1 to end-flag
end-read
read file-name    record at end imperative-statement-1
```

This causes the next available record of the specified file to be transferred to the area of memory allocated to the file. Only if the end of the file is encountered when attempting to read another record is the statement following end executed. This imperative-statement may comprise a number of statements before the end-read.

```
read trans-file into temp-rec
  at end set end-of-file to true
end-read
```

The into option causes the record read to be copied into the specified identifier, temp-rec. The statement above is equivalent to the two statements:

```
      read trans-file
        at end set end-of-file to true
        not at end move trans-rec to temp-rec
      end-read
```

This assumes that `trans-rec` is the record description of `trans-file`.

rewrite - replaces the last record read from the file with the current contents of the record area assigned to the file. It assumes that the file has been `opened` for `i-o`. The format of the statement is:

```
      rewrite record-name [from identifier-1]
```

The `from` option has the same effect as that in the `write` statement described above.

Examples

```
      rewrite employee-rec
```

This overwrites the last record read from the file by the current contents of the area of memory allocated to the file, that is, the current contents of the record held in memory.

```
      rewrite stock-rec from temp-area
```

This issues a `move` statement to transfer the contents of `temp-area` to `stock-rec` prior to writing `stock-rec` to the file.

close - this is used to terminate the processing of input and output files. The format of the `close` statement is shown below:

```
      close file-name-1 [, file-name-2 ] ...
```

A file must be `open` before it can be `closed`. In order to start reading an `opened` sequential file from the beginning, first `close` the file and then `reopen` the file for `input`.

Examples

```
      close members-file
      close trans-file, master-file
```

Relative files

Relative files allow either random access or sequential access, depending on the form of the `select` statement used in the `input-output section` of the `environment division` (see 'Relative files' in the earlier section on the `environment division`). When a relative file is to be accessed as if it were a sequential file, then the input-output statements are the same as those appropriate to sequential files as described in the preceding section; these will not, therefore, be described again. Statements that are appropriate to the processing of relative files are:

```
open
read
write
rewrite
delete
close
```

open - as for sequential files.

write - transfers a record from memory to an output device.

There are two general formats for relative files, the appropriate format depending on the access mode required. The first format is used for relative files which are to be accessed as sequential files. The second format is appropriate to relative files accessed randomly.

1. <u>write</u> record-name [<u>from</u> identifier-1]

```
        {before}              {identifier-2}
   [ {after } advancing {integer    } lines ]
        {page         }
   end-write
```

2. <u>write</u> record-name [from identifier-1]
   [<u>invalid</u> key imperative-statement-1]
   [<u>not</u> <u>invalid</u> key imperative-statement-2]
   <u>end-write</u>

When the second format is used, the requested record number must be transferred to the relative key identifier associated with the file prior to issuing the write statement. This identifier must be defined in the working-storage section as a numeric field. The invalid key clause is invoked if the record to be written already exists in the file, in which case the imperative statement is executed. The rewrite statement (see later) is used if a record is to be overwritten.

In addition, the file must have been opened for i-o (input-output) prior to executing the write statement.

If statements (imperative-statement-2) are to be executed after the write then not invalid must be used, otherwise they will only be executed when the invalid key condition arises. This is a frequent cause of run-time errors in COBOL programs.

Examples

```
move rec-pos to rel-key-1
write customer-record
   invalid key display "This customer already exists"
end-write
```

Here, `rel-key-1` is the field which has been identified as that containing the relative key for the file. The record `customer-record` will be released to the output device if the record position identified by `rel-key-1` is unoccupied, otherwise the message 'This customer already exists' will be displayed on the screen. The `display` statement is the imperative-statement in this instance.

```
write summary-rec from ws-summary
   invalid key move 4 to error-num
      display "Can't write to this record"
end-write
```

The `from` clause causes the contents of `ws-summary` to be transferred to `summary-rec` prior to attempting to write this record. This time, if the `invalid key` clause is invoked, the `move` statement is executed followed by the `display` statement.

rewrite - this is identical to `write` except that the specified record position must *exist* in the file, irrespective of whether or not it is empty. Thus `rewrite` is usually used when an existing record is to be updated or modified in some way. The general format for `rewrite` is:

```
rewrite record-name [from identifier-1]
        [invalid key imperative-statement-1]
        [not invalid key imperative-statement-2]
end-rewrite
```

When a relative file is being accessed sequentially, the `invalid key` clause is not used. (See the description of `rewrite` for sequential files). As with the `write` statement, in order to use this statement, the file must previously have been `opened` for `i-o`.

Example

```
move stock-num to rel-key-2
rewrite stock-rec
   invalid key display "No such stock item on file"
end-rewrite
```

The stock file has a `relative key` called `rel-key-2` to which has been moved the stock item's position in the file. If the `rewrite` fails because this position is outside the limits of the file, the message "No such stock item on file" is displayed.

read - This transfers a record from the file medium to the file record area in memory, making it available for processing. The two possible formats allow a relative file to be read either sequentially or randomly.

```
1.   read file-name record [ into identifier-1 ]
         at end imperative-statement-1
         [not at end imperative-statement-2]
     end-read
```

This format is used when the file is to be read sequentially and has been opened for input or i-o. For examples, see sequential files.

```
2.   read file-name record [into identifier-1]
         [invalid key imperative-statement-1]
         [not invalid key imperative-statement-2]
     end-read
```

This format is used only when the file has been opened for i-o, that is, for random access. The position of the required record must previously have been transferred to the relative key assigned to the file.

The invalid key clause is invoked if the record position specified is outside the bounds of the file, that is, the record specified does not exist in the file.

Example

```
move id-num to rel-key-3
read master-file
  invalid key display "record number", rel-key-3,
                      " does not exist"
  move 3 to err-flag
end-read
```

The record in position id-num is to be read from the backing storage device assigned to file master-file. If this record does not exist, the invalid key clause is invoked causing the two statements in this clause to be executed. The field rel-key-3 is the relative key field for the file as defined in the select statement for the file.

delete - this is used to remove a record from a random disk file. The format is:

```
delete file-name record
   [invalid key imperative-statement-1]
   [not invalid key imperative-statement-2]
end-delete
```

The file must have previously been opened in the i-o mode, and must not be a sequential file. In addition, the delete statement must have been preceded by a successful read statement for it to be successful. The invalid key clause must be used.

Example

```
move member-code to rel-key-5
read members-file
   invalid display "no such member"
end-read
delete members-file record
   invalid display "no such member - can't delete"
end-delete
```

close - as for sequential files.

Indexed files

Indexed files are very similar to relative files in that they also allow both sequential and random access. The main difference between the two types of file is that an indexed file has a separate index file associated with it. This index allows you to assign non-numeric keys to files and, as explained in indexed files in the section on the environment division, the record key must form part of the record description for the file. Because of the close similarities between relative files and indexed files, the statements appropriate to them are also almost identical. The main difference between relative and indexed file processing for random access is that before accessing a record.

(i)   for relative files the record position must be contained in the relative key field defined in the working-storage section and

(ii) for indexed files the record identifier (key) must be contained in the record key defined in the record description of the file.

Thus, all of the statements described for relative files are identical for indexed files, except for a small addition required for the read statement, and this is explained below.

Statements that are appropriate to the processing of indexed files are:

```
open
read
write
rewrite
delete
close
```

`open` - as for sequential/relative files.

`write` - as for relative files.

`rewrite` - as for relative files.

`read` - This transfers a record from the file medium to the file record area in memory, making it available for processing. The two possible formats allow an indexed file to be read either sequentially or randomly.

```
1.   read file-name next record [ into identifier-1 ]
         at end imperative-statement-1
        [not at end imperative-statement-2]
     end-read
```

This format, with the inclusion of the word `next`, is used when the file is to be read sequentially in the `dynamic` access mode and has been `opened` for `i-o`.

Example

```
    read customer-file next record
      at end
          move "y" to end-of-file
    end-read
```

This reads the next available record of the indexed file `customer-file` as if it were a sequential file.

```
2.   read record-name [into identifier-1]
        [invalid key imperative-statement-1]
        [not invalid key imperative-statement-2]
     end-read
```

This format is the same as that for relative files.

`delete` - as for relative files.

`close` - as for sequential/relative files.

Summary of permissible statements

Table 38.2 summarises permissible file-handling statements for each type of file, its organisation, access mode and open mode.

Access mode	open mode	sequential				relative				indexed			
		i	o	i-o	e	i	o	i-o	e	i	o	i-o	e
sequential													
	read	■		■		■		■		■		■	
	write		■		■		■		■		■		■
	rewrite			■				■				■	
	delete							■				■	
random													
	read					■		■		■		■	
	write						■	■			■	■	
	rewrite							■				■	
	delete							■				■	
indexed													
	read					■		■		■		■	
	write						■	■			■	■	
	rewrite							■				■	
	delete							■				■	

Table 38.2. *Summary of permissible file handling statements*

The abbreviations used in the table have the following meanings:

i	input
o	output
i-o	input-output
e	extend

A shaded square indicates that the operation is possible.

So, for example, the table shows that for a sequential file opened for i-o, the read and rewrite statements are permitted, but the write and delete statements are not.

Stages in the development of a COBOL program

In general terms, the stages involved in producing an executable COBOL program are as follows:

1. Write the source code using a program/text editor. The documentation that accompanies a COBOL compiler will specify the type of text file that the compiler requires as input. Some compilers, of which Micro Focus COBOL is an example, will supply a program editor as part of the COBOL system; others will recommend suitable editors.

2. Compile the program. The compiler will check the source code and issue an error report if it detects any syntactic or semantic errors. An example of a typical error report is shown below.

```
Line# Col# Err# Lvl Messages

000420 26 0004    f   file not selected in the input-output section.
000590  1 0057    w   warning line numbers out of sequence.
000600 43 0005    f   occurs limited to one level.
000740 34 0006    f   subscripted items cannot be redefined.
000750 27 0051    w   warning more than 30 characters in a word.
000810 54 0007    f   picture items must be elementary.
000820 36 0017    f   value of file-id missing.
000840 20 0018    f   subscript literal contains illegal character.
000950 22 0020    f   occurs clause is illegal at 01 level.
000980 60 0021    f   value is illegal with occurs.
000990 28 0050    w   warning literal truncated right end.
001030 last line read by the compiler.
```

Each line of the report supplies a number of pieces of information relating to an error that has been detected. The first piece of information is the number of the line containing the error; next is the position within the line (`col#`) at which the error was detected; then there is a code number assigned to the error; following this is the type, or level, of error - `f` (fatal) means that the compiler has been unable to produce the object code and the program must be corrected and recompiled, and `w` (warning) indicates that the error is not as serious, has not prevented object code generation and the program may still function correctly when run; finally there is a short explanation of the cause of the error.

3. Identify and correct compilation errors. The source code must be corrected and the program recompiled. Steps 2 and 3 may have to be repeated a number of times until the program compiles successfully.

4. Link the program. This is the process of linking subroutines required by the program into the object code. These subroutines form part of a library of procedures which are referenced by the compiler at compile time. Some compilers may not

require this stage to be performed as a stage separate from compilation.

5.   Run the program. This stage may produce run-time errors, that is errors which only become apparent when the program is first executed or at some later date during the testing phase. Detection of the cause of a run-time error might again necessitate correction of the source code and recompilation of the program.

Example programs

The example programs in this section implement three of the program design examples in Chapter 36. Program #1 is used to create a file of car details and illustrates screen handling and the creation of sequential files. Program #2 prints, in tabular form, the contents of a sequential file created with the first program and illustrates the process of producing a printed report. Program #3 asks the user to enter a target car price, which is then used to display a tabulated list of cars within £1000 of the target price; the program illustrates the technique of searching a sequential file for records which match a criterion.

The pseudocode and structure charts which illustrate the logic of these programs can be found in Chapter 36. Each of the following COBOL implementations reflects the logic of its pseudocode and structure chart. The comment lines in each program listing enable its logical structure to be clearly seen.

Program #1. Creating a sequential car file through a screen mask

```
000001   identification division.
000002   program-id.    create-file.
000003   author. Nick Waites.
000004   date-written. April 1998.
000005*  remarks. Creates sequential car file
000006
000007   environment division.
000008     configuration section.
000009       source-computer. ibm-pc.
000010       object-computer. ibm-pc.
000011     input-output section.
000012     file-control.
000013         select car-file assign to disk,
000014             organization is line sequential.
000015
000016   data division.
000017   file section.
000018
000019   fd car-file
000020       label records are standard
000021       value of file-id is "c:\work\car.dat".
000022   01 car-rec.
```

```
000023        03 make                pic a(10).
000024        03 model               pic x(10).
000025        03 ins-group           pic 99.
000026        03 cost                pic 9(5)v99.
000027
000028
000029     working-storage section.
000030     01 verify-rec             pic a value is "y".
000031         88 rec-ok             value is "y", "Y".
000032     01 another-rec            pic a value is "y".
000033         88 no-more-recs        value is "n", "N".
000034
000035     screen section.
000036     01 car-details.
000037        03 blank screen foreground-color is 6
000038                        background-color is 1.
000039        03 line 5 col 20 value is
000040            "Create Cars Master File".
000041        03 line 9 col 20 value is
000042            "Make (e.g. Ford):".
000043        03 line 9 col 48 pic a(10) using make.
000044        03 line 11 col 20 value is
000045            "Model (e.g. Mondeo):".
000046        03 line 11 col 48 pic x(10) using model.
000047        03 line 13 col 20 value is
000048            "Insurance Group (e.g. 7):".
000049        03 line 13 col 48 pic 99 using ins-group.
000050        03 line 15 col 20 value is
000051            "Cost (e.g. 8450.50):".
000052        03 line 15 col 48 pic 9(5).99 using cost.
000053
000054     01 verify-line.
000055        03 line 18 col 20 value is
000056            "OK to save this record? (Y/N):".
000057        03 line 18 col 52 pic a using verify-rec.
000058
000059     01 another-line.
000060        03 line 20 col 20 value is
000061            "Enter another record (Y/N)?".
000062        03 line 20 col 48 pic a using another-rec.
000063
000064     procedure division.
000065     para-1.
000066
000067* — Open file ─────────────────────────────
000068         open output car-file
000069
000070* — Allow entry of records until user ──
```

```
000071* — chooses not to enter another record —
000072        perform test after until no-more-recs
000073
000074* — Initialise all variables in car record —
000075* — and display input mask                  —
000076          initialize car-rec
000077          display car-details
000078          accept car-details
000079
000080* — Allow user to save or abandon current record —
000081          display verify-line
000082          accept verify-line
000083          evaluate rec-ok
000084            when true
000085                write car-rec
000086          end-evaluate
000087
000088* — Ask if user wants to enter another record —
000089          display another-line
000090          accept another-line
000091        end-perform
000092
000093* — Close car file and terminate program ——
000094        close car-file
000095        stop run
000096    end program create-file.
```

Program #2.   Reading, displaying and printing the sequential car file

```
000001    identification division.
000002     program-id.   read-file.
000003     author.        Nick Waites.
000004     date-written. April 1998.
000005* remarks.  Reads Car file, displays, prints all records
000006
000007    environment division.
000008    configuration section.
000009        source-computer. ibm-pc.
000010        object-computer. ibm-pc.
000011    input-output section.
000012    file-control.
000013        select car-file assign to disk,
000014            organization is line sequential.
000015        select printer-file assign to printer.
000016
000017    data division.
```

```
000018   file section.
000019
000020   fd car-file
000021      label records are standard
000022      value of file-id is input-file.
000023   01 car-rec.
000024      03 make              pic a(10).
000025      03 model             pic x(10).
000026      03 ins-group         pic 99.
000027      03 cost              pic 9(5)v99.
000028
000029   fd printer-file
000030      label records are omitted.
000031   01 printer-rec          pic x(80).
000032
000033   working-storage section.
000034   01 report-heading.
000035      03 filler            pic x(33) value spaces.
000036      03 filler            pic x(15) value
000037         "Car File Report".
000038      03 filler            pic x(32).
000039   01 detail-line.
000040      03 p-make            pic x(10).
000041      03 filler            pic x(5) value spaces.
000042      03 p-model           pic x(10).
000043      03 filler            pic x(5) value spaces.
000044      03 p-ins-group       pic x(2).
000045      03 filler            pic x(5) value spaces.
000046      03 p-cost             pic z9999.99.
000047
000048   01 blank-line           pic x(80) value spaces.
000049   01 end-of-file          pic a value is "n".
000050      88 eof               value is "y".
000051   01 file-name.
000052      03 input-file        pic x(20) value spaces.
000053
000054   procedure division.
000055   para-1.
000056
000057*  — Prompt user to enter name of file to be read —
000058      display erase
000059      display "Enter name of INPUT file :"
000060         at line 10 col 10
000061      accept input-file
000062
000063*  — Open named file and printer file ——————
000064      open input car-file
000065      output printer-file
```

```
000066
000067* — Print report headings ─────────────────────
000068     write printer-rec from report-heading
000069     write printer-rec from blank-line
000070          after advancing 3 lines
000071
000072* — First read of car file ──────────────────
000073     read car-file
000074       at end set eof to true
000075     end-read
000076
000077* — Send car details to printer and screen ──────
000078     perform test before until eof
000079       move make to p-make
000080       move model to p-model
000081       move ins-group to p-ins-group
000082       move cost to p-cost
000083       write printer-rec from detail-line
000084       display detail-line
000085
000086* — Read next car record ──────────────────
000087       read car-file
000088         at end set eof to true
000089       end-read
000090     end-perform
000091
000092* —Close car file and terminate program ─────────
000093     close car-file
000094     stop run
000095   end program read-file.
```

Program #3.   Searching the sequential file for cars within certain price range

```
000001   identification division.
000002     program-id.    search-file.
000003     author.        Nick Waites.
000004     date-written. April 1998.
000005* remarks.        Accepts approximate price and lists cars
000006*                 within + or - £1000 of the price
000007
000008   environment division.
000009   configuration section.
000010     source-computer. ibm-pc.
000011     object-computer. ibm-pc.
000012   input-output section.
```

```
000013   file-control.
000014      select car-file assign to disk,
000015      organization is line sequential.
000016
000017   data division.
000018   file section.
000019   fd car-file
000020      label records are standard
000021      value of file-id is "c:\work\car.dat".
000022   01 car-rec.
000023      03 make           pic a(10).
000024      03 model          pic x(10).
000025      03 ins-group      pic 99.
000026      03 cost           pic 9(5)v99.
000027
000028   working-storage section.
000029   01 end-of-file       pic a value is "n".
000030      88 eof            value is "y".
000031
000032   01 price             pic 9(5) value zero.
000033   01 display-line.
000034      03 filler         pic x(5) value spaces.
000035      03 s-make         pic a(10).
000036      03 filler         pic x(5) value spaces.
000037      03 s-model          pic x(10).
000038      03 filler         pic x(5) value spaces.
000039      03 s-ins-group    pic 99.
000040      03 filler         pic x(5) value spaces.
000041      03 s-cost         pic z9999.99.
000042
000043   procedure division.
000044   para-1.
000045
000046* — Open file ———————————————————————
000047      open input car-file
000048
000049* — Prompt user for required car price ———
000050      display erase
000051      display "Enter approximate price of cars to list:"
000052      accept price
000053
000054* — First read of file ————————————————
000055      read car-file
000056         at end set eof to true
000057      end-read
000058
000059* — Compare each car cost with input price and —
000060* — display those records within £1000 of price —
```

```
000061        perform test before until eof
000062          evaluate cost >= price - 1000 and
000063                   cost <= price + 1000
000064            when true
000065              move make to s-make
000066              move model to s-model
000067              move ins-group to s-ins-group
000068              move cost to s-cost
000069              display display-line
000070          end-evaluate
000071
000072* - Read next car record ─────────────
000073          read car-file
000074            at end set eof to true
000075          end-read
000076
000077        end-perform
000078
000079* - Close file and terminate program ──
000080        close car-file
000081        stop run
000082   end program search-file.
```

Reserved words

COBOL contains a large number of words which are recognised by the compiler as key words having special meanings. These reserved words must be spelled correctly and used in the correct context according to the syntax of the language. They are listed here so that you know which combinations of characters to avoid when deciding on your program identifiers, and also to give you an idea of the true complexity of the full COBOL language.

The list of reserved words includes the additions introduced in COBOL 85 (the successor to COBOL 74) which attempts to bring COBOL more in line with the current trend towards structured programming.

accept	access	add
advancing	after	all
alphabet	alphabetic	alphabetic-lower
alphabetic-upper	alphanumeric	alphanumeric-edited
also	alter	alternate
and	any	are
area	areas	ascending
ascii	assign	at
attribute	author	auto-skip
beep	before	beginning
binary	blank	block

bottom	by	call
cancel	cd	cf
ch	character	characters
class	clock-units	close
cobol	code	code-set
collating	column	comma
common	communication	comp
comp-0	comp-1	comp-3
computational	computational-3	compute
configuration	contains	content
continue	control	controls
converting	copy	corr
corresponding	count	cseg-memory
currency	data	date
date-compiled	date-written	day
day-of-week	de	debug-contents
debugging	debug-item	debug-line
debug-name	debug-sub-1	debug-sub-2
debug-sub-3	decimal-point	declaratives
delete	delimited	delimiter
depending	descending	destination
detail	disable	disk
display	divide	division
down	dseg-memory	duplicates
dynamic	egi	else
empty-check	enable	end
end-add	end-call	end-compute
end-delete	end-divide	end-evaluate
end-if	end-multiply	end-of-page
end-perform	end-read	end-receive
end-return	end-rewrite	end-search
end-start	end-string	end-subtract
end-unstring	end-write	enter
environment	eop	equal
erase	error	escape
esi	evaluate	every
exception	exit	extend
external	false	fd
file	file-control	file-id
filler	final	first
footing	for	from
generate	giving	global
go	greater	group
heading	high-value	high-values
identification	if	in
index	indexed	indicate
initial	initialize	initiate
input	input-output	inspect

installation	into	invalid
i-o	i-o-control	is
just	justified	key
label	last	leading
left	length	length-check
less	limit	limits
linage	linage-counter	line
line-counter	lines	linkage
lock	low-value	low-values
memory	merge	message
mode	modules	move
multiple	multiply	native
negative	next	no
not	number	numeric
numeric-edited	object-computer	occurs
of	off	omitted
on	open	optional
or	order	organization
other	output	overflow
packed-decimal	padding	page
page-counter	perform	pf
ph	pic	picture
plus	pointer	position
positive	printer	printing
procedure	procedures	proceed
program	program-id	purge
queue	quote	quotes
random	rd	read
receive	record	records
redefines	reel	reference
references	relative	release
remainder	removal	renames
replace	replacing	report
reporting	reports	rerun
reserve	reset	return
reversed	rewind	rewrite
rf	rh	right
round	rounded	run
same	screen	sd
search	section	security
segment	segment-limit	select
send	sentence	separate
sequence	sequential	set
shell	sign	size
sort	sort-merge	source
source-computer	space	spaces
special-names	standard	standard-1
start	status	stop

string	sub-queue-1	sub-queue-2
sub-queue-3	sum	suppress
symbolic	sync	synchronized
table	tallying	tape
terminal	terminate	test
text	than	then
through	thru	times
to	top	trailing
true	type	unit
unstring	until	up
upon	usage	use
using	value	values
varying	when	window
with	words	working-storage
write	zero	zeroes
zeros		

Exercises

Example Program #1

1. Using example Program #1 as a model, write a data entry program for a file that you have designed. Plan the appearance of the screen mask on squared paper before writing the program so that you can calculate the coordinates for each prompt and input.

2. Modify example Program #1 such that when a field is to be entered, the corresponding field of the previous record is displayed, allowing the user to just press <ENTER> to accept this data rather than enter new data; this can save time when certain fields do not change from record to record, or when only certain fields of an incorrect record are to be changed.

   Sometimes the COBOL compiler will facilitate this type of operation by providing special options in the accept statement, otherwise you must provide your own code. A possible approach to programming this facility is to reserve an area of working-storage for a copy of the input record to be used as a buffer for each field to be entered. Each field of the new record, in turn, is read into its buffer; if the buffer contains one or more characters constituting new data, its contents are transferred to the corresponding field of the actual record description in the file section; if the buffer is empty because the user has pressed <RETURN> without entering any data, no action is taken, thus allowing the previous contents of that field to remain.

3. Write a program to validate a sequential file such as that created by example Program #1. Each record should be subjected to as many checks as possible to ensure

that the data has been entered correctly. Here is a list of possible validation checks with brief descriptions of their purposes:

(i)   *Alphabetic/numeric class test* to ensure that fields do not contain invalid characters.

(ii)   *Range check* to ensure that numeric data is within certain prescribed limits.

(iii) *Code check* to determine whether a code field contains one of a limited number of special codes.

(iv)   *Presence check* to ensure that a field's contents are present, that is, the field has been entered and is not empty.

(v)   *Control totals* which are pre-calculated totals of numeric fields (typically monetary fields); these are compared with the same totals calculated during computer processing. For example, in the example sales file, the sale value field for all the source records could be totalled prior to entry to the computer - this would be the control total. The validation program would then keep a running total of this field as the records are processed. When the whole file has been validated, the control total would be compared with the calculated total as a check that no mistake had been made during the data entry phase.

4.   Implement a selection sort or an insertion sort in COBOL using either your own file or one created with example Program #1. Sorts are described in detail in Chapter 35.

Example Program #2

1.   Write a program to print a report of one of your own files, using example Program #2 as a guide.

2.   Modify example Program#2 so that the report will show a grand total of the costs of all cars on file.

3.   Modify example Program #2 to allow for the report spanning more than one page. You should arrange that the page number appears at the bottom of each page and that the page column headings are printed at the top of each new page.

Example Program #3

1.   Write a program to search one of your own files, using example Program #3 as a guide.

2.   Modify example Program #3 to allow searching using other criteria, in addition to entry of a price, for example, a particular make or insurance group.

Assignment programme

The following tables detail the location of each assignment, the Principal Objectives it covers and the most relevant Chapters.

The Principal Objectives for each Unit are also given in the table. Apart from the assignments in this section, it should be noted that some Principal Objectives are also achievable through the completion of Exercises and COBOL projects; the page numbers of these are also provided.

Unit title: Information Systems		Principal Objectives	
1.	Understand the reasons for different forms and sizes of organisation in the public and private sector.		
2.	Describe the principal functional areas common to most organisations and their interrelationships in various types and sizes of organisation.		
3.	Understand the need for various types and levels of information in organisations.		
4.	Identify the manual and computerised methods by which an organisation may store and process its information.		
5.	Identify and describe essential features of data processing applications.		
6.	Appreciate the physical and operational changes necessary for computerisation of a business system.		
Assignment Title	**Page**	**Objectives**	**Relevant Chapters**
1. Weaving a web	642	1, 2, 3, 4	Ch. 1, 2, 3
2. Moving house	643-644	2, 3, 5	Ch. 3, 4, 14, 15
3. Educating rITa	644-645	2, 3, 4, 6	Ch. 2, 8, 13, 15, 24, 25
4. Revamp	645-647	5	Ch. 6, 9, 10, 11, 12, 13.
5. Protection racket	647	6	Ch. 13

Unit title: Introduction to Programming		Principal Objectives	

1. Appreciate the different categories of software.
2. Appreciate simple problem specifications and develop appropriate program designs.
3. Appreciate the structure and elements of a structured high level programming language.
4. Implement a simple program design in an appropriate structured high level language.
5. Produce appropriate documentation.

Assignment Title	Page	Objectives	Relevant Chapters
6. Job applications	648	1	Ch.16
7. Testing angles	648-649	4, 5	Ch.29, 37

Unit title: Computer Systems		Principal Objectives	

1. Appreciate the relationship between the basic hardware and software components of a computer system.
2. Describe the operation and characteristics of typical peripheral and storage devices.
3. Understand how data is represented and manipulated within a computer.
4. Understand how data is processed within a computer.
5. Identify and describe the features and applications of networks and distributed systems.

Assignment Title	Page	Objectives	Relevant Chapters
8. Paper mountain	649-650	2	Ch. 19
9. Fine wines	650-651	2	Ch. 19
Exercises	249-250	3	Ch. 21
10. 7-segment display	651	3	Ch. 22
Exercises	294	4	Ch. 23
11. Booking for sunshine	652	5	Ch.24

Unit title: Quantitative Methods		Principal Objectives	

1. Perform a range of arithmetical calculations and understand the result of approximate calculations.
2. Use algebra to express quantitative ideas and processes.
3. Interpret and manipulate data presented in tabular form.
4. Use geometrical terminology to provide pictorial definitions.
5. Plot graphs of simple algebraic functions, and use computerised graph plotting techniques to present statistical information.
6. Understand statistical techniques and interpret results from simple statistical packages.
7. Apply simple accounting concepts as a basis for analysis of financial problems.

Assignment Title	Page	Objectives	Relevant Chapters
Exercises	353-355	1	Ch. 26
12. Denary to binary	653-654	2	Ch. 27
13. Picture shows	654-655	3	Ch. 28
14. Corker of a job	656	4, 5	Ch. 29
Exercises	404-406, 430	5, 6	Ch. 30, 31
Exercises	453-454, 460	7	Ch. 32, 33

Unit title: Programming concepts and practice		Principal Objectives	

1. Compare the characteristics of different computer programming languages.
2. Understand the different types of data structure and manipulate data within these structures.
3. Appreciate the role of language processors.
4. Appreciate alternative methods of program implementation.
5. Understand the principal features of operating systems.
6. Understand and apply current program design methods.
7. Understand the basic structure of the COBOL language.
8. Define appropriate data descriptions.
9. Apply appropriate program constructs.
10. Handle simple data manipulation processes.
11. Use appropriate input-output facilities.
12. Apply the techniques used and aids available for testing programs.
13. Demonstrate the ability to document computer programs to agreed standards.

Assignment Title	Page	Objectives	Relevant Chapters
15. Language development	657	1	Ch.16
16. Waste not, want not	657-658	2	Ch.34
Exercises	148	3, 5	Ch.16
Exercises and Projects	637-638, 658-662	6-13	

Assignment 1

Weaving a web

Your County Council is developing a Web site to attract businesses to the area. The Council also wishes to encourage people to move there. A number of Web pages will feature case studies of various organisations, designed to demonstrate the variety of employment opportunities and to attract employers to the County. You are part of a team gathering the data for these Web pages and your particular tasks are as follow.

Tasks

1. Research organisations in your County and choose six, two for each of the following classifications: *manufacturing*; *public service*; *commercial*. Create a table showing the six organisations classified as indicated and include a brief description of the main *purpose(s)* of each.

2. Select two of the organisations with which you are particularly familiar, or are able to research sufficiently to provide the following information. For each organisation:

    (i)   describe its *distinct identity*. Apart from a written description, this should include the organisation's logo or a graphical image which you feel best describes its distinct identity.

    (ii)   Draw and annotate an *organisation chart*, showing its functional and management structure.

3. Choose one of the organisations from Task 2 and select a minimum of three internal functions and one external function.

    (i)   Describe the *purpose* of each function and the *tasks* it routinely carries out. Also, identify and briefly describe the purpose of *standard documents* used in the completion of the tasks The descriptions should be supported with appropriate graphical illustrations.

    (ii)   Describe four examples of information provided by any of the functions in (i) which illustrate the need for different *types* of information to assist decision-making at different *levels* in the organisation.

    (iii) Describe two distinct examples of difficulties caused by inaccurate information at each of the levels identified in (ii).

Assignment 2

Moving house

McManus, Lorimar and Barnes is a firm of estate agents based in Portsmouth. The partners believe that recent loss of business results from problems in the matching of prospective purchasers with properties for sale. A brief outline of the property sales procedures follows.

(a) The initial request from a client wishing to sell a property is dealt with by one of the four partners. The partner arranges to visit the property and in consultation with the client, records the details of location, type, price range, number of rooms and so on.

(b) The property details are transcribed onto one of two source documents, depending on whether the property is residential or used for business purposes. This work is carried out by staff in the Property Registration section.

(c) A copy of the property registration from is passed to Property Sales section, where staff categorise the property according to basic criteria, including location, type, size, quality, number of rooms and price range. These basic details are transcribed onto record cards, which are then used as the initial point of reference when a prospective buyer makes an enquiry.

(d) In order to match prospective buyers with properties for sale, a Buyer Clients file is maintained. Details of suitable properties are sent on a mailing list basis to each client.

Mr. Jones is preparing a report on the existing procedures, to present to senior partners. The firm intends to approach a computer consultancy firm with the intention of computerising the property and client recording procedures. The report will be used as a basis for a detailed analysis by the consultancy firm.

It is envisaged that the computerised system will include Property, Buyer and Offer files. The Property file will record details of all properties for sale, the Buyer file will include contact details and property requirements of prospective buyers and the Offer file will hold details of offers made by particular buyers for particular properties. The need for a separate file for offers arises from the facts that there will be numerous offers for a single property and each buyer may put in offers for several properties at the same time.

You are employed by the estate agency, as a trainee office manager and Mr. Jones has asked you carry out the following tasks towards production of the report.

Tasks

1. Using the information provided, produce details of the work activities carried out in each of the functional areas, in tabular form.

2. Draw an information flow diagram which includes the functions already identified in Task 1 and the clients who deal with the agency, namely, vendors and prospective buyers. Each information flow should indicate direction of flow and the nature of the information passing from one function to another.

3. Suggest possible structures for the Property, Buyer and Offer files, which will allow the agency to closely match buyer requirements available properties and keep track of offers. The structure for each file should identify all field names and example contents for each field. The field or fields which form the primary key should also be identified.

4. Briefly describe the file processes which would allow buyers to be informed of suitable properties.

5. Briefly describe the file processes needed to produce a letter, addressed to a buyer, informing him or her of the outcome of their offer for a property. It is assumed that the vendor will accept the highest offer.

6. List and briefly explain any changes in office layout that computerisation will require.

7. List and briefly explain the effects computerisation is likely to have on the staff in the agency.

Assignment 3

Educating rITa

Newborough County Council accommodates its various departments in a purpose-built Civic Centre in Newborough. IT provision is based on linked networks throughout the Centre. Some stand-alone microcomputers are still in use, although it is planned to include them in the network in the near future. The network servers are located in a secure location and adjoining workrooms are used by the specialist computing and IT staff, who are part of the IT Services department.

You are employed as a personnel officer at Newborough County Council and the Personnel Manager has asked you to prepare a slide presentation. The IT Services Manager is concerned that the work of the Department, as a servicing unit for the whole organisation, is understood by other staff in the Civic Centre. It is intended that newly appointed staff are given a tour of the various departments, so that they can gain a wider view of the Council's work. The slide presentation seeks to support this aim.

Tasks

1. Prepare the slides, using presentation software. The presentation should make extensive use of graphics and text descriptions should be brief. The display should cover the following sections:

    (i)   An introduction to the general role of IT Services;

    (ii)   the roles of its specialist staff in supporting the work of the Council.

    (iii)   the benefits arising from distribution of the processing function through the Council's computer network, in contrast to an earlier central facility.

    (iv)   the IT services it can provide, for example, electronic mail, Internet access, ISDN and other network services, document processing and so on.

    (v)   The responsibilities the Council and its employees have in respect of the Data Protection Act. Use illustrative examples appropriate to the Council's activities.

    (vi)   The threats to security of computer systems and the information they hold and the measures which are taken to combat those threats. (You are not given this information and will have to make appropriate suggestions)

2. Present the display to the group and be prepared to answer questions on its content.

Assignment 4

Revamp

Revamp Limited is an electrical contracting company. There are two directors, one of whom is responsible for management of jobs on site and estimating for possible contracts, the other being occupied with pricing, cost control and general maintenance of the company's accounts. The company employs a workforce of around fifty, but there are periods, usually in winter, when fewer are employed. All systems are manual at present, but it is in the particular area of cost control where the manual system fails to provide management with information, which is vital to the profitability of the company. In addition, pricing of jobs is time-consuming and savings could be made by using computers. The Revamp directors have asked MicroSystems Limited, computer dealers and consultants, to carry out an investigation of the job and cost control systems with a view to their computerisation. MicroSystems employ you as a trainee systems analyst and have given you nominal control of this project. The following information is provided by Revamp.

Existing operation of job costing and control system

The system provides an estimate of costs, including profit, relating to individually identifiable jobs or contracts. The estimate, or price, quoted to the main contractor or customer is generally maintained when the job is completed, so it is vital that the original estimate does not fall short of the actual costs incurred.

The job costing does not present any great problems to the business (except that it is time-consuming), but during a job's progress there is insufficient time to closely monitor costs. This can result in the original cost being exceeded before the job is complete. Although the original price is usually fixed, if the situation mentioned should occur, it may be possible to negotiate with the customer or contractor before the job has progressed too far.

Procedures for pricing or job costing

Having received a request from a customer for a job quotation, the responsible director visits the site and estimates the quantities of materials and labour needed to complete the job.

The estimated quantities are used to calculate a job cost, by reference to price catalogues.

The job is given a unique number and a record of the job is kept in the job file.

Procedures for cost control

Once the job is accepted, invoices for purchased materials are charge to the relevant job. A supply is 'tied' to a job by recording the job number on the invoice. As well as charging materials to a job, labour (including overheads) is also charged, labour being treated as just another supplier. When the job is completed, an invoice for the quoted price is sent to the customer and provided that the amount is greater than the actual cost, a profit has been made.

Task

1. Produce a Feasibility Report on the job costing and cost control systems, including:

    (i)   an outline description of the applications, suggesting the overall business and system objectives they are designed to meet;

    (ii)   a more detailed description of the system's existing operation, its good and bad points and the means by which a new system could improve upon it;

(iii) a description of the new system's envisaged operation and its expected costs and benefits;

The study should concentrate on the application and the scenario already outlined.

2. Produce a System Specification, including the following sections.

(i) Nature of the system (processing method).

(ii) Output specification, providing samples of screen and printed outputs.

(iii) File design, including organisation and access methods.

(iv) Input specification, detailing transaction types and source documents.

(v) Processing tasks, including updating of files and generation of various reports.

(vi) Validation, backup and access control measures.

Assignment 5

Protection racket

You have been asked to write an article for the staff magazine at HFC Ltd, an employment agency, on ONE of the following issues.

1. Viruses, their types, their effects and the measures which can be taken to protect the systems in HFC Ltd against attack.

2. Hacking, the motives of hackers and the measures which HFC Ltd can take to protect their systems.

3. The Internet and the opportunities and dangers its use could bring to HFC Ltd.

The article should be between 800 and 1200 words and may include graphical illustrations.

Assignment 6

Job applications

Software Training Ltd provides a range of training courses for prospective system and applications programmers, using a range of different languages and operating systems. You work for the company as a publicity assistant. You are asked to prepare a 'flyer' advertising the company's courses.

Task

1. Research job advertisments for systems and applications programmers and identify the operating systems and application areas to which they relate. Select two from each for use in the flyer.

2. Prepare notes on the essential differences between applications and systems software.

3. Prepare the flyer, using the notes from Task 2 and incorporate the information found in Task 1 to clarify the differences between these types of software. Also use the information from Task 1 to illustrate opportunites for each category of programmer.

Assignment 7

Testing angles

A program is required to read in three numeric values representing the three sides of a triangle. The numbers are to be entered from a keyboard one after the other, separated by one or more spaces and followed by pressing the Enter key. The program outputs a number of messages regarding the type of triangle that the three numbers represent:

    ❑   Invalid data: these values cannot be used to form a triangle;

    ❑   Invalid data: non-numeric input;

- ❑ Scalene;

- ❑ Isosceles;

- ❑ Equilateral;

- ❑ Obtuse;

- ❑ Right-angled.

It may print out more than one message. For instance, if the three values were 3, 3, 5, the program should say that the triangle is 'Obtuse' and 'Isosceles'.

Tasks

1. Use appropriate black box testing methods to devise test classes and test cases which would test the program thoroughly.

2. For each test case specify the expected output from the program.

3. You should assume that the program has code to validate the input so that it can detect invalid inputs. Your test data should cover every possible output from the program for invalid and valid data.

You will need to research the characteristics of each type of triangle in order to devise test data that represents each possible type of triangle.

Assignment 8

Paper mountain

Everest Equipment Limited is a medium-sized company, based in Swansea and specialising in the manufacture of clothing and accessories for walking and climbing enthusiasts. The company has a factory on the outskirts of town, where most of the goods are manufactured. The manufactured clothing and accessories are sold to specialist retail shops throughout the United Kingdom and about half of their production is for the export market. The company employs 20 office staff and 105 factory staff. All computer systems are networked. The LAN workstations are used for a variety of purposes, including costing, planning and computer-aided design. Large volume, monochrome, hard copy output is required for the main information processing applications, although this is primarily text. High quality colour graphical output is required for product design applications and for the production of the staff magazine and company reports. Final product designs need to be printed on paper sizes up to A0.

Everest employs you as an IT support technician. Judith Conlon, IT Services Manager, has asked you to research available hard copy devices which satisfy the various needs of Everest.

Task

Research suitable printing devices prepare a presentation (printed or on screen), detailing the following:

(i)   Classification of main printing technologies.

(ii)   Principles of operation of each class.

(iii)   Two example product specifications for each class, including quality (resolution), printing speeds.

(iv)   Recommendations on products suitable for requirements of Everest.

Assignment 9

Fine wines

Fine Wines Limited is a medium-sized company, with a chain of off-licence shops in the Somerset area. Its Head Office and central warehouse are in Frome. A local area network at the Head Office is used for most of the company's accounting and administrative applications. Warehouse staff can update stock files, for stock issues and receipts, through terminals connected by an ISDN link to Head Office. Each week, the company's lorries deliver ordered goods to the shops; the order has been prepared a week previously. When the goods are delivered, the driver collects the completed order forms for the following week. The drivers return these order forms to the Frome office, where they are keyed in and processed. Orders and delivery instructions are transmitted over the ISDN link to the warehouse and printed.

Compudata, a Bristol software house, employs you as a trainee systems analyst. Fine Wines Limited have approached Compudata regarding the improvement of the order collection procedures. It is apparent that the data collection could be automated, because the Fine Wines order forms are designed with pre-printed item lists and choices of quantities to be ordered. A shop manager simply has to tick chosen quantity boxes next to selected items on the list. Your team leader, Ken Barlow, has given you the task of preparing a preliminary report for presentation to Fine Wines Limited.

Task

1. Prepare a preliminary report for Fine Wines Limited, outlining the use of optical mark reading (OMR) to automate order collection. Explain how the present forms may be utilised and how shop managers should complete them. Identify any necessary extra equipment.

2. Describe an alternative to the OMR proposal.

Assignment 10

7-segment display

The diagram shows the layout of a seven segment display commonly used in calculators. Each segment of the display can be emphasised by applying logic 1 to the input to that segment. By simultaneously emphasising the appropriate segments, the device can be used to display the digits 0 to 9.

Task

Design seven logic circuits, one for each segment, such that when four signals representing a binary coded decimal (BCD) digit are applied to each circuit, the appropriate digit is displayed.

The truth table will have the following form.

inputs (BCD)	digit	outputs
A B C D		a b c d e f g
0 0 0 0	0	1 1 1 1 1 1 0
0 0 0 1	1	0 1 1 0 0 0 0
etc	....	.....
1 0 0 1	9	1 1 1 1 0 1 1

Assignment 11

Booking for sunshine

Sunshine Holidays Limited operates a chain of travel agencies. The company's Head Office, in Leeds, accommodates a minicomputer system, which is used for all the company's main information processing applications. At present, the only computer provision at each agency is a Prestel unit, for checking on travel and holiday vacancies. The company recognises that it needs to modernise its systems, and in particular, provide each agency with on-line communications to Head Office and specialist travel databases through other networks. As a representative for NetSystems, you are to prepare a report, which suggests ways in which the needs of Sunshine Holidays Limited can be met.

Task

As a group assignment, prepare a presentation on the following:

1. General introduction to define *wide area network (WAN)* and *local area network (LAN)*, together with an explanation as to why the company will need both. Illustrate the broad configuration of the network connections between the various parts of Sunshine Holidays Limited and other network systems.

2. Identification and explanation of the functions of hardware components needed for each LAN.

3. Annotated diagrams showing the different shapes or topologies which can be used to connect these LAN components.

4. Brief explanation of the alternatives for data communications through wide area networks, including ISDN connections, multiplexed and packet switching systems and so on. Suggest, with reasons, an appropriate choice.

5. Comment on the importance of protocol standards, particularly for connection to different networks outside of those used by Sunshine Holidays Limited. Quote some of the protocols used on different types of network.

6. Briefly outline the seven levels of the OSI model, using examples of their use for network and data communications standards.

7. Suggest ways in which the networks may be used to improve the communication and information processing systems within the company.

Assignment 12

Denary to binary

An iterative technique for converting binary integers to denary was presented in this chapter as an illustration of the use of the subscript notation. There is a similar algorithm for the reverse process, that is, denary to binary conversion. The algorithm is as follows:

```
LET N be a positive integer. To find its binary
representation (an an - 1 .....a1 a0), let b0 = N
and iteratively calculate,
b1 = (b0 - a0)/2
b2 = (b1 - a1)/2
This is, in general
bk = (bk-1 - ak-1)/2
where ak = 1 if bk is an odd number, and
ak = 0 if bk is an even number.
The procedure terminates when bk = 0.
```

The algorithm produces the binary coefficients in reverse order, that is the least significant digit, a_0 is produced first and the most significant digit, a n is produced last.

Tasks

1. Using a range of denary numbers investigate the operation of the algorithm; show how each digit of the binary number is produced.

2. Write a program, based on the algorithm, to accept a denary number and convert it to binary. The output from the program should be a binary number with its digits in the correct order (the algorithm above produces the digits in reverse order).

Developmental task

A method of determining whether a number is odd or even is to divide it by 2 and if there is no remainder, the number is even. The problem is how to do this in a programming language. Here is the basis of one possibility using 13 as an example:

(i)   divide the number by 2: $13/2 = 6\cdot5$

(ii)   remove the fractional part: $6\cdot5 \rightarrow 6$

(iii)   multiply this by 2: $6\times2 = 12$

(iv)   since this is not the same as the original number, the original number must have been odd. If the result was the same as the original number, it would have been even.

The programming language that you use will determine the precise coding required for this, so you should investigate the facilities that your particular language provides. Look through the language manual for suitable instructions. (Some languages provide MOD and DIV functions for integer division; MOD gives the remainder and DIV the integer quotient of the division. Other languages allow conversion from real numbers to integers).

Assignment 13

Picture shows

In Chapter 28, some examples were presented to illustrate calculations on arrays using simple 2-dimensional graphics. Though it was not mentioned at the time, the examples were thinly disguised matrix multiplications. For the present purposes, a matrix may be regarded as a 2-dimensional array, and multiplying a co-ordinate pair by a 2×2 matrix has the effect of transforming the co-ordinates. This can be represented by the following notation

$$(xt, yt) = (x, y)\begin{pmatrix} a & c \\ b & d \end{pmatrix}$$

which states that the point (x,y) transforms to the point (xt, yt) when multiplied by the matrix (array):

$$\begin{pmatrix} a & c \\ b & d \end{pmatrix}$$

The matrix operation shown above produces the equations

$$xt = ax + by$$

$$yt = cx + dy$$

The choice of a, b, c and d determines the particular transformation to be performed on the point. The application of this process is that standard transformations of shapes may be performed by applying certain, standard types of transform matrices. Some of these matrices are shown below. A transformation of a shape is performed by applying the transform matrix to each point in the shape. Some interesting effects can result.

1. Identity (no effect) $\begin{pmatrix} 1 & 0 \\ 0 & 1 \end{pmatrix}$

2. Scaling $\begin{pmatrix} S1 & 0 \\ 0 & S2 \end{pmatrix}$ (S1 is the x and S2 the y scaling factor)

3. Reflection about the x-axis $\begin{pmatrix} 1 & 0 \\ 0 & -1 \end{pmatrix}$

4. Reflection about the y-axis $\begin{pmatrix} -1 & 0 \\ 0 & 1 \end{pmatrix}$

5. Y shear $\begin{pmatrix} 1 & S \\ 0 & 1 \end{pmatrix}$ (S is the shear factor)

6. X shear $\begin{pmatrix} 1 & 0 \\ S & 1 \end{pmatrix}$

Tasks

1. Using graph paper draw a simple (but interesting) geometrical shape consisting of straight lines and note the position of each point of the shape in x-y co-ordinates.

2. Apply a transform matrix to the points in your shape and draw the transformed points on graph paper. Repeat for different transforms.

Developmental task

Most books on interactive computer graphics will explain the use of matrices in 2-dimensional transformations. Read up on the subject (such books are usually packed with good illustrations of the effects that can be achieved) and try to find out how to perform a rotation of a figure through a specified angle.

Assignment 14

Corker of a job

The kitchen floor shown alongside is to be covered in cork tiles. The tiles are square and come in packs of 10. The usual procedure when laying tiles is to start at the centre of the room and work outwards towards the walls. At the edges of the room, the tiles have to be cut to fit, which means that parts of some tiles will be wasted. After the tiles have been glued down, they are sealed in three coats of varnish. Finally, decorative wood strips are fixed along the floor where the tiles meet the wall . Tiles cost £4·59 per pack, a 1 litre can of varnish costs £5·60 and a 2 litre can costs £9·80.

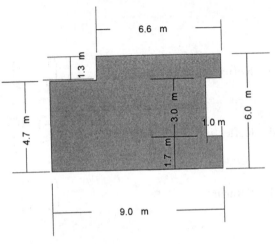

Tubs of adhesive cost £11·50 and cover up to 40 square metres of floor. Wood strips come in 2 metre lengths and cost £1·20 each.

You have been put in charge of buying the materials for the job.

Tasks

1. Calculate the area of the floor.

2. If each tile is 30 cm square, what area, in square metres, will each pack be able to cover?

3. Assuming that there will be 10% wastage and that only complete packs of tiles can be purchased, calculate how many packs of tiles will be required.

4. If a litre of varnish can cover 20 square metres of floor, calculate how many 1 litre and 2 litre cans of varnish will be required.

5. How many wood strips will need to be purchased?

6. What will be the total cost of materials for the job?

7. What percentage of each of each type of material do you estimate will be wasted?

Assignment 15

Language development

This assignment is concerned with programming languages, the problems they are designed to solve and their input-output and processing facilities.

Tasks

1. Reearch the history of programming languages and draw an annotated 'time line' to illustrate the points when particular programming languages were introduced. The annotations should distinguish between assembler level and high level programming languages, perhaps by colour coding.

2. Select two languages from Task 1 and analyse their facilities for handling input-output, controlling iteration and selection and performing arithmetic. Design code examples to illustrate the facilities in each language. Also identify the particular problem area for which each is designed to solve. Present all the information in tabular form.

3. Comment on the relationship between each languages facilities and the problem area with which it is associated.

Assignment 16

Waste not, want not

A list of stolen credit card numbers is to be stored in memory using a linked list. It is necessary to be able to display the numbers in ascending order of magnitude without first having to sort them. Numbers will be frequently added to the list and deleted from it. The amount of storage space allocated to the numbers is limited , so it is important that it is utilised as efficiently as possible. The numbers are to be stored as a linked list.

Tasks

1. With the aid of examples, explain how items will be added to and removed from the linked list of credit card numbers. Carefully show how the various pointers are

altered, and draw diagrams to illustrated the structure of the data before and after changes have been made.

2.   When an item is deleted from a linked list, the storage space released can be re-used by means of a linked list of free space. This involves linking together all of the free space nodes. With the aid of diagrams, show how you could use this idea to reduce the amount of memory required for the storage of the numbers.

3.   Write pseudocode for the algorithms in Task 2.

Cobol project 1

Video rental company

A video rental company wishes to put a computer system into all of its outlets. The software is required to perform the following functions for each outlet:

1.   Record the details of each video tape title in stock.

2.   Record the details of each of its customers.

3.   Keep track of the current videos on loan.

4.   Calculate the charge to be made to customers returning video tapes.

The structure of each file is as follows:

Video tape file

Field	Purpose
Tape identifier code:	Numeric code which uniquely identifies each tape
Charge code:	Charge for one day's hire
Title:	Full name of video
Category:	Comedy/Thriller/Horror etc
Certificate:	PG/Universal/15/18 etc
Hire count:	Number of times tape has been hired
Cost price:	Purchase price
Current return:	Running total of income from tape
Status:	Whether the video is currently on hire or on the shelves
Membership number:	The membership number of the current/last customer to hire the video
Hire date:	When the video was hired

Customer file

Field	Purpose
Membership number:	Unique identifier
Address:	
Telephone number:	
Date:	When customer joined club

Programs required

1. Update customer file:

    (i)   Add new customer;

    (ii)   Modify customer details.

2. Update video tape file:

    (i)   Add video to file;

    (ii)   Delete video from file;

    (iii)   Modify video details.

3. Record loan: Set video status flag to indicate the video is on loan.

4. Acknowledge return of video(s) and calculate hire charge.

5. List details of videos that have been on hire for more than two days.

6. Display list of all videos in stock.

The system works as follows:

Customers are given a membership card when they join the club. This card has the customer's membership number on it and must be produced when hiring videos.

The details of each hired video are entered through the keyboard before the customer leaves the shop. These details comprise the customer's membership number (entered once only, no matter how many videos are hired) and the video identifier code. The customer record is retrieved first in order to confirm that the membership number and address match (the customer is asked to give his/her address so that the assistant can check it against the computer display). The video title is retrieved from the Video Tape File, using the identification code and displayed on screen for visual confirmation that the code and title match, and the hire date is automatically retrieved from the system. The details of the hire are displayed on the screen and the assistant checks them before storing the record. The status field is set to indicate that the video is on hire.

When a video is returned, its code number is entered and the video record is retrieved and the relevant data is displayed. The assistant checks that the details are correct before confirming that the video has been returned. The computer then calculates the hire charge, based on the return date and the hire date. The charge is accumulated for each video returned. The video record is written back to the Video File with the status field set to a code representing that the video is available for hire. The customer then pays the appropriate fee.

Every morning the Video File is processed so that all videos that have been on loan for more than two days are printed out, together with customer details retrieved from the Customer file. The shop assistant will then take the appropriate action.

If a customer enquires about a video, the complete list of videos currently in stock is displayed in alphabetical order. The display shows the video title, its status, category, certificate and charge code.

The same principles described here could also be adapted to a CD hire club.

COBOL project 2

Computer literacy

Design a system which will allow you to store the titles and authors of articles on computing. (The first program in Chapter 38 and Program Example #3 are rudimentary information retrieval programs based on this idea). Your system will be required to perform the following functions:

(i)   Store details of the articles.

(ii)   Retrieve details of all articles relating to a certain topic, or by a certain author, or containing a certain keyword.

(iii) Print a report of the above records.

(iv)   Browse through the whole file.

The articles file will need to store the following details for each article:

Field	Purpose
Title	The full title of the article
Author(s)	The author or authors
Publication	The periodical in which the article appeared

Date	When the article was published
Categories	A list of codes indicating the areas that the article covers
Hire date:	When the video was hired

You will need to design a menu program to allow the user to decide how to use the system. It should give the user the opportunity to:

- ❑ Display the possible category codes.

- ❑ Enter one or more codes and obtain a list of articles on the screen.

- ❑ Print the list.

- ❑ Enter an author and obtain a list of articles by that author.

- ❑ Print this list.

- ❑ Entering a keyword and obtaining a list of articles whose titles contain the keyword.

- ❑ Print this list

- ❑ Browse through the file record by record.

- ❑ Print the displayed record.

In addition, you will need a program to allow you to enter article details to create and add to the file.

A similar system to this could be devised for Estae Agents, the file being based on house details instead.

COBOL project 3

Club records

Design a system for use by clubs to keep track of their membership. The system will need to perform the following functions:

(i)   Store member details.

(ii)   Modify member details.

(iii)   Record payment of annual subscriptions.

(iv)   Send reminders to members whose subscriptions are overdue.

The members file will need to contain the following details:

Field	Purpose
Name	Member's name
Title	Mr/Mrs/Miss etc.
Address	Member's address
Telephone number	
Date of birth	
Date of joining club	
Membership number	To keep track of how many members there have been since it started
Sex	Whether male or female
Status	Senior or junior member
Subscription	Amount paid in the current year
Other information	Special details relating to type of club

Your system will allow authorised users (access should be restricted by using ID codes) to retrieve a member's record and modify it if, for instance, there has been a change of address. You should be able to use the file as a mailing list so that reminders can be generated automatically when subscriptions are overdue. A report program will provide a list of all current members. A further program will allow the recording of subscriptions.

Glossary

Absolute address. The actual machine address of a memory location.

Access. The process of seeking, reading or writing on a storage device.

Access mechanism. A mechanism for moving the read-write heads to a position at which data can be read or written, for example, the moveable head mechanism in a magnetic disk unit.

Access method. The method used to retrieve data from a storage system, for example, serial, sequential or random access.

Access time. The time taken to retrieve data from a storage device, that is, from the moment the instruction is executed to the moment when the data is placed in memory.

Access table. A table look-up method used for accessing elements of string arrays.

Accumulator. A storage location, sometimes a special register in the arithmetic-logic unit of the processor, in which arithmetic operations are performed on numbers and where results are temporarily stored.

Addend. The addend constitutes one of the operands in an addition and is added to the augend.

Adder. Electronic circuitry in a computer capable of carrying out addition. It accepts three inputs, the addend, augend and carry to produce two outputs, the sum and carry.

Address. An identifier for a memory location in which data is stored. It may also be that part of an instruction which specifies the location of an operand.

Addressing. The means of assigning data to storage locations and subsequently retrieving them according to a key.

ALGOL. ALGOrithmic Language; a high level programming language suited to mathematical and scientific applications.

Algorithm. A computational procedure or series of instructions for the solution of a particular problem.

ALU. An acronym for arithmetic-logic unit, a component part of the CPU or processor; used for arithmetic operations and logical comparisons of, stored data.

Analogue signal. A signal, such as that produced by the human voice, which is transmitted along a channel of, for example, the telephone network.

Analogue/digital converter (ADC). A device for converting analogue signals to the digital form useable by a digital computer. For example, the temperature measurements taken from a furnace can be digitized by an ADC and monitored by computer.

AND operation. A Boolean logical operation applied to two operands. If both are equal to 1 (TRUE) then the result or output is 1 (TRUE).

Applications software (programs). Programs to deal with user applications, for example, stock control or word processing. They may be packaged or specially written.

Arithmetic shift. A shift of the digits in a location or register to affect a multiplication or division of the number. For example, in binary notation, a left shift of 'n' places is equivalent to dividing the number by 2 to the power 'n'.

Array. A block of storage locations occupying a known area of memory and accessed using a base address and offset from the base.

Artificial intelligence (AI). The ability of a computer to take on some attributes of intelligence, for example, learning and improving its performance through the use of repeated experience.

ASCII code. A set of character codes standardised under the American Standard Code for Information Interchange.

Assembler. Translator program to convert assembly language instructions into their machine code equivalents.

Assembly language. A machine-orientated programming language which uses mnemonic codes (memory aids) to identify instructions. Programs written in assembly language must be translated into machine code by an assembler program before execution.

Asynchronous transmission. The transmission of characters along a channel at irregular intervals, for example, those produced by keyboard operation.

Audit trail. A mechanism, usually built into the applications software, to allow the tracing of a transaction's history from input through to output. Auditing is an essential part of any accounting application as a guard against accidental or deliberate misuse of data.

Augend. One of the operands used in addition which is replaced by the result of the addition.

Auxiliary storage. Synonymous with backing store, for example, magnetic tape or disk.

Base address. An address in a program instruction which forms the starting point for relative addresses and allows the calculation of the absolute or machine address.

Base address. The starting location for an array.

BASIC. A high level programming language suitable for on-line program development and popularly used to introduce beginners to programming techniques. Acronym for Beginner's All-purpose Symbolic Instruction Code.

Batch. A collection of transactions awaiting processing as a single unit.

Batch file. A facility available with the MS-DOS operating system for the automatic execution of regularly used sequences of commands.

Batch processing. A method of processing transactions which allows accuracy control totals to be associated with each batch. Each

batch is dealt with as an entity, so that one error causes the rejection of the whole batch for correction and resubmission. Used where delay in updating is acceptable to users. Contrast with real-time.

Batch total. A total produced from selected values in a batch, for example, invoice quantities. Used to control the progress of a batch of transactions through each stage of processing. Totals are checked at each stage.

BCD. Abbreviation for binary coded decimal notation. Each decimal digit is coded with four binary digits.

Binary number system. A number system with the base or radix of 2 and in which only two digits are used, one and zero.

Binary search or chop. A method of searching a sequenced table or file. The procedure selects the upper or lower half based upon an examination of its midpoint value. The selected part is then similarly halved, and so on until the required item is detected.

Binary tree. A form of tree data structure in which each node has a left pointer and a right pointer to other nodes in the tree.

Bit. Contraction of binary digit (0 or 1). A bit is the smallest element of data or instruction representation in a computer. Bits are usually handled in groups of, say, 8, 16 or 32, depending on the architecture of the computer.

Block. A group of logical records transferred between memory and peripherals as a unit. Also known as a 'physical' record.

Blocking factor. The maximum number of logical records which can be fitted into a block.

Block marking. A function in word processing packages, for marking sections of text for special attention, such as moving, deleting or copying.

Boolean algebra. A system of algebra developed by the mathematician George Boole. Its application to computers lies in its facility for expressing the logical operations carried out by a computer.

Branch instruction. An instruction which specifies the address of the next instruction, normally out of program sequence. A branch may be conditional or unconditional. Also known as a jump instruction.

Bubble memory. A non-volatile memory device which uses magnetized 'bubbles' to represent binary data.

Bucket. Area of direct access storage such as disk which may consist of a number of blocks of data and can be addressed as a unit.

Buffer. A temporary storage area for data being transmitted between devices and components of a computer system. Buffers are used in terminals, storage and other peripherals and in the CPU. They can compensate for speed differences between relatively slow peripheral devices and the CPU.

Bug. A defect or malfunction in a computer program or system.

Bus. An electrical connection within a computer system and along which data is passed.

Byte. A group of bits handled as a unit by a computer system. Generally, a byte is formed from eight bits.

CAD. An acronym for Computer-Aided Design. A designer makes use of a computer, screen and light pen or similar device as aids to design.

Cambridge ring. A network configuration developed at Cambridge University and used in local area networks.

Cell. In relation to spreadsheets, a single location identifiable by co-ordinate references.

Central processing unit (CPU). The components of a computer system with the functions for control and processing, namely the control unit and the arithmetic/logic unit. Often known as the 'processor'.

Character codes. A code use to represent characters, for example, ASCII.

Check digit. An additional digit appended to a number to provide a self-checking device for transcription errors, for example, the modulus 11 check digit.

Circular or cyclic shift. The shifting of bits from one end of a location to reappear at the

other, for example, a right shift of 2 moves the two bit values from the two rightmost positions to the two leftmost positions.

Cluster. A cluster is a group of disk sectors. A file may occupy a number of non-contiguous clusters.

COBOL. A high level programming language used for programming business and file processing applications. Acronym for COmmon Business Orientated Language.

CODASYL. An acronym for COnference on DAta SYstems Languages. Responsible for standards in Codasyl database management systems.

COM. An acronym for Computer Output on Microforms. Data is recorded in a physically condensed form and can be viewed with a special projector.

Compiler. A program which translates high level source code into the object or machine code of the target machine.

Concentrator. A device for concentrating transmission from a number of low speed lines into a high speed line.

Conditional branch instruction. Program control is 'branched' out of its normal sequence when specified conditions occur.

Constant or literal. A value which is set at compilation time and does not change during program execution.

Control characters. Perform special functions, for example, carriage return on a printer.

Control total. A total accumulated on a batch of data to be processed. The computer accumulates the same total during data entry and checks its consistency. Used in batch processing.

Control unit. The functional component within the Central Processing Unit (CPU) of a computer which fetches instructions one by one, interprets them and 'triggers' the appropriate action.

Controlled redundancy. Used in connection with relational databases and refers to the duplication of certain key data items which allow connections to be made between different relations or files in a database.

CPU. Acronym for Central Processing Unit. It is the 'brain' of the computer, incorporating the control unit and the arithmetic-logic unit (ALU).

Credit note. A document which signifies that a customer's account is to be credited by a given amount, thus reducing the customer's indebtedness to the supplier.

Creditor. A person or organisation which owes money to a business for goods or services supplied on credit.

CSMA/CD. Acronym for Carrier Sense Multiple Access with Collision Detector. A method of access control used on broadcast computer networks such as the 'bus' network.

Current instruction register (CIR). A register in the CPU for the storage of the current instruction for decoding and execution.

Cylinder. A grouping of tracks in the same vertical plane, as for example, in a disk pack. Synonymous with seek area - all the tracks available whilst the read-write heads are in one position. The concept of the cylinder is used in addressing indexed sequential files.

Database. A collection of inter-related data stored together on a direct access storage medium to serve one or more applications.

Database Management System (DBMS). The programs required to control the use of a database. For example, Relational DBMS and Codasyl DBMS.

Data capture. The collection of data at the source point by automated means, for example, optical mark reading, point-of-sale (POS) terminals.

Data collection. The process of gathering raw data for preparation and computer processing, for example, the collection of timesheets for a payroll run.

Data control. The process of controlling the accuracy and completeness of data during the data processing cycle. In batch processing, for example, this includes verification and validation (batch totals etc.). The responsibility for day-to-day control lies with the data control staff in the Data Processing Department or Management Information Services.

Data format. A description of the length and form of data values.

Data independence. The property of a database which allows the alteration of its overall logical or physical structure without changing the applications' views of the data.

Data item. The smallest unit of data that has meaning as information, for example, name, date of birth in a personnel record. Synonymous with 'field'.

Data transmission. The electronic transmission of data via a telecommunications link.

Data word. A unit of computer storage containing an item of data.

Debug. To remove errors from a computer system, for example, syntax or logic errors in a computer program. The process is usually supported by software utilities such as a trace or debugger.

Desktop publishing (DTP). A computer system with facilities for combined text and graphics presentation, 'cut and paste' and font selection, which are necessary for publishing.

Digitiser. A device to convert analogue signals into a sequence of digital values. For example, maps or pictures can be digitised for computer storage and processing.

Direct access storage. A facility which allows data to be retrieved directly from a storage device without reference to the rest of the file, for example, magnetic disk.

Directory. Used by the operating system to record the names of files, their size and the date they were created or last updated.

Disk pack. A set of disks mounted on a central spindle and accessible as a unit by read-write arms.

Distributed processing. A system where computer power is not centralized, but is distributed to geographically separate branches of an organization, or amongst user systems within the same branch. This can be facilitated through the use of networked computers.

Double buffering. Where the input-output buffers are used in tandem to speed data throughput.

Double-precision arithmetic. Computer arithmetic using storage locations double the usual length to increase accuracy.

Drivers. Files which enable a package to make use of the particular capabilities of different peripherals, for example, screen and printer drivers.

Dry running. A process of checking the logic of a computer program by hand and off-line.

Duplex or full duplex. Simultaneous transmissions of data in both directions with the use of two channels.

EBCDIC. An acronym for Extended Binary Coded Decimal Interchange Code. It is an 8-bit code used mainly on IBM equipment.

Electronic Mail. The transmission of mail by electronic means via a computer network. There is usually a 'mailbox' facility for the storage of messages awaiting collection.

Electrostatic printer. A printer which uses electrostatic charges to 'fix' characters to the paper.

Encryption. The transformation of data passing through a communications link into an encoded form which prevents its interpretation by unauthorized persons 'tapping' the line.

Exchangeable disk. Hard disk storage which is removable.

Execute phase. The part of the 'fetch-execute' cycle in which the instruction is executed.

Expert system. A computer system programmed using artificial intelligence techniques to provide information or decisions relating to some narrow area of human expertise, for example, house conveyancing, house plant care, medical diagnosis. Also known as 'knowledge-based' systems.

Exponent. The power to which a base is raised.

Relevant to floating point arithmetic.

Expression. A logical or mathematical statement represented symbolically.

Facsimile Transmission (FAX). The transmission of a copy of a document via a telecommunications link. Usually, it is transmitted in digital form.

Feasibility study. A study carried out by systems analysts and interested parties to ascertain possible solutions to an information processing problem.

Fetch-execute cycle. The activity of the CPU in fetching, decoding and executing program instruction one by one in a cycle.

Fibre optics. A means of transmitting data in light form.

Field. A subdivision of a record containing an item of information. Synonymous with data item.

Fifth generation computers. A combination of advanced hardware and software; characteristics include, faster processors, the use of multiple processors for 'parallel' processing, natural language processing and more human-orientated input-output devices, such as speech synthesizers, voice recognition devices and 'mice'.

File. A collection of logically related records, for example, a stock file or a personnel file.

File allocation table (FAT). A table used by the MS-DOS operating system and stored on disk to record the allocation of disk clusters to individual files.

File organisation. Methods of organisation records in a file, for example, serially, sequentially or randomly.

File server. A local area network node which handles workstation access to shared storage and controls the exchange of files between network users.

Fixed length record. A record with a fixed physical length in terms of the number of bit positions it occupies.

Fixed point arithmetic. Arithmetic without taking account of the radix point position.

Numbers are treated as whole numbers for the purposes of calculation. The programmer has to keep track of the radix point to control calculations.

Floating point arithmetic. Arithmetic using floating point numbers, the absolute value of which are determined by a mantissa and an exponent.

Flowchart. A diagrammatic representation showing the flow of control in a computer system.

Footprint. The physical desk or floor space needed by a computer system or peripheral.

Format - disk. A process which establishes the sector size on a disk for a particular operating system and establishes a file allocation table (FAT) and root directory.

FORTRAN (FORmula TRANslator). A high level programming language particularly useful for programming scientific and mathematical applications.

Fourth generation languages (4GLs). Higher level languages which allow applications to be generated with the minimum of procedural programming; includes Applications Generators.

Frequency division multiplexing (FDM). The separation of different data streams with the use of different frequency bands for each.

Front-end processor (FEP). Usually a minicomputer handling incoming and outgoing communications traffic for a mainframe computer, which is left free to carry out the main processing tasks.

Functional area. A section or department within an organisation with a particular function, for example, sales or accounts.

Gate. An electronic circuit which accepts a number of inputs and provides the requisite output. The output will depend on the function of the gate. Synonymous with logic gates, for example AND and OR gates.

Gigabyte. One thousand million bytes.

Graph plotter. A computer output device which produces graphical material under computer control. There are two main types, the flat bed and the drum plotter.

Half-duplex. Data transmission in both directions, but not simultaneously.

Hashing. A technique using an algorithm to generate disk addresses for records within a random file. The technique aims to achieve an even distribution of records and to minimise overflow.

Hash total. A control total used in batch processing. Totals are derived from values such as account numbers and arc thus meaningless apart from their control function. Also known as nonsense totals.

Hexadecimal ('Hex'). Number system with the base 16. Uses digits 0 to 9 and then A, B, C, D, E and F. Often used as shorthand for binary codes in technical manuals for computer systems and by programmers who make use of assembly language.

High level language. A language remote from any particular machine code. Each instruction in a high level language usually equates with a number of machine code instructions.

Hit rate. A percentage figure expressing the proportion of records in a file 'hit' during a processing run.

Host computer. A computer providing a central service to a number of other computers in a network.

Icon. A symbol on a screen menu representing a program option.

Iliffe vector. A table look-up method for accessing array elements.

Immediate address. The operand is held in the address portion of an instruction word, so no further access to memory is needed.

Indexed sequential. A method of organising a file on a direct access storage device such as disk, where records are organised in sequence according to a primary record key and indexes provide a means of referring to records directly.

Indirect address. An instruction word

contains an address, not of the operand but of another address which itself contains the address of the operand. This process can be repeated so that the actual operand is obtained through several levels of indirect addresses.

Infix notation. An expression places the operator between the operands, for example X + Y.

Information flow diagram. A diagram which identifies the flows of information between different functional areas of a business.

Initialise. To set variables to an initial value at the beginning of program execution.

Instruction address register (IAR). Keeps track of locations where instructions are stored. It is incremented each time an instruction is received, so that it has the address of the next instruction. Also known as Program Counter (PC) and Sequence Control Register (SCR).

Instruction format. The layout of an instruction word - the number of bits allocated to each part.

Instruction set. The set of all machine instructions available with a particular computer.

Instruction word. A memory word containing an instruction.

Inter-block gap (IBG). The physical gap between blocks of data on magnetic tape to allow the starting and stopping of the tape between block transfers.

Interpreter. A translator program which interprets and directly executes program statements. Contrast with compiler.

Interrupt. A break in the activity of the central processor caused by an external event. For example, the completion of an input/output operation by a peripheral results in an interrupt to the processor to return to the original routine. During the input/output operation, the processor can be occupied with other processing until interrupted.

Iterate. Commonly, to undertake a series of steps repeatedly, usually until a certain condition or result is achieved. More correctly, a process of calculating a result through a repeated series of steps, in which successive approximations are made until the desired result is achieved.

Jump instruction. Synonymous with branch instruction.

Karnaugh map. A method of representing logical relationships in table form.

Key-to-disk. A method of encoding source data onto magnetic disk prior to input and processing.

Kilobyte (kb). A unit of computer storage - 1024 bytes.

Latency. The rotational delay which occurs as the read-write head waits for a revolving magnetic disk to bring the required block of data into the read-write position.

Least significant bit (LSB). The rightmost digit in a group of bits.

Light pen. A 'pen-like' input device which uses a photo-electric cell to indicate positions on a screen, for example, to select items from a menu on screen.

Line printer. A printer which effectively prints a line of text at a time.

Linked list. A data structure in which nodes have pointers to other nodes in some sequential order.

Linker. A program which incorporates any necessary machine code routines, from a library of standard routines, into an object program after compilation.

LISP (LISt Processing). A programming language where data elements are used in 'lists'. Its main application is in the field of artificial intelligence.

List. A simple data structure consisting of a sequence of elements.

Local area network (LAN). A network of connected computers confined to a small area, say to a group of buildings on one site.

Logical operator. One of the logical functions, AND, or OR, NOT etc. used on variables.

Logical shift. A shift of bits in a location which takes no account of numeric value. Contrast with arithmetic shift.

Logo. A high level language designed by Seymour Papert to encourage an 'active' approach to computer-aided learning through the use of 'turtle' graphics. Shares many of the features of LISP.

Low-level language. A machine-orientated programming language as opposed to a problem-orientated high level language. Generally, each low level language instruction has a single machine code equivalent.

Machine code or language. The pattern of bits directly executable by a computer.

Macro-instruction. An instruction in a source language (high level or low level) which, when compiled, produces a number of machine code instructions.

Magnetic disk. A disk-shaped backing storage medium which provides direct access. Each magnetisable surface is divided into tracks and sectors addressable by the computer. Each addressable location may contain one or more logical records.

Magnetic tape. A serial access backing storage medium. It consists of a reel of plastic tape with a magnetisable coating to allow the representation of data. Generally, records are stored and accessed sequentially because the medium is non-addressable.

Magnetic ink character recognition (MICR). An input method whereby a reading device 'recognises' stylised characters printed in magnetisable ink. Used almost exclusively by the banking industry to read coded data from cheques.

Main memory. The primary memory of a computer system which stores programs and data currently being processed by the CPU. Contents are lost when the power is switched off and so is supplemented by backing storage.

Mantissa. The fractional part of a floating point number. The absolute value is determined by the value of the exponent.

Masking. The extraction of specified bits from a group of bits with the use of a 'mask'.

Master file. A file which contains permanent or semi-permanent information on a subject. Usually affected by transactions during the updating process.

Megabyte (mb). Roughly one million bytes - a measurement of computer storage.

Memory address register (MAR). Provides the location address of the specific memory word to be read from or written to via the memory buffer register (MBR).

Memory buffer register (MBR). Whenever the contents of a memory word are to be transferred in or out of memory, they pass through the MBR. This applies to data and instructions.

Message switching. A technique of switching messages between nodes in a network. Usually carried out by a mainframe or minicomputer at the 'hub' of the network.

Microprocessor. A central processor (control unit and arithmetic-logic unit) on a single chip.

Millisecond (ms). One thousandth of a second.

Minuend. In subtraction, the number from which another number (subtrahend) is extracted is known as the minuend.

Mnemonic. A memory aid generally used for representing machine code operations in assembly language, for example, LDA for LoaD Accumulator.

Modem (MOdulator-DEModulator). A device for converting the digital signal produced by a computer into an analogue form suitable for transmission along a telephone line. Also capable of carrying out the reverse process for incoming data.

Most significant bit (MSB). The leftmost bit in a group of bits.

Multiplexer (MUX). A device which transmits data arriving from several sources along a single transmission medium, by modulating the carrier wave for each data stream. Two major methods of producing separately identifiable signals are time division and frequency division multiplexing.

Multiprocessing. The use of multiple processors for executing programs.

Multiprogramming. The processing of several jobs apparently at the same time. Programs and data relating to jobs are partitioned in memory and the CPU makes use of its high speed to switch control between them. This is possible because when a job is occupied with input or output, the CPU is free to carry out other tasks.

Multi-tasking. The concurrent processing of several tasks, relating to a single user, in memory at the same time.

Multi-user. A facility to allow more than one user to use a computer at the same time. Requires that the operating system can share the computer's resources and protect users' files from other users.

NAND gate. A logic gate with two or more inputs and whose output is 0 if all inputs are 1 and 1 if any inputs are 0.

Nanosecond. One thousand millionth of a second.

Network. A number of computers connected together for the purposes of communication and processing.

Node. An element of a data structure containing data and pointers to other nodes.

Node. A component in a computer network, for example, one microcomputer station in a local area network.

Non-volatile memory. A storage medium which continues to hold data after the power is removed, for example, ROM, EPROM and PROM. Contrast with RAM which is volatile.

NOR gate. A logic gate with two or more inputs whose output is 0 if any input is 1 and 1 if all input values are 0.

Normalise. In floating point arithmetic the representation uses a mantissa and exponent. A normalised number is one conforming to this representation (standard form).

NOT gate. A logic gate with a single input and a single output. The input is inverted so that if the input is 0 the output is 1 and vice-versa.

Object program. The machine code or object program produced after compilation of the source program. The object program is executable on the target machine.

Octal. A number system using the base eight. The octal system uses the digits 0 to 7 and each digit position represents a power of eight.

Offset. The displacement required from a base address in order to access a particular element of an array.

One address instruction. The instruction word only allows reference to one operand address.

Opcode. The part of an instruction word which defines the operation to be performed.

Operand. A data item to be operated upon. The instruction word may contain the actual operand or an address which refers to the operand directly or indirectly.

Operating system. The basic suite of programs which supervise and control the general running of a computer system.

Optical character recognition (OCR). The recognition by an OCR device of characters (usually stylised) by measuring their optical reflectance.

Optical disk. A high capacity storage device (measured in gigabytes) which makes use of laser technology to record and read data on the disk.

Optical mark reading (OMR). Process whereby an OMR device identifies values on a pre-printed document by the position of pencil marks. Usually, boxes on the document are indicated as representing particular values and each can be indicated by a pencil mark in the relevant box.

OSI model. Open Systems Interconnection model. Developed by the International Standards organisation, it lays down standards for network systems.

Parallel processing. The technique of executing a number of computer instructions in parallel. A number of interconnected processors called transputers are needed to do this. Most computers only have one processor and carry out instructions one after the other.

Parallel running. When a new system is implemented, the old system is continued until the users are satisfied that the new system is functioning correctly and reliably.

Parallel transmission. The transmission of bit groupings in parallel.

Parity. A minimal form of error checking in data transmission, whereby an extra bit is added to a group of bits to make the total number of bit 1s even (even parity) or odd (odd parity). The parity is checked after each transmission.

Partition. A division of memory, either disk or RAM.

Pascal. A high level, block-structured programming language named after Emile Pascal, a French mathematician.

Picosecond. One million-millionth of a second.

Pilot testing. A method of system implementation which only applies a new system to a portion of the live data. The remainder is processed by the old method until the users of the pilot data are satisfied concerning the system's accuracy and reliability.

Plotter. Flat bed or drum graph plotter.

Pointer. An arrow or 'finger' in the cursor position which allows the selection of menu options on screen, possibly with a 'mouse'.

Port. A place of entry to or exit from a central processor, dedicated to a single channel, for example, a printer port.

Primary key. A data item which ensures unique identification of an individual record.

Print server. A local area network node which shares its printer facility amongst all users on the network. Print jobs are queued and may be executed in turn or according to assigned priorities.

Processor. See central processing unit.

Program counter (PC). A register which contains the address of the next instruction to be executed. Synonymous with sequence control register (SCR) and instruction address register (IAR).

Program specification. A specification produced by a systems analyst as part of a system specification and detailing all the requirements of the related applications software.

Program testing. The process of running a program with test data to check the correctness and completeness of output.

Prolog. A programming language based on mathematical logic. It is used extensively in artificial intelligence (AI) applications and is particularly suitable for database applications. Adapted by the Japanese for programming their 'fifth generation' computers.

PROM (Programmable Read Only Memory). A chip which can be 'blown' or programmed by the user to produce non-volatile memory store (ROM).

Protocol. A set of rules governing the format of messages transmitted in computer networks. Compatibility needs to be established between communicating devices so that they can 'talk' to each other.

Query language. A language designed for users to make ad hoc enquiries of a database.

Queue. A linear list data structure in which elements are added at one end and removed from the other end.

Radix. The base of a number system, for example, the radix for the binary number system is 2, for the decimal system, 10.

RAM. Random access memory - the main memory of the computer.

Random access. A facility for accessing a storage medium for any record or data item, without reference to the rest of the file. Also known as direct access. Main memory and disk storage provide this facility.

Read only memory (ROM). Storage medium which allows only 'reading' and not 'writing'.

Record. A group of related data items forming

an entity. A subdivision of a file.

Register. A storage location, usually within the CPU with special (for example Program Counter) or general purpose functions (storage of intermediate values during processing).

Relation. A two-dimensional array or table forming a 'flat' file. Terminology associated with relational databases.

Relational algebra. A language providing a set of logical operators for manipulating 'relations' (files) in a relational database.

Relational database. A database made up of relations or two-dimensional tables.

Relative addressing. A method of addressing where each address is relative to a 'base' address. Each address is given a 'displacement' value to relate its position to the base address. By altering the''base', a program can be relocated in memory. If the base address is taken as the address of the current instruction, this is known as self-relative addressing.

Repeater. A signal amplifier, which passes packets of data onto the next node in a network.

Reverse polish (postfix notation). A form of expression where the operators succeed the operands. For example, the expression $(W + X) * Y + Z$ in infix notation, becomes $WX + Y * Z +$.

Reverse video. A reversing of background and foreground colours on a VDU screen to highlight selected characters.

Rewrite. To overwrite an existing record with an updated version of it. This is only possible with direct access storage.

Ring network. A network topology where computers are connected in a ring structure. Evolved in Cambridge and known as the Cambridge ring.

RISC. An acronym for Reduced Instruction Set Computer in which the decoding circuitry is limited to the most frequently used instructions, thus producing smaller, faster processors.

RPG (Report Program Generator). A high level programming language designed to allow trained users (as opposed to specialist programmers) to generate reports from computer files.

Schema. The overall logical definition of a database.

Search. The scanning of data items for those in accord with specified criteria, for example, salaries in excess of 10,000 in a Personnel file.

Sector. A subdivision of a track on a magnetic disk. Constitutes the smallest addressable unit on a disk.

Seek time. The time taken for moveable read-write heads to move to the selected track or cylinder on a magnetic disk.

Self-relative address. An address calculated by adding a 'displacement' value to the address of the current instruction. That is, the address is in a position relative to the address of the current instruction. See also relative address.

Sequence control register (SCR). See program counter.

Sequential access. The retrieval of records according to the sequence of their organisation, for example, a customer file stored in Customer Account number order.

Sequential organisation. A method of storing a file so that records are sequenced according to a primary record key, for example, a Stock Code.

Serial access. Retrieving records in the order that they are physically stored, in other words, as they come.

Serial organisation. Simply, records stored one after the other, not necessarily in sequence, for example, an unsorted tape file.

Serial transmission. Transmission of data, usually via a telecommunications link, whereby the 'bits' follow one another in a serial fashion. Contrast with parallel transmission.

Sign and magnitude. Integer numbers represented in a computer with the most significant bit as the sign (0 for positive and 1 for negative).

Simplex. Transmission of data in one direction

only.

Source program. A program written in a programming language (high or low level). It must be translated into machine code before execution.

Spooling (Simultaneous Peripheral Operation On Line). Making more efficient use of hardware during input-output operations by using faster peripheral devices in parallel with normal job processing, as a temporary substitute for slower devices. For example, output destined for printing may be spooled to an area of disk and dumped from there to the printer while the processor is left to carry on with other tasks.

SQL. Structured query language. A non-procedural 4th generation programming language.

Stack. A linear list data structure allowing access to elements only at one end of the list.

Star network. A network topology, whereby a main 'host' computer at the 'hub' services a number of peripheral systems.

Stop bit. A bit used to indicate the end of a character in asynchronous transmission.

Structured programming. A programming design technique which makes use of control structures such as 'IF ... THEN ... ELSE' and 'DO ... WHILE ...' to combine and control separate functions within a program. Only three basic control structures are used; sequence of operations, selection of alternative operations and repetition or iteration.

Subroutine. A self-contained routine, coded once within a program, which may be 'called' at any point during the main program. After execution of the subroutine, control is returned to the instruction immediately following the call.

Subschema. A limited logical view of a database derived from the schema (overall logical database view) to be used by an applications program.

Subtrahend. One of the two operands in a subtraction which is subtracted from the 'minuend' to give a result.

Synchronous transmission. The transmission of data in 'streams'. The sender and the receiver devices are synchronised so that individual characters are identified within the stream. No start or stop bits are needed. Special 'SYN' characters are transmitted periodically to maintain the synchronisation. Contrast with asynchronous transmission.

Syntax. The formal rules of grammar and structure governing the use of a programming language.

Syntax error. Where the syntax rules are broken in program coding. Generally, such errors are indicated by a compiler or interpreter.

Systems analysis. The study of an activity with a view to its computerisation.

Systems software. Program purchased as part of a computer system and which are concerned with the general running of the hardware and not with specific applications. Examples include, operating systems, utilities and compilers.

Teleworking. Working from home with the use of a computer link to the actual office.

Test data. Data specially prepared for the testing of program output for accuracy and consistency with the requirements of the program specification.

Three address instruction. An instruction format which allows for three addresses.

Timesharing. The technique, often used with interactive systems, whereby the CPU shares out its time amongst a number of users, with the aim of giving good response times to each. The allocation of time is known as 'time slicing'.

Token ring network. A local area network industry standard. Its main proponent is IBM.

Top-down design. Designing a program according to its overall logic, in terms of its identifiable components and then defining those components in further detail and so on, until the required level of detail is obtained.

Trace. A software facility which traces the path of a program's execution. Useful in the detection of logic errors.

Transaction file. A file containing transactions to be used in the updating of a master file.

Transaction logging. The recording of transactions on a separate serial file at the same time as they update the relevant master files.

Translator. A program for the translation of source code into object or machine code, for example, a compiler, an interpreter or an assembler.

Transputer. A processor with serial links to allow communication with other transputers. The basis of parallel processing computers.

Tree. A non-linear list in which each node has a number of pointers to other nodes in a hierarchical structure.

Two address instruction. An instruction format which allows for two addresses.

Update. A process whereby a master record is amended by a transaction to reflect the current position.

Utility. A program which performs a common task such as sorting a file or copying a disk.

Validation. A process, usually carried out by a validation or 'data vet' program, to check that data falls within specified valid criteria, for example, that hours of overtime worked fall within a range from 0 to 20.

Verification. The process of checking the accuracy of data transcription, usually in a data encoding operation such as key-to-disk, prior to batch data input. Commonly, verification involves the re-keying of the data by another operator and the verifier machine compares keys depressed with data already stored.

Videoconferencing. The conducting of a conference through the use of computers, video cameras and telecommunications links.

Virtual memory. An extension of main memory to include on line disk storage, such that a programmer can regard the total memory space as being available for a program. Programs are written in segments or pages and are called into main memory as required.

Voice output. The technique of simulating the human voice by computer means.

Voice recognition. A technique to allow computer input to be supplied directly by a human voice.

Volatile. A property associated with computer memory, whereby it loses its data when power is removed.

Wide area network (WAN). A network which makes use of the telecommunications network to link computer systems over a wide geographical area.

WIMP. Acronym for Windows, Icons, Mice and Pull-down menus, all of which are commonly used in user-friendly, menu driven packages.

Word. A unit of memory storage addressed as a single unit.

Write. To transfer data from main memory to a storage device such as disk. If the transfer is to an output device it is known as printing.

Write protect. A mechanism to prevent accidental or deliberate overwriting of a disk's contents.

Index

Information Processing
Third Edition

Geoffrey Knott Nick Waites   August 1997   352 pp

ISBN 0 907679 97 8   Soft Cover £15.95

The new edition of this popular text demonstrates the importance of computerised Information Processing in modern organisations. The text has been extensively revised to keep students aware of the most recent changes and developments. It assumes no previous knowledge of the subject and is suitable for National, Advanced, Higher National and undergraduate programmes which have an Information Processing requirement. Business, Finance and Management courses will find the text highly relevant. The text also meets the requirements of Members of the Association of Accountancy Technicians (AAT), who are studying for Paper 6, Elements of Information Systems.

Each chapter is followed by exercises designed to test the reader's retention of facts and understanding of ideas developed within the text.

A programme of 25 problem-based assignments provides assessment coverage of all the topics in the book and could form the basis of a teaching programme. Each assignment indicates the chapters which are of particular use for its completion.

The 18 chapters provide coverage of the following topics:

- information in organisations
- computer systems
- computer software
- information processing methods
- role and structure of an Information Technology (IT) Services department
- data communication systems
- MS-DOS, Windows 3.x, Windows 95, Windows NT and OS/2 operating systems
- financial accounting software, illustrated with the Quickbooks package
- financial modelling and simulation using a spreadsheet

- business applications
- input, output devices and storage systems
- computer files
- information processing controls
- computer networks
- office information technology systems
- general -purpose software packages
- system investigation, design and implementation
- organisational and social issues relating to computerisation.

A glossary of commonly used computing and IT terms is also included.

Information Technology Advanced Level GNVQ3
Second Edition

Nick Waites Geoffrey Knott   September 1997   768 pp

ISBN 0 901888 01 0   Soft Cover £16.95

This book covers the 8 Mandatory Units of the Information Technology GNVQ, Advanced Level:

- Information Technology Systems
- Using Information Technology
- Organisations and Information Technology
- Communications and Networking

- Systems Analysis
- Software
- Information Technology Projects and Teamwork
- Database Development

In depth coverage of
- Program Design
- Programming

is also provided, these being the subjects of two important Optional Units.

The book is divided into three parts, as follows.

Knowledge Resource

This provides the underpinning knowledge needed for all the Units in the book and covers the following subject areas:

- Information in Organisations
- Information Technology Applications

- Data Handling Systems
- Computer Files
- Systems Analysis and Design
- Data Control and Security
- Privacy and Computer Fraud
- Health and Safety
- Software
- High Level Languages

- Program Design
- Relational Database Management Systems
- Data Modelling
- Project teams
- Computer Types
- Computer Hardware
- Computer Systems Architecture
- Networks
- Data Communications
- Measurement and Control Systems

Skills Resource

This part supports the practical aspects of the Units and includes detailed guidance in the features and use of:

- Word Processors
- Spreadsheets and Spreadsheet Graphics
- Graphic and Computer Aided Design
- Relational Databases

- Local Area Networks
- Data Communications
- Computer-based Control Systems
- Pascal Programming Language

Study Programme

A study programme, sectioned according to the Mandatory Units, provides complete coverage of the Performance Criteria. Each activity identifies the Units, Elements and Performance Criteria it covers and the sections of the Knowledge and Skills Resources which support completion of the activity.